AMERICAN ORIENTAL SERIES

VOLUME 65

STUDIES IN LITERATURE FROM THE ANCIENT NEAR EAST

BY MEMBERS OF
THE AMERICAN ORIENTAL SOCIETY

DEDICATED TO SAMUEL NOAH KRAMER

AMERICAN ORIENTAL SERIES

VOLUME 65

AMERICAN ORIENTAL SOCIETY

New Haven, Connecticut

1984

STUDIES IN LITERATURE FROM THE ANCIENT NEAR EAST

BY MEMBERS OF
THE AMERICAN ORIENTAL SOCIETY

DEDICATED TO SAMUEL NOAH KRAMER

EDITED BY

JACK M. SASSON

AMERICAN ORIENTAL SOCIETY

NEW HAVEN, CONNECTICUT

1984

Published earlier without indices as
Journal of the American Oriental Society
Volume 103, Number 1

ISBN 0–940490–65–X

Phototypeset by Eisenbrauns
Winona Lake, Indiana, United States of America
1982+1984

Articles

SAMUEL NOAH KRAMER

SPECIAL ISSUE

STUDIES IN LITERATURE FROM THE ANCIENT NEAR EAST, BY MEMBERS OF THE AMERICAN ORIENTAL SOCIETY, DEDICATED TO SAMUEL NOAH KRAMER.

Edited by

JACK M. SASSON

EDITOR'S PREFACE

On September 28, 1983, Samuel Noah Kramer will be 86. He will also have passed 55 years as an active member of the American Oriental Society. Because of his many contributions to the well-being of the Society, he was elected as its president during 1967-1968. The Society and the Editorial Board of the Society's *Journal* recognize this event by dedicating to him this special issue of the JAOS: *Studies in Literature From The Ancient Near East*. In offering their contribution to this publication, members of the *American Oriental Society* individually pay tribute to a scholar who has committed his energy to recovering and disseminating Sumer's literary heritage.

In editing this special issue I have benefited from the support of Ernest Bender and of Stanley Insler. Contributors were quick to respond to my queries, and Eisenbrauns was generous in its advice. Julia Hardy graciously bore the brunt of assisting me. Rachel Frew and Kathryn Logan of the University of North Carolina's Music Library aided my searches in a not altogether familiar territory. The Research Council of the University of North Carolina assisted this publication with welcome funds.

The firm EISENBRAUNS has been very helpful in solving technical problems arising from this issue. I am beholden to Jim Eisenbraun and his staff.

JACK M. SASSON

THE FORM AND MEANING OF A BABYLONIAN PRAYER TO MARDUK

I. Tzvi Abusch

Brandeis University

Mesopotamian hymns and prayers often evoke a response of boredom; more than one reader has found himself wondering whether these texts are not simply collections of phrases that were strung out indiscriminately.[1] Perhaps; still it is no less possible that the sense of meaninglessness and dreariness is due to mechanical reading and presentation. Understanding the artistry and thought of a Babylonian psalm—especially one which represents a new form and thus gives evidence of creativity—underscores the vitality of Mesopotamian psalmody; this study of the poetic form and theological meaning of a well-known and relatively simple prayer, the Marduk šuilla *BMS* 9 obverse and duplicates,[2] may serve, then, as an appropriate tribute to Professor Samuel Noah Kramer: for Kramer has sought repeatedly to draw the attention of scholars and general readers alike to the vigor and excitement of Mesopotamian literature.

The composition will be treated as a self-contained unit. First the introductory hymn (1–9) will be explicated, particular attention being paid to some of the techniques used by the composer and the ideas he wished to convey thereby (I). Then several irregularities in the remainder of the text (10–27) will be noted, and the sections (10–12; 22–24) responsible for these irregularities will be studied (II). A consideration of lines 10–12 and 22–24 suggests the possibility that the composition is arranged concentrically. This possibility is examined: the central prayer (13–21) is analyzed, the relation of lines 13–21 to 10–12 and 22–24 explored, and the introductory hymn and concluding benediction drawn together. The structure of the text is presented in diagram form (III). An historical observation concludes the discussion.

I. The šuilla begins with a hymn of praise to Marduk:

1. *gašru šūpû etel Eridug*
2. *rubû tizqāru bukur* ᵈ*Nudimmud*
3. ᵈ*Marduk šalbābu murīš E*ʾ*engura*
4. *bēl Esag̃ila tukulti Bābili*
5. *rā*ʾ*im Ezida mušallim napišti*
6. *ašarēd Emaḫtila mudeššû balāṭi*
7. *ṣulūl māti gāmil nišī rapšāti*
8. *ušumgal kališ parakkī*
9. *šumka kališ ina pī nišī ṭāb*

These nine lines[3] constitute a distinct unit. The unit opens with the invocation *gašru šūpû etel Eridug* (1)

---

[1] Cf. W. W. Hallo, *JAOS* 97 (1977), 582–85 (review of M.-J. Seux, *Hymnes et prières aux dieux de Babylonie et d'Assyrie*), esp. 582f.

[2] This šuilla is cited as Marduk no. 2 in the lists of šuillas compiled by W. Kunstmann, *Die babylonische Gebetsbeschwörung* (*LSS* nf 2), 94 and Werner Mayer, *Untersuchungen zur Formensprache der babylonischen "Gebetsbeschwörungen"* (Studia Pohl: Series Maior 5), 395. For a list of exemplars and other bibliographical information, see Mayer, *Untersuchungen*, 395; the unpublished British Museum duplicates listed there have since appeared in copy in O. Loretz and W. R. Mayer, *ŠU-ILA-Gebete* (*AOAT* 34), nos. 26–29. This šuilla was known by its opening line: *gašru šūpû etel* (var. *etelli*) *Eridu*. This incipit is cited in l. 11 of the list K. 2832 + 6680 col. I (W. L. King, *Babylonian Magic and Sorcery*, p. xix and Mayer, *Untersuchungen*, 399) and follows there immediately upon the entry: *gašru šūpû ilitti Eridu* (9). Kunstmann, *Gebetsbeschwörung*, 95, and Mayer, *Untersuchungen*, 399, take l. 9 as referring to an otherwise unattested or unidentified prayer (Kunstmann: Marduk 7; Mayer: Marduk (?) X). However, since one MS of Marduk no. 2 (Loretz and Mayer, *ŠU-ILA*, nos. 28 (+) 29:3′) preserves the reading *gašru šūpû ilitti Eridu* (the better reading is *etelli*; *ilitti* is due to an auditory error which resulted in metathesis: *etelli* → *ilitti*), the incipit *gašru šūpû ilitti Eridu* in K. 2832 + 6680 I 9 may simply refer to a version of Marduk no. 2 that had *ilitti* instead of *etelli* in its opening line. If such is indeed the case, it might explain why the scribe of K. 2832 + 6680 associated the two incipits and entered them together.

[3] The division into nine lines is supported by almost all MSS. On two points do we encounter variation: l. 8 is joined

and ends with the statement *šumka kališ ina pī nišī ṭāb* (9). To be sure, l. 10 also contains an invocation: *Marduk bēlu rabû*; but this invocation recurs in l. 22. It is the opening of a summary statement (10–12; 22–24) recited once between the introductory hymn (1–9) and the prayer and again between the prayer and the concluding benediction.[4] L. 10, then, begins a new section and is not part of the introductory hymn. Besides, l. 9 is itself bound up with what immediately precedes it. Ll. 8 and 9 are bound together by their content:

> The single great one of chapels everywhere,
> Your name is lovingly hymned by the people everywhere.

They are bound even more closely by their sound; note the alliteration of the first two words of 8 and of 9: *ušumgal kališ* . . . ; *šumka kališ*. . . . And we may even wonder whether the play does not extend backwards from *ušumgal* of l. 8 to *gāmil* of l. 7. It is possible, moreover, that the boundaries of the hymn are signalled by its first and last lines:

> *gašru šūpû etel Eridug* (1)
> *šumka kališ ina pī nišī ṭāb* (9)

gašru at the beginning of l. 1 and *šumka* at the beginning of l. 9 call to mind *gašru* at the beginning and *gašru lū šumka* at the end of the speech to enlist aid in Anzu.[5] Furthermore, the occurrence of Eridug[6] at the end of l. 1 and of *nišī ṭāb* at the end of l. 9 appears to be more than just a coincidence: dùg and *ṭāb* are, respectively, the Sumerian and Akkadian words for "good"; eri, "city," and *nišī*, "people," encapsulate the two poles of Marduk's activities in the poem: in the first stanza the focus is on the city of his youth, and in the third stanza it is on the people for whom he cares and who admire him in his maturity. Other Sumero-Akkadian wordplays in the hymn[7] lend credence to this observation. However, we need not belabor these uncertain boundary markers, for the definition and unity of the hymn are rendered sufficiently clear by the thematic makeup and structure of ll. 1–9.

The hymn comprises nine poetic lines. These nine lines are to be arranged into three-line stanzas;[8] the basic unit is the triplet.

> I. Famed mighty one, chieftain of Eridu,
> Exalted prince, first-born of Nudimmud,
> Raging Marduk, restorer of rejoicing to Eᵓengura.
> II. Lord of Esağila, hope of Babylon,
> Lover of Ezida, preserver of life,
> Lone one of Emaḫtila, multiplier of living.
> III. Protection of the land, savior of the multitudes of people,
> The single great one of chapels everywhere,
> Your name is sweetly hymned by the people everywhere.

Each stanza conveys a picture of Marduk. Each picture is full-blown and self-contained, and yet each differs from the others. Marduk's actions and concerns, the groups with which he interacts, and the areas in which he operates change from one stanza to the next. But the hymn is not a series of disjointed images. It retains a sense of constancy while portraying a changing figure. This is all the more impressive in view of the brevity of the hymn and the static form of description. The hymn integrates a series of different pictures and tells a story of the expansion of the activities and concerns of a single god. Earlier roles presage later ones; later roles do not require the

---

with l. 9 in *STT* I 55 and with l. 7 in the *bīt mēseri* version IV R^2 21* no. 1(c)rev. (= G. Meier, *AfO* 14 [1941–44], 140–43); this is due to the brevity of l. 8. More significant, IV R^2 21* splits up l. 5 and joins 5a with 4 and 5b with 6. Besides destroying the parallelism of ll. 4, 5, and 6, this division obscures the scholastic wordplays upon which our text turns (see below). One must assume that the scribe of IV R^2 21* was unaware of, or had no regard for, the devices used to convey the meaning and was more concerned with compressing the text into a smaller number of lines. It is unfortunate that the line division of IV R^2 21* has been perpetuated by *BMS* 9 obv., F. Delitzsch, *Assyrische Lesestücke*[5], 85, and K. K. Riemschneider, *Lehrbuch des Akkadischen*, 155f.

[4] For this characterization of ll. 10–12 and 22–24, see below, section II.

[5] For Anzu, see J. S. Cooper, *JAOS* 97 (1977), 508–11 (example A); W. W. Hallo and W. L. Moran, *JCS* 31 (1979), 82–87, ll. 37–44, 58–65, and 79–86.

[6] See Th. Jacobsen, *JCS* 21 (1967), 162 n. 14 for a discussion of the form and meaning of the name "Eridug." It is of no consequence for our interpretation of *BMS* 9 whether "the good city" is the original meaning of the name or the result of ancient etymologyzing.

[7] See below.

[8] For a different stanza arrangement, see A. Falkenstein and W. von Soden, *Sumerische und akkadische Hymnen und Gebete*, 297f.

rejection of earlier ones; rather, they incorporate and expand on them.

To understand how the composer has achieved his goal, we must take note of the picture and thought of each stanza, see some of the ways in which the stanzas are joined together, and try to imagine the progression of images and the overarching conception of the hymn.

In the first stanza Marduk is presented as a young aristocrat residing in his parents' estate and acting on their behalf. He is a warrior-prince, a well-endowed son who is accorded social prerogatives and placed under filial obligations. He performs heroically in the service of his family; still, he remains a local figure. He serves his family within the confines of his ancestral town and home. Yet the way forth is prepared by his role as *murīš Eʾengura* (3). The third stanza presents a very different scene: here Marduk is the supreme god. He takes care of the land and its people and is rewarded for his care. The first and third stanzas seem to clash. But for all their differences, they also balance and parallel each other. Both operate within the bounds of the concrete. The first describes Marduk's place in a specific city, family, and temple; the third describes Marduk's relation to the land, its people, and its sanctuaries.[9] All the same, the universalism of the third stanza contrasts with the particularism of the first, and Marduk's domination of the country in the third contrasts with his dependent status in the first.

The third stanza is obviously an outgrowth and widening of the first one. But how was the transition achieved? The conecting piece is provided by ll. 4–6: this stanza constitutes the pivot of the text; it draws the first and third stanzas together and creates a whole. In the second stanza, Marduk is presented as the god of Babylon and its environs. The role of lord of Babylon, Esag̃ila, Ezida, and Emaḫtila forms a crucial episode in his life. It fits nicely between his role in the first stanza as the young god of Eridu and his role in the third as supreme god of the land. This does not exhaust the meaning and function of the second stanza: this stanza gives the hymn a distinct slant. But to understand the stanza and its place in the poem, we must first take note of a series of anomalies in ll. 4–6 and explain them. The stanza reads:

4. *bēl Esag̃ila tukulti Bābili*
5. *rāʾim Ezida mušallim napišti*
6. *ašarēd Emaḫtila mudeššû balāṭi*

The epithets are standard enough; yet the sequence and conjunction are striking and unexpected. It is sufficient to take note of a similar section of a Nabû šuilla to appreciate our own stanza:

14. *ašarēd Bābili rāʾim Esag̃ila*
15. *ṣulūl Barsip tukulti Ezida*
16. *šāʾimu šīmāti mušallim napišti*
17. *murrik ūmī qāʾišu balāṭi*[10]

This address to Nabû shares many elements with our stanza but orders them in a more conventional way: Epithets describing the god's relation to city and temple are joined together and appear in the order city-temple (14–15); these epithets are followed by epithets describing the god's relation to human life (16–17). These two distinct sets of epithets are presented separately and are not mixed together. Turning back to our own stanza, we now note the following: Line 4: The expected and logical procedure would have been to mention first the city Babylon and then the temple Esag̃ila. Certainly the first stanza has prepared us for the order city-temple by presenting Marduk first as *etel Eridu* and then as *murīš Eʾengura*. Instead, l. 4 presents Marduk first as *bēl Esag̃ila* and only then as *tukulti Bābili*. Lines 5–6: Coming to these lines from l. 4, we notice immediately the absence of a city name. Moreover it would have been more usual and natural for the two epithets describing the god's relation to temples of Borsippa to be joined together in one line and the two describing his relation to human life to be joined together in another. Instead, the sets of epithets are split up, and epithets describing his relation to temples in Borsippa are juxtaposed to those describing his care for human life.

Far from being mere hackwork, the second stanza is tightly knit and ingeniously constructed. The order is intentional and expresses the central notion of the hymn. The purpose of the stanza is not simply to depict Marduk as the lord of Babylon. Even more it serves as a transition and provides the vehicle for Marduk's development from the local god of Eridu into the supreme caretaker of mankind, and it does so

[9] More specifically, note the city in l. 1, the country in l. 7; elevated princely status in l. 2, elevated divine station in l. 8; the applause of the family in l. 3, the applause of all people in l. 9.

[10] E. Ebeling, *Die akkadische Gebetsserie "Handerhebung"*, 110:14–17.

by expressing a thought basic to the composer's theology and art: the god's place in the temple is intimately related to his ability to care for the people; his power to care for human life derives from his rootedness in the temple. The connection between the god's relation to temple and his relation to people is expressed first of all by the juxtaposition of temple and mankind:

> Lover of Ezida, preserver of life,
> Lone one of Emaḫtila, multiplier of living.

The two are thus put on a par. But the connection is more than just mechanical. There is an internal, organic connection, and here a mere scholastic play serves to draw together god, temple, and man. The composer relies on a knowledge of the equations zi : *napištu* and ti.la : *balāṭu* to convey his meaning. Here, far from being an orthographic convention that obscures the Akkadian text, the use of Sumerograms is a literary device meant to express or, at least, enhance the composer's message.[11] *napišti* translates and is written in all but one manuscript with ZI[12] and plays on the temple name, "Ezida," a name translated elsewhere as *bīt napišti māti.*[13] *balāṭi* translates and is written in almost all manuscripts with TI.LA[14] and plays on the temple name, "Emaḫtila."[15] Thus in l. 5 Ezida shares zi with *napišti* and in l. 6 Emaḫtila shares ti.la with *balāṭi*:

> *rā'im Ezida mušallim napišti* (ZI[D])
> *ašarēd Emaḫtila mudeššû balāṭi* (TI.LA)[16]

The placing of the temple name in first position in ll. 5 and 6 explains furthermore the order of l. 4: *bēl Esağila tukulti Bābili.*[17] Esağila is placed before

[11] The literary use of ideograms might suggest a written—rather than an oral—form of composition. Note, however, that a learned composer could certainly see and exploit the connection between Ezida and *napištu* and between Emaḫtila and *balāṭu* without recourse to writing. If this šuilla was originally composed orally, the scribe who introduced the writing ZI for *napišti* in l. 5 and TI.LA for *balāṭi* in l. 6 is to be credited with preserving and rendering explicit the aforementioned connections.

[12] + *ti/tì*; *STT* I 55: *na-piš-ti.*

[13] For this translation, see *RLA* I 188; cf. Ebeling, *AGH*, 124:8: *zēr Ezida bīt šikin napišti ša ilī rabûti.*

[14] The exceptions are Loretz and Mayer, *ŠU-ILA*, no. 26: TIN and *KAR* 59: *ba-l*[*á*?-*ṭi*].

[15] While completing this study, I located E. Lehmann and H. Haas (eds.), *Textbuch zur Religionsgeschichte*² (1922), and noted that whereas in the 1912 edition (101f.) Landsberger had apparently not noticed any wordplays, in the 1922 edition (307f.), he comments on 6b: "Anspielungen auf die vorangehenden Tempelnamen" (307 n. 7).

[16] The use of Sumero-Akkadian equations as a poetic device and as a way of expressing thought is not particularly surprising in this hymn; the composer seems to have been acquainted with bilingual literature. Note, for example, that whereas the combination Babylon, Esağila, Ezida, and Emaḫtila in our text is relatively uncommon in Akkadian prayers, it occurs with greater frequency in Sumerian and bilingual liturgies: See, for example, the Sumerian Marduk šuilla J. S. Cooper, *Iraq* 32 (1970), 58f.: 5–8 (disregard the additions of the Nabû adaptation MS D) and the Marduk Kiutukam IV R^2 29/1 obv. 27–30 // *STT* II 182 (+) 183 obv. 6'f: lugal tin.tir.KI lugal é.sağ.íl.la : *šar* (*STT*: [x]x) *ba-bi-lì* (*STT*: KÁ.DI[NGIR.RA.KI]) *be-el é-sağ-íla*; lugal é.zi.da lugal é.maḫ.ti.la : *šar* (*STT*: xx) *é-zi-da be-el é-maḫ-ti-la.* Babylon - Esağila - Ezida - Emaḫtila formed the original kernel out of which was constructed the expanded and convoluted Babylon section (Babylon, Esağila, Borsippa, Ezida, Emaḫtila, Etemenanki, Edaranna) of such eršemmas and balags as M. E. Cohen, *Sumerian Hymnology: The Eršemma* (HUCA suppl. 2), 29:7–13; 118b:8–14; 127:12–18; 113f:21–25 (= R. Kutscher, *Oh Angry Sea* [YNER 6], 63: 26–30 [Kutscher's MS Haa = Cohen's MS B]. Eturkalama in l. 27 between Esağila and Borsippa must be misplaced; elsewhere, it occurs before Babylon [e.g., Cohen, *Eršemma*, 133:37; 144:22; 147:17; 148:21].), M. E. Cohen, *Balag-Compositions* (SANE 1/2), 18:88–92; 19:134–38; 30:17–21 (cf. S. Langdon, *Sumerian and Babylonian Psalms*, 104, 108, 120). In these lists, Borsippa introduces Ezida and Emaḫtila; it is set on a level with Babylon and introduces its temples as Babylon introduces Esağila. The secondary nature of this longer list is suggested by the separation of the Babylonian Etemenanki and Edaranna from Esağila and their citation after Ezida and Emaḫtila, by the joining together of Esağila and Borsippa in one line in the Balags cited above (Babylon // Esağila - Borsippa // Ezida - Emaḫtila, etc.), and by such adaptations as Cooper, *Iraq* 32, 58 MS D, which attest directly to the insertion of Borsippa (6a) between Esağila (6) and Ezida - Emaḫtila (7f.).

[17] I do not wish to imply that the order Esağila - Bābili is found only in this hymn; see simply Ebeling, *AGH*, 68:5f: *šarrat Esağila . . . bēlet Bābili . . .*, and 54:3 // 112a4: *Esağila liḫdūka Bābili lirīška* (corrected reading: Seux, *Hymnes*, 304 and n. 26 and Mayer, *Untersuchungen*, 336 1c). The first example is addressed to Zarpanītu and is found on

Babylon in order to open the stanza with a line beginning with a temple, a stratagem facilitated by the mention of the temple E$^{\supset}$engura at the end of l. 3. By placing the temple first and the city second in l. 4, the composer both provides a precedent for beginning ll. 5–6 with a temple-name, as well as cushions the shock of these lines, for not only do ll. 5–6 begin with temples, but they also replace references to cities with references to mankind.

The second stanza presents an important episode in the life of Marduk and sets forth a period of growth and transition. It plays a special role in the poem. It links the first and third stanzas and creates a unity. The first stanza leads into it; the third emerges out of it. The second stanza is a center: it draws the text to itself and then sets in motion the progressive loosening of tightly-knit connections. The tightening and loosening, the narrowing and widening come to expression not only in the choice and order of themes but also in the choice and order of metrical and grammatical units. These forms arrange themselves into concentric patterns with the second stanza forming the center. A primitive count of the number of syllables in each stanza indicates that whereas the first and third stanzas contain approximately the same number of syllables: ca. 30, the second has a different number: ca. 35. This pattern sets off the second stanza by giving it special marking and balances the first and third stanzas. On a grammatical level, too, we find a marking off of stanzas. But the grammatical structure does more; it is more flexible and therefore able to convey the meaning of the text. The grammatical units form a concentric pattern. The second stanza is more tightly drawn than the first and third, and it forms a center. The first is relatively loose at the beginning; it tightens up and becomes more particular as it approaches and links up with the second. The third becomes looser and less particular as it moves away from the second, until at the end it is looser and more general even than the first line of the poem. A diagram of the text demonstrates this point. A characterization of the syntactic structures encountered in the hymn should make clear our interpretation: a construct chain is the tightest form of linking two words; a noun plus attributive adjective is a looser form; a sentence with an adjective in predicate position is the loosest form. A proper noun is the most particularizing substantive; a general noun is less particularizing; an adjective is the least particularizing. The grammatical scheme is as follows:

Stanza I	1a nominalized adjective + adjective	1b construct chain
	2a general noun + adjective	2b construct chain
	3a proper noun + adjective	3b construct chain
Stanza II	4a construct chain	4b construct chain
	5a construct chain	5b construct chain
	6a construct chain	6b construct chain
Stanza III	7a construct chain	7b construct chain augmented by adjective modifying 2nd member of chain, "*nišī*"
	8 construct chain expanded by a second bound form, "*kališ*," before *rectum*	
	9 stative sentence composed of nominal subject and adjectival predicate, separated by adverb, "*kališ*," and prepositional phrase (preposition + construct chain whose 2nd member is "*nišī*")	

The last line is the only real sentence; it is the most expansive form in the hymn and describes the delights of praising the god, thus stating the essence of a hymn: *šumka kališ ina pī nišī ṭāb*.

We have witnessed the loosening of Marduk's local ties and the widening of his orbit, his change from a local to a national god, from a god who serves his divine parents to one who cares for the people of the land. We watch the broadening of Marduk's scope and note that the composer has managed to preserve the god's connections with the concrete. A desirable and even necessary achievement: while extending his care to more and more people, Marduk must remain rooted, for only thus can he remain the master of his home, the object of a cult, and the possessor of the power to help people. But seeing all this only makes us more aware of the difficulties that faced the poet. To describe a god's growth and not to let go of the link between the god and the concrete world and to manage even to extend the god's links are not easy tasks. For our poet the difficulty was if possible even greater. Locality, temple, and community were connected in the first stanza; but locality then served as a stepping stone to the temple and receded into the distance. Temple then served as a stepping stone for reaching the people and then began slipping away.

---

the reverse of *BMS* 9; the second is part of the concluding benediction of the prayer to Nabû from whose introduction we cited an example of the more usual order! For Marduk, see G. Wilhelm, *ZA* 69 (1979), 39: *ina qibīt* ^{d}*Marduk āšib Esağila u Bābili.*

The second stanza asserted that temple and human life were connected but conveyed this thought by means of an interlocking structure which could easily fly apart. The third stanza provides a climax and the poet's solution: the first stanza emphasized city and temple; the second, temple and human life; the third stanza serves both to broaden Marduk's focus of concern and action as well as to bring together again locality, temple, and human community—but this time on a higher level of generalization: Marduk is the supreme god; he takes care of the land and its people and is rewarded for this care. This is expressed clearly in the wording and structure of this last stanza. L. 7 is composed of two distinct halves and these two parallel each other:

7a. *ṣulūl māti*	Protection of the land,
7b. *gāmil nišī rapšāti*	Savior of the multitudes of people.

Ll. 8 and 9, for their part, also parallel each other:

8. *ušumgal kališ parakkī*	The single great one of chapels everywhere,
9. *šumka kališ ina pī nišī ṭāb*	Your name is sweetly hymned by the people everywhere.

What draws the stanza together and brings together the loose pieces of the poem is the relationship of l. 7 to ll. 8 and 9: each half of l. 7 stands in direct relation to one of the two following lines: 7a to 8, 7b to 9: he who covers the land (7a *ṣulūl māti*) attains dominion over all chapels therein (8 *ušumgal kališ parakkī*); he who saves the widespread people (7b *gāmil nišī rapšāti*) is joyfully praised by the people everywhere (9 *šumka kališ ina pī nišī ṭāb*).

Marduk is the shelter of the land and protector of the people; as his due for being caretaker of the land, he becomes the single great one of chapels everywhere; as his due for being the protector of the people, his name is lovingly hymned by people everywhere. A climax worthy of Marduk. Instead of living in only one temple and being a subordinate member of a group of gods, he has become master of all sanctuaries and the object of praise of diverse human constituencies. Marduk has changed, but always the new has been drawn back into an original if constantly widening circle of places, temples, and communities. True, he has had to extend his care to the whole land and to more and more people. The power to care derives from his place in the temple; but his desire to care may be motivated by the knowledge that in this way he will acquire more chapels and more veneration. In any case, Marduk has been provided with the elements that comprise the identity of a national god: land, people, residences, and service. One may even consider the possibility that what Marduk is to the gods in *Enūma Eliš*, he is to mankind in our hymn. But then there is the expected reversal: in *Enūma Eliš*, the gods receive *parakku*s in Babylon; in our hymn Marduk receives *parakku*s all over the land. He has been transformed into a great god who grants life and receives homage in return. And this thought, we shall see, is not restricted to the hymnic introduction; it is taken up and developed in later sections of the prayer.

II. In explicating the hymn, we discerned thematic and formal levels of expression and saw how the composer merged the various modes of expression to convey meaning. Not surprisingly, his art and thought extend beyond the hymn; especially in its later portions, the composition shows a number of innovations and forms a new structure.

Following the hymnic introduction, the remainder of the šuilla reads:[18]

10. ^{d}*Marduk bēlu rabû (ilu rēmēnû →*) Ø
11. *ina qibītika (kitti → kabitti →) ṣirti lubluṭ lušlimma*

[18] Phonetic variations and standard *attalû*-insertions (*BMS* 54:1′–4′, *PBS* I/2 108 obv. 1′–8′, Loretz and Mayer, *ŠU-ILA*, no. 27 obv. 11–14) are ignored. The few variants that require mention in the context of the present study are included in the transcription and discussed at appropriate places below. Contrary to the impression given by some editions, manuscripts are often internally consistent in their treatment of case endings; others represent definite stages of transition. I follow the MSS that have merged sing. nominative and accusative and have retained a separate genitive; the forms *qabâ* and *šemâ* are found even in those MSS that read *magāru* (*STT* I 55, *KAR* 23 + 25, *PBS* I/2 108). The claim that "in the literary dialect these CVC signs [*i.e.*, CVM] are used only for forms in which the /m/ ending is historically correct" (E. Reiner, *A Linguistic Analysis of Akkadian*, 60) requires modification in light of such writings as SIG_5-TIM (*KAR* 59) / MÍ.SIG_5-TIM (*KAR* 23 + 25) for *damiqtī* (accus. + 1. sing. poss. suff.; cf. SIG_5.MU [*STT* I 55]) in l. 16 and ZI-TIM (*BMS* 9, *PBS* I/2 108) for *napištī* (accus. + 1. sing. poss. suff.) in l. 22; cf. ZI-TIM-*ia* (*BMS* 9) / ZI-TIM-MU (*PBS* I/2 108) for *napištiya* (genit. + 1. sing. poss. suff.; cf. *na-piš-ti-ia* [*KAR* 23 + 25], ZI-*ti-ia* [*STT* I 55], ZI-*ia* [IV R^2 21*]) in l. 23.

12. *luštammar ilūtka*
13. *ēma uṣammaru lukšud*
14. *šuškin kittu ina pīya*
15. *šubši amāt damiqti ina libbiya*
16. *tīru u nanzāzu liqbû damiqtī*
17. *ilī lizziz ina imniya*
18. *ištarī lizziz ina šumēliya*
19. *ilu mušallimu idāya / ina idīya lū kayān*
20. *šurkamma qabâ šemâ u magāru*
21. *amāt aqabbû* (*kīma* →) *ēma aqabbû lū magrat*
22. ^{d}*Marduk bēlu rabû napištī qīša*
23. *balāṭ napištiya qibi*
24. *maḫarka namriš atalluka lušbi*
25. ^{d}*Enlil liḫdūka* ^{d}*Ea lirīška*
26. *ilū ša kiššati likrubūka*
27. *ilū rabûtu libbaka liṭibbū*

The text deviates from the norm and in so doing poses some difficulties of interpretation. The normal structure of a šuilla is a) introduction: hymn, b) body: prayer, c) conclusion: promise of thanksgiving or divine benediction.[19] In the main, our šuilla follows this form: it contains an introductory hymn (1–9), a prayer (13–21), and a concluding benediction (25–27). However, some elements are repeated and do not appear where expected. Thus in addition to the hymn, prayer, and benediction, the text also contains two other invocations (10; 22a), two other prayers (11; 22b–23), and two other concluding promises of thanksgiving or service (12[20]; 24). And the arrangement of these duplicate elements seems to give the text a somewhat confused and disjointed appearance: the second invocation (22a) appears after the main prayer and is separated from the hymnic introduction (1–9) and the first invocation (10);[21] the prayer in ll. 13–21 is separated from the prayer in l. 11 by a promise (12) and from the prayer in ll. 22b–23 by an invocation (22a); the first promise (12) appears surprisingly before the main prayer (13–21) and is separated from the second promise (24) and final benediction (25–27).[22] Furthermore, the prayer in ll. 13–21 seems to differ in tone and purpose from the prayer in ll. 11 and 22b–23: ll. 13–21 present a request for success; ll. 11 and 22b–23 contain the request for life itself. Even on formal grounds, the prayer in ll. 13–21 is set off from preceding and following sections. It begins and ends with a similar theme and identical words—*ēma uṣammaru lukšud . . . amāt aqabbû ēma* (←*kīma*) *aqabbû lū magrat*; these lines thus form a border and mark the outer limits of the segment.

Noting seemingly divergent themes and structural irregularities may on occasion lead to the identification of a new pattern. Such is the case here. The difficulties are the result of innovation. Although the text deviates from the usual liturgical pattern, it does not lack a meaningful order. We have here a new form, the recognition of which resolves the very difficulties which led to its recognition. Examining the list of difficulties, we note that the source of the formal and thematic incongruities is located in ll. 10–12 and 22–24. This is hardly fortuitous. Each of these sections constitutes a capsulated šuilla, and the two sections parallel each other to the extent even of playing on the same words and sharing identical forms:

Invocation: 10	22a
^{d}*Marduk bēlu rabû* (*ilu rēmēnû*)	^{d}*Marduk bēlu rabû*
Prayer for Life: 11	22b–23
ina qibītika kitti[23] *lubluṭ lušlimma*	*napištī qīša, balāṭ napištiya qibi*
Promise of Service: 12	24
luštammar ilūtka	*maḫarka namriš atalluka lušbi*

[19] See Kunstmann, *Gebetsbeschwörung*, 7–42.

[20] The occasional occurrence of a thanksgiving-formula in a prayer that concludes with a benediction is noted and l. 12 cited by Kunstmann, *Gebetsbeschwörung*, 40 and n. 4; cf. Mayer, *Untersuchungen*, 331 and n. 42 and 347f.

[21] The first invocation (10) is not cited here because it follows immediately upon the hymn.

[22] The second promise (24) is not cited here because it immediately precedes the benediction.

[23] On grounds of usage, *kitti* and *ṣirti* are to be preferred over *kabitti*. On the whole, *kitti* appears to be the original reading: a) whereas *ka-bit-ti* (IV R^2 21*) and *ṣir-ti* (*BMS* 9) are found only in Nineveh, *kit-ti* is found in MSS from Babylonia (*PBS* I/2 108; Loretz and Mayer, *ŠU-ILA*, no. 26: *kit-tú*), Aššur (*KAR* 59; *KAR* 23 + 25: *kit-*[*ti*]), Sultantepe (*STT* I 55), and Nineveh (*BMS* 54). b) It is easier to explain the development of *kabitti* from *kitti* than from *ṣirti*. Limiting ourselves to simple linear models, we suggest the development 1. *kitti* → 2. *kabitti* → 3. *ṣirti*: 1) *kitti* is chosen perhaps under the influence of *kittu* in l. 14. 2) *kit-ti* → *ka-bit-ti*: we note a) *qibītika* is written in several ways in our MSS including *qí-biti-ka* (*KAR* 23 + 25: [*q*]*í-biti-ka*; *STT* I 55: [*qí*]-*biti-ka*). The signs KIT and BIT are similar and can be identical in NB; and b) *ka* of *kabitti* is easily explained as a dittography of the suffix *-ka* of *qibīti-ka*. Accordingly, the

Each set of consecutive lines constitutes a summary statement. These statements, moreover, form discrete units and are set off from the introductory hymn and concluding benediction, on the one side, and the core prayer on the other. The structure of the text seems to be:

1–9	I	Introductory Hymn
10–12	A	Capsule Šuilla: a) invocation; b) prayer for life; c) promise
13–21	II	Prayer for Success
22–24	A′	Capsule Šuilla: a′) invocation; b′) prayer for life; c′) promise
25–27	III	Concluding Benediction

What seems to be emerging is a different šuilla design, a design created by the inclusion of two related summary statements of invocation, prayer, and thanksgiving, the first placed between the hymnic introduction and the prayer, the second between the prayer and the concluding benediction. We may account, then, for the present form of the text by assuming that the (original) prayer (13–21) was (secondarily) framed by two related summary statements.

But having recognized that ll. 10–12 and 22–24 form an envelope construction, we must still ask: Why were these summary statements included? This question gains in significance to the extent that the inclusion constitutes the creation of a new pattern or, at the very least, the use of an unconventional one. It may be easier to find an answer if the question is rephrased: What purpose do the summary statements serve? A partial answer is provided by the observation that the summary statements repeat the central thought of the hymn—the greatness of Marduk and the reciprocal relationship between the god and mankind. If anything, the summary seems to carry the thought even further; by the very baldness of its formulation, the summary articulates this thought in sharper terms and renders it more explicit than does the hymn itself:

O Marduk great lord,
By your affirmative decree may I live and be well,
I will then constantly praise your godhead (10–12)

O Marduk great lord,
Grant me my life; decree for me a healthy life,
In joyfully serving you regularly will I then find satisfaction. (22–24)

The summary links up with the hymn; one may even go so far as to state that each set of parallel lines of the summary statements corresponds to one of the three stanzas of the hymn:

Hymn		*Summary A*		*Summary A′*	
1–3	‖	10	‖	22a	the person of Marduk
4–6	‖	11	‖	22b–23	the granting of life (*balāṭu, napištu*) by Marduk
7–9	‖	12	‖	24	the praise of Marduk

The summary statements draw together the introductory hymn and the body of the prayer.

III. Lines 10–12 and 22–24 carry forward the thought of the hymn: Marduk is the great god who grants life and receives homage in return. These lines are important for the ideas they convey; they are no less important for the place they occupy in and the effect they have on the composition. They form a circle: on its inner side (12 + 22), this circle surrounds the core prayer—the center of the text (13–21); on its outer side (10 + 24), it runs along the inner border of the introductory hymn (1–9) and of the concluding benediction (25–27). The circle affects the meaning of the parts it touches and forms a bridge between the outer hymn and benediction and the inner prayer, thus drawing the parts of the composition together and creating a circular structure. For once the frame has

---

development *kitti* → *kabitti* requies only the repetition of *ka* and the misreading of *kit* as *bit*, perhaps under the influence of a preceding BIT: *qí-biti-ka ka-bit-ti*. 3) *kabitti* is hypercorrected to *ṣirti*. Note, however, that this reconstruction remains provisional; a final assessment must await the determination of the precise nature and direction of relation between our text and the genetically related Nabû šuilla *BMS* 22:1–29 and duplicates. Compare the variant readings *ina qibītika kitti/kabitti/ṣirti* of our text with the parallel lines (9f.) of the Nabû text: *ina amātika kitti ina siqrika kabitti ina qibītika rabīti*; if the Marduk composition is dependent on the Nabû one, our variants may reflect the break-up of a ἓν διὰ τριῶν and the preservation of its parts in different MSS; if, on the other hand, the Nabû composition is dependent on the Marduk one, the ἓν διὰ τριῶν may simply be the result of a conflation of several variants.

been set in place, the text no longer follows a linear design but is arranged concentrically. Ring composition becomes the architectonic principle of the text, and the world of gods and the world of men touch and interact where the movement inward from an outer divine orb and outward from a human center attain equilibrium and meet.

This characterization is in line with observations made in our analysis of the hymn and summary statements. 1. Cohesion and integrity. The hymn and the two summary statements parallel each other and share a common theme. Furthermore, each summary constitutes a miniature šuilla (invocation ‖ hymn; prayer ‖ prayer; promise ‖ benediction); by linking up with and recapitulating the crucial parts of the šuilla, each summary signals a joining together of the parts of the whole šuilla and suggests the notion of unity. 2. Circular structure: the introductory hymn (1–9) follows a concentric pattern. The same pattern obtains in the body of the šuilla (10–24) in that the summary statements form a frame around a core prayer (13–21) which itself begins and ends with a similar line (13:21). At this stage of exposition, however, the value of these earlier observations is presumptive not demonstrative. Thus for the above characterization to be more than just an assertion, we must now try to set out the structure in some detail and understand how it gives direction to the movement of ideas and shapes new images. We start at the center and work our way outwards. We begin by asking what is achieved by the innovative technique of constructing a frame and setting the core prayer within it. This question may be answered by forming some impression of the core prayer as an independent entity and then noticing the nature and consequence of the interaction of core and frame.

In ll. 13–21, the petitioner sets out his requests:

13. Whatsoever I seek may I attain,
14. Ordain (the response) 'done!' to my speech,
15. Fashion (the response) 'agreed!' to my thought,
16. May courtier and attendant seek agreement on my behalf,
17. May my god stand at my right,
18. May my goddess stand at my left,
19. May the guardian-deity be constantly at my side,
20. Grant me (the power) to speak, to be heard, and to meet with consent (so that)
21. Whatsoever words I utter may meet with consent.

Though not ordered sequentially, his wishes form more than just a random list of requests. The common concern is achievement and success. This text-segment conveys a picture of effective behavior, a picture which possesses scenic (though not yet dramatic) coherence. To what shall we ascribe the coherence? Certainly the existence of a common theme contributes to the creation of a structured scene, but if there were nothing more than this common theme, the text would probably just ramble and give the impression of discontinuity. Thus alongside a common theme there must be a structural principle giving form to the segment. The occurrence of a frame (10–12; 22–24) around the section, the similarity of the first and last lines (13:21) and their possession of features found nowhere else in the segment[24] suggest that even if there is a linear stanza arrangement we also have a concentric structure.

Support for seeing a concentric arrangement in our text is provided by the observation that ancient readers also seem to have understood the text in this way. This is suggested by two variants: line 10: ᵈ*Marduk bēlu rabû ilu rēmēnû* is read by all MSS except the *bīt mēseri* text IV R^2 21*, which deletes *ilu rēmēnû*; line 21: *amāt aqabbû kīma aqabbû* is read by all MSS except IV R^2 21* and Loretz and Mayer, *ŠU-ILA*, no. 26, which replaces *kīma* with *ēma*. The minority readings ᵈ*Marduk bēlu rabû* and *amāt aqabbû ēma aqabbû* are secondary. They reflect an attempt to harmonize, and thereby emphasize the relation of, the parallel lines 10 ‖ 22a and 13 ‖ 21: by the deletion of *ilu rēmēnû*, the invocation ᵈ*Marduk bēlu rabû* of l. 10 is rendered identical with the parallel invocation ᵈ*Marduk bēlu rabû* of l. 22;[25] by the replacement of *kīma* with *ēma*, the first (13) and last (21) lines of the core

[24] Subjunctive and first-person verb forms.

[25] I cannot exclude the possibility that the shorter form is due to haplography: . . . GAL<-*ú*/*u* DINGIR *réme*/*re-mé-nu*>-*ú*/*u*. The original, longer form of the line may derive from a prayer which begins with the invocation ᵈ*Marduk bēlu rabû ilu rēmēnû*. Note that a Marduk šuilla with this opening line is attested in all its occurrences immediately after our šuilla (cf. Kunstmann, *Gebetschwörung*, 95, no. 8; Mayer, *Untersuchungen*, 397, no. 18); in view of the observation made below that l. 10 is part of a written equivalent of a "presentation scene," see also the inscribed prayer cited below, n. 34.

prayer are rendered even more alike (*ēma uṣammaru . . . ēma aqabbû . . .*).

But however welcome such supporting testimony is, we need not rely on it, for the demonstration of concentric symmetry here is simple enough. If the text is unfolded from its outer edge inward and corresponding lines are placed alongside each other, corresponding lines are seen to be essentially identical in meaning and structure, and to parallel each other and form segments of the same circle.

13:21	*ēma uṣammaru lukšud*	:	*amāt aqabbû ēma* (←*kīma*) *aqabbû lū magrat*
14–15:20	*šuškin kittu ina pīya, šubši amāt damiqti ina libbiya*	:	*šurkamma qabâ šemâ u magāru*[26]
16:19	*tīru u nanzāzu liqbû damiqtī*	:	*ilu mušallimu idāya/ ina idīya lū kayān*
17:18	*ilī lizziz ina imniya*	:	*ištarī lizziz ina šumēliya*

An outer ring (13:21)[27] encircles an inner ring (14–15:20) which in turn encircles a chiastic staircase quatrain (16–19).[28] In ll. 13:21, the petitioner himself is the actor; in ll. 14–15:20, he shares the role of actor; in ll. 16–19, the role of actor is assumed by divine guardians. Ll. 17–18 form the actual center. Each line is more nearly identical with the other than are any other two adjoining or concentrically balanced lines. Jointly they share features with the two surrounding lines. *lizziz* of ll. 17–18 both draws on the same root as *nanzāzu* of l. 16 and concretizes and specifies the general and non-transitive *lū kayān* of l. 19. Ll. 16–19 are drawn together by these shared features and by the studied contrast of single members in ll. 17–18 with groups of two in ll. 16 and 19. Ll. 17–18 have single subjects and single indirect/locative objects, while l. 16 has two subjects and l. 19 has a dual indirect/locative object:

tīru u nanzāzu		*liqbû damiqtī*
ilī	*lizziz ina imniya*	
ištarī	*lizziz ina šumēliya*	
ilu mušallimu	*ina idīya* / *idāya*	*lū kayān*

Ll. 17–18 separate entities which appear in groups of two in ll. 16 and 19: *ilī* and *ištarī* (17–18) individualize (and define the divine nature of[29]) the preceding *tīru u nanzāzu* (16), and *ina imniya* and *ina šumēliya* (17–18) split *idāya* (19) into its two component parts. By associating each of the "sides" with a single god, the subsequent joining of the two sides in the dual *idāya* then allows and renders credible the merging of the individual *ilu* and *ištaru* into the group concept *ilu mušallimu* in a picture which would be spatially impossible—*ilu mušallimu idāya lū kayān*—were the speaker (and the modern reader) not caught up in the transformation. Fused together in this way, ll. 16–19

---

[26] Note that all finite verb forms in ll. 14–15 and 20 begin with /š/: *šuškin, šubši, šurkamma.*

[27] Various translators (Landsberger, *Textbuch*[1], 102 and *Textbuch*[2], 308; von Soden, *SAHG*, 298; Seux, *Hymnes*, 291; and Mayer, *Untersuchungen*, 348) separate l. 13 from l. 14 and connect it to l. 12. However, the concentric structure of ll. 13–21, the parallelism of ll. 13 and 21, the fact that l. 12 constitutes a promise and forms a proper ending of the statement ll. 10–12, and the parallelism of ll. 12 and 24 all indicate that l. 13 is joined to l. 14ff. Furthermore, an occurrence such as Ebeling, *AGH*, 62:37a does not contradict —rather it seems to confirm—this conclusion. This Ištar šuilla (*AGH*, 60–63) also contains a line identical with our l. 21: 34 (...) 37a: *amāt aqabbû kīma aqabbû lū magrat* (...) *ēma uṣammaru lukšud.* The composer of this šuilla has reversed the order of lines identical with the opening and closing lines of our core prayer. This reversal indicates, I believe, that ll. 13 and 21 belong together and form a single circle and that the circle may be rotated 180°. This Ištar šuilla also contains promise and benediction and displays some affinity with the Marduk šuilla.

[28] The connection of l. 16 with l. 19 and the unity of ll. 16–19 are underscored by such a passage as Ebeling, *AGH*, 22:5–8: *ilī lizziz ina imniya, ištarī lizziz ina šumēliya, ilu mušallimu ina idīya lū kayān, tīru manzāzu liqbû damiqtī.*

[29] A decision whether the *tīru* and *nanzāzu* refer to palace officials or to divine figures is not cut and dry: note, for example, that Landsberger treated them as "untergeordnete Götter" in the first edition of *Textbuch* (102 n. 1), but as "Palastbeamte" in the second edition (308 n. 1). I prefer the former characterization; cf. Mayer, *Untersuchungen*, 255 n. 56: "Da dieser Wunsch [*i.e.*, *tīru u nanzāzu liqbû damiqtī*] jeweils neben Bitten steht, die sich auf 'Schutzgeister' beziehen . . . , hat man vermutet, *tīru* und *nanzāzu* seien hier ebenfalls der Kategorie der Schutzgottheiten zuzurechnen. . . . Wenn das zutrifft, wäre hier das Modell des königlichen Hofstaates auf die Welt der Götter übertragen."

form a scene of divine guardians surrounding a petitioner on all sides.[30]

The core prayer may be diagrammed as follows:

13 21
14–15 20
16 19
17–18

This analysis of ll. 13–21 is confirmed by the grammatical structure of the segment. Note especially that every line contains a form of the "volitive" mood; the concentric structure finds expression in the pattern of distribution of precatives and imperatives.

13:21	*lukšud*	: *lū magrat*	precative *lu-*/*lū*
14–15:20	*šuškin, šubši*	: *šurkamma*	imperative
16:19	*liqbû*	: *lū kayān*	precative *li-*/*lū*
17:18	*lizziz*	: *lizziz*	precative *li-*[31]

13 *luprus* *lū parsat* 21[32]
14–15 *purus* *purus* 20
16 *liprus* *lū parrās* 19
17 *liprus* *liprus* 18

The use of the techniques of ring composition and hysteron proteron result in the creation of a concentrically symmetrical form. Circles are balanced in an inverted order around a still point, and our attention is directed first inward toward the center and then back to the border (13:21) and beyond, to lines 10–12 and 22–24. Around the prayer, ll. 10–12 and 22–24 form a further circle. This outer frame accentuates the concentric structure of the core prayer. It also changes the meaning of the prayer for success and itself receives a definite setting. In ll. 10–12 and 22–24, a suppliant petitions Marduk for the gift of life. In this setting, the core prayer is transformed into a request for the kind of assistance, skills, and reception that the suppliant imagines he needs to present his petition effectively and to be granted whatever he asks for; a prayer for mundane success becomes a prayer that prepares the suppliant for a successful audience with Marduk. What previously only possessed scenic coherence now possesses dramatic coherence. From being a snapshot, the core prayer is transformed into a story, a description of movement toward a journey's end. The meeting of petitioner and god is that end, and this meeting takes the form of the petitioner's address to Marduk in ll. 10–12 and 22–24.

By joining together 1) scenes of meeting and addressing Marduk (10–12 : 22–24) with 2) those of preparation and introduction (13–21), the composer creates a scene comparable to the "presentation scene"[33] so often represented on cylinder seals, and it is hardly a coincidence that the most common and basic wish expressed in prayers engraved on Cassite seals is the wish for a long life.[34] We now have a scene with a frame and an apex. The frame—10–12 : 22–24—represents both culmination and context, and the apex—16–19—represents the point from which the action moves. The petitioner asks that protective, minor gods accompany him and speak well of him to the god (16–19), that he himself be granted the ability of being able to address the god convincingly (14–15 : 20), and that whatever he requests from the god be granted him (13:21). Standing before Marduk and surrounded by his gods, he then presents his petition (10–12 : 22–24): he addresses Marduk respectfully, as a loyal subject addresses his overlord (10:22a); he asks Marduk to grant him the boon of life (11:22b–23); and he declares his personal allegiance to Marduk and his desire to continue serving the god faithfully (12:24).

Minor gods give way to the great god; intimacy with interceding guardians is replaced by the feeling

---

[30] Note that a verbal strand seems to run through our passage; . . .*kittu* (14) . . .*amāt damiqti* (15) . . .*liqbû damiqtī* (16) . . . *kayān* (19) . . . *qabâ* (20) . . . *amāt aqabbû* . . . *aqabbû* (21) . . . .

[31] For other grammatical features that are shared by corresponding lines, note 13:21: conjunction + 1st pers. subjunctive verb form and 17:18: preposition + noun + 1 sing. poss. suff.

[32] Note the gradual loosening of grammatical structure: *lu-* ... *li-*... *li-*... *li-*... *lū* + masc. absol.... *lū* + fem. absol. It almost appears as if each side is building up one difference: 17–13: *u* (*li-* → *lu-*), 18–21: independent form (*li-* → *lū* + predicative stative); the segment would thus form a circle that begins and ends with *lu-*/*lū* + (13/21).

[33] Cf. the characterization of this scene by H. A. Groenewegen-Frankfort, *Arrest and Movement*, 166.

[34] Cf. H. Limet, *Les légendes des sceaux cassites*, 46; furthermore, compare ll. 10–12 with such inscribed prayers as Limet, *Légendes*, 83, no. 6.5. (As an aside, note that *a-mi-ri* of 95, no. 7.9:2 does not refer back to Marduk; it is the subject of the following *liqbi*: "May the one who beholds me speak well of me.")

of majesty and the call to praise that Marduk inspires. The suppliant has drawn near to Marduk and asked for life. We witness the direct meeting of man and god. But now we have reached the introductory hymn (1–9) and concluding benediction (25–27) and the god disengages and draws away. The conflict between divine involvement and separateness is recognized and resolved. The distancing allows man and god to retain their separate identities and thus preserves the possibility of an ongoing relationship. However much Marduk cares for man, he is finally a member of a different community. At the moment of direct contact, the text looks outward and beyond the world of man and reasserts the god's divine nature.

The first-person voice of the suppliant is silenced. The introduction and conclusion present Marduk's withdrawal from man and his reentry into the world of the gods. Human praise gives way to divine praise in hymn and benediction. The praise of the individual man in ll. 10–12 is replaced with that of mankind in general. Marduk then draws back from caring for and being praised by men everywhere (7–9) and turns first to his cities Borsippa and Babylon (4–6) and returns finally to his family and home in Eridu (1–3). Care of the god and the joy man feels in his service (22–24) are replaced by the joy Marduk feels when he returns to his own world and receives the greeting and praise of Enlil and Ea, the gods of the heaven and the abyss (25), of the gods of the universe (26), and of the great gods (27).

Forming the outer ring, hymn and benediction, though internally concentric, stand in parallel symmetry to each other, a symmetry best exemplified by shared words:[35]

1–3 ‖ 25	^d^*Marduk...murīš E*ᵓ*engura* (3); ...^d^*Ea lirīška* (25)
4–6 ‖ 26[36]	
7–9 ‖ 27	*šumka...ina pī nišī ṭāb* (9); *ilū rabûtu libbaka liṭibbū* (27)[37]

Moving from the center, we have made our way to the outer edge of the composition. The following diagram sets out in schematic form the structure of the text and may serve to summarize and conclude this last portion of our exposition:

					lines
	1				1–3
Hymn	A 2				4–6
	3				7–9
		1			10
Meeting with Marduk		B 2			11
		3			12
			1		13
			2		14–15
			3		16
Preparation for meeting			C	X	17–18
			3′		19
			2′		20
			1′		21
		1′			22a
Meeting with Marduk		B′ 2′			22b–23
		3′			24
	1′				25
Benediction	A′ 2′				26
	3′				27

The way we chose to study the Marduk šuilla was determined, in the first instance, by several difficulties which we encountered in the text itself, and this approach has served us well. But there is more than one way of reading a text, and much has also been left unsaid. Our composition, as we have noted, has a form different from most other šuillas. Precisely because we have eschewed historical questions and modes of inquiry and have treated the composition as an independent creation, it is necessary to remark at this point that our study also suggests that the composition did not stand in isolation. Some of the compositional features that characterize our text and distinguish it from other šuillas are also found in various degrees of development in prayers to other members of Marduk's circle.[38] The composition, moreover, is genetically related to the Nabû šuilla *BMS* 22 : 1–29.[39] The Marduk šuilla was composed, I should guess, sometime before the reign of Adad-

[35] What looks like a standard benediction is only one variation among many (see Mayer, *Untersuchungen*, 336f.); if it is granted that intention and choice played some part in the formulation, then the connections between hymn and benediction are all the more striking.

[36] The parallelism of ll. 4–6 and 26 is posited for systematic reasons; I am unable to isolate specific points of contact between ll. 4–6 and 26.

[37] Cf. ll. 14–15: . . . *ina pīya*, . . . *ina libbiya*.

[38] Cf. Ebeling, *AGH*, 60ff.; 68ff.; 106ff.

[39] See Kunstmann, *Gebetsbeschwörung*, 99 s. Nabû 2: "Stilistisch auf das engste verwandt mit dem Gebete Marduk 2." For a new edition, see Mayer, *Untersuchungen*, 473–75.

apla-iddina; it appears to have been a product of a theological and literary movement that centered around the figure of Marduk. Such questions, though, are best left for another occasion; here, we must be satisfied with having recovered an aspect of the form and a fragment of the meaning of a prayer.*

* I have enjoyed conversations with M. Brettler, S. Kaufman, W. L. Moran, and P. Stark on various aspects of the text.

ETHNOPOETRY AND THE ENMERKAR EPICS

ADELE BERLIN
UNIVERSITY OF MARYLAND

AS A FORMER STUDENT OF PROFESSOR SAMUEL NOAH KRAMER, under whose guidance I first read Sumerian epics, it is a privilege and pleasure to offer here a paper which continues his tradition of comparative studies of epic literature.[1] It is limited to a discussion of the tales of Enmerkar and Lugalbanda, and addresses itself to ways of viewing these tales from a folkloristic perspective.

Little is known about the origin of the Sumerian epics. An oral stage is assumed, in conformity with current views in comparative literature, but, of course, this is not recoverable.[2] Our only knowledge of the epics comes from written texts. There are hints of a written epic tradition from as early as the Fara Period,[3] but it is not until the Ur III Period that we find clear evidence of a heroic epic tradition. Furthermore, as has often been noted, the early rulers of Ur III, Urnammu and Shulgi, themselves claim kinship with the ancient heroes of Uruk who are the epic heroes.[4]

What is the significance of this claim? Since there is a strong likelihood that Urnammu was actually a native of Uruk, Sumerologists often assume that the epics were preserved (or composed—at any rate, took written form) because of Urnammu's personal origin. That is to say, had it not been for this link with Uruk, these epics would not have been preserved; and conversely, there may have been cycles of other cities which were not preserved because the Ur III rulers had no attachments to these cities. This position is stated most unambiguously by J. Renger: "The . . . heroic epics of Enmerkar and Lugalbanda owe their continuing existence to the fact that . . . the Third Dynasty of Ur originated in Uruk, the city of these epic rulers."[5] But this is putting the cart before the horse. It seems more reasonable that the Ur III rulers, whether or not they had actual ties to Uruk, claimed Uruk origins because of the existence and acceptance of the epics. First of all, the epics do not preserve local traditions, as Renger suggests. With the exception of *Gilgamesh and Agga*, none of them depicts local rivalries, but rather they show Uruk opposed to a foreign enemy. They are thus implicitly nationalistic, in a broad sense, with Uruk symbolizing the entire nation (as will be discussed below). One need not hail from Uruk in order to identify with its past.

Uruk as a symbol of national supremacy was reinforced by historical events closer to the time of Ur III; the overthrow of the Gutians and the re-establishment of Sumerian hegemony is credited to Utuhegal of Uruk (Dynasty V). Thus Uruk became a paradigm of Sumerian national strength, and its ancient heroes

---

[1] "Heroes of Sumer: A New Heroic Age in World History and Literature," *PAPS* 90 (1946), 120–30; "Sumerian Epic Literature," *La Poesia Epica e la sua Formazione*, 1970, 825–37.

[2] On the oral composition of Sumerian literature see B. Alster, *Dumuzi's Dream*, 1971, 15–27; W. Millar, "Oral Poetry and *Dumuzi's Dream*" in *Scripture in Context: Essays in the Comparative Method*, 1980, 27–57; V. Afanasjeva, "Mündlich Überlieferte Dichtung ('Oral Poetry') und schriftliche Literatur in Mesopotamien," *Acta Antiqua* 22 (1974), 121–35; J. Laessøe, "Literacy and Oral Tradition in Ancient Mesopotamia," *Studia Orientalia Ioanni Pedersen . . . Dicata*, 1953, 205–18.

Earlier theories of oral composition are coming under criticism; cf. R. Finnegan, *Oral Poetry*, 1977, 68–72; G. S. Kirk, *Homer and the Oral Tradition* 1976, 113–28; J. A. Russo, "Is 'Oral' or 'Aural' Composition the Cause of Homer's Formulaic Style" in *Oral Literature and the Formula*, 1976, 31–71; D. Bynum, *The Daemon in the Wood: A Study of Oral Narrative Patterns*, 1978.

[3] Cf. J. D. Bing, "Gilgamesh and Lugalbanda in the Fara Period," *JANES* 9 (1977), 1–4.

[4] References are found in J. Klein, "Šulgi and Gilgameš: Two Brother Peers (Šulgi O)," *Kramer Anniversary Volume* [*AOAT* 25], 1976, 271 note 1.

[5] "Mesopotamian Epic Literature," *Heroic Epic and Saga* 1978, 28. Cf. also C. Wilcke, *Das Lugalbandaepos*, 1969, 1.

paradigms of national leaders. By claiming kinship with Lugalbanda and Gilgamesh, Urnammu and Shulgi were doing more than proving they were the legitimate successors of Utuhegal (whom Urnammu overthrew); they were viewing themselves as the spiritual heirs to the ancient rulers of Uruk, i.e., embodiments of traditional leadership *par excellence* (regardless of Urnammu's actual lineage).[6] Theirs was a time of extraordinary nationalism, and they called upon the epic tradition to promote it. The epics continued to be preserved, not because they record the lives of actual forebearers of Ur III kings, or historical events, but because they are an expression of national aspirations.

EPIC AND ITS SUB-TYPES. In a systematic description of ethnopoetic genres,[7] which I use as a model for this study, Heda Jason discusses the characteristics of the epic genre and outlines several sub-genres. Her main sub-genres are mythic epic (positive forces struggle with negative forces in the creation of the world order), carnavalesque epic (a kind of parody of the epic), and heroic epic (which tells of a struggle against a family, tribal, or national enemy, real or fabulous). Heroic epic, which is our concern here, has several sub-types: historical epic, national epic, and universal epic. A final subdivision is romantic epic, which may be classed as a sub-group of either historical or national epic. The components of the epic genre would be thus diagrammed as follows:

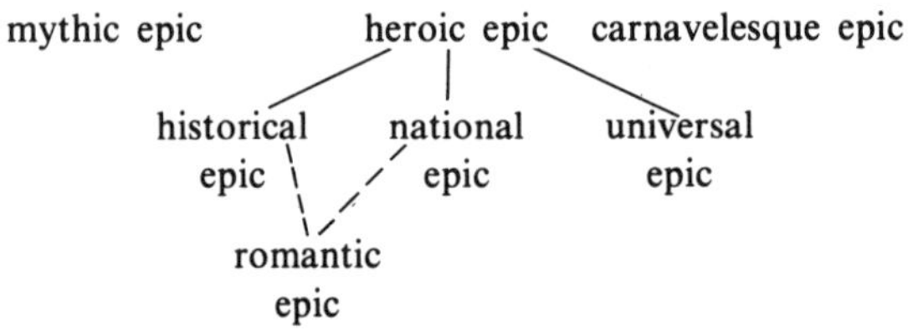

While all heroic epic involves a struggle of significant proportions, its sub-types are distinguished in the following manner:

In *historical epic* "historic or pseudo-historic personages act, and real particular historic events may be described. The themes . . . are struggles against family and national enemies, but the details have no broad symbolic value" (31).

In *national epic* "the characters and events are poetic generalizations of a nation and its enemies, and the struggle between the two. This epic describes typical symbolic events and personages, and not historical particulars. Its theme is the national struggle as a whole" (31).

In *universal epic* "the hero represents . . . humanity as a whole, and is supported by sacred and mythic forces in his struggle with monstrous remnants of mythic hostile forces. The hero himself is of half divine parentage. In this group of epics the mythic world is finally overcome by man" (31).

"*Romantic epic* tells about wooing a bride, or about couples separated by an enemy and reunited after heroic exploits of the husband. The enemy may be real . . . or a fabulous being. Here many fairy tale, novella, and legend plots may be utilized" (31).

A work is assigned to its genre primarily on the basis of the mode in which it is written. By mode Jason means "man's relation to his world as it is manifested in ethnopoetic work" (17). Three modes are distinguished: the realistic, the fabulous, and the symbolic. The realistic mode is centered on humans in the real world. Relations among fellow humans dominate, and no forces outside the human world interfere with human affairs. The only power is that of human strength and morality. In the fabulous mode "man confronts various worlds of the fantastic" (18). This mode may contain numinous or marvelous elements—it is a spiritual or fairy tale world. In the symbolic mode the entities "have no properties at all and are used as symbols of properties of real entities" (25–6). While heroic epic is, in general, set in the realistic mode (18), it may include fabulous and symbolic elements (31). Actually, as we shall see, not all types of heroic epic are equally realistic. Romantic epic comes closest to being in the fabulous mode.[8]

---

[6] The political motive of claiming legitimacy has been recognized by others, e.g. Klein, *loc cit.*; D. O. Edzard in *The Near East: The Early Civilizations* 1967, 135; W. W. Hallo, "The Coronation of Ur-Nammu," *JCS* 20 (1966), 137. I appreciate the rulers' personal political motivation, but see ramifications far beyond this.

[7] *Ethnopoetry*, 1977. Page numbers cited throughout refer to this work. The terminology which Jason has developed can be found in concise form in *Ethnopoetics, A Multilingual Terminology*, 1975. Her approach was outlined in "A Multidimensional Approach to Oral Literature," *Current Anthropology* 10 (1969), 413–26. Also of interest are "The Story of David and Goliath: A Folk Epic?" *Biblica* 60 (1979), 36–70, and "The Poor Man of Nippur: An Ethnopoetic Analysis," *JCS* 31 (1979), 189–215.

[8] Jason's chart (51) places romantic epic in the fabulous-marvelous mode [the chart erroneously reads "miraculous"].

We turn now to the Enmerkar and Lugalbanda epics of Sumer: *Enmerkar and the Lord of Aratta* (ELA), *Enmerkar and Ensuhkešdanna* (EE), *The Lugalbanda Epic* (LB), and *Lugalbanda-Hurrum* (LH).[9] The main theme of ELA concerns relations between man and his fellow man (the enemy). The power of the hero comes not from superior strength, but from his cleverness. The general tone of ELA places it well within the realistic mode, in which man confronts man on the human level. It is clearly a heroic epic, and can further be designated as a national epic, as opposed to a historical epic, for although there may be a historical kernel of truth behind the plot, it would be straining credibility to suggest that such a contest of wits as is described actually occurred. The events, and quite possibly the characters—especially in light of the fact that the lord of Aratta is not named—are poetic generalizations of a nation and its enemy.[10]

The mode of EE is somewhat difficult to ascertain. It seems to be basically in the realistic mode, but has more intrusions from the marvelous than the other three epics (see note 8). It contains talking animals and a transformation combat. Marvelous helpers, a sorcerer and a sorceress, intervene on behalf of human rivals, and the issue between them is decided through magic. The plot indicates that this is a romantic epic, since it involves the wooing of a bride (in this case the goddess Inanna). It is not surprising that EE sounds like a fairy tale, for romantic epic is close to heroic fairy tale.[11]

In LB the realistic mode predominates, with some elements of the marvelous being present. The hero, Lugalbanda, obtains superhuman swiftness and endurance from the Anzu-bird (a mythical or marvelous creature), which later enables him to go alone on a dangerous journey in order to obtain aid from the goddess Inanna for Enmerkar and the army of Uruk. LB seems to be a national epic: It is the need of the nation in its struggle against its enemy which forms the background and motivates the plot, even though the interest in the conflict is subordinated to the interest in the hero, Lugalbanda, who never engages in direct combat with the enemy. As in the *Chanson de Roland*, the action focuses on events outside of the main campaign.

The plot of LH has similarities to that of LB. Lugalbanda sets out with Enmerkar's army to conquer Aratta, falls ill on the way, and is left for dead by his comrades. He revives, prays to the gods, and is restored to health. The dream which follows, and the subsequent offerings to various deities, seem quite realistic. I would tentatively classify this text as in the realistic mode (based on incomplete knowledge of the text and the fact that its end is not preserved). LH also seems to be a national epic, similar to (if not actually part of) LB.

Mode, the relationship which pertains between man and his world, is an important indicator of ethnopoetic genre. At least three of the texts examined here were found to be in the realistic mode—the expected mode for epics. The fourth text, EE, may be either realistic or marvelous. Its mode, along with its plot, point to the fact that it is a romantic epic, a sub-group of national or historical epic. The others are national epics, since they depict a national struggle in supernatural proportions, not strictly adhering to actual historical events. Thus all of the Enmerkar-Lugalbanda epics can be said to be, at this point in our analysis, national epics. This will be confirmed in the analysis of the contentual aspect. Not all Sumerian epics are national epics, however. The Gilgamesh epics, with the exception of *Gilgamesh and Agga*, lack the background of a national struggle and reflect more universal concerns of mankind battling against the forces of evil or mythical forces. This suggests that they are universal epics. Perhaps this explains why Gilgamesh

---

But in *Ethnopoetics, A Multilingual Terminology*, 50, she states that romantic epic is in the realistic mode.

[9] Textual editions of ELA, EE, and LB are as follows: S. Cohen, *Enmerkar and the Lord of Aratta* (Dissertation, Univ. of Pennsylvania, 1973); A. Berlin, *Enmerkar and Ensuhkešdanna, A Sumerian Narrative Poem*, 1979; C. Wilcke, *Das Lugalbandaepos*, 1969. Plot summaries are found in S. N. Kramer, *The Sumerians*, 1963, 269–75; *La Poesia*, 825–28; C. Wilcke, "Sumerische Epen," *Kindlers Literatur Lexikon*, VI, 2111–15. J. Renger in *Heroic Epic and Saga*, 28–32 summarizes only "The Enmerkar Epic" (ELA) and "The Lugalbanda Epic" (LB).

[10] I am not suggesting that Enmerkar did not really exist, but that here he is serving a supra-historical role. He appears not as his historical self, but as a generalized hero of Uruk. Cf. B. Alster, "The Paradigmatic Character of Mesopotamian Heroes," *RA* 68 (1974), 50.

[11] Romantic epic and heroic fairy tale have much in common. For a more detailed comparison of the two see Jason, *Biblica* 60 (1979), especially 61–5. See also A. E. Alexander, *Bylina and Fairy Tale, The Origins of Russian Heroic Poetry*, 1973.

found his way into later, non-Sumerian epics, while Enmerkar and Lugalbanda did not. Gilgamesh, from the outset, lent himself to more universal concerns than did the other heroes of Uruk.

NARRATIVE STRUCTURE. The narrative structure refers to the patterning of the plot and is independent of the texture of the work. One of the most general levels of structural analysis seems to be that of V. Propp. Originally developed for Russian fairy tales, it has been successfully applied to a wide variety of non-Russian and non-fairy tale compositions.[12] H. Limet has analyzed the structure of some of the Sumerian epics and found that they correspond to Propp's model.[13]

For a more specific group of texts, including some Sumerian, Akkadian, Hittite, Indian, and Russian epics, Jason has worked out a proposed structural model for an epic struggle.[14] The central theme of these texts is the struggle of a deity, or of a part-human, part-divine hero against a monster. Although the theme is the combat of a hero against a monster, Jason generalizes: "the core model is the struggle between hero and adversary,"[15] and is thus able to include epics concerning human rivals, such as *Gilgamesh and Agga.* Jason does not mention the Enmerkar-Lugalbanda epics, but it seems likely that this model fits at least some of them. It is not my intention to analyze the whole model, or to do a proper structural analysis of the Enmerkar-Lugalbanda texts. I will merely list the functions of the model that clearly fit ELA and EE. None of Jason's texts contain all of the functions, as the model is a composite of the functions of many texts, but it is apparent from a cursory glance that ELA and EE contain enough functions to be "epic struggle" texts. It is not immediately apparent whether LB and LH do also. The functions (and the numbers assigned to them by Jason) that are of most interest are:

3. Either the hero or the adversary may take the initiative against the other
4. Adversary demands surrender from community
5. The community responds—it may be either willing or unwilling to surrender
6. The summoning of a messenger
7. Hero asks permission from the community or a helper to oppose adversary
8. The community or helper advise either to oppose or not to oppose
9. Hero either accepts or does not accept advice
13. Hero prepares for encounter with adversary
14. First encounter—hero (or adversary) attacks adversary (or hero)
15. Adversary defeats hero
16. Hero/community takes council against adversary
17. Hero sends for help (through messenger B)
18. Messenger B/community summons help from helper/hero
19. Helper extends help to hero
20. Hero and helper attack adversary
21. Hero and helper overcome adversary
22. Triumph—community grants triumph to hero (or does not grant triumph).

Of interest to Sumerologists in this model are the dominant roles of messengers and community counsel, which, as can be seen in this context, are not peculiarities of Sumerian society, but functions of stories of epic struggles.

CONTENTUAL ASPECT. The contentual aspect deals with contentual terms, which are the distinctive elements or attributes of the content. Jason classifies them as anthropomorphic terms, zoomorphic terms, spatial dimension, and temporal dimension. I will discuss only selected parts of these four terms.

A. Anthropomorphic Terms: attributes of human characters.

1. *Physical appearance.* There is almost a total lack of physical description of human characters in these epics. We have no idea of the appearance of Enmerkar, Lugalbanda, or anyone else. When a person is described, it is in terms of actions of which he is either the performer or the recipient. For example, messengers are described as running like birds or fleet animals. The sick Lugalbanda is unable to eat fat and cheese (LB 229–230). The hero may be described in terms of the favors shown to him by deities (e.g. EE 91ff.). The most "heroic" description is that of Enmerkar given by the messenger to the lord of Aratta: "My king who is fit for lordship from his birth, The

[12] This has been possible in part due to a mistranslation of one of Propp's terms. On this see H. Jason and D. Segal, *Patterns in Oral Literature*, 1977, 313–20.

[13] "Les chants épiques sumériens," *Revue belge de philologie et d'histoire* 3 (1972), 3–24.

[14] "Ilja of Murom and Tzar Kalin. A Proposal for a Model for the Narrative Structure of an Epic Struggle," *Slavica Hierosolymitana*, V-VI (1981) 47–55.

[15] *Ibid.*, 48.

lord of Uruk, the *sagkal*-dragon living in Sumer, who pulverizes mountains like flour, The stag of the tall mountains endowed with lordly antlers, (Beautiful as) the mother-goat (after) being cleansed with soap and plucked, Whom the 'unfailing cow' had given birth to in the very highland" (ELA 180–184). This may be not so much an epic description as part of the protocol which preceded the actual message. And even here the description is in terms of action. Also described are reactions or emotional states, for example, the confusion of the sorcerer (EE 248), the depression of the lord (ELA 236) and his elation when he finds a fitting reply (ELA 239–241). Arrivals always seem to be happy (ELA 299, 417, LB 346).

One expects an epic hero to be of great physical strength, but this is not so in these works. Enmerkar's prowess lies in sending and answering verbal challenges and outwitting his opponent. Lugalbanda does possess superior physical abilities, but only insofar as they enable him to traverse the distance from Aratta to Uruk. In fact, to the extent that there is description of humans, most of it is lavished on the messenger and not the hero.[16]

The Sumerian poets were not incapable of physical description. It does occur in reference to deities, fabulous beings, and cities. For example, Inanna has mascara-ed eyes, a white garment, a shining tiara (ELA 590ff.); Anzu's body is described in detail (LB 120–124). The magnificence of Uruk is told at the beginning of ELA and EE, and that of Aratta is found at the end of LB.

2. *Distribution of the anthropomorphous terms.* In historical and national epics, according to Jason (141), the hero and his adversary are human. Numinous beings may take part, in secondary roles. The gods are the numinous beings in the Sumerian epics, and they clearly have secondary roles. In universal and romantic epics the hero is human; the adversary and/or princess to be won are mythic or marvelous beings. This is the case in EE, where the "princess" is the goddess Inanna. (And compare Huwawa, the adversary in the universal epic, *Gilgamesh and Huwawa.*)

3. *Fabulous beings.* "The epic is an exceptional genre in that it does not possess its own class of fabulous beings but uses beings from other genres. The epic uses both marvelous and numinous beings of all sorts.[17] In historical and national epics all of them play a secondary role, participating in conflicts which are wholly human. They act as helpers of humans who are the principal actors" (156). What could better describe our compositions with helpers like the Anzu-bird (LB) and a sorcerer and sorceress (EE). The gods also serve as helpers.

B. Zoomorphic Terms: attributes relating to animal characters.

As in the case of anthropomorphous beings, epics may contain both realistic and fabulous animals. The Sumerian epics lack the most common epic animal, the hero's horse, which had not yet been domesticated. They do feature a number of fabulous animals. In LB there is the Anzu-bird and its young. In EE there are talking cows and sheep, and a series of domestic and wild animals produced by a magic transformation. Domestic and wild animals are often opposed to each other in various genres, and usually the domestic are "ours" and the wild are "theirs" (163). In EE the reverse is true; the wild animals are produced by the representative of Uruk, and are the natural predators of the opponent's domestic animals. The seizing of the domestic animals by the wild signals the winning of the transformation combat.

C. Spatial Dimension.

Jason has organized the locations in which different genres are staged into a spatial model of concentric circles radiating out from the narrator. The closest is "our settlement," the immediate surroundings of the narrating community, known in detail by all. "Our district" is the district in which "our settlement" is located. It reaches as far as most members of the community travel in their everyday lives (e.g. to market, to a local shrine). Places and distances within it are known here, too. A more abstract spatial location is "our country." The natural and social order of

---

[16] Cf. ELA 106ff., 156ff., 297ff., 348ff., 413ff., 507ff., EE 40–52.

[17] It is not a question of these elements having been added to a historical core, as one might conclude from Kramer's statement that "the poet does not hesitate to introduce fanciful, folkloristic motifs that can have no basis in historical fact" (*La Poesia*, 831). These elements are indigenous to the epic genre. In fact, the process has been shown to be the reverse, at least in Russian epics, by A. Alexander, who concludes that "The epic event appears to be not a distortion of a historical event, but rather an analogue of a fairy tale event" (*Bylina and Fairy Tale*, 85). He explains earlier that "Historical personal names and place names are present in the *byliny*, but the epic action appears to follow that of the fairy tale rather than history" (*ibid.*, 67).

"our country" is similar to "our settlement," and it is perceived as a more or less uniform area; real settlements within it and distances between them are not known or remain vague. "This world" includes the rest of the human world. "The afterworld" is the area where the souls of the deceased exist. Deities may also live here. "The in-between space" is the area between the human world and the afterworld. Fairy tales take place here; it is the abode of fabulous beings. In addition to these areas there are symbolic locations which may occur in "our country," "this world," or "the in-between space." Symbolic locations may be real or imaginary, but are not normally visited by members of the narrating community. For example, Kiev symbolizes Russia in the *bylina*, but the peasants from northern Russia who have preserved the *bylina* have never been there.

Heroic epic is staged in "our country," an area of settlements with indefinite space between them (197). Real distances between settlements are ignored, so that even in the realistic mode characters can hop from one to another without much concern for geography. In most epics "our country" is opposed to "their country," and the hero travels back and forth between the two.

In the Enmerkar-Lugalbanda epics Uruk seems to function both as "our settlement" and as a symbol for "our country." Opposing it is the enemy's settlement/country, Aratta. Various other geographic locations—cities, mountains, and rivers —are mentioned in the epics; S. Cohen has listed them and identified most of them.[18] From a folkloristic point of view it would be interesting to see how these locations fit into the spatial world of the epics. Discretion should be used when one seeks geographic information from epics, since they do not always correspond to physical reality. For example, the epic tradition knows where Aratta is and what it looks like; but it is doubtful if members of the Sumerian narrating community had ever been there. In the case of Aratta we have, so far, only literary references; the name has yet to appear in an economic, administrative, or geographic document.[19] It may, indeed, have been a real city in the vicinity of Hamadan,[20] but in the epics it functions symbolically, as enemy territory, rather than realistically.[21]

In most epics, the plot is staged in "our country"—the enemy comes and attacks it and is fought against. Rarer are instances where "our" heroes go to the enemy's country (198). The Sumerian epics are in the minority in this matter. Enmerkar initiates the sending of messages to Aratta in ELA. In LB the Urukians are besieging Aratta, instead of the reverse. However, in EE Ensuḫkešdanna, the lord of Aratta, initiates the hostilities and the decisive magical contest takes place near, but not in, Uruk (in Eresh).

Epic space can extend beyond "our country" and "this world" to the "afterworld," from where one sees the gods acting and interfering in human affairs (198). In universal epic the principal battle takes place in a semi-mythic location which seems to be in "the in-between space." One of Jason's examples of this area is the abode of Humbaba (198). While man can travel back and forth between the human world and "the in-between space," the creatures indigenous to "the in-between space" remain there; they do not enter the human world but vanish from the tale when the human hero does so. While none of our epics is a universal epic, there is at least one view of what may be "the in-between space." This is the home of the Anzu-bird in LB. Lugalbanda entered this realm and received help from the bird; but when Lugalbanda left this realm to rejoin his comrades, the Anzu-bird could not follow. The bird led Lugalbanda to the edge of this "in-between space" and then "The bird hurried back to its nest, Lugalbanda set out for his brothers" (lines 218–219). Lugalbanda re-entered the human world, and the Anzu-bird is not mentioned again.

D. Temporal Dimension.

Just as it is possible to reconstruct a community's spatial perception of the world from the body of its ethnopoetic works, so is it possible to reconstruct its temporal perception. Every society has its own ethnopoetic timeline—the past events and their relative order which occur in folk literature. This time-line does not include every event that has occurred, or even every event of which people are aware. The events that enter the ethnopoetic time-line are chosen on the basis of their meaningfulness to the society, its

---

[18] *Enmerkar and the Lord of Aratta*, 41–61.

[19] *Ibid.*, 61.

[20] S. Cohen, *Enmerkar and the Lord of Aratta*, 55–61; Y. Majidzadeh, "The Land of Aratta," *JNES* 35 (1976), 105–14.

[21] B. Alster notes that in at least one context Aratta "represents the mythical city from where wisdom and art was [sic] brought down" (*Studies in Sumerian Proverbs*, 1975, 128 note 32).

social system, and its main concerns. For example, it has been found that in tales of Jews from Arab lands, the two destructions of the Temple (586 B.C.E. and 70 C.E.) are telescoped into one; and the expulsion from Spain (1492 C.E.), a major historical event known to the community who still consider Spain their land of origin, is absent. Thus one cannot learn actual history from an ethnopoetic reconstruction, but rather a traditional history of significant events—those events which have become points around which different genres of ethnopoetic literature adhere. From myths, epics, and tales, one can reconstruct a list of important events and order them chronologically. But the Sumerologist must be warned that this yields a *subjective* history, though in some ways more interesting than an objective history. Likewise, one must distinguish between the setting of a work and the time in which it was actually composed. For example, myth is set in mythic time, which precedes human time—the setting of the epics; but it does not follow from this that the myths were composed before the epics.

Jason distinguishes three basic categories of time: 1) Human time (historical time) which flows regularly. Human time begins at the end of the mythic epoch and ends at the eschatological age. 2) Mythic time, flowing time-in-the-making. Mythic time begins before time exists, and continues through the establishment of ordered time. 3) Fabulous time, which flows slowly or not at all. Miraculous, demonic, and marvelous beings live in varieties of fabulous time.

Epic is set in human time but occasionally contains bits of fabulous time. Since heroic epic purports to describe historic events, it is clearly set in a particular period in the national time-line—in the specified distant past (as opposed to fairy tales, which are in the unspecified distant past).

The setting of some of the Enmerkar-Lugalbanda epics gives a partial national time-line and the place of the epics on it. The most complete setting is in LH, which reviews events before Enmerkar and puts Enmerkar's epoch into perspective. Its story takes place after heaven had been separated from earth (the beginning of time), after agriculture and architecture had been undertaken (the beginning of civilization), after *en*-ship and kingship had been made to shine forth in Uruk (the founding of Uruk), after the lord of Uruk had been foremost in battle (the rise of Enmerkar; several more references follow).[22]

ELA begins with the building of Uruk and its temple, and Aratta and its temple. The builder of Uruk is Enmerkar himself, so the story can be said to begin with "It was in the days when Enmerkar was building Uruk . . ." That is, it is set in the same general time period as LH (perhaps at the beginning of this period), but does not relate itself to earlier periods on the national time-line.

LB begins *in medias res*, but there is a flashback near the beginning of the poem describing a long-ago period when the Anzu-bird first built its nest. The story, of course, does not take place then (that would be mythic time), but a later unspecified time when Lugalbanda finds the Anzu's nest.

After praising the glory of Uruk, EE begins the story with the enigmatic phrase, "At that time the day was lord, the night was sovereign, Utu was king" (line 14). I have suggested that, although the exact meaning is uncertain, it sounds like "Once upon a time, a long time ago"—i.e., it takes the audience far back to an unspecified (unhistorical) time in the past.[23] It closely resembles a Yemenite Jewish opening cited by Jason (90):

> There was not and there was never
> Neither a judge nor a king,
> Only God the Supreme, He existed . . .

This is the least specific setting of the four epics. But it is a romantic epic, and thus conforms to the expectation that "romantic epic is less definitely set and tends more towards the period in which the fairy tale is set" (218).

The settings of the epics are structured in what appears to be a formulaic opening structure, diagrammed as follows:

ELA	EE	LB	LH
introductory hymn	introductory hymn	main action	--------
u₄-ri-a "in those days" ancient setting	*u₄-ba* "at that time" ancient setting	*u₄-ba* "at that time" ancient setting	*u₄-ul* "in olden times" ancient setting
u₄-ba "at that time" main action	-------- main action	-------- main action	*u₄-ba* "at that time" main action

[22] The text and translation of this passage are found in Cohen, *op. cit.*, 18.

[23] Cf. A. Berlin, *Enmerkar and Ensuḫkešdanna*, 63, 64.

The time in which the epic is set is to be distinguished from the time within the epic itself. Although the epics are set in a "real" period (historical or human time), and some even place themselves in relation to other, more distant events or eras, time within the epics is fabulous. Events occur but the passage of time is ignored. Heroes do not age; the epoch does not end. Enmerkar is still the king; Aratta is still the enemy. Time seems to stand still, freezing us into an unending "heroic age." A similar observation was made by D. S. Lixačev in reference to the Russian epics:

> The folktale in no way defines the past with regard to the general flow of history . . . The time of action in the *byliny*, on the other hand, is distinctly localized in a conditional epoch of Russia's past which could be called "the epic epoch" . . . The "epic epoch" represents a kind of ideal antiquity which knows no direct transition to later times. In this epoch Vladimir rules "eternally", the heroes live eternally, many events take place. This, unlike fairy-tale time, is history, but a history without transition to other epochs. The place of this history is "island-like".[24]

CONCLUSION. The Sumerian epics have been found to share the mode, narrative structure, and contentual aspects of other epics. They are, then, correctly viewed as epics in their own right, and not just as forerunners to later Mesopotamian epics (as is sometimes implied in discussions of the Akkadian *Epic of Gilgamesh*). Now that the basic generic similarities have been established, it remains for the distinctive features of Sumerian epics to be elicited: how do Sumerian epics differ from other Sumerian compositions? I have tried to indicate in a few instances where one may begin such investigations.

Sumerologists have always referred to these poems as epics, but have not always appreciated what that generic identification implies. They have persisted in asking historical questions of these non-historical writings—questions such as when did Enmerkar live, where was Aratta, what politico-economic relations are reflected in the poems. These are the preoccupations of modern "scientific" scholars, but they are not the questions that the epics are addressing. It is, of course, possible to learn history, geography, economics, etc., from fictional literature; but it is a mistake to stop there. Epics are not poeticized history. They use history-like elements for a purpose which is essentially nationalistic. The more fundamental question is what do these poems teach us about the world view of the Sumerians: their values, their role models, their conceptions of the past, and, by extension, their conception of their national destiny.[25]

[24] Quoted in Alexander, *Bylina and Fairy Tale*, 90. The original source is *Poètika drevnerusskoj literatury*, 1967, 234.

[25] I wish to thank Dr. Heda Jason who discussed the manuscript with me and prevented a number of errors in the area of folklore.

BABYLONIAN BALLADS: A NEW GENRE

J. A. Black

The Oriental Institute

The poem edited here, written in an elaborate "monumental" script on a tablet of unknown provenience now in the British Museum, is not quite like anything else in Akkadian.[1] Rather, its content (if not its style) is reminiscent in general terms of certain Sumerian literature, and so it is appropriate to inscribe this short study to the honour of Samuel Noah Kramer, the editor of balbales of Inana and Dumuzi and of the Sacred Marriage cult songs.

On palaeographic and linguistic grounds the tablet is possibly to be dated to the Middle Babylonian period, hardly any earlier.[2] However, it chances that the composition is listed, by its first line, in an ancient library catalogue, and that the tablet's catch-line is the next entry in the catalogue. Now the preservation of such a catalogue, that is a list of the first lines of a collection of literary works, is both illuminating and infuriating, shifting the beam of our attention, as it were, to the large extent of Mesopotamian literature which by accident has not yet been recovered. The tablet from Aššur published over sixty years ago as *KAR* 158 is a case in point.[3] Its partially damaged text originally listed the incipits of nearly 400 songs and hymns, of which some 275 are preserved. Of these at least two-fifths are in Sumerian and the remainder in Akkadian, and apart from the poem below, none of the Akkadian works (and only two or perhaps three of the Sumerian) is otherwise known to us.[4]

The first section of *KAR* 158 lists ninety-three titles of Akkadian *zamārū*—"songs," a rather general word[5]—which are divided into three named series. Each series (ÉŠ.GÀR) is further divided into sets (*iš-ka-ra-a-tu*) of five or six titles each. The first series, *Māruma rā*ʾ*imni* ("O young man loving me"), of which our poem appears as the third title of its second set, also bears the (presumably stylistic) designation *akkadīta*.[6] The

[1] I am indebted to the kindness of I. Finkel for drawing the tablet to my attention in the first place, and to the Trustees of the British Museum for permission to publish it. My treatment has benefitted greatly from discussion with, and references generously communicated by, A. Kilmer, S. Parpola and E. Reiner, and to them I am especially grateful.

[2] In view of the special interest attaching to the script in which the tablet is written, and the virtual absence of other means of dating the composition, detailed palaeographic notes have been appended to the commentary.

[3] *KAR* 158 has no colophon, and, although the tablet was certainly excavated at Aššur, the excavation number (as happens) has been lost (this much is clear from Weidner's account, see *AfO* 16 (1952/3), 205, 206, 207)—so that it is not possible to know exactly where in the site it came from. It was assigned, solely on the basis of the ductus of its script and of its general appearance, to the library collection probably begun by Tiglathpileser I (1114–1076) and continued by Tukultī-Ninurta II (890–884; see Weidner, *AfO* 16, 199), but it seems incautious to attempt to date it with any precision.

[4] *KAR* 158 ii 52 is the balbale of Inana edited by S. N. Kramer in *PAPS* 107, no. 9, see Civil, *JNES* 26, 90 n. 27: ba-lam ba-lam hi-iz^{sar}-àm a ba-an-dug$_4$; *KAR* 158 iii 11 is the adab of An, *VAS* 10 199 ii 9—iii 7, see Falkenstein, *ZA* 49, 88 no. 2: an urú^{ru} gal dingir-re-e-ne; *KAR* 158 iii 11 is perhaps the hymn beginning e-i lugal-mu SA[L(?) . . .], *VAS* 2 3 iii 22ff., see Falkenstein, *ZA* 49, 103 n. 3, but the broken sign certainly looks more like SAL than kiri$_4$(KA). I am inclined not to accept the identification, suggested to me by Anne Kilmer, of *KAR* 158 ii 6 *za-mar* ^{d}*iš*$_8$*-tár šar-ra-ti a-za-am-mu-ur* with the OB text *CT* 15 1-2 (edited by Römer in *WdO* 4 12–28), of which the incipit is [*za*]*-ma-ar* ^{d}*be-le-et-ì-lí a-za-ma-ar*. So many religious hymns begin "I sing of . . ." or "Let me sing of . . ." that unless the coincidence is absolute, it is quite likely that a different hymn is involved. For instances of this sort of incipit cf. *KAR* 158 i 20 *bukur bin Anim luzmur dunnaka*, also i 21, i 22 (*bēlu luzmur zamār ilūtika*), i 30, ii 30.

[5] *Zamāru* is used for instance of Sumerian tigi compositions (*KAR* 158 iii 16, 28) and of adab hymns (ibid. iii 46, viii 11).

[6] *KAR* 158 i 42f.: [6 *iš-ka-ra*]-⸢*a*⸣-*tu* 31 *za-ma-ru* MEŠ [ÉŠ.GÀR *ma-ru-ma*] ⸢*ra*⸣-*im-ni ak-ka-di-ta* "six sets, in all 31 songs, series *Māruma rā*ʾ*imni, akkadīta*." That this does not mean "in Akkadian" is evident from the other entries throughout the catalogue and in the summary at the end, where compositions in Akkadian or Sumerian respectively are so designated using the words *ak-ka-du-ú* (MEŠ), URI^{ki}, *šu-me-ru* (MEŠ). All of the first three series are marked *akkadû* in the summary. Parallel to *akkadīta* is the term *ištarūta* (^{d}*iš*$_8$*-tár-ú-*

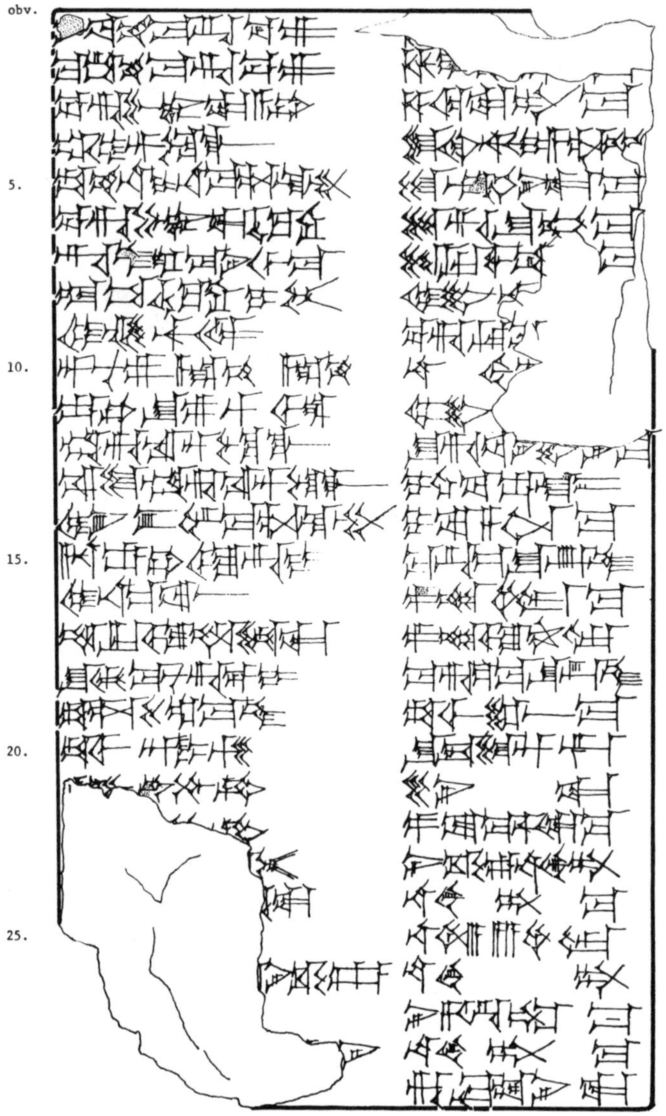

Figure 1. Obverse. BM 47507.

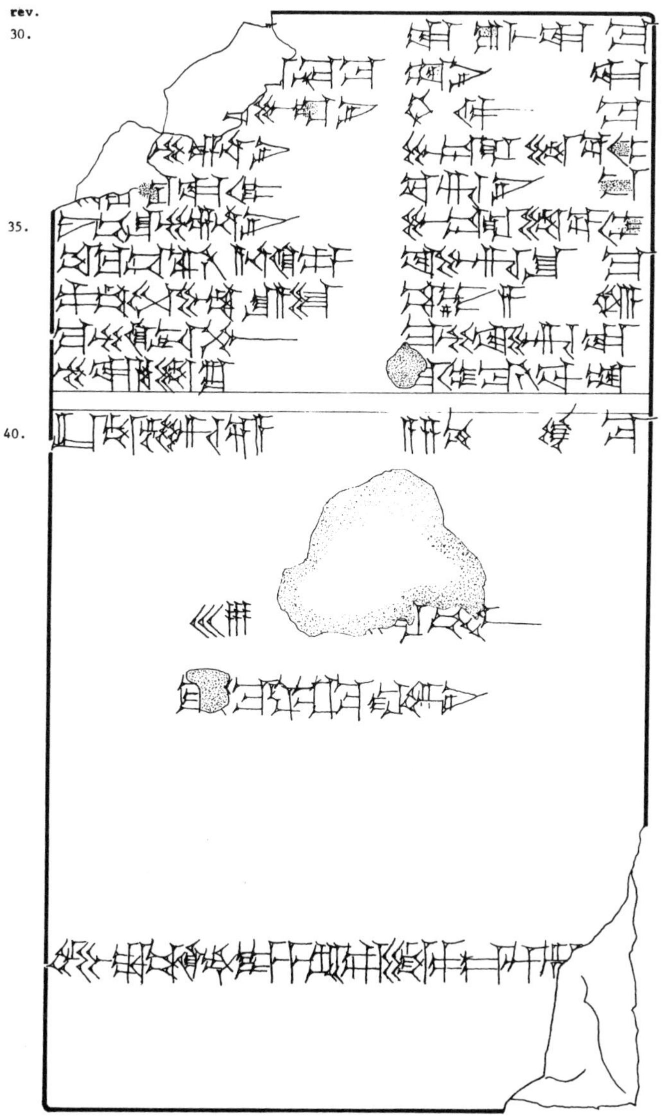

Figure 1. Reverse. BM 47507.

BM 47507

second series is *Murtāmī* ("The lovers"), and this is followed by *Rēʾî rēʾî* ("My shepherd, my shepherd"). The genres of the other compositions listed in the catalogue are mixed, some familiar to us and others known only from their mention here, some religious, in particular hymnic, and others (for instance some, but by no means all, of these *zamārū*) apparently secular, or at least not explicitly religious. Most, even of the series *Māruma rāʾimni* and of *Rēʾî rēʾî*, appear to be hymns, addressed to a variety of gods and goddesses; but the second set (if not the first two sets) of each of these series is different: the titles all seem to be secular, what one might call "pastoral" and amatory, e.g.

Māruma rāʾimni	"O young man loving me" (viii 3)
[Erba]mma rēʾû harmi Ištarma	"Come in, shepherd, Ištar's lover" (i 6)
[Uršā]na rēʾâ azammurma	"I shall sing of the brave shepherd" (i 7)
Ana nahši rēʾî aṣajjah	"I smile at the lusty shepherd" (ii 7)
U rēʾî ana bīti ruʾam	"Now bring me home my shepherd" (ii 8)

ta) which likewise follows the titles of the third series, *Rēʾî rēʾî* (ii 11, 19, 28, 36, 46), and so also, perhaps, the term *šumera* appended to the tigi and adab songs (and consistently so spelled, see iii 9, 17, 29, 38). Presumably *ištarūta* does not mean "song about Ištar" or the like, since the songs of *Māruma rāʾimni*, to judge from our text and the other incipits, were also about Ištar, and some songs of *Rēʾî rēʾî* concern deities other than her. One imagines then that *akkadīta*, *ištarūta* and possibly *šumera* are terms (adverbs?) relating to the style or perhaps the manner of performance, but whose meaning is unfortunately not yet recoverable. The adjective *akkadû*/*akkadītu*, when it does not refer to the Akkadian language, describes a style of manufacture of e.g. boats or implements. There seems to be no basis for the suggestion made in *CAD* A/1, 272b s.v. *akkadû* that *akkadīta* is for *mīnūta akkadīta* "Akkadian metre" (nor for the implication that *minûtu* might mean "metre").

These share a similarity of language, vocabulary and tone with the compositions called *irātu* listed later in the catalogue.[7] The *irātu* are divided into species by the names of the strings of the lyre—*ša kitme*, *ša ebbūbe*, *ša pīte* etc., as A. D. Kilmer pointed out some years ago—probably identifying the modes or keys in which they were composed.[8] They have titles like

Kî ṣêhāku ana nahši	"How I smile at the lusty man" (vii 7)
Ūm ēn imnija išhiṭanni	"When my right eye twitched" (vii 8)
Mūša māru ušamšakku	"I'll let you stay the night, young man" (vii 13)
Ana mušīti annīti ana lilâti annâti	"Tonight, this evening" (vii 23)
Kê nahšat kê namrat	"How vigorous she is, how flushed" (vii 25)
Rāmka lu sû ṣīhātuka lu hurāṣu	"Your love is a jewel your smiles are gold" (vii 43f.)
Hadīš akša šarru	"Come joyfully, my king" (vii 50)

and so on. However, the incipits of the amatory songs of *Māruma rāʾimni* and *Rēʾî rēʾî* differ from the *irātu* in being explicitly concerned with the love between Ištar and Dumuzi, "the Shepherd." Now poetry on this theme is well-known in Sumerian: there are a number of compositions, some brief, some more extended, dealing with self-contained episodes in the courtship and love of the pair.[9] But apart from the poem presented here, and the other titles from the catalogue, no Akkadian examples are known; and no Sumerian poem known to me is directly related to them. In fact *Erbamma rēʾû* and those suggestive single lines are the only traces of a whole genre of Akkadian verse which is lost to us.

This *zamāru*, then, was presumably intended to be sung, and for that reason, and because of its brisk narrative style and secular tone, I call it a ballad.[10] I do not mean to make any further implications about its possible popular origin. But it is not an extended poetic dialogue, like the refined "conversation about love" between a young man and a young woman, published most recently by M. Held.[11] And it is worlds apart from the various "divine love lyrics," which are distinctly cultic in setting, and are even accompanied by a ritual tablet.[12] The "love lyrics," on the whole, are not narrative but lyrical in style, and the very characteristic vocabulary employed by the *zamārū* ballads and by the *irātu* is absent. Their metrical structure is much more varied, more highly wrought and more lyrical, where *Erbamma rēʾû* is

[7] E.g. the use of *māru*, lit. "son," and *šarru*, lit. "king," both to refer to the male beloved, the use of the relatively rare *akāšu* for *alāku* "to go," *nahšu* "lusty," *ṣâhu* "to smile coquettishly," the use of the 1st person plural for the singular, etc.

[8] *AS* 16, 267f.

[9] References to these are conveniently gathered together in the notes to S. N. Kramer, *The Sacred Marriage Rite*, chapters 3, 4 and 5, and Th. Jacobsen, *The Treasures of Darkness*, chapter 2.

[10] Some justification is required for introducing (purely as a matter of convenience) a modern term to describe a genre of ancient literature. It is clear (and to my knowledge without parallel) that the compositions making up the series *Māruma rāʾimni* and *Rēʾî rēʾî* (and possibly also *Murtāmī*) were not homogeneous. The compositions listed for the second (and hypothetically the broken first) sets of *Māruma rāʾimni* (*KAR* 158 i 4–8), probably the first (if the series title is the incipit) and hypothetically the second sets of *Murtāmī* (i 45ff.), and the second, and hypothetically the first, sets of *Rēʾî rēʾî* (ii 5–9) were, to judge from their incipits, poems of the type I am calling "ballads": they are amatory, pastoral, probably concerned with love of Ištar and Dumuzi, and are different from the other "songs" listed in these series, which appear to be formal hymns addressed to various deities. So the designation *zamāru* used by the compiler of the catalogue for all the compositions is not helpful when it is specifically the amatory compositions that we wish to characterise. In any case it is never clear exactly what the relations are between ancient genre-names and distinctions, based on style and content, made by ourselves. A ballad is "a simple, spirited poem . . . in which some popular story is graphically narrated" (*Oxford English Dictionary*); "a narrative composition in verse of strongly marked rhythm . . . having narrative combined with lyrical and sometimes dramatic elements" (*Webster's Third New International Dictionary*), and also "a popular song of a romantic or sentimental nature" (*American Heritage Dictionary*).

[11] M. Held in *JCS* 15 (1961), 1–26.

[12] See W. G. Lambert, 'Divine Love Lyrics from Babylon' in *JSS* 4 (1959), 1–15, 'Divine Love Lyrics from the Reign of Abī-Ešuh' in *MIO* 12 (1966), 41–56, and 'The Problem of the Love Lyrics' in H. Goedicke and J. J. M. Roberts, edd., *Unity and Diversity* . . . (1971), 98–126.

written throughout in the regular line of four lifts with medial caesura. The frequent use of the enclitic *-ma* lends an unstudied, vernacular note to the verse.

The partial translation below indicates the obscurity of the poem's content. Even allowing for the broken or unintelligible passages, the action described in the ballad seems oddly disjointed, within so short a compass. Nonetheless this is an impression produced by other works of Mesopotamian narrative literature dealing with themes of which the details must have been already familiar to their audiences. Unsignalled switching from one speaker to another, too, especially in a song or ballad, is entirely understandable as an artistic device, particularly if the text is not regarded as a sequence of lines upon the printed page but as merely the libretto of a live musical performance, with all the possibilities of dramatic expression which that involves.[13]

At first reading the text appears to be a narrative, partly in the first person. But is the entire action presented as having in fact happened to Ištar—or did she imagine some of it? Some of the narrative hiatuses are resolved if we read the first part as an imaginative monologue, and with that in mind the following summary is offered. It is undoubtedly inexact in details, but I feel that the general tone of the composition is just as whimsical as this. Ištar (cast as an infatuated but reticent young girl) imagines to herself inviting her lover into her parents' house to spend the night (ll. 1–2). (Such a thing would of course be unthinkable for an unmarried girl.) She makes this sound more reasonable to herself by assuring Dumuzi (in her imaginary conversation with him) that her parents genuinely like him. Her father approves of him (l. 3) and her mother had greeted him hospitably before (ll. 4f.). In her heightened state of emotion she apostrophizes the bolt and the wooden door by which he entered when he came, wishing that they might admit him of their own accord (l. 7), and confidentially confesses to the door her love for Dumuzi—*annû arâm arâm* "Yes indeed, I love him, I love him" (l. 10). Her lively fantasy depicts the scene as he arrives—his words as he walks in (l.12), his reception (ll. 13f.). She reflects on his frequent visits, which are inconvenient and annoying to his fellows (ll.15ff.), and on his constant offers of presents. She next imagines to herself how she would intimately, perhaps even lasciviously, address him (ll. 21ff.), encouraging him to relax, take off his sandals, eat and forget his shepherdly tasks for the moment. We are prevented from knowing just what this dereliction of duty might have led to because of damage on the tablet. Then (following the gap, in l. 36) the ballad switches to third person narrative. Ištar's reverie is ended, and the narrator describes what she actually does: summoning her courage, she pays a visit to Dumuzi's sheepfold, and says to him (and for "says to him" the poet chooses one of the commonest and most banal of all formulaic lines of Babylonian poetry) how pleasant the stream is that runs past his sheep-pens. The temptation to see bathos in this is irresistible. After all her passionate declarations of love for Dumuzi—to herself —and her imagined conversation with him in which she addresses him as *nahšu* "lusty," all she can manage to say when confronted with him in person is "How pleasant it is here." Nonetheless, beneath the watery reference of her remarks, a sensual undercurrent may flow.

⸢er⸣-ba-am-ma re-e-ú	*⸢ha⸣-[ar-mi ^{d}iš$_{8}$-tár-ma*	Come in, Shepherd, Ištar's lover,
ma-ša-am-ma re-e-ú	*ha-⸢ra-am ^{d}ištar⸣*	Spend the night here, Shepherd, Ištar's lover,
e-re-bu-uk-ka a-bi	*ha-di ka-šum-ma*	At your entering, my father is delighted with you,
um-mi ^{d}nin-gal	*tu-ul-ti-ya-al-⸢kum⸣*	My mother Ningal invites you to recline.
ša-am-na i-na ma-al-la-tim	*tu-mah-hi-ir-ka-ma*	She offered you oil in a bowl.
e-re-bu-uk-ka sik-ku-ru	*li-ri-šu-kum-ma*	When you enter, may the bolts rejoice over you,
dal-tum ra-ma-ni-ši-ma	*li-ip-pi-ta-[kum]-ma*	May the door open of its own accord.

[13] For a striking modern example, see the ballad "Wo die schönen Trompeten blasen" in the collection *Des Knaben Wunderhorn.*

at-ta sik-ku-ru i-ṣu	*mi-in* ⌜*ti*⌝-[*de* (?)]	You, bolt, and wood—what do you [know?]
mi-nam ti-de	*e-re-eb* ⌜*ma*⌝[	What do you know— . . . .
an-nu-ú a-ra-am a-ra-am	*na-ah-*⌜*šum*⌝[	Yes indeed! I love him, I love him! The lusty . . . .
kal-bi-šu ú-maš-ši-ra	*mi-in* [	He has left his dogs, ...
mah-ri-iš ^{d}*nin-gal*	*šu-ri-ba-*⌜*ni-in-ni-ma*⌝	"Show me into the presence of Ningal!"
iš-tu mah-ri-iš ^{d}*nin-gal*	*i-ru-ba kal-la-sa*	When he had entered the presence of Ningal . . . . ,
mi-ir-sa im-ma-al-la-tim	*i-zu-za-nim-ma*	The women divided up the *mirsu*-cake in a bowl.
a-na kal-bi ù re-i	*ma-ri-iṣ šu-nun-dum*	The swain is troublesome to the dogs and shepherds.
mi-na iz-zu-rù	*ú-bíl ub-lam-ma*	Why did they excoriate him? He fetched and brought,
il-lik ù il-li-ka	*ú-bíl ù ub-lam*	He went and came, he fetched and brought
šu-ul-ma-nu re-e-i	*ma-ri-iṣ-ma šu-nun-dum*	Shepherds' greeting-gifts—the swain is a nuisance.
ša-al-mat um-ma-tum	*ša-lim šar-rum-ma*	The pack (?) is safe, the "king" is safe,
ša-lim ^{d}*dumu-zi*	*šu-da-tu* ^{d}*ištar*	Dumuzi is safe, the beloved of Ištar.
⌜*x x pu-ṭur*⌝ *pu-ṭur*	*še-ni-ka*	. . . . loosen, loosen your sandals,
]⌜*pu-ṭur*⌝	*pa-sú-ma-ti-ka-ma*	. . . . unpack your fowling-nets,
] *ṣu*	*ni-ik-kal na-ah-šum*	. . . . we shall eat, o lusty one,
]*x ka*	*na-ah-šum-ma*	. . . . o lusty one,
]	*na-kar a-a ub-lam*	. . . .
] *ni-ik-kal*	*na-ah-šum*	. . . . we shall eat, o lusty one,
]	*ni-za-ar-riq*$^{!}$*-ma*	. . . . we shall sprinkle (?),
] ⌜*x*⌝ *ni*	*na-ah-šum-ma*	. . . . o lusty one,
]	*ri-gim ṣe-ni-ka*	. . . . the noise of your flocks,

rev.

]⌜*x*⌝	*ka-lu*$^{!}$*-me-ka-ma*	. . . . your lambs,
] ⌜*ri*⌝-*gim-ma*	*ṣe-ni-ka*	. . . . the noise of your flocks,
] ⌜*su*⌝-*pu-ra-ni*	*hi-ṭi-ma*	. . . . neglect the sheepfolds,
] ⌜*mu*⌝-*un-na-ni*	*bu du ra li e mi*	. . . .
⌜*mu na ra ra*⌝ *ka mi*	*pá-ri*<*-ir*$^{?}$*-*>*ma*	. . . .
ni-bi-šu mu-un-na-ni	*bu du ra li e mi*	. . . .
ta-ku-uš iš-tar a-na qé-reb	*su-pu-ri-šu-ma*	Ištar went to his sheepfold,
pa-ša NIM-*pu-ša šu-a-tu*	*ta-az-za-kar*	She opened her mouth and said to him,
ma-mu ki ṭa-bu	*ma-mu su-pu-ri-ka*	"How pleasant are the waters, the waters of your sheepfold,
mu-ka ha-li-lu	⌜*ma*⌝-*mi-ma tar-ba-ṣi*	Your waters are burbling, the waters of the cattle-pen."

---

ur-ša-nam re-e-a	*a-za-am-mur-ma*	I shall sing of the brave Shepherd.

39 [MU].⌜ŠID.BI.IM⌝ — total 39 lines

⌜ÉŠ.GÀR⌝ *ma-ru-um-ma ra-im-ni* — series "O young man loving me"

IM.GÍD.DA *ta-qí-šum* DUMU me-me-^{d}en-líl-le PA É ^{d}MÙŠ — library tablet of Taqīšum son of Meme-Enlil, *šāpiru* of the temple of Ištar

Commentary. The dimensions of the tablet are 2 1/8" × 3 1/2". The language of the poem exhibits a number of features of the so-called "hymnic-epic" literary dialect, for instance the use of the adverbial in *-iš* as a periphrasis for a prepositional phrase (*mahriš* in 12f.) and the (here intermittent) use of the t- prefix for third person feminine (4f., 36f., but not 14). Mimation is occasional. A number of "rare" words occur (*šunundum*, *šu-da-tu*, *hālilu*), but this may be an impression due more to the lack of other texts of the same genre than to any preciosity of the poet.

1. The remainder of the first line is restored from the catalogue *KAR* 158, i 6, where the incipit is listed; the first part of which, conversely, is restored from the present line. Dumuzi is frequently described as the *harmu* of Ištar, notably in the collection of incantations beginning *atti Ištar ša harmaša Dumuzi*, see W. Farber, *Beschwörungsrituale an Ištar und Dumuzi . . .* (1977).

2. The scribe, who carefully distinguishes *ša* and *ta*, has here written *ma-ša-am-ma*. This, it seems, can only represent an imperative of the verb *mašû* B "to spend the night." (Clearly it cannot be derived from any of the other verbs *mašû* A "to forget," **mâšu* "to check" or *mašāʾu* "to abduct.") So far *mašû* "to spend the night" is attested only once, in a commentary (2*R* 47 r. i 60) where it has been regarded as an artificial back-formation from the common *šumšû* (itself a denominative from *mūšu* "night"). *Šumšû* occurs in the incipit of an *irtu*-song at *KAR* 158 vii 13. "Come in, Shepherd, and spend the night" fits the context well, so perhaps a G stem *mašû* (pret. **imša*) should be regarded as established.

Note here and throughout the song the liberal use of the enclitic *-ma*, especially at line ends, where it is useful in completing the necessary final trochee. But it is also used in some places where a final trochee already obtains (e.g. lines 3, 5, 12), in which case its use may either be attributed to musical considerations lost to us or be considered a rhythmic feature of some sort.

The traces at the end of the line suggest *haram* ^{d}*Ištar*. This variant form of the construct (probably also to be restored in line 1) is found at En. el. I 113, 117 (*ha-ra-am-ki*).

3. For the dative object over which one rejoices, cf. PN *aštaprakkum hu-du-ú-*[*š*]*um* "I have sent PN to you, be well disposed towards him" *TCL* 17 68:7 (OB letter).

4. The form *tultīalkum* can hardly be derived from *šiālu* "to pour," in view of the prefix. With no *qātāša* it is unlikely to be the Št of *eʾēlu*—for *tušteʾel* "she wrings her hands (in despair)." Also excluded is the Št stem of *niālu*, *uštanīl*: but the occurrence of forms such as OB *at-ta-ti-ya-al* (*TCL* 17 56:21) and NB *lu-ul-ti-il-šu* (*YOS* 3 19:29), which are probably to be derived from *itūlu*, suggests that *tultīal* may be the Š present of *itūlu* (formed exceptionally like the "strong" G present *iqtīaš*). This should then mean "she causes you to lie down, invites you to recline," which fits the context well, although a dative pronominal suffix is less expected than an accusative. The change *-št-* to *-lt-* confirms the *terminus post quem* for dating the text.

5. *Mahāru* is used here in its nuance of "have someone accept (an offering)" (*CAD* usage 7a). Here as in 4 the *tu*-prefix for 3sg. f. is a characteristic of the literary dialect.

Mallatu is the sort of bowl used in making an offering: Gilgameš fills a carnelian *mallatu* with honey and a lapis lazuli one with ghee in connection with funerary offerings to Enkidu (Gilgameš VIII 47).

6. For a similar idea cf. the inscription of Nabonidus: when you enter E-babbar, Šamaš, *bābāni nērebī papāhī u šubāti uddušam pahukku kīma a-a-ri lirīšūku* (*VAB* 4 258:17).

7. In *lippetâmma* note the use of the N theme to mean "open (of one's own accord)," reinforced by *ramanišima* (for expected *ramanšama*).

8. *i-ṣu* is *iṣu* "wood (of the door)" rather than *īṣu* "too small." It is a commonplace to link the door and the bolt, e.g. in the Descent of Ištar *amahhaṣ daltum sikkūru ašabbir* (*CT* 15 45:17 and dupl.). Apostrophe of the door recalls the genre of Classical love poetry παρακλαυσίθυρον "doorstep lament," see for example, among many others, Ovid Amores I 6, especially 73f.

10. *Annû* is a form of *anna* "yes." Apart from some early personal names, *nahšu* "lusty" is recorded virtually only in the context of this poem and others like it (cf. the incipits *ana nahši rēʾî aṣajjah KAR* 158 ii 7 and *kê ṣêhāku ana nahši* ibid. vii 7).

11. Presumably these are Dumuzi's dogs, most likely sheep dogs (see Gilg. VI 63 and *CAD* s.v. *kalbu*). Possibly, however, they were hunting dogs, cf. the allusion to fowling in line 22.

12. *Mahriš* is here a periphrasis for the commoner *ana mahar*, characteristic of the dialect. *Šūribāninnima* at the line end seems fairly clear.

13. *ka-la-sa* cannot, in the context, be *kallassa* "her daughter-in-law." Some confusion is possible: an adverb might be expected here.

14. *Mirsu* is a "confection of dates, butter, oil etc.," one variety of which seems to be associated with shepherds: see Hg. B VI 67ff., and cf. *mirsa* [*ana k*]*aparrāti ša Dumuzi tašakkan* "you set out *mirsu*-cake for the shepherd boys of Dumuzi" *LKA* 70 i 25, see TuL 50.

Izūzā must be 3rd ps. pl. fem. of *zâzu* (note that the t-prefix is not observed here), and if it describes what the two women did to the *mirsu-cake* (presumably divided it up, cut it up for consumption) it implies a usage of *zâzu* not hitherto recorded, but not impossible from its attested meanings, see *AHw* s.v. *zâzu*(*m*) G II 4.

15. *Šunundum* here and in line 18 is a word not previously recorded except in lexical works, where it is equated with

qarrādu or *amīlu*, see Malku I 22, *CT* 18 13 iv 21 and *CT* 18 16 iii 5 (broken), or with *raʾīmu* (An VIII 67, see *CAD* s.v. *amīlu*. It is possibly *not* the same word as *šanūdu* (*AHw* s.v. *šanūdu* I). Presumably it refers to Dumuzi, *rēʾû* to the other shepherds. *Marāṣu* here seems to be used in its sense (with *ana*) of "be annoying, troublesome, displeasing to" (*CAD* mng. 3), despite the presence of *šalmu* in 19f.

16. It seems best to translate here "why did they excoriate him?" (*nazāru*) than to take IZ-ZU-*rù* as a form of *naṣāru*.

19. The parallelism of the adjective suggests that *um-ma-tum* and ŠAR-*rum* are somehow equated or contrasted, so if *ummatu* were taken as a "pack" (of marauding wild beasts, cf. [*lu-ú-na*]-*ki-is ummātišunuma napištašunu lu-ú-b*[*al-li*] *BWL* 194 a 27 (Fable of the Fox), where the dog boasts how he protects the flocks from wild predators), then it may be better to read *sarru* "the criminal," the implication being that while the shepherd Dumuzi is otherwise occupied in courtship, his flocks are exposed to the dangers of *ummatu* and *sarru*, who are thus "safe" from disturbance. However, the use of the word *šarru* "king" as an epithet of the male beloved is paralleled in Babylonian amatory verse in *šarrī tanittukka* (*KAR* 158 ii 43), *ārid kirî šarru hāṣibu erēni* (ibid. vii 28) and *hadīš akša šarru* (vii 50) (although possibly in all these in the vocative) and it is probably so used here.

20. The word written *šu-da-tu* here is the same as that registered in the following passages from lexical works:

muš-ta-mu = *šu-da-*[*d*]*u* (var. *šu-ta-*[x]) Malku III 40
šu-da-du = *ra-i-mu* (i.e. *raʾīmu*) *CT* 18 13 iv 20 = An VIII 65,

and is to be connected with *mudadu* "beloved," occurring only in personal names. Since it is certain to be Dumuzi who is here described as the beloved of Ištar, we must assume that the scribe either wrote *šu-da-tu* for *šu-da-dú*, or misread *-ad* as *-tu*. This is the first record of the word in a literary composition.

21. The request "loosen your shoes" is here addressed (by implication of the masculine suffix) to Dumuzi. Note *paṭāru* said of *šēnu* in a bilingual proverb in *BWL* 263 r. 12. The traces at the beginning of the line look like ⌜*e-ru*⌝ (?)

22. As the masculine suffix shows, *pa-sú-ma-ti-ka* cannot be the word denoting a woman's veil. It is the hitherto unattested plural of *pasuttu*, *pasuntu*, glossed as a "fowler's net" at Hh. VI 36, demonstrating that word's connection with the verb *pasāmu*. *Paṭāru* must therefore mean something like "unpack" your nets.

27. The last sign but one seems to be RIQ although apparently incomplete. The verb must thus be *zarāqu*, a word which denotes sprinkling or strewing, mostly as a ritual action. Its presence here is difficult to explain.

30. It is difficult to determine what signs were written here (see palaeographic notes). The plausible reading *kalūmēka* "your lambs" was suggested to me by S. Parpola.

31. It looks as if the enclitic *-ma* has been attached to the construct ⌜*ri*⌝-*gim*, ungrammatically, if this is the same phrase as in 29, *rigim ṣēnīka* "the noise of your sheep." Cf. *māmīma tarbāṣi* in 39, again perhaps *metri causa*.

32. The plural *supurānī* does not appear to be attested elsewhere.

33, 35. These lines, which may be identical, are obscure. *Munnanni*, so read, may be the D imperative of *menû*, "love me." Read *munnâni*, it is the pl. imper., with ventive, of the D stem of *manû* ("count!" possibly referring to animals). *bu-du-ra* is possibly *budduru*, glossed as *guzullu*, *bilti ša qanāti*, a bundle of load of reeds, at Hg. II 219f., in *MSL* 7 68. Alternatively one might read *bu-du-ra* as *puṭṭura* and *le-e-mi* as a stative of *lēmu*/*lewû* "unwilling" (almost always constructed with infinitive)—"is unwilling to loosen." In either case the reference of the line remains opaque.

34. This whole line is obscure. It is possible that not NI but IR is the penultimate sign.

36. Except in Old Assyrian, where it appears to be colloquial, *akāšu* is a rather literary or poetic word. The verb here, as in the next line, has the *t*- prefix characteristic of the dialect. *Akāšu* occurs again within this genre in the *irtu* listed at *KAR* 158 vii 50, *hadīš akša šarru*.

37. There is no doubt that the scribe here wrote not *te-pu-ša* but NIM-*pu-ša*, in error. As so often, beauty of script is no guarantee of accuracy of copying. For the collected occurrences of this common formulaic line, see Sonneck, *ZA* 46 225ff.

38. *Malīlu hālilu* is a "piping flute" (Craig *ABRT* I 15:6, see *CAD* s.v. *malīlu*) and the adjective is used to qualify "water" in an incantation: A TÚL *ha-li-lu-ti* (*AMT* 52,1:4), so I translate "burbling." See *CAD* s.v. *hālilu* A, B (probably the same word).

40. The catch-line restores *KAR* 158 i 7.

Colophon. Taqīšum is probably a hypocoristic form of a name like Taqīš-Gula. In the curious name Me-me-^{d}En-líl-le, Me-me can hardly be a writing (without determinative) for the goddess Gula, since this would produce a name with two theophoric elements and no predicate. ME = *išippu* and LÚ.ME.ME = *āšipu* seem equally unlikely to be involved here, and in any case neither is attested in personal names. This, together with the unidiomatic -le at the end of the name, suggest that this may be the concocted name of a fake Sumerian scribal "father," which suits well with the archaising script of the tablet. The title *šāpir bīt Ištar* (PA É ^{d}MÙŠ, probably to be so read) is not found elsewhere and can be paralleled only from Old Babylonian texts dated in the reigns of Samsuiluna and later rulers: *ša-pir* É *YOS* 13 2:3 (Aṣ), 365:3 (Sd), PA É *YOS* 13 154:11 (Ad), PA É ^{d}MAH *BE* 6/2 30:1 (Si).

Palaeographic notes. The tablet was carefully written by a rather precise scribe imitating or practising monumental script. Simpler, more cursive forms occur, especially in the subscription, where he presumably reverts to his everyday hand. The script in general has an air of painstaking artificiality about it. Apart from those signs given special notice below, most are of standard Babylonian cursive forms.

Ba is regularly distinguished from *ma* by the angle of the lower horizontal, *ta* from *ša* by the presence (in *ša*) of two small verticals crossing the two horizontals. *Li* and *tu* are very distinct. The form of *ka* throughout, with diagonals or horizontals inscribed in the first trapezoid, is commoner in MB or monumental Babylonian than in NB cursive.

Line 3, 3rd sign. The *bu* here and in lines 6, 32, 33, 35, 36, 37, 38 is the standard form. These in line 21 (3rd and 5th signs), with the oblique strokes at the beginning crossing each other, are of a form not found after MB.

Line 3, 7th sign. The form of *bi* here and in line 15 (4th sign) is characteristic of OB or MB monumental script; contrast the standard cursive forms in 35 and 41.

Line 4, 2nd sign. The *mi* here and in 8, 9, 11 (?), 14, 16 and 39 is a typical OB form, with two horizontals followed by four.

Line 4, 4th sign, cf. 12, 13. The writing of the SAL part of *nin* without a first vertical is an archaic (OB-MB) feature.

Line 4, 7th sign. The form of *ul* with two oblique strokes at the end is virtually confined to monumental inscriptions; contrast the standard cursive form in 18.

Line 4, 10th sign, cf. 5 and 14: a typical monumental form of *al*.

Line 6, 9th sign, and 7, 8th sign. These forms of *li* are unique. Contrast in 17, 33, 35, 39 a more common form consisting of four Winkelhaken followed by something resembling *ta*. In the subscription, line 43, a slightly more complicated form is found in which the "*ta*" has four horizontals.

Line 8, 7th sign. The *ṣu* here has only single oblique strokes at the end: contrast the more usual *ṣu* in 23.

Line 10, 11 sign, cf. 24, 26, 28. The form of *ah* in which the NUN is entirely inscribed in the other strokes is not cursive after OB, and rarely found after MB at all.

Line 14, 11th sign, cf. 37 (where the *nim* is erroneous but indubitable). *Nim* with oblique strokes crossing each other is much commoner as a monumental form.

Line 16, 8th sign, cf. 25. These standard form of *ub* should be contrasted with the characteristically monumental form in line 17.

Line 20, 7th sign. The *da* here and in 38 are elaborately written signs, and may be contrasted with the cursive form in the subscription (line 43).

Line 25, 2nd sign, and 37. Monumental forms of *kar*.

Line 27, 4th sign. This seems to be an incomplete form of *riq*.

Line 30, 2nd sign. *Ba* and *zu* seem to be excluded as possibilities by the straightness of the lower horizontal: but the line is written cramped over the edge. What appears to be the middle vertical could just possibly be damage, so that *ku*, but more likely *lu*, would be reasonable, even though there is no trace of the left-hand vertical. The sign is not wide enough for *ma*: the shape certainly suggests *lu*.

Line 36, 8th sign. The *ki* here and in 38, with final vertical, are slightly different from that in the subscription (line 43) with its tendency to a lozenge shape. The lozenge shape is not found after MB.

Taken together, the evidence thus suggests a date in the MB period, or conceivably even very late OB, despite the variety of sign forms used by the scribe.

THROUGH A GLASS DARKLY
ESARHADDON'S RETROSPECTS ON THE DOWNFALL OF BABYLON

J. A. BRINKMAN

ORIENTAL INSTITUTE, CHICAGO

THE READER OF ESARHADDON'S BABYLON INSCRIPTIONS is inevitably struck by a curious omission: the downfall of the city is recounted without reference to its harsh destruction by the Assyrian army ten years earlier. (This is roughly comparable to an historical account of the final days of World War II in the Pacific neglecting to mention use of atomic weaponry.) Esarhaddon's texts deal in detail with the disastrous fate of the old capital; but they lay the blame on a natural cataclysm, a severe flood. This blatant revisionism for recent history seems singularly futile: after the passage of only ten years very few adult inhabitants of Mesopotamia were likely to have forgotten the ruthless decimation of Babylon by Esarhaddon's father. Yet these texts were found mostly at Babylon (where memories would be sharpest) in connection with Esarhaddon's repair of his father's ravages. What purpose would such drastic rewriting be expected to serve?

To appreciate the ideological background implied by this question, we should try to understand the concrete historical circumstances and the issues of policy involved. Esarhaddon came to the throne at the end of 681, in a time of turmoil following his father's assassination.[1] Sennacherib, for the greater part of his reign, had been preoccupied by Babylonia and the political problems it posed.[2] He had conducted several lengthy and costly campaigns against Babylonia and its Elamite allies,[3] had lost his eldest son to Babylonian-Elamite machinations, and had finally captured and destroyed Babylon after a protracted siege. Though *de facto* monarch of Babylonia for ten of his twenty-four years on the Assyrian throne, he seems never to have formally acknowledged this role: in contrast to his predecessor and his two successors he did not authorize the use of Babylonian royal titles in his titulary.[4] He not only distanced himself ideologically from the southern kingdom, but he eventually allowed the land around Babylon itself to become derelict and depopu-

---

* The abbreviations used in this paper generally follow the system of *The Assyrian Dictionary of the Oriental Institute of the University of Chicago*, vol. N/2 (1980), v-xix, or of "Keilschriftbibliographie, 42" in *Orientalia* N.S. 50 (1981), 1*–6*, with the following exceptions:

ARINH	=	F. M. Fales, Ed., *Assyrian Royal Inscriptions: New Horizons in Literary, Ideological, and Historical Analysis* (Rome, 1981 [appeared 1982])
Asarh.	=	R. Borger, *Die Inschriften Asarhaddons Königs von Assyrien* (Graz, 1956)
Death in Mesopotamia	=	B. Alster, Ed., *Death in Mesopotamia* (Copenhagen, 1980)
HKL	=	R. Borger, *Handbuch der Keilschriftliteratur* (Berlin, 1967–)
LAS	=	S. Parpola, *Letters from Assyrian Scholars to the Kings Esarhaddon and Assurbanipal* Kevelaer-Neukirchen-Vluyn. I. (1970). II A (1971).

[1] According to the Babylonian Chronicle, Sennacherib was killed on X–20–681, and the revolt in Assyria did not end until XII–2 (*TCS* 5 81 iii 34–37). Esarhaddon's inscriptions list his own accession date as XII–8 (Borger, *Asarh.*, p. 45 §27 Ep. 2 i 87); the chronicle gives the day as "18[(+10)]" (*TCS* 5, 82 iii 38). On Sennacherib's murder, see the recent note by Parpola in *Death in Mesopotamia*, 171–82.

[2] For a general discussion see *JCS* 25 (1973), 89–95.

[3] Discussed by L. Levine in "Sennacherib's Southern Front: 704–689 B. C.," an article currently scheduled to appear in *JCS*. Note that the tradition of lengthy or successive campaigns in Babylonia goes back some time to Shalmaneser III (851–850), Shamshi-Adad V (814–811), Ashur-dan III (771–770, cf. 769 and 767), Tiglath-pileser III (731–729), and Sargon II (710–709).

[4] Later Babylonian tradition reciprocated by describing the years 688–681 as kingless (Babylonian Chronicle iii 28 in *TCS* 5, 81), echoed also in the ἀβασίλευτα designation given the years 704–703 and 688–681 in the "Ptolemaic Canon." Note the new study of Sennacherib's titulary by Liverani, *ARINH*, 225–57, which of course does not deal with omissions; it would be useful to expand Liverani's coverage so as to make comparisons possible between monarchs (and between countries) and to note sequential position, systems of honorifics and epitheta, and omissions as well.

lated. Soon after Sennacherib's death, Esarhaddon expressly reversed his father's anti-Babylonian policies.[5] He made it a top priority of his reign to conciliate the Babylonians, to rebuild their city, and to function as an active dual monarch of both Assyria and Babylonia.[6] His Babylon inscriptions may be regarded as a forceful programmatic statement for the reconstruction of the city.[7]

Esarhaddon's policies are known to us primarily as refracted through official statements formulated by his scribes.[8] In essence, we read what the scribes wrote, with their selectivity, distortions, fabrications, and slant, in their words, and with their rhetorical emphases. Our task in interpreting these texts is perhaps not so much to reconstruct the singular "event history" (*histoire événementielle* in a Braudelian sense) which afforded the occasion for writing—though this too may be a legitimate occupation for the historian—as to understand the broad range of the message, both overt and subliminal, communicated through the scribal formulation. It is important to be aware of and to appraise the scribal filter through which the information comes to us.

The scribes at Esarhaddon's court produced a body of royal inscriptions that differed significantly from those of his father and grandfather. Although Esarhaddon was an active and frequent campaigner, his scribes generally eschewed royal military accounts arranged in explicit chronological order: neither the annals form nor numbered campaigns were normally used in their narratives.[9] The scribes also evinced a heightened awareness of hemerology, celestial signs, and other omen lore: the king was recorded as having performed major actions on specifically propitious days;[10] significant attention was paid to astronomical

[5] It has sometimes been suggested that Esarhaddon changed his father's policies towards Babylonia because both his mother (Naqi'a-Zakûtu) and his primary wife (Ešarra-ḫamat) were Babylonians. In fact, there is no clear evidence that either of these two women was Babylonian. Similar is the case of Šamaš-šum-ukīn's mother (if different from Ešarra-ḫamat); 5 *R* 62 no. 2:6, sometimes adduced as proof that she was Babylonian by birth (e.g., Borger, *Asarh.*, 88 commentary, *BiOr* 29 [1972], 34), is at least ambiguous and may mean nothing of the kind (e.g., *CAD* A/1 340; Landsberger, *WO* 3 [1964–66], 77 n. 116). On the other hand, it is likewise difficult to explain first Sennacherib's and then Esarhaddon's reversals of the policies of their fathers towards Babylonia simply as reactions against the no longer asserted will of a domineering parent.

[6] Esarhaddon adopted Babylonian royal titles (e.g., *šakkanakku* of Babylon, king of Sumer and Akkad) in his official titulary and planned to return the divine statue of Marduk to Babylon (Knudtzon, *Gebete*, nos. 104–106, as contrasted with *ibid.*, no. 149 alluding to Šamaš-šum-ukīn; see also the sources mentioned in note 7).

[7] Including actions already accomplished and those still contemplated. A scrupulous distinction between past and future actions was not always observed in Esarhaddon's inscriptions, as may be seen from his claims that he had restored the Marduk statue to Babylon (actually accomplished under his successor Šamaš-šum-ukīn): *Asarh.*, 74 §47:18–19, 88–9 §57 rev. 8–21. It is also difficult for us to distinguish plans from accomplishments in the Babylon inscriptions because we are not sure of the date when they were written. Those texts which have dates preserved have a unique Babylonian-style formula: accession year of Esarhaddon (A^1, C^2, E^3) and even month Ayyaru of the accession year of Esarhaddon (G); that this is not to be taken in a literal Babylonian sense is amply demonstrated by the fact that Esarhaddon's accession year (681) had no Ayyaru (his father died only eight months later, and his official accession year was less than a month long—see note 1 above for the sources) and by the fact that the Babylon inscriptions themselves (Ep. 10) refer to the resettling of the city only after eleven years had elapsed following the destruction (which would be 679 even by an inclusive reckoning). Note that Borger interprets the "accession year" in this case to mean 680 (*BiOr* 29 [1972] 34–35). A satisfactory solution has yet to be worked out to this problem.

[8] There are also ways of approaching Esarhaddon's policies other than through an analysis of their explicit formulations. One means would be to check contemporary letters, especially passages where there might be less ideological posturing (e.g., portions of *ABL* 418 written by Ubāru, Esarhaddon's newly appointed governor of Babylon, who reports on how he was welcomed by the Babylonians on his arrival, how the king was praised for returning spoil taken by his father, and how certain factions allegedly welcomed the resettlement of the area—all with some propaganda value; also *ABL* 1216, commented on by Labat, *RA* 53 [1959], 113–8 and Parpola, *Death in Mesopotamia*, 179–80 n. 41). Another would be an analysis of the archeological evidence for Esarhaddon's reconstruction of the city; (with the evidence presently available, this does not seem particularly promising).

[9] Unlike the common chronological use of *palû* in the texts of Sargon II and of *girru* in the texts of Sennacherib, Esarhaddon's inscriptions only rarely use such numbered division (e.g., *girru* in Nin. D and E).

[10] E.g., Borger, *Asarh.*, 21 §11 Ep. 26a: 41–42, 40–5 §27 Ep. 2 i 20.

and terrestrial omens as prognostications of both good and ill;[11] and concrete references were made to specific stars and planets and their influence on human affairs.[12] In contrast to the royal texts of Sargon and Sennacherib, Esarhaddon's inscriptions in general were more concerned with the phenomena of the divine and increasingly focused on the observance of omina.[13]

Because of the Assyrian tradition of authorial anonymity, we do not know the names of those who drafted Esarhaddon's royal inscriptions. But, thanks to the patterns of survival in the archives containing royal correspondence,[14] we are unusually well informed about scribes and scholars attached to the Assyrian court in Esarhaddon's time.[15] The names and letters of many of these are preserved, including the illustrious *ummânu*'s Nabû-zēru-līšer and Ištar-šum-ēreš, father and son, whose names are also enshrined in an Assyrian synchronistic kinglist.[16] Esarhaddon's court scribes frequently discuss hemerology, astrology and other omen sciences, extispicy, magic, and medicine in their letters to the king;[17] and it is obvious from both sides of the correspondence that these were interests shared between king and courtiers.[18] Thus, while the scribes may have been responsible for the wording of Esarhaddon's royal inscriptions, they were nonetheless reflecting their master's predilections for hemerology and omen lore in their introduction of these elements into the royal texts. One can debate possible reasons behind Esarhaddon's preferences and whether the scribes and scholars reinforced some of his specific tendencies or casts of thought, but it is clear that Esarhaddon was not merely a passive bystander in the quest for prognostication. It may also be significant that there is strong evidence in this reign for a revival of the substitute-king ritual,[19] which was designed primarily to avert the effects of inauspicious omina. Esarhaddon and his scribes were much exercised by interpreting the intervention of the divine in human affairs.

With this background in mind, let us turn to an examination of the pertinent passages in Esarhaddon's inscriptions concerning the downfall of Babylon. Borger's ground-breaking edition, *Die Inschriften Asarhaddons Königs von Assyrien*, published in 1956, stimulated many supplementary text publications; but this volume is still basic to our work even though the list of scattered additions has become cumbersome. The Akkadian text itself has yet to be changed significantly[20] and need not be reproduced here; but the

---

[11] *Ibid.*, 12–17 §11 Eps. 2, 6, 12–13.

[12] *Ibid.*, 17 §11 Ep. 13.

[13] In my choice of terms to describe Esarhaddon and his scribes, I am trying to avoid the condescension of modern hindsight in labelling their attitudes as "superstitious," "obsequious," or the like. Such judgements should be made only after a balanced appraisal of Esarhaddon in relation to his time and not just inferred because the accidents of survival have preserved for us the archival correspondence of Esarhaddon and his experts on divination and astronomical omina (see Parpola's discussion cited in the following note). It is quite possible that Esarhaddon's attitudes were colored—consciously or unconsciously—by his valetudinarianism or by his awareness of the untoward deaths of his very able father and grandfather. It is also possible that the court was much more omen-oriented during Esarhaddon's reign. But at least part of the pertinent argumentation is built *e silentio* (we have not yet found comparable archives from Sargon's or Sennacherib's reign, though parts of Sargon's political archives have been recovered); and further studies must try to compensate for that deficiency. The cautions raised by Parpola, *LAS* II A, 46–7 are well taken.

[14] Ably summarized by Parpola in *ARINH*, especially 119–24.

[15] *LAS* II A, *passim*.

[16] *LAS* I, nos. 1–33; II A, 32–33, 41–42. Synchronistic kinglist: Istanbul A. 117 iv 13 (*AfO* 3 [1926] 71; *RLA* 6, 120). Note that later tradition sometimes placed the sage Aḫiqar in Esarhaddon's reign: "[in the ti]me of King Esarhaddon, Aba-Enlil-dari, [whom] the Arameans name Aḫuqar, was *ummânu*" ([*ina tarṣ*]*i* ^{md}*Aššur-aḫ(u)-iddin šarri* ^{m}a-ba-^{d}50-da-ri *ummânu*" [*ša* L]Ú *aḫ-la*-MI-*mu-ú iqabbû* ^{m}*a-ḫu-*ʾ*-qa-a-ri:* van Dijk, *UVB* 18 [1962], pl. 27:19–20 and p. 45, Seleucid *apkallu-ummânu* list). See further the pertinent remarks by Jonas Greenfield, *JAOS* 82 (1962), 292–3, especially concerning the Elephantine material (which also puts Aḥiqar in the early seventh century, but under Sennacherib). Both attributions may be true, as we know in the case of Ištar-šum-ēreš, who worked successively under Esarhaddon and Ashurbanipal.

[17] *LAS* II A, 22–23.

[18] *LAS* II A, *passim*.

[19] *LAS* II A, 54–65, followed by Bottéro, *Akkadica* 9 (1978), 2–24; cf. also earlier remarks by Landsberger, *Brief*, 40–51. For the use of the substitute-king ritual in the last years of Adad-nirari III (810–783), see Parpola, *JSS* 21 (1976), 173.

[20] Though there are of course numerous minor changes. One should note the additional materials added by Version G (*AfO* 24 [1973], 118–9 and pl. 14) in Episodes 3c^2, 3c^3, and 4b and the whole new section to be inserted after Episode 3c^3; yet all of these are quite fragmentary and are at present

critical apparatus and its bibliography are largely superseded and so are revised below in an abbreviated chart to facilitate reference to the text publications which have appeared since 1956. This chart is followed by a schematic summary of the contents and coverage of the various manuscript traditions. It should be noted that the critical apparatus and summary are concerned only with those texts (Borger's Bab. A-E and Bab. G-"H") and passages (Borger's §11 Episodes 2-9) that deal with Esarhaddon's description of the downfall of Babylon.

Esarhaddon's Texts Bab. A-E, Bab. G-"H": Textual Apparatus

Material	*Sigla and Museum Numbers*			*Primary Publication*	*Provenience*
P	*Version A*	A^1:	BM 78223=	*CT* 44 3	(Babylon)
"			A^1a: (formerly priv. coll.)+	"	"
"			A^1b: 88–5–12,78+	"	"
"			A^1c: 88–5–12,77	"	"
P		A^2:	MAH 15877	unpublished	-----
P		A^3:	VA 8420 (Assur 8000)	unpublished	Assur
P		A^4:	BM 60032 (82–7–14,4442)	*AfO* 24, 117	-----
P		A^5:	BM 132294 (1958–4–12,28)	*AfO* 24, 117–8	-----
T	*Version B*	Ba:	K. 192 (+)	*BA* 3, 311–3	Nineveh
T		Bb:	K. 4513	Bauer *Asb.* pl. 41	"
P	*Version C*	C^1:	BM 78224 (88–5–12,79)	*CT* 44 4	(Babylon)
P		C^2:	BM 78221+78222 (88–5–12,75+76)	*CT* 44 5	(Babylon)
S	*Version D*		60–12–1,1	1 *R* 49	Nineveh
P	*Version E*	E^1:	BM 78225 (88–5–12,80)	*CT* 44 6	(Babylon)
P		E^2:	BM 78248 (88–5–12,103)	*CT* 44 7	(Babylon)
P		E^3a:	BM 78246 (88–5–12,101)+	*CT* 44 8	(Babylon)
"		E^3b:	AO 7736	*AfO* 18, pls. 21–2	(")
P		E^4:	BM 42688 (81–7–1,430)	*AfO* 24, pl. 13	-----
P		E^5:	BM 34899 (Sp. 2,411)	*CT* 51 78	(Babylon)
P	*Version G*	Ga:	1904–10–9,1(+)	*CT* 34 1–2	Nineveh
"		Gb:	BM 122617+127846 (1930–5–8,6)	*AfO* 24, pl. 14	"
T	*Version "H"*		82–3–23,55	*AfO* 24, pl. 14	Nineveh

Notes to Chart

Material. P=prism. S=stone. T=tablet.

Sigla. Note that A^3 and A^4 in *HKL* 2, 18 are relabelled here as A^4 and A^5 to conform with the numbering in *Asarh.*, p. 10 (where there is already an A^3). The designations *a* and *b* for different parts of E^3 and G are introduced here. Bab. H in *HKL* 2, 18 is referred to here as "H" to distinguish it from *WVDOG* 4, 17 no. 7 and pl. 6 no. 3 (already labelled as Bab. H in *Asarh.*, p. 29).

Provenience. There is a minor slip in *Asarh.*, p. 10, where Versions B, E, and G are said to come from Nineveh; this should be corrected to B, D, and G. Borger infers that the texts with 88–5–12 accession numbers (A^1b+c, C^1, C^2, E^1, E^2, E^3a) came from or near Babylon on the occasion of a purchasing expedition by Budge; Landsberger, *Brief*, p. 19 n. 18 seems to hint that they might have come from Sippar. In this respect, I have followed Borger throughout this paper.

Sources for this Chart. Borger, *Asarh.*, pp. 10–11; *AfO* 18 (1957–58), 113–8; *AfO* 19 (1959–60), 148; *BiOr* 21 (1964), 143–8; *HKL* 2 (1975), 18–9. Millard, *AfO* 24 (1973), 117–9 and pls. 13–4. Nougayrol, *AfO* 18 (1957–58), 314–8 and pls. 21–2. Pinches, *CT* 44 3–8. Walker, *CT* 51 78.

of little direct use for historical purposes. G middle col. 28′–29′ and "H":9′–12′ are either a new transition between Eps. 2 and $3c^1$ or are part of the lost beginning of Ep. $3c^1$. The enigmatic Episode $3a^2$(=$3c^2$) is further elucidated by Borger, *BiOr* 21 (1964), 144, and Millard, *AfO* 24 [1973], 117 and pl. 14, but is still not satisfactorily solved. A fuller bibliography is given in the list of sources following the textual apparatus chart.

ESARHADDON §11 EPISODES 2–9: SUMMARY OF CONTENTS AND COVERAGE OF THE VARIOUS VERSIONS

Episode/ Fassung	*Contents*	*Versions*						
2	In the reign of an earlier king, there were evil omens in Sumer & Akkad.	A		C	D		G	… "H"
3a[1], 3b	The inhabitants continually prevaricated.	A		C	D			
3c[1]	There were crimes, injustice, dishonoring parents, etc.		… B				G …	"H" …
3a[2], 3c[2]	(The inhabitants) mistreated their gods and goddesses [uncert. mng.]	A	B	C			G	
3c[3]	They left off regular offerings and cult observances.		B				G	
3′	[contents undetermined]						G	
4a	They took the treasure of Esagila and used it to pay Elam.	A		C	D			
4b	They took the property of Esagila and Babylon, etc. [longer vers. of 4a.]		B				G …	
5a	Marduk became angry and decided to destroy land and people.	A		C	D			
5b	[Longer, more literary version of 5a.]		B				… G	
5c	Before my (Esarh.'s) time, Marduk became angry with Esagila & Babylon.					E		
6	There were evil omens in heaven and on earth (with description).		B				G …	
7a	The Araḫtu overflowed and turned the city into a ruin.	A	B	C …	D			
7b	Esagila and Babylon became a wasteland.					E		
7c	Reeds and poplars grew in the abandoned city; birds & fish lived there.						… G …	
8a	Its gods and goddesses flew up to heaven.	A	B		D			
8b	Its gods and goddesses left their shrines and went up to heaven.					E		
9a	Its inhabitants fled for refuge to an unknown land.	A						
9b	Its inhabitants sought concealment in an unknown land.		B					
9c	Its inhabitants were distributed as slaves among foreigners.				D	E		

Legend. In the "Versions" column, letters in a horizontal line indicate that the episode is attested in the listed versions; thus Ep. 2 is at least partially attested in Versions A, C, D, G, and "H" (but not in B or E). A vertical line indicates manuscript continuity between episodes; thus in Version A, Ep. 2 is immediately followed by Eps. 3a[1], 3a[2], 4a, 5a, etc. Dots indicate where a version breaks off (B is broken before Ep. 3c[1], "H" after Ep. 3c[1], etc.).

Before commenting on the contents of these passages, it is worth making a few general remarks on the textual tradition itself. First, despite the editorial convenience of editing the inscriptions together, it must be stressed that we are dealing here with multiple texts, not just recensions of a single text. Though one may dispute about fine points of textual families and more or less duplicate recensions, there are certain clearly observable patterns. Version A, the text taken as standard for most of Episodes 2-9, devotes 32 lines to the downfall of Babylon.[21] The other versions dealing with the same theme run the gamut from total agreement to total disagreement with Version A: Version C (100% agreement),[22] Version D (77%),[23] Version B (38%),[24] Version G (20%),[25] Version E(0%).[26] Version E, though complete, has no text here in common with any of the other versions except D,

[21] Counted according to text A[1].

[22] I.e., Version C shares all parts of Eps. 2–7 in common with A until it (C) breaks off. This does not mean verbal and orthographic invariation, but simply the sharing of the same basic text for each episode (2, 3a[1], 3a[2], 4a, 5a, 7a, though only one word of the last is preserved).

[23] 7.5 lines of Version A differ from D, which omits Ep. 3a[2] and substitutes Ep. 9c for 9a. (This and the following divergences are reckoned in terms of lines in Version A, as counted in prism A[1]; needless to say, the percentages are only approximate indications of shared text.)

[24] Version A has 12 lines in common with B, namely Eps. 3a[2](=3c[2]), 7a, and 8a (with a substantial variant in the last). The preserved part of B begins at the concluding section of Ep. 3c[1].

[25] Out of a possible 25 lines (Eps. 2–7, before Version G breaks off), A has only 6.5 lines in common with G, namely Ep. 2 and Ep. 3a[2]. Version "H" matches Version G in its only preserved parts (Eps. 2, 3c[1] [?]) and could conceivably be part of or related to B or G; it and B have no overlapping text, but they are the only two Babylon inscriptions written on tablets. Because of their essential similarity, "H" is here subsumed under G and will not receive separate treatment.

[26] Episodes 5c, 7b, and 8b are unique to E; Ep. 9c is shared with D only.

with which it shares 3.5 lines (Ep. 9c).[27] In general, in these passages, versions A, C, and D have many affinities,[28] as do versions B and G.[29] Version E has a very shortened description of the downfall of Babylon, slightly over half the size of that in Version A (17.5 lines versus 32 lines). Second, the contents of some of these versions may be geographically conditioned. The more literary episodes (3c[1], 5b, 6, 7c) occur only in recensions found at Nineveh,[30] and these include the detailed description of lawlessness in Babylon (Ep. 3c[1]) and the portrait of the abandoned city as a swamp inhabited by birds and fish (Ep. 7c). Is there a reason why these more graphic passages are lacking in the versions found at Babylon? A brief perusal suggests that the manuscript traditions of these texts as a whole—not just the passages studied here—would repay more detailed study, with greater attention paid to a wide variety of factors, including patterns of variants, selectivity, geography, and style. The results could be illuminating both from a literary and from a historical point of view.

When one turns to a consideration of the contents of these passages, the overall picture is clear, despite variations in details. It may be outlined as follows:

Divine Alienation

1. There were evil omens. (Eps. 2, 6: all versions except E)
2. The Babylonians were guilty of crimes, including misappropriation of temple property for payment to Elam. (Eps. 3–4: all versions except E)
3. Marduk became angry and decided to destroy Babylon and its people. (Ep. 5)[31]

Devastation

4. Babylon is destroyed and becomes a wasteland. (Ep. 7)
   Versions A, B, C, D: the Araḫtu overflows and causes the destruction. (Ep. 7a)
   Version E: Esagil and Babylon become a wasteland and turn into fallow land. (Ep. 7b)
   Version G: (beginning broken) description of flora and fauna in the abandoned city. (Ep. 7c)
5. The gods leave and fly up to heaven. (Ep. 8, broken away in Versions C and G)
6. The people go off. (Ep. 9, broken away in Versions C and G)
   Version A: for refuge to an unknown land. (Ep. 9a)
   Version B: for concealment to an unknown land. (Ep. 9b)
   Versions D and E: into slavery under foreigners. (Ep. 9c)

The structure of these passages becomes more intelligible when they are viewed as counterpoint for the rest of the inscription (which deals with Esarhaddon's beneficence):

Divine Reconciliation

1. There were good omens and favorable astronomical phenomena; the gods became reconciled with Sumer and Akkad. (Eps. 12–17, reversing Eps. 2, 5, and 6)

Reconstruction

2. Babylon and its temples were repaired. (Eps. 18–31 and 34–35, reversing Ep. 7)
   Version G: The poplars and reeds were cut down, the Euphrates returned to its old bed. (Ep. 18, reversing Ep. 7c, both in Version G only)
3. The divine statues were refurbished and returned from Assur and Elam; cult personnel and offerings were reinstated. (Eps. 32–33 and 36, reversing Ep. 8)

---

[27] Most of Version E for the whole inscription is in fact unique. As far as I am aware, it shares only Eps. 1b and 9c (with D), 20–22 (with A and D and partially with B and C), and 40–41a (with A, C, and AC).

[28] This is also true elsewhere in the later parts of these versions (Ep. 10–41), where the texts often overlap. Version C seems to be unique only in Eps. 29–30 and 34a, Version D only in Eps. 23 and 37b.

[29] If we broaden our enquiry to the whole texts rather than just these passages, B and G exclusively share Eps. 3c[1] (putative, not yet overlapping), 3c[3], 4b, 5b, and 6 towards the beginning of the text, but nothing thereafter (this may be skewed by the fact that G is broken away between Eps. 18 and 39b). B shares some episodes with combinations of A, C, D, and/or E (Eps. 3c[2] [also with G], 7a, 8a, 13, 15a, 16, 20, 22, 24), but it also has several unique passages (Eps. 9b, 10b, 12c, 17b, 19b, 26b, 34b, 27 in that order). G too shares passages with A, C, and/or D (Eps. 3a[2], also shared with B, and 12a), but also has more sections that are unique (Ep. 3′[=*AfO* 24 (1973) pl. 14, BM 122617+127846, right col. 8′–14′]; Eps. 7c, 18, 39b, and what is presumably 40b [*ibid.*, left col., placement uncertain; but cf. Millard's remarks, *ibid.*, p. 119 about lines 10–11 (thus, rather than 11–12) as compared with Ep. 40:11–12]).

[30] In the sense that these episodes are only in texts found at Nineveh (i.e., Versions B and G), but not all texts from Nineveh have them (D does not).

[31] The decision to destroy is omitted in Version E.

4. The Babylonians were brought back, their privileges were reinstated, and they were given an honored place among nations (Ep. 37, reversing Ep. 9)

Thus the themes *divine alienation—devastation: divine reconciliation—reconstruction* delineate the body of these texts (Episodes 2–37); the rest (Episodes 1, 38–41) is essentially introduction and conclusion.

Noteworthy of course is the prominence given to the divine role in both destruction and reconstruction. There are first favorable and then unfavorable omens on earth and in the heavens. The Babylonians are guilty of all manner of crimes, including sins of commission and omission vis-à-vis the temples and their cults. Marduk becomes angry and decrees destruction; the deities later relent and allow rebuilding. The gods and goddesses leave their shrines and go up to heaven; the divine statues are subsequently brought back from Assyria and Elam. Considerable attention is given to divine participation in each step of the *alienation—devastation* : *reconciliation—reconstruction* cycle. In fact, much of the treatment could be said to be "theologically" oriented in the sense that religious perspectives clearly dominate over what we would consider dispassionate "factual" reporting. The impression gained from the inscriptions is that their primary concern is religious explanation rather than historical narrative.

Thus we return again to the question posed at the beginning of this paper. What purpose was served by Esarhaddon's revised account of the downfall of Babylon? First, it must be observed that purely theological constructs and motivation aside, the account is mostly true or at least probably so: Babylon was in the habit of paying Elam for military assistance,[32] the Araḫtu and its effluent canals seem to have played a major part in the destruction of the city,[33] the gods (i.e., their statues) did leave the city,[34] and so may have many of the people.[35] In such matters, the scribes were not lying, although they were exercising considerable selectivity (e.g., omitting any reference to Assyrians as throwing debris into the Araḫtu or bringing away divine statues). In many respects, they were reflecting the interests of their patron, Esarhaddon, and their fellow scribes in charting divine intervention in human affairs; and the Babylon inscriptions as a whole, though concerned with the reconstruction of the city, came to embed the *destruction—reconstruction* motif deeply in the broader *alienation—destruction* : *reconciliation—reconstruction* cycle and to orient it as a religious explanation (answering the question "why") rather than as an historical narrative (answering the question "how"). The explanation was probably not designed to deceive a particular audience, but rather to satisfy the predilections of an elite group of literates who formed a fellowship of authors and readers.[36] If some embarrassing details were lost in the telling, e.g., the involvement of Sennacherib in the initial devastation, then this would—not entirely incidentally—remove the onus from Esarhaddon in so quickly reversing his father's work.[37] The retrospects on the destruction of

[32] *JNES* 24 (1965), 161–6, though focused primarily some decades earlier, also adduces material from the early seventh century (*ibid.*, 166).

[33] *OIP* 2 84:52–54 (Bavian inscription).

[34] Whether through being smashed (*OIP* 2 83:48, 137:37) or being carried off is immaterial; the divine statues were no longer present in a meaningful sense.

[35] Sennacherib's texts speak mainly of slaughter (*OIP* 2 137:37, cf. 83:45–46), but there is no *prima facie* reason to doubt Esarhaddon's statement that he brought back some of the exiled population (Ep. 37).

[36] The value of the texts as apologia or religious ratiocination/justification for what could otherwise be viewed as sacrilegious acts on the part of the Assyrians would not of course be coincidental. But, in contrast to Cogan's view in *Imperialism and Religion,* 12–3, I do not think that this religious explanation need necessarily have been the product of a "Babylonian priesthood and/or party." The extrapolation of divine causation behind political and military events seems to have been a general pre-condition of Mesopotamian politico-religious thought, and such apologias could theoretically have arisen in Assyria or Babylonia and won acceptance in either land. (This too is reflected in the remarks of B. Albrektson, *History and the Gods*, 91 and 102; but he imputes primarily political motives for these inscriptions and presupposes a larger audience for the texts than was probably literate.) The downfall of Babylon and Marduk's subsequent "exile" would naturally have been viewed as taking place on divine initiative and would have been regarded as a manifestation of Marduk's anger. But the same theme could be verbalized in a variety of forms by various authors writing under different reigns; a survey of such forms has been presented recently by J. J. M. Roberts, *CBQ* 38 (1976), 9–10.

[37] In dealing with questions of motivation, one is inevitably guessing in attempting to assign priorities within what must have been a complex, multi-layered process, the complexities of which would not have been fully evident even to the actors themselves. An analysis, such as the present essay, will tend to stress one or more aspects in trying to arrive at an appreciation of the ancient situation.

Babylon served a precise purpose in Esarhaddon's Babylon inscriptions: within a narrative structured around divine involvement in human affairs, the former debasement of the city and its abandonment by god and man acted as a perfect literary foil for its glorious resurrection under Esarhaddon and the restoration of its exiled deities and citizens.

ENLIL AND NINLIL: THE MARRIAGE OF SUD*

MIGUEL CIVIL

ORIENTAL INSTITUTE, CHICAGO

0. PRELIMINARY REMARKS[1]

THIS ARTICLE IS AN EDITION OF A RELATIVELY COMPLETE MYTHICAL TALE, known since 1967 (*JNES* 26, 200ff.). The publication by O. R. Gurney of a Neo-Assyrian bilingual tablet in 1964 with a substantial part of the first third of the text (*STT* 151–54) prompted a reexamination of unpublished duplicates from Nippur and two published pieces (*VAS* 10 177 and *HAV* 16) that resulted in a preliminary, and in many points incorrect, proposal of reconstruction (*JNES* 26, 201). Subsequent work led to the identification of further duplicates and to an almost complete recovery of the text. Noteworthy among the new texts are two tablets from Susa made available by the late Maurice Lambert, and three Kouyunjik pieces identified by W. G. Lambert. There remain a number of partially broken lines, some weak spots (notably from line 137 on), and two very short gaps (lines 52–56 and 124), but the main outline of the plot is now clear. The tale had a wide diffusion attested not only by the relatively high number of sources preserved and their geographical distribution, but also by its long survival through Middle-Babylonian times and into the Assyrian libraries. We hope that this edition, although limited in scope because of space restrictions, will please Samuel Noah Kramer who has done more than anyone else to revive Sumerian mythology and without whose inspiration this work would not have been started. To him it is respectfully dedicated.

1. CONTENTS AND STRUCTURE

1.1. *Dramatis personae*

1.1.1. *Nidaba.* She is the Lady of the city of Ereš, wife of Ḫaia, and mother of Sud. Nidaba's roles are in accordance with what is known of her elsewhere in the literature (Falkenstein, *AnOr* 30, 110f.; Sjöberg, *TCS* 3, 148f.; H. Behrens, *Enlil und Ninlil* 18f. lines 13f.; and see below for the most important literary sources). She appears in the text under three names: Nidaba(k), Nanibgal, and Nunbaršegunu. The pronunciation of the name Nidaba is not directly attested in syllabary sources; both Proto-Ea 678ff. and Ea VII iv 15′ff. (with Aa VII/4:92ff.) omit the goddess's name from the NAGA-section. Akkadian reads her name as Nissaba: *ni-is-sà-ba* Proto-Diri Nippur J 32, *ni-is-sa-a-ba* EN_1 14, *ni-sa-ba* *CT* 17 34:28. The reading Nidaba, preferred here, is based only on the sign name ni-da-ba in Diri IV 69. The name Nidaba is considered a compound of nin + x in Emesal Voc. I 21f.: ^{d}gašan-NAGA = ^{d}NAGA = DAM.BI MUNUS (sc. of Ḫaia); the pronunciation of NAGA in Emesal in the divine name is not yet clear. The second name Nanibgal (wr. AN.AN.NAGA, less frequently AN.NAGA.GAL) is attested in Proto-Diri Nippur J 33′ as *na-ni-ib-gal* (Akk. subcolumn); it could give a clue to a more accurate form of the original name since it would seem that it corresponds to nidaba + gal, but no interpretation is possible without additional evidence. In the present tale as well as in some OB texts the names Nidaba and Nanibgal obviously designate the same person in many cases, but in the tradition of the list An = *anum* they are kept apart: Nidaba, with nine additional names including nun-bar-še-gùn-nu, is listed as wife of Ḫaia in I 281ff., while Nanibgal (with the two spellings mentioned above) appears in I 326f. as the wife of Ennugi/Urimaš and as gu-za-lá of Enlil. The present tale seems to give another solution (see 1.1.7) which results in the following family tree:

Nidaba I - Nanibgal + Ḫaia

Enlil + Sud

Nidaba II - Ašnan

*Copies are by W. G. Lambert. See his remarks appended to this article.

[1] In addition to the usual abbreviations, note UGN = UD.GAL.NUN orthography.

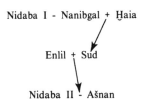

The main literary sources dealing with Nidaba are:

1) The section 89–91 of the Zà-mì hymns (R. D. Biggs, *OIP* 99, 48, with UGN parallels, see J. Krecher, *BiOr* 35, 156).

2) A short Ur III text: 6N–T680 = NBC 11107, to be published by D. Reisman.

3) The hymn nin mul an-gin$_7$, edited by W. W. Hallo, *CRRA* 17, 123ff.[2]

4) Išbi-Erra's hymn bur-šu-ma gal to Nidaba, edited by D. Reisman, *AOAT* 25, 357ff.[3]

5) An eršemma-song: L 1489 (*ISET* 1 162).

6) A širnamšub-song, edited by M. E. Cohen, *JAOS* 95, 602ff.

7) One of the hymns (no. 42) of the Collection of Temple Hymns (A. Sjöberg, *TCS* 3 48f.) is dedicated to Nidaba's temple in Ereš.

1.1.2. *Ḫaia, husband of Nidaba and father of Sud.* Originally, the name may have been a variant spelling of é-a and therefore identical with Enki, but Ḫaia and Ea are already considered two different deities in the early OB period. Note that while offerings are made to Ḫaia, especially in Ur, in the Ur III period, at that time Ea appears only in personal names. The sole text dealing directly with Ḫaia is the Rim-Sin hymn en géštu maḫ šu-du$_7$, edited by H. Steible, *Ein Lied an den Gott Haja.*

1.1.3. *Sud.* She is the daughter of Nidaba and Ḫaia who, after marrying Enlil, becomes Ninlil. Originally the deity of Šuruppak, where she is often mentioned in the ED period, Sud appears very rarely in texts from other periods or places.

The reading sud, first pointed out by R. Scholz in 1933 (*ZA* 41, 304), is supported by the complement in -da in ED: nam-máḫ-^{d}sùd-da *NTSŠ* 294 r.3, and in the ED and Sargonic personal names: inim-zi-^{d}sùd-da (DP 1; *BIN* 8 15:11), a-nun-^{d}sùd-da (*NTSŠ* 65+; 165), ^{d}sùd-da-zi-dè (*BIN* 8 181:8), etc., and -dè: di-^{d}sùd-dè-mu (Grégoire, *AAS* 203:6). The known syllabic spellings are su-ud (line 170 of the present composition; *PBS* 10/2 13 r.10, cf. E. Bergmann, *ZA* 64, 38f.), su-de (*VAS* 2 11 r. iii 12), and sù-ud (AN = *anum* I 169); late canonical texts write ^{d}sù-ud-ág (see below). By Ur III times Sud no longer appears in personal names, and receives offerings only on very rare occasions, e.g., *AASF* 92, 681:2f.; AO 4682:11f. (*TCL* 2 1), *YOS* 3 512:9. Literary texts dealing with Sud are:

1) *WVDOG* 43 36, which ends in a litany with the refrain ^{d}sùd-kam$_4$.[4]

2) Lines 180f. of the Zà-mì Hymns (*OIP* 99 51):
nun kù šuruppak BAN
nun ^{d}sùd zà-mì.

3) The balag-like text *TRS* 15 1 of OB date.

An isolated mention of Sud is found in A 33632 (Ur III Nippur, perhaps an incantation):
i′ 2′ nu mu dumu-m[u ...] n[a ...]
^{d}sùd^{ki} ⌜x⌝ [. . .] ZU.A[B? ...]
4′ a-e íd-da-b[i ...] in-[...]
kar babbar-ra SI.A b[a-...].

After Ur III the name survives, except for *TRS* 15 1, only in stereotyped phrases:

a) ù-mu-un sa-a-zu ^{d}sùd dumu nun *CT* 42 3 v 9 (dupl. *MAH* 16088, quoted *OLZ* 1961 370, has var. sa-za), written [. . .] sa-za su$^{!}$-de dumu nun in *VAS* 2 11 r. iii 12, for which the late canonical texts have: umun sa-a ^{d}sù-ud-ág dumu nun-[na] *SBH* IV 92f.; and ^{d}sùd dumu nun làl-e šà-ba *CT* 42 3 v 26, for which the late dupl. *SBH* 48 and 5R 1+ give also ^{d}sù-ud-ág, showing how unfamiliar the late scribes were with Sud's name. Both phrases belong to a standard litany found in several balags. I can offer no explanation for the repetition of the name in the same litany.

b) ^{d}sùd dumu nun a ^{urudu}šen-díli kù-ga TA[5] *VAS* 2 8 iv 9′ with the syllabic dupl. su-ud dumu nu-un e še-en-di-li kù [. . .] *PBS* 10/2 13 r.10, in a litany of the balag zi-bu-ù zi-bu-ù. The phrase is quoted in a širnamšub of Inanna: ^{d}sùd AŠ a ^{urudu}šen-díli kù-ga a-da-mìn mu-ne-ne *CT* 42 13 35 (cf. *PAPS* 107, 503). The implications of "water of the holy washing bowl" are unknown, although a connection between Sud and water seems apparent in A 33632 quoted above; note also the refrain bar a gá-gá (or a bar gá-gá) at the beginning of *WVDOG* 43, 36, and the relationship with the abzu in A 33632 and in *BA* 5 no. 1b 18, and dupl.: ^{d}sùd dumu nun abzu dúr-(ra nam-mi-gub).

1.1.4. *Enlil.* The god of Nippur who marries Sud.

1.1.5. *Nuska.* Enlil's adviser and representative (sukkal), he acts as emissary.

1.1.6. *Aruru/Ninmaḫ.* Sister of Enlil, she is a mother goddess whose name is sometimes applied metonymically to other female deities with childbear-

---

[2] Add to the sources CBS 15141, N 3041 + N 3042, and several small frags. from Ur (some bilingual).

[3] Sources D, E, and F are part of the same tablet; add CBS 15175, *TIM* 9 7, 11.

[4] Not an UGN text despite *OIP* 99 37; see Krecher, *BiOr* 35, 156.

[5] TA indicates repetition of the refrain in some OB tablets and thus its function is similar to (KI).MIN or to the blank spaces in later tablets.

ing functions. Nidaba, for instance, is called ^{d}a-ru-ru kalam-ma "the A. of the land" in a hymn (*CRRA* 17 124:8); see line 152.

1.1.7. *Ašnan* is the personification of grain. In earlier texts Ašnan plays an active role in the mythology; later on, as shown by the Debate between Laḫar and Ašnan, she is simply a divine hypostasis of grain. The former role is exemplified by the myth *OIP* 99 283 (with numerous dupls. in the same volume), which deals with, among other topics, her seven sons (of which no trace is found in the later mythology). Note also her inclusion in the Zà-mì Hymns (102f.). The god lists fail to give a clear picture of Ašnan's ancestry. In the Debate between Laḫar and Ašnan, Ašnan comes out from among the gods but it is not obvious how. In the present tale, it would seem that Ašnan is identified with Nidaba II and thus is the offspring of Enlil and Ninlil-Sud. See remarks to line 157.

1.1.8. Other deities playing secondary roles are: a) En-bàd-tibira^{ki}, spelled here en-ba-tibira (line 153), practically unknown, possibly identical with the lugal-bàd-tibira^{ki} of An = *anum* VI 68.[6] Perhaps more relevant are the names ^{d}tibira kalam-ma and ^{d}tibira dingir-re-ne given to Aruru in An = *anum* II 26f. See commentary to line 153. b) Iškur, the weather god that waters the crops.

1.2. *Geographic Setting*

The geographic frame does not play any significant role in the story and no special passage is devoted to its presentation. Shifts in locale are handled implicitly or as a matter of fact. The action takes place in Nippur, Enlil's town, and Ereš, mostly in the second locality. The reading of the town's name is given as e-re-eš (Diri IV 70; Hg B to Hh XX–XXII 27), e-reš (Aa VII/4:95), or [e-ri-i]š (Ea VII iv 21′). The earliest mention of the town is in the list of geographic names *OIP* 99 21 i 7 = *WVDOG* 43, 23 i 7 = *UET* 7 80 i 8. The archaic Uruk recension of this list (cf. *JNES* 36, 293f.) already includes Ereš (M. W. Green, personal communication). An Abū Ṣalābīkh administrative text in extremely poor condition (*OIP* 99 505) lists amounts of še GÁN PAD gur for different people; the last name is lugal éreš^{ki}. In the same place and period, Ereš is mentioned in the Zà-mì Hymns (line 89) as Nidaba's home town. It is infrequently found in ED and Sargonic times, mostly in Nippur texts and in personal names (see simply *Rép. Géog.* 1, 49 s.v.). The temple hymn no. 42 (*TCS* 3 46f.) is dedicated to the Ezagin temple in Ereš. In the Ur III period an ensi of Ereš is mentioned in a transaction that takes place in Nippur, dealing with a large amount of grain, in the 36th year of Sulgi (*ʿAtiqot* 4, 52), From the fourth month of the following year we have the inventories from two temples in Ereš: the temple of Ninḫursag (A 5834) and the one of Ninegal (*YOS* 4 296). Both texts mention Ur-^{d}nin-mug as the ensi. After this date, no more is heard of Ereš during that period. The inventories and the amount of grain could point to some critical situation, whether due to economic or military causes we cannot tell, that ended the history of the town. In the 15th year of Sinmuballiṭ (1797 B.C.), the year formula commemorates the building of the walls of Ereš, possibly a reconstruction attempt, unsuccessful in all likelihood. In literary texts, Ereš plays an important role in one of the episodes of the tale of Enmerkar and Ensuḫkešdanna (lines 170ff.; ed. by A. Berlin, 1979) as Nidaba's city and home of the old woman Sagburru. Ereš is called in this tale uru^{ki} ul "an ancient town" (line 253) and "city beloved by Ninlil" (ibid.). Otherwise, it is only occasionally mentioned in connection with Nidaba (*CCRA* 17 125:33; *ISET* 1 162:5; *CT* 44 18 r.i′ 18′; N 4196 r. 2′). R. D. Biggs (*OIP* 99, 24) and N. Postgate (*Iraq* 38, 160f.) have suggested that Abū-Ṣalābīkh is a good candidate for Ereš. For another suggestion, Ğarin between Šuruppak and Uruk, see Th. Jacobsen, *Iraq* 22, 176. Nothing definitive can be said with the information now available. If the gú-e/gú-ri/gú-še deictic system is based on river orientation, line 70 = 99 could indicate that Nippur and Ereš were on opposite banks of the Euphrates, a not too helpful detail.

1.3. *Structure of the Tale*

1. Introduction of the Protagonists	
1.1. The Woman (Sud)	
1.1.1. The Mother (Nidaba)	1
1.1.2. The Father (Ḫaia)	2
1.1.3. Intercourse	3
1.1.4. Birth of Sud	4
1.1.5. Sud grows into womanhood	5–8
1.2. The Man (Enlil)	
1.2.1. A bachelor	9–10
1.2.2. Journey in search of a wife	11–12
1.2.3. Finds woman in Ereš	12a–14
2. Meeting of Enlil and Sud	
2.1 First proposal of Enlil	
2.1.1. Enlil's proposal	14–16
2.1.2. Sud's answer (rejection)	17–21
2.2. Second proposal of Enlil	

[6] *CT* 15 18:8 does not refer to this deity, as proposed by Tallqvist, *AGE* 351. The passage should be translated "The lord no longer inhabits (the town) of Badtibira"; bàd-tibira^{ki} is in the locative, not genitive case.

2.2.1. Enlil's proposal 22–25
2.2.2. Sud's refusal to answer (rejection) ... 26
3. Enlil's plans to win the woman
3.1. Sending of emissary to the mother
3.1.1. Enlil's reaction to rejection 27
3.1.2. Instructions to the emissary (Nuska) 28–30
3.1.3. Text of message 31–40
3.1.4. Further instructions (gift for Sud) ... 41–43
3.1.5. The emissary goes to Ereš 44–47
3.1.6. Delivers message to the mother ...... 48–...
(short gap)
3.2. Mother's answer
3.2.1. Mother addresses emissary ....–60
3.2.2. Responds to emissary 61–67
3.2.3. Dictates letter to Enlil 68–73
3.3. Emissary delivers gift to Sud
3.3.1. Mother offers drinks to emissary 74–76
3.3.2. Gives instructions to daughter 77–81
3.3.3. Sud pours drink for emissary 82
3.3.4. Emissary delivers gift 83–85
3.4. Emissary returns to Nippur
3.4.1. Trip to Nippur 86
3.4.2. Emissary presents himself to Enlil ... 88–89
3.4.3. Repeats mother's speech and letter ... 90–102
3.4.4. Enlil is pleased by the answer 103
4. Enlil sends bridal gifts
4.1. Description of gifts
4.1.1. Wild and domestic animals 104–13
4.1.2. Milk and honey 114–17
4.1.3. Fruits 118–23
4.1.4. Metals and precious stones 124–27
4.2. The arrival of the caravan in Ereš
4.2.1. Description of the caravan 128–29
4.2.2. Delivery of the presents .... 130–...
(short gap)
5. Mother prepares daughter for wedding
5.1. Mother addresses Sud 137–38
5.2. Advice and blessings 139–45
6. Wedding
6.1. Sud is taken into the temple by Aruru .. 146–47
6.2. Intercourse 148–49
7. Enlil addresses his wife
7.1. Decrees the fate of his wife (Ninlil-Sud) 150–56
7.2. Decrees the fate of their daughter (Nidaba II-Ašnan)
7.2.1. As a personification of crops 158–64
7.2.2. As patron of the scribal art 165–68
8. Conclusion
8.1. Sud becomes Ninlil 170–74
8.2. Doxology 175

1.4. *Themes and Motifs*

1.4.1. Underlying the tale is the synchretistic theme of the identification of Sud, an Ereš deity, with Ninlil, Enlil's consort in Nippur. It contains, no doubt, the solution to some conflict between local pantheons whose nature is not apparent from the extant religious texts and that goes back to prehistoric times. It is possible too that the existence of two Nidaba's may have been a theological conflict of long standing. Our tale provides a solution, while the late list An=*anum* provides a different one (see 1.1.1). Besides the theme of the birth of a deity, one can point out other familiar themes such as the divine journey, the allotment of duties and powers among deities, Enlil's supremacy, etc. It is not possible to present here an analysis of the various motifs interwoven with the general plot of a marriage between deities, but some of these motifs require at least a brief comment.

1.4.2. The straightforward marriage plot is complicated by a case of mistaken identity. Enlil finding Sud "standing in the street" (sila-a gub-ba) mistakes her for a prostitute. Nowhere are we explicitly told that Sud is taken for a kar-kid, but the expression sila-a gub-ba,[7] the way she is treated by Enlil, and the repeated use of the verb šu—kár "to smear the reputation,"[8] as well as the need for the insult to be corrected by marriage, leave no doubt that Enlil took her for a lady of the street.

1.4.3. A second motif is the carrying of gifts with the left hand. Nuska is instructed by Enlil (line 42) as follows: "do not go to her (i.e., Sud) empty-handed, take her a treasure with your left hand." Complying with these instructions, "the emissary opened his left hand and gave her the treasure" (line 38). This motif does not seem to be attested in Mesopotamian narrative texts, but there are inklings in didactic texts about beliefs associated with the use of different hands.

The term for "left hand" used here is šu ki-ta "lower hand" instead of the regular šu gùb-bu. This

---

[7] See remarks to line 15.

[8] The translation *ṭuppulu* of šu--kár "to dirty one's reputation, to soil someone (physically)" is now firmly established (OB Lu A 333; C3 16; D 241; Antagal C 232; cf. Antagal e i 10′ff. and Erimhus VI 202), and confirmed by šu-kár--ak = *ḫesû* C (OB Lu D 12). My translation in *JNES* 26 205, as well as the proposals of Wilcke, *JNES* 27 237 n.16 and Sjöberg, *JCS* 25 132 are to be modified accordingly. Note that *UET* 6 275 has šu--kar and not šu--kár as stated in the last two contributions. See also F. R. Kraus's discussion of the derived *ṭupullû* in *RA* 64, 145.

term and its expected counterpart šu an-ta, or šu an-na, seem to be restricted to side designations with ethical implications as shown by the following passages:

a) *STT* 398 side b ii′ 4′ff. (Group Voc., unidentified):

á zi-da	"right side/arm"
šu an-na	"upper hand"
šu *gu$_7$ (text NAG)	"eating hand"
á gùb-bu	"left side/arm"
šu ki-ta	"lower hand."

The Akkadian translation is broken away but the meanings are clear.

b) *ZA* 6 243:38 (Commentary to an unidentified text): ŠU^{II} AN.TA *im-na* : ŠU^{II} *šap-lit* : *šu-me-lu.*

c) *CT* 24 24:44f. (Group Voc. appended to a copy of An=ANUM):

[(x) š]u an-ta = *i-mit-tu*

[(x) š]u ki-ta = *šu-me-lu.*

d) *RA* 17 121 ii 13′ff. (Bilingual religious instructions):

ninda gur$_4$-ra kíd tur-bi ú maḫ-a *in e-pe-e qir-*[*ša* (or *kir-ṣa*) *ṣuḫ-ḫi-ir*]

šu an-ta-zu ul$_4$-bí-íb	*ak-la ru-ub-*[*bi*]
šu ki-a(for -ta)-zu	*im-nu-uk šu-uḫ-*[*miṭ*]
gú-gíd-da ak-ab	*ka-bit-tuk it-*[. . .].

"In baking, make the dough compact, the loaves large. Be quick with your right hand, [keep away(?)] your left."[9]

In the ritual position of prayer seen, for instance, in Gudea statues, the right hand is on top and the left underneath. It seems preferable, however, to seek the origin of this terminology in the "good manners" dictated by traditional taboos. From the references a) and d), above, it appears that the rule, traditional in the Near East, that food be eaten only with the right hand was already operative in the old days. The concept of the pure right and the impure left is further illustrated by Antagal C 240ff.:

[šu] silig (for zalag)	= ŠU KÙ-*tum*	"pure hand"
[šu] silig-ga	= *im-nu*	"right hand"
[šu] níg-gig	= ŠU *ma-ru-uš-tum*	"bad hand, taboo hand"
[šu] níg-gig-ga	= *šu-me-lu*	"left hand."

In the context of the tale, the nature of the present, called "treasure" (gi$_{16}$-sa), is unknown. It may have been described in the missing parts of lines 85f. or it may have simply been left unspecified as something well-known to the audience. In any case, it is different from the bridal gifts described in lines 104ff., and it does not seem to have been anything edible. I would surmise that Enlil persists in believing that Sud is a prostitute and therefore the presents given to her, an impure person, have to be offered with the left hand. There seems to be no Mesopotamian evidence for other implications of the use of the left hand found in other cultures, such as secrecy or ruse; it would be rash to exclude them a priori from our tale, but I believe that the interpretation proposed above is sufficient.

9 Note that the Sumerian and Akkadian lines do not correspond one-to-one. One could restore *it-*[*id*] "watch," with a more general meaning.

2. SOURCES

2.1. *Nippur*

A 3N-T150 = UM 55-21-265 ...... 1–44.
One-column tablet (lines 1–44), complete. From TA 181 X 4.

B 3N-T371 = IM 58450 (cast and photo) .... 1–20, 27–30.
One-column tablet (lines 1–30), damaged, with several fragments incorrectly glued together. From TA 205 XI 2, wall 4.

C Ni 4412* (*ISET* 1 93) + Ni 4477* (*ISET* 1 96 and unpubl. copy by Kramer; photo) .... 11–19, 34–49, 58.
Fragment from the middle of a one-column tablet (lines 1–58?).

C$_1$ CBS 3956 (*STVC* 112) .... 14–19, ...?
Very small center fragment.

D N 2431* .... 33–44.
Small fragment, obverse. MB?

E UM 29-15-255B .... 36–48, 57–71.
One-column tablet (lines 36–71), lower edge missing, reverse heavily damaged.

F N 2203* .... 39–40, 60–63.
Small fragment, MB. Irregular text: line 40 is followed immediately by 60ff.

G UM 29-13-495 .... 40.
One-line MB oblong exercise tablet.

H 3N-T902, 91 (*SLFN* pl. 2) .... 57–64, 81–84.
Upper fragment from a one-column tablet (lines 57–84). From TA 205 XI 2.

I 3N-T503 = IM 58526 (cast) ..... 65–86.
Lower half of a one-column tablet. From TA 205 XI 2.

I$_1$ N 2690 .... 67–70, 77–79.
Left edge fragment from a one-column tablet.

J UM 29-13-345 .... 70=100.
One-line MB oblong exercise tablet.

K 3N-T903, 107 (*SLFN* pl. 2) ...... 72-78, 84-88.
Right side fragment from a one-column tablet, near the bottom. From TA 205 XI 2.

L 3N-T385 = A 30229 .... 88-110, 117-51, 154-67?
Lower right third of a two-column tablet. From TA 205 XI 1.

M 3N-T476 = IM 58506 .... 89-95, 110-18.
Upper left corner of a one-column tablet (lines 89-118). From TA 205 XI 2.

N 3N-T902, 99 (*SLFN* pl. 1) .... 96-102, 104-06.
Center fragment of a one-column tablet, near the bottom. Compatible with source M. From TA 205 XI 2.

O N 2692* .... 81-84.
Very small fragment, probably obverse.

P UM 29-16-483* .... 108-16, 157-64.
Center fragment from the reverse of a two-column tablet.

Q CBS 13104 (*HAV* 16) .... 157-73, 175.
One-column tablet (lines 157-end), lower right corner missing.

R N 3035 .... 14-19, 34-41.
Fragment from a one-column tablet.

2.2. *Susa*

S_1 Sb 12521 (copy of obv. by M. Lambert,[10] photo, coll.) .... 60-74, 92-113.
Large fragment from a one-column tablet. Ten-line marks.

S_2 Sb 12361 (copy by M. Lambert, photo, coll.) .... 143-77.
Oblong tablet, practically complete.

2.3. *Origin unknown (Sippar?)*

T VAT 1352 (*VAS* 10 177) 28-46, 95-99, 138-58
Lower left corner of a two-column tablet (despite Zimmern's remarks in VAS 10 p. x), very poorly preserved. Not collated.[11] Number of lines (46) at the bottom of col. i.

[10] These tablets are part of a group of Sumerian literary tablets from Susa whose join edition by M. Lambert and myself, finished shortly before his death, will appear in the near future. It will include copies of sources S_1 and S_2.

[11] Dr. E. Klengel kindly tells me that "die Tafel durch Salz zerstört ist und leider auch keine Photonegativ von ihr existiert" (letter of 10/9/74).

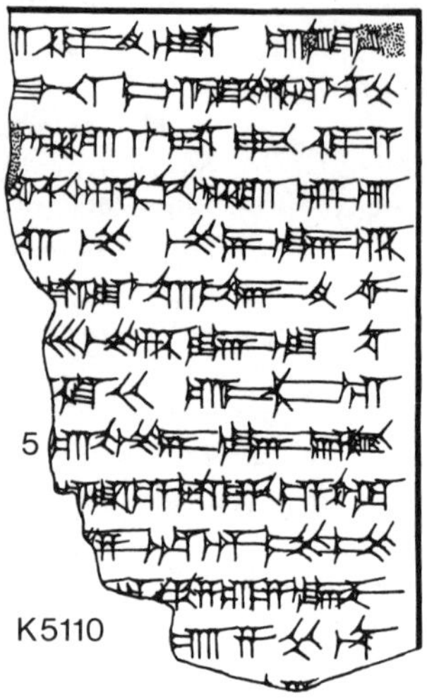

Plate 1.

2.4. *Neo-Assyrian*

U K 5110* (copy by W. G. Lambert, pl. 1) .... 1-7.
Upper right corner of a one-column tablet, bilingual.

V_1 *STT* 151 (+)

V_2 *STT* 152 +

V_3 *STT* 153 (+)

V_4 *STT* 154 .... 7-13, 15-51.
One-column tablet with a max. of 57 lines (colophon included), with the upper and lower edges missing, bilingual. V_2 and V_3 join immediately (rev.) and join back-to-back V_4 (obv.). This source is simply designated as V in the critical apparatus.

W K 5243 + K 5885* (copy by W. G. Lambert, pl. 2) .... 68-75.
Large fragment from the obverse of a one-column tablet, bilingual.

X K 17725* (copy by W. G. Lambert, pl. 3) .... 69-72.
Very small fragment, only Sumerian as far as it is preserved.

The Neo-Assyrian version was divided into three tablets. Sources U and V belong to the first tablet, W and X to the second. Nothing has been recovered from the third tablet. No colophons have been preserved to confirm this division.

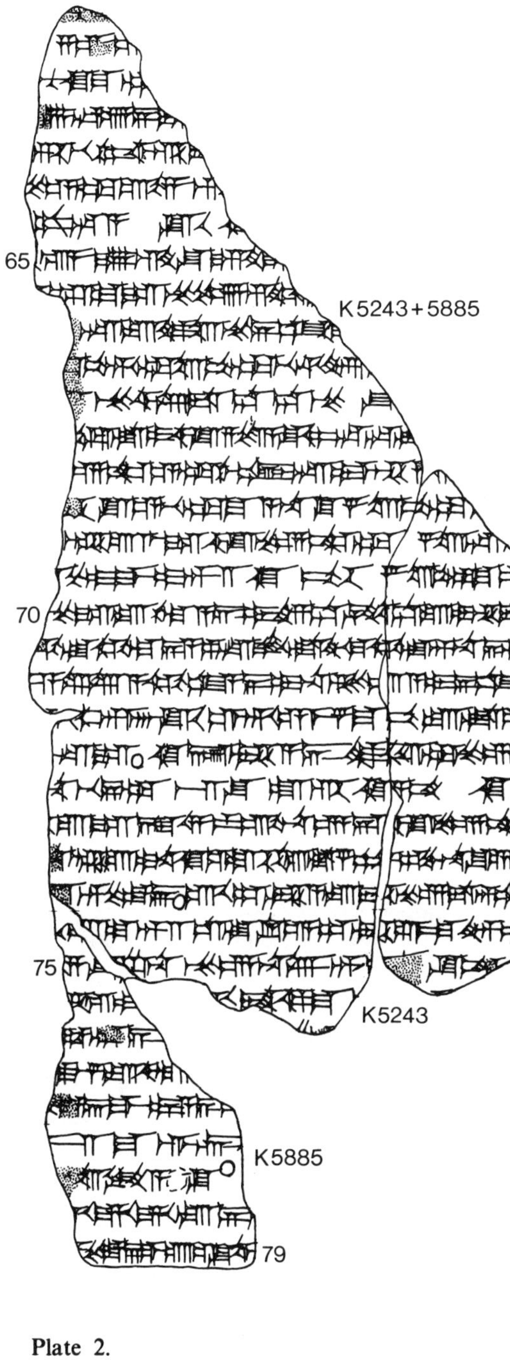

Plate 2.

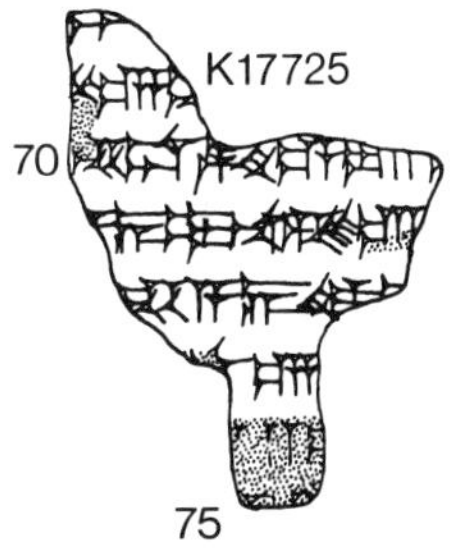

Plate 3.

Note that source C ends and H begins at the hypothetic cutoff point between the NA tablets I and II, while other sources, for instance E, straddle this point.

[In the preparation of the edition, the originals of the Nippur tablets have been used, unless stated otherwise. The Susa tablets have been collated by me. I have relied on copies for the NA texts and for source T.]

2.5 *Remarks on the Present Edition*

The Nippur sources are combined in a single line since their variants are mostly of a secondary orthographic nature. Where source T differs appreciably from the Nippur text, it is presented separately. The Susa and NA recensions always rate a separate line.

Among the many important questions that are not discussed because of lack of space, that of the differences between recensions is the most important. The NA recension, particularly the Sultantepe tablet (source V), has many morphological and syntactic errors which, for the most part, are not pointed out specifically. Note that in line 22 the scribe erroneously reverses interlocutors.

The translation may be considered too free by many colleagues. I consider it unfortunate that the common practice, used for most exotic languages, of giving first a morpheme by morpheme translation and then a current translation that respects the syntax and idioms of the target language has never gained currency in Sumerological work.

The translation follows, wherever possible, the Nippur recension. When this recension is not available or is incompletely preserved, the source that seems to fit better the plot has been followed.

3. TEXT

1 [x x x x zi-d]è-eš g̃ar-ra u$_6$-di ḫi-li gùr-ru AB
[ ] ⸢u$_6$⸣-di ḫi-li gùr-ru U
[*á*]*š-bat ana tab-rat ku-uz-ba na-šat*

2 [x]⸢x x⸣ dumu nun a-ba e-ne-gin$_7$ an ^{d}en-líl-da zag-du AB
[a]n ^{d}en-líl-lá-da zag-di-a U
[*i*]*t-ti* ^{d}*a-nim u* ^{d}*en-líl šit-nun*

3 [x x ^{d}ḫa]-ià a kù-ga ⸢šà-ga⸣[1] mu-ni-in-ri AB
[ ] šà-mu mu-ni-in-ri U
[*el*]-*le-tu ina* ŠÀ-*bi ir-ḫe-ši*

4 [x x x] ⸢d⸣nun-bar-še-gu-nu ⸢zi⸣-[dè-e]š mu-ni-in-tu-ud AB
[ ]-eš mu-ri-in-tu-ud U
[ ] *ki-niš ú-lid-si*

5 [x x] ⸢x⸣-na mu-ni-in-bùlug̃ ⸢ubur ga dùg⸣ mi-ni-in-gu$_7$ AB
[dùg]-ga mu-ni-in-sub$_x$ (DAG.KISIM$_5$ × GA) U
[*t*]*u-le-e ṭa-biš e-niq*

6 [x x k]i sikil-la ba-gur$_4$-gur$_4$ ḫi-li ma-az ba-an-d[u$_8$-du$_8$][1] AB
[-a]z ba-an-du$_8$-du$_8$ U
[*ku-uz-b*]*a ul-ṣa ú-za-in-ši*

7 [x x] ⸢x⸣ ^{d}nidaba-⸢ka⸣-ke$_4$ ká é-za-gìn-na AB
[ ] é-za-gìn-na U
(traces)

8 [x] ⸢x x⸣áb maḫ sig$_7$-ga-⸢gin$_7$⸣ u$_6$-e àm-ma-gub AB
[ ] ⸢maḫ sig$_7$⸣ [ ] V
lit-ti ṣir-ti ⸢*x*⸣ [ ]

9 ⸢u$_4$⸣-ba ^{d}en-⸢líl⸣-le é-kur-ra dam nu-mu-na-ba-àm AB
[^{d}e]n-líl-lá-ra é-kur-ta
[ ] V
[ ] *a-na* ^{d}*en-líl ina* É.KUR *áš-*[*šá-ta*]

10 ^{d}nin-líl-le mu-ni ki-ùr-ra pa [nu-u]m-mi-in[1]-è-àm AB
[ ]-líl-lá mu-ne é-ki-ùr-ta
[ ] V
[ ] *i-na* É.KI.ÙR *šum-šá*
[ ]

11 zag an-ki ki-en-gi níg̃in-na-ba igi ⸢x⸣ [x n]a-me sag̃ [m]i-[ni]-⸢ib⸣-í[l] AB
[ ] ki-i-in-gi nig̃in-na-šè ugu na-me gú [ ] V
[ ] *u* KI-*tim a-na nap-ḫar ma-a-ti* [ ]

12 kur-gal ^{d}en-líl-le kalam kin-kin-da-ni éreš^{ki}-a[1] b[í$^{?}$-(in)]-gub ABC
[-lí]l-lá kalam kin-kin-na-šè éreš^{ki} [ ] V
[ ] *ra-bu-ú* ^{d}MIN *ma-a-tum ina ši-te-ʾ-*[*i-šu*]

TEXTUAL FOOTNOTES

3. 1) A: -⸢ga⸣; B:-zu.

6. 1) This line in A is written on the left edge.

10. 1) A: [nu-u]m-mi-in-; B: nu-mu-um-m[i-.

12. 1) B: -a; B om.

12a [t]illa$_4$ nir-g̃ál-bi [ ] V
[ ] *su-la-a e-te*[*l-liš*]

13 igi i[1]-ni-in-bar munus šà-ga-na-ke$_4$ im-ma-ni-in-p[à-d]è ABC
[ ] ⸢šà-ga⸣- [ ] V

14 mu-un[1]-na-te šà-ḫúl-la diri-na inim mu-un-da-bal-e[2] ABCC$_1$

15 {túg}pàla[1] nam-nin-a ga-ba-ab[2]-du$_7$-un e-sír-ra un-gub-bu ba-[x] ABCC$_1$
(traces) V

16 nam-zil-zil á-šè nir im-te-g̃ál lú téš nu-tuku-tuku-un[1] ABCC$_1$
[ ]-zu-šè nir im-[ ] V
[*a-na du-m*]*uq-qí-ki ki-i tak-la-k*[*u*]

17 {d}sùd-e {d}en-líl-ra á nam-tur-ra-ta inim mu-na[1]-ni-ib-gi$_4$-gi$_4$ ABCC$_1$
[{d}s]ùd {d}en-líl-lá {KA} á nam-tur-ra-[ni-ta] V
[{d}MIN] *ana* {d}*en-líl a-na i-di meṣ-ḫe-ru-ti-šá a-m*[*a-ta*]

18 me-e ká-me-a še-er-ma-al-bi da-gub a-ba šu mu-un[1]-kár-kár ABCC$_1$
[ ] ká-me-ke$_4$ nir-g̃ál-e ba-da-gub a-b[a] V
[*a-na-k*]*u ina* [*b*]*a-bi-ni e-tel-liš az-za-az-zi man-nu* [ ]

19 za-e ta-z[u i-bí(?) m]u-ma-al ta[1]-aš gú-uš[2] im[3]-di-di-in ABC
[ ]-zu ne-a [x-z]u mi-ni-in-g̃ál ugu-g̃u$_{10}$-[ ] V
at-t[*a*] ⸢*e*⸣*-ka-a* [ ]*-ka šá-kin-ma a-na* [ ]

20 [b]í-ib-lá[1] i-bí-g̃u$_{10}$-ta ABC
šul [x] ⸢x⸣-a K[A x b]í-in-lá ig[i] V

⸢*eṭ-lu*⸣ [(traces)]
⸢*um x*⸣ [ ]

21 [a]-ša-an-gàr mu-⸢un⸣-ak-ne mùrgu mu-un-na-ne[1] AC
[a-š]a-aš-a-an-gar mu-un-⸢x-x⸣ [b]í-in-si-eš V
[ ] ⸢*x*⸣ *um-mi-ia ú-šam-ga-*⸢*ru*⸣ *l*[*i-ib-b*]*a-te-ia i-ma-al-lu-u*

22 [mìn-kam-ma-šè {d}en-líl-le {d}s]ùd m[u-un]-na-ni-ib-gi$_4$-gi$_4$ A
[{d}]sùd {d}en-líl-lá-ra gù mu-u[n-n]a-dé-e V
šá-niš {d}MIN *ana* {d}MIN *i-šas-si*

23 [-b]é mu-na-da-gub-àm A
[i-gi-in-z]u ⸢inim⸣ mu-un-na-ab-bé mu-un-na-an-d[a-gub]-ba V
tu-šá-ma a-ma-ta i-qab-bi-ši it-ta-zis-si

24 ⸢g̃en?⸣ ga-ra-ab-dug$_4$ inim mu-⸢un⸣-da-bal-en nitlam-g̃u$_{10}$ ḫé-me-en A
[-r]a-ab-dug$_4$ inim mu-un-d[a-]-e nitlam-g̃u$_{10}$ ḫé-me-en V
[ ] *lu-uq-bi-ki šá a-ta-mu-*[*ú*] *ḫi-ir-ti-ma-an at-ti*

25 ne su-ub-ma-ab nin$_9$ igi sag$_9$-sag$_9$-g̃u$_{10}$ ur$_5$ šu-zu-šè na-nam A
[ne] su-ub-ba-ab nin igi sig$_7$-ga[u]r$_5$ šu-zu ḫé-na-g̃ál V
[*iš-q*]*in-ni a-ḫa-ti šá pa-nu-šá dam-*[*qu š*]*u-ú gi-mil-la-ki*

26 inim ka-ka-na nu-um-ma-ra-è igi-ni-šè é-a ba-ku$_4$ A
[ini]m ka-ka-na nu-um-ma-ra-[è i]gi-a-ni-šè é-a ba-an-ku$_9$ V
[*a-ma*]*-tum i-na pi-i-šú ul u-ṣa-*[*a ana pa*]*-ni-šú a-na* É *i-te-ru-ub*

27 en gal-an-zu šà ní-te-na-ka dum-dam mu-un-da-ab[1]-za AB
[en g]al-an-zu šà ní-te-en-na-k[a!] mu-un-da-ab-za V
[*be-lu*]*m mu-du-ú ina* ŠÀ*-bi ra-ma-ni-š*[*u ri(?)*]*-im-ma uḫ-taš-ša-ši*

---

13. 1) A: i-ni-in-; C: m[i-.
14. 1) A: -un-; C om. 2) A: mu-un-da-[; B: mu-da-bal-e; C: mu-na-ab-ba-⸢x⸣-[(x)].
15. 1) AC: NAM.NIN; B:].A. 2) AC$_1$: -ab-; C om.
16. 1) B: nu-un-tuku; C: nu-tuku-tuku-un.
17. 1) B: -na-; AC om.
18. 1) A: -un-; BC om.
19. 1) AC: ta-aš; B: ta-a-[. 2) A: -uš; C: -eš. 3) A: im-; C: ì-.
20. 1) AC: -lá; B: -⸢x⸣ (perhaps su[d).

---

21. 1) A: mu-un-na-ne; C: -g]e-eš.
27. 1) A: mu-un-da-ab-; B:]-íb-[.

28 gù ba-an-dé u$_4$-ul a-ra-zu ^{d}nus-ka á-ba mu-un-da-áĝ-e ABT
[gù b]a-an-dé-e ul-la a-ra-zu ^{d}nus[ka x-d]a á mu-un-da-an-áĝ V
[*a*]*n-ni tés-li-tu* ^{d}*nuska* [ ] *ú-ma-ʾ-ár*

29 ga-e-gi$_4$ éreš^{ki} uru ^{d}nidaba-šè uru^{1} ki-ùr maḫ-bi^{2} ABT
[ ] éreš^{ki} uru ^{d}nidaba ur[u ki]-ùr maḫ^{3}-b[i]-im V
[ ] *ana e-reš* URU *šá* ^{d}NIN.PI.
[*šá du*]*-ru-uš-šu-šu ṣi-i-ru*

30 nam-ba-ra-gi$_4$-dè-en^{1} níĝ a-ra-ab-bé-en-na-ĝu$_{10}$^{2} e-ne-er ⌈ù⌉-ne-dè-daḫ ABT
[-g]i$_{(4)}$-⌈e-dè-en níĝ a-ra-ab⌉-b[é]-⌈en-na-ĝu$_{10}$e⌉-ne-er ù-mu-⌈e⌉-[daḫ] V
[*la tap-p*]*a-rak-ki šá a-qab-b*[*u-k*]*a a-na šá-a-šá* [*šu*]*-un-ni-*⌈*šim*⌉*-m*[*a*]

31 ĝuruš-me-en igi-íl-la-ĝu$_{10}$-dè mu-e-ši-in-gi$_4$-i[n] AT
[ĝuruš-m]e-en igi-íl-la-[ĝ]u$_{10}$-dè {er} lú m[u-š]i-íb-gi$_4$-gi$_4$ V
[*eṭ-lu a-n*]*a-ku a-na* Í[L *i*]*-ni-ia áš-pu-rak-ki*

32 dumu-munus-zu nam-dam-šè ga-tuku gi-na-zu šúm-[ma-ab] AT
[ ]-dam-šè ga-tuku gi-⌈na$^{!}$⌉-zu šúm-ma-ab V
ma-rat-k[*i*] *a-na áš-šu-ti lu-ḫu-uz* [*ki*]*t-t*[*a*]*-ki id-din*

33 mu-pà-da-ĝu$_{10}$ ga-mu-ra-ab-íl níĝ -dé-⌈a⌉-[ĝu$_{10}$] ADT
[g]a-mu-ra-ab-íl [ní]ĝ-ì-dé-a-ĝu$_{10}$ šu te-ma-ab V
a-n[*a*] *zi-kir šu-m*[*i*]*-ia lu-uš-ši-ki-im-ma bi-ib-la muḫ-rin-ni*

34 ^{d}en-líl-me-en pa-bíl-ga^{1} ù-tu^{2}-da an-šár maḫ-[di e]n an-ki-⌈a⌉-[me-en] ADTR
[-e]n pa-bíl-ĝu$_{10}$ ù-tu-ud-da an-šár maḫ-di en an-ki-a-me-en V
[*pi*]*-ri-ʾ-i i-lit-*[*ti*] ⌈AN.ŠÁR⌉ *ti-iš-qa-ru be-el* AN*-e u* KI*-tim a-na-ku*

35 [(x) d]umu-zu^{1} mu-ni ^{d}nin-líl ḫé-im kur-kur ḫé-im-me-KAS$_4$$^{?}$ ADTR
[-z]u mu-ni ^{d}[nin-líl]l ḫé-im kur-kur-ra ḫé-im-mi-in-dug$_4$ V
[ ]*-tu šum-šá* [^{d}*nin*]*-líl-ma ma-ta-a-tum liq-ba-a-ši*

36 ĝá-ĝeš-šú-a nam-èrim-na-šè sag-e-eš ga-na-rig$_7$ ADETR
[na]m-èrim-na-[šè] sag-ge-e-eš ga-an-na-rig$_7$-g[a] V
[MIN *ana i*]*-ši-it-ti a-na* [*š*]*i-rik-ti lu-uš-ruk-ši*

37 ki-ùr-ra^{1} ama$_5$ ki-áĝ-ĝá-ni-šè^{2} níĝ-ba-aš ga-na-an-ba ADETR
[a]ma$_5$$^{!}$ ki-áĝ-ĝá-a-ni-šè níĝ-ba-aš ga-an-na-an-ba V
[É.KI].ÙR *maš-tak na-*⌈*ra*⌉*-mi-ia a-na qiš-t*[*i*] *lu-qí-is-si*

38 é-kur bára-maḫ-ĝá^{1} ḫu-mu-da-an-tuš^{2} nam ḫé-im-mi-íb^{3}-tar-re ADETR
é-kur bára-maḫ-ĝu$_{10}$ ki-ĝu$_{10}$ ḫu-[ ]-ni-íb-tar-re V
i-na É.KUR *pa-rak-ki-ia ṣi-ri* [(traces) *ši*]*-ma-a-ti* <*li*>*-šim*

39 ^{d}a-nun-na dingir gal-gal-e-ne-er^{1} me ḫé-im-mi-íb^{2}-ḫal-ḫa ACDEFTR
^{d}a-nun-na dingir gal-gal-la-e-ne-er me ḫ[é-š]i-in-ḫal-ḫal V
ana ^{d}*a-nun-na-ki* DINGIR.MEŠ GAL.MEŠ *par-ṣi li-za-ʾ-iz*

40 ù za^{1}-ra zi sag-gi$_6$-ga^{2} šu-zu-šè ga-mu-u$_8$^{3}-ĝar ACDEFGTR
ù za-ra zi sag-gi$_6$-ga šu-zu-šè ga-mu-un-ĝál V
ka-a-ti nap-šat ṣal-mat qaq-qa-di ana qa-t[*i-ki lup-qí-i*]*d*

---

29. 1) A: uru; B om. 2) A: -bi; B: -bi-šè.

30. 1) AB: -en; T om. 2) A: -bé-en-na-ĝu$_{10}$; B: -du]g$_4$-ga-ĝu$_{10}$.

34 .1) A: -ga; T om. 2) AD: -tu-da; T: -tu-ud-[.

35. 1) R: [(x) d]umu-zu; T: dumu NI TÚG zu$^{?}$

37. 1) AE: ki-ùr-ra; T: é-ki-ùr. 2) ADE: -šè; T om.

38. 1) A: -ĝá; E: -a. 2) ADE: -tuš; T: -ti. 3) AD: -íb-; E om.

39. 1) AE: -er; D om. 2) A: ḫé-im-mi-íb-; D: ḫé-en-ne-eb-[; E: ḫe-e[n-; T:]-ne-éb-[.

40. 1) AE: -ra; FG: -a-ra; T om. 2) ADE: -ga; T om. 3) AD: ga-mu-u$_8$-; T: ì-. F has lines 60ff. immediately after line 40.

41 du-a[1]-zu-dè munus ḫi-li-a[2] pà-da-ĝu$_{10}$
ama-a[3]-ni ḫa-ra-ra[4]-ab-lá-e ACDETR
ĝen-na-zu-dè munus ḫi-li pà-da-ĝu$_{10}$
ama-a-ni ḫa-[ ] V
ina a-la-ki-ka sin-niš-tú šá ina ku-uz-bi a-ta-tu um-m[a]

42 sù-ga nam[1]-ši-du-un šu ki-ta-za[2] gi$_{16}$-sa de$_6$-an[3]-na ACDET
sù-ud-bi na-an-ši-du-un šu ki-ta-zu gi$_{16}$-sa [ ] V
ri-qiš la ta-lak-ši ina š[u-me]l-ti-ka [ ]

43 u$_4$ na-àm[1]-zal-zal-e-en[2] ul$_4$-la-bi inim-ma[3]-ni gur-ma-ab[4] ACDET
u$_4$ na-an-zal-e ul$_4$-la-bi inim-m[a-ni]-ra-ab V
l[a]

44 ukkingal ^{d}nuska á-áĝ-ĝá ^{d}en-líl-lá[1] šu ba-an[2]-ti-a-ta ACDET
ukkingal ^{d}nus[ka] V

45 u$_4$ ⸢x x⸣ nam-zal[1] éreš^{ki}-šè[2] ĝìr-ni[3] na-àm-mi[4]-gub CET
[ ]-in-[ ] V
[ ]-*ta*-[ ]

46 é-za-gìn ki-tuš ^{d}nanibgal-šè[1] mu-na-da-an-ku$_4$-ku$_4$[2] CET
[ ] V
[ana É].⸢ZA.GÌN⸣ šu-bat ^{d}MIN i-ru-um-[ma]

47 [x x] ⸢x⸣ zi ^{d}nanibgal ⸢bára⸣-ga-na ki mu-na-ni-ib-za CE
[k]i-a mu-un-ni-íb-za V
[p]a-rak-ki-šá uš-te-ke-ni

48 [x x ^{d}en-l]íl-lá-ka [x-x]-⸢x⸣-gub èn mu-mu-ni-ib-⸢tar-tar⸣-[re] CE
[m]u-ra-an-tar-tar-re V
iz-ziz-ma ŠU? ⸢^{d}EN.LÍL.LÁ x⸣ [ ]

49 [ ] a-na ⸢a⸣-[ ] C
[ ] ⸢é⸣-kur-ra a-na ⸢a x x⸣ [ ] V
[ ] ⸢x⸣-e-nu šá É.KUR [ ]

50 [ma]ḫ-mu-a igi in-[ ] V

51 [ ] en-na m[u-] V

52 [ ]

53 [ ]

54 [ ]

55 [ ]

56 [ ]

57 [ ] KA ⸢x⸣ [ ] EH

58 [g]a[1] KA [( )] ⸢^{d}⸣sùd lá-a ma-ra-ab-[x] CEH

59 níĝ ⸢ma⸣-[ab-bé-en]-na-zu de$_6$-ma-ab ⸢x⸣ [ ] ⸢x⸣-ab-gi$_4$ EH

60 in-ga-[n]a[1]-daḫ ^{d}nanibgal sukkal-ra[2] inim m[u-na-a]b-sag$_9$-sag$_9$[3] EFH
^{d}nidaba [ ]
inim mu-un-⸢x⸣-[ ] S$_1$

61 ad-gi$_4$-gi$_4$ lugal-bi-ir túm-⸢ma?⸣ igi-níĝin mùš nu-túm-mu EFH
⸢ad⸣-[ ]-ma? ig[i] S$_1$

62 a-ba za[1]-gin$_7$ kur-gal-da u$_4$-da šà-kúš-ù EFH
a-[ ] S$_1$
[a-ba] za-e-k[e$_4$] W
[man]-nu ki-ma k[a-a-ti]

63 kin lug[al] šubur bí-in-dab$_5$-ba me[1] a-na a-da-mìn ì-ak EFH
ki[n]-aš a-⸢da⸣-[ ]-e S$_1$
[kin l]ugal šubur NI-d[a] W
[šip]-ri be-lum ar-d[a-tú]

---

41. 1) AT: -a-; CE om. 2) AE: -a; T om. 3) ET: -a-; ACD om. 4) A: -ra-; CE: -ra-ra-.

42. 1) A: nam-; E: n]a-an-; T: ma-an-. 2) A: -za; CD: -a-zu; E: -zu. 3) A: -an-; C: -a-.

43. 1) AT: na-àm-; C: nam-; E: na-ab-. 2) AE: -e-en; T om. 3) AC(collated)DE: -ma-; T: -a-. 4) A -ab; C: -a-a[b].

44. 1) ACE: -lá; T: -le. 2) ACDT: -an-; E: -e-.

45. 1) T: -e; C om. 2) CE: -šè; T om. 3) CE: gìr-ni; T om. 4) C: na-am-mi-; E nam-[; T: nam-mi-ni-[.

46. 1) CE: -šè; T: ke$_4$? ma. 2) C: mu-na-da-an-ku$_4$-ku$_4$; E:]-ku$_4$-ku$_4$; T: ba-an-du-[x].

58. 1) Uncertain, the -g]a could be]-⸢x⸣-SAL (H).

60. 1) E: -⸢na⸣-; F:]-an-. 2) E: -ra; H: -⸢a?⸣-r[a. 3) In F this line follows line 40.

61–73. These lines are repeated in 90–102; see there for restorations and additional variants.

62. 1) F: za]-a-; E: za-.

63. 1) E: -e; H om.

64 [níĝ mu-e-dug$_4$-ga-z]a gi-na ⸢ḫél⸣-[im níĝ-lul nam-me-a] H
níĝ [ ]-lul-[la] nam-me-a S$_1$
[níg m]u-e-dug$_4$-ga-za g[i-na] W
[*šá*] *taq-ba-a lu-u k*[*i-in*]

65 [maḫ diri lú šu-gi$_4$-gi$_4$ a-b]a ḫul [ba-an-gig] I
[ ] a-ba ḫul ⸢ba⸣-[ ] S$_1$
[ma]ḫ diri lú gi šu-gi$_4$-g[i$_4$] W
[*ṣ*]*i-ra at-ra mu-ter gi-mil-l*[*i*]

66 [ur$_5$ šà mu-ni-in-ḫú]l ga-nam ì-[UD bí-dug$_4$] I
[ ]-UD b[í-] S$_1$
[(x) x é]-zu-ta ur$_5$ šà mu-ni-íb-ḫú[l] W
[*x*]-⸢*x*⸣ *bi-ti-ka ŠÀ-bi ka-bat-ti iḫ-d*[*u*]

67 níĝ-dé-⸢a⸣ mu-pà-da de$_6$-de$_6$-d]a šu-kár i[m-ma-ab-gi$_4$-gi$_4$] II$_1$
[-g]i$_4$-gi$_4$ S$_1$
[níĝ-dé]-⸢a⸣ mu-pà-da túm-túm-mu šu-[ ] W
[*i-na b*]*i-ib-li-i ù za-kar šu-mi ba-ba-l*[*i*]

68 ù-n[a-dug$_4$] ⸢ùšbar⸣-ĝu$_{10}$ ḫé-me-en níĝ šà-za ak [e-še] EII$_1$
[ ]-zu ak-a e-še S$_1$
[ù-mu]-un-ne-e-dug$_4$ SAL.ušbar$_6$-zu ḫé-me-en ⸢níĝ šà⸣-[ ] W
[*qí-b*]*i-šú lu e-met-ka-ma a-na-ku šá ŠÀ-bi-ka-m*[*a*]

69 kur-gal $^{[d]}$en-líl-⸢ra⸣ ù-na-a-dug$_4$ níĝ šà-za ak e-še EII$_1$
[ ]-zu [ ] S$_1$
[kur-gal] ^{d}en-líl-lá-ra ù-mu-un-ne-dug$_4$ níĝ šà-zu a[k] WX
[*a-n*]*a KUR-i GAL-i* ^{d}*MIN qí-bi-šú šá ŠÀ-bi-ka-ma e-*[*pu-uš*]

70 gú-ri-ta nin$_9$-a-ni ḫé-en-ĝen gú-e-ta ḫé-en-da-ĝen EII$_1$J
[-t]a ⸢ḫé-im⸣-ši-ĝen S$_1$
[gú]-še-ra-ta nin$_9$-a-ni ḫé-im[1]-ĝen gú-e[2]-ta ḫé-en-da-a[b-x] WX
[*u*]*l-tu ul-la-ni a-ḫat-su lil-li-kam-ma ul-tu an-na-ni li-r*[*u-ub*]

71 $^{[d]}$a]-ru-ru e-ri-ib-a-ni na-nam é ḫé-n[a]-ra-ab-lá-lá EI
[-d]a-ab-lá-e S$_1$
$^{⸢d⸣}$*a-ru-ru a-ru*$_5$-íb-a-ni ḫé-na-nam é-a ḫé-ni-íb-lá-[ ] WX
$^{[d]}$ ⸢*be*⸣*-let* DINGIR.MEŠ *lu-u mar-ti e-me-šá-ma bi-ta li-kal-lim-*[*ši*]

72 [lugal-zu-úr ki-ùr maḫ]-a-ni ur$_5$-gin$_7$ dug$_4$-mu-na-ab IK
[ ] dug$_4$-mu-na-ab S$_1$
[en]-zu-ra ki-ùr maḫ-a-ni ur$_5$-gin$_7$ dug$_4$-mu-un-na-[ab] WX
[*a-n*]*a be-lí-ka ina* MIN*-šu ṣi-ri ki-a-am qí-bi-š*[*um*]

73 $^{[d}$en-líl-ra itima kù si(?)-ga-n]a ù-ga-na-dè-daḫ IK
[-d]è-daḫ S$_1$
$^{[d}$e]n-líl-ra itima kù sìg-ga-na un-ĝá ù-mu-un-ne-DU-⸢x⸣ WX
[*a-n*]*a* ^{d}*en-líl i-na ki-iṣ-ṣi-šú el-li šá-qum-*[*m*]*e ap-pu-na šu-un-ni-šum-m*[*a*]

74 [ ]-ra á mu-da-an-áĝ-⸢ta⸣ IK
[ ]-⸢áĝ⸣-e S$_1$
[(x)] ⸢x⸣ ^{d}nidaba sukkal èš-maḫ-a-ta á mu-un-da-an-áĝ-a-t[a] WX
[*ka*]*b-*⸢*ta*⸣*-at* ^{d}MIN *iš-tu suk-kal* ÈŠ.MAḪ *ú-ma-*ʾ*-i-*[*ru*]

75 [-g]ub ^{d}nuska dúr bí-in-ĝar IK
$^{[\text{ĝeš}}$g]u-za šu-niĝin-na mu-un-na-šub ^{d}⸢nuska!⸣ dúr bí-i[n-ĝar] W
[*ku-u*]*s-si-i* [*mit-ḫar-t*]*i id-di-ma* $^{⸢d⸣}$[*nuska*]

76 $^{[\text{ĝeš}}$ban]šur ⸢kir$_4$⸣-zal-[ ] W
[*pa*]*-áš-šur ta-ši-la-*⸢*a*⸣*-*[*ti*]

77 ^{d}nanibgal [gù mu]-⸢na⸣-an-dé na mu-ni-ib-de$_5$-ge II$_1$K
$^{[d}$na]nibgal dumu-a-ni g[ù] W
$^{[d]}$MIN *ma-rat-sa* [ ]

78 lú tur-ĝu$_{10}$šà n[á k]ù-ga-zu ama$_5$ dùg II$_1$K
[dumu-ĝu$_{10}$] šà ná-a KU [ ] W
[*mar-t*]*i qer-biš ta-ni-*[*il-*]

79 é-ĜEŠTU.^{d}NIDABA-ka-kam [ ] è-a-me-en II$_1$
$^{[d}$n]anibgal é-ĜEŠTU. $^{[d}$NIDABA] W

70. 1) W: -im-; X: -en-. 2) W: -è-; X: -e-.

80 [ ] ⸢x kin⸣-ti-la kù-zu gal-an-zu-⸢àm⸣ I

81 [x] ⸢igi⸣-ni-šè na-an-DU-DU kaš dé-mu-na-ni-ib HIO

82 [dug$_4$-g]a ama-na-šè šu bí-in-luḫ zabar šu-na bí-in-g̃ar HIO

83 [šu k]i-ta-ni sukkal mu-un-ši-in-⸢bar⸣ gi$_{16}$-sa mu-na-an-šúm HIO

84 [ ]-⸢x⸣-ka-ni níg̃-nam gar-gar igi-[ni]-šè mu-na-an[1]-gub HIKO

85 [ ] umbin níg̃-ba šu bí-in-ti IK

86 [nib]ru^{ki}-šè g̃ìr ba-an-dab$_5$ IK

87 [ ] ⸢x⸣ ^{d}en-líl-ra [ki] mu-un-⸢su⸣-ub[1] KL

88 ⸢x x x-e?⸣ nin-ga[l]-⸢x⸣-ni- in-dug$_4$ KLM

89 á mu-da-ág̃-e [ ]-⸢x⸣-gi$_4$ LM

90 ad-gi$_4$-gi$_4$ lugal-b[i-ir túm-ma igi-níg̃in mù]š nu-túm-mu LM

91 a-ba za-gin$_7$ [kur-gal-da u$_4$-da šà]-⸢kúš⸣-ù LM

[-d]a šà k[úš-] S$_1$

92 kin ⸢lugal šubur⸣ b[í-in-dab$_5$-ba me-e a-na a-da]-mìn ì-ak[1] LM

[ ] a-da-<mìn> ì-[ ] S$_1$

93 ⸢níg̃ mu-e-dug$_4$-ga⸣-[za gi-na ḫé-i]m níg̃-lul nam-me-a LM

[ ]-im níg̃-lul-la nam-[me-a] S$_1$

94 ⸢maḫ⸣ di[ri lú šu-gi$_4$-gi$_4$ a-ba] ḫul ba-an-gig LMT

[ ]a-ba ḫul ba-an-gig S$_1$

95 ⸢x x⸣ [u]r$_5$ šà mu-[ni-in-ḫúl ga-nam ì]-UD bí-dug$_4$ LNT

[-i]n-ḫúl ga-na ì-UD bí-dug$_4$ S$_1$

96 níg̃-dé mu-pà-da[1] [de$_6$-de$_6$-da šu-kár i]m-ma-ab-gi$_4$-gi$_4$ LNT

[d]é-dé-da šu-kár-bi gi$_4$-gi$_4$ S$_1$

97 ù-na-dug$_4$ ùšbar-g̃u$_{10}$ ḫé-[me-en níg̃ šà]-za ka[1] e-še LNT

[ ] ḫé-me-en níg̃ šà-zu ak-a e-še S$_1$

98 kur-gal ^{d}en-líl-ra ù-[na-a-dug$_4$ níg̃ šà]-za ak e-še LNT

[ ]-na-a-dug$_4$ níg̃ šà-zu ak-a e-še S$_1$

99 [gú-r]i-ta nin$_9$-a-ni [ḫé-en-g̃en] gú-e-ta ḫé-im-ta-g̃en LN

[ ]-⸢ri-ta⸣ {a-ni} nin$_9$-a-ni ḫé-g̃en ki-bi ga-àm-ši-g̃en S$_1$

100 [^{d}a]-ru-ru e-ri-i[b-a-ni na-na]m é ḫé-na-ra-lá-lá-e LN

⸢^{d}⸣a-ru-ru SAL.UD-a-ni na-nam é ḫé-im-da-ab-lá-e S$_1$

101 [lugal-z]u-úr ki-ùr [maḫ]-a-ni-a ur$_5$-gin$_7$ dug$_4$-mu-na-ab LN

lugal-zu ki-ùr maḫ-a-ni ur$_5$-gin$_7$ dug$_4$-mu-na-ab S$_1$

102 [^{d}en-líl-ra itima kù si(?)]-ga-ni ù-ga-na-dè-daḫ L

^{d}en-líl-ra itima kù si-ga-ni ur$_5$-gin$_7$ ù-ne-dè-daḫ S$_1$

103 [ ] ba-dùg ^{d}en-líl šà-ga-na ḫúl-ḫúl-e im-DU LN

su-na inim ba-dùg ^{d}en-líl šà-ga-a-ni ḫúl-ḫúl àm-⸢DU⸣ S$_1$

104 [ ] sag̃ mu-ni-íl kuš$_5$ mu-tag-tag-ge LN

kur igi-nim-ma sag̃ mi-ni-in-íl PIRIG mu-un-tag-tag-ge S$_1$

105 [x x máš-an]še <níg̃>-úr-4-e edin ní-ba lu-a L

máš-anše níg̃-úr-4-e edin-na ní-ba lu-a S$_1$

106 [-z]u ḫur-sag̃ g̃ál-la-ba šu im-ma-ni-tag L

šid nu-zu ḫur-sag̃ íl-la-ta šu mu-tag-tag-ge S$_1$

107 am lu-lim am-si dàra maš-dà az šeg$_9$ šeg$_9$-bar-ra LP

am lu-lim am-si dàra maš-dà az šeg$_9$ šeg$_9$-bar-re S$_1$

108 su-a ka$_5$-a[1] su[2]-a-ri ur-šub$_5$ udu-kur-ra áb-za-za ^{ugu}ugu$_4$-bi LP

su-a ka$_5$-a su-a-ri ur-šub$_5$ udu-kur-ra áb-za ^{ugu}ugu$_4$-bi S$_1$

84. 1) IO: -na-an-; I: -un-.

87. 1) K: -⸢su⸣-ub; L:]-za.

92. 1) Sequence as in M and S$_1$; L has line 93 before 92.

96. 1) Perhaps -m[u? in N.

97. 1) L has -ka here but ak in next line.

108. 1) L: -a; P om. 2) L: sa$_5$-; P: su-.

109 gud niga á gur-gur-ra ⸢gù-bi⸣ bí-in-sì-⸢sì⸣ LP
gud [gu]r$_4$-gur$_4$-ra gù-bi bí-in-za-za S$_1$
110 šílam amar-bi am si ḫal-ḫa sàm[an] MP
[ ]
sàman za-gìn lá-lá S$_1$
111 u$_8$ sila$_4$ ùz máš zur-zur-re [ ] MP
[-r]a
a-da-mìn ne e-ne [ ] S$_1$
112 máš gal su$_6$-lá umbin súd-súd sila$_4$$^?$ ⸢x⸣ [ ] MP
[s]ud
sila$_4$ udu ⸢x⸣ [ ] S$_1$
113 udu nam-en-na-ba[1] si ba-ni[2]-in-sá ^{d}en-[líl éreš^{ki}-šè] MP
114 ga-àr gal-gal ga-àr gazi ga-àr tur-[tur] MP
115 ga nunuz-te šeĝ$_6$-ĝá ga i-ti-ir-d[a] MP
116 làl ḫád làl ḫáb ku$_7$-ku$_7$-da ḪI [x] ⸢x x x⸣ [( )] LM
117 [x x] ⸢x⸣ gur-gur gal-bi s[i b]a-ni-sá ^{d}en-líl ⸢éreš⸣[^{ki}-šè] LM
118 [x x] zú-lum ĝeš-pèš ^{ĝeš}nu-úr-ma gal ^{ĝeš}⸢x⸣-[(x)] L
119 ⸢^{ĝeš}mi⸣-par$_4$ ^{ĝeš}šennur ^{ĝeš}ḫa-lu-úb ^{ĝeš}lam ^{ĝeš}⸢al-la-nu-um⸣ L
120 zú-lum dilmun-na gur-da dab$_5$-ba an zú-lum za-gìn-na L
121 ^{ĝeš}nu-úr-ma gal pú-ta šu-su-ub-ba ^{ĝeš}ĝeštin ga-ra-an gal nim L
122 ĝeš kur gi-rin-na ^{ĝeš}šà-^{ki}kiri$_6$ ^{ĝeš}ḪI UD ⸢x⸣ [ ] en-te-en-e gù-peš-a L
123 gurun ^{ĝeš}kiri$_6$-a si ba-ni-in-sá ^{d}e[n-líl ére]š^{ki}-šè L
124 ḫa-šum ḫa-ra-li kur ki su[d] èrim-ma níĝ šà [ ] L
125 ^{na_4}du$_8$-ši-a kù-sig$_{17}$ kù-[babbar] L
126 gú-un igi-nim-[ma ( )] L
127 gú-un dugud-da-bi si b[a-ni-in-sá] ^{d}en-líl éreš$^{k[i}$-šè] L
128 mu-pà-da eĝer-bi níĝ laḫ$_4$-[ ] ^{d}nin-maḫ sukkal a-⸢ab⸣-[x] L

113. 1) P: -ba; M om. 2) M: ba-a[b-; P. ba-ni-in-.

129 saḫar ĝìr-bi ^{IM}mùru šeĝ-ĝá-gin$_7$ an-šà-ga i-ib-[ú]s L
130 éreš^{ki}-šè nam-mi-ni-in-tùm níĝ-dé-a gal-[ga]l ^{d}nanib[gal ( )] L
131 šà bar uru-ba im-mi-in-⸢si⸣-s[i$^?$] šu nam-peš-peš-d[am] L
132 tak$_4$-tak$_4$-bi ĝìr-⸢bar$^?$⸣-ra ⸢x⸣ [ ] kur-bi [ ] L
133 AN ⸢sig$_7$$^?$-ga x⸣ [ ] L
134 [ ] L
135 ú.⸢x⸣ [ ] BI [ ] L
136 ú.A ⸢x⸣ [ ] ^{túg}aktum [ ][1] L
137 ùšbar ^{d}en-líl-lá mu[nus] ^{d}ašnan [ ] L
⸢ùšbar⸣$^{bar?}$ ^{d}en-líl-le munus šu ba-kár-kár ^{d}nanibgal mí mu-un-e T
138 [z]ur-ra-[-b]i mu-un-KU-[ ] [x] mu-[un-na]-an-DU-a-aš L
nin zur-zur-ra-ke$_4$ mu-un-tak$_4$-tak$_4$ gù mu-un-na-an-dé T
139 [^{d}en]-líl] [dam]-ta[m-m]a -ni [ḫé-m]e-en dùg-[g]a ḫé-ne-da-ab-bé L
^{d}en-líl-le dam$^!$ šà-ga-ni ḫé-me-en dùg-ge-eš ḫé-en-da-ab-dé T
140 ⸢sag$_9$-sag$_9$-ge⸣ gú-da ḫu-mu-rí-in-lá [ba]d-bad-⸢e⸣ ḫa-ra-NE L
sì-sì-ke gú-da ḫu-mu-ni-bal-e ki-áĝ bad-bad ḫa-ra-NE T
141 ḫ[i-li e-n]e-bi šu [n]am-bar-re-en-zé-en ⸢u$_4$⸣ sù-ud ba [r]e-en-zé-en L
ḫi-li-a e-ne-bi šu nam-bal-àm ḫé-im T
142 mìn-na-ne-ne du$_6$-ta NE-⸢NE⸣-en-zé-en u$_4$-da-ta tu-ud-en-zé-en L
[d]u$_7$-da zal-zal-le-zé-en ⸢mu x⸣ [ ] S$_2$
mìn-na-ne-ne ⸢x⸣ NE-NE mu-da NE-NE-zé-me-en T
143 ⸢é-a⸣ ku$_4$-ra tuš[1]-ù-dè igi-[zu-š]è ḫé-ĝál ḫé-im a-ga-zu-šè

136. 1) There is a] KA [on a tiny fragment of L, glued upside down, that could belong to this line.

143. 1) The sign is not ZU as shown by a comparison with the -zu- of a-ga-zu-šè immediately underneath.

kir$_4$-zal ⸢ḫé⸣-i[m] L
[k]u$_4$-ra-ba-ni igi-zu-š[è ḫé-g̃]ál ḫé-im [ ] S$_2$
é-e ku$_4$-ra KU-⸢x⸣ igi-zu-šè ḫé-g̃ál ḫé-im a-ga-zu kir$_4$-zal ḫé-im T

144 gìr-ús-sa-zu-ne un si ḫa-ra-[ab-sá] un ní-ba ḫa-ra-⸢x⸣ L
[-z]u-šè un-e si ḫa-ra-ab-si un ní-bi ḫa-ra-⸢NE⸣ S$_2$
gìr-ús!-a-zu-šè un! ⸢si⸣ ḫa-ra-sá un ní-bi ḫa-ra-NE T

145 nam i-ri-tar-ra-g̃u$_{10}$ ḫé-im-*ši[1]-g̃ál sag̃-íl-la ⸢é⸣-maḫ-šè g̃en-na L
[ ]⸢i⸣-ri-tar-ra-zu ḫé-im-ši-g̃ál sag̃-íl-la èš-maḫ-[ ] S$_2$
nam e-tar-re-zu? níg̃ nu-kúr-ru sag̃-íl é-maḫ-šè g̃en-[x] T

146 šu-ni im-ma-an-dab$_5$ ^{d}a-ru-ru èš-maḫ-šè mi-ni-in-kar L
[ ]-ni mi-ni-in-dab$_5$ ^{d}a-ru-ru èš-maḫ-a-šè mi-[ni]-i[n-] S$_2$
šu!-ni im-ma-dab$_5$ ^{d}a-ru-ru èš-maḫ-šè [ ] T

147 é-kur za-gìn-na mu-ni-in-ku$_4$ ì-sag̃ igi-ni mi-⸢ni⸣-[in]-dé[1] S$_2$
é-kur é ^{d}en-líl-ke$_4$ mu-un!-ši-íb-ku$_4$ ⸢x⸣ [ ] T

148 é ki-ná ⸢g̃eš-ná gi-rin⸣-[ ] tir ^{šim} $^{g̃eš}$erin-gin$_7$ [ ][1] L
é ki-ná g̃eš-ná gi-rin-n[a] tir erin-na-gin$_7$ dùg S$_2$
⸢x-ná⸣-a [g̃e]š-ná girin-n[a] $^{g̃eš}$tir ^{šim}[ ] T

149 ⸢^{d}en-líl⸣ nitlam-a-ni g̃ìš [m]u-ni-in-ḫi-li-[ḫi-li] L
^{d}en-líl SAL.UŠ-a-ni g̃ìš-a-⸢ni⸣ [(x) i]m-mi-in-⸢nir⸣ mu-ni-ib-ḫi-li-ḫi-li S$_2$
^{d}e[n-lí]l nitlam-a-ni g̃ìs b[í?-] T

150 [ ]-ka mu-[ ] L
bára nam-^{d}en-líl-lá-ka-ni mu-⸢ni⸣-[in-x-(x) š]u$_{12}$ mu-ni-in-gub[1] S$_2$

151 en dug$_4$-ga-ni URU × URUDU nin munus tam-[t]am-*ma-ni nam ḫé-r[i-i]b-tar-re S$_2$
en-dug$_4$-ga-a-⸢x x⸣-ru nin [ ] T

152 ^{d}nin-tu-re nin ù-tu nin dùg-bad mu-še$_{21}$ m[u-ri]-in-sa$_4$ S$_2$
^{d}nin-tu! munus nu-ù-t[u] T

153 ⸢^{d}⸣[e]n-ba-tibira mùš-me mi-ni-in-sig$_7$ igi-x dím-[d]ím S$_2$
[^{d}en-ba!-tibira! mùš-m[e] T

154 [nam(?)- nu-gig-ga níg̃-nam munus-e]-ne [lú igi] nu-bar-re-dam L
[n]u-gig-ga níg̃-nam munus-e-ne lú igi nu-bar-re S$_2$
⸢x x x⸣ níg̃-nam [ ] T

155 ki-ni g̃ar me *ki[1]-ti-⸢le sag$_9$-ge sag-e⸣-[eš ri]g$_7$ LPQ
[k]i-ni ì-gál gi-ti-l[e] ⸢x⸣ sag̃-e ḫé-na-ri[g$_7$] S$_2$
⸢ki x x⸣ [ ] T

156 u$_4$-da-ta munus EDIN.BAR ḫé-im munus bar lú é ḫé-im PQ
[u$_4$]-da-ta munus EDIN.B[AR] ḫé-im [mu]nus lú nin é-e-ke$_4$ S$_2$
⸢u$_4$!⸣-d[a!] T

157 lú dam sì-ga-g̃u mu-un-ù-tu kù ^{d}nidaba-ke$_4$ PQ
lú dam-tam-ma-g̃u ù-tu-d[a?] kù ^{d}nidaba-ke$_4$ S$_2$

158 ^{d}ašnan ^{d}ašnan mú zi ki-en-gi-ra ḫé-im PQ
^{d}ašnan ^{d}ašnan zi kalam-ma ḫé-im S$_2$

159 ab-sín-na ki-sikil sag$_9$-ga-gin$_7$ ní pa-è[1]-ak-za LPQ
[ ] ki-sikil sig$_7$-ga-gin$_7$ [n]í pa-è-ak-dè S$_2$

160 ^{d}iškur kù-g̃ál ú-a-zu ḫé-im a ki-ta mi-ri-in-dé[1] LPQ
[ ]-g̃ál ú-a-bi ḫé-me-en a ki-ta nag̃-nag̃ S$_2$

161 zag mu-a gu sag̃ gibil-gibil-za[1] še sag̃ gibil-gibil-za[1] LPQ
[ ] še sag̃ mú-mú-dè gu sag̃ mú-mú-dè S$_2$

---

145. 1) The tablet has -te- for -ši-.

148. 1) Line in S$_2$ and T; L om.

155. 1) Q has DI- for ki-.

159. 1) Q: -è; L:]-e.

160. 1) L: -r]i-ib-gu$_7$(clear); P: -r]i-in-dé; Q: -ri-ib-dug$_4$.

161. 1) L: i-za; Q: -za.

162 ^{d}en-líl ^{d}nin-líl-bi kúrku-a ḫé-mu-⌜ni⌝-[t]u-tu-[d]è-eš[1] LPQ

163 lú li-bí-in-dug$_4$-ga-g̃u$_{10}$ lú érim-bi hé-im[1] lirum$_4$ un-bi tu-lu-ab LPQ

[ ]-in-dug$_4$-ga-zu lú NE.DU-bi šà-nam lirum$_4$ un-bi dul-la-ab S$_2$

164 buru$_{14}$ ezen gal ^{d}en-líl-l[á-ke$_4$] sag̃ an-šè mi-ni-[íl] L$^{?}$Q

[bu]ru$_{14}$ ezen gal ^{d}en-líl-lá un ur$_5$-sì-ge ḫé-me-en S$_2$

165 nam-dub-sar-ra dub mul-la gùn-a gi-⌜dub-ba g̃eš-dub-dím⌝ Q

166 níg̃-kas$_7$ šid zi-zi-i g̃á-g̃á éš ⌜za-gìn x⌝ [ ] Q

167 sag̃-$^{g̃eš}$gag gi-1-ninda bulug sì-k[e] Q

[ ] gi-ninda-na bulug si-ga e-pa$_5$ dab$_5$-dab$_5$-bé S$_2$

168 šu mi-ri-in-du$_7$ énsi [ ] Q

[šu m]i-ni-in-du$_7$ énsi-ke$_4$ úlul (GÁN.GÁN)-la šu-zu im-mi-in-g[i] S$_2$

169 munus sag̃-íl nun-gal-e-ne

[ ] Q

⌜munus⌝ sag̃-íl kur-ra zag-dib igi-íl-la-zu-dè pà-dè S$_2$

170 u$_4$-da-ta ^{d}⌜sùd⌝ [ ] $^{[d]}$nin-líl [ ] Q

u$_4$-ta $^{⌜d⌝}$su- ^{d}en-líl lugal-bi ^{d}nin-líl nin-bi ḫé-im S$_2$

171 dingir ⌜mu⌝ nu-tuku ⌜mu⌝ gal tuku ú-gu$_7$ rig$_7$-ga S$_2$

172 ⌜x⌝ [x x]-na bára ⌜zag$^{?}$ an-né⌝ gar nidba šúm-šúm-mu S$_2$

173 [sa]g̃$^{?}$ èn-tar-bi [x x x x]-ga za-⌜e⌝ nam ḫé-tar S$_2$

174 [è]š nibru^{ki} sag̃-e-eš rig$_7$-ga-ba S$_2$

175 ⌜šìr kù mí-dug$_4$-ga⌝ [(...)] ^{d}en-líl ^{d}nin-líl-bi-[da zà-mí] Q

šìr kù mí-dug$_4$-ga dug$_4$-ge-⌜e⌝ ^{d}en-líl lugal kur-ra-ke$_4$ [zà-mí] S$_2$

---

162. 1) LP: -NI; Q: -d]è-eš.

163. 1) L: -im; P: -me-en.

4. TRANSLATION

1 [The Lady] faithfully standing [in . . .], full of admirable charms,

2 [. . .], the noble son, who compares with An and Enlil like him?

3 [Ḫa]ia, the [. . .], put the holy semen into her womb.

4 Nunbaršegunu faithfully gave birth to [. . .],

5 Raised her in her [. . .] and nursed her at the breasts of good milk.

6 [The . . .] of the young girl grew, she became full of charms and delight.

7 In the [. . .]of the house of Nidaba, in the gate of the Ezagin,

8 [. . .] stood as an object of admiration, like a large, beautifully shaped cow.

9 At that time no one had given Enlil a wife in the Ekur.

10 The name of Ninlil was not yet known in the Kiur.

11 After having traveled through Sumer and to the ends of the universe, he . . .

12 Enlil, the Great Mountain, in his search throughout the land, stopped at Ereš.

13 He looked around and found the woman of his choice,

14 Approached her and overflowing with joy engaged her in conversation:

15 "I want to outfit you with the cape of ladyship; after standing in the street, you will be [. . .].

16 How I believe in your beauty, (even if) you are not a honorable person."

17 In her youthful inexperience Sud answered Enlil:

18 "(If) I want to stand proudly within our gate, who dare give me a bad reputation?

19 What are your inte[ntions]? Why do you come here?

20 Young man, the conversation(?) is finished, out of my presence!

21 [Others . . .] have already tried to deceive my mother and made her angry."

22 Enlil spoke to Sud a second time,

23 Once more conversing with her and standing close to her:

24 "Come, I want to speak to you, I will have a talk with you, please be my wife.

25 Kiss me, my darling of the beautiful eyes, the matter rests in your hands."

26 The words had scarcely left his mouth that she went into the house in front of him.

27 The Lord, all-wise in his own heart, cried out.
28 He said: "Quick, please, Nuska, I will give you instructions about this,
29 I want to send you to Ereš, Nidaba's city, the city whose grounds are august.
30 Do not tarry. Repeat to her what I am going to tell you:
31 'I am an unmarried man, I send you a message concerning my wishes.
32 I want to take your daughter as wife, give me your consent.
33 I want to send you presents in my name, accept my bridal gifts.
34 I am Enlil, the offspring of Anšar, I am the noblest, the Lord of heaven and earth.
35 Let the name of your young daughter become Ninlil, let it be spread throughout all foreign countries.
36 I will present her the Gagiššua as her storehouse,
37 I will give her a present of the Kiur as her favorite private quarters.
38 Let her live with me in the Ekur, the august royal dwelling. Let her (also) decree fates.
39 Let her apportion the duties among the Anunnas, the great gods.
40 And, as for you, I will place in your hands the life of the black-headed people.'
41 When you get there, the luscious woman of my choice will stay close to her mother.
42 Do not go to her empty-handed, take her a treasure with your left hand.
43 Waste no time. Bring me back her answer speedily."
44 When Nuska, the Head of the Council, had received Enlil's instructions,
45 He wasted no time [. . .], he arrived at Ereš.
46 Entered the Ezagin, Nanibgal's residence,
47 [. . .], prostrated himself before her on her throne.
48 Enlil's [emissary] stood [before her], she asked him (about the message).
49–59 [*too broken for translation*]
60 He repeated to her. Nanibgal spoke flatteringly to the emissary:[12]
61 "Advisor, fit for his king, ever observant,
62 Who, like you, could give counsel daily to the Great Mountain?
63 What could I contest in the king's message which (his) slave has received?
64 If there is truth in what you have told me—and may there be no falsehood—
65 Who could reject the one who bestows such exceedingly great favors?
66 [The message] from your House gladdens our hearts and livers. Let us consider that amends have been made.
67 By bringing the bridal gifts and his personal presents the insult is wiped away.
68 Tell him: 'Let me be your mother-in-law, do what you wish.'
69 Tell Enlil, the Great Mountain: 'Do what you wish.'
70 Let his sister come from over there and I will go from here.
71 Let Aruru become my daughter-in-law, let her be shown the household
72 Inform thus your Lord in his august Kiur,
73 Repeat this to Enlil in the privacy of his holy bedchamber."
74 After the noble Nidaba, from the August Shrine, had given her instructions to the emissary,
75 She set out the chair of honor and seated Nuska on it.
76 [She set] a table of rejoicing, [. . .].
77 Nanibgal called her daughter and gave her advice:
78 "My little one, sleeping indoors [. . .] your pure [. . .], the private quarters are better (for you).
79 (Only) I may leave the House-of-Nidaba's-Wisdom.
80 [He . . .s] the finished work, he is knowing and wise.
81 [. . .] go to his presence and pour him beer."
82 [According to the instructions] of her mother, she washed (his) hands and placed a cup in his hands.
83 The emissary opened his left hand, gave her the treasure.
84 [. . .] he piled up everything and set it before her.
85 [. . .] she took the gift with fingertips.
86 [Nuska, the emissary, . . .] took the road back to Nippur.
87 [. . .] he kissed the ground before Enlil.
88 . . . , the great Lady, had said to him [. . .],
89 She gave instructions [. . . that he repea]ted:
90 "Advisor, fit for his king, ever observant,
91 Who, like you, could give counsel daily to the Great Mountain?
92 What could I contest in the king's message which (his) slave has received?
93 If there is truth in what you have told me—and may there be no falsehood—

[12] Lines 61–73 are repeated in 90–102; the translation gives the combined text and does not reflect the state of preservation of the text.

94 Who could reject the one who bestows such exceedingly great favors?
95 [The message] from your House gladdens our hearts and livers. Let us consider that amends have been made.
96 By bringing the bridal gifts and his personal presents the insult is wiped away.
97 Tell him: 'Let me be your mother-in-law, do what you wish.'
98 Tell Enlil, the Great Mountain: 'Do what you wish.'
99 Let his sister come from over there and I will go from here.
100 Let Aruru become my daughter-in-law, let her be shown the household
101 Inform thus your Lord in his august Kiur,
102 Repeat this to Enlil in the privacy of his holy bedchamber."
103 The message made his body feel good, brought great rejoicing to Enlil's heart.
104 He raised his head toward the Upper Country, animals came running:
105 Quadrupeds, from goats to donkeys, that multiply freely in the desert.
106 The uncountable ones that are in the mountain were chosen:
107 Wild oxen, red deer, elephants, fallow deer, gazelles, bears, wild sheep, and rams,
108 Lynxes, foxes, wild cats, tigers, mountain sheep, water buffaloes, monkeys,
109 Thick-horned fat cattle that bellow,
110 Cows and their calves, wild cattle with widespread horns, led by blue ropes,
111 Ewes and lambs, goats and kids, romping and fighting,
112 Large kids with long beards, scratching with their hooves, lambs, [. . .],
113 Sheep fit for a lord, Enlil directed toward Ereš.
114 Large cheeses, mustard-flavored cheeses, small cheeses, [. . .],
115 Various kinds of milk products, [. . .],
116 White honey, dry honey, the sweetest, [. . .],
117 [. . .] thick and large, Enlil directed toward Ereš.
118 [. . .], dates, figs, large pomegranates, [. . .],
119 Cherries, plums, ḫalub-nuts, pistachios, acorns,
120 Dilmun dates packed in baskets, dark-colored date clusters,
121 Large pomegranates seeds plucked from their rinds, big clusters of early grapes,
122 Exotic trees in fruit, trees from orchards, [. . .] grown in winter.
123 Fruits from the orchards, Enlil directed toward Ereš.
124 Ores(?) from Ḫarali, a faraway land, [. . .] in storehouses, goods, [. . .],
125 Topaz, gold, silver, [. . .],
126 The products of the Upper Country, [. . .],
127 Heavy loads of them, Enlil directed toward Ereš.
128 After the personal gifts, the transported goo[ds . . .], Ṉinmah and the emissary [follow].
129 The dust from their march reaches high amidst the sky like rain clouds.
130 Before they had finished bringing the enormous bridal gifts for Nanibgal to Ereš,
131 The city was full inside and out, to spread out [. . .]
132 The remainder on the outlying roads [. . .], the piles [. . .].
133–36 (*too broken for translation*)
137 (Nuska) treated nicely Nanibgal, the mother-in-law, the woman slandered by Enlil,
138 (But) the lady disregarded the flatterer, spoke to her (daughter):
139 "May you be Enlil's favorite wife, may he treat you well.
140 May he embrace you, the most beautiful of all, may he tell you: 'Beloved, open wide!'
141 Never forget charms and pleasure, make them last a long time.
142 You two make love on the 'hill,' have children afterwards.
143 Entering the House and living there, may abundance precede you, may joy follow you.
144 Let the population line your way, let the people . . . spontaneously.
145 May the fate I have decreed for you come to pass, go with head held high into the August House."
146 Aruru grasped her hand and took her away into the August Shrine,
147 She made her enter the Ekur of lapis lazuli, poured the best perfume over her face.
148 In the sleeping quarters, in the flowered bed pleasing like a cedar forest,
149 Enlil made love to his wife and took great pleasure in it.
150 He [sat] on the throne of his Enlilship, and stood up to bless her (his wife).
151 The Lord whose word is pure(?) decrees the fate of the Lady, the woman of his choice:
152 He gives her the name Nintu, the Lady-Who-Gives-Birth and the Lady-of-the-Open-Legs.
153 He makes beautiful Enbadtibira's face, . . .

154 The [functions of the] nu-gig, everything pertaining to women that no man must see,
155 He gives to her a place set for her, honor, and a favorable protective spirit.
156 From now on, let a woman be the . . . , let a foreign woman be mistress of the House.
157 My beautiful wife gives birth to holy Nidaba.
158 Let Ašnan, the growing grain, be the life of Sumer.
159 When you appear, like a beautiful young girl, in the furrows,
160 Let Iskur, the water master, be your provider, he will make water gush from the ground for you.
161 The beginning of the year is in your new flax, in your new grain.
162 Let Enlil and Ninlil procreate as desired.
163 Let the one I do not mention be the enemy, let the strength of his people diminish.
164 (While) the harvest, the great festival of Enlil, raises its head to the sky.
165 The scribal art, the tablets decorated with writing, the stylus, the tablet board,
166 To compute the accounts, adding and subtracting, the blue measuring rope, the [. . .],
167 The head of the (surveyor's) peg, the measuring rod, the marking of the boundaries, the preparation of canals and levees,
168 Are fittingly in your hands. The farmer repays you the favor in the fields.
169 Woman of pride, surpassing the mountains, choosing what you desire.
170 From now on, Sud, Enlil is the king, and Ninlil is the queen.
171 The deity without name has now a famous name, makes gifts of pastures.
172 . . . gives constantly offerings.
173 Its caretaker, . . . , may you decree the fate.
174 When (all that) is offered in the Nippur shrine,
175 A holy song of praise is said. [Praise be] to Enlil and Ninlil.

5. COMMENTARY

1. If the missing incipit of this composition were listed in the Nippur literary Catalogue, the only still unidentified beginning that gives a plausible restoration seems to be nin me zi-da (Cat N2 23 [*BASOR* 88, 14ff.]). For the relationship between Nidaba and the me's, compare nin (= Nidaba) me-ni-da me nu di-a "the Lady with whose me's no me's can compare" Ed C 74; me gal-gal-zu ki-bi [ḫa]-ma-gi$_4$-gi$_4$ *AOAT* 25, 363:117; me gal 50-e šu-du$_7$-a *CCRA* 17, 124:5; ^{d}nidaba-bi-da me šu sukud-rá 6N–T780:2. However, the text, at least as understood by the Akkadian translator, requires here a locative. Furthermore, the resulting sequence zi-da zi-dè-eš seems awkward from the point of view of Sumerian stylistics. No definitive restoration seems possible under the circumstances.

5. The sign DAG.KISIM$_5$×GA, known with the values ag/kan (Ea IV 60; Sb II 248) and ubur (Proto-Ea 830, Ea IV 65, Sb II 247; and syllabic spellings, e.g., *CT* 15 23:5, *PRAK* C 124 r.3; BM 100046:8 [*AnSt* 30, 7]), must have here the value sub$_x$, so far unattested, replacing the normal spelling with KA×GA (*enēqu, naṣābu*).

6. The placement of this line suggested in *JNES* 26, 262 has been proved wrong by B and U. Note that Sumerian uses a verb of state at the end while Akkadian has a factitive.

11. The restoration of the end of the line is most uncertain:
A igi ⌜x⌝(begins with Winkelhaken) [(x) n]a-me sag ⌜x⌝ [. . . .]
B [m]i-[ni-i]b-í[l].
A reading igi u[gu n]a-me sag . . . íl (without negative in the verb) does not seem satisfactory.

15. Enlil obviously mistakes Sud for a prostitute because he finds her "standing in the street." It is clear that saying sila-a gub-ba of a woman indicates that she is a prostitute: ki-sikil sag$_9$-ga sila-a gub-ba, ki-sikil kar-kid dumu ^{d}inanna "the beautiful girl standing in the street, the young prostitute daughter of Inanna" (incipit of an incantation BL IV, dupl. *JCS* 8 146:1f.) Cf. Falkenstein, *ZA* 56, 118 and Finkelstein, *JAOS* 86, 362f. In the Code of Lipit-Eštar, kar-kid is followed regularly by tillá (xvii 12ff., 50ff.).

16. The verb nir--gál takes regularly the comitative infix that for unknown reasons is spelled -ta- or -te- with more frequency than expected. It also governs a NP with comitative although constructions with dative (in the case of persons) or terminative (in the case of inanimate nouns) are also attested: za-a-ar nir ḫu-mu-u$_8$-dè-gál *SRT* 12:33; nam-dingir-zu-šè nir im-te-gál Enlil hymn 132. The verb nir--gál is not easy to translate (cf. *JNES* 31, 386f.) and the usual translation "to trust" often does not fit the context properly. The general idea here is that Enlil's decision is based on his evaluation of Sud's charms which override the ethical considerations resulting from her profession.

19. The deictic system with gú is regularly used in this composition (see line 70 = 99). The NA version here has misunderstood it and writes ugu-mu-[šè "toward me" for the older gú-uš/eš "to here."

21. KA×NE = mùrgu (Ea III 121; UM 29-13-648 ii 12; *MSL* 14 519 iv 3) or urgu (Proto-Ea 323; Sag B 347). Sumerian uses the construction mùrgu--dug$_4$/e: KA×NE zi ù-ne-[dug$_4$ . . .] UM 29-16-10:1 while its dupl. *VAS* 17 44:13′ has KA×NE-gin$_7$ na-a-dug$_4$; KA×NE dug$_4$-dug$_4$-ga-

a-ni Dimmani 39 (*TMH* NF 3 42); cf. further KA×NE-ni ù-dúb šu táb-e "her anger, burning coals that scorch the body" *ZA* 65, 180:17. The Akkadian idiom is *libbātu malû* (see simply *CAD* L 164 *libbātu*, b); note that the NA version modifies the Sumerian text to fit the Akkadian idiom.

23. Despite the penetrating analysis of C. Wilcke in *JNES* 27, 229ff., the "irrealis" meaning of i-gi$_4$-in-zu is ill-suited to many contexts including the present one. A simple "furthermore," "moreover," or "once more" seems to render better the intended nuance.

26. A colloquial translation of the Sumerian idiom would be "she closed the door in his face."

30. It is assumed here that Akkadian has a form of *naparkû* "to tarry" that fits very well the context, although Sum. gi$_4$ is not known in this meaning (one would expect rather to have it translated by *parāku*).

33. For mu-pà-da, see Finkelstein *JCS* 22, 75 n. 5 (based exclusively on this passage, it seems); the objections of F. R. Kraus, *RA* 65, 99ff., especially 110, are valid, and I prefer to translate "personal gift," "gift in someone's name." The *a-na* at the beginning of the Akkadian translation, for which Kraus proposes with hesitation an emendation *a-na-<ku>*, is obviously incorrect and has to be considered as one of the many mistakes of the NA scribe. Perhaps it has been inserted by false analogy with *ana širikti šarāku* or *ana qišti qâšu* (lines 36f.). The incorrect affix -ma-ab in V is probably due to an incorrect interpretation of a Babylonian cursive BA misread as MA.

41. For the verb lá with a dative of person, cf., for instance, gal-an-zu-me-en šul nu-zu-ra a-na-aš mu-un-na-lá "I am a wise person, why then do I keep close to an ignorant youth?" Man and his God, 44.

42. For the term šu ki-ta to designate the left hand, see 1.4.3.

45. The restoration proposed in *JNES* 26, 204, although plausible in itself, is not supported by a closer examination of the sources.

52ff. The reverse of C_1 has to be placed here:

1′	[	]-íb-[	]
2′	[	] ⸢x⸣ bar-šè ⸢x⸣ [	]
3′	[	] ⸢x⸣-ga [	]
4′	[	nid]aba-ka-šè ére[š	]
5′	[	] dug$_4$-⸢ga⸣ mu-u[n-	]
6′	[	] ⸢x⸣ [	].

The end of the fragment may be identical with 57f.

58. A *verbum dicendi* is probably to be restored at the end. The meaning of the imperative lá-a is not clear because of the lack of context; cf. line 71.

66. The verb UD is to be taken here as *ubbubu* in the legal sense of "to clear from debts, accusations, etc."

67. The verb šu-kár--gi$_4$, lit. "to return the slander," is used here in the sense of "to make amends for the slander, to wipe out the insult." Compare Dialogue 2:152: ki šu-kár-gi$_4$-zu gizkim nu-ra-ab-tuku "he has not given you recognition of your amends for the slander." The expression is reminiscent of šu-gar--gi$_4$ "to repay a favor," and could very well be a, perhaps ironical, analogical formation based on it.

71. Since the Sumerian speaker orientation in the use of kinship terms is different from English, the possessive -ni cannot be translated by "his" in this passage without paraphrasis or without changing the possessive. Aruru is Enlil's sister and her new relationship to Nidaba's house is described by Enlil's mother-in-law as e-ri-ib, here to be translated as "son-in-law's sister" from the perspective of Nidaba, but as "husband's sister with a specific function in the marriage rite" in relation to Enlil (hence the "his" possessive in Sumerian). For additional references for e-ri-ib, see Sjöberg, *HSAO* 219f. (add there *STVC* 131 r.2). From the present line and from lines 146f. it appears that the husband's sister had an important role in marriage rites. Aruru-Ninmaḫ goes to Ereš with the bridal gifts caravan (line 128).

75. This type of chair is mentioned in Hh IV 119 (*MSL* 5 160 with a misprint *pit-* for *pít-*). The logogram šu-nigin fits a derivation from *paḫāru*, compare ^{giš}gu-za-níg-nigin-na = *kussi puḫri* "seat in the assembly" Hh IV 101, but a form *pitḫurtu* is unattested elsewhere and the evidence for it in Hh IV 119 is orthographically difficult once the spelling *pit-* has been eliminated. I would prefer to read *mit-ḫar-ti*, for which nigin is also a possible correspondence. The meaning is not clear; it could refer to the physical shape of the chair or designate a chair of "equal rank" to the seat or throne of Nidaba. In any case, the context implies a "seat of honor."

82. Hand washing is a preliminary to proper eating or drinking: šu nu-luḫ-ḫa ka-e tùmu-da níg-gig-ga-kam "to have to bring to the mouth unwashed hands is an abomination" Prov. 3.161 in R. S. Falkowitz, *Sumerian Rhetoric Collection*, 240 (with a different translation).

104. Note the syntactic order Object + Verb + Subject + Terminative NP, used in all clauses until line 127, which puts the focus on the size of the gifts. Because of the uncertainties of the zoological and botanical vocabulary, the translations in the list of gifts are given just for literary effect and are not intended to give specific identifications. For kuš$_5$--tag, see *AS* 20 134ff. where my remarks do not emphasize sufficiently the difference between kuš$_5$--tag "to run at a fast gait, to trot, etc." and kuš$_5$ ki--tag "to drag."

106. The verb šu--tag with locative-terminative means "to choose" and corresponds to Akk. *lapātu* for which this

meaning is not explicitly accepted in the dictionaries. Compare šu-dug$_4$-ga DN and *lipit qāti* (*CAD* L 87b *lapātu*, 4′k) a ritual gesture to express choice.

114f. Given the uncertainty of the Sumerian terminology about dairy products, the translations are only approximative; those of line 115 have been replaced by a general gloss.

116. Reading ḫád from Aa III/3:87; see Ḫh XXIV 4f. and *MSL* 11 163 vi 20; 164 19 ii 2. The honey làl-ḫáb = *matqu, lallaru* Hh XXIV 2f., here with the spelling with ḫab, confirming the reading. See Sjöberg, *ZA* 63, 54f. for ta-ḫáb which in some cases has been misread for làl-ḫáb. Clear examples: mu-ná làl-ḫáb-ba bí-in-ná-e *PAPS* 107 523 r.6; é ki ná-a lál-ḫàb dug$_4$-ga-ba *ISET* 1 32:11.

124. The word ḫa-šum/sum$_6$ is spelled ḫa-zé-en in *SLTN* 61:136 (cf. *JCS* 28, 184). (Ḫ)arali is known as a source of gold (*UET* 6 1 ii 1; *CAD* A/2 227 *arallû*, e). The term ḫa-šum has been translated here by a neutral "ore," but it could very well designate a precious stone.

137ff. The text of these lines is especially uncertain because of the unreliability of the copy of source T, the peculiarities of S$_2$, and the fragmentary condition of L. In line 137, I assume that, despite the absence of -ra after ba-kár-kár in T, it is a relative clause. The clear Ašnan in L is difficult to explain.

138. It is assumed that zur-zur-ra-ke$_4$ is a genitive with ellipsis of the regens. The dative infix -na- refers to Sud. The translation follows T since L, with a diverging text, is too poorly preserved.

139. dam-tam-ma = *ḫāʾiru* A Lu III 199, but can be said of either spouse; see Finkelstein, *JCS* 22 73 ad 6 (the new dupl. Si 277 [*OrNS* 50, 92, with note] has dam-nitadam). The var. of T, dam šà-ga-ni, is a paraphrasis that confirms nicely the meaning of dam-tam. See line 157, where dam-tam of S$_2$ corresponds to dam-sì-ga of Q.

140. The verb bad-bad = *puttû* is taken here in a sexual sense as in the more usual combinations with dùg and úr.

141. e-ne here is not the 3rd pers. pronoun but rather the first element of such compounds as e-ne--dug$_4$/di or e-ne--sù-ud; its meaning seems clear (note the association with ḫi-li) although no Akkadian translation seems to be known.

142. The du$_6$ (for the term, see *TCS* 3 50f.) is also the birthplace of deities in Laḫar-Ašnan 39, and -ta is a locative of remote deixis. The verb NE-NE, with the var. zal-zal in S$_2$ (through a var. *NI-NI?) perhaps here corresponds to Akk. *ḫelû*.

144. The meaning of the verb NE at the end of the line remains uncertain.

145. The verb gál with infix -ši- means "to come into being (somewhere)," see Ninmešarra 10 (with a divergent interpretation in *YNER* 3 15, see also 74); here it refers to the actual realization of the fate.

149. The expected verb is gìš--dug$_4$, but S$_2$ seems to have gìš--nir, perhaps a hybrid formation (giš--dug$_4$ × dùg--nir, both synonyms).

151. The translation follows S$_2$; in T the first sign after -ga-a- could be -n[i] and the second looks like A; perhaps this apparent A and the following RU are a miscopy for URU×IGI. The sign URU×URUDU is perfectly clear in S$_2$, but in all probability it should be considered as a graphic variant of URU×IGI attested elsewhere: Gud cyl. A xvii 8, B xviii 8; Temple hymns 64; etc. If this interpretation is accepted, it requires the insertion of a nu- before the URU×URUDU, read silig, since the rhetorical usage of this word, with very few exceptions, shows a strong preference for negative forms. A positive form, furthermore, would not fit the context. For silig "to cease, to stop" in general, see *TCS* 3 64. Note that the equation silig = *naparkû*, first suggested by Thureau-Dangin in 1904 (*ZA* 18, 140 n.3) and now traditional in Sumerological literature (e.g., *TCS* 3 64, *SGL* 1 45ff., *SGL* 2 118ff., Behrens, *Enlil und Ninlil*, 101, Steible *FAOS* 1 42, etc.), although almost certainly semantically correct, apparently has no explicit lexical basis. The only way to avoid the insertion of the negative would be to take silig (presumably read *zilig) as *ellu* or the like as, for instance, in Lugal-e 5 or Antagal C 240f. (quoted in 1.4.3). Note in this connection the equation zulug(NAR) = *namru* Aa VII/4:135, Nabnitu XXI 250, Nigga bil. B 185 (cf. Proto-Ea 582), which gives a "complete" series zalag/zilig/zulug. However, zalag is not as appropriate stylistically as nu-silig as a qualification of Enlil's word. On S$_2$ the sign between -tam- and -ni looks more like GIŠ than MA, but GIŠ-NI (giz-zal) does not make sense in the present context.

152. I assume that Enlil here does not bless his sister Nintu (presumably for her role in the wedding) but rather addresses his new wife and gives her the name Nintu, as well as the other names, because she has become a birth-giving deity. For the names, see An = *anum* II 37f.; ama-tu-ud-da and ama-dùg-bad, with gloss du-ba-da and translation *ummu pe-ta-at bir-ki*.

153. For en-bàd-tibira, see 1.1.8. The sign which follows igi has the outline of LAGAB with some imprecise traces of wedges inside.

154. The missing sign before nu-gig-ga is possibly nam-; níg seems less likely.

155. The phrase ki-NI-gar, with var. ki-NI-NI-gál in S$_2$, can be the verbal phrase "to set her place," i.e., "a place of her own," but in view of the context one may wonder whether it is not a variant phrase of ki-bi-(in)-gar = *pīḫatu* "(administrative) responsibility."[13] Such a meaning would fit the context well, although I do not have supporting

[13] Note that since *pīḫatu* designates an administrative responsibility associated with a determined district or region, the difference between the literal translation and one based on *pīḫatu* is more apparent than real.

evidence for the spelling ki-NI-gar. Here me = *dūtu*. Source Q has DI- instead of ki-; for /kitil/, see *CAD* L 61a, *lamassu* and 66a, *awīl lamassi*, lex. sections.

156. Despite the var. A.BAR.EDIN for A.EDIN in *ITT* 1 1436, it is not obvious that EDIN.BAR is a kinship term (as suggested by Sjöberg, *HSAO* 219ff.); note that the present tale uses e-ri-ib in line 71. In ED texts there is a profession or status term BAHAR.BAR (ref. M. Lambert, *Sumer* 10, 163 sub bar-bir$_4$; and *WVDOG* 43, 29:12) applied, it seems, to males. Note that some words which are spelled with BAHAR in early texts seem to be written with EDIN in later times; thus, for instance, BAHAR.BÚR (*WVDOG* 43, 56 vi 15) seems to correspond to EDIN-búr of Proto-Lu 392 and Rim-Sin 8:36: ki-bi bàd nu-dub gú-gìr-bi edin-búr-bi ḫé-šub (the term designates something in or around the city walls; gú-gìr here is probably *pilšu* and not *padānu* [Grégoire, *RA* 69, 191]). It is thus not impossible that BAHAR.BAR corresponds to EDIN.BAR. The few occurrences of edin-bar do not provide any clue: edin-bar sù-ga-ka lú im-mi-in-nú-ù-da "people have to sleep in the naked desert" Ur-Nammu's Death 192; in *WVDOG* 43, 36 iii 13 edin bar tab-ba, bar--tab is probably the verb attested elsewhere with a meaning "to banish into, to exile" as in a-ne-ne lú edin bar-tab-ba al-me-a-ke$_4$-eš "they, being persons banished to the desert . . ." 6N–T638 i 8 (Ur III Lugalbanda epic). Note, furthermore, the expression edin-bar lagaš^{ki} in BL 175:22 (cf. *BA* 5 1b 7): edin-bar lagaš^{ki} ba-ḫul-(a-šè), where the context requires a toponym; this fact is not so clear in Eršemma 10:12 edin-bar lagaš^{ki}-mèn me-er-(ra-mu-dè a-ba mu-un-šed$_7$-dè) "I am the . . . of Lagaš, who will calm me down when I am angry?," where a term qualifying a person seems indicated (note, however, the parallel preceding line which has èš é-50 etc.).

157. While source S$_2$ could be understood as a vocative: "Oh, my favorite wife, born of Nidaba," source Q can only mean, with a Subject+Verb+Object syntactic order, that Enlil's wife has given birth to Nidaba, i.e. Nidaba II. I want to stress that this line, with its textual ambiguity, is the only basis for the theory of the two Nidaba's proposed in 1.1.1 and 1.1.7. It must therefore be considered for the moment as at best a likely hypothesis. Note that the god lists are curiously reticent about Ašnan's parentage. For the variant dam-tam : dam-sì-ga (presumably for sig$_5$), see remarks to line 139.

158. The first time, Ašnan has to be taken as a divine name, the second as a term for "grain."

161. Note that zag mu-a is not a locative here.

162. The verbal phrase occurs in Gud cyl xx 17f.: (Gatumdug) sig$_4$-bi kur-ku$_4$-a mu-ni-tu(d) "she creates the brick walls as desired." For KA.AN.NI.SI = *kúrku* "desire, wish," see Sjöberg, *AS* 16 65ff. and *TCS* 3 153. We have here a likely word play with /kurku/ "(yearly) flood," and even possibly with kurku(ME.^{d}NIDABA) Diri IV 69.

165. It is assumed that all the scribal implements listed here are given to Nidaba II and not to her grandmother. For giš-dub-dím, see Ḫh IV 21 and its Ḫg A 35 as well as OB Lu A 465 (cf. D 305). The Akkadian equivalent should be **gišda/ubdimmu*, probably identical with *muštaptinnu* (*CAD* M/2, 285b s.v.), as shown by the Ebla vocabulary *MEE* 4 403: giš-dub-dím = /*mašdabdinu*/. The reading = NI.LAGAB-*di-im-mu* in Hg A 35 is incorrect; NI.LAGAB may have resulted from a carelessly written DUB or from GIŠ.DUB. The term designates a wooden implement used to fashion tablets and, occasionally, to spank unruly students: (the student who calumniates a classmate) giš-dub-dím-ta ^{giš}tukul-l-àm ù-ba-ab-ra "after being spanked with a tablet board, like with a mace," will be thrown in chains and jailed in the Edubba for two months (Dialogue 3:183); cf. also Rules of the Edubba A 11′: [. . .] giš-dub-dím-ta ra-ra.

168. Although ensí could conceivably be used here in its Ur III meaning, it more likely reflects the semantic shift to "farmer" attested in OB times.

169. Note the textual differences between Q and S$_2$; the translation follows the latter.

175. The second part of the doxology shows again textual differences between Q and S$_2$.

APPENDIX

Further Notes on ENLIL AND NINLIL: THE MARRIAGE OF SUD.

W. G. LAMBERT

It is an honour to be invited to contribute to the present edition both in view of the jubilarian, and in view of the distinction of his former student. While the writer identified and copied the LA fragments from Nineveh, he has seen no more of the other tablets than is published. Thus he cannot comment on the main, OB-period text, but will concentrate on some more general issues.

First, the dramatis personae. The editor follows the sign-name in Diri for the standard form of the name of Sud's mother: ME.^{d}ŠE+NAGA = *i-ši-ib-ni-da-ba-ku* (*CT* 11 49 16), though he quotes other evidence favouring Nis(s)aba. There is in fact much more evidence for the latter. The earliest item is from Fara, *SF* 77 ii 11: NAGA.SÁ nu.su.bu.šè. As noted by Jestin (*ZA* 51, 37ff.), M. Lambert (*RA* 47, 84f.), and R. D. Biggs (*OIP* 99, 39), this text is remarkable for supplying phonetic renderings. Then there is ^{d}ni-is-sa-bi four times (not in every case quite complete) in a LB literary fragment (J. J. A. van Dijk and W. Mayer, *Bagh. Mitt.*, Beiheft 2, no. 91); also ^{d}ni-is-sa-ba-an in the Meskene version of the Weidner List (*RHA* 35, 186), and all the phonetic writings of the common noun in Akkadian, *nissabu* (see *AHw* and *CAD* sub voce). Thus the evidence from ED to LB is unanimous for Nis(s)aba apart from the sign-name in Diri. This is known from one LA copy only (unless there is unpublished material). Of course there is no difficulty in assuming two forms of the word, due to phonetic interchange of dental and sibilant, but it must be observed that the LA sign-form DA, especially in some Assur and Nimrud hands, is easily confused with ŠA, and the two signs are very similar in NB and LB script also. Thus it is possible that *-ni-da-ba-* in this case is a scribal error for *-ni-ša-ba-*. On this evidence the present writer prefers the majority opinion of the ancient witnesses.

As to meaning, Civil accepts that the Emesal writing ^{d}gašan.ŠE+NAGA (in litanies as well as in the Emesal Vocabulary) presumes that the meaning is nin+sab(a) "Lady of Sab(a)." Already in Uru'inimgina's time the name is treated as a genitive construction: ^{d}NAGA.ke_4 nam.tág.bi gú.na ḫé.íl.íl (*Corpus*, Ukg. 16 ix), as often later. This fits with the Emesal evidence very well. Also it must be observed that when a dialect attests the interpretation of a name, this is different from an interpretation from a learned, scribal source. It implies that that interpretation was generally accepted among speakers of the dialect. (There is evidence that spoken Sumerian of the early Second Millennium was much akin to Emesal.) Thus one must assume that about the end of the Third Millennium this interpretation of the name Nissaba was the general view in Sumer. The grammatical construction of the name as known from about the middle of the Third Millennium makes it very probable that the same interpretation was also current then. It may be objected that this interpretation may be folk-etymology only, but this objection reveals confusion of method. In studying Sumerian religion the important thing is what meaning or meanings the ancients assigned to names. For the purposes of study of Sumerian religion that is the meaning. Modern philologists talk about "original" meanings, but in the case of Sumerian we have no cognate languages nor earlier language out of which Sumerian evolved, so serious Sumerian etymology is in most cases a pipe-dream only for the present. That is a loss for study of the Sumerian language, but little loss for study of Sumerian civilization. Here the sense assigned by the Sumerians (right or wrong by our standards) is the important thing. Thus the present writer leaves to others to decide what Nissaba meant in the Uruk period, if it was then current. The doubled *-ss-* of the majority of phonetic writings is explained from the ancient etymology of the name as "Lady of Sab(a)." What sab(a) means is unknown. While it might be a place or a cult installation, it might be other things too.

With Sud, it seems that two quite distinct goddesses bear the name. In the litany *CT* 42 3 iv–v etc. ^{d}SU.KUR.RU occurs twice, which happens with no other god or goddess. The section containing the first occurrence is lacking from a shorter version edited by E. Bergmann in *ZA* 56, 13ff., but that does not change the situation. The first time she occurs in a line with preceding: ù.mu.un.sa.a.zu/za, herself bearing the epithet dumu nun. The second time she occurs in a line on her own described as dumu nun and as làl.e.šà.ba. The OB forerunner to An = Anum, *TCL* 15 no. 10 gives ^{d}nin.sa.za as a name of Šamaš, and ^{d}sud.ág as a name of Aya his spouse (ll. 176, 178). The late version of this litany reads ^{d}sù.ud.ág in both cases, though only in the first case does it render it "Aya," in the second case it repeats Sudag in the Akkadian. So at least from the period of the First Dynasty of Babylon the Umunsazu/a and Sud of the litany were understood as Šamaš and Aya. One could nevertheless argue that this identification is wrong, and that this Sud is, historically speaking, goddess of Šuruppak. Against this view two arguments must be set. The first is that there is no problem in assuming an abbreviation of a divine name. Just as Dumuzi-abzu often appears as Dumuzi and so causes potential confusion with Tammuz, so Sudag could appear as Sud. The second is that the apparent total lack of a god Ninsazu/a from the Fara texts strongly opposes any suggestion that his spouse was goddess of Šuruppak. It is of no significance that in the litany Sud bears the epithet dumu nun at both occurrences, since it occurs with many other deities. But the other epithet with the second occurrence of Sud is significant. It is làl.e.šà.ba, the meaning of which has not so far been elucidated. The late version changes it to a[m]a é.šà.ba, which is rendered *um-mi ŠU-MA*. This gives the impression of being the replacement of the difficult OB reading with something simpler! Curiously both E. Bergmann (*ZA* 56, 39) and J. Krecher (*Kultlyrik*, 124) tacitly emend the text to làl.é.šà.ba, but that is wrong despite *TCL* 15 1 24 because in Proto-Lu làl.e.šà.ga appears as a professional title (*MSL* XII 41 228), the meaning of which is given in Malku = šarru I 128: *làl-šà-ga-ku* = *šab-su-tum* "midwife" (*JAOS* 83, 427). Thus the second Sud in the litany was a divine midwife.

This connects with Sud in the myth under consideration. Previously almost nothing was known of her character, but, after marrying her, Enlil assigns her place in the universe (literally "decrees her destiny": line 151), the first point of which is to make her the Mother Goddess by giving her the name Nintur, and lines 153–154 can be interpreted to continue this theme. The phrase [ĥam?].nu.gig.ga need not refer to prostitution, but to midwifery, because the OB Atra-ḫasīs I 290 portrays the midwife at work in the house of the *qadištu* (= nu.gig): *ša-[ab]-sú-tum i-na bi-it qa-di-iš-ti li-iḫ-du*. If this is correct, line 154 of Enlil and Ninlil indicates that men were not welcome at childbirth in Sumer and Babylon. Line 153 is obscured by the uncertainty of reading at the beginning, but Civil already noted that tibira occurs in names of the Mother Goddess to indicate her activity in the growth of the unborn child, cf. also ^{d}šà.zu.dingir.re.e.ne and ^{d}nagar.šà.ga in the same context. Note further that while mùš.me can bear the meaning of *zīmū*, it can also be rendered *būnu*, which could allude to the foetus, while sig_7

can mean "make grow." dím.dím in the second half of the line is very clear, and as described the sign X could conceivably be BUL, cf. sà.an.sur BUL = *šá-as-*[*su-ru*] "womb." This final point must await the discovery of fully preserved copies, but the general point is certain. Sud as the mother goddess both engages in procreation herself and presides over procreation generally. Thus the title làl.e.šà. ba of the litany fits.

In the present writer's opinion another attribute is given in lines 157–158. Civil notes the grammatical significance of the variant readings, but his choice (and interpretation of it) does not yield the utmost clarity because it results in two goddesses Nissaba in this one text, something for which (as he stresses) there seems to be no other evidence. Also we are apparently forced to identify the second Nissaba with Ezinu/Ašnan, though this is not formally stated. The grammar of the Nippur copy is difficult, but if there is no objection to an object with agentive ending after the verb, there can hardly be objection to taking the noun with agentive as the subject and assuming that the verb lacks the subjunctive ending, which appears in the other copy. This would yield:

> May my beautiful wife, whom Nissaba bore,
> be Ezinu/Ašnan, the growing grain, the life of Sumer.

Nissaba is mentioned because, being associated with grain herself, it is appropriate that her daughter should bear the name "Grain." By this interpretation there is no granddaughter of Nissaba with the same name, only the daughter Sud, who was married by Enlil, and who made her "Grain" be giving her the extra name.

Finally, Civil's observation about the significance of right and left hands in Antagal is a very important discovery, though perhaps it does not explain everything. The passage in *RA* 17 has to be emended to yield a left hand, which the Akkadian translation does not accept, and we do not understand the Sumerian phrase sufficiently to be sure that the Akkadian is wrong. Also in the epic, while Civil is surely correct to stress that Enlil first mistook Sud as a prostitute, her reaction to his first advances must surely have disabused him of the idea. There is a perfectly obvious reason why Nusku kept the gift in his left hand. He was sent to arrange the marriage with Sud's mother, and when she agreed he was to produce a hidden gift to seal the arrangement. No doubt he used his right hand for other purposes. Perhaps, like Ninšubur, he carried a sceptre as a symbol of office. Thus the less-used left hand served to hold the concealed gift. And one wonders what Nissaba would have said if the manner of production of the gift had misrepresented her daughter's character!

THE SUMERIAN SARGON LEGEND

JERROLD S. COOPER
THE JOHNS HOPKINS UNIVERSITY

WOLFGANG HEIMPEL
UNIVERSITY OF CALIFORNIA, BERKELEY

COLLABORATION IN THE PUBLICATION OF TEXTS AMONG ASSYRIOLOGISTS IS RARE. S. N. Kramer's solicitation of comments from colleagues and publication of these comments and criticisms alongside his own work are exceptional acts, especially among the senior generation of Assyriologists. One recalls the appendix of Landsberger to *Schooldays*, the remarks of Jacobsen at the end of *Gilgamesh and Agga*, and Jacobsen's lengthy contribution to the monumental dissertation of Kramer's student Edmund Gordon, *Sumerian Proverbs*. This was preceded by Kramer's own unique experiment with Sumerian proverbs: In 1952, he presented forty-eight proverbs and their translations to the third Rencontre Assyriologique Internationale. Because of the difficulties proverbs present, he had circulated his transliterations in advance among twenty colleagues, soliciting their translations and comments, and his translations reflected the contributions of the eight colleagues who responded. And many of us recall being present at scholarly meetings where Prof. Kramer would present some unusual text he had recently discovered, freely admitting that there was much he didn't understand, and offering to send his copy and transliteration to all interested (and qualified : "only the cuneiformists among you") parties.

The present collaboration originated when Cooper and Heimpel discovered that they both had worked on the unpublished Sargon-Urzababa tablet 3N T296. Cooper had learned about it from M. Civil and Å. Sjöberg when he was preparing an edition of the *Curse of Agade*[1] and he studied it from the casts in the University Museum, discussing it with both Civil and Sjöberg. Heimpel had copied the original during a stay in Baghdad. Civil, who has the publication rights to the tablet, had already completed his own edition of the text, but nevertheless agreed to let Cooper and Heimpel publish the text here, since other commitments have delayed the revision of his manuscript for publication. He kindly made his transliteration, translation and copy available, as well as a lexical note on gú-ne-sag-gá. The present article was hammered out in discussions and correspondence between Cooper and Heimpel, utilizing Civil's material. Where there is irreconcilable disagreement between the two authors, both opinions have been included. In anticipation of Civil's more comprehensive publication, the present study has been kept brief.

THE TEXT. The existence of a Sumerian literary account of Sargon's rise has been known since the publication by Scheil in *RA* 13 of a fragment from Uruk, subsequently republished as *TRS* 73 (AO 7673; see pl. 1), and studied by Güterbock, *ZA* 42, 37f. This fragment is the lower left hand corner of a two column (per side) tablet, containing the end of the first column and the beginning of the fourth column of the composition. The one-column tablet 3N T296 does not overlap *TRS* 73, but rather seems to be a nearly immediate continuation of *TRS* 73 i, as *TRS* 73 iv seems to pick up very close to where 3N T296 ends. The story, or this portion of it, then, is nearly complete, and a hypothetical four-column edition of the text can be reconstructed as follows:

i = *TRS* 73 obv.	ii = 3N T296 obv.
iii = 3N T296 rev.	iv = *TRS* 73 rev.

Only the first and last 15 or so lines, and perhaps some transitional lines between cols. i and ii, and iii and iv, are missing.

THE STORY. The composition opens with a description of a prosperous Kish ruled by Urzaba. But the gods have decreed an end to the rule of Kish, and their new favorite, Sargon, is introduced. The bulk of

[1] To be published in Spring, 1983, by the Johns Hopkins Press.

Plate 1a. AO 7673 obverse.

the composition, contained on 3N T296, relates the events foreshadowing Sargon's displacement of Urzababa, and possible efforts by Urzababa to forestall the inevitable. The episode involving the Esikil and the chief smith is particularly obscure, but if some kind of trap for Sargon was being laid, it was certainly not successful. When Sargon reappears in Urzababa's palace, the king is horrified and writes a message about Sargon to Lugalzagesi, presumably another trap for Sargon. But we are told at tablet's end that this will backfire and lead to the death of Urzababa himself.

In *TRS* 73 iv, Lugalzagesi is questioning a messenger, presumably Urzababa's from Kish, about Sargon's refusal to submit to Lugalzagesi. If the composition ends with that column, there is scarcely room enough to give the messenger's response and then very summarily to relate events back in Kish and Sargon's triumph. If, however, this tablet is only the first half of the composition, the second tablet would recount the foretold death of Urzababa, the succession of Sargon and the battle in which Sargon finally defeated Lugalzagesi and established his hegemony over all of Babylonia.

The composition is full of grammatical and syntactic peculiarities that suggest a later Old Babylonian origin. This is also supported by the frequent quotations from and allusions to other Sumerian literary texts, and the fact that only one exemplar has turned up from Nippur. But, this may just be a degenerate version of a text composed in the Ur III period; only the future discovery of more literary texts from that period and from other sites will enable us to know for certain.

HISTORY AND THE HISTORICAL TRADITION. The inscriptions of Sargon tell us nothing of his career before he became King of Agade. The various traditions about Sargon preserved in Sumerian and Akkadian literary, historiographic and omen literature

Plate 1b. AO 7673 reverse.

have been recently collected and discussed by Brian Lewis.[2] Our composition agrees with the Sumerian King List[3] and the Weidner Chronicle that Sargon began his career as an official of Urzababa, the King of Kish. Whether it agrees with any other traditions of Sargon's early life cannot be said because of the break in *TRS* 73, but that tablet gives the name of his father, La⁾ibum, and so contradicts the birth legend's account of his paternity.[4]

Urzababa is known only from historical-literary texts. These and the Sumerian King List agree that he was Sargon's superior, whom Sargon replaced as sovereign of northern Babylonia, and thus was a contemporary of Lugalzagesi. This last is well known from his own inscriptions,[5] an inscription of Uru⁾inimgina of Lagash,[6] inscriptions of Sargon,[7] and contemporary administrative documents.[8] The son of a ruler of Umma, Lugalzagesi became king of Uruk and suzerain over Sumer. By defeating Lugalzagesi, Sargon, already in control of the north, gained hegemony over all Babylonia. Thus, unlike the *Curse of Agade*, which flagrantly contradicts much of what we know from contemporary sources, the composition presented here is faithful to the outlines of history. But, by their very nature, the details of the composition suggest that they are invented, and the composition must be classed

[2] *The Sargon Legend*, Chaps. 3–4. [See also J. Westenholz's article, below, *Ed.*]

[3] See the contribution of P. Michalowski in this volume.

[4] Lewis, op.cit. 42ff., quoted here in the comm. to *TRS* 73 obv. 10f.

[5] See Cooper, *Sumerian and Akkadian Royal Inscriptions*, I (forthcoming), Um 7.

[6] Ibid. La 9.5.

[7] Hirsch, *AfO* 20 Sargon b 1, 6, 7.

[8] Powell, *HUCA* 40 1ff.

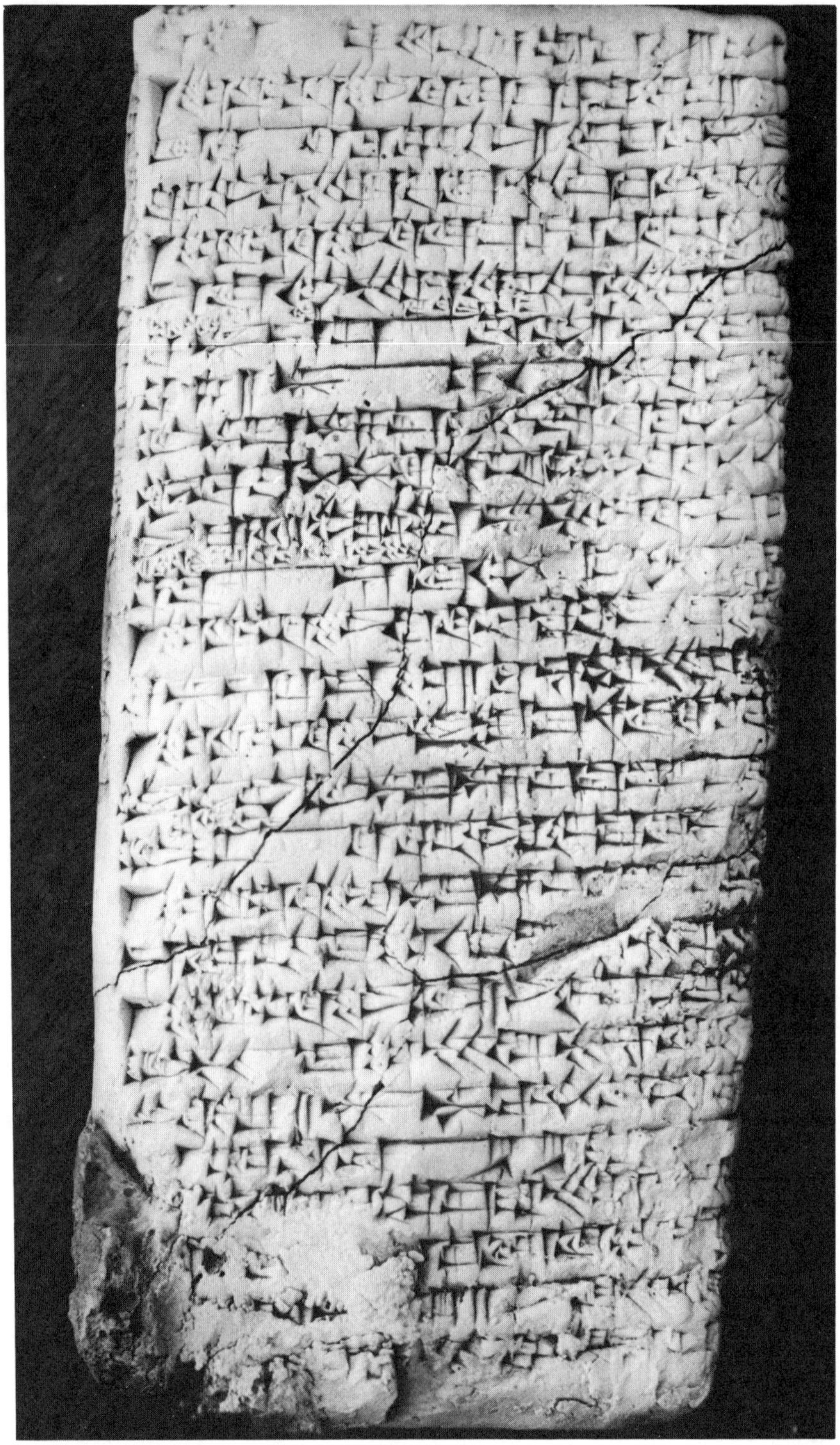

Plate 2a. 3N T296 obverse.

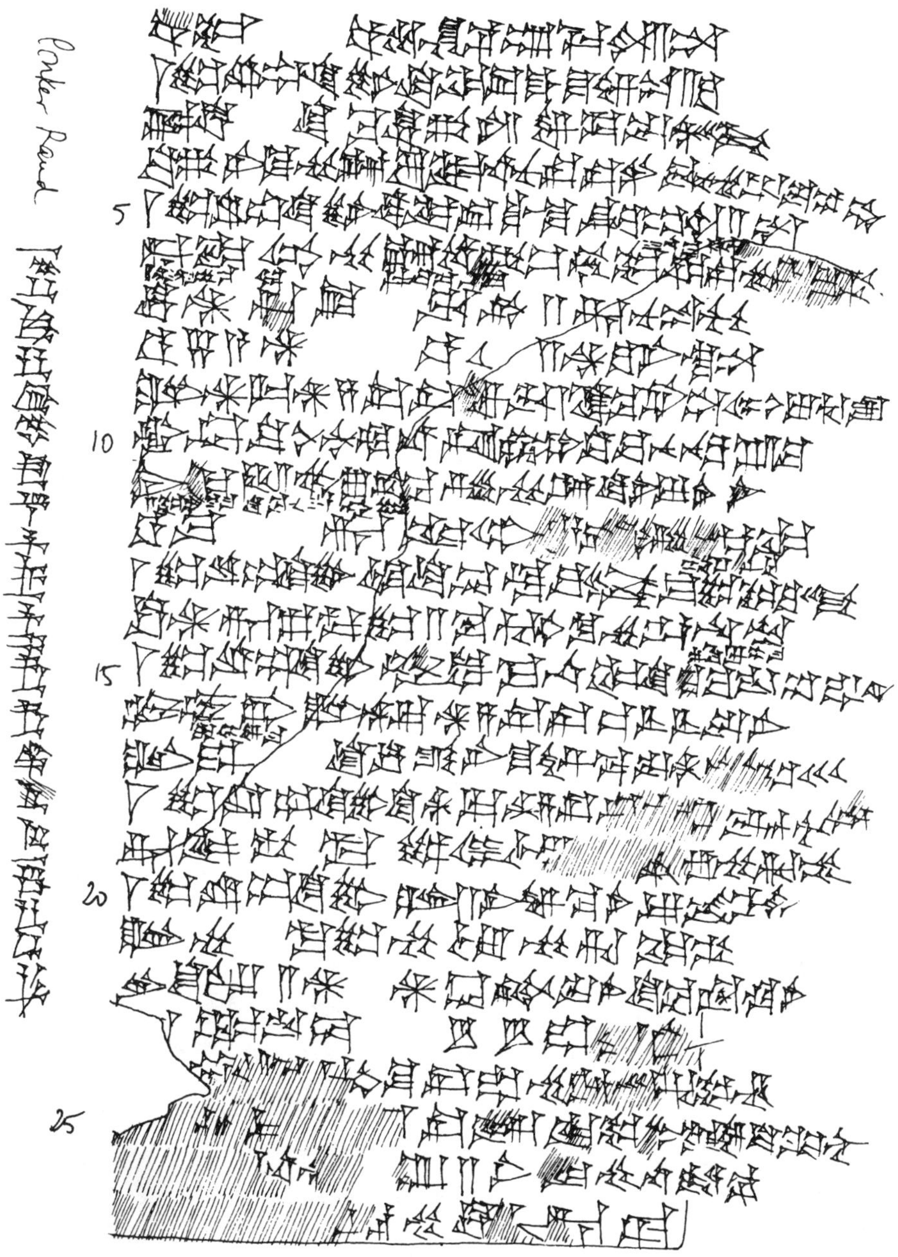

Plate 2b. 3N T296 obverse.

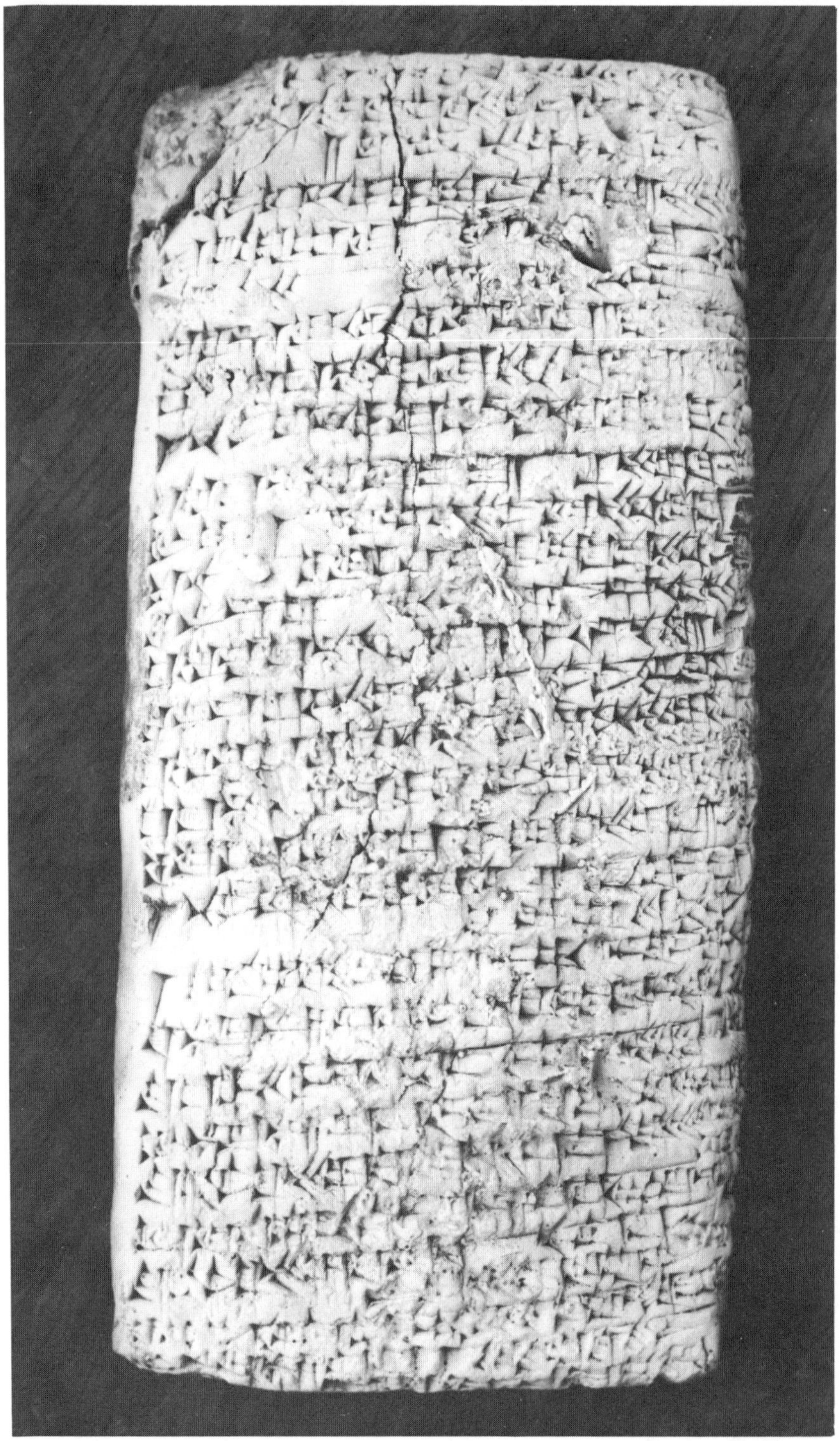

Plate 3a. 3N T296 reverse.

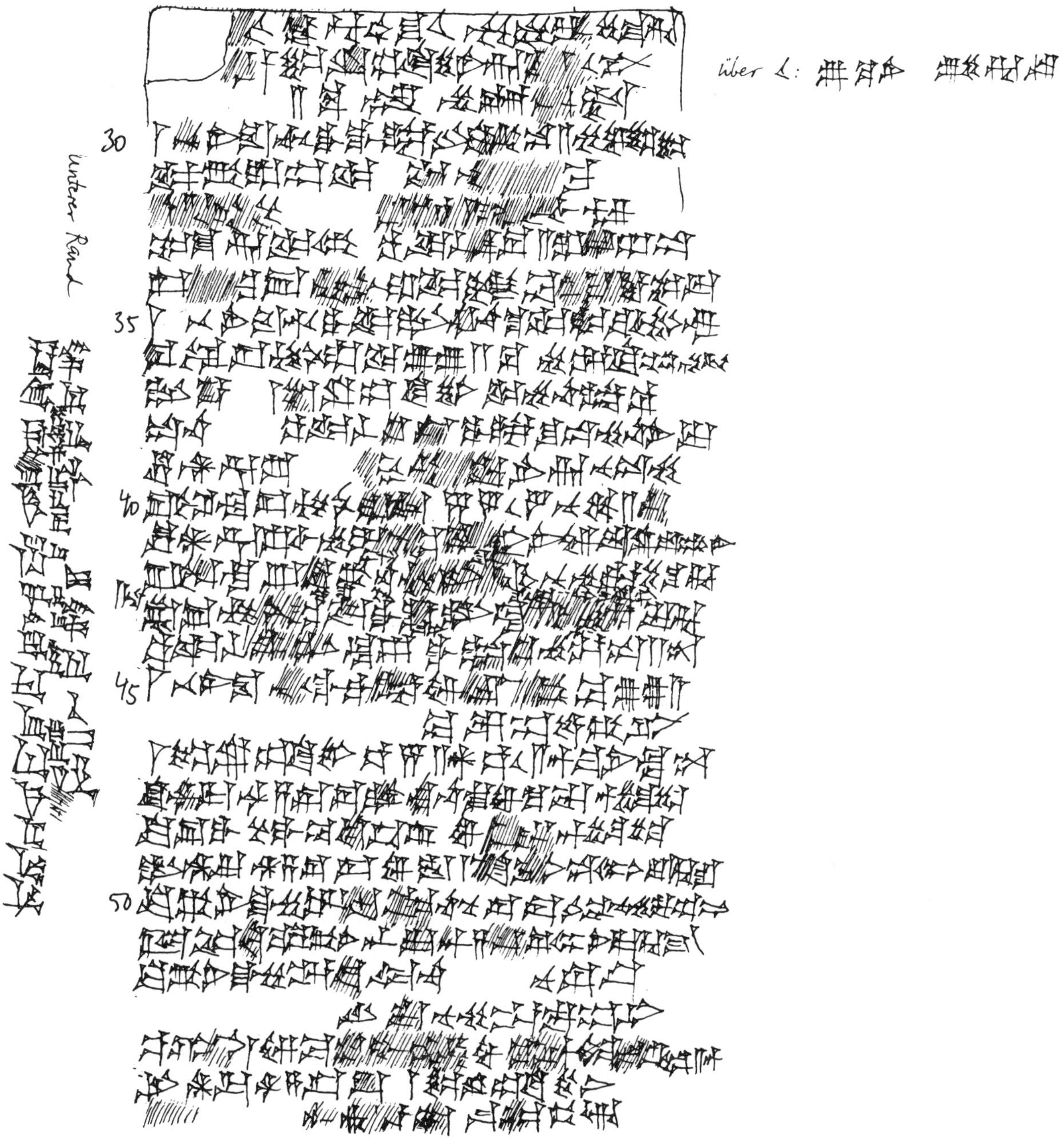

Plate 3b. 3N T296 reverse.

with the *Curse of Agade*, the Sumerian city laments, the Akkadian Sargon and Naramsin romances, and other historical-literary texts. Many, if not all, of those texts have a didactic tendency, and a similar message can be detected in this text as well: destiny determined by the gods is unavoidable and not to be resisted. The reluctance of Urzababa, and probably Lugalzagesi, to acquiesce to the divinely sanctioned ascendance of Sargon is used to dramatize that ascendance, just as the opposition of Naramsin to Enlil in the *Curse of Agade* is used to dramatize Agade's fall and destruction.[9] The text edited here can thus be seen as one of a series of literary-historical compositions that relate, within a similar ideological framework, the downfall of every major Mesopotamian hegemony prior to the Old Babylonian period: Uruk and Kish (this text), Agade (Curse of Agade) and the Third Dynasty of Ur (Ur Laments).

GLOSSES. Lines 5, 6, 11, 12, 14, 16, 27, 35, 40, 42, 43, and 55 have minutely written Akkadian glosses (41 alone has a Sumerian pronunciation gloss). They are often legible only because we know what to expect, and they sometimes translate the Sumerian more freely than literally.

TRANSLITERATION AND TRANSLATION. The transliteration of *TRS* 73 is based on Cooper's collation of the tablet.[10] The transliteration of 3N T296 is based on Cooper's study of the cast, the copies and transliterations of Civil and Heimpel, and final careful collation of the cast by Cooper.[11] The many lexical and grammatical difficulties of the text, and problems in reconstructing the narrative, will be discussed in the Commentary.

TRANSLITERATION

TRS 73 obv.

1′ èš má-⸢gur$_8$-gi⸣[m]
2′ gir$_4$ maḫ-bi x[ ]
3′ íd-bi a ḫúl-la da-[rí]
4′ a-gàr-bi ^{giš}al-e ri-e-dè ⸢gán⸣[ ]
5′ é kiš^{ki}-a uru líl-la-gim maš-gán gi$_4$-[gi$_4$-dè]
6′ lugal-bi sipa ur-^{d}za-⸢ba$_4$-b⸣[a$_4$]
7′ é kiš^{ki}-a-ka ^{d}utu-gim àm-è
8′ nam-lugal-la-na bal-bi šu kúr-ru-dè é-gal-l[a] LAM-bi sud$_4$-rá-x[(x)]
9′ an ^{d}en-líl inim kù-ga-ne-ne-a zi-dè-eš x[x x]
10′ ki u$_4$-bi šar-ru-um-ki-in uru-ni ur[u]
11′ ad-da-ni la-i-bu-um ama-n[i]
12′ šar-ru-um-ki-in šà du$_{10}$-ga mu-[ ]
13′ mu im-ta-tu-ud-da-aš x[ ]

3N T296
obv.

1 u$_4$-NE u$_4$-te-en-e um-ma-te-a-ta
2 ^{m}šar-ru-um-ki-in sá-du$_{11}$ é-gal-šè im-DU-a-ba
3 itima kù ki-tuš kù-ga-ni-a im-ma-da-an-nú
4 šà-ga-ni-šè mu-un-zu eme-na nu-gá-gá lú-da nu-mu-un-da-ab-bé
5 ^{m}šar-ru-um-ki-in sá-du$_{11}$ é-gal-šè šu ba-ab-te-a-ta
i-na ma-ḫa-ri
6 MÙŠ.KA.UL mu-un-sì-ga ^{giš}gú-ne-sag-gá mu-un-dab$_5$-bé
a-na QA.ŠU.DU$_8$ × GUL *ip-qí-du-šu-ma*

---

[9] See Cooper, *Curse of Agade*, Chap. 3.

[10] I would like to thank Mme. B. Leicknam of the Musée du Louvre for making the collation possible, and for excellent photographs of the tablet.

[11] Thanks to Å. Sjöberg of the Babylonian Section, University Museum, Philadelphia, for making the cast available for study. The photographs of the tablet, made from field negatives in the files of the Oriental Institute, were obtained too late for use in preparing this article.

7 kù ^{d}inana-ke$_4$ da-bi-a mùš nu-túm-mu
8 u$_4$ 5-àm u$_4$ 10-àm ba-zal-la-ta
9 lugal ^{d}ur-^{d}za-ba$_4$-ba$_4$ im-da-lá ki-tuš-bi-ta mi-ni-ib-ḫu-luḫ
10 pirig-gim šà pap-ḫal-la-na kàš biz$^{!}$(or biz$^{!}$-biz)-biz šà-ba úš lugud SI.A-ba
11 ì-⌈kúš⌉ ku$_6$ a mun lu-ga-gim zi mu-un-di-ni-ib-ir-ir
a-ne-eḫ-ma šu ki-ma nu-un as-li
12 u$_4$-ba MÙŠ.KA.UL (eras.) é$^{?}$[12] ^{d}ezinu-ka
i-na x x (x)
13 ^{m}šar-ru-um-ki-in ù-sá-gim la-ba-nú ma-mú-dè ba-nú
14 kú ^{d}inana-ke$_4$ ma-mú íd mud-šè mu-un-gir$_5$-gir$_5$
ú-ṭe$_4$-eb-bi-šu
15 ^{m}šar-ru-um-ki-in dum-dam-ma-na KA ki-⌈šè⌉ ba-da-ab-ra-⌈aḫ⌉
16 dum-dum-bi lugal ^{d}ur-^{d}za-ba$_4$-ba$_4$ giš-tuk-tuk-da-ni
ra-mi-im-šu
17 lugal-ra ki kù-ga-ni-šè im-ma-da-an-⌈sun$_5$⌉-ne-eš
18 ^{m}šar-ru-um-ki-in ki ^{d}ur-^{d}za-ba$_4$-b⌈a$_4$-šè im-ma⌉-da-an-sun$_5$-ne
19 MÙŠ.KA.UL$^{!}$(GA) ma-mú gi$_6$-ù-[(na x) n]a ⌈ù⌉-mu-re-du$_8$
20 ^{m}šar-ru-um-ki-in lugal-a-ni im-ma-ni-ib-gi$_4$-gi$_4$
21 lugal-mu ma-mú-mu ù-mu-re-du$_{11}$-ga
22 lú ki-sikil diš-àm an-gim sukud-da-ni ki-gim dagal-la-ni
23 [suḫ]uš$^{?}$ bàd-da-gim gar-gar-ra (eras.?)
24 [íd] ⌈maḫ íd mu⌉d-šè gá-ra mu-un-⌈gir$_5$⌉-re-dè-en
25 [(x)] ⌈x⌉ $^{[d]}$u[r-^{d}za-b]a$_4$-ba$_4$ nundum KA bí-in-⌈kú⌉ ní šà-⌈šè⌉ ba-gíd
26 [x x]x na A[N x] sukkal-a-ni ⌈gù⌉ mu-na-dé-e
27 [n]⌈in$_9$-e⌉-mu kù ^{d}inana-ke$_4$
rev. *ú-ba-ni ú-še-ri-ib*
28 [x x]x x mud-šè u-mu mu-un-ku$_4$-re
29 [x]x ^{m}šar-ru-um-ki-in MÙŠ.KA.UL íd maḫ mu-un-gir$_5$-gir$_5$
30 ^{m}be-lí-iš-ti-kál gal-simug lú šà-ga DU-a-mu im sar-sar
31 inim ga-ra-ab-du$_{11}$ ⌈inim-mu⌉ [ḫé]-dab$_5$
32 ⌈na-ri-ga⌉-mu ⌈gizzal ḫé-em⌉-ši-ak
33 ne-éš MÙŠ.KA.UL zabar-⌈šu⌉ - gá a-ra - ⌈x⌉-ab-túm
34 é-[sikil-l]a é ⌈nam⌉-tar-ra-ka alan-gim ⌈kùš-kùš-a⌉ sì-bí-ib
35 ^{m}be-lí-iš-ti-kál inim lugal-la-na-šè sag-kéš ba-ši-in-ak
uš-ta-sí-iq
36 é-sikil é nam-tar-ra-ka kùš-kùš-a si mu-un-sá
37 lugal-e ^{m}šar-ru-um-ki-in gù mu-na-dé-e
38 gin-na zabar-⌈šu⌉-gá gal-simug-šè$^{!}$ túm-mu-na-ni-ib
38a ^{m}šar-ru-um-ki-in é-gal ^{d}ur-^{d}za-ba$_4$-ba$_4$ im-ma-da-ra-ab-è (from edge)
39 kù ^{d}inana-ke$_4$ ⌈zà zi-da-⌉ni mùš nu-túm-mu
40 é-sikil-la é nam-tar-ra-ka 5 nindan 10 nindan nu-te-a-⌈na⌉
ID/DA.AB/TA/DU.NI/HI.NI/IR
41 kù ^{d}inana-ke$_4$ igi mu-u⌈n-na⌉-nigin gìr-ni im-da-ru
ú x x (x) ru
42 é-sikil -la é kù-ga na-nam lú mud nu-mu-un-ku$_4$-re
a-na [(?)] *mu* (x)$^{?}$*el* x ⌈*ša*⌉*da-mi*⌈*ú-ul*⌉ *i -ru-ub*
43 ká é nam-tar-ra-ka gal-⌈simug$^{!}$⌉ lugal-la-{ke$_4$ gaba⌉ mu-un-da-ri
šu bi/ub x x (x)
44 zabar-⌈šu lugal⌉-la-ke$_4$ gal-simug-⌈šè⌉ mu-un-DU-a-ta
45 ^{m}be-lí-iš-⌈ti⌉-kál gal-simug im-⌈da⌉-lá alan-gim kúš-kúš-a ba$^{!}$-da-ab-sì-ga-bi
46 ^{m}šar-ru-um-ki-in u$_4$ 5-àm u$_4$ 10-àm ba-zal-la-ta

[12] Heimpel reads é-DIN (with Civil).

47 ki ^{d}ur-^{d}za-ba$_4$-ba$_4$ lugal-la-na-šè im-ma-da-an-ku$_4$-ku$_4$
48 šà é-gal kur gal-gim ⸢ki-ús⸣-sa im-⸢ma-da⸣-an-ku$_4$-ku$_4$
49 lugal ^{d}ur-^{d}za-ba$_4$-ba$_4$ im-da-lá ki-tuš-⸢bi⸣-ta mi-ni-ib-ḫu-luḫ
50 šà-ga-ni-šè mu-un-zu eme-na nu-gá-gá lú-da nu-mu-un-da-ab-bé
51 itima-ka ki-tuš kù-ga-ni ^{d}ur-^{d}za-⸢ba$_4$⸣-ba$_4$mi-ni-ib-ḫu-luḫ
52 šà-ga-ni-šè mu-un-zu eme-na nu-gá-gá lú-da nu-mu-un-da-ab-bé
53 u$_4$-bi-ta im-ma ⸢gub-bu ḫé-gál⸣ im ⸢si-si⸣-ge ba-ra-gál-la-àm
54 lugal ^{d}ur-^{d}za-ba$_4$-ba$_4$ ^{m}šar-ru-um-ki-in ⸢dingir-re-e⸣-ne šu-du$_{11}$-ga-ar
55 im-ma gub-bu níg ní ba-ug$_7$-a-ta
tu-up-pa iš-ṭù-ur-šu ša šu-mu-ut ra-ma-ni (-[*šu*]?)
56 unu^{ki}-ga lugal-zà-ge$_4$-e-si šu ba-ni-ib-tag$_4$-tag$_4$

TRS 73 rev.
1 dam$^{!}$ lugal-zà-ge$_4$-si-⸢da im⸣-[ ]
2 nam-munus an-dùl-šè mu-ni-ba x[ ]
3 lugal-zà-ge$_4$-si kin-gi$_4$-a nu-[ ]
4 gá-nam-ma sig$_4^{!}$ é-an-na-šè gìr mu-un-g[ub]
5 lugal-zà-ge$_4$-si šà-ga-ni nu-un-z[u] ugu kin-gi$_4$-a nu-mu-un-du$_{11}$-du$_{11}$
6 en-na ugu kin-gi$_4$-a na-mu-un-du$_{11}$-du$_{11}$ igi dumu nun ba-an-da-bad
7 en-e u$_8$ bí-in-du$_{11}$ saḫar-ra ba-an-da-tuš
8 lugal-zà-ge$_4$-si kin-gi$_4$-a-ar im-ši-in-gi$_4$
9 kin-gi$_4$-a šar-ru-ki-in gú nu-mu-un-⸢sì⸣-s[ì]
10 gam-gam-ma-ni šar-ru-ki-in ⸢lugal⸣-z[à$^{?}$-ge$_4$$^{?}$-si$^{?}$]
11 šar-ru-ki-in lugal-z[à-ge$_4$-si]
12 a-na-aš-àm š[ar-ru-ki-in]
13 (traces only)

TRANSLATION

TRS 73 obv.
1′ The sanctuary, [like] a cargo-ship [ ],
2′ Its great furnace [ ].
3′ [So that] its canals would fore[ver flow with] waters of joy,
4′ So that the hoe would be wielded in its agricultural tracts, the fields [ ],
5′ So that the house of Kish, (which had been) like a ghost town, would be turned back into a settlement,
6′ Its king, the shepherd Urzababa,
7′ Rose like the sun over the house of Kish.
9′ (But) An and Enlil, by their holy command, authoritatively [*ordered*]
8′ That his royal reign be alienated, that the palace's *prosperity* be removed.

10′ At that time, Sargon—his city was the city [ ],
11′ His father was Laʾibum, his mother [ ]—
12′ Sargon, happily [ ].
13′ Because he was so born [ ]

3N T296
1 One day, after evening had arrived,
2 Sargon, when the offerings had been brought to the palace—
3 He (Urzababa) having lain down in the holy bed-chamber, his holy residence,
4 He understood, but would not articulate it, nor speak about it with anyone—
5 Sargon, having received the offerings for the palace—
6 *He (Urzababa) had made the cupbearer responsible (for the offerings)*—he (Sargon) took charge of the drinking chest.
7 Holy Inana was unceasingly working *behind the scenes.*

8 After five or ten days had passed,
9 King Urzababa . . . , he was frightened in that residence,
10 Like a lion, he was dribbling urine, filled with blood and pus, down his legs,
11 He struggled like a floundering salt-water fish, he was terrified there.

12 At that time, the *cupbearer*, in the *temple* of Ezinu,
13 Sargon, lay down not to sleep, but lay down to dream.
14 Holy Inana, in the dream, was drowning him (Urzababa) in a river of blood.
15 Sargon, screaming, gnawed the ground.
16 When king Urzababa heard those screams,
17 He had them bring him (Sargon) into the king's presence.
18 Sargon came into the presence of Urzababa, (who said:)
19 "Oh *cupbearer*, was a dream revealed to you in the night?"
20 Sargon replied to his king:
21 "Oh my king, this is my dream which I will have told you about:
22 "There was a single young woman, she was high as the heavens, she was broad as the earth,
23 "She was firmly set as the [*bas*]*e* of a wall.
24 "For me, she drowned you in a great [river], a river of blood."

25 [ ] U[rzab]aba chewed his lips, became seriously afraid,
26 He spoke to [. . .]. his chancellor:
27 "[ ] my royal sister, holy Inana,
28 "[ ] is going to put my finger into a . . . of blood,
29 "[*The*]*n* she will drown Sargon, the *cupbearer*, in a great river.
30 "Belištikal, master smith, man of my choosing, who can write tablets,
31 "I will give you orders, let my orders be carried out!
32 "Let my instructions be heeded!
33 "Now then, when the *cupbearer* has delivered my *bronze cups* to you,
34 "In the Esikil/pure temple, the temple of destinies, *cast them in moulds* as if for figurines!"

35 Belištikal paid attention to his king's orders, and
36 He readied *moulds* in the Esikil/pure temple, the temple of destinies.
37 The king spoke to Sargon:
38 "Go and deliver my *bronze cups* to the master smith!"

38a Sargon left the palace of Urzababa,
39 Holy Inana was unceasingly ⌜at his right side⌝.
40 When he had not come within five or ten *nindan* of the Esikil/pure temple, the temple of destinies,
41 Holy Inana turned around toward him and blocked his way, (saying:)
42 "Is not the Esikil/pure temple a holy temple? No one (polluted) with blood should enter it!"
43 At the gate of the temple of destinies, he (Sargon) met the master smith of the king.
44 After he delivered the king's *bronze cups* to the master smith—
45 Belištikal, the master smith, . . . , having *cast them in moulds* as if for figurines—
46 Sargon, after five or ten days had passed,
47 Came into the presence of Urzababa, his king,
48 Came right into the palace, firmly founded as a great mountain.
49 King Urzababa . . . , he was frightened in that residence,
50 He understood, but would not articulate it, nor speak about it with anyone,
51 In the bed-chamber, his holy residence, Urzababa was frightened,
52 He understood, but would not articulate it, nor speak about it with anyone.

53 In those days, writing on tablets certainly existed, but enveloping tablets did not exist;
54 King Urzababa, for Sargon, creature of the gods,
55 Wrote a tablet, which would cause his own death, and
56 He dispatched it to Lagulzagesi in Uruk.

TRS 73 rev.
1 With the wife of Lugalzagesi . . . [ ],
2 She . . . [ ] her feminity as a shield [ ],
3 Lugalzagesi would not [*reply*] to the envoy, (and said:)
4 "Come now! Would he step within Eana's masonry?"
5 Lugalzagesi did not understand, so he did not talk to the envoy,
6 (But) as soon as he did talk to the envoy, the eyes of the prince's son were opened.
7 The lord said "Alas!" and sat in the dirt,
8 Lugalzagesi replied to the envoy:
9 "Oh envoy, Sargon does not *yi*[*eld*],
10 "When he submits, Sargon [ ] *Lugalz*[*agesi*],
11 "Sargon [ ] Lugalz[agesi],
12 "Why does S[argon]?"

ALTERNATIVE TRANSLATION FOR 3N T296 (*HEIMPEL*)

When on that day evening had come,
and when Sargon had brought the meal for the palace,
he (Urzababa) was lying down in the pure chamber, his pure dwelling.
He 'knew it to his heart,' did not set it on the tongue, spoke with nobody.
When Sargon had received the meal for the palace,
and when he had put on the MÙŠ.KA.UL, he took hold of the tray.
Pure Inana did not move from his sides.
5 days, 10 days went by.
King Urzababa withdrew. He was frightened 'of that dwelling.'
'Like a lion' sprinkling the inside of his legs with urine in which there was plenty of fresh blood
he moaned and gasped like a struggling salt-water fish.
On one of these days, the MÙŠ.KA.UL, Sargon, lay down in the winehouse of Ashnan—
not that he wanted to sleep, he lay down for a dream.
In the dream, pure Inana 'submerged' into a blood river.
Sargon shouted "hither" in his agitation.
As Urzababa heard that agitation
they came hurrying before the king to his pure place.
Also Sargon came hurrying to Urzababa's place.
"MÙŠ.KA.UL$^{!}$, ..."
Sargon turned to his king:
"My king, in my dream which I am telling you now
there was a person, one young woman. She was high like heaven. She was broad like earth.
She was set like the foundation of a wall.
She submerged you for me into a mighty river, a river of blood."
. . . Urzababa bit his lip. 'Fear reached to the heart.'
To . . . , his vizier, he said:
". . . , my noble sister, pure Inana
into . . . blood she 'entered' my finger.
. . . Sargon, the MÙŠ.KA.UL, she submerged in a mighty river."
"Belishtikal, chief smith who writes down my wishes,
let me tell you, heed my word,
pay attention to my counsel.
Now, when the MÙŠ.KA.UL has brought to you the bronze of my hand,
Pour it into the ingot mould like a statue in the Esikil, the house of fate."
Belishtikal obeyed the word of his king.
He prepared the ingot mould in the Esikil, the Esikil, the house of fate.
The king said to Sargon:
"Go, bring the bronze of my hand to the chief smith."
Pure Inana did not move from his right side.
He had not come to within 5, 10 Nindan of the Esikil, the house of fate,
when pure Inana ..., blocked his path.
"Is not the Esikil a pure house? A blood (stained) person does not enter it!"
He met the chief smith of the king at the gate of the house of fate.
When he had handed the bronze of the hand of the king to the chief smith,
Belishtikal, the chief smith, withdrew and poured it like a statue into the ingot mould.
etc.
53ff. [I cannot give a running translation.]

PHILOLOGICAL COMMENTARY

TRS 73 obv.

1′ff. For the similarities between this text and the first section of the Curse of Agade, see Cooper, *The Curse of Agade*, chapter 3.

6′f. Cf. Curse of Agade, 40f. lugal-bi sipa ^{d}na-ra-am-^{d}sin $bara_2$ kù a-ga-dè^{ki}-šè u_4-dè-éš im-è. "Its shepherd, Naramsin, rose like the sun upon the holy throne of Agade."

8′. LAM = *ešēbu*?

10′f. Cf. lines 2–4 of the Akkadian Sargon Legend:[13]

ummi ēnetu abi ul īdi
aḫi abīja irammi šadâ
āli Azupirāni ša ina aḫi Puratti šaknu
My mother was an *ēntu*-priestess, my father I did not know,
My uncle inhabits the mountains,
My city (of birth) was Azupirānu, which lies on the bank of Euphrates.

[13] Lewis, *The Sargon Legend*, 24f.

3N T296

1. The same line occurs in Hendursaga (*AOAT* 25, 148) 77 and Marriage of Martu (*SRT* 8), i 19, 34. Cf. Shaffer *Sumerian Sources*, 68:158, and S. Cohen, *Enmerkar and the Lord of Aratta*, l. 98 with commentary.

2. Our text exhibits a clear predilection for subordinating clauses with nominalization and following ablative case marker (cf. lines 1, 5, 8, 44, 46, 55). The meaning of this subordination is in all cases temporal. Temporal subordination in the form of -a-ba occurs only in line 2 where it is obviously chosen in order to avoid repetition of -a-ta (cf. l. 44).

3. The intrusive nature of these lines is especially awkward, but the subject must be Urzababa, for it is he who sleeps in the itima kù (l.51) and has the awful premonitions of his own downfall (4 = 50 = 52). Similar premonitions of Naramsin are expressed in the same words in the Curse of Agade, 87 and 93a. Note the play on this line in *TRS* 73 rev. 5.

6. MÙŠ.KA.UL occurs in no other text, but the gloss SILÀ.ŠU.DU$_8$ "cupbearer" (what is the x GUL which follows it?) immediately identifies Sargon's function at Urzababa's court according to the literary-historical tradition (see above). Heimpel understands MÙŠ.KA.UL as the direct object of mu-un-sì-ga, and speculates that the MÙŠ is the emblem MÙŠ worn by kings and en's, and Sargon is wearing some such emblem in his function as cupbearer, and that, by extension, the wearer of the emblem (here Sargon) was called by the emblem's name (cf. Muškešdaʾana, the en of Aratta).

Civil has contributed the following note on ^{giš}gú-ne-sag-gá (see already *JNES* 31, 386): "The meaning 'cupboard,' or 'chest to keep the drinking utensils' for gú-ne-sag-gá (the reading of the second sign is not completely certain and perhaps it would have been wise to transliterate gú-NE-) is based on the following evidence:

1) The curse formula in *UET* 1 15:3ff. (a fragment of an obsidian cup) reads: tukum-b[i] gú-ne-sag-[gá-ta] íb$^!$-ta-[an-zi-zi] é-níg-ga-[ra-(ni) ì-íb-ku$_4$ ...] 'if he takes (this cup on which the text is inscribed) out of the g. and takes it into (his) storehouse.'

2) The g. is associated with drinking: (beer) gú-ne-sag-gá-ka a-gin$_7$ ḫé-ni-bal-bal IšD A 162; gú-ne-sag-gá mu$^?$ me-te-aš [ḫ]é-im-mi-ib-gál L 2:23 in the context of a drinking party (see the remarks in *JNES* 31, 386); during the hot summer people ^{giš}gú-ne-sag-gá-ke$_4$ mu-un-kin-kin èn-tar mu-ni-gál 'they look constantly for the g. and take good care of it' EE 245; GG 68 mentions the g. after the banšur 'table'; two ^{giš}gú-ne-sag-gá are mentioned in an inventory among furniture and utensils, Pinches Berens, 89 ii 18; 1 ^{giš} gú-ne-sag-gá kaš(?) gin esír-é-a-bi 4 sìla *BIN* 9 451:6f.

3) The g. of some gods are mentioned in Ur III texts and normally it is drinking and cooking utensils that go into them: cups (gal) for the g. of Nanna *UET* 3 376; 1 dára a nag-nag and one níg-ì-dé-a 'oil cruet(?)' in the shape of a reclining calf encrusted with lapis lazuli and gold for the same destination in *UET* 3 378 and 101, respectively; copper kettles for the g. of Alamuš(LÀL) *UET* 3 378; other mentions of the g., e.g., 6N-T362, do not specify the destination. A Pre-Sargonic possible mention of the g. remains doubtful: 1 GAR-ne-sag-gá^{urudu} ^{kuš}šagan-bi 1-am$_6$ *VAT* 4856 in *Or* 16 39 (transliteration only).

4) The man in charge of the g., (lú) gú-ne-sag-gá-(ak), is often mentioned in administrative texts: BM 12245:1 (*CT* 10 49); H 6246 (*MCS* 1 22); Nies *UDT* 59:54; *BM* 21399:12 (CT 9 37); note that among the personnel (gìr-sì-ga) of the libation place ki-a-nag en-en-e-ne-ka in *RTC* 4 1 ii 5 there is at least one lú-gú-ne-sag-gá mentioned between the doorman and the brewer, confirming once more the association of the g. with drinking."

While the g. usually contained drinking utensils, the presents given to the g. of Nanna by the king and queen seem to be a different kind of object. *UET* 3 101:1f (1 ninda-ì-dé-a / amar-nú-a na-za-gìn guškin gar-ra) is probably "1 pastry ninda-ì-dé-a ("bread with oil poured over it") with a gold set lapislazuli figure of a reclining calf." The latter may be the ornament of the former. Also the other presents, the gold set lapis-lazuli ^{giš} KU (*UET* 3 378:1), the "small KU of red gold" (*UET* 3 376:4), and the "drinking ibex" (*UET* 3 378) may be ornaments. *UET* 3 741 mentions the g. of a šabra together with bronze vessels and utensils which are also attested in connection with cupbearers (see below to 33ff.).

7. Cooper translates da as *puzru* (Proto-Izi II 104 [*MSL* 13 44]); Heimpel follows l. 39.

Inana was the chief goddess of Kish, as she would be of Agade (as she was also of Lugalzagesi's Uruk), and thus on one level was the wife of the current king, Urzababa. The activity of Inana here on Sargon's behalf means that she is preparing to change royal husbands in accord with the decision of An and Enlil in TRS 73 obv. Her disengagement from Urzababa is one of the foreboding indications of his reign's approaching end. A similar process can be observed in the Lugalbanda Epic. Enmerkar sees in the misfortune in which he finds himself before the walls of Aratta a sign that Inana has abandoned Him:

> Now and here my *ḫili* has ended. . . . Like a child who, hating his mother, leaves the city, has my noble sister, pure Inana, run away from me to the brickwork Kulaba. . . . Would I (now) enter the brickwork Kulaba, my lance would be taken from me then, my

shield would be broken by her then. (Wilcke, *Lugalbanda*, 306–320)

Thanks to his powers gained from Anzu, Lugalbanda makes the trip from Aratta to Uruk at the speed of thought, and is well received by Inana:

> As she looked at the shepherd Amaᵓushumgalana, she looked at pure Lugalbanda. As she spoke to her son, the lord Shara, did she speak to pure Lugalbanda. (Wilcke, *Lugalbanda*, 350–353)

Inana has shifted her loyalties from the reigning king, whose powers are on the wane, to the eventual successor who has impressed her as fit to be king.

8. Cf. 1. 46.

9 = 49. For im-da-lá, note Gragg, *AOATS* 5 65. In the *Lamentation over Sumer and Ur* 58, An frightens Sumer in its residence (an-né ke-en-gi ki-tuš-ba bí-in-ḫu-luḫ).

10. The verb after kàš might also be su_x (TAG)-bé (So Civil); cf. *MSL* 14 413:221 su-bu TAG = *ša-ta*[-*x*], probably to be restored *šatānu*, "to urinate." For úš lugud, cf. *MSL* 12 185:52 (OB Lu B) lú šà úš lugud dé-dé = *ša libbašu dama u šarka malû*. Whereas this refers to the presence of blood and pus in the man's insides, šà in our line must be prepositional and refer to blood and pus in the urine (unless -ba is an error for -ga-na).

11. See Heimpel, *Tierbilder*, 79.2; for the gloss, cf. *eslu* "bloated."

12. Heimpel, with Civil, reads é-DIN ᵈezinu-ka.

13. For this dream introduction, see *SGL* 1 75f.; Civil, *AOAT* 25, 92.

14f. Because Sargon, in line 24, tells Urzababa that "For me, she drowned you," the person being drowned in line 14 must be Urzababa, not Sargon. Sargon's frightened reaction in line 15 is not caused by fear for his own life, but by the realization of his master's downfall and his own ascendance, and the risks this will entail.[14]

15. Cooper understands zú-ra-aḫ "to gnaw, chew"; Heimpel gù-ra-aḫ "to scream."

19. The ù- prefix here is problematic.

22f. Whereas the initial version of the dream in l. 14 identifies the protagonist as Inana, Sargon's retelling is both more poetic and more oblique, echoing the appearance of Ningirsu in Gudea Cyl. A iv 14ff.:

> šà ma-mú-da-ka lú diš-àm an-gim ri-ba-ni
> ki-gim ri-ba-ni
> a-ne sag-gá-ni-šè dingir-ra-àm
> á-ni-šè anzu ᵐᵘšᵉⁿ-dam
> sig-ba-ni-a-šè a-ma-ru-kam
>
> In the dream there was a single man, huge as heaven,
> Huge as the earth,
> He, by his head was a god,
> By his wings, the Anzu-eagle,
> By his lower body, the Deluge.

24. The ambiguity of the direct object is resolved here only by gá-ra "for me," since the accusative pronominal suffix -en translated "you" can also be translated "me," just as the accusative infix /n/ in l. 14 could theoretically refer either to Sargon or Urzababa.

25. The traces at the beginning seem to exclude ⌈lugal⌉. For nundun-kú, see *CAD* s.v. *našāku*. For ní šà-šè ba-gíd, cf. *OECT* 5 28f.:2 lugal-mu ní nu-te ní nu-gíd-i "My king need not fear or worry," and *TIM* 9 6:14f. = 32ff.:

> e-ne ma-an-du_{11} šà-šè nu-gíd
> gá-e in-na-an-du_{11}-du_{11} ba-kéš šà-šè ba-gíd
> *šī iqbīamma ana libbim ula ašdud*
> *anāku aqbīšimma iktaṣar*
> *ana libbim ištadad*
> She spoke to me, but I didn't take it seriously;
> I spoke to her, and she *payed attention* and took it seriously.

28f. Despite Urzababa's premonition of his downfall in 1.4 and his frightened reaction to Sargon's dream in 1.25, which shows that he well understood the dream's meaning, he publicly reinterprets the dream here to bode well for him and ill for Sargon. This intentional flounting of divine will is similar to Naramsin's reaction in the *Curse of Agade* to the god's decision to bring *his* dynasty to end. But whereas Naramsin's efforts to resist were directed against the source of the decision, Enlil's temple Ekur in Nippur, Urzababa's efforts will be directed here against the agent of the gods, Sargon. In his dream interpretation, Urzababa does not just switch victim and beneficiary, but rather splits the action of Inana in two: she will dip Urzababa's finger into blood, and will drown Sargon in a great river. The íd maḫ íd mud of 1.24 are separated, and another verbal clause is created, using ku_4(-r) possibly because of its partial homonymy and synonymy with the original verb gir_5.

30. Bēliš-tikal, "trust in the lord," uses the post-Old Akkadian imperative form. Cf. šarriš-takal on a seal of Naramsin's reign (*AfO* 22 16 No. 10) with the name šulgiš-tikal in Ur III (*MAD* 3 295).

31f. For the instructional formula, see Alster, *Studies in Sumerian Proverbs*, 29ff.

33ff. The activity to be performed by the smith is the least intelligible part of the composition. Is this a kind of Nam-

[14] See Cooper in the *Iwry Festschrift* (forthcoming).

burbi to counteract the message of the dream, or a trap being laid for Sargon? Since, at the end of the activity, Urzababa is rather shocked to see Sargon again (1.49), it must be a trap, but what kind? The zabar-šu which the cupbearer Sargon is to bring to the smith is probably a cup of some sort. The element zabar in this word does not necessarily mean the material bronze. According to Bauer, *AWL* 182 xi 11 the zabar-šu could be made of "pure silver." In *OIP* 14 103 on the other hand, 3 zabar-šu are contained in 32 zabar-ḫi-a. The conflicting indications can be harmonized by assuming that the object was originally and typically made of bronze, yet it acquired a ceremonial or ornamental use in which it could also be made of more precious materials. Our text demonstrates that the word contains a genitive. According to *OIP* 14 103, the zabar-šu belonged to a set of bronze utensils which were given to a certain Me-ša-kan. The latter is a cupbearer according to *OIP* 14 100. His set in 103 includes 7 different kinds of objects. Only three are vaguely identifiable, i.e. *ma-ša-lum* as "mirror" or "palette" (so *CAD* s.v. *mušālu* A; but possibly to be connected with *mušālu* B "esophagus" and explained as drinking tube); *za-ḫum* as a container of liquids (*AHw* "Schale"; Limet, *TMP* "aiguière" following Deimel *ŠL "Kanne"); gal*-KA×ŠU as a variety of container of liquids (Salonen *HAM* I s.v.; Heimpel, *ZDMG* 120 [1970], 186). A similar set is characterized as ŠU SILÀ.ŠU.DU$_{8}$ in *BIN* 8 145, another (*UET* 3 741) is related to the gú-ne-sag-gá of a šabra. Comparable is also *MVN* 3 152 which details gifts of a governor for Anunītum, among them a copper "mirror" and a "copper of the hand" (urudu-šu). The word zabar-šu is found in prominent position in the forerunner to Hh XII (*MSL* 7 231:2) and to be expected in Gap A of the canonical version.

The association of cupbearer and the zabar-šu insures that our text is indeed talking about the same zabar-šu found in the texts just cited, despite the grammatical difficulty of zabar-šu-gá in lines 33 and 38. If zabar-šu is "bronze (vessel) of the hand," "my z." should be *zabar-šu-ak-mu>zabar-šu-mu, whereas zabar-šu-gá means "the bronze of my hand, bronze in my possession" (*zabar-šu-mu-ak).

kùš-kùš is translated in lexical lists by Akk. *rāṭu* "pipe, tube, gutter, ditch," but seems, in fact, to mean *rāṭu* mainly in specifically metallurgical contexts. The lexical evidence is as follows:

ku-uš = Ú = *rāṭum*	Proto-Aa 231:1 (*MSL* 14 98)
$^{(urudu)}$kùš-kùš = *rāṭu*	Hh 10:383 and 11:423 (*MSL* 7 98 and 147)
kùš-kùš = *rāṭ nappāḫi*	Erimḫuš 2:55 and Imgidda Erimḫuš A r.5′ (*CAD* s.v. *nappāḫu*)
ku-ku-uš = ^{urudu}Ú.Ú = *rāṭu*	*JAOS* 65 225:65 (Diri 6)

In Hh 10 and 11 it is followed by $^{(urudu)}$níg-sa-sa, the furnace grate, and in Diri it is preceded by ^{urudu}ama-TÙN = *agarinnu* "crucible" (or "mould"?), and followed by *qurqur erî* "coppersmith." The association with crucibles and furnace grates suggests something used in the melting and casting process, which fits well in our text, where the smith is pouring (sì = *šapāku*) the zabar-šu into kùš-kùš "as if for a statuette" or image of some kind. Mould fits best here and copper and bronze moulds as well as stone or clay moulds were used in antiquity for casting bronze.[15] Despite the determinative URUDU in some references, non-metallic kùš-kùš are certainly intended in Hh 10 (the metal kùš-kùš is in Hh 11), and the *rāṭu* used by a *nappāḫu* in the newly published piece of Gilgamesh 5[16] seems to be a crucible, and hence stone or clay.

A meaning "mould" in our composition would also fit the similar passage in the *Curse of Agade* 127f.:

> a-gàr maḫ a-eštub^{ku_6} dagal-la-gim
> é-kur-ra ^{urudu}gí-dim gal-gal-bi kùš-kùš-a bī-in-sì-sì
> As if for great tracts of land with wide-spreading carp ponds.
> He cast large spades in moulds for the Ekur.

Naramsin is manufacturing spades to dig up the Ekur precinct, as if he were digging carp ponds. The same spade (^{urudu}gí-dim) appears in the list of tools on the OB forerunner to Hh 11 immediately following ^{urudu}kùš-kùš-e-dím (*MSL* 7 225:117f.), which we can tentatively translate as "mould-made (tool)." Finally, in the *Lamentation Over Sumer and Ur*, 232, we can now restore [ala]n-gim kuš-kùš-a dé-a-me-eš ì-[sì]-ge-dè-en-dè-en "We are spilled out like figurines being cast in moulds."

Heimpel thinks kùš-kùš are ingot moulds (cf. Goetze, *JAOS* 65, 235: "the furrow in front of the crucible into which the molten metal flows, in which it hardens, and from which it is taken out in the form of ingots"), which is supported by the presence of *rāṭu* for gold, silver and copper in an Old Babylonian list of key numbers for various standardized containers and vessels (*MCT*, 134:22ff.). If *rāṭu* is a standardized ingot mould, its association with the standard of capacity (in the form of a vessel) *ḫiburnu* in Frankena, *Tākultu*, 25 i 39 would also be explained. kùš-kùš-a sì "to pour into ingot moulds," then means, more freely, "to melt down." The *Curse of Agade* passage cited above can be

---

[15] Tylecote, *A History of Metallurgy*, 32f.

[16] Von Weiher, *Ba Mi*, 11 93:19.

translated "That which produces (dím, not -gim) the large arable tracts (lapped) widely by carp waters, (namely) the Ekur's large spades, were poured into the ingot mould (i.e. melted down)," and the *Lamentation* passage can be rendered "Like statues poured into the ingot mould, we will be killed" (restoring ug$_6$, not sì).

What is the Esikil? It certainly cannot be the temple of that name dedicated to Ninazu/Tišpak in Ešnuna, and it is not known as a temple of Inana or a temple in Kish. Should we rather translate "pure temple?" The temple's epithet "temple of destinies" may well be connected with the activity Urzababa is ordering to be done there, in an effort to alter *his* destiny.

41ff. Inana's attempt to prevent Sargon from entering the temple must be in order to save him from Urzababa's trap. Why is Sargon polluted by blood? Does it refer to the dream, or to his future as a warrior? The outcome of this encounter is that Sargon delivers the bronze cups to the smith at the entrance to the temple, but does not actually enter it.

53ff. Line 53 parodies the famous passage in *Enmerkar and the Lord of Aratta* 503ff.:[17]

> en kul-aba$_4^{ki}$-a-ke$_4$ im-e šu bí-in-ra inim dub-gim b[í-i]n-gub
> u$_4$-bi-ta inim im-ma gub-bu nu-ub-ta-gál-la
> ì-ne-éš ^{d}utu u$_4$-dè-a ur$_5$ ḫé-en-na-nam-ma-àm
> en kul-aba$_4^{ki}$-a-ke$_4$ ini[m dub-gim b]í-in-gub ur$_5$ ḫ[é-en-na]-nam-ma

> The *en* of Kulaba pressed some clay and wrote words on it as if on a tablet—
> In those days, writing words on tablets had not existed,
> But now, with the sun's rising, so it was!
> The *en* of Kulaba wrote words as if on a tablet, and so it was!

[17] S. Cohen, *Enmerkar and the Lord of Aratta*, 85f.

The translation of im si-si-ge follows a suggestion of Civil's; cf. im-si = *imšukku*, si = *arāmu* (*CAD* svv.).

Urzababa must now be trying to anger Lugalzagesi, the overlord of southern Babylonia, against Sargon, hoping that Lugalzagesi will somehow do away with Sargon. Line 55 tells us that this plan will backfire, leading to Urzababa's own death, because, no doubt, the tablet written by Urzababa was seen by Sargon, and since tablets in those days were not sealed in envelopes he could read the message and take appropriate countermeasures.

55. For ní-ug$_7$, cf. Alster *Šuruppak*, l. 32 ní-zu nam-mu-ug$_7$-e "Do not kill yourself." But Urzababa is not actually committing suicide, only precipitating his own death through his treachery toward Sargon.

TRS 73 rev.

1. The DAM has one too many verticals.

4. The sign is LUM, as copied.

5. This line parodies lines 4,50 and 52 of 3NT 296. See the commentary to 1.4 of that tablet.

9. The last sign is SUM, as copied, not GAM$^!$ or ⌜ŠUB⌝. The beginning of a second SUM is visible before the break.

SOME REFLECTIONS ON NUMERALS IN SUMERIAN TOWARDS A HISTORY OF MATHEMATICAL SPECULATION[1]

I. M. Diakonoff

Institut Vostokovedenija, Leningrad

The Sumerian numerals have more than once since Samuel Noah Kramer's undergraduate days been the object of discussion, but still there is much that is puzzling about them. Unfortunately, the recent, comprehensive treatment of the subject by M. Powell became accessible to me only when this paper was practically finished.[2] My study was induced by D. O. Edzard's recent paper, where he treats the Sumerian numerals as listed in a school tablet from Ebla, and supplies much material upon which to reflect.[3]

Apparently, all that can be gleaned from the Sumerian material itself has by now been weighed and summed up, and since Sumerian has no known related languages, comparative historical research is impossible. Therefore I shall try to put the data in a typological context, comparing Sumerian numerals to numerals in other archaic languages.

In order to escape subjectivity in using the latter term, I shall define as 'archaic' any language which, on the lexical level, has no or only poorly developed means of expressing abstract ideas, and on the grammatical level, is based on the opposition 'action vs. state' (or 'transitive action' vs. 'intransitive action and state'). Such an opposition implies (a) that the subject of action (or of transitive action) is expressed by a specific oblique (ergative) case, while the subject of state, including the state resulting from an action, is expressed by the direct or absolute (usually zero) case, and (b) that a grammatical category of the direct object as distinct from the subject of a state does not exist in the syntax, nor that of the accusative case in the morphology.[4]

In an archaic language there are no adequate means, either lexical or grammatical, to express such abstract ideas as 'time', space', 'subject', 'object', 'cause', 'beauty', 'liberty', 'invention', 'multiplication', 'division' and many others, some of which appear to us elemental, as, e.g., the distinction between 'darkness', 'calamity', 'illness', and 'pain', etc., or between 'good', 'enjoyable', 'kind', 'happy', 'useful', 'lucky', etc. However, human thought is impossible without inductive thinking, i.e., thought which proceeds from particular facts to a generalization. In the absence of means to express general ideas, one resorts to generalization by tropes (metaphors and metonymies). All myths are actually generalizations of the empirical facts of life through tropes, and, like all tropes, they are pregnant with man's emotional attitudes to the facts. The development of lexical and grammatical means to express general ideas opens the way, on the one hand, for scientific thought, which has as its goal a non-emotional cognition of objects, and on the other, for specifically artistic thought, whose goal is the emotional cognition of man's attitude toward and relation to objects.

---

[1] In this paper some of the Sumerian words will be quoted in a form laying bare their morphological structure. These will be quoted in slanted slashes.

[2] M. A. Powell, *Sumerian Numeration and Metrology*, (Dissertation, University of Minnesota, 1971).

[3] D. O. Edzard, "Sumerisch 1 bis 10 in Ebla," *Studi Eblaiti* 3 (1980), 121–7.

[4] According to Klimov (G. A. Klimov, *Tipologija jazykov ergativnogo stroja*, Moscow, 1980, 55, 63ff.), an ergative language is one that is based on the opposition 'transitive': 'intransitive' and which has an oblique 'ergative' case for the subject of the transitive verb, and a zero 'absolute' case for the subject of the intransitive verb (also usually for the object of the transitive). Klimov labels 'active' any language which is based on the opposition 'action : state', with the actor in the ergative and the object of action, or subject of the state, in the absolute case. I do not think this term is felicitous, especially when one recalls that precisely these languages were only recently called 'passive' (thus, e.g., E. A. Speiser when referring to Hurrian). I think that the term 'active' should be reserved for languages based on the opposition 'active : passive' (='nominative languages', i.e., such as have a nominative case for any subject, both of action and of state, and an accusative for the object of the transitive action, and which use the passive construction alongside of the active, being able to visualize the action either from the point of

Sumerian is an archaic language in which abstract ideas were in the making: this is why both Sumerian language and Sumerian mythology are so interesting. It has no means to express a subject-object relation, and very inadequate means to express the idea of time etc. Abstraction of human activities is incarnated either in the materially perceived me, i.e., the internal 'laws', or 'order of things'—which can be loaded into a boat and unloaded from it. (Admittedly, the boat is a divine one.) Or they can be expressed through the (equally materially perceived) nam, which can be translated as an abstract term, 'fate',[5] although it can be 'cut' (cf. ^{d}nam-tar 'the nam-cutter', nam-tar-a 'the cut-off nam'). nam is represented by the pictograph of a bird (like the Egyptian *bꜣ*, supposedly 'soul'). Even 'to kill' is, in Sumerian, expressed naturalistically as sag̃-g̃iš-ra(ḫ) 'head stick-break'.

This paper will discuss the Sumerian numerals from the point of view of their place on the road of development of abstract thinking, starting from Edzard's data on the Sumerian numerals written on a school tablet in Ebla.[6] Looking through the Ebla list, one notices that the numerals from '1' to '10' end in /-u/ (with the exception of '5', where the reading, as pointed out by Edzard, is rather obscure, and of those numerals which are quoted with a suffixed copula). This /-u/ appears sporadically also in the earlier published syllabic spellings of numerals (mainly known from Proto-Ea, Aa, and Ea), but otherwise it is either absent or replaced by /-a/.

A noticeable feature of the Sumerian numerals is that they usually have at least two different forms: one with a suffix, the other without it. The Ebla text lists the following suffixed numerals:

1 - Aš.*t*., not transcribed, presumably /*aš-u/
2 - /min-u/
3 - /iš-am/ (probably </*êš-u-àm/)
4 - /lim(m)-u/
5 - /i + Vowel/ (see below)
6 - /i-aš-u/ (= 5 + 1)
7 - /u-min-u/ (</i-min -u/=5+2)
8 - /ûs(s)-am/ (</ûs-(u-)àm/*i-wes-u/=5+3)[7]
9 - /i-lim-u/ (=5+4)
10 - /hawim-u/

Edzard thinks that the sign 'I' which stands for '5' in the list, is to be read /ya/. It certainly is not to be read /i/, for which the sign Ì is used. However, in accordance with the Old Akkadian usage, to which the scribal usages of Ebla are certainly closely related, and also in accordance with Edzard's own examples of Semitic syllabic spellings from Ebla,[8] it is more probable that /ia/ should be transcribed by the 'A'-sign, which was also in Old Akkadian used to spell /ia/ and /aia/.[9] Actually, in the Ebla tablet itself, A-ŠU 'six' is doubtless to be read /iašu/, and it would be strange if the scribe should use two different signs in two adjoining lines for transcribing the same syllabic value /ia/in the same initial position. Therefore we must probably adopt some other reading for 'I', and I suggest it should be /iyi/, which seems to be

view of the logical subject, or from the point of view of the logical object). For Klimov's 'active', I suggest 'fientive'; however, I am not quite convinced that the division of archaic languages into 'fientive' and 'ergative' proper is useful, because most 'fientive' languages oppose not only action to state but also transitive action to intransitive. Unless a language has the same morphological means to express both the subject of a state resulting from an action (=our object of action), and the subject of a state *per se*, it cannot be called 'ergative' in the strict sense of the word. In practice it is very difficult to draw a line between 'fientive' and 'ergative' languages. Note that many so-called 'ergative' languages (e.g., Georgian) have many features of an emerging nominative construction; other allegedly 'ergative' languages (e.g., a number of Middle Indian and Middle and Neo-Iranian languages) are the result of a secondary decomposition of 'nominative' languages, and are in no way archaic. They are to be carefully distinguished from the genuine, archaic 'fientive-ergative' languages, such as Sumerian, Hurrian, Paleo-Asiatic, Burušaski, Tibetan, some of Cushitic, and the reconstructible Common Afrasian and Common Indo-European. Also the North (Western and Eastern) Caucasian ergative languages, although in many respects more developed than Sumerian (e.g., in the system of tenses), are in other respects archaic.

[5] Falkenstein's etymology of nam</*ana-àm/ 'what is it' is wrong because nam is a substantive, and can be construed with a noun in the genitive (cf. A. Falkenstein, *Das Sumerische* [*HdO*, I Abt., 2 Bd. 1–2 Abschn., Lief. I] 1959, 35).

[6] No.TM.75 G.2198.

[7] $iš_{11}$-(š)a-am might conceivably also be read $eš_{11}$-(š)a-am, in accordance with all later evidence; eš- contracted </*eweš/, cf. n. 18 below, hence our transcription /êš-/, /îš-/. The suffix -u is elided in the copula.

[8] *a-mì-núm* = /*yamīnum*/ 'right', *a-mì-tum* =/*yamittum*/ 'right side/hand'. The variants *i-mì-tum*, *i-sa-lum* probably stand for /*yemittum*/,/*yešarum*/, *i-ti* for /*yiddin*/.

[9] I. J. Gelb, *Old Akkadian Writing and Grammar*, 1961. Sign List s.v.

supported by other Eblaite material.[10] Thus I propose a reconstruction of the first five Sumerian numerals from Ebla as follows:
1 - / *aš-u /, 2 - / min-u /, 3 - / î / êš-u /, 4 - / lim-u /, 5 - / iyi / < / *i-u /. The form / eš-u /[11] is actually attested in the later texts.

Elsewhere the Sumerian numerals are encountered: (a) without a suffix, as, e.g., 1 - / aš /, 2 - / man,min /, 3 - / êš /, 4 - / lim /,[12] 5 - / *i /;[13] (b) with the suffix / -a /, as e.g., 1 - / *aš-a /, 2 - / min-a /, 3 - / êš-e / (harmonized < / *êš-a /),[14] 4 - / lim-a /[15] (/ -a / > / -u /, influenced by the labial / -m- /), 5 - / ia /; (c) with the copula -àm, when used as an attribute or predicate.

Thus we may reconstruct four parallel series of forms:

	Suffixless	/ -u /	/ -a /	With copula
1	/ aš /	/ *aš-u /	/ aš-a /	/ *aš-am /
2	/ man,min /	/ min-u /	/ min-a /	/ min-am /[16]
3	/ êš /	/ êš-u /	/ êš-e / (< *eš-a /)	/ ê / îš-(š)am /
4	/ lim /	/ lim-u /	/ lim-a / (> / lim-u /)	/ limmu(< / *lim-um / < / *lim-am /)
5	/ *i / (not attested)	/ *i-u /	/ i-a /	/ i-am /[17]
6	/ *i-aš / > / âš /[18]	/ i-aš-u /	/ *i-aš-a / (not attested)	/ i-aš-am /
7	/ i-min / > / u-mun /	/ i-min-u / > / i / u-mun-u /[19]	/ i-min-a /[20]	/ i-min-am /[21]
8	/ *ûs / (not attested) ·	/ ûs-(s)u /	/ ûs-(s)a /	/ us-(s)am /
9	/ *i-lim / (not attested)	/ i-lim-u /	/ i-lim-(m)u / < / *i-lim-a /	/ i-lim-(m)u(m) /

The numerals for '10' should perhaps be reconstructed as / *haw /, / *hû /, / *hâ /, but I will discuss this in more detail below. The next non-compound numerals are niš, or neš '20', and '60' g̃eš.

In the compound forms it is usually the suffixless form that is present, thus / i- / in '5+x' compounds, / -min / in the 'x+2' compounds (ni-min < / *niš-min / '20X2'=40; likewise / -(h)aw-u / > / -û / in the 'x+10' compounds, as in / ušû / (< / *niš-û / - '20+10'),[22] / ni(mi)n-û / '50' (< / *ni(š-min-haw-u / '20X2+10') with stress on the last syllable; also / ni- / in nimin, ninnû should perhaps be treated as the

[10] 'I' in the Ebla text might perhaps be read as / ii,iyi /, with harmonization of the vowels < / *iu /. This would point to a stress on the first syllable. However, in the numerals compounded with '1' to '9' and in '10' the stress is apparently on the first syllable of the second element.

[11] Ea I, 321 (var.) (*MSL* 14, 192).

[12] Powell thinks that the actual Sumerian word for 'one' is diš, and seems not to be quite certain about aš, but tending to regard it as not a numeral properly speaking. The compound numerals seem, however, to indicate clearly, that aš, as well as diš, is the numeral 'one'.

[13] Only in Proto-Ea 169, 170, var. (*MSL* 14, 38); elsewhere always in the suffixed form / limu /,/ lim(m)u /.

[14] Aššur MA Excerpt, 28′, 32′ (*MSL* 14, 262); *WO* I (1950), 374, III 29′.

[15] Ibid. 30′. Powell's suggestion that the forms eš-še, lima may be ordinals can hardly be accepted.

[16] Gudea Cyl. A XXI, 1–11; Edzard, op. cit. 123 n. 8.

[17] Ibid.

[18] In the later periods seems to have been read / âš /, thus coinciding with the word for 'one', probably except for the tone. I use a circumflex to denote a contracted vowel; it would very likely have a contoured (circumflex) tone.

[19] For explanation of the *u*-vocalism cf. Edzard, op.cit., 124, and see below.

[20] See Powell, apud Edzard, ibid., 124 n. 19, (Ea II 170).

[21] VII-nam is well attested, cf. e.g., g̃eš-imin-(n)am *SAKI* 48, 6, 18; the omission of -àm in Gudea Cyl. A XXI 1–11 may be accidental (contra Edzard, op. cit., 123, n. 8; W. Heimpel, *Or.* 39 [1970], 492–5).

[22] This is the etymology advocated by A. P. Riftin, "Sistema šumerskich čislitel'nykh," in *Jazykovednye problemy čislitel' nykh*, 1927, 187. Initial **n*- dropped as in nindá//inda, or ES èm, àm for EG níg; vowel harmonization because of loss of the consciousness of the compound nature of the word; stress on the last syllable. Powell, 48, n. 1, explains the form ušu as < *eš-u but is unable to account for the reversal of the elements (the smaller numeral should follow the larger).

short form of niš '20'.[23] The /-u/ or the /-a/ suffix at the end of the compound form, when present, belongs to the compound as a whole, not to the second of its components. This is probably because the compound numeral is treated as a syntagm with only one expiratory stress. A numeral coupled with an enumerated object is also a close compound with a single stress, hence we find such forms as bán-de-eš '1 bán', ba-an-mi-in '2 bán', bùr-mi-in '2 bùr', ba-an-eš '3 bán'. In compound numerals involving multiplication we find that the lesser numeral almost invariably (with the exception of the very ancient nimin 'twice twenty') is in the suffixed form, thus g̃eš mi-na (60×2)=120, g̃eš eš-(š)e (60×3)=180, g̃eš-u-a-šá-a[24] (60×6)=360,[25] geš ú-mi-na (600×7)=4200, geš-ú-sa (60 ×8)=480.[26] The cited form g̃eš-ú-li-mu-ku [60×(5+4)]=540 is an error.[27] The numeral '600' is spelled syllabically as ni-šu which probably is also an error. Elsewhere the attested form is /g̃ešu/=/*g̃eš-u/ '60×10'. It had also a special name, *nēr*, which is attested only as an Akkadian numeral but surely must have had a Sumerian origin.[28]

The numerals of the type involving addition ('10+digit', '60+digit') probably originally had the digit in the suffixless form, so that /*u-min/ was '12', and /g̃eš-min/ was '62'. However, the two series of forms (suffixed and suffixless) tended to get mixed up. Thus /limu/ '4' was originally a suffixed form, as well as /*ûsu/ '8' and /*hû/</*haw-u/ '10'. However, they were used in the same way as the suffixless forms, presumably because the /-u/-series had ceased to exist as such and passed on its specific function (whatever it was) to the suffixless form. Hence the latter now appeared in the form: 1 -/aš/, 2 -/man/, /min/, 3 -/êš/, 4 -/lim(m)u/, 5 -/i/ia/, 6 -/âš/, /-uaš/, 7 -/umun/, /umin/, /imin/ etc., 8 -/ûs(s)u/, 9 -/ilim(m)u/, /ulim(m)u/, 10 -/(h)û/. Of these at least /lim(m)u/, /i/ulim(m)u/ and /(h)û/ appeared also in the /-a/-series (probably by phonetic reasons: /a/>/u/ in the presence of a labial). This finally led to the loss of semantic differentiation between the three series. Thus we find in the word-list such forms as g̃eš-eš for '(60×3)=180,[29] ba-an-iá '5 bán',[30] ba-mi-na(<*bán-min-a) '2 bán', ba-eš$_{6}$-(š)e '3 bán' and even ba-ḫi-ia either for '*bán-ḫà' or '*bán-iá ('5' or '10' bán).[31]

Already A. Deimel[32] has asked how the Sumerians distinguished between '62'(60+2) and '120'(60×2), since both the numerals to be added and those to be multiplied were simply put one beside the other, the smaller always following the bigger one (/g̃eš-u/= 60×10=600, but /i-lim(m)u/ 5+4=9, and /*ni-min-u/ 20×2+10=50); and thus both '62' and '120' should have been pronounced /*g̃eš-min/. I have suggested that originally '62' was /*g̃eš-min/, but '120' was /*g̃eš min-a/; but at a later period the form /g̃eš-min/ seems certainly to be used also for '120'. Deimel's question thus remains on the agenda.

The answer is probably that multiplication was kept apart from addition by the use of different tones. Sumerian was certainly a tonal language, or else the many homonyms would have made spoken Sumerian quite unintelligible. The tone co-existed in Sumerian with expiratory stress.[33] The latter leads to vowel

---

[23] Loss of final *-š cf. in ES mu = EG g̃iš; g̃iš-dar-a >g̃idrī 'stick' (A. Falkenstein).

[24] /-uašâ/ by alliteration with /-uminâ/, /-ûsâ/, /-ulimmu/, cf. on this phenomenon below. The form shows that '6' was pronounced /iaš-/, not /*yaš/. See Aššur MA Excerpt, 35′–38′ (*MSL* 14, 212). Edzard (op. cit. 122, n. 6) translates /-uminâ/ incorrectly as '2×600'; the text clearly has '7×60'.

[25] Ibid., 35′.

[26] Ibid., 37′.

[27] Ibid., 38′. *MSL* regards -ku as a scribal error, but perhaps it stands for -ka.

[28] Ibid. 39′. The Sumerian /g̃/ is, as is well known, sometimes transcribed as /n/ in the word-lists, thus ki-in for /kig̃/, although sa-ag for /sag̃/, di-in-gi-ir for (presumably) /dig̃ir/, cf. ES dèm-me-er. Cf. also Akkad. *nisānu*<Sum. ne-sag̃. Likewise Akkad. *nēr* should perhaps be derived<Sum. /*g̃ìr/ in the sense of 'bone' (counting alternatively 'sticks' g̃iš and 'astragals, bones' g̃ìr?). Cf. also note 59.

[29] Ea II 248 (reconstructed; *MSL* 14, 258).

[30] Ea I 325 (*MSL* 14, 193).

[31] Aššur MA Excerpt, 24′–27′ (*MSL* 14, 200).

[32] A. Deimel, *Šumerische Grammatik der archaischen Texte*, 1924, 180.

[33] This was seen by Riftin, op. cit., 183, n. 2 and shown explicitly by A. Falkenstein, *Das Sumerische*, 31; developed by Diakonoff, *Jazyki drevnej Perednej Azii*, 1967, 52. Cf. 'dele-dele>'dedle 'gi-lam>'gilim, 'nam-a-zu >'nam-zu, /*ana-m-g̃u/ 'what is mine?'>'nam-g̃u 'what is it?', 'g̃iš-dar-a 'broken tree'>g̃idri 'stick' (the examples are from Falkenstein). It seems that in roots/stems with an initial vowel the stress could fall on the second syllable, cf. /*e'wen-líl/>ES/*Umun-líl/>^{d}Mul-lí/; ^{d}ǎmar-u'tu(k)> ^{d}*Marduk*. There may have been changes in the position of the stress in affixed forms.

contraction, which the tones do not; they are more apt to influence the quality of a vowel than its quantity. We suggest that the well known harmonization of the vowels inside a Sumerian bisyllabic root[34] points to the invariability of the tone inside the root morpheme. Vyačeslav Vs. Ivanov pointed out to me that in Sumerian each morpheme might have had a tone of its own, while the word as a polysyllabic whole or a close syntagm would have had a single expiratory stress. The point beyond which the harmonization of vowels inside a verbal form no longer obtains must thus be the point where the tone changed. Characteristically, the harmonization of the vowels can be extended to the suffixes (as -túm-ed-a>-túm-ud-u etc.) but not to the prefixes (the harmonization of *ḫé-mu->*ḫu-mu- etc. has nothing to do with the vowel of the root and the tone lying on it).

If our suggestion that digit numerals in the compounds of the type '10 + digit', '60 + digit', belonged to another series than those in compounds '10 × digit', '60 × digit', then it is probable they too would have had different tones. If in the course of development the suffixless and the suffixed forms could be mixed up, this means that the sense-distinguishing function was not so heavily laid upon the suffix and there probably was also some other phonemic phenomenon bound up with this function. This must have been the tone. When the same function is expressed by two different means, one of the morphs is redundant and apt to be lost. In this case probably the suffix proved redundant, and the sense-distinguishing function was laid entirely upon the tone.

However, the fact remains that originally Sumerian had three parallel series of numerals (not counting the form with the copula), and these forms must each have had a special semantic of its own. As we have seen, the suffixless form was probably used in a nominal syntagm to qualify a measure or an enumerated object, or as an element in the compound numeral. Hence the full form should be expected when the numeral was used outside of syntactical context, i.e., for abstract counting. In a list, like the Ebla text, we naturally encounter the form for the abstract count ('one, two, three, four, five'). In a vocabulary we are nearly as likely to find forms extracted from real contexts. Therefore, our guess is that the suffixed form of the numerals in the Ebla text (/-u/-series) represents the abstract count. We have now to look for typological analogies.

The use of suffixed forms for numerals in abstract counting is a feature known in quite a number of archaic languages. Selecting at random, to begin with, three archaic languages—Burušaski in Kašmir,[35] Laki in Daghestan[36] and Ket on the Yenisey[37]—I found this phenomenon in all three: Burušaski adds a suffix *-i* to the numerals when used for abstract counting (and also when applied to a certain limited class of nouns), Laki a suffix *-wa*/*-ma* (also used for inanimate beings) and Ket a suffix *-s'*/*-am*/*-əm* (the suffix *-s'* being also used with adjectives not qualifying a noun, i.e. *in abstracto*).

Especially interesting is the situation in Chukchi, the archaic language which is typologically perhaps the most similar to Sumerian in Eurasia.[38] Besides being, like other archaic languages, an ergative one, Chukchi has verbs compounded with the subject of resulting state (=object) plus the verb proper (like Sumerian šu-····-tag, ik-····-tak₄ etc.: cf. Chukchi *qora-nmə* '(to) reindeer-kill' etc.). Although Chukchi does not resume the case-forms of the indirect object inside the verb, as does Sumerian, it can include the object itself in a compound verb: *t-ačyğy-ply-tko-ak* 'I paid (*ply-*, lit. 'ended') (the) debt (*ačyğy*)'; *t-* is roughly equivalent to Sumerian šu- in compound verbs. More-

[34] The rule has no exceptions; instead of erim, erín, erin, èri, edin etc. read, of course, erem, erén, eren, erè, eden etc. The seeming exceptions are either compounds (uğken< /uğ-ken/) or borrowings (ni-is-kum, Niburu); lately I have been able to show that also ḫašḫur 'apple(-tree)' and anšu, anše 'donkey' are borrowings from an Eastern Caucasian language, perhaps Qutian, of which Udi, spoken in two villages on the border between Georgia and Azerbaijan, seems to be a relic: EC *ᶜ*a(n)č-qIwir* 'apple-pear' (cf. German *Granatapfel*!) and **ḥənčwV* 'horse, donkey'; EC **q̇ut'ī-*>Udi *udi*. Elsewhere I will try to show that Old Sumerian *t* is /t'/, while *d* is /t/, and *š* is, at least in a number of cases, /č/.

[34a] Powell (p. 58) suggests that the additive compounds had the stress on the first syllable, while the multiplicative ones on the second. This might have been a possible solution, were it not for such additive compounds as ninnu< *ni+min+u, ušu<niš+u which have obviously the stress on the ultimate syllable.

[35] G. A. Klimov and Joy Edelman, *Jazyk burušaski*, 1970, 46.

[36] For information on Laki I am indebted to my friend M. A. Dandamaev, a native speaker of the language.

[37] J. A. Krejnovič, "Ketskij jazyk," in *Jazyki narodov severa, I* (ed. by J. A. Al'kor), 1934, 232.

[38] V. G. Bogoraz, "Luoravetlanskij (Čukotskij) jazyk," ibid., 25 sq.

over, Chukchi has a 'women's language' which, like eme-sal in Sumerian,[39] differs from the language of men in phonetics, in retaining certain archaisms,[40] and insignificantly in the vocabulary.[41] The category of the plural of the noun is, as in Sumerian, imperfectly developed (a general plural is used only in the absolute case; there is a special suffix for group plural, more or less corresponding to the Sumerian -ḫá).

Chukchi has special forms for numerals in abstract counting or not included in syntagms, and other forms for numerals when included in a syntagm: *g̃irə-q* '2', *mytlyg̃-en* '5', *myng̃yt-ken* '10' (abstract counting), but *g̃irä-muri* 'we two', *mytlyg̃-qlekken* '100' (lit. '5×20'), *myng̃yt-kaletol* 'ten roubles'. A numeral with copula is used to express ordinals: *g̃irə-q-äu-rkyn* 'two-is-he/it' = 'second', *mytlyg̃-kau-rkyn* 'five-is-he/it' = 'fifth'.

Thus the use of suffixed forms of numerals for abstract counting is well enough attested in archaic languages so that we may assume that such was the role (or one of the roles) of suffixed numerals also in Sumerian. There remains the question of why there were two different series of suffixed numerals. The /-u/-series can confidently enough be assigned to the abstract count, but also the /-a/-series seems originally to have been used for numerals when not part of a close syntagm and hence, probably, likewise for abstract counting. Two explanations can be suggested. Either the difference was one of dialect, or the form depended on the character or class of the enumerated objects. The first alternative seems at first glance to be the more probable, because one would think that in abstract counting the character of the object would hardly matter; however, there is a possibility that there may have been two different ways of counting, say, animate and inanimate beings, even *in abstracto*. Turning to typological parallels, we find in our 'control' languages the following picture: Burušaski uses different forms of numerals for different classes of nouns[42] even in abstract counting; Laki, which has three genders, uses one form for masculine, another for feminine, and a third for inanimate beings (including girls, as in German), the latter also being used for abstract counting; Ket has one form of the numeral 'one' for animate, and another for inanimate objects, the latter also included in the abstract counting series. Chukchi has no genders or nominal classes.

The most curious numeral system which I have ever encountered is that of Gilyak, or Nivkhi, a language spoken on the river Amur.[43] Here the forms of the numerals are subdivided into no less than twenty-four classes, thus the numeral '2' is *mex* (for spears, oars), *mik* (for arrows, bullets, berries, teeth, fists), *meqr* (for islands, mountains, houses, pillows), *merax* (for eyes, hands, buckets, footprints), *min* (for boots), *met'* (for boards, planks), *mir* (for sledges) etc., etc. Of course, the root is *m(i)-* in all cases.

Thus it is quite possible that the /-u/-forms and the /-a/-forms of the numerals in Sumerian might have been, at least originally, used for different classes of objects. Moreover, the system of distinguishing the forms of numerals depending upon the class of objects enumerated might have been at an early period still more developed; this would account for the invention of different numerical signs for areas, capacities etc., and in the Proto-Literate period, even for barley and wheat. Note that a differentiation of the numerals by classes of enumerated objects, which appears as a rather cumbersome outgrowth in Gilyak where it applies to all numerals, seems to be much more frequent in the case of 'one' and 'two'.[44] Note also that there are only two words certainly meaning 'one' in Sumerian, viz./aš/, and /deš/; dele and ge/gè/gi₄ can only with reservation be regarded as numerals, and other phonetic values for the single wedge probably have nothing to do with the numeral 'one'.[45] I

[39] On eme-sal as the language of women see I. M. Diakonoff, "Ancient Writing and Ancient Written Language," in *Sumerological Studies in Honor of Thorkild Jacobsen* [*AS* 20], 1974, 113–16.

[40] Cf. ES/umun/, /aman-/ (in /Aman-ki/) for EG /ên/</*ewen/.

[41] E.g., ES gašan 'lady' for EG nin.

[42] Klimov, Edelman, *Jazyk burušaski*, 37. The 'classes' are actually genders; but genders are often called 'classes' when they do not include the categories 'masculine' and 'feminine', and especially when they are more than three. Burušaski has four 'classes', North Caucasian also usually four.

[43] J. A. Krejnovič, "Ņivkskij (giljakskij) jazyk," in *Jazyki narodov severa*, 201–4. A similar phenomenon exists in Micronesian languages; these also have special forms for numerals in abstract count.

[44] Thus even in the non-archaic Russian: 'one' is *raz* in abstract count, but *o'din* in context.

[45] dele belonged to the group count, on which more below. Powell (p. 19 sq.) has shown that gè(-da) means 'whole' in the UR III administrative text and is also used for 'one' in reciprocal tablets (on the ternal count see below). However, it seems probable that originally gè did not mean 'one' but 'single line (wedge) in writing'; it could conceivably be used for 'reed' or 'stick' (in counting) and hence for 'unit' (of count), cf. below on niš '20', g̃eš '60' and /*g̃ìr(?)/ '600'; g̃eš as a reading for the vertical wedge has, as is convincingly shown by Powell, only the meaning 'sixty' but not 'one',

would suggest that /aš/ was the reading of the figure '1' expressed by a horizontal wedge (e.g., for measures of surface), /deš/ for the vertical wedge; it was probably also the original reading of the 'Mister'-sign and hence listed in Ea II 53 sq., 203 sq. (*MSL* 14,256) together with /aš/ and /dele/ as the reading of AŠ and Aš-*t*. (cf. the ED and Akkadian use of the horizontal wedge to note units in lists of persons). However, there is no evidence that the DIŠ-sign could ever be read either /aš/ or /dele/.

Are there any traces of differentiation of other numerals according to the enumerated object? Except for the Ebla text, in the Sumero-Akkadian manuals known to us there does not exist any coherent and complete list of the phonetical values of the numerals. The readings must be gleaned from items unsystematically placed at different points in the word-lists; these are partly readings assigned to combinations of measure and numeral, or to compound numerals. Very probably, the quotations in the word-lists originate from individual and often not uniform contexts. The data are to be found in Proto-Ea, Aa and Ea, more seldom in other lexical lists.

By systematizing and arranging the data, we come to the following conclusion:

1. *Quintal-vigesimal system, vertical signs:*[46] 1 - /deš/, 2 - /min/,[47] 3 - /êš/ (</*eweš/),[48] 4 - /lim/,[49] 5 - (?)/i/[50] etc. Note that digits may have suffixed forms, but 'ten', 'twenty' 'sixty' have none; the reason may be that the abstract count was in practice not extended beyond the two hands.

ES variant: 1 - /*de/,[51] 2 - /nim/,[52] (-a-form /im-a/), 3 - /am(m)uš/.[53] The numerals beyond '3' are unknown.

2. *Quintal-vigesimal system, horizontal signs:* 1 - /aš/, 2 - /man/(? - also /min/, secondary?),[54] 3 - /êš/, 4 - /lim/,[49] 5 - /ia/.[55] Use of suffixed forms as in system 1.

3. *Group count:* 1 - /dele/ 'only one, alone; (as) a whole';[56] 2 - /tab/[57] (also /min/)—'both, double,

---

although it also might have meant something like 'stick' or 'notch'. Note, that g̃eš is never equated with g̃iš 'tree, stick' and is reflected in ES as muš (but g̃iš as mu!) and thus probably was distinguished by another tone, and possibly by another final phoneme, although it was transcribed in Akkadian uniformly as -*š*; sag̃ta(k) means 'triangle, cuneiform element in writing', lit. 'head of wedge', *sag̃-dà-(k).

[46] Slanted signs do not constitute a separate system of numerical signs in the Sumero-Akkadian word-lists. Whether they originally existed as a system, or were just a variant of the other two, is not clear to me, but we learn that two Winkelhaken had the syllabic values man and mìn. However, the fact that three Winkelhaken had the value eš may not be relevant because here eš stands also for *maʾdūtu* 1'(verbal plural' (Aa II/ 4–12, 179, *MSL* 14, 284); cf. also three horizontal wedges to which the same meaning is attached (Proto-Aa 165, *MSL* 14, 96).

[47] Ea II 246, *MSL* 14, 258; cf. *mi-na* Aššur MA Excerpt, 27′, 31′, 40′, *MSL* 14, 262.

[48] The derivation of eš(êš)</*eweš/ is based upon the ES form /amuš/(am-mu-uš) = EG eš$_6$ ES III 134 sq. (*MSL* 4, 40) which is a regular development of /*amaš/); ES /*amaš/, in its turn, is the regular correspondence of EG /*eweš/, cf. ES ^{d}A-ma-an-ki = EG ^{d}En-ki, and also ES u-mu-un = EG en(/ên/</*ewen/), with *a*>*u* because of the labial.

[49] Thus only in the variant of Proto-Ea 169, 170 (*MSL* 14, 38); elsewhere only /lim(m)u/.

[50] Only the suffixed -*a*-form is attested.

[51] The ES vocabulary (ES III 131, *MSL* 4, 39) has [de]-ed, but the -d is probably a variant of the ES numeral suffix -da/-de, cf. de-da variant to ES III 130, [de-le/-de = EG dele, ibid.; (?) [mu-uš-di-t]a (or [mu-uš-t]a) = ES g̃eš, g̃eš-ta '60'; ES III, 134 (*MSL* 4, 400; ES de-ta = EG deš in 'Enkidu and the Netherworld' (= *AS* 10, 7.1.68; Powell, 52); de-da *SBH* 109, No. 56:87 f. ES de = EG deš; for the loss of -š cf. n. 23.

[52] Cf. ES [mu-uš-n]im = EG g̃eš-min, ES III, 135 (*MSL* 4, 40); but ES i-im-(m)a (a-form) = EG min ES III 132; ES [áb mu n]im-m[u]-uš bal 'three years old cow' = EG áb mu eš$_6$, ES II 92 (*MSL* 4, 19), includes nim(m)uš 3' which is an alliterating form of /amuš/, influenced by nim '2'.

[53] See n. 48.

[54] Both the variants màn and min$_6$ are attested for the horizontal sign by Ea II 66, 125 sq. (*MSL* 14, 250), and Aa II/1 = 9, 14 (reconstructed, *MSL* 14, 272); in the latter case min$_6$ has the form and sense of tab, see below; man and mìn are also both attested for slanted signs or Winkelhaken; but /man/, like /aš/, is never used for the vertical sign.

[55] Ea II 133 (*MSL* 14, 253) attests the value ia$_x$ (!) for the horizontal '1'. No other attestation in the word-lists *MSL* 14.

[56] Akkad. *wēdum*; also *mitḫariš*, Ea II 63 (*MSL* 14, 149); Proto-Aa 100, 1 (*MSL* 14, 93). Hence the 'distributive' plural in *-dele-dele>-dedle 'all of them', one by one'. Cf. Powell, 20[a] etc.

[57] Two horizontal wedges: ta-ab Aa II/1–9, 2 (*MSL* 14, 272) = *šinā, kilallān*; but also mi-in ibid. 14 = *šinā, tu'āmu, kilallān*; mi-in and ma-an Ea I 17 sq., (*MSL* 14, 20), 126–127 (*MSL* 14, 252); reading ta-ab, mi-in given also for two Winkelhaken, Ea II 218–219 (*MSL* 14, 256); tab is obviously the word specific for the group count, while min$_6$ has strayed into the group count from the usual numeral system.

twin, companion'; 3 - eš₄ 'three together, troika'; 4 - tab-tab 'all four' (as in an-ub-da-tab-tab-(b)a 'all four corners of the world'; the reading *an-ub-da-limmu-ba, although supported by Proto-Ea 170 which has the reading li-im-mu for the four horizontal wedges, must nevertheless be regarded as wrong, and the reading of Proto-Ea 170 be assigned to System 2); 5 - /*i/ 'all five of them'. (Actually the reading /i/ is not ascribed *expressis verbis* to any of the numerals in the word-lists: Ea II, 133 reads the horizontal sign as iaₓ(!). However, a reading /i/ must have existed for *some* numerical sign with the value '5', and it was this sign which ultimately was responsible for the emergence of the syllabic value *i*. The verbal values i = *naʾādu* ('praise', originally perhaps 'raise hand'?) and i = *waṣû* (//éd, è)[58] are obviously secondary. My guess is that /i/ originally was '5' in the group count. The latter may not have been continued beyond '5'.

4. *Ternal count*. This very curious and archaic system is attested by a very few texts. The *Sitz im Leben* of this count is uncertain. However, I would venture to suggest hypothetically that the ternal count was reserved for strictly household usage and employed mostly by women.

It is best preserved in Antagal C (v. Lambert, *JSS* 14 [1969], 246); very close to it is the version of *NBGT* IV, 34 sqq (*MSL* IV, 100): 1 - ge (*NBGT* IV has instead me-er-ga, which probably is ES);[59] 2 - daḫ ('addition'; *NBGT* IV has daḫ-ḫe, but also adds two other forms, TAG₄-a-bi which apparently is the ordinal, and AN-ga-am);[60] 3 - PEŠ (*NBGT* IV adds the ordinal PEŠ-be); 4 - PEŠ-ge 'three+one' (*NBGT* IV has PEŠ-bala 'three passed', and adds the ordinal PEŠ-gi₄-bi 'three, one it (is)' which shows that bala 'passed' could freely be replaced by ge/gi₄ 'one'); 5 - PEŠ-bala-gi₄ 'three passed, one'; 6 - PEŠ-bala-gi₄-gi₄ 'three passed, one, one'; and 7 - PEŠ-PEŠ-gi₄ 'three, three, one'. PEŠ is possibly to be read /weš/ or /weš/, a variant of the archaic /*ewes/š/, the prototype of ES /am(m)uš/.[61]

A similar count is presented in a corrupted form by the text 'Enki and Ninḫursag'; here '7' is erroneously

placed before '5', while '2' and '6' are omitted, and '3' is represented by the ordinal PEŠ-bi.

Another variant of the ternal count is represented by a text discussed by W. G. Lambert, ibid., 243–47. It is a count of days and has -be for /ge/: 1 - be, 2 - be-be, 3 - PEŠ, 4 - PEŠ-be, 5 - PEŠ-be-be, 6 - PEŠ-PEŠ, 7 - PEŠ-PEŠ-be, etc. up to the very artificial looking '12': PEŠ-PEŠ-PEŠ-PEŠ. Here be is not the pronoun -be/-bi but is the ge of the other texts. Since /b/ is one of the ES equivalents of EG /g/,[62] the whole count is presumably in ES.

It is clear that, except for the actually not numerical daḫ 'addition', the ternal count operates only with two numerals, ge/gè/gi₄/be 'one' and PEŠ 'three', and with the auxiliary word bala 'passed' which can be used after 'three' for the unit. Any combination of these three elements is allowed, thus PEŠ-ge = PEŠ-bala, and PEŠ-bala-gi₄-gi₄ = PEŠ-PEŠ etc.

The Sumerian ternal count does not stand alone in the languages of the world. A rudimentary ternal count is known, e.g., in Yukagir, an isolated language of North Eastern Siberia. It has not been satisfactorily explained. As to the usual Sumerian quintal-vigesimal system, it has long been understood that it is based on counting fingers, 'five' being equivalent to 'hand' or 'fist', or simply to 'all the fingers on the hand'. 'Ten', by the same token, must have meant 'both hands', and 'twenty'—'all four limbs', or 'the whole man'. However, in Sumerian itself the numerals in question, viz. /i/ '5', /huwimu/ (thus in Ebla) or /*(h)aw/ '10', and /neš/ '20' do not have any such connotation and have only a numerical value. Typological analogies show, however, that the finger-count is not a pure hypothesis, but is encountered as a real fact in the history of human mentality. In the Old World this is evidenced by Chukchi and other Paleo-Asiatic languages, which we have already quoted earlier for analogies with Sumerian.

Thus, in Chukchi, after 'one', 'two', 'three', and 'four' (the numerals '2, 3, 4' being, curiously enough, formed from the same root: g̃irə-q, g̃ir-o-q, g̃ir-a-q) comes the numeral 'five' which is an adjective, mytlyg̃en, lit. 'that-of-hand'; 'six' is 'one-(plus-)that-of-hand', 'seven' is 'two-(plus-)that-of-hand'. 'Eight', however, is 'just-that-of-three', or 'only-third'—am-g̃iroot-ken (cf. Sumerian /ûs(s)u/ which also does not quite fit into the system), 'nine' is 'one-behind-that-of-both-hands', and 'ten' is 'that-of-both-hands'—myng̃yt-ken. The numerals '11' to '19' are not exactly

---

[58] Ea II 135 (*MSL* 14, 253); Proto-Aa 16 (*MSL* 14, 119).

[59] Probably ES for EG =g̃ír in the sense of 'bone', 'astragal' + a suffix -ga which we also encounter in '2'.

[60] Probably read am₄-ga-am, with am₄ ES for nim like ám-, èm- for níg-. On the suffix -ga cf. n. 59.

[61] Compare the loss of the initial vowel, e.g., in ES ᵈMul-lil</*Ewen-líl/.

[62] E.g., EG dùg= ES ze-eb.

known for Sumerian. In Chukchi '11' is 'that-of-both-hands, one redundant', '15' is a derivative of 'foot', and '20' is 'that-of-man'—*qlikken*; '30' is 'that-of-man, that-of-both-hands redundant', '40' is 'two-of-that-of-man', '50' is 'two-of-man, that-of-both-hands redundant', '60' is 'three-of-that-of-man', etc. The highest numeral is 'man-of-man', i.e. '20×20'=400. For counting above 400 the Chukchi use, e.g., 'that-of-both-hands-of-hand-of-man' i.e. '10×5×20=1000' etc., but this is a neologism (more usually replaced by the Russian word for 'thousand'); formerly all numbers higher than 'man-of-man' were called 'limit of knowledge'.

The system is similar to the other Paleo-Asiatic languages. Note the curious, very archaic system in Asiatic Eskimo (Yuhit):[63] 'one, two, three, four, hand' (lit. a derivative of 'hand'); '6' is 'going across' (cf. Sum. bala in the ternal system!); then follow 'two going across', 'third on the other side', 'fourth on the other side', and 'ten' is '(hands) up!'. The following count is semantically the same as in Chukchi. The ordinals are formed by the modal case of the cardinal numeral plus the copula.

One can easily see the similarity to the structure of both Sumerian systems, the quintal-vigesimal and the ternal (bala!). The Yuhit numerals do not actually belong to a ternal system, but the latter, as mentioned above, is attested in another Northern Asiatic language, Yukagir, where, however, the inner semantic of the numerals is not evident.

Not in all respects are the Paleo-Asiatic languages more archaic than Sumerian. Thus both Chukchi and especially Yuhit have got farther than Sumerian in the development of tenses (and hence in the means to express time); and Chukchi has a rather sophisticated set of word-formational affixes for, e.g., qualitative adjectives, *nomina instrumenti*, abstract nouns, etc. In the 20th century it has adapted itself quite satisfactorily for the expression of modern notions, although much is, of course, borrowed from Russian. But in the matter of counting, the Paleo-Asiatic languages are developmentally clearly behind Sumerian, at least as we know the latter from historical times. There are no vestiges of the connotation 'hand' and 'both hands' in the Sumerian numerals 'five' and 'ten' (the latter, according to Riftin, originally meant 'multitude', 'set' or 'group').[64] The word for 'twenty' niš or neš may actually at one time have meant 'man' (if read /g̃iš/, cf. g̃ìš), but this is exceedingly difficult to prove. Nevertheless, there can hardly be any doubt that the Sumerian system of numerals as we know it, was at least formed at a stage of mentality not very different from that which was responsible for the creation of the Chukchi and the Yuhit systems.

The tens in Sumerian constitute something of a half-developed vigesimal system, since '20' is niš and not '2×10', and the following tens up to 'fifty' are based on 'twenty'. They were also counted on the fingers, since the series does not go beyond the first five tens. Next comes an entirely new number, 'sixty', which is beyond the range of both the quintal and the vigesimal systems. 'Sixty' is g̃eš (ES muš). The phonemic sequence /*g̃i/eš/ may stand for a number of homonyms, and it is difficult to decide what was the

---

[63] V. G. Bogoraz, "Juitskij (aziatsko-eskimosskij) jazyk," in *Jazyki narodov severa*, 116.

[64] According to Riftin, op. cit. 188, the original form of the Sumerian numeral '10' was /ḫa/. The values listed by Aa II/14=12, 36–38 (*MSL* 14, 281), also in Ea II 146–149, (*MSL* 14, 253) are (besides u), also a (=a$_6$), ḫu-u (=ḫù) and ḫa-a (=ḫà). Riftin thought that the word originally meant 'much' or 'all' (actually, the Aa vocabulary lists the meaning *maʾdūtu* 'many, plural' for ḫà). Riftin identified ḫà 'ten; plural' with ḫá (ḪI.A), the morpheme of the 'sorting plural' of inanimate objects : udu-ḫá '(all) sheep according to their different groups or kinds'. This suggestion of Riftin must now be emended. In the Ebla text TM.75.G.2158 the syllable in question is expressed by the sign u$_8$ which, as shown by Edzard, op. cit. p. 126, should be read /ha/, in Akkadian also /*ḥa*/, but not /ḫa, γa/ with velar fricative, and, according to the spelling rules of Ebla, also /hai/,/haw/. Thus the word for '10' in Sumerian should be reconstructed as /haw, hau/; the initial aspirate was later lost or not spelled out, which is the reason for the existence of the later variant readings a$_6$,u // ḫà,ḫù. There exist also other proofs of the existence of a phoneme /h/ in Old Sumerian, later lost or spelled in the same way as /ḫ/, e.g. the sign É (*'à*) was originally pronounced /ha/ or even /hai/, hence Hebrew *hêḵal*, Aramaic *haiḵəlā* 'temple' but Akkadian *ēkallu* 'palace'. Cf. also the Akkadian (!) name of the Sumerian god ᵈEn-ki, viz. ᵈ*É-a*, read in Old Akkadian **Ḥà-ia*$_x$ /*ḥāi(a)*/; later (on Hurrian evidence) it was read *E-i-a-*. Another case of the spelling ḫ//zero for Old Sumerian /h/ are probably the readings ḫar,àr for the sign ḪAR (/har/?). This shows that some Sumerian spellings with *ḫ* may have to be read with /h/; hence the spelling of the plural morph as -ḫá need not invalidate its identification by Riftin with /ha/ '10'. Riftin also notes that 'three', eš, must have originally also meant 'multitude', hence its use as plural marker in stative predicates.

original literal meaning in this case. Possibly it simply meant 'unit', or 'the big unit'.[65]

The subsequent development of the system of numerals in Sumerian attests to a serious intellectual progress. The loss of the differentiation between the abstract count and counting concrete objects which is reflected in the loss of relevance of the distinction between suffixed and suffixless forms of the numerals was, no doubt, a step towards the generalization of the idea of number. But more important was the development of a very original and logical system of the higher numerals, which had occurred already at an earlier date.

The first order higher than '60' is '60×10'=600 /*g̃eš-u/ '60×10', or /*g̃er/?). It belongs halfway to the earlier series. The next is 60×60=3600 and is called šàr; this term obviously means 'round, circle', but in the specific sense of 'multitude'. The notion of 'circle' as something able to encompass a great multitude is stressed by the fact that the still higher round numerals are all 'circles', including šàr-gal 'the big circle (multitude)', and šàr-šu-nu-tag 'the unattainable (lit. 'untouchable') multitude'.[66] This is the 'limit of knowledge' already known to us from Chukchi, but note how far it has receded! The new idea that the 'encompassed multitude', or 'circle' can be used as the base for a new series of numerals and counted in the same way as digits are, was certainly a major achievement in abstract thinking.

A few words concerning the phonetic form of the digit numerals. Edzard[67] has correctly noticed the frequent tendency to alliteration of neighboring numerals in different languages, like **fioþwor*, **finf*, '4', '5' in Germanic (for **hwaþwor*, **finhw*), *quattuor*, *quinque* '4', '5' in Latin (for **quattuor*, **penque*), and *devjat'*, *desjat'* '9', '10' in Russian (from Proto-Slavonic **nevã*, **desãtĭ*). In Sumerian this feature appears in /u-min-u/, /ûs(-u)/ of the Ebla text,[68] but also in g̃eš-u-a-šá-a, g̃eš-u-mi-na, g̃eš-ú-sa, geš-ú-li-mu-ku(!) '60×6', '60×7', '60×8', '60×9' (for /*g̃eš-iaš-a/, /*g̃eš-i-min-a/, /*g̃eš-ûs-a/, /*g̃eš-i-lim-u/) in the MA Aššur Excerpt from Ea.[69]

There is also another frequent characteristic feature of numerals in many languages, viz. that of rhyming neighboring numerals.[70] In Eblaite Sumerian it is found in the rhyming pair '9', '10' -/i-lim-u/, /hawim-u/.[71] As we have mentioned before, the original form of the numeral '10' was perhaps /*haw/, with the suffixed forms /*haw-u/>/*hû/ and /*haw-a/>/*hâ/. I think that Riftin's suggestion connecting Sumerian '10', attested with the phonetic values u,ḫù,a₅,ḫà with the adjective -ḫá (ḪI.A) 'multitude' expressing the sorting plural holds good; he also suggested the sense 'multitude' also for /êš/ '3', used as a plural marker in predicates of state.[72] Thus, 'three' (/êš/, /*eweš/), 'ten' (/hau,hâ/) and perhaps also 'twenty' and 'sixty' had possibly also been 'multitudes' in their own time, like šàr '3600' at a much later period.

To conclude: first, one counts on the fingers—or, more properly, one counts the fingers; then one applies the numerals of the finger count to different objects, perhaps trying, like the Gilyaks, to keep the count concrete, even developing different forms of numerals for different objects—either of all numerals, or at least of 'one' and 'two'; then one develops the idea of numeral in the abstract and, correspondingly, there emerges a series of numerals for abstract count. Later Sumerians seem no longer to have distinguished the abstract series as such, but still there are duplicate numerals—with a suffix and without one. Having developed the idea of numerals in the abstract, one no longer resorts to tropes, as 'hand' for 'five', or 'man' for 'twenty', or 'going over the water' for passing from 'five' to 'six'. But the quintal-vigesimal system, or at

[65] If 'five', 'ten', 'fifteen' and 'twenty' might conceivably be derived from words meaning 'hand', 'both hands', 'foot' and 'man', no such naturalistic trope is probable in the case of 'sixty' and 'six hundred'. There is a possibility that these numerals were named after some helps for counting, as notches, sticks, stones, astragals etc. Cf. n. 45.

[66] F. Thureau-Dangin, *JA* 1909, 106 n. 1.

[67] Op. cit., 124 and n. 21.

[68] In spite of doubts expressed by M. Powell and other scholars /ûs-/ '8' is probably </*i-'wes/, /*i-e'wes/. The difficulty is in the final sibilant, which here is invariably attested as Akkadian *-s*, while it is Akkadian *-š* (actually /-č/) in /êš/ '3'. But we still are rather ignorant of the actual situation as regards Sumerian sibilants. For Akkadian sibilants see now I. M. Diakonoff, *Assyriological Miscellanies, I*, 1980, 7–12 (unfortunately, the publication abounds in misleading misprints).

[69] Aššur MA Excerpt, 35′–40′ (*MSL* 14, 262).

[70] Also noted by Edzard, but not applied to the Sumerian numerals. Cf. In Russian: *pjat'*, *šest'* '5', '6' < *pěkŭ(tĭ), *šes(ĭ); *sem'*, *vosem'* '7', '8' < *sem(t)ĭ<*septm̥; *os(t)ŭ; *devjat'*, *desjat'* '9', '10' (<*nevã, *desãtĭ).

[71] Edzard suggests the reading hà-wu-mu which is possible but not necessary.

[72] Cf. n. 64.

least the vigesimal system, continues to be alive.[73] One operates with 'units' and 'multitudes', a 'big unit' or a 'multitude' being equivalent first with 'three', then with 'ten', then with 'sixty', then with a *saros*, etc. There appears the idea that a 'multitude' can be operated in the same way as a digit, but not only as a visually evident multitude, like the two hands, but also as a multitude which can no longer be visualized, like the *saros*. And the positional system of notation of arithmetical figures comes at last—for its time the greatest triumph of abstract thinking, since it was developed by the Sumerian scribes at a period when the linguistic means of expressing ideas were still so very archaic.

I hope these reflections will make clearer the ways in which the Sumerian man marched towards knowledge. They may also help to reconstruct Sumerian as it was spoken. Were this to be achieved in full measure, then Sumerian poetry, to which Sam Kramer has given a new life, would become even more enjoyable to those who try to understand its language and its message.

[*Addendum*. Similar phenomena can apparently also be observed in Afrasian languages. Thus, e.g., Egypt. *dy* 'five' is an adjective <* *i̭ad* - 'hand', and Semitic *ḫamš* - 'five' is connected to the verb *ḫmš* 'to crook, bend (hand, fist)'; also Berber $s^{V}mm^{V}s$ 'five' is the same word deformed by assimilation to the neighboring numerals beginning in *s*-.]

---

[73] Empirically it is known that the vigesimal system is especially typical in the languages which have an ergative construction of the sentence. However, there does not seem to be any causal connection between the vigesimal system and the ergative. Joy Edelman has convincingly shown that the vigesimal system appears in those languages which do not (or did not at the period of the creation of the counting system in question) have different words for 'fingers' and for 'toes', or else the vigesimal system was introduced from a substratum or adstratum, see *Voprosy jazykoznanija* 5 (1975), 30–7. Of course, basing a numeral system on the counting of fingers and toes as well as structuring a sentence ergative-fientively have a common ground, viz., in an archaic mentality.

OF SLINGS AND SHIELDS, THROW-STICKS AND JAVELINS

Barry L. Eichler

University of Pennsylvania

In a review of E. Salonen, *Die Waffen der alten Mesopotamier*, D. O. Edzard noted almost fifteen years ago the confusion prevalent in the scholarly literature concerning the meaning of the Sumerian term ^{kuš}E.ÍB-ùr(-mè).[1] This confusion stemmed from the cuneiform lexical evidence which equated the term to both Akkadian *arītu* and *kabābu*. Today, the standard reference works agree that *arītu* is to be translated, 'shield'.[2] They differ, however, in the meaning of *kabābu*, with some translating the term as 'shield', but with others translating the term as 'sling'.[3] Since the appearance of the *CAD* entry *s.v. kabābu*, the Sumerian term ^{kuš}E.ÍB-ùr(-mè) has been translated more commonly as 'shield'. Nevertheless a certain ambivalence still exists today, with the most recent discussion of the term opting for 'sling' in two contexts while acknowledging that the term may elsewhere by rendered 'shield'.[4] It is hoped that the following examination of the lexical, literary and pictorial evidence may clarify this matter and may serve as a token of my appreciation and esteem for a beloved master of Sumerology who, through his forthright pioneer translations of Sumerian literature, has taught his students to meet the ever-changing state of knowledge with intellectual honesty and realism.

LEXICAL EVIDENCE

In the lexical series SIG$_7$.ALAN = *nabnītu*, the Sumerian term ^{kuš}E.ÍB-ùr-mè corresponds to Akkadian *arītu* and *kabābu*.[5] In the commentary ḪAR-gud to ḪAR-ra, ^{kuš}E.[ÍB.ÙR.M]È is equated to Akkadian *tukšu*, *arītu* and *kabābu*.[6] These terms also appear together in the Akkadian synonym list *malku* = *šarru*.[7]

In a Ras Shamra administrative list of personal names and weapons, written in alphabetic Ugaritic with Akkadian summation tallies,[8] the Ugaritic term ql^c corresponds to Akkadian *kabābu*. In 1939, on the basis of Semitic comparative etymology, F. Thureau-Dangin translated Ugaritic ql^c 'sling' and concluded that *kabābu* together with *tukšu* and *arītu* were Akkadian synonyms with the meaning 'sling'.[9] However, with the appearance of C. G. F. von Brandenstein's discussion of the term *arītu* in 1943[10] and subsequent contextual evidence from Akkadian literature, the interpretation of *arītu* as 'shield' became assured. Nevertheless, the interpretation of its "synonym" *kabābu* as 'sling' remained widely accepted on the strength of its Ugaritic correspondent ql^c. In 1958, B. Landsberger discussed the Akkadian term for 'sling' and noted that Ugaritic ql^c should not be con-

---

[1] *OLZ* 63/11–12 (1968), 559. The orthographic addition of -mè occurs only in post-Old Babylonian lexical and literary references. For other orthographic variants of the term, see below n. 12.

[2] *AHw*, 68, *s.v. arītu(m)* II; *CAD* A/2, 269, *s.v. arītu* A; E. Salonen *Waffen (StOr* 33), 129; *contra*: F. Thureau-Dangin, "Kabâbu, arîtu, tukšu," *RA* 36 (1939), 57–60.

[3] For 'sling', see *AHw*, 414, *s.v. k/gabābu(m)* but note the recent correction in 1565; E. Salonen *Waffen* (*StOr* 33), 134, 136; *CAD* A/2, 527, *s.v. azmarû.*

For 'shield', see *CAD* K, 1, *s.v. kabābu*.

[4] J. Klein, *Three Šulgi Hymns: Sumerian Royal Hymns Glorifying King Šulgi of Ur* (1981), 79, 138, with discussion on p. 102 in his commentary to lines 187–188.

[5] Nabnitu IV 154 (*MSL* 16, 82; note that the manuscript E = *CT* 12 39a:7 reads -mè and not -me), and Nabnitu XXIII 186 (*MSL* 16, 217; note that manuscript A = *CT* 19 20a:10 reads -mè and not -me, while manuscript B = *CT* 19 23b:5 reads -me$_6$).

[6] *MSL* 7, 151:178.

[7] Malku III 23f. cited in *CAD* K, 1, *s.v. kabābu*.

[8] This text, designated as text no. 321 in C. H. Gordon's *Ugaritic Textbook* (*AnOr* 38) and transliterated in 207–9, was first published by F. Thureau-Dangin, "Une tablette bilingue de Ras Shamra," *RA* 37 (1940), 97–118.

[9] *RA* 36 (1939), 57–60.

[10] *Hethitische Götter nach Bildbeschreibungen in Keilschrifttexten* (*MVAG* 46/2), 1943, 40f.

nected with the Semitic words for 'sling' but with Egyptian *qrᶜw*, Coptic *gl* 'shield'.[11] Landsberger's interpretation of the Ugaritic term *qlᶜ* as 'shield' restores the integrity of the lexical evidence in which *kabābu*, *arītu* and *tukšu* are synonyms. Thus Sumerian ^{kuš}E.ÍB-ùr-mè may be lexically equated to both *arītu* and *kabābu* and translated as 'shield'.

Despite the attractiveness and force of Landsberger's interpretation, Sumerian ^{kuš}E.ÍB-ùr-mè has continued to be rendered both as 'shield' and 'sling' in Sumerian literary passages. In order to understand this ambivalence, these Sumerian literary contexts must be examined.

LITERARY EVIDENCE

Evidence from Sumerian literary texts has tended to complicate the issue. Of the seventeen literary references to the term ^{kuš}E.ÍB-ùr(-mè) which have been collected,[12] the context of only one passage attests strongly the meaning 'shield' rather than 'sling'. In this passage the term occurs in metaphoric association with igi-tab 'blinker'. Lipitištar in a self-laudatory royal hymn exclaims:[13]

> ^{kuš}E.ÍB-ùr-igi-tab-ugnim-ma-me-en
> I am the ^{kuš}E.ÍB-ùr, the 'blinker' of the troops.

The metaphor 'blinker' seems to refer to one's ability to direct and guide the gaze of others thus ensuring their resolve in executing one's commands.[14] Although both ^{kuš}E.ÍB-ùr and igi-tab bear the determinative for leather objects, their association makes sense only if ^{kuš}E.ÍB-ùr is rendered 'shield', thus sharing the metaphoric nuance of a barrier, obstructing unwanted

---

[11] "Akkadisch *aspu* = "Schleuder", *assukku* = "Schleuderstein," *AfO* 18 (1957–58), 379 n. 8. Cf. the same identification made independently by R. Grafman *apud* A. Rainey, "The Military Personnnel of Ugarit," *JNES* 24 (1965), 22 n. 97. This identification, however, does not resolve the etymological issue. The earliest attestation of Egyptian *qrᶜw* is from the Nineteenth Dynasty (ca. 13th century B.C.E.) and it is not the common word for shield in Egyptian. Furthermore, J. Černý considers Coptic *gl* to be a loanword from Semitic (*Coptic Etymological Dictionary* [1976], 326). Are the Ugaritic, Egyptian, and Coptic terms for 'shield' etymologically related to the Hebrew noun *qlᶜ* (*Exodus* 27:9 *et passim*) which refers to the outer hangings forming the enclosure of the tabernacle (cf. W. Gesenius, *Hebräisches und Aramäisches Handwörterbuch*, 715)? The common semantic relationship could be based on the fact that both served as protective barriers or that both were of plaited construction—one of reeds and the other of linen thread. It is possible that the Hebrew term for sling may also be semantically related to the late attested Hebrew verb 'to twist, plait' (J. Levy, *Wörterbuch über die Talmudim und Midrashim*, volume 4, 316–8). Such a semantic association occurs in Sumerian as seen from Inanna and Ebiḫ 41 = 100 (ms. B. Eichler) á-sìg ebiḫ$_2$(ÉŠ.MAḪ)-gin$_7$ ga-na-ab-sur-sur 'I shall *fling* the slingstones like (with) a big rope'. The Sumerian verb sur, here translated as 'fling', is equated with Akkadian *zâru* 'to twist' and *ṭamû ša ṣubāti* 'to spin cloth' (cf. the Biblical expression *qlᶜ b*ʾ*bn* [*Judges* 20:16] to describe the flinging of a slingstone). Although Å. Sjöberg has interpreted the Inanna and Ebiḫ passage differently in that he considers the term for 'slingstones' to be a mistake for 'sling' (*JCS* 21 [1967], 275 n. 3; cf. *CAD* A/2, *s.v. assukku* with translation 'I want to plait a sling like a big rope'.), the semantic relationship between the term for sling/slingstone and the verb 'to twist, plait' is assured. Similarly, the English word 'to sling' exhibits a semantic derivation from the Anglo-Saxon verb 'to twist, wind' (*Webster's New International Dictionary of the English Language*, Volume 2 [1939], 2365, *s.v.* sling. Reference courtesy of Mark Hall). Thus it seems plausible that the Hebrew term for 'hangings' and 'sling' may be derived from the Semitic verb 'to twist, plait' from whence the Ugaritic term for 'shield' is also derived.

[12] Nine references are quoted below in the main text of this article. The remaining references are cited in the following footnotes: 23, 26, 27, 28, 34, and 36.

In the above literary references, the preponderant orthography of the term is ^{kuš}E.ÍB-ùr. The omission of ùr occurs in one manuscript of Lipitištar 77 (*TuM* NF 4 13:77) in two mss. of Angim 143 (Cooper, *AnOr* 52, p. 82) and in the Susa version of Death of Urnammu 92 (courtesy of M. Civil). One manuscript of Lugalbanda 386 reads ^{kuš}e-bu-ùr (*OECT* 1, pl. 8 iv 12, collated). In three of the four Šulgi royal hymns the term is consistently written ^{kuš}ÍB-ùr (D 188, O 18, X 65, *contra* the emendation in *MSL* 9, p. 16 re: *SLTN* 79:18). The addition of -mè to the preponderant orthography occurs only in post-Old Babylonian texts as noted by Cooper, *AnOr*, 52, p. 128 n. 2.

[13] Lipitištar A 77 (Römer *Königshymnen*, 35, and ms. Farber-Flugge in the University Museum).

TuM NF 4 13:77 has the variant
^{kuš}E.ÍB igi-tab-ba-ugnim-ma-me-en
TuM NF 4 14–15 III 7′ has variant
^{kuš}E.[ÍB]-ùr igi-tab-unkin-na-me-en

[14] Cf. Wilcke, *Lugalbanda*, 83 n. 344.

external elements. These two terms also appear in literary association in Lugalbanda-Ḫurrum, in describing Utu:[15]

^{kuš}E.ÍB-ùr-ra ki-ús-sa igi-tab-unken-na
^{kuš}E.ÍB-ùr-ra é-nì-ga-ta è igi-tab-guruš-a
He is the one who set the ^{kuš}E.ÍB-ùr upon the ground, the 'blinker' of the Assembly,
He is the one who brings forth the ^{kuš}E.ÍB-ùr from the magazine, the 'blinker' of the young warriors.

In this passage, only the term 'blinker' is used metaphorically and the association with ^{kuš}E.ÍB-ùr does not seem primary. Nevertheless, in view of their literary association in the Lipitištar verse, a translation 'shield' rather than 'sling' seems preferable. There is a third occurrence to be grouped with the above references which also employs the term ^{kuš}E.ÍB-ùr as a metaphor of the assembly. Šulgi O, in praising the Ekišnugal shrine of Ur states:[16]

bàd-nigín-na uru-ki-gá-ra-bi utúg ^{giš}tukul ki-ús-sa
unken-gar-ra un-ša-ra-ba ^{kuš}ÍB-ùr ki-ús-sa
Its city, built within the encircling walls, is an utúg-mace, a weapon, firmly founded,
The multitude in its convened assembly is a ^{kuš}ÍB-ùr, firmly founded.

On the basis of the two previous passages and the metaphoric imagery of protection and stability, the translation 'shield' seems more appropriate also in this context despite the fact that the preceding verse likens the city to a weapon.

In the remaining collected literary references, the term appears in contexts requiring a type of offensive weaponry, thus suggesting a translation 'sling' rather than 'shield'. A notable example is a passage from the Lamentation Over Sumer and Ur, describing the enemy's weaponry in its assault on Ur:[17]

[ur]í^{ki}-ma ^{urud}ḫa-zi-in-gal-gal-e igi-ni-[šè ù-SAR ì-ak-e]
^{giš}gíd-da á-mè-ke$_4$ si ba-sá-sá-e-ne
^{giš}ban-gal-gal GIŠ.ŠUB ^{kuš}E.ÍB-ùr-ra téš im-da-kú-e
ti-zú-ke$_4$ muru$_9$-šèg-gá-gin$_7$ bar-ba mi-ni-in-si
na$_4$-gal-gal-e ní-bi-a pu-ud-pa-ad im-mi-ni-íb-za
At Ur, the large axes are brandished[18] before them,
The spears, 'the arm of battle', are thrust directly (to their mark),
The large bows, the GIŠ.ŠUB, the ^{kuš}E.ÍB-ùr are all devouring,
The barbed arrows fill its outskirts like rain clouds,
The large (sling?-)stones one after the other[19] fall thuddingly.

Similarly, a Šulgi royal hymn depicts the manner in which the king will attack and defeat the enemy, enumerating a variety of projectile armaments to be employed in the impending battle:[20]

é-mar-uru$_5$-mu-ù nì ga-àm-ta-si
^{giš}ban-mu-ù muš-ḫuš-gin$_7$ guruš$_3$ ḫa-ma-búr-búr-re
^{giš}ti-zú igi-mu-šè nam-gin$_7$ ḫé-gír-gír-re
gi-bar-bar-ra su-din^{mušen}-dal-a-gin$_7$
ka-mè-bi-a ḫa-ma-an-dal-dal
im-^{kuš}da$^{!}$-<lu>-úš-a un-ba ḫa-ma-šeg$_x$(IM.A.AN)
im-dug-ge na$_4$-šu-gin$_7$
murgu-ba dub-da-ab ḫa-ma-ab-[za]
ki-bal-a un-tar-tar-ra-[x x]
GIŠ.ŠUB ^{kuš}ÍB-ùr-mu-[ù] buru$_5$-gin$_7$ ga-àm-mi-íb-ur$_4$?
I will fill my quiver,

[15] *TuM* NF 3 10:225–226. Cf. Wilcke, *Lugalbanda*, 82f. lines 225–226.

[16] J. Klein, "Šulgi and Gilgameš: Two Brother-Peers (Šulgi O)," *Kramer Anniversary Volume* (*AOAT* 25), 276f. lines 17–18.

[17] *PBS* 10/2 19:11–15 with restoration based on *UET* 6/2, 132:25–29. Cf. Wilcke, *Lugalbanda*, 192 lines 378–382 and the translation of S. N. Kramer in Pritchard, *ANET*^{3}, 618 lines 384–388 based on his ms. in the University Museum.

[18] Cf. Wilcke, *Lugalbanda*, 192 n. 471 who understands ù-sar—ak in this context as a variant of u$_4$-sar—ak 'to describe a semi-circle' referring to the swinging of the ax, rather than its usual meaning 'to make pointed, sharpen'. It is clear from this context and that of Lugale XIII 23 $^{\text{na}_4}$ú-ru-tum mi-tum-gin$_7$ ù-sar ḫé-aka-ne (ms. van Dijk, Lugale, 579) that ù-sar—ak connotes not only the brandishing but also the wielding of the weapon against the opponent.

[19] For this meaning of ní-bi-a, see Heimpel, *Tierbilder*, 153f. Cf. S. Cohen, *Enmerkar and the Lord of Aratta* (University of Pennsylvania Ph.D. dissertation, 1973), 158.

[20] Edition of Šulgi D by J. Klein, *Three Šulgi Hymns*, 78 lines 179–188 with translation in 79.

My bow will distend, ready to shoot like a raging serpent,
The barbed arrows will flash before me like lightening.
The barbar-arrows like flying bats,
Will fly into the "mouth of its battle."
Slingstones will rain down on its people,
Heavy clay lumps, like "hard-stones"
Will fall thuddingly on their back.
The crushed(?) people of(?) the rebellious land,
I will cut down with my GIŠ.ŠUB and ^{kuš}ÍB-ùr like locust.

In another Šulgi royal hymn, Inanna blesses the king, promising him divine assistance in battle, and declares that he is ideally suited for kingship. Describing his military prowess, she states:[21]

^{giš}meddu(TUKUL.AN)-ma á-íli-dè ba-ab-du$_7$-ù
^{giš}tukul-a du$_{10}$-bad-bad-du ba-ab-du$_7$-ù
ti-⸢sù⸣-^{giš}ban si-sá-e-dè ba-ab-du$_7$-ù
GIŠ.ŠUB ^{kuš}ÍB-ùr-ra zà-kéš-du-a ba-ab-du$_7$-ù
To hold high the mitum-weapon in (one's) arm, you are suited.
To run fast with(?) the battle mace, you are suited.
To guide straight the barbed(?) arrow and bow, you are suited.
To hold fast the GIŠ.ŠUB and ^{kuš}ÍB-ùr, you are suited.

As in the above three passages, the term ^{kuš}ÍB-ùr is paired most frequently with the GIŠ.ŠUB weapon, occurring together in seven references.[22] The verbs associated with this pair are those common to weaponry and acts of destruction:

si—sá: *šutēšuru* 'to aim, direct'.[23]
ur$_4$: *eṣēdu, ḫamāmu* 'to reap > cut down, collect'; *ašāšu* 'to catch with a net, engulf'.[24]
kú: *akālu* 'to consume, devour'.[25]
tùm/tun: *tabālu/ḫatû* 'to carry off/ to smite'.[26]

The term also occurs three times in parallel context with ^{giš}gíd-da 'spear'[27] and twice with gu$_4$-si-AŠ 'battering ram'.[28] This latter association again underscores the premise that the term ^{kuš}E.ÍB-ùr is part of the assault and siege weaponry as evident from the verse in the Uruk Lament:[29]

uru gu$_4$-si-AŠ ^{kuš}E.ÍB-ùr ba-su$_8$-ge-e[š] bàd-bi mu-un-si-il-si-[il-le-eš]
The battering ram and ^{kuš}E.ÍB-ùr advanced against the city; they split open its fortification walls.

The above literary references seem to indicate that the term ^{kuš}E.ÍB-ùr is an offensive weapon. The ambivalence found in scholarly literature in translating this term may thus be attributed to the dichotomy between the lexical evidence suggesting a preferred meaning 'shield' and the literary evidence suggesting a

[21] Edition of Šulgi X by J. Klein, *Three Šulgi Hymns*, 138 lines 62–65 with translation in 139.

[22] The other four passages are Šulgi E 224, Angim 143, Lugale 163, and Elevation of Inanna iv B 17.

[23] Lugale 163 GIŠ.ŠUB ^{kuš}E.ÍB-ùr-e (later version ^{kuš}E.ÍB-ùr-mè) si bí-in-sá kur ba-gul ba-sal: *til-pa-na ù ka-ba-ba uš-te-eš-š* [*ir* . . .] "He aimed his GIŠ.ŠUB and ^{kuš}E.ÍB-ùr, the mountain was destroyed, was flattened." (ms. J. J. A. van Dijk in the University Museum; cf. Cooper, *AnOr* 52, 157). Elevation of Inanna IV B 17–18 $^{\text{il-lu-ru}}$GIŠ.ŠUB ^{kuš}E.ÍB-ùr-mè šu si-sá-da-zu ulu$_3$ ḫa-ra-an-^{du}du$_9$-^{du}du$_9$-dè: *til-pa-nu u ka-ba-bu i-na šu-te-šu-ri-ki me-ḫu-u li-su-ru-ki* "When you direct the GIŠ.ŠUB and ^{kuš}E.ÍB-ùr-mè, may the storms rage for you (cf. B. Hruška, *ArOr* 37 [1969], 488).

[24] Šulgi D 188 quoted above.

[25] Lamentation Over Sumer and Ur 386 quoted above.

[26] Angim 143 é ki-bal tùm-tùm(NIM × KÁRA-NIM × KÁRA) GIŠ.ŠUB ^{kuš}E.ÍB-ùr-mu mu-da-an-gál-[la-àm] with NA ms. reading é ki-bal tun-tun GIŠ.ŠUB ^{kuš}E.ÍB-ùr-mè-mu [mu- . . .] "I bear those which carry off (NA ms. smash) the houses of the rebellious land, my GIŠ.ŠUB and ^{kuš}E.ÍB-ùr." (Cf. Cooper, *AnOr* 52, 82f.).

[27] Lugalbanda 319–320 which are parallel to lines 385–386:
^{giš}gíd-da-mu u$_4$-ne ba-DU
^{kuš}E.ÍB-ùr-mu u$_4$-ne e-ne ba-an-zur-zur-re
"My spear on that day will be *set aside*,
My ^{kuš}E.ÍB-ùr on that day will she shatter." (cf. Wilcke, *Lugalbanda*, 118ff, 124f.).
Death of Urnammu 91–92:
^{giš}gíd-da ^{kuš}lu-úb dag-si-mè-a i-mi-tum-ḫuš-an-na
^{kuš}E.ÍB-ùr-ki-ús-sa á-nam-ur-sag-gá
"A spear, leather bag, military *takšium*, the awesome *imittum*-weapon of An,
A firmly founded ^{kuš}E.ÍB-ùr, the valorous arms." (cf. Kramer, *JCS* 21 [1967], 114, 118).

[28] Uruk Lament 5:12, see below with n. 29; and Išmedagan A 250–251: gu$_4$-si-AŠ (x) ⸢x⸣ e ⸢x⸣-da-me-en ^{kuš}E.ÍB-ù[r] (x) ⸢x⸣ ka-ba DU-me-en (H. deGenouillac, *TCL* 15, pl. XXIV 3–4; ms. B. Eichler in the University Museum. Cf. Römer, *Königshymnen*, 52).

[29] UM 29-16-409 + UM 29-16-428 rev. I 26′ (Uruk Lament 5:12, ms. M. Civil in the University Museum).

preferred meaning 'sling'. Fortunately, the pictorial evidence now to be considered will help bridge this apparent dichotomy.

PICTORIAL EVIDENCE

In 1971, A. Parrot published a small incised stone slab from Mari dated to the late Early Dynastic period,[30] bearing the earliest representation of a siege scene in Mesopotamian art.

War scene from Mari (after A. Parrot, *Syria* 48 [1975], Pl. xiv)

The slab depicts a Sumerian soldier holding a large siege-shield resembling the Neo-Assyrian long top-curved shield[31] in his right hand and a long spear-like weapon in horizontal position in his left hand. Behind him is another Sumerian soldier drawing a "Scythian" bow in an upward position. Y. Yadin has argued convincingly that this scene does not depict an infantry combat in the open field but rather a siege assault upon the enemy's fortifications.[32] From this unique representation of Sumerian siege warfare, it is clear that this type of shield was considered to be an integral part of the Sumerian offensive weaponry and should be identified with ^{kuš}E.ÍB-ùr.

With this conception of ^{kuš}E.ÍB-ùr as a siege-shield, other literary references in which the term occurs alone become more readily comprehensible. In a hymn to Ninurta with a prayer to Šusin, Ninurta boasts of his anticipated military success:[33]

> an-za-kár-zu ^{kuš}E.ÍB-ùr ù-bí-lá saḫar-re-eš ga-mu-dub$^{!}$-dub
>
> After I have placed the siege-shield at your tower, I will turn it into heaps of dust.

The ^{kuš}E.ÍB-ùr thus symbolizes the entire system of siege and assault on fortifications. In a similar vein, Inanna is addressed in the exordium of Inanna and Ebiḫ as:[34]

> mè-gal-gal-la ḫúb-dar-ak ^{kuš}E.ÍB-ùr ki$^{!}$-ús-sa
>
> The one who darts forth[35] in the great battles, pressing the siege-shield upon the ground.

---

[30] "Les fouilles de Mari, dix-neuvième campagne (printemps 1971)," *Syria* 48 (1971), 253 ff, pl. XIV:4.

[31] E.g., B. Hrouda, *Die Kulturgeschichte des Assyrischen Flachbildes*, (1965), 91 with plate 24, nos. 8–11, and p. 202.

[32] "The Earliest Representation of a Siege Scene and a 'Scythian Bow' from Mari," *IEJ* 22 (1972), 90ff *contra*: A. Parrot, *Syria* 48 (1971), 269.

[33] Å. Sjöberg, "Hymns to Ninurta with Prayers for Šūsin of Ur and Būrsin of Isin," *Kramer Anniversary Volume* (*AOAT* 25), 416f, line 69.

[34] Ni 3052 (*SLTN* 13) + Ni 9722 (*ISET* 2 pl. 13) obv. 3 (Inanna and Ebiḫ 3, ms. B. Eichler in the University Museum).

In addition to these two passages, ^{kuš}E.ÍB-ùr occurs alone in an offensive military context in Temple Hymns 441 (Sjöberg, *Temple Hymns*, 42): šen-šen-na SA$_4$-gin$_7$ DU á-maḫ ^{kuš}E.ÍB-ùr$^{!}$-ra (CBS 19767 rev. III 26 = manuscript B after maḫ reads -bi ⌜x x x x⌝, *contra*: Sjöberg, *Temple Hymns*, 42 n. 441:2).

[35] The verb ḫúb-dar—ak occurs in a similar context depicting Inanna's action in battle, as a variant of húb-sar—ak, in Inninšagura 20: e-ne-di-bi šen-šen mè ḫúb-sar-AK-dè (variants ḫúb-dar-AK, ḫúb-dar-AK-bi) nu-kúš-ù gìri-né ^{kuš}e-sír ši-ni 'Her(!?) joy (is) the fight, to

The nuance of the verb ki—ús-sa in this context seems to denote an aggressive action of assault rather than a defensive posture.[36]

The identification of ^{kuš}E.ÍB-ùr with the siege-shield depicted on the Mari slab may provide a key in understanding the orthography of the term. The first element of the term, ^{kuš}E.ÍB, to be equated with ^{kuš}gur$_{x}$(E.ÍB) = *miserru* 'belt, girdle',[37] seems to refer to the broad leather thongs which gird the plaited reed construction of the shield. The second element ùr, to be equated with ùr = *ūru* 'roof', seems to refer to the curved top of the shield which provided a protective roof for the soldier. Although this understanding further enhances the identification of ^{kuš}E.ÍB-ùr with the depicted shield, it offers no new evidence for the pronunciation of the Sumerian term.[38]

. . . battle, untiring, strapping on her sandals,' (*ZA* 65 [1975], 180, 203 with commmentary on p. 213 leaving the verb untranslated). It is impossible to ascertain the semantic distinction between ḫúb-sar and ḫúb-dar. From the terms húb-sar: *lasāmu*, ḫúb-šú: *lasāmu*, ḫúb-DU: *rapādu* (cf. C. Wilcke, *AfO* 23 [1970], 85 n. 4), lú-ḫúb-bi: *ḫuppû*, it is clear that the ḫúb element conveys the basic meaning evident from its original pictograph. Hence all of the terms convey types of leg or foot movements. On the basis of the Inanna and Ebiḫ and Inninšagura contexts, a meaning 'to spring forth, dart, or sprint' would seem probable. Unfortunately, the very difficult Samsuiluna hymn *PBS* 10/2 11 passages, line 13: un-gú-ri-a ḫúb-dar du$_5$-mu-ra-an-aka and line 20: bal-a-ri gú-ri ḫub-dar aka-dè (*AOAT* 25, 178), do not provide a lucid context to test the proposed meaning. The context, however, does not rule out the proposed semantic range of meaning. In the Inanna and Enki passages I v 29 and II v 40 (G. Farber-Flügge, *St. Pohl* 10, 28, 56) the term nam-ḫúb-dar occurs in association with nam-kar-kid 'prostitution'. Perhaps in these contexts nam-ḫúb-dar may refer to playful dance movement. Such an interpretation would not disassociate this context from the battle contexts, since warfare and movement in battle is often likened in Mesopotamian literature to game and play (cf. *CAD* M *s.v. mēlultu*, *mēlulu* and Landsberger, *WZKM* 56 [1960], 121ff; 57 [1961], 23).

[36] Cf. G. Farber-Flügge's interpretation of this passage (*AOAT* 25, 179). The verb ki—ús-sa 'to press upon the ground' also occurs with the siege-shield in Šulgi E 223–224 (*YBC* 4660 obv. 30–31, ms. of J. Klein in the University Museum) denoting aggressive action:

ki-šu-mar-za-^{d}inanna-ka
GIŠ.ŠUB ^{kuš}E.ÍB-ùr u$_4$-gal-gin$_7$ ki la-ba-ni-ús-a
Against the cult (and) ritual places of Inanna
I did not allow the GIŠ.ŠUB and siege-shield to be set down.

The verb again occurs in the Death of Urnammu 92 (see above, n. 27) and in Lugalbanda-Ḫurrum 225 (see above). In the latter passage, Wilcke interprets the verb as indicating an anti-war posture by putting down one's shield (*Lugalbanda*, 83 with n. 344). In light of the above passages, this interpretation is open to question. The occurrence of the verb ki-ús-sa in Šulgi O 18 (see above) is not relevant since it does not refer to the siege-shield but rather represents a common refrain within the hymn.

[37] *AHw*, 658, *s.v. misarrum* and *CAD* M/2, 110, *s.v. miserru*. For the pronunciation of E.ÍB as gur$_x$, see *MSL* 7, 130 and *MSL* 9, 16.

[38] The most recent discussion on the pronunciation of the term is that of J. Cooper who finds the arguments in favor of a pronunciation /ebur/ to be unconvincing and provisionally adopts the reading ^{kuš}gur$_x^{\text{ùr}}$ or ^{kuš}gu$_x$-ùr (*AnOr* 52, 128, cf. J. Klein, *Three Šulgi Hymns*, 102). Unfortunately, the evidence is far from conclusive in support of this pronunciation. Despite the exceptional variant ^{kuš}E.ÍB for ^{kuš}E.ÍB-ùr (see above, note 12), a pronunciation /gur/ with the resultant homonymy of the term for 'belt' and 'siege-shield' seems difficult, especially with the use of the complicated sign ùr as a phonetic complement. The more common orthographic variant ^{kuš}ÍB-ùr (*ibid.*) would also argue against the pronunciation /gur/ in support of /ebur/.

In a personal communication, Piotr Steinkeller has offered new evidence for the solution of this problem. This evidence is provided by a Pre-Sargonic economic text from Lagaš which lists various weapons including the weapon E.ÙR (*Nikolski* 1, 281 I 2, 5, 8 II 1, 4, 7, 10 *et passim*) which Steinkeller identifies with the term for siege-shield. If the identification is correct, this earliest attested spelling of the term proves that the term for 'shield' and 'belt' are not homonymous, and supports the pronunciation /ebur/ as suggested by Sjöberg and Wilcke. Regarding the question of the pronunciation underlying the orthography e-ùr and e-éb-ur, Steinkeller states: "The simplest approach would be to assume that the word was pronounced /ebur/ or /epur/. However, while this interpretation admits the possibility of e-ùr being an archaic spelling of /ebur/, it leaves unanswered the spelling e-éb-ur, which is hardly compatible with the rules of the Sumerian writing system. For this reason, I would favor a different solution, namely, that the original pronunciation of the word was /ewur/, which later, perhaps under the influence of Akkadian, developed into /ebur/. (For the intervocalic change *w*>*b* in Old Akkadian, see the examples of ^{urudu}*ḫa-ú-da* and ^{urudu}*ḫa-bù-da* and the evidence cited by I. J. Gelb, *MAD* 2^2, pp. 122–123). Following the

The pictorial evidence from the Mari siege scene also seems to bear upon another issue, that of the meaning of GIŠ.ŠUB. Based upon the collected Sumerian literary references, the siege-shield occurs in most frequent association with the GIŠ.ŠUB weapon. In the Mari scene, the bearer of the siege-shield is also holding a spear-like weapon. Could this be a representation of the GIŠ.ŠUB weapon?

The Sumerian term GIŠ.ŠUB[39] is equated with Akkadian *tilpānu*[40] which in late lexical commentaries is given the synonym *qaštu* 'bow'.[41] In the most recent discussion of the term, J. Cooper concludes that the evidence from Sumerian literary texts does not allow the meaning 'bow' to be assigned to GIŠ.ŠUB but rather supports the more generally accepted translation 'throw-stick' (i.e., boomerang).[42] The literary references cited by Cooper indeed demonstrate that GIŠ.ŠUB is a weapon which is hurled at the struck victim, thus excluding the meaning 'bow'. Notable is the passage from Gilgameš, Enkidu and the Netherworld in which Gilgameš counsels Enkidu prior to his descent:[43]

> GIŠ.ŠUB kur-ra nam-mu-e-sìg-ge
> *til-pa-na a-na* KI^{ti} *la ta-na-suk*
> lú GIŠ.ŠUB ra-a nam-mu-e-nigin-dè-eš
> *ša i-na til-pa-na maḫ-ṣu i-lam-mu-ka*
> Do not hurl a GIŠ.ŠUB in the Netherworld, (for)
> Those who were struck down by a GIŠ.ŠUB will surround you.

It should be noted, however, that none of the marshalled literary evidence indicates that the hurled weapon is a 'throw-stick'.[44] This translation seems to stem mainly from the interpretation of the lexical equation GIŠ.ŠUB^{illulu}-nigin=*sāḫertu* 'that which turns'[45] as referring to a weapon which returns to its thrower.[46]

Despite the slightness of the evidence this meaning has been widely accepted.[47] There are two considerations, although admittedly weak, which render somewhat problematic the acceptance of the identification of the hurled weapon GIŠ.ŠUB with a throw-stick. The first is that the throw-stick is not depicted on any Mesopotamian battle representations.[48] The second is that a late bilingual magical text precludes such a meaning by describing GIŠ.ŠUB as a piercing weapon. The passage from the sag-gig-ga-meš series states:[49]

> GIŠ.ŠUB-búr-gin$_7$ nì-nam mu-un-ši-in-lá-e
> *ki-ma til-pa-a-nu ba-aš-me mím-ma šum-šú i-šaq-qir*
> (The demon) pierces everything like a ... GIŠ.ŠUB (Akk. like the GIŠ.ŠUB of the *bašmu*-monster).[50]

In the absence of compelling positive evidence to identify GIŠ.ŠUB with throw-stick, the spear-like weapon from the Mari siege scene should be examined more closely. This weapon may represent either a spear or javelin. Both are very similar in appearance but differ in size, weight and manner of manipulation.[51] The spear is a thrusting weapon sim-

---

latter interpretation, e-éb-ur could be explained as an awkward adaptation of the old spelling, which reflected the changed pronunciation of the word, but, at the same time, preserved the old signs."

[39] For the uncertainty concerning the pronunciation of this term, see the discussion of J. Cooper, in *AnOr* 52, 128 where he adopts the reading ^{giš}ilar.

[40] *MSL* 6, 88:65f. and *MSL* 14, 100:599.

[41] *MSL* 6, 109:61f. and *MSL* 14, 324:30.

[42] *AnOr* 52, 127. Cf. E. Salonen *Waffen*, 145, 147f, and *AHw*, 1359, *s.v. tilpānu(m)*.

[43] Gilgameš, Enkidu and the Netherworld, 189f = Gilgameš Epic XII, 17f. (cf. A. Shaffer, *Sumerian Sources of Tablet XII of the Epic of Gilgameš*, University of Pennsylvania Ph.D. dissertation [1963], 74f., 108).

[44] The literary evidence is assembled by J. Cooper, *AnOr* 52, 127.

[45] MSL 6, 89:78. It should be noted that, here too, the ḪAR-gud commentary adds to the equation a correspondent entry *qaštum malītum* 'full bow' (= fully equipped(?), cf. *AHw*, 597, *s.v. malû* I, 1)d.).

[46] Cf. D. O. Edzard, *OLZ* 63 (1968), 559 who also notes that the original shape of the RU sign may have depicted a boomerang (cf. *MSL* 2, 76, 140).

[47] See above, note 42. Almost all current editions of Sumerian literary texts prefer the translation 'throw-stick', 'throwing-stick' and 'Wurfholz' to the only other alternate translation 'bow'.

[48] B. Hruška, *ArOr* 37 (1969), 511 and D. O. Edzard, *OLZ* 63 (1968), 559. Cf. B. Landsberger's comments re: *gāmlu*, S. I. Feigen, "The Date List of the Babylonian King Samsu-Ditana," *JNES* 14 (1955), 157 n. 72.

[49] *CT* 17, pl. 26 lines 46f.

[50] Cf. *CAD* B, 141, *s.v. bašmu*, lexical section, where it is suggested that the Akkadian translation misunderstood BÚR as ušum. For the piercing nuance of the verb *šaqāru*, cf. the verse *uṣṣu mušaqqer libbi u ḫašê* 'The arrow that pierces the heart and lungs' (*AnOr* 37 [1969], 488:2).

[51] Cf. Y. Yadin, "Goliath's Javelin and the 'Menor Orgim'," *PEQ* (April 1955), 58 n. 2 in which he distinguishes between the Hebrew terms *rwmḥ* 'spear' and *ḥnyt* 'javelin'. The asso-

ilar to a very long stabbing sword. The javelin is smaller and much lighter, functioning like a large arrow. It is hurled by hand and served as a medium range weapon.[52] Closer scrutiny of the Mari siege scene reveals that the soldier's hand is placed on the forward section of the shaft, close to the leaf-shaped blade. This indicates that the held weapon is too light to be a spear and must therefore be a javelin. The predominant pairing of the siege-shield in Sumerian literature with the GIŠ.ŠUB weapon strongly suggests the identification of this hurled weapon with the javelin.[53] It should be noted that a type of javelin had a loop and a cord would round the shaft. The swift unwinding of the cord would give it a spin, thereby allowing it to be hurled a greater distance with greater stability.[54] Such a javelin may have been called GIŠ.ŠUB^{illulu}-nigin=*sāḫertu* 'that which turns'.

In view of the above discussion, the siege scene depicted on the Mari stone slab could have fittingly borne the Sumerian line from the Lamentation Over Sumer and Ur:[55]

> ^{giš}ban-gal-gal GIŠ.ŠUB ^{kuš}E.ÍB-ùr-ra téš im-da-kú-e
>
> The great bows, javelin and siege-shield are all-devouring.

---

ciation of javelin with shield is attested also in the Bible (cf. I *Chronicles* 12:4 for the pair *ṣnh wḥnyt*).

[52] Y. Yadin, *The Art of Warfare in Biblical Lands*, 1 (1963), 10.

[53] A preliminary examination of the occurrences of the term *tilpānu* in Akkadian references indicates that a translation 'javelin' in these contexts is not to be excluded.

[54] For evidence of its use in Biblical and Classical times, see Y. Yadin, *ibid.*, 10; volume 2, 355; and especially his article in *PEQ* (April 1955), 58–69.

[55] See above, and n. 17. It is interesting to note that the Akkadian line from Sargon's Eighth Campaign (*TCL* 3, 320): *nāš qašti kabābi u azmarê*, 'the bearers of bow, siege-shield, and lance' would have been an equally appropriate caption.

NOTES ON "LUGALBANDA AND ENMERKAR"

ROBERT S. FALKOWITZ
CORNELL UNIVERSITY

IN 1971, SAMUEL NOAH KRAMER OFFERED A DETAILED ANALYSIS of the ambiguities of the plot of "Lugalbanda and Enmerkar" in a review[1] of Claus Wilcke's edition of the tale.[2] While he acknowledged that Wilcke's *editio princeps* required modifications to his own earlier views of the story, Kramer offered a critique of Wilcke's interpretation. Kramer concluded that while no single interpretation solved all difficulties, Assyriologists would now be able to judge the evidence for themselves.

My interest in this composition arose during a close examination of all tablets in the University Museum, Philadelphia, belonging to "Lugalbanda and Enmerkar."[3] I take this opportunity to publish the resulting notes as well as to reflect on the structure of the story.

Discussions of the plot of "Lugalbanda and Enmerkar" have centered on three problems: 1) the relationship of this tale to other heroic tales about Lugalbanda and Enmerkar; 2) the relationship of the first half of the story to the second half; and 3) the interpretation of the different versions of the second half of the story.[4] The primary contribution I would like to make here is a redefinition of the issues related to these three areas of inquiry. This would be especially useful for the third question, where Wilcke's and Kramer's views are stalemated.

One Lugalbanda Epic or Two? Wilcke, pp. 5–8, has suggested that "Lugalbanda and Enmerkar" may be only the second half of a composition, the first half being the tale which he named "Lugalbanda im Finstersten des Gebirges," Kramer calls "Lugalbanda, the Wandering Hero," while others speak of it as "Lugalbanda and Hurrum(-kurra)" as well as "Lugalbanda and Enmerkar I."[5]

Both Kramer and J. Klein[6] have adequately rebutted all of Wilcke's arguments in favor of one "epic" except the question of why "Lugalbanda and Enmerkar (II)" seems to start *in medias res*. That is, how did Lugalbanda become lost and what is the origin of Enmerkar's difficulties?

The story appears to start *in medias res* from an occidental point of view. Many non-Western and even occidental narratives appear to us to start abruptly. Consider this case. According to a given story, a certain king mounts an expedition against a distant city, lays siege to it without success, and finally finds victory through the extraordinary efforts of one of his lieutenants. There is also a story about this lieutenant and his wanderings through hostile regions in his attempt to find his family and friends. Furthermore, we cannot understand why the lieutenant was lost and wandering unless we know the first story about the war. Shall we dare call the Iliad and the Odyssey two halves of one epic? The case for only one Lugalbanda

---

[1] *Acta Orientalia* 33 (1971), 363–78 (hereafter cited as "Kramer, p. . . .").

[2] *Das Lugalbandaepos* 1969 (hereafter cited as "Wilcke, p. . . ."). A list of reviews of Wilcke's edition, as well as some collations and additional texts, was published by Wilcke himself in *Kollationen zu den sumerischen literarischen Texten aus Nippur in der Hilprecht-Sammlung Jena* [Abhandlungen der Sächsischen Akademie der Wissenschaften zu Leipzig, Phil.-hist. Kl., Band 65, Heft 4], 1976 (hereafter cited as "Wilcke, *Kollationen*, p. . . ."). Add to this H. Sauren, *OLZ*, 68 (1973), 580–86; and the comments by S. Cohen, "Enmerkar and the Lord of Aratta," Dissertation University of Pennsylvania, 1973 (hereafter cited as "Cohen, *ELA*[2]"), 7, 9, 19–21, 23–25. Among the various reviews, J. Bauer's is very useful for his many corrections to typographical errors and readings. J. Klein's supplements Kramer's discussion of ambiguous lines. M. Civil's contains references to new texts, a few philological notes and general comments on text editions.

[3] Together with Prof. Åke W. Sjöberg, whose guidance and advice I gratefully acknowledge here. More than a few of his suggested readings have been incorporated in this paper.

[4] See notes 1 and 2.

[5] As distinct from our story, called "Lugalbanda and Enmerkar II" (or simply "Lugalbanda and Enmerkar"). This numeration does not imply an organic unity between the compositions.

[6] *JAOS* 91 (1971), 297.

story is no more compelling. Thus, it may be that the problem of one or two epics as a "solution" to the "difficulty" is based on a false, ethnocentric question.[7]

By assuming that explicit explanations of the situation at the start of the story are required, however, we cannot hope to understand the artistry, narrative principles and the structure of the story on its own terms. In a traditional social context where heroic tales are performed orally, such as those studied by contemporary ethnographers, the audience would have been familiar with both the story itself and the implicit background. We cannot know for sure if this information was lost when the Sumerian vernacular died out, nor if *any* tradition preserved this information to the time of our Old Babylonian copies of the story. The Old Babylonian student or scribe might have found this story, taken out of its performance context, to be as obscure as modern Western interpreters find it.

The Two Halves of "Lugalbanda and Enmerkar." Wilcke analyzed the plot of "Lugalbanda and Enmerkar" on two levels. On the broader level, he considered the tale as having two halves, the first concerning Lugalbanda and Anzu, the second concerning Lugalbanda and Enmerkar (p. 14). Within these halves he described the story as containing sixteen "episodes" plus the doxology (pp. 9–14). However, his division of the episodes into halves does not follow his criteria for the division on the broader level. He puts in the first half the first eight episodes, in which Lugalbanda is either lost or alone. The ninth episode, I, which describes Lugalbanda rejoining his brothers and friends, is included in the second half, even though Enmerkar does not appear until the tenth episode.

In *AfO* 24 (1973), 50, Wilcke argued that the first line of episode I, line 220, is also found as entries P31 and L50 in the literary catalogues. He also suggested that this might indicate that line 220 is the first line of a hypothetical two tablet recension of the story, while admitting that the evidence for such a recension is weak and circumstantial, at best. Finally, he pointed out in *AS* 20, 244 n. 60, that the entries in the literary catalogues may also refer to the incipit of "Nanshe and the Birds."[8]

In the following analysis of the structure of "Lugalbanda and Enmerkar," I accept the division into two halves, but I include Wilcke's episode I as part of the first half. I interpret the literary catalogue entries as probably referring to "Nanshe and the Birds," having no relationship to "Lugalbanda and Enmerkar," and as being no evidence for either a two tablet recension or a dividing line of the plot of the story. According to my interpretation, the first half of "Lugalbanda and Enmerkar" concerns the augmentation of Lugalbanda's own powers, for his personal benefit. The second half concerns his use of these augmented powers for the benefit of his urban-based Uruk society. Both halves have what I call a mythic, *rite de passage* structure, and are patterned as mirror images to one another.

The setting of the first half is the kur, a distant place. As Jestin and others have pointed out,[9] kur symbolized the chaotic realm where cultural organization does not obtain. That kur is a distant place (line 1: ki sù-rá) indicates that the point of view of the story is the urban Mesopotamian culture from which the kur is distant. It is a place lacking kin (lines 3–4) and acquaintances (line 5). As we know, Lugalbanda had been separated from his brothers and friends.

Without any guidance, Lugalbanda devises a plan to return to his society (lines 6–7). In comparable situations in Mesopotamian literature, a woman or a being with female attributes (mother, female goddess, Enkidu) usually tells the hero how to act. Otherwise, Enki gives this information. Lugalbanda plans to gain the assistance of the monster Anzu who lives in the area. However, Anzu is an inimical, dangerous and sacred being, normally unapproachable. Lugalbanda first plans to put Anzu into a state in which normal relationships do not hold, drunkenness: "(Then) Anzu, intoxicated from drinking beer, may show me where the Urukites have gone" (lines 25–26).

---

[7] C. Wilcke discusses formal aspects of prologues in *Sumerological Studies in Honor of Thorkild Jacobsen* [Assyriological Studies 20], 1976, 239–45. He mentions "Inanna's Descent," "Inanna and Shukaletuda," "Nanna's Journey to Nippur" and "Gilgamesh and Huwawa" as narratives doing without prologues and starting *in medias res*. I would also include the "Lamentation over the Destruction of Sumer and Ur" (="Second Ur Lament"). Wilcke considers the first 115 lines of this composition as a prologue (p. 240), but they are organic parts of the narrative. Note also Wilcke's division of Akkadian epic texts into those with and those without formal indications of the narrator at their beginnings (*ZA* 67 [1977], 214–17).

[8] Read D. Foxvog for D. I. Owen there.

[9] *BiOr* 27 (1970), 365–66; Y. Rosengarten, *Trois aspects de la pensée religieuse sumérienne* 1971, 7–38; B. Alster, "Enki and Ninhursag. The Creation of the First Woman," *Ugarit-Forschungen* 10 (1978), 15–27.

The setting is then further described by a comparison with two symbols, Enki's "eagle-tree" and Inanna's "carnelian mountain." The top of the latter is so high its shadow spreads even over the highest points. Its roots are like a hydra(?) (muš-SAG.KAL) which is compared in turn to the seven-mouthed stream of Utu. This emphasis on great height and roots shows the mountain to be an *axis mundi*, the path of Inanna's powers moving from heaven to earth to the underworld. The "eagle-tree" is also an *axis mundi*, recalling both the eagle of Etana flying up to heaven and the tree of Inanna in "Gilgamesh, Enkidu and the Netherworld," with the eagle in its branches and the serpent in its roots. These comparisons show the spot to be most sacred, where great powers come into play.[10]

Following a discussion of the natural history of Anzu (lines 36–49), Lugalbanda puts his plan into effect. He realizes that Anzu is so dangerous one cannot simply offer him beer; he must be approached in steps. First, cultic acts are performed for the young of Anzu, treating them like gods (lines 51–60). When Anzu returns to the nest he is very upset that his young do not respond to his three calls. When aroused, Anzu's power is so great that he completely controls the situation, not even giving Lugalbanda a chance to carry out his plan to offer beer. Anzu describes himself in terms which must have terrified Lugalbanda, hiding by the nest. Anzu uses typical divine terms, implying that no one can alter the fate he determines, whether it be good or bad, a fate determined by Anzu's destructive or beneficial power. Lugalbanda certainly had no desire to be picked up in Anzu's talons, like an ox. The tension mounts when Anzu announces that he will determine the fate of whoever had been to the nest, be he a human or god. Relief comes with the pronouncement, "He (the man) will have no opponent at all in the mountains. You will be a man given strength by Anzu" (lines 109–110).

Lugalbanda's next speech describes the structure within which Anzu might help him. Anzu was given his power by the gods. His grandfather or uncle (pa-bíl-ga) made the division of lots, or fates. Anzu says that his father Enlil made particular assignments to him (lines 100–2), including that of being a great door in the mountains. Now, Anzu too can grant power by determining a good fate. Thus, Anzu will be a father to Lugalbanda as Enlil was to Anzu.

Anzu makes four speeches to Lugalbanda telling him to be on his way. In each he uses metaphors which Lugalbanda apparently cannot understand, for he remains gestureless after each speech. Finally, Anzu gives up and asks Lugalbanda what he wants: "I will determine for you the fate you desire" (line 166). Lugalbanda answers in terms which both he and we can better understand. He desires strength and speed, powers described in terms of divine or sacred power. He wishes the speed of sunlight, like Inanna; the power of Ishkur's seven storms. He wishes to be like fire and lightning, both primary symbols of sacred or divine power. He wishes to be able to go where he desires, and not to have quarrels when he returns to his city. If granted this, he will put up a statue of Anzu to spread his fame. Anzu agrees and grants all that Lugalbanda has asked.

As they part from this liminal place, Anzu going up, Lugalbanda going down (lines 205–6), Anzu adds some advice: Lugalbanda should keep secret the powers he received from Anzu. Anzu then goes to his nest and Lugalbanda makes his way, using his new powers, back to his brothers and friends. They describe him as one back from the dead, like one who had been killed in battle and separated from his troops (line 228). In response to his brothers' and friends' questions about how he survived (lines 225–37), Lugalbanda obeys Anzu and keeps secret his amazing experiences. Instead, he misleads them by failing to tell the whole truth (lines 238–43), saying essentially that he survived as a wild animal would. Lugalbanda is then formally reintegrated into society by a meal (line 249). With the arrival of the group at the outskirts of Aratta, the first half ends.

The first half, then, has the structure of a rite of passage. It starts in a sacred place in the wilderness, apart from society. Lugalbanda is in a state of weakness, abandoned by his brothers and friends. He performs cultic acts and undergoes an ordeal (waiting for Anzu's favorable reply). Next, he receives secret information and new powers. Lastly, he rejoins his society with a status of new, though secret, power. Thus was Anzu described as a doorway, the liminal place through which Lugalbanda had to pass in order to gain the power necessary to return to his brothers and friends.

Just as it was necessary for Lugalbanda to mediate his approach to Anzu, his reentry into society was mediated through the microcosm of his own band of brothers and friends. But once he rejoins the en

---

[10] S. Cohen, *ELA*^{2}, 19–21 understands this section as a flashback which explains the background of the opening, *in medias res*. How this would be true and the symbolism he sees here needs further explanation. For example, if the "eagle-tree" of Enki symbolizes Enmerkar and the troops, why is it at Sabum?

Enmerkar, the leader of the Urukites, he finds that Enmerkar and the Urukites are in a situation paralleling Lugalbanda's own situation at the beginning of the story. Thus, the stage is set for Lugalbanda to use his new powers on behalf of his society, Uruk.

Enmerkar is laying an unsuccessful siege of Aratta.[11] He decides to send a message to Inanna for help. At first he cannot find a volunteer, but Lugalbanda finally offers himself. The message recounts how Inanna organized the territory of Uruk from a presumably chaotic state into its constituents of swamp, water, dry land, poplars and reed thicket. From Kulaba, Inanna chose Enmerkar to be en (lines 295–96), the leader of Uruk who would perform the sacred marriage rite with Inanna. Then, Enki gave Enmerkar the power to utilize the territory, to use the reeds, to build and to adjudicate for fifty years (lines 301–2). The Mardu were brought up in the land so walls had to be built. However, now Enmerkar's successful leadership and his hi-li have come to an end (line 306), for, Inanna has abandoned Enmerkar (the en of Uruk) and gone (back) to Kulaba (line 310). This abandonment has had two consequences. Because Inanna has ceased to perform the sacred marriage rite with Enmerkar (ceased to "love" him), Enmerkar has lost the power, authority and hi-li which the en normally has. Without this power he is superfluous to society and he cannot even understand the function he ought to perform in his society, that is, the connection between himself and the city. Inanna performs the sacred marriage with only one en at a time ("loves" only one en at a time). It seems that at present she favors the en of Aratta.[12] Thus, Enmerkar bemoans (lines 311–14):

> Should she love his city, she would hate me.
> Why do you (Inanna) connect the city with me?
> Should she hate his city, she would love me.
> Why do you connect me with the city?

It is hoped that Inanna's answer to this message will lead to a restoration of favor for Uruk.

Having received his instructions, Lugalbanda rejoins his brothers and friends and then goes alone on his mission. Thus, once again, this group mediates between society and isolation. He miraculously undergoes the ordeal of crossing seven mountain ranges, arrives at Uruk, then Kulaba before midnight, delivers the message to Inanna and receives her answer.

The second half has the same *rite de passage* structure as the first. Lugalbanda is separated from society, he undergoes an ordeal, he performs cultic acts (line 349), and he receives information which gives him power. Thus, each of the halves of "Lugalbanda and Enmerkar" has the same internal relationship of episodes. However, with respect to each other, there are certain inversions or other differences. The first half brings Lugalbanda toward Enmerkar; the second half takes him away. The first half starts in a sacred place in the wilderness; the second half ends in a sacred place in the city, Kulaba. The first half concerns the bestowal of power as it affects the individual; the second half concerns its effect on society at large. This last point serves to explain why the story ends before Lugalbanda returns to Enmerkar with the answer, and why there may be a feeling that the story ends before its true conclusion.

The key to understanding the structure of the story is the rather obvious fact that the story is about Lugalbanda. The last line says: "Sacred *Lugalbanda*, praise!" However, the second half of the story is nested within another story about the vicissitudes of Enmerkar and Uruk. The shifting balance of power between Uruk and Aratta is also chronicled in "Enmerkar and the Lord of Aratta" and "Enmerkar and Ensuhkeshdanna." We see a glimpse of this ongoing struggle in "Lugalbanda and Enmerkar." Here, the balance of power is tipped toward Aratta. Thus, Uruk is in a difficulty characterized by a breakdown in the chain of power. The link between Inanna and Enmerkar is weakened and the link between Enmerkar and Uruk is weakened, so Enmerkar can neither effectively carry out the siege of Aratta nor even raise a volunteer from among his troops. The very fabric of Uruk society seems to be in decay. Only Lugalbanda, with an independent source of power, is able to act effectively on Uruk's behalf. Only Lugalbanda, who has power, is able to approach a much greater source of power, Inanna, and receive great power from her.

---

[11] Following Wilcke's interpretation. Kramer's view that they are in Uruk is incompatible with the analysis offered below. The difficult lines 254–57, from which a military action is inferred, are paralleled, in part, in Shulgi D 177–185 (see J. Klein, *Three Šulgi Hymns* 1981, 101–2), where a military context is clear.

[12] This either-or principle is also at the heart of "Enmerkar and Ensuhkeshdanna" and "Enmerkar and the Lord of Aratta." Note in particular "Enmerkar and Ensuhkeshdanna" 275–76, where the en of Aratta admits to the en of Uruk, "You are the beloved en of Inanna, you *alone* are exalted. Inanna has truly called you for her sacred lap, you are her beloved."

So important is this power for the restoration of order among the Urukites that Lugalbanda swears an oath never to let the great me's, which he will bring from Inanna in Kulaba, leave his hand (line 289).[13]

Lugalbanda is a sort of culture hero. He is not, to be sure, of the type that first brings fire or any other aspect of culture to humankind. Rather, through his efforts the balance of power may be tipped in favor of his own society, away from Aratta. Having received Inanna's response, he possesses the knowledge and power which may be used to bring an end to the vitality of Aratta (line 408). But the story ends before that power is transmitted to Enmerkar and before the story ceases to be a tale about Lugalbanda and becomes a tale about Enmerkar and Uruk.

Versions of the Second Half. Key evidence for the divergent interpretations of the second half offered by Kramer and Wilcke has been based on differences between texts A and AA (from Nippur) on the one hand, and text T (not from Nippur, of uncertain provenience) on the other. The argument centers on line 328 which, in A and AA says Lugalbanda is going to Aratta, but in T says he is going to Kulaba. Kramer argues that A and AA are right while T is wrong. Wilcke argues the opposite.[14] The hypothesis upon which both of their reconstructions are based appears to me to be in error. What is called line 328 in T is not a variant of what is called line 328 in A and AA. The context of the line in T is not the same as the context in A and AA. The unit of variation between the versions is much larger than the line. None of the texts have "Aratta" or "Kulaba" as an erroneous variant of the "true text." A and AA have one version of the tale, T another. A structuralist, for example, would accept both versions as valid in the context of the whole work.

Different versions of tales are well known from Old Babylonian Sumerian texts. There is a Nippur and an Ur version of "Gilgamesh, Enkidu and the Netherworld." The end of "Inanna's Descent," such as it is preserved, likewise varies in Ur and Nippur tablets. That text T, not from Nippur, has a version differing from the Nippur tablets A and AA should be no surprise. Even among the Nippur tablets of our story there are many variations—on the bases of line omissions and additions, the order of lines, the order of various speeches, and many orthographic variants.[15] Therefore, rather than impute errors to the ancient scribes, it is better to seek the inner logic of the extant versions.

Text T contains the general story described above, including lines 247–417. It follows the version of A and AA until line 270. Then, in T, Enmerkar seeks a volunteer to return to Kulaba. First he goes to the KA-kešda-igi-bar-ra troops,[16] then the army (ugnim) and then the first group again. In view of Enmerkar's failure to get a response, Lugalbanda volunteers. Enmerkar agrees to his desire to go alone. At least part of their communication takes place in the é-gal, Enmerkar's residence (be it tent or palace).[17] Lugalbanda emerges and joins his brothers and friends (lines 322–25). The next three lines say: "Send it (the message) to Uruk for the en / For Enmerkar the child of Utu / I will go alone to Kulaba. No one should go with me. Thus did he speak to them." I do not believe that lines 326 and probably 327 belong to the direct address of Lugalbanda to his band. Enmerkar has agreed that only Lugalbanda will go to Uruk and Kulaba, so only Lugalbanda can be the subject of the imperative in line 326. In the version of text T there is no problem with interpreting this line as a quotation by Lugalbanda of Enmerkar's command, now related to the brothers and friends. However, in the version of texts A and AA this is impossible, for line 328 says he is going to Aratta.

Wilcke offers two possible solutions. On page 121 he translates: "Für den Herrn schicke (Leute) nach Uruk!" But I see no possible candidate for such hypothetical people (Leute). His second solution (p. 211) is to make lines 326–28 a speech by the brothers and friends containing Lugalbanda's statement to Enmerkar (line 328) as a quote. However, as Wilcke says, the grammar of line 328 requires Lugalbanda to be speaking to the band (a-gin$_7$ mu-un-*ne*-du$_{11}$).

---

[13] I touch here on a theory of sacred power in ancient Mesopotamia which I will develop at length in future studies. The key point here is that Sumerian me means "sacred power," exactly the power discussed in this article.

[14] For a fair summary of all the arguments, see Kramer's review.

[15] Wilcke, 24–28.

[16] I do not know the meaning of the term. Should it refer to Lugalbanda's brothers and friends, my interpretation would require revision.

[17] The semantic range of é-gal is wider than simply "palace." See Å. W. Sjöberg, *AfO* 24 (1973), 19–20 and n. 3 for é-gal as a temple. W. W. Hallo, in *JCS* 31 (1979), 161–65, argues for its use as a place of detention, among other meanings, although I doubt that the term bears any relation to the American cant term "big house."

I suggest that line 326 is addressed from the narrator to the reader or audience. It serves to remind us that there is no doubt about Lugalbanda's destination—it is Uruk-Kulaba. And it underscores the misinformation Lugalbanda gives in texts A and AA (see below).[18]

Returning to text T, Lugalbanda's brothers and friends remember his separation and ordeal in the first half and, surprised that he insists on going alone through the mountains, ask "*Why* will no one join you?" (line 329). Lugalbanda will make the trip using the powers given him by Anzu. Not only would his brothers and friends not be able to keep up, they would find out about his new powers and he might be forced to reveal Anzu's secret. So he makes the journey alone, miraculously arriving before midnight. He gives Inanna Enmerkar's message and gets her response.

The version of texts A and AA is more elaborate in the section where it differs from T. Enmerkar seeks a volunteer first among the army, then the KA-kešda-igi-bar-ra troops and then repeats his request to both groups. After Lugalbanda volunteers, his agreement with Enmerkar occurs before an assembly, also in the é-gal. Enmerkar's message is the same, but when Lugalbanda emerges and joins his brothers and friends, he misinforms them. Texts A, AA and T all state that Enmerkar's orders were to "return to Uruk." However, the brothers and friends were not in the assembly and could not have known the nature of Lugalbanda's mission. In line 328 he tells them "I will go alone to *Aratta*. No one should go with me" With this deceit Lugalbanda forestalls any need to explain how he could return to Uruk or Kulaba or how, the last time he rejoined his group, he had deceived them about how he survived in the mountains. With this second deception, structurally in the same place as the first, Lugalbanda can again follow Anzu's advice and keep his powers secret.

The response of the brothers and friends is not the plaintive "Why?" of text T, but a warning that he will not benefit from the various protections afforded the group as a whole. And note that they do not revive the comparison of Lugalbanda to one killed in battle and separated from the troops (line 329a - T only). For this is exactly the description given by the brothers and friends of his earlier abandonment (line 228).[19] In the version of A and AA they believe he is now about to go on a mission to Aratta, where they are laying siege, so no such comparison is warranted. Thus, Lugalbanda's first deception was his agreement with his group's suggestion that he survived in the mountains by acting like the wild animals. Now he lies to them about his destination. In both cases he preserves the secret of his powers.

Two problems arise in this reading. In line 335 the brothers and friends call his destination a "great hur-sag̃ where one does not go alone." In the context of T all parties involved understood this as a reference to the seven mountain ranges Lugalbanda would have to cross. In the version of A and AA the line is much richer, for the brothers and friends are referring to Aratta. Lugalbanda knows this is their intended meaning but, from his own point of view, he takes it to refer to the true destination, the mountain ranges.[20] The poignant ambiguity of the term hur-sag̃ (gal) is further heightened by the irony of the statement. Lugalbanda is the living proof that one *can* go alone in the hur-sag̃ gal. Thus, line 335 helps to further delineate two conflicts. Lugalbanda wishes to help Enmerkar and the Urukites, but in a fashion which does not force him to reveal his secret. Lugalbanda's brothers and friends do not wish to hinder his efforts, but do not want him to be subjected to double jeopardy, tempting his luck in the mountains twice.

Line 344a would seem to put the lie to this interpretation. Found only in text A, it reads: [xx u]n-íl aratta*ki[x] ba-te. This is restored by Wilcke as [igi mu-u]n-íl arattaki[-aš] ba-te on the basis of the parallel lines "Enmerkar and the Lord of Aratta" 172–74=510-12.[21] It appears to state that Lugalbanda is arriving in Aratta, not Kulaba. Either text A has yet another version, line 344a is to be taken metaphorically, or line 344a is to be understood as an erroneous insertion. I am unable to interpret the differences between A and AA as attesting to two

[18] The existence of apostrophe in Mesopotamian literature is yet to be studied. Frequently, it may be an indication of the written text being a modified notation for an oral performance.

[19] Text T does not cover this section, so arguments about what the version of T said there are moot.

[20] Aratta, or its ziqqurat, may be described as a hur-sag̃. Ziqqurats are commonly described as lofty or towering (see Å. W. Sjöberg, *TCS* III, 50). Ninhursag's temple in Kesh is called a hur-sag̃ gal (*TCS* III, 176:9). Aratta is described as a hur-sag̃ in "Inanna and Ebih" 47 (*PBS* X/4, 9 rev. 20 =*SEM* 107 I:8=*UET* 6/1, 13:14); also as hur-sag̃ gal perhaps in "Enmerkar and the Lord of Aratta" 243.

[21] Wilcke, 25. ki omitted by Wilcke, 122.

different versions with respect to this line.[22] "Aratta" may possibly be understood as an epithet for Kulaba meaning "honored" or the like.[23] Should this be the case, then we may understand "Aratta" in the same way in line 328, where in the version of A and AA Lugalbanda says he is going to Aratta, meaning the "honored (city, Kulaba)" while his band understands him literally. This interpretation would save Lugalbanda from a bold-faced lie.

While one should always feel uncomfortable arguing that the text is in error, there is some justification here. First, line 344a occurs in only one text. Second, erroneous insertions of lines do occur in this composition. In lines 360–87 Lugalbanda gives Enmerkar's message to Inanna, paralleling lines 294–321, where Enmerkar tells Lugalbanda the message. Line 322 says that Lugalbanda then left the é-gal. Text AA repeats this line after line 387, as if it were part of the message. It is clearly an error there, for Inanna is still speaking to Lugalbanda after this line. It is not far-fetched to agree with Wilcke, p. 25, that line 344a is an erroneous insertion in text A. Third, acceptance of line 344a as correct and literal does not yield any clear and consistent interpretation of the rest of the text. Instead, it yields a stalemate of contradictions.

Conclusion. The three questions addressed in this study have mutually dependent solutions. Once it is established that "Lugalbanda and Enmerkar" is a self-standing heroic tale, we may see how the internal structure relates to the characterization of the hero. Our story contains two halves, the first concerned with the personal uses of power, the second with the social uses of power. These uses of power can create conflicts and tensions in the relationship between the hero and society and there are many ways in which these tensions may be depicted or resolved. Thus, two major versions of the second half of the story are known. One, the richer and more complex of the two, highlights the multiple roles of the hero by means of the ambiguities of language, deceit and desire. The other, insofar as it is preserved, emphasizes the positive role of heroic power. It makes little reference to the personal and social conflicts which reveal the human frailties of the hero.

[22] Other differences among the Nippur texts (see Wilcke, pp. 24–28) are yet to be analyzed in terms of different versions rather than in terms of error versus fidelity.

[23] See Wilcke, 40 and Kramer, 375 n. 32.

APPENDICES

A. *New Texts.* A list of texts not used in Wilcke's edition may be found in M. Civil, *JNES* 31 (1972), 386, with additions and corrections to this list in S. Cohen, *ELA*², 7 n. 15,[24] as well as the list, with line numbers identified, in Wilcke, *Kollationen*, 14. The following list includes those tablets whose line numbers have not yet been indicated, as well as additional new texts, made known to me from a list by M. Civil:

UM 29–13–198	55–58, 61; 100–7
N 2628	3 unidentified lines, 231–41
N7278	271–72
3N–T919, 450 (*SLTF*[25] pl. 8)	220–30; 246a??, 247, 250–58
3N–T919, 478 (*SLTF* pl. 9)	111–22

Other possible texts are 2N–T669 and Ni 4059, neither of which I have seen.

Contrary to C. J. Gadd, the obverse of *UET* 6/1, 48 (Text Y) is partially preserved, but difficult to read. A few broken signs from column I probably belong to lines 79–81. Column II preserves lines 125–32 (see the notes to these lines).

B. *Joins.* Texts M, O and UM 29–16–441 join (joiner unknown to me, already reported by S. Cohen, *ELA*², 7 n. 15). UM 29–16–449 is part of this tablet, continuing rev. I and II (see the photograph).

C. *Notes on Individual Lines.* Although Wilcke collated many texts,[26] it is not always clear if his readings are based on published copies or collations. I will try to clarify such ambiguities below, as well as other ambiguities which arise from noting text "variations" by means of a critical apparatus.[27]

[24] For convenience I repeat here some of his comments. UM 29–16–141 is a contract tablet from the reign of Samsuiluna. UM 29–16–433 belongs to "Lugalbanda and Hurrum."

[25] J. W. Heimerdinger, *Sumerian Literary Fragments from Nippur* [Occasional Publications of the Babylonian Fund, 4], 1979.

[26] Wilcke, p. x; *Kollationen*, 15.

[27] Mr. C. B. F. Walker kindly collated *UET* 6/1, 48 for me. Prof. O. R. Gurney provided me with collations of W. B. 162. My thanks to both.

3 - For the reading na—di$_5$-di$_5$ see H. Behrens, *Enlil und Ninlil*, Rome (Biblical Institute Press, 1978) 76–77. **18** - AA seems to have KÙ.ZI-ga, not KÙ.GI-ga. Were the word for gold /kusig/ (see M. Civil, *JCS* 28 [1978], 183–84), this might not be an error. **21** - Read sagi (SILA.ŠU.DU$_8$)-a kaš sá-sá-da-ni DU.DU nu-kúš-ù "the cupbearer never tired from mixing beer" (see already M. Civil, *JNES* 31 [1972], 386). Compare with "Enki's Journey's to Nippur" 101: dug ku-kur-ru kaš du$_{10}$-du$_{10}$-ga duh-bi bí-in-sá-sá "In the *kukurru* container he mixed (for brewing) its bran mash for good beer." sá-sá is Akkadian *šutahhuqu* "to mix." **22** - It is not clear that the DU in CCC belongs to this line. **24** - The translation by Wilcke "froh dasitz" for ul ti is too general. The term refers to the elation of alcohol intoxication. The only citation where this is not clear is "Enki and Ninhursag" 179 (if ti is correct), where the use is metaphorical. **27** - Perhaps inim—sì-sì, as in lines 6–7. **29** - A and DD have DAR for gùn. **30** - Preformative hé- has asseverative force. DDD: ugu$_3$ possible. **34** - The comparison of the muš-SAG.KAL to roots here and in "Temple Hymns" 39: 498 (correct Wilcke's commentary on p. 144), and the mention of the seven-branched river in line 35 indicates to me that the muš-SAG.KAL is a many-(perhaps seven-)headed hydra. Illustrations of the hydra include H. Frankfort, *Stratified Cylinder Seals from the Diyala Region*, 1955, ## 478, 497; J. Pritchard, *ANEP*, pl. 218 fig. 671; all three in P. Amiet, *Glyptique mésopotamienne archaïque* [CNRS] 1961, ## 1393, 1394, 1492 (my thanks to Prof. Edith Porada for pointing out to me two of these illustrations). **45** - A has KA×BALAG; I has KA×ŠU? un-gi$_4$. **46** - EE, G and H have KA×BALAG I has kur; FF and G have kur-ra; AA and FFF omit entirely; Wilcke's reading kur-kur in FFF is not clear in his copy. **47** - See M. E. Cohen, *JCS* 25 (1973), 203–10 for kuš$_2^{ku_6}$ as a tortoise. The -e after kušu$_2^{ku_6}$ is the problem. Perhaps it is a locative-terminative: "The claws are those of an eagle upon (i.e. grasping) a kušu$_2$." This concurs with lines 48–49. If kušu$_2$ is "tortoise" a comparison with the claws of a tortoise *or* eagle might make sense, but the grammar would remain unclarified. **48–49** - "In fear of them (the talons) the wild steer runs alone to the base of the mountains, the deer runs for its life to its own mountains."

53 - DUH ends in four Winkelhakens; DU$_8$ ends in six. See *VAS* 17, 33:19–20. A, AA and FFF have duh-duh, rhyming with dah; F has du$_8$-du$_8$. Prof. Sjöberg pointed out the rhyme to me. Ni 4228 (*ISET* 1, 83): [xxx] gi-izi-eš-ta-ba [xxxxx] / [xxxx]x[xxx]. **55** - Bauer's emendation of KA to kú (*ZDMG* 123 [1973], 381) would involve *five* texts which have not been shown to belong to one manuscript family. Ni 4228 (*ISET* 1, 83) has a new line between lines 55 and 56: [xxxxx n]i? ù bí-in-gan[xx(x)]. **57** - H: tuš/dúr means "to be seated (for a meal)." See line 12 and my comments to RC 3.41 in forthcoming edition. **60** - See line 96 where BM 123396 (bilingual) has uzu as first sign. **62** - "He waited at the unknown hašur of the mountain." The tree is unknown in Uruk, being so isolated in the wilderness. The tree also emphasizes the cosmic nature of the spot as an *axis mundi*. See also line 129. **64** - B$_2$ (Akkadian): *ú-kab-[bi-ir]*. **67** - The dead metaphor dé "to pour," used for making sounds, is here revivified. I saw ad, not zé (against M. Civil, *JNES* 31 [1972], 386. C. B. F. Walker indicated that the difficult Y reads as copied. **68–69** - B$_2$ (Akkadian): *i-z[i-iz]* (see Å. W. Sjöberg, *StOr* 46 [1975], 311–12). **70** - AA: mušen-e gùd-šè KA×X u̥n-gi$_4$. L: [xxxxx] GA-bi-*šè KA×X um-gi$_4$. **77**- Ni 4228 (*ISET* 1, 83): gù ba-ni-in-⌜x⌝[xx] for gù nu-um-ma-ni-ib-gi$_4$. **78** - Ni 4228 (*ISET* 1, 83): copy appears to have [xxx] e-em-gar m̥u-na ba-gi̥[(x)] although collation may yield a reading [xxx ni]r im-gar ḁn-na ba-(erasure?) t[e]. **79** - Why does the verb te take -e in line 78 and -a in line 79 (except in M)? **81** - Ni 4228 (*ISET* 1, 83): [x b]i-a nir-ra gar-ra-bi-š[è]. nir-ra here, for a-nir in A and AA, may argue against [. . . ni]r in line 78. **82–83** - "Inanna and Ebeh" 116–19, quoted by Wilcke, p. 159, as evidence for the Anunna gods dwelling in the mountains, is not really relevant. Insofar as they were worshipped at Ebeh and Ebeh was mountainous terrain, the Anunna were there, too. For gods native to the mountains see A. Falkenstein, *SGL* I, 116. The epithet dingir hur-sağ-ğá in line 82 of our text probably refers to place of birth. **87** - A: du$_8$-du$_8$; AA, L and M: duh-duh. Wilcke, p. 161, explains this line by rejecting a meaning "lion" for pirig̃. W. Heimpel, *Tierbilder in der sumerischen Literatur*, 1968, 299–307, argues for a broader meaning for du$_7$-du$_7$ than "to gore." Å. W. Sjöberg, *OrSuec* 22 (1973), 112 (to line 11) is undecided. In Ershemma 23:10 (*CT* 15 pl. 15 *l.* 10): ^{d}iškur pirig̃-an-na gud mah pa-è-a "Ishkur, divine beast?, radiant, sublime ox," indicates that pirig̃ has a semantic range broader than "lion." In the early religious history of Mesopotamia it would have been natural to describe a god such as Ishkur as a monster—part lion, part ox. By the Old Babylonian period the tendency toward replacing monstrous aspects with anthropomorphic or metaphorical descriptions was well established. **88** - AA: ba-ra-an-tum$_4$; L: [ ] *na(?) *a-*ba[. . .]. **89** - AA: anzu^{mušen}gùd-ba a-<ba ba->ra-an-tum$_4$. **90** - AA: hé-em-ma-te-g̃á-dam? **92** - A and AA: im-duh-duh. I do not see the traces of im before AK in Wilcke's copy of AA (pl. III ii 36). Could the signs read i̥m-aka by Wilcke be kin ak "The place was made a kin, like a god's dwelling, splendidly decorated." For kin as a room, see Å. W. Sjöberg, *TCS* III 52 (to line 10). **94** - A and F write BAPPIR for ŠIM. **96** - MM: uz[u x l]i-a . . . ; BM 123396 (*CT* 51, 181) I 1': uzu mu-du[. . .] // *mu-un-du-li*[. . .].

100 - A and AA: g̃iš-igi-tab-bi. UM 29-13-198 rev. 1: [xxx e]n-líl-lá-kam. **101** - A: ⌜*tu̥m⌝. UM 29-13-198 rev. 2: [xxx e]n-líl-lá mu-u[n xxx]. **103** - šu--bal has the sense of transferring the fate of one thing, as decreed by Anzu, to another thing, thereby changing fate. **104** - It is not clear on the tablet or in the copy that AA has *a-⸢*ba⸣, not a-ba-a. Why do A and J have a-ba in line 103 and a-ba-a in line 104? Is the -a an emphatic copula? Does it show influence from the phonetic environment? Note that UM 29–13–198 has a-ba in both lines. **107** - M: [. . . i]n-ku$_4$-k[u$_4$ . . .]; UM 29-13-198 rev. 8: [xxx] nam-ba-ni-in-ku$_4$[xx]. **108** - MM: lú-u$_{18}$-ḷụ. **109** - A: na]m-mu-rí-in-du$_{12}$-du$_{12}$; AA: nam erroneously omitted; MM omits this line. **111** - 3N–T919, 478: šà-húl, with AA. **113–114** - mí--e is "to treat carefully," not "to flatter," which may be inim--sa$_6$-sa$_6$. See Gudea Cylinder A VII 16: g̃iš-e mí im-e "He (Gudea) treated the wood with care." **115** - 3N–T919, 478 obv. 5′: Second sign is *NANGA(LÁL.LAGAB). **118** - M: [PA.GIŠ].GIBIL-ga-zu N[UN? (x) ha]l-hal-la-ke$_4$; A: also N[UN? . . .]; 3N–T919, 478 rev. 3: [xxxx *z]u *nun-hal-hal-la-ke$_4$ "Your grandfather/uncle is a prince (dividing) all the lots," **119** - Ni 4518 (*ISET* 1, 83) I 3′ needs collation. **120** - Ni 4518 I 4′: [xxxxxx] im-ši-lá-lá-en nu x [x?]; 3N–T919, 478 rev. 5: sa-àm ši-im-lá-lá-en nu-mu[x]. **121** - A: KI-šè umbin-zu am-kur-ra šilam-kur-ra g̃iš-és-a[d . . .]; M+: ⸢xxxx⸣ [xxxxxxx] / és-⸢ad⸣[. . .]; Ni 4518 I 5′–6′: [xxxxx] kur-ra šiḷam!-kur-ra murg[u-zu] / sar-ra-me-e[n?] (assuming the horizontal line at the beginning of 6′ is not a wedge). See Å. W. Sjöberg, *ZA* 65 (1975), 216 (to line 27) for reading of this line. "Your talons are like a trap lain on the ground for wild mountain oxen and cows."

123 - If ti-ti is translated "Brustkorb" with Wilcke, how does it differ from gaba? Why not "ribs" as a metonym for "chest." **125** - Ni 9600 (*ISET* 1, 115) I′ 5′: ša-du$_{11}$-ba[. . . as in AA. Y obv. II 1: x[. . . .]. **126** - Y obv. II 2: dam-ẓụ[. . . .]. **127** - Y obv. II 3: za-ạ ad-da-g̃[á. . . .]. **128** - A: nam-ba-e-ni-k[u$_4$. . . ; AA: probably enough space in lacuna for only nam-[ba-n]i-in-ku$_4$-ku$_4$; Y obv. II 4–5: ḍi$_4$? x̣? lá-zu-ne [šeš-mu-ne-ka] ṇạm-ba-ṇi-ịṇ-ku$_4$-k[u$_4$]. Strictly speaking, Wilcke's comments about this line, based on the natural history of eagles, are not relevant (p. 171). Anzu is not an eagle, but a monster which is only part eagle. **129** - Y obv. II 6–7: x̣ x̣ x̣ x̣ [h]a?-šu-ụṛ? / . . . . **130** - Y obv. II 8: [xxx]⸢x⸣ hé-me-ḍa-⸢x̣⸣. **131** - Wilcke's composite line needs some clarification. A: [x m]u ga-mu-ra-du$_{11}$ nam-tar-ra-mu ga[. . .]; AA: silim-mu ga-mu-ra-an[-g̃á]-g̃á? nam-tar-ra-mu ga-mu-ra-⸢x⸣[-tar]-ra-a; MM: ⸢x⸣-mu ga-mu-ra-ab-g̃á-g̃á? ⸢xxx⸣[. . .]; Y obv. II 9: [xxx m]u-e-ra-[du$_{11}$]. Here, Lugalbanda means that the manner in which he greets Anzu determines how Anzu will react to him. Thus, Lugalbanda will effectively determine his own fate. See. J. Klein, *JAOS* 91 (1971), 299, for Lugalbanda talking to himself here. **132** - MM: mu-un-ši?[xx]; Y obv. II 10: [xxx] bi mu-r[a x(x)]. **137** - Compare the MA in line 141 of AA (III 35) to the putative pèš(MA) in this line (III 31). The sign here is probably a defective hašhur, not pèš. **138** - AA: g̃iš-má húl-la <an>-dùl!-[ak?]-a-gin$_7$ "Like a boat joyfully providing shade." A: also húl, not ukuš$_2$. **139** - A: du$_8$-duh; AA: not clear; LL: du$_8$[. . .]. **140** - Both sag̃-íl-la and gin-na are imperatives. **141** - LL:]ki-ág̃-g̃á[, as in AA. **142** - Y: [x]-*dumu-ki-ág̃-^{d}[inanna..]. Dumu is preceded by the end of a horizontal wedge, such as the end of dingir. Insufficient space for [^{d}šara$_2$] at beginning. **143** - Y: [xx *z]u u$_4$-gin$_7$ *U[D . **145** - A: Collation does not reveal a reading muš-šà-tùr. šà is possible, but there is an erasure and a definitive reading is not possible. Only G has a clear šà. Y: [. . . r]a-ra x[..], x as copied, not BI. **146** - A: KA×BALAG̃-ku$_5$; AA: KA×X-ku$_5$.

151 - Y: Copy accurate, end is hé-en-gub[x]. **153** - Y: Probably uru^{*ki}, not uru-šè **156-157** - A (both lines) and N (line 157): ša-ra-a[g . . .]. In a context with oil (ì) and milk (ga), perhaps ša-ra-ag is the verb meaning "to dry; to remove, diminish" (see J. Krecher, *SKLy*, 190–92 for references and discussion). Note that šár in the same line probably excludes ša-ra as a syllabic writing (for this writing in other contexts, see Å. W. Sjöberg, *MNS* I, 114–15). A and G have ga, not gara$_2$. **158** - No text preserves -dè at end. **159** - A: ends with inim-m[a . . .]. N: ẓi (or ṇam-)ṃ[u]-na-ab-gi$_4$; M+: . . .]ni-ib-gi$_4$-gi$_4$. **173** - Y omits first clause. **176** - Ni 9600 (*ISET* 1, 115) II 3′: lugal in copy, collation may yield gi$_4$. M+ (UM 29–16–449 II′ 6′): . . . s]á-bí-ib. **177** - A: no emendation necessary. AA and M+: ga-duh. **178** - Ni 9600 II 5′: [. . .]dè-en-na; M+: . . .] ku$_4$-dè [. . .]AN. **179** - Ni 9600 II 6′: [. . . húl-]le. **184** - AA: anzu^{mušen}-dè k[ù lug]al-bàn-da ⸢x⸣[x(x)]-dé-e. **191** - AA: bar-ra-g̃[á . . .]. **194** - P: duh-a; Q: du]h-a or d]u$_8$-a.

202 - Q: $^{PA.PA}_{PA}$! mí àm-me in copy. Wilcke read MUL($^{AN.AN}_{AN}$).SAL.A.AN-me. No comments in Wilcke, *Kollationen*, p. 15. **205** - Q:]MI^{mušen}. **207** - All texts duh. **208** -All texts duh. **214** - S: ku-li-zu-*ni-*ir na[m . . .]. **215** - S: šeš-zu-*ni-*ir pa nam[. . .]. **218** - Q and QQ: NIGIN$_2$. NIGIN$_2$ (not ligature). **219** - Read im-ma-gub-bé. **223** - UM 29–16-432 obv. 1′: [lugal-]bàn-da KA-kešda-gar-ra-šè / murub$_4$-bi-a mu [xx]. **224** - UM 29–16–432 obv. 2′: šeš-a-ne-ne gù ba-ab-ra-ra-ra-a[š x(x)] eren$_2$-e gù ab-ra-ra-aš. **225** - UM 29–16–432 rev. 2-4: Three lines corresponding to 247, 246, 244, follow 225: gú-ni-«da» gú-da mu-un-lá-lá-e [xx] / i-gi$_4$-in-zu burus$_5$-dè u$_4$-gíd-da teš-b[i xx] / ^{d}lugal-bàn-da šeš-a-ne-ne ku-l[i-ne-ne]. **228** - 3N–T919, 450 obv. 10′: [. . . gi]n$_7$ eren$_2$ hé-e[n x]. **231** -N 2628 4′: nu omitted. **232** - N 2628 6′ is an added line after line 232: [x]ba-ra-àm-gi$_4$ [xxx(x)]. **237** -N 2628 11′: [xxx g]in$_7$ me-nag̃-a [xxxx]. **238** - After this line N 2628 has three lines of unsure placement, 13′–15′: [xxxx] tùr [xxxx] / [xxxx] ⸢šeš?⸣ [xxxx] / [xxxx b]i? [xxxx]. **241** - A: um-mi-ús; AA: um-ma-ni-ib-ús; QQ: um-mi-ni-ús.

242 - AA: Perhaps gúm-gam$_x$(GÚM) àm-mi-ni-i[b-za . . . **243** - A: i-li-i-a-nu-um; QQ: i-li-nu-um. **246** - QQ: ì-gi$_4$-i[n]-zu. In 3N–T919, 450 (*SLTF* pl. 8) rev. 1′, the line before line 247, reads: [xxxxx]⌜ni⌝-in [-ú?-ús?]. **247** - 3N–T919, 450 rev. 2′: [xxxxx]un-su[xx] (not enough space to parallel other texts here.

253 - 3N–T919, 450 rev. 8′: [xxx]aš àm-d[a xxx]. **257** - AA: im-ma?-⌜x⌝ [. . .]. **259** - Does U have ama-bi-ir? (Wilcke, p. 87 n. 365c). **261** - AA: a-šà igi ba-ab-hul n[í . . .]; U: [. . . m]u? ab-hul. **264** - QQ and T: ul$_4$(GÍR-*gunû*). **272** -Omitted in T. See line 278 for restoration. **274** and **280** - AA: ugnim written KI.ZU(or LU).ÚB.GAR. **284** - AA: un-g̃á omitted. **291** - N: . . .] ki hé-ús-⌜sa-ba⌝. **295** - A: . . .]*ni-pàd-dè-en. **297** - A: . . .]⌜ma⌝-dé-a.

302 - The rhyme of dù and di recalls the rhyme of duh and dah in line 53. Wilcke seems to take di as a phonetic variant to dù in his translation. Why not di "to render judgements"? Reading silim is possible, but the rhyme is lost. **303** - A: ba, not GADA. T: nigin$_2$-*n[a-(a-)]ba (O. Gurney's collation). **313** - Second gig is error for ág̃ in A. See parallel line 379. **335** - Gurney's collation indicates that Langdon's copy of T is largely accurate, implying a reading lú ka-aš gal, not Wilcke's hur-sag̃ aš gal (III 2:  ; III 11: 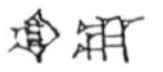). I suspect the absent-minded scribe wrote the first half of the line while thinking of the second half. Another interpretation would take ka-aš as a writing for kaš$_4$, yielding a translation "(Even) a great runner ought not go alone." However, such syllabic writings are not otherwise known in T, whereas the scribe was confused in lines 298–99. hé-mú-a is expected at the ends of both (compare 364–65), but 298 ends only in mú-a while 299 ends only in hé. I see no relationship to the term lú-ka-aš-ka-sa in Ershemma 165:10 and 16 (*CT* 15, 19).

364 - T and W: g̃iš-asal$_2$. **368** -See line 302. **372** - W: i-da-lá-ba. **374** - T: è-a-*g[in$_7$] (Gurney's collation). **379** - A: ki ha-ra-an-ág̃; W: u$_4$-da g̃á-ra ki ha-ba-ki-ág̃ uru-ni hul ha-ba-an-gi$_4$. **385** - W: ba-DU. **391** - AA: peš$_x$-peš$_x$-bi (KI.A.KI.A-bi). **393** - AA: ú-i-a-nu!-kur-ra; T: ú-i-li-a[. . .].

400 and **402** - šinig in all texts. **403** - W: <<ù-ba>> mu-ni-in-bu. Prospective preformative not expected. **408** - W: ù-ni-in-til in copy. Aratta^{ki} in all texts.

D. *Plates.*

UM 29–13–198 obv. and rev.	Plate 2
UM 29–16–432 obv. and rev.	Plate 2
N 2628 obv. only; rev. destroyed	Plate 2
CBS 7977(0)+CBS 7979(M)+UM 29–16–441 (+)UM 29–16–449 rev. only	Plate 3
X 84 (Y)	Plate 1

obv. rev.

Plate 1. X 84 (Y)

UM 29–16–432 obv., rev.

N 2628 obv. only
rev. destroyed

UM 29–13–198 obv., rev.

UM 29-16-441

CBS 7977

CBS 7979

UM 29-16-449

Rev. only; obv. of new texts destroyed.

Plate 3.

FORM AND REFORMULATION OF THE BIBLICAL PRIESTLY BLESSING

MICHAEL FISHBANE

BRANDEIS UNIVERSITY

NUM 6:23–27 CONCLUDES A CYCLE OF PRIESTLY INSTRUCTIONS to the people of Israel with an additional instruction to the Aaronids. It opens with a comment to these priests, delivered by Moses, "In this manner shall you bless (*tĕbārăkû*) the Israelites," and then proceeds with the blessing itself:

(v. 24)	May YHWH bless you and protect you;	*yĕbārekĕkā Y. vĕyišmĕrekā*
(v. 25)	May YHWH brighten His countenance toward you and grant you grace/favor;	*yāʾēr Y. pānâv ʾēlêkā vîḥunnekkā*
(v. 26)	May YHWH raise His countenance toward you and give you *šalom*.	*yiśśāʾ Y. pānâv ʾēlêkā vĕyāśēm lĕkā šālôm*

At the conclusion of this blessing, another instruction follows, in v. 27: "And when they shall put (*vĕśāmû*) My Name over the Israelites, I shall bless them (*ʾabārăkēm*)."[1] It is at once apparent that in both form and content the narrative instruction in v. 27 balances that found in v. 23, and thus provides a stylistic envelope to the poetic blessing.[2] In addition, the final instruction in v. 27 clarifies the encased benediction in at least two respects. First, it serves to emphasize that while the Aaronids articulate the Priestly Blessing (PB), it is YHWH alone who blesses; and second, it serves to emphasize that the core of the blessing is not simply the specification of the blessings—central as this is—but rather the ritual use of the sacred divine Name, thrice repeated. The PB is thus realized to be a series of optative expressions (e.g., "May YHWH bless . . . ; May YHWH brighten His countenance . . . ; May YHWH raise His countenance . . .") referring to actions which YHWH, alone, will perform. The priests, by contrast, are merely the agents of the blessing: they articulate it; but their words, in themselves, do not effect reality. Moreover, from a purely semantic standpoint, one must admit that the precise force of the priestly articulation is somewhat ambiguous. While it is clear that the PB is composed of three cola, each of which has two verbs, or stated actions (though the relative length of the first bi-colon to the second varies),[3] it is not clear whether six separate actions are intended. The transitional *waw* in each colon may be considered to be copulative (i.e., bless

[1] The Sam reading is *wśymw*; probably a pl. imperative in order to balance the command-instruction in v. 23. Comparably, the LXX transposes v. 27 to the end of v. 23, and thereby tightens the nexus between the verses. However, v. 27 is resultative, and so no verse transposition is necessary; see *infra* also for comments on the formal symmetry of the MT which reinforces this point. In any event, the precise meaning of v. 27, and its relationship to the previous prayer, is an old crux. See the most recent review by P. A. H. de Boer, "Numbers 6:27," *VT* 32 (1981), 1–13. However, his reconstruction, which claims that *ʿal*, "over" is a misreading of an original divine epithet "The Most High of the Israelites" is problematic because it leaves the verb without an object and it is gratuitous because it is the divine name YHWH which recurs in the blessing itself.

[2] The narrative framework is, moreover, textually linked to the blessing; cf. the stem *bārēk* in vv. 23–24, and the stem *śîm* in vv. 26–7.

[3] These 'asymmetries' have resulted in different dubious reconstructions. Cf., for example, the proposal of D. Freedman, "The Aaronic Benediction (Numbers 6:24–26)," in *No Famine in the Land, Studies in Honor of John L. McKenzie*, edited by J. Flanagan *et al.*, 1975, 35–8, who reconstructs the piece to produce a new, more 'symmetrical' structure (but one hardly less symmetrical overall than the MT); or the proposal of O. Loretz, "Altorientalischer Hintergrund Sowie Inner- und Nachbiblische Entwicklung des Aaronitischen Segens (Num 6:24–26)," *UF* 10 (1978), 116, who, on the basis of metric criteria, isolates the 'original' components of the blessing from later accretions (though, thereby, a new asymmetry is introduced, since the *waw*-clause is retained only for the first blessing!).

and protect; brighten *and* grant; etc.) or the second verb may be merely the result of the first so that the transitional *waw* indicates consequence (i.e., the blessing *is*—in its result—protection; the brightening of the divine countenance *is*—in its result—grace or favor; etc.). The second option suggests that the second action stated in each colon is but the concrete manifestation of a beneficent divine state.[4] So regarded, the PB would articulate three blessings, not six.

In addition to its formal presentation in Num 6:24–26, there are hints elsewhere in Scripture that the PB was enunciated by the priests on various occasions. Thus in what appears to be a deliberate reference to the PB in Lev 9:22, it is said that Aaron, after the appointment of the priests, raised his arms and "blessed" the people (cf. Num 6:23); and in Deut 10:8 and 21:5 it is stated that the Levitical priests have been set aside as a special class, to serve YHWH "and to bless in His name (*ûlĕbārēk bišmô*)" (cf. Num 6:27). Apart from these circumspect allusions, it is certain that the PB had an appreciable impact on the liturgical life of ancient Israel. This certainty is not derived from the repeated requests in the Psalter for divine blessing, for the manifestation of the radiant divine countenance (cf. the refrain in Ps 80:4, 8, 20), or for grace and favor (cf. Pss 25:16; 86:16). For these expressions often occur piecemeal in the psalms, and may as much derive from common metaphorical usage as from the PB as the direct source. Certainty of the impact of the PB on ancient Israelite piety can rather be ascertained only where the clustering of terminology leaves no reasonable doubt as to the source. Ps 67:2, for example, provides just such a positive case; for in this instance the psalmist opens his prayer with the invocation, *ʾĕlohim yĕḥānnēnû vîbārăkēnû yāʾēr pānâv ʾittānû—selāh*: "May Elohim have mercy/show favor and bless us; may He cause His countenance to brighten among us—selah." In this piece, it is not only clear that priestly liturgists—or their lay imitators—have been inspired by the language and imagery of the PB; but they have reused it with minor modifications. The verbs have been selectively chosen and regrouped innovatively; and there is a use of verbs from both halves of each of the PB's cola, suggesting that, for the liturgists of Ps 67:2, the PB consisted of six separate actions (cf. *supra*). In v. 3 (and its sequel) the desired consequences of divine grace, blessing and luminosity are spelled out ("that all the earth may know Your ways").

Among other clear examples of the impact of the PB on the liturgical life of ancient Israel, as reflected in the Psalter, Ps 4 may be noted—particularly since it provides a literary form manifestly different from that found in Ps 67. In this last, the PB is first (partially) cited and only applied thereafter. By contrast, the key terms of the PB are, in Ps 4, spread throughout the piece, serving at once as its theological touchstone and as its ideational matrix. The psalmist first calls upon YHWH to "favor me (*ḥānnēnî*)" and hear his prayer (v. 2); then, after citing those disbelievers "who say: 'who will show us (*yarʾēnû*) good," the psalmist calls upon YHWH to "raise over us the light of Your presence (*nĕsāh ʿālēnû ʾôr pānêkā*)" (v. 7);[5] and finally, the psalmist concludes with a reference to *šālôm* (v. 9).

The various and abundant references to the PB in the Psalter, but particularly the recurrence of similar language there and in many biblical genres, where a direct use of the language of the PB cannot be posited as its source, suggest that such imagery as 'shining the face' in favor, or 'raising the face' in beneficence, and so on, were widely diffused throughout the culture. And more: the various and abundant use of such imagery in ancient Near Eastern literature,[6] particularly from Mesopotamia[7] where it recurs in a wide range of genres, suggests that ancient Israel absorbed such imagery as part and parcel of its rich patrimony. The source of the diffusion of this imagery, the channels of its transmission, and the relevant dates and periods can hardly, at this point, be reconstructed with any confidence. Nevertheless, two particular Mesopotamian documents may be invoked with decided interest in this context. A close comparison of them, in conjunction with the biblical PB, reveals a remarkable similarity of language and literary form. These

[4] Cf. P. Miller, "The Blessing of God," *Interp* 29 (1975), 243, and the authorities cited.

[5] In this context *yarʾēnî* is a pun on PB *yāʾēr*; and *nĕsāh* is a play on *yiśśāʾ* (if it is not simply an orthographic error). I find no basis for the emendation of M. Dahood, *Psalms* I [Anchor Bible] 1966, 26, which introduces new problems.

[6] For Ugaritic literature, cf. *UT* 1126:6.

[7] For Akkadian literature, cf. the examples collected and discussed by E. Dhorme, "L'emploi métaphorique des noms de parties du corps en hébreu et en akkadien," *RB* 30 (1921), 383ff.; A. L. Oppenheim, "Idiomatic Accadian," *JAOS* 61 (1941), 256–8; *idem*, "Studies in Accadian Lexicography, I,"

correspondences are so strong, in fact, that whatever the ultimate Near Eastern sources for the aforenoted biblical imagery in its various reflexes and genres, an indubitable prototype for the liturgical form and language of the PB may be recognized.

Of the two Mesopotamian texts which offer striking parallels to the biblical PB, the first is from a 9th century *kudurru*-inscription.[8] In it, Nabu-apla-iddina, the king of Babylon, bestows priestly revenues upon one Nabu-nadin-šum, the priest of Sippar. Upon doing so, *im-me-ru zi-mu-šu*, "his countenance brightened" (iv 39); and *it-ru-ṣa bu-ni-šu*, "he turned his attention (to the priest)" (iv 42); and *ina bu-ni-šu nam-ru-ti zi-me-šu ru-uš-šu-ti*, "with his bright gaze, shining countenance" (iv 43–44) . . . *arad-su i-rim*, "he granted his servant (the priestly dues)" (v 13). As Y. Muffs has fully explained in his analysis of terms of volition in gift-giving contexts, the metaphorical expressions used in this official grant document are actually technical legal idioms conveying such notions as thinking about, considering and intending (to give a gift).[9] Thus, behind the florid style lies a technical genre and vocabulary denoting the grace and benefaction of a superior to his underling—here a priest. The document, with its metaphorical language, is then a legal instrument establishing the transfer of revenue rights. The parallels with the biblical PB are readily apparent; for also in Num 6:24–26 there is described the (hoped for) moods of a superior's attention and consideration, in cognate terms like *yāʾēr pānâv*, and the PB climaxes with its reference to the gift of *šālôm*, the favor of peace or well-being.[10]

Even more striking in its linguistic and formal resemblance to the PB is a neo-Babylonian document from the 6th century.[11] It describes how the goddess Gula,

> (19) *pa-ni-šu tu-saḫ-ḫi-ram-ma* (20) *ina bu-ni-šú nam-ru-ti* (21) *ki-niš tap-pal-sa-an-ni-ma* (22) *túš-ri-im-mi ra-am-ma*
>
> turned her countenance toward me (viz., Nabunaʾid); with her shining face she faithfully looked at me and actually caused (him; i.e., Marduk) to show mercy.

Of obvious note here is the formal sequence of turning and bestowing a shining countenance, followed by the bestowal of mercy by Marduk (*túš-ri-im-mi ra-am-ma*); for this strikingly corresponds to the idioms found in the biblical PB.[12] This formal nexus suggests that while the Akkadian and Hebrew idioms in these documents circulated as independent phrases in each cultural sphere this particular formal clustering in Mesopotamia may have influenced their structuring in Israel. But this is far from certain; for the biblical PB may just as well reflect an independent combination of shared Near Eastern idiom groups. Whatever the case, all three texts—the two Mesopotamian, the one Israelite—are applied to *different* situations. Accordingly, it must be stressed that the formal clustering of idioms in the biblical PB is as much an expression of the ancient Near Eastern literary history of this pattern, broadly viewed, as are the biblical reformulations of this pattern in Pss 4 and 67, more narrowly viewed.

The examples of Pss 4 and 67 aside, over a generation ago L. Liebreich proposed another possible reformulation of the PB in the biblical Psalter.[13] He asserted that the entire ensemble referred to as the 'songs of ascent,' Psalms 120–30, reuses the key language of the PB; and that it is this last which gives the

Orientalia n.s. 11 (1942), 123f.; and see the two examples to follow.

[8] L. W. King, *Babylonian Boundary-Stones and Memorial-Tablets in the British Museum*, London, 1912, No. 36.

[9] *Studies in the Aramaic Legal Papyri from Elephantine* [Studia et Documenta ad Iura Orientis Antiqui Pertinentia, VIII], 1969, 130–4. I have largely followed Muff's translation; cp. that in *CAD*, I, 155a.

[10] Hebrew *šālôm* appears to combine Akkadian *šulmu/šalmu* ("be well; unimpaired; at peace") and *salimu/sullimu* ("be favorable; gracious"); cf. M. Weinfeld, "Covenant Terminology in the Ancient Near East and its Influence on the West," *JAOS* 93 (1973), 191f., and n. 31, and the references cited.

[11] The transcription and translation follows H. Lewy, "The Babylonian Background of the Kay Kâûs Legend," *AnOr* 17^2(1949), 51f.

[12] Muffs, *op. cit.*, 132f., n. 2, has pointed out the relationship between *tušrimi* (the bestowal of mercy) and *irīm* (the giving of a gift) in the *kudurru*-inscription cited earlier; and has also compared this latter term to Susa *īnun*—to which corresponds the Hebrew verb *ḥānan*. These links and correspondences establish an even closer nexus between the Mesopotamian texts and the PB than the terminological and sequential parallels noted above.

[13] "The Songs of Ascent and the Priestly Blessing," *JBL* 74 (1955), 33–6.

ensemble its coherence. Moreover, Liebreich made the strong claim that all this reflects an interpretation or reapplication of the old PB for the post-exilic community. In his words, we have in "this group of Psalms . . . the earliest interpretation of the Priestly Blessing, an interpretation that may be considered to be the precursor of the homilies on the Priestly Blessing in Midrashic literature."[14] Quite apart from the omission of Pss 4 and 67 as early examples of the reapplication of the PB, Liebreich's contention appears intriguing. But secondary reflection suggests that it is ill-advised given the commonplace nature of the words and verbs emphasized, and, especially, given the fact that these words and verbs do not occur in clusters which either dominate or transform the meaning of the psalms in question. Thus, it is one thing to say that certain well-known liturgical and theological terms and idioms were liberally used in the 'songs of ascent'—even by priestly liturgists—in order to convey the sense of blessing and peace so much hoped for by the post-exilic community. But it is quite another matter to assume, on the basis of references to blessing and protection, that any one of the psalms—let alone the ensemble—is an interpretative reuse of the PB.

However, the dismissal of Liebreich's suggestion does not mean that reinterpretations of the PB do not exist in post-exilic biblical literature. Indeed, to the contrary, Mal 1:6–2:9 is a great (and hitherto unnoticed) counterexample. As we may now observe, Malachi's vitriolic critique of cultic and priestly behavior in the post-exilic period is, at once, a systematic utilization of the language of the PB and an exegetical transformation of it. With great ironic force, the prophet turns to the priests and says:

> Where is your fear of Me (*môrāʾî*), says YHWH of hosts, to you, priests who despise My Name (*šĕmî*) . . . You offer polluted meat upon My altar . . . (and) bring it to your governor. Will he accept you, or will he be gracious/favorable to you (*hayiśśāʾ pānêkā*)? . . . So, now, beseech the countenance of God (*ḥallû-nāʾ pĕnē-ʾēl*) that He may have mercy upon us (*vîḥānnēnû*); . . . will He be gracious/favorable to you (*hayiśśāʾ mikkem pānîm*)? Would that there was one among you to close the door (of the Temple), that you not kindle (*tāʾîrû*) My altar in vain (*ḥinnām*) . . . I will not accept your meal-offerings . . . (for) My Name (*šemî*) is awesome (*nôrāʾ*) among the nations (1:6–14).

After this condemnation, Malachi levels a harsh statement of ensuing divine doom upon the priests:

> If you do not hearken . . . and give glory to My Name (*šĕmî*), says YHWH of hosts, I shall send a curse (*mĕʾērāh*) among you and curse (*vĕʾārôtî*) your blessings (*birkôtêkem*) . . . Behold, I shall . . . scatter dung upon your faces (*pĕnêkem*) . . . and raise you (*vĕn-āśāʾ ʾetkem*) to it[15] . . . For you know that I have sent you this covenant, that My covenant be with the Levites . . . and My covenant was with them (viz., the Levites) for life and peace (*haššālôm*); and I gave them fear that they might fear Me (*môrāʾ vay-yîrāʾēnî*) and . . . My Name (*šemî*). A true Torah was in their mouth; . . . but you have turned from the path . . . and so I shall make you contemptible . . . for you do not guard/protect (*šōmĕrîm*) My ways; but (you rather) show partiality/favor (*venōśēʾîm pānîm*) in (the administration and teaching of) the Torah. (2:2–9)

From this translation and transcription, it is immediately evident that all the key terms of the PB are alluded to or otherwise played upon in the prophet's diatribe. On the one hand, the dense clustering of these terms makes it clear that Mal 1:6–2:9 has more than casual, terminological similarities with the PB. Indeed, the transformed uses and reapplications of these terms indicate that Malachi's oration is *exegetical* in nature. In brief, the prophet has taken the contents of the PB, delivered by the priests, with its emphasis on blessing, the sanctity of the divine Name, and such benefactions as protection, gracious/favorable countenance, and peace—*and negated them*! The priests have despised the divine Name and service, and this has led to a threatened suspension of the divine blessing. Even the governor will not give his gracious acknowledgement of the offerings. The only hope is in YHWH's gracious acknowledgement and mercy. The gift in the PB of a brightened divine countenance which leads to grace/favor (*yāʾēr Y. pānâv ʾelêkā vîḥunnekkā*), and the raising of the

---

[14] *Ibid.*, 33. Loretz, *op. cit.*, 118, has claimed that the PB already contains exegetical expansions; but first, his 'exegetical expansions' are not exegetical in any meaningful sense, and further, the whole enterprise rests on his reconstruction of the text's strata, and this is dubious. See *supra*, n. 3.

[15] Cf. LXX.

divine countenance (*yiśśāʾ Y. pānâv ʾelêkā*) which leads to peace or well-being, are punningly countered by the prophet's wish that the priests no longer ignite (*tāʾîrû*) the altar in vain (*ḥinnām*), and by the anticipated divine curse (*mĕʾērāh . . . vĕʾārôtî*). Indeed, the priests' perversion of their sacred office is such that they who asked YHWH to raise His countenance (*yiśśāʾ Y. pānâv*) in boon for the people now "raise the countenance" (theirs and others) in overt partiality and misuse of the Torah and its laws (*nōśĕʾîm pānîm battôrāh*). Given this state of things, how can the priests hope that YHWH will raise His countenance in beneficence? In truth, says the prophet, the priests have spurned the divine gift—entrusted to them —of *šālôm*, so that what will be "raised" for them, or against their "faces" (*pĕnêkem . . . vĕnāśāʾ ʾetkem ʾēlâv*), will be the polluted refuse of their offerings—nothing more. Those who neglect their office, and do not "guard knowledge" (*yišmĕrû-daᶜat*) or "guard/protect" (*šōmĕrîm*) YHWH's ways, can hardly be permitted, implies the prophet, to invoke the Lord's blessing of protection (*vĕyišmĕrekā*) upon the people of Israel.

A more violent condemnation of the priests can hardly be imagined. Nor does the ironic texture of the diatribe stop with the preceding lexical and conceptual cross-references between Mal 1:6–2:9 and the PB. On closer inspection, one will observe that the prophet's speech is replete with interlocking puns that condemn the priests 'measure for measure.' Note, for example, the initial ironic appeal to "beseech" (*ḥallû*) God, which is countered by the reference to the priests's desecrations (*mĕḥallĕlîm*);[16] the initial reference to the "governor" (*peḥāh*), which is echoed in the punishment of utter blasting and ruination by God (*hippaḥtem*);[17] the failure of the priests to fear YHWH's awesome (*nôrāʾ*) presence, which leads to the extinguishing of the altar lights (*tāʾîrû*) and the onset of divine curses (*mĕʾērāh . . . vĕʾārôtî*);[18] and the priestly condemnation (*bôzêʾ*) of the divine Name, which leads to the condemnation of the priestly offering (*nibzeh*) and the priests themselves (*nibzîm*).[19]

Both through the reworking of and plays on the language of the PB, and through internal puns like those just suggested, the ironic *bouleversement*, or inversion, of the priests' language, actions and hopes is textured. Indeed, in this way, the priests' cultic language is desacralized and their actions cursed. By unfolding the negative semantic range of most of the key terms used positively in the PB, the rotten core and consequences of the language and behaviors of the priests echoes throughout the diatribe. Contrast, for example, PB *yāʾēr Y. pānâv ʾēlêkā* and Malachi's *vĕnāśāʾ ʾetkem ʾēlâv* or *nōśĕʾîm pānîm*; or PB *yāʾēr* vs. Malachi's *tāʾîrû* or *mĕʾērāh*; or PB *vîḥunnekkâ* vs. Malachi's *ḥinnām*; and others. The prophetic speech of Malachi, itself spoken as a divine word, is thus revealed to be no less than a divine exegesis and mockery of the priests who presume to bless in His Name. The sacerdotal language of the PB is, in this way, systematically inverted and desecrated. The priests, bearers of the cultic PB and sensitive to its language, could not have missed the exegetical irony and sarcastic nuance of the prophet's speech.

A final comment concerning the relationship between form and content in Mal 1:6–2:9 may be added to the foregoing reflections. As against the fairly balanced and symmetrical style of Num 6:23–27, the reuse of it in Mal 1:6–2:9 is imbalanced and unsymmetrical. If, to explicate this point, the formalized style of the positive blessing in the PB is the objective literary correlative of the hopes for protection, well-being, mercy and sustenance expressed therein, then the disorder of Malachi's condemnation—its narrative effusiveness, its redundancies, and its disjointed and scattered allusions to the PB—is the corresponding correlative of the fracture and disruption of harmony forecast in the threats and curses. The transformation of the sacerdotal blessing into a curse is thus expressed not only on the manifest level of content, but on the deeper level of structure and form as well. The original language of sacral blessing has thus been scattered and desacralized—an objective correlative of the content. In this way the deep ironical core of Malachi's speech inheres in its destabilizing liturgical mockery: a mockery which curses the forms and language of order, cosmos and blessing as entrusted to the priesthood. The *Mischgattung* created by this interweaving of liturgical language with prophetical discourse thoroughly transforms the positive assurances of the former into the negative forecasts of the latter. One may even wonder whether Malachi's diatribe has its very *Sitz im Leben* in an antiphonal outcry in the gates of the Temple—one that corresponded to, perhaps was even simultaneous with, the recital of the PB in the shrine by the priests. Viewed thus, the mounting crescendo of exegetical cacaphony in the prophet's speech served as an anti-blessing, as a veritable con-

[16] Mal 1:9, 12.

[17] Mal 1:8, 13.

[18] Mal 1:10, 14; 2:2.

[19] Mal 1:6, 12; 2:9.

trapuntal inversion of the sound and sense of the official PB.

It would take us well beyond the scope of this study to follow the many threads of the exegetical afterlife of the PB in post-exilic Israel and Judaism. Nevertheless, several established points, and several new ones, may be briefly considered. Thus, to start from the known, it may be recalled here that the Rule Scroll from Qumran contains particularly striking reuses of the biblical PB. Of particular importance for the present discussion is the fact that, as in Malachi's discourse, these are systematic reinterpretations of Num 6:23–27. However, by contrast with Malachi's variation, which contains covert or embedded exegesis, the variations in the Rule Scroll are explicit and lemmatic: each phrase is cited and its meaning(s) given. Positive blessings and esoteric knowledge and salvation are bestowed upon the elect of the community, while curses and ignorance and doom are the lot of the less fortunate (cf. 1 QS II, 2–9). This reapplication of the PB to wisdom and Torahistic piety is in itself a remarkable incorporation of the main ideological and pietistic trends of Qumran theology into the biblical PB. What is even more striking, as M. Gertner has already noticed,[20] is that the reapplication of phrases of the PB to wisdom and Torahistic piety *already* occurs in late biblical literature—specifically, in Ps 119:135, where the psalmist says *pānêkā hāʾēr bĕʿabdekā vĕlammĕdēnî ʾet-ḥuqqêkā*, "Brighten your countenance toward your servant and teach me your laws." In this version, the brightened divine countenance serves to bestow neither grace nor sustenance nor even wisdom *per se*. The request is rather for the beneficence of divinely guided Torah instruction. And since Torah instruction was an exoteric feature of the community, one may further wonder whether the request to God to teach the supplicant Torah is not, in fact, a request for instruction in the deeper meanings of the laws—their esoteric, even exegetical side. It may not be accidental that in this psalm, which is an eight-fold acrostic, all eight verses beginning with the letter *pê*, of which Ps 119:135 is one, have some terminological or punning connection to the language of the PB (note especially, *yāʾîr*, v. 130; *pĕnēh-ʾēlay vĕḥānnēnî . . . šĕmekā*, v. 132; and *ʾešmĕrāh*, v. 134).

In following the threads of the PB beyond the Hebrew Bible, one may point to several other remarkable reapplications of it. In the Gospels, for example, a very compelling instance of an exegetical reuse of the PB occurs in the liturgical piece found in Luke 1:67–79, the Benedictus. As Gertner has shown, this piece, ostensibly comprised of two sections (vv. 67–76, 76–79), in different styles and rhythms, and with seemingly different content, is, in fact, a complex reinterpretation of the ancient PB.[21] However, in "the narrative framework" of the birth legend, "this midrashic homily had to be shaped as a piece of liturgy and not as a didactic sermon. For although its content is a doctrinal interpretation of a scriptural text its function in the context of the legend is a liturgical exposition of the child's destiny."[22] In readapting his material, opines Gertner, "Luke has reworked here extant homiletical material, adapting it to his requirement and creating a truly Christian version of an older Jewish midrash."[23] Just what that older version was, we can only guess.

One final instance of exegesis of the PB in the Tannaitic period may be noted here—both because it exemplifies the tradition to which the homiletician of Luke 1:67–79 was heir, and for purely formal reasons. For in the preceding discussion, two distinct types on the spectrum of literary form have been isolated. One type was embedded exegesis, in which the language of the PB underpins a reinterpretation or reapplication of it; the other was called lemmatic exegesis, in which citations from the PB are directly followed by reinterpretations. A third type may be added. In it, the entire PB is first cited and then followed by a comprehensive paraphrase. The example I have in mind occurs at the conclusion of the central *Amidah* prayer of the Jewish liturgy. Quite remarkably, it has gone virtually unnoticed that the great prayer for peace, the so-called *Sim Shalom* prayer, which follows the recitation of the PB, is nothing short of an exegetical paraphrase of the old biblical blessing and a reapplication of its contents in terms of peace.[24] Other thematics occur, as well: the Torah, for example, is considered a gift of God's mercy and a manifestation of the effulgent divine countenance. But this aside, it is the topic of peace which dominates the prayer starting from the opening line, which connects

20 "Midrashim in the New Testament," *JSS* 7 (1962), 276.

21 Ibid., 273–4, 277–8.

22 Ibid., 274.

23 Ibid.

24 Cf. Liebreich, op. cit., 36, who refers to "references" in the *Sîm Shalom* prayer "to other parts of the Blessing"; though he does not see that the prayer is an exegetical adaptation of the PB.

with the final line of the PB (*vĕyāśēm lĕkā šālôm*) just recited. The *Sim Shalom* prayer, which now follows, together with its ancient variant, the *Shalom Rab* prayer,[25] is thus an ancient homiletical meditation on selected thematics of the PB for the laity. Even to this day, the PB is only recited by the communal precentor or by descendents of the ancient family of Aaron. To them, as of old, belongs the PB; to the people belongs the prayer for peace:

> Grant peace (*śîm šālôm*), goodness and blessing (*bĕrākāh*); mercy (*ḥēn*), and grace and compassion. For by the brightening of Your countenance (*bĕʾôr pānêkā*), You have given us, O Lord, our God, a Torah of life, and the love of kindness, and charity, and blessing (*ûbĕrākāh*), and compassion, and life and peace (*šālôm*). So may it be pleasing in Your eyes to bless (*lĕbārēk*) Your people, Israel, at all times with Your peace (*bišlômekā*).

[25] This prayer is also an exegetical adaptation of the PB, linked to it verbally; cf. L. Finkelstein, "The Development of the Amidah," *JQR* 16 (1925), 31f.

SELF-REFERENCE OF AN AKKADIAN POET

Benjamin R. Foster
Yale University

"The Poem of the Righteous Sufferer" is a late second millennium B.C. Akkadian poetic monologue in which a noble gentleman, once prosperous, important, and happy, relates how the god Marduk for no apparent reason turned his lot to one of poverty, abasement, and disease. He suffers for a period longer than usual, during which his piety, though tried, remains firm. Later, through the intervention of personages who appear to him in dreams, he is restored to favor, wealth and health. He concludes by praising Marduk, the all-knowing god, who caused him his woes.

The poem consists of four tablets of about 120 lines each.[1] Of the presumed 480 or more lines of the complete text, nearly ninety percent are preserved in whole or in part. Of these, exact placement of substantial portions of Tablet III and of a number of lines preserved only in an ancient commentary is uncertain.[2] The arrangement of the text of Tablet IV is still not agreed upon.[3] Moreover, numerous passages, lines, and words are obscure or are susceptible to differing interpretations.

Even with these problems, preservation and understanding of the text are sufficient for critical observations on its poetics. Many topics invite discussion, for example, the intricate parallelism, the ornamented and recondite language, the symmetrical scheme of the text. I have chosen to discuss means by which the speaker refers to himself, because they are peculiarly apt both for appreciating the quality of the poet's artistic achievement and for their special significance in relaying his message. I offer this with warm personal thanks and admiration to the *apkallu* of Sumerian poetry, though perhaps not heedful enough of his sage injunction, "don't get fancy!"

Four means of self-reference may be distinguished here. The first is an overt means whereby the poet either refers to himself by name or selects words or particles that linguistically refer to the speaker.[4] The latter may be either active (independent, subjective pronouns or fientic verbs), or neutral, possessive or passive (pronominal or lative suffixes).[5] The second means of self-reference may be called "distancing" and includes use of second and third person to refer to the first person speaker.[6] The third means is the speaker's choice of verb forms, the temporality or activity of which are intended to point to him. The fourth is poetic devices invigorated by the author so that they extend and refine his self-reference beyond single words to include whole passages. These devices I consider under two rubrics: rhyme and assonance on the one hand, and "cinematics" on the other. What might be considered a fifth device, the relationship between the form of the text and the author's self-reference, will be considered briefly in conclusion.

---

[1] The standard edition of the text is by W. G. Lambert, BWL. I keep in mind Kramer's reminder that it is easier to follow with interpretations where others have done the basic epigraphic and philological work (review of F. H. Taylor's *Babel's Tower*, *Crozer Quarterly* 22 [1945], 270f.). Additional pieces of the text have been published since *BWL* by Leichty, *Studies Finkelstein*, 145, and particularly by Wiseman, *AnSt* 30 (1980), 104ff. I have published a few suggestions to that text separately in *RA* 75 (1981), 189. I am grateful to Kathleen Good for suggestions and bibliography.

[2] Commentary edited by Lambert in the apparatus to *BWL*, copy plates 15–17.

[3] I have accepted the ingenious solution to the problems of Tablet IV put forward by Vogelzang, *RA* 73 (1979), 180.

[4] P. Ricoeur, "Creativity in Language," *Philosophy Today* 17 (1973), 99.

[5] See E. Benveniste, "La nature des pronoms," = *Problèmes de linguistique générale*, 1966, 254.

[6] I have misappropriated this term from Ricoeur, "The Hermeneutical Function of Distanciation," *Philosophy Today* 17 (1973), 129ff. The question of whether or not the speaker in the text is the author or pseudo-author (in critical terms) seems to me insoluble. Note that the narrator knows the "truth" of the story from the beginning, so there is no *Bildung*; however, the author is not omniscient, as in so much Mesopotamian narrative poetry, and thereby presents no extra-perceptual scene of his tormentor, as even Job does. For critical discussion of the problem of first person "hero," see G. Genette, *Figures* III, 1972, 255ff., and especially p. 252.

On the level of overt self-reference, one can already appreciate the originality of the author. The poet, Šubši-mešre-Šakkan, refers to himself by name, a practice known in other highly original works of Akkadian poetry.[7] Yet here his self-naming is done with a characteristic twist: the author is addressed by name in a dream in the third person, and thus does not introduce himself directly. In fact, this is the most remote modulation of self-naming to be found in all Mesopotamian tradition.[8] The reference comes in a significant passage. There Marduk is named for the first time since the opening hymn of the poem (I.31), and then the author in the immediately succeeding line.[9]

The author's use of the independent personal pronoun 'I' is likewise original: it occurs but once in the entire preserved text. This is remarkable not only for a text in the first person but for Akkadian narrative poetry in general, for, at least in what may be called the "heroic style," the independent pronominal forms are often used. The context of this refurbished word requires attention. A thirteen-line series of subordinate clauses (II 10ff.), all referring to a hypothetical 'third' person, none with a first person referent, climaxes in the only use of the independent nominative first person *anaku*, one of two uses of the first person stative, and is followed immediately by a preterite in the first person and the word for 'self': *anaku amrak/ aḫsusma ramān*. This is the greatest concentration of self-reference in the poem. The effect of this is carried over by a unique repetition of one word from the end of one line (23b) to the beginning of the next (24a). One can only conclude that the poet has deliberately avoided elsewhere the most obvious means of self-reference available to him, and saved it for dramatic effect.[10]

Considering first person fientic verbs, one finds what amounts to patterning. The poet contrives to mention himself at the onset of his text, even before Marduk, the object of his speech:

1) *ludlul bēlu nēmēqī ilu muš[taʾilu?*]
2) [ ]*-bit mūši mupaš[šir urru]*
3) [d]*Marduk bēlu nēmēqī [ilu muštaʾilu*]
4)]*-bit mūši mupaššir ur[ru*]

1) Let me praise the lord of wisdom, de[liberative?] god,
2) [Who restrains?] the night, who rel[eases the day],
3) Marduk, lord of wisdom, [deliberative? god],
4) [Who restrains?] the night, who releases the da[y].

The usual arrangement of such a pair of parallel lines: epithet/epithets: god's name/epithets, has been altered for the sake of self-reference.[11] Thereby the god's name seems to replace a self-reference of the poet rather than an epithet of the god, and is at the same time object of the reference.

Equally striking is the patterning of first person fientic verbs in the remainder of the tablet. The next one occurs in line 50, a passive, one of but thirteen examples of first person verbs in over eighty lines of self-predicating text. The majority of these are intransitive. The speaker's powerlessness to act is thereby adroitly conveyed. By contrast, his protective gods, spirits and genius all act against him in a passage beginning with five preterite verbs (I.43–7). Note also that this passage contains third person fientic verbs in

---

[7] The best example of this is, of course, the Erra epic, in which overt self-reference of the poet is reserved to the end.

[8] For example, Kabti-ilani-Marduk uses the third person, Erra V 42ff.; Saggil-kinam-ubbib the first (Theodicy = *BWL*, 63ff.).

[9] III. 41. *mašmaššumma nāši līʾu[m]*
42. [d]*Marduk-ma išpuran[ni]*
43. *ana* [I]*Šubšī-mešrē-Šakkan ubilla ṣi[mra?]*

41. There was an exorcist carrying a tablet!
42. "It is Marduk who sent me!
43. To Šubšī-mešrē-Šakkan I bring hither suc[cor?] . . ."

The absence of a verb of speaking seems to convey the abruptness of the address. Comparable pairing of the deity and the petitioner by name is found in lines 197ff. of the Gula hymn of Bullutsa-rabi (= Lambert, *Or NS* 36 [1967], 128).

[10] Note but a single occurrence of the oblique *iāti*, II.49, whereby an emphatic passage of introspection separates general observations on the wheel of fortune (34–47) from the passage dealing with the onset of his physical disintegration.

[11] For comparable use, one has to look back to the Agušaya story (see most recently Wilcke, *ZA* 67 [1977], 181ff.), in which Ištar seems to be the "replacive" (or object!) for *lunaʾʾid*. This text too abounds with self-references of the author, some of which Wilcke points out, 183ff. Generally in the texts he chooses with "Ankündigung der Erzähler" the initial self-reference occurs in the second part of the first line.

twelve lines, as many as the poet has given himself in over eighty. This usage, taken with the preceding, renders on a deep verbal level the hostile action against the helpless speaker.

In the second tablet, the speaker asserts himself in a brief flurry of activity. He seeks the aid of gods and men (II.4–8); he refers to his past good deeds (II.23, 29–32), and at last confesses his incomprehension (II.33, 48). Whereas his previous afflictions were loss of status and wealth and vulnerability to threats, now physical attacks begin, first in the form of disease, and for seventy lines the speaker takes no further action. Thus the only first person is an N-stem (II.70). When at last he falls bedridden (II.95), the first person preterite at the beginning of the new scene seems dramatic, as it marks a turning point in the speaker's disintegration.

In the third tablet, he seems to have lapsed into a coma, whereupon he sees a vision. In this and in two succeeding dreams, his redemption is begun in the form of divine intervention and cleansing. Disease and misfortune retreat, and, at the beginning of Tablet IV, Marduk himself takes action in a passage strongly reminiscent of I.43ff., in that twelve or more lines are built on preterite third person verbs. At last the poet himself bursts once more into the text, giving prayers and offerings (thirteen first person verbs in twenty lines).

Suppletive patterning is found with first person pronominal suffixes to verbs. In the first tablet they abound, but in the second there are scarcely any until he describes his torments again, 100ff. After that they vanish until his redemption in Tablet IV. One may note as well that for a text in the first person, the "ventive" is used with surprising rarity, as opposed to the "heroic style," where it is used with surprising frequency. In some cases, one suspects meter is the reason for its use (e.g., I.84f.; cf. GAG §§82b), but in others, its use seems striking and effective, if only because one has seen it so infrequently (e.g., III.34).[12] By such sparing use, one may suggest, the poet has reinvigorated the "personal" aspect of this form. Finally, the first person stative/permansive is rarely used (I.78, II.22). Neither of these examples is of the active type.[13]

Author-based second person, the inversion of first person reference, is found only in the hymnic introduction addressed to Marduk (I.29, 31), and this case is open to question.[14]

From these observations one may ask how is it that this text seems so intensely personal when use of grammatical self-reference is so sparse and depends on the least overt means? Three answers to this question may be offered. One is the poet's judicious patterning of grammatical self-referential elements. The second depends upon one's interpretation of the two categories of self-reference yet to be discussed. The third is the form and medium of the text itself.

As for grammatical distancing, the poet is referred to in the third person in the context of his own discourse, all in cases of direct speech of others about him (I.59ff., II.116). The first example occurs in the "conspiracy" passage discussed below, and contributes to the vividness of this passage. In II.116 we have a stative devoid of time: *ki ḫābil* "how oppressed he is!" The dream sequence is notable for containing both the only use of the third and second person in direct address to the author (III.43, 35).[15] These examples are more remarkable than they seem at first sight, for comparable distancing of speech is not common in Akkadian poetry, a further measure of the poet's inventiveness.[16]

---

[12] While one can suggest lexical rather than poetic reasons for use of the "ventive," in most significant cases the same verb can be found with or without the ventive ending in different contexts, so the lexical argument cannot be used (cf. *atūr* I.78, 1st person, but *itūra* I.84, 3rd person!); parallel: *errub bitušša* (I.62), *īrubamma* (III.33, said of the dream apparition); cf. also *irruṣa* (II.112), etc.

[13] For the "active" stative, see Rowton, *JNES* 21 (1962), 233ff.

[14] In line 31 *at-ta* is questionable. Note the third person at the end of line 32 and the problematic grammar of 31 if a dependent clause is assumed.

[15] *la tapallaḫ* "fear not!" For this as a usual exhortation of apparitions, see Oppenheim, *Dreams*, 200.

[16] Literary instances of a putative first person in the third are mostly incidental (e.g., Gilgamesh OB Yale iv 14ff.), but sometimes modulation of person can be used with great effect (e.g., Erra I, which I hope to treat elsewhere). Deliberate switching of person or standpoint in a text (*enallange*) is a rarer form of distancing, and sometimes (*ipso facto*) seen as a secondary accretion. Examples include Ninmešarra 143ff. (= *YNER* 3, 34 and remarks of Hallo, p. 63), or, a clearer case, the funerary inscription of Adad-guppi (= Gadd, *AnSt* 8 [1958], 46ff.) composed, as tradition of the region seems to have demanded, in the first person (cf. Hawkins, *AnSt* 30 [1980], 139ff.; *CRRAI* 16, 213ff., or, the statue of Idri-Mi), but switching to the third person at the moment of her death (note the remarks of Landsberger, *TTKY* VI No. 5

The poet's use of time of the verb may be considered. The time of the action portrayed in the text ("Erzählte Zeit") is past.[17] This is clear from I.43ff., where the poet tells of the onset of his disaster in a series of twelve preterites. Use of the preterite for narrative continues throughout the poem: the conspiracy opens with the preterite (I.56 *ikkaṣirma*), is vividly described in the present (I.57ff.), and ends with the preterite again (I.65 *ikṣurūnimma*). The section dealing with his rejection by family, friends, and community (I.84–92) likewise begins with a preterite (*itūra*, I.84), switches to present in the middle (I.86ff.), and ends again on the preterite (I.92). When rejection becomes slander and criticism (I.93–7), the author again ends with a pair of preterites (*ul arši, ul amur*). When slander turns to outright aggression (I.99–104), the whole section is marked with preterites, but now in the third person. When describing his own reaction to all this, he switches to the present again (I.107f.: *adammuma, ušaṣrap*), and uses *t*- and *tan*-forms (I.105f.: *šutānuḫu, qitaʾʾulu*).

Like balance between past and continuous is found in Tablet II. The tablet, like the first, may or may not open with a first person preterite verb, but in any event time moves forward a year.[18] The next three lines contain three present forms, conveying the speaker's assessment of the situation in which he finds himself, and reverts to the preterite when he describes the actions he took to find out the causes of his misfortune.

These examples are sufficient to demonstrate that the author uses the present to draw the reader into the time of his discourse. Since he uses the present in moments of introspection and in statements about his feelings, or for vivid narration, and, insofar as the present tense and autobiographical narrative are inherently contradictory, one can assign the present tense of the verb particular self-referential value.[19]

Use of verbal *t*-infixes poses one of the most difficult problems for students of Akkadian poetry. Grammarians assign two axes of meaning to the same infix, a theory suported by the possibility of having two *t*-infixes in the same verb. The one main axis is ethical, reflexive, or medio-passive;[20] the other is temporal.[21] When, as is usually the case, only one infix is found, choice between the ethical and temporal meanings can be difficult to make, especially in poetry. While the passive force of the *t*-infix is well attested in the text, the perfect or ethical force is used rather sparingly in conjunction with preterites and presents, and this commands one's attention.

T-forms tend to occur in clusters (I:73–6, three instances, no other clear case in the whole tablet!); II.71–81 (five instances), II.89–91 (three instances), II Si 55.10ff. (at least five instances). In I.71–81 and 89–91 the *t*-forms (perfects) replace presents, but in I.73–6 and II Si 55.10ff. they replace preterites. This illustrates the capacity of the perfect to serve both past and present, or its "participation in two contrasting spheres" as Jacobsen put it.[22]

The two spheres in question here, I suggest, are the time of the action portrayed in the discourse (preterite), and the time of the discourse itself (present). How else can an alternation like *ēme* in I.71 and *ēteme* in I.79 be explained? The self-referential nature of such usage is obvious.

Turning now to the fourth category of self-reference, the use of certain suprasegmental poetic devices, one may look closely at two "poems within the poem."

= *Halil Edhem hatira Kitabi* I [1947], 141). Intriguing use of person switch is found in mathematical problem texts, wherein the first person speaker of the problem (= the master) is referred to in the third person (by the teacher) in the solution, itself cast in the second person to the student (so Thureau-Dangin, *RA* 33 [1936], 56).

[17] I borrow from Günter Miller, "Erzählzeit und erzählte Zeit," *Festschrift Paul Kluckhohn und Hermann Schneider* . . . , (1948), 196ff., especially p. 202. For further discussion of this from a critical point of view, see for example Gennet, *Figures*, 228ff.; A. A. Mendilow, *Time and the Novel* (1952) and E. Benveniste, "De la subjectivité dans le language," *Problèmes*, 263.

[18] Reading II.1 as *šattamma* (*CAD* B, 52; *AnSt* 30 [1980], 106) has the merit of dispensing with the intratextually unparalleled verbal logogram read by Lambert (*akšud*[ud]), but does not seem to me to make such good sense with the following lines. For 119 I suggest *a?-kàš?-šad a-na ur-ru iš-ši-ra da-me-iq-tum* "I will attain to daylight and good will befall me."

[19] Mendilow, *Time*, 106f. has pointed out that first person narrative by its nature is written backwards from the present, and so has difficulty creating the illusion of presentness that the third person can enjoy, in that the action is naturally felt as having already taken place.

[20] For ethical *t*-forms, see *GAG* § 92.

[21] For the problem of temporal *t*-forms, see Goetze, *JAOS* 56 (1936), 297ff.; von Soden, *GAG* § 80, *Studi Semitici* 4 (1961), 42f.; *AS* 16 (1965), 104; Gelb, *BiOr* 12 (1955), 110.

[22] Jacobsen, *MSL* 4, 7*.

I. 41–50:

41) *ultu ūmu* ^{d}En[. . .] nu [. . .]
42) *ù qarrādu* ^{d}En.[ ] *pūsu*[ ]
43) *iddanni ilī šadāšu īmid*
44) *ipparku* ^{d}*ištarī ibēš*
45) *islit šēd dumqī ša idīja*
46) *iprud lamassīma šanamma išeʾʾ*[*e*]
47) *innitịr baltī duʾūti utammil*
48) *simtī ipparis* (var. *-iš*) *tarāna* (var. *-i*) *išḫiṭ*
49) *iššaknānimma idāt piritti*
50) *ušteṣī ina bitīja kamāti arpud*

41) From the day [the lord . . .]
42) And the most valiant hero [the lord . . .]
43) My own god threw me over and disappeared,
44) My own goddess broke rank and vanished,
45) My guiding genius at my side veered off,
46) My protective spirit broke away in search of another,
47) My manliness dwindled, my presence was sapped,
48) My fairest qualities were lopped off (var: took wing) and leapt for cover.
49) Horrifying signs began to beset me,
50) I was forced from my house, I ran about outside.

The limits of this poem are marked off by Marduk's action and the speaker's flight.[23] Between these two limits, all but two of the lines begin with a verb, and of the two remaining, one has a verb in second position. This patterning of verbs, used here to emphasize the abrupt onset of the author's misfortune, is not repeated until his redemption in IV.1ff. Within the two-line frame provided by 41f. and 49f., there are three sets of parallel lines, fully replacive and partly antithetical. On the level of sound, the parallel lines are tied to each other and to their frame by rhyme and assonance: *ipparku*/*iprud*/*arpud*; *islit*/*išḫiṭ*/*piritti*. The vowel coloring of the passage is overwhelmingly i/a over u:

i	=	45%	u	=	14%
a	=	32%	e	=	7%
ia	=	2%			

A level of contiguous dimensional logic is added. Between the framing lines is a regular descent from Marduk to personal god to protective spirits to internal physical vitality and vigor (*baštu*) to its external manifestation (*simtu*). The poet describes what would today be called his "whole person," highest spiritual perception to basic sexuality, using peculiarly Mesopotamian terms.[24] Perhaps a hint of contiguous dimensional logic is found as well in the arrangement of the verbs. Nearly all have to do with forsaking, fleeing, and loss. They are found regularly deployed at the opposite ends of the lines, in effect diffusing the action from the center in mirror image of the fleeing elements, away from the downwards central progression of the passage's speaker-centered logic. The first person verb at the end of the frame is the logical outcome of the third person (Marduk) with which it began, as well as the exocentric third persons following thereafter. The motivation for all this phonic, semantic, logical, and dimensional art is none other than the self-reference of the author. This is why the passage has such internal unity and is so effective poetically.

One case proves no argument, so a second may be considered (I.69–83):

69. *tuššu u napraku ušamgarū elīja*
70. *muttallu pīja apātiš īteš ʾu*
71. *šaptāja ša ittaṣbarā ḫašikkiš ēme*
72. *šapūtum šāgimātī šaqummeš* x-*še*-[. . .]
73. *šaqātum rīšaja iknuš qaqqar*[*šu*?]
74. *libbī kabbarā piritti utan*[*niš*]
75. *rapaštum irātī agašgū itteʾ*[*i*]
76. *šādiḫā aḫāja kila*$^{?}$*tta ītaḫzā*
77. *ša eṭilliš attallaku ḫalāl almad*
78. *šarrāḫākuma atūr ana rēši*
79. *ana rapši kimāti ēteme ēdāniš*
80. *sūqa abaʾʾama turruṣa uzunāti*
81. *errub ekalliš iṣappurā īnāti*
82. *āli kī ajjābi nikilmanni*
83. *tušāma nakrāti nandurtu mātī*

69. Falsehood and libel they were trying to lend credence against me,
70. My mouth, once proud, was muzzled like a . . . ,
71. My lips, which used to discourse, became those of a deaf man,
72. My stentorian shouts . . . struck dumb,
73. My proudful head shunted earthward,

[23] As read by Lambert, the poem was framed by words of the same root (*daliḫtamma*, *dalḫa* in 51), a neat parallel for the second example, but the Nimrud piece seems to exclude this reading. Note that Lambert sees no reference to Marduk's role in the speaker's suffering in this passage, but I have read that into 41f.

[24] A. L. Oppenheim, *Ancient Mesopotamia*, 1970, 198ff.

74. My stout heart turned shaky for terror,
75. My broad breast brushed aside by a novice,
76. My splendid arms seized limp,
77. Walking proudly once, I learned slinking,
78. I, so grand, turned servile.
79. To my vast family I became a loner,
80. As I went through the streets, ears were pricked up,
81. I would enter the palace—eyes were squinting at me.
82. My city was glowering at me like an enemy,
83. Belligerent and hostile would seem my land.

Here the passage is framed by similar-sounding words at the beginning of the framing lines (*tuššu, tušāma*). Within this frame, the verb patterning is more subtle than that of the first example. A passage of seven lines dealing with speech, head, heart, chest, and arms is laid out on the pattern attribute: organ, organ: attribute. The vertical contiguous progression from top down recalls the similar progression of the first example, but continues beyond the seven-line section with an elegant conceit: as the reader is prepared for a reference to legs, the poet switches to walking, and proceeds to ever widening concentric horizontal circles: his kin, the public street, the government, the city, and at last his country. There the frame ends. The ends of the framing lines mirror the overall progression: *elīja/mātī.*

The rhyme in this passage is outstanding. The syllables *ati* are found seven times in fifteen lines, including two occurrences in the last line, and thereupon disappear from the text until a single, non-rhyming occurrence twelve lines later. Patterning of vowel sounds is rather similar to that of the first sub-poem:[25]

a =	46%	u =	17%
i =	25%	e =	8%
ia =	4%		

Within the framing is yet another definition of the author's person, beginning with his power of speech as the center of his self-presenting being, proceeding vertically through his physical self, and, when reaching the legs, proceeding to the outer limits of his place in humanity. One notes that the spiritual man begins with god and ends with his inmost being and its outer signs, while worldly man begins with speech and ends with the limits of his land. This poem completes the definition begun in the preceding one, and, like it, finds its unity and beauty in the self-reference of the poet.

As for the "cinematic" technique, topical examples of it have already been considered in the use of present and perfect in alternation with preterite and stative. Expansion of this device to include a whole passage forms one of the most remarkable episodes in Akkadian poetry (I.59–64):

59. *šumma ištēnma napištašu ušatbakšu*
60. *iqabbī šanū ušatbī tērtuš*
61. *ša kīma šalši qīptašu aṭammaḫ*
62. *errub bituššu rēbū itammī*
63. *haššu pī hašē šubalkut*
64. *šeššu u sību ireddū šēduššu*

59. If the first "I'll make him waste his life"
60. Says the second, "I'll take over his command"[26]
61. While likewise the third "I'll get my hands on his post"
62. "I'll force his house" vows the fourth
63. As the fifth fills his lungs[27]
64. Sixth and seventh follow in his train!

The poet surprises seven conspirators talking among themselves. The first four are just saying what they will do, the fifth is about to chime in, while sixth and seventh have not yet begun to speak. The effect of the first two speaking at once is conveyed by one verb of speech seeming to serve two speakers, themselves interchangeable by being placed in an either-or construction.[28] By contrast, the speeches of third and fourth come hard upon each other without a verb of

[25] Of course variants alter the count somewhat, so the precise percentages are of less importance than their overall proportion.

[26] The putative author seems to have achieved political or military distinction (Lambert, *BWL*, 296f., 21f.), and, in fact, uses an elaborate military metaphor in this passage, hence my "militarization" of this term.

[27] Literally, "agitates the lungs' opening" (with pun on lung/fifth, here feebly conveyed by "fills/fifth"). I take this bizarre expression to refer to a sharp intake of breath preceding an excited attempt to intervene in the conversation.

[28] Contra Borger, *JCS* 18 (1964), 51 and Lambert, *ad loc.*, I see no reason not to take *šumma* in its usual sense "if." As for II.28, *ikribī šarri šī ḫidūtī / ù nigūtašu ana dameqti šumma*, one may speculate that *šu-ma* is meant, parallel to *ši* in the preceding line. In II.88 *ašnan šumma daddariš alaᵓᵓut* "if" fits well: "If it be grain, I choke it down like stinkweed."

speaking intervening. The reader is plunged thereby into the midst of the talk, not only by the use of the present in the subjective manner already alluded to, but by the very grammatical logic of the lines. What atrocities the last three speakers will perpetrate is left to the imagination of the reader, an intriguing variation of the classical figure aposiopesis.[29]

The self-referential devices studied above fall into two main categories: those inherently self-referential, including appropriate parts of speech and elements of inflection, and those of assigned self-reference, including manipulation of time, framing and dimensional logic, and patterning of sounds. One is struck by the sparing use of the inherently self-referential devices and the increased impact they thereby acquire. Of the assigned ones, the first acquired its value as a means of discourse, the second, as a means of self-presentation, but what of the third? Assigning cognitive extra-phonemic value to sounds, as has been done by some poets and linguists, goes beyond the limits of this analysis.[30] Yet one can see in the poet's use of sound patterning in the two inner poems treated here a coloring or modulation the effect of which is supra-segmental self-reference. It is the author's assignment of literary value to neutral elements that helps make the text poetry in a modern understanding of that term.[31]

One further point: Can one see deliberate self-reference in the form of the text itself? The outer framing element of the text is a hymn, a form which, unlike narrative poetry, presupposes for its effect a concerned, identifiable speaker. This hymnic quality adds authorial speaking voice in a way even a first-person narrative could not. Yet, this very quality is a vitiation of simple self-presentation in that a hymn, unlike first person narrative, requires an explicit "thou" as well as an "I," also concerned and identifiable, but not usually the reader.[32] So even the form, which ostensibly stresses the speaker, by its nature divides that stress and attention with a "thou" who relegates the reader to third place. One may suggest that the author's avoidance of straight self-presentation, such as autobiography or pseudo-inscription would allow him, in favor of a hymnic format, is of a piece with his avoidance of conventional, overt means of self-reference. One concedes, however, that self-naming of the petitioner or speaker in hymns and prayers is occasionally found.[33] To balance the hymnic frame, the inner portion of the text is a story narrative,[34] but with abundant present

[29] This refers to rhetorical silence, e.g., "If you don't give me the money, I'll . . ."

[30] One has occasionally argued that u-sounds are inherently masculine, large and dominant, i-sounds small, feminine, and dependent, and (presumably), that a-sounds lie partway in between. For discussion of this in linguistics, see O. Jespersen, "Symbolic Value of the Vowel I," *Philologica* I (1922), 15–33; E. Sapir, "A Study in Phonetic Symbolism," *Journal of Experimental Psychology* 12 (1929), 225–39. The idea was taken up for Semitics by A. Gazor-Ginzberg, "Simbolism u::i kak vyraženie pola (roda) i razmerov v semitskih yazykah," *Palestinskij Sbornik* 21 (1970), 100–10. A variant notion was adduced by Jacobsen, *JNES* 19 (1960), 114ff. While such an analysis of vowel quality fits these passages, I do not offer it as a literary interpretation.

[31] Cf. Ricoeur, *Philosophy Today* 12 (1968), 129.

[32] A Mesopotamian attempt to avoid this is the hymn of self-praise (divine or royal), where "I" is fused with "Thou," perhaps to gain unique authority for the speaking voice, but liturgical reasons have been suggested as well (von Soden, *RA* 52 [1958], 132); for discussion see Lambert, *OrNS* 36 (1967), 107ff. One is struck by the fact that neither the author nor Marduk ever speaks directly in this text. Gods' speaking is a theme as old in cuneiform literature as the stele of the vultures; that Marduk never speaks in the narrative lends him remoteness no description could emulate. On the other hand, that the author says nothing direct in his own discourse is but another example of his apparent occlusion. Gods were sometimes expected to be the "reader" of their hymns and prayers; see Gadd, *Iraq* 25 (1963), 177ff.; Hallo, *JAOS* 88 (1968), 75ff.

[33] For examples of named petitioners in prayers, see Lambert, *JAOS* 88 (1968), 130ff.; Gadd, *Iraq* 25 (1963), 177ff. (here, curiously, introduced narratively, rather than precatively, in the third person, cf. Gadd, p. 177 note 3).

[34] While space does not permit analysis of this complicated aspect of the text, we have here the continuity and conflict basic to the notion "story," and, on the broadest level: setting (the hymn! = I.1–40), initiating event (II.4ff. = 112ff. etc.), consequences (II.49ff. etc.), reactions (II.33 etc.), and so forth, as well as final resolution (H. Gese's "happy-ending model": Gattung des Klageerhörungs-paradigmas, cf. *Lehre und Wirklichkeit in der alten Weisheit* [1958], 61ff.). In simplest terms, see B. Bruce, "What Makes a Good Story," *Language Arts* 55 (1978), 460–66; on a more sophisticated level, with extensive bibliography, see T. A. Van Dijk, ed., *Story Comprehension* = *Poetics* 9/1–3 (1980). Note that the classical criterion of "epic narrative," that it begin "*in medias res*," is met in our text, in that the author's antecedent

tense exclamations or introspective moments. These present a critical problem: are they "internal monologue," that is, addressed by the author, fictively at least, to himself,[35] or are they addressed to the reader, and hence metaleptic in intent, in that the author has broken the narrative screen,[36] or are they addressed to Marduk himself? In any case, they are exceptionally direct instances of self-reference.

Much of the poetic quality and originality of the Poem of the Righteous Sufferer lies in its being a highly self-referential piece and in its attainment of this not so much by overt means as by effect. Self-effacement on all levels of discourse from morphemics to outer form of the whole text is the very means by which it attains its personal quality, and serves to convey its message of submission and uncertainty subliminally as well as expressly.

Self-reference is scarcely the only topic of interest in the Poem of the Righteous Sufferer. Besides poetics per se, the place of this work within cuneiform literature both of the penitential and self-presentory type needs further work. The message or thought content of the text merits study for its own sake as well as for its relationship to other, comparable, texts.[37] Yet, I submit, the poet's self-reference leads directly to critical appreciation of his genius and thereby justifies itself as a fruitful topic of inquiry.

---

behavior is described only after his fall (contrary to the Job story, for example).

[35] While this is generally conceded to be a modern invention, its properties seem here foreshadowed: "one explanation of the vividness that this technique is capable of achieving lies in the effect of presentness produced by the fact that such writing is in the present tense [as opposed to autobiography, BRF]; it gains thereby in immediacy what it loses for most readers by its use of private and esoteric forms of expression, association and symbols which hinder easy identification with the protagonists," Mendilow, *Time*, 113. Note also that our text uses the restricted point of view as well.

[36] For metalepsis, or intrusion of the real author, see Genette, *Figures*, 243ff.

[37] For discussion of this topic, see J. J. Stamm, *Das Leiden des Unschuldigen in Babylon und Israel* (1946), 16ff.; J. Gray, "The Book of Job in the Context of Near Eastern Literature," *ZATW* 82 (1970), 251–69.

THE TRIBULATIONS OF MARDUK
THE SO-CALLED "MARDUK ORDEAL TEXT"

TIKVA FRYMER-KENSKY
ANN ARBOR, MICHIGAN

ONE OF THE BEST KNOWN, MOST DISCUSSED AND LEAST UNDERSTOOD TEXTS FROM MESOPOTAMIA is *KAR* 143 + duplicates, customarily (but wrongly) labelled as the "Marduk Ordeal Text." This text is cast in the form of a cultic commentary, similar to *KAR* 307 (Ebeling, *TuL*, no. 7) and *TuL* nos. 8 and 10, but written in the Assyrian dialect. The text was first edited by Zimmern in *Zum babylonischen Neujahrsfest* [Zweiter Beitrag, *BSGW* Phil. Hist. kl 70/5], 1918, as text no. 1. Zimmern interpreted the text as an account of the "Passion and Triumph of Bel-Marduk" at the Spring New Year's festival, and drew numerous parallels between this text and the passion accounts of the New Testament (12–14). This mode of interpretation was continued by Langdon, *The Epic of Creation*, 1923, who entitled the text "The Death and Resurrection of Bel-Marduk" (36–64). While Pallis in *The Babylonian Akitu Festival*, 1926, rejected numerous Christological parallels, he continued to stress the death of Bel, the lamentation over him, his subsequent restoration and the rejoicing over his resurrection (pp. 200f).

A different interpretation was offered by P. Jensen, "Bel im Kerker und Jesus im Grabe," *OLZ* 27 (1924), 573–80, who argued that the death of Bel is never explicitly mentioned, and that the few statements that might indicate his death had been falsely interpreted. According to Jensen, the text is an account of how Bel was taken captive and held a prison for trial for no apparent offense, and eventually released. Jensen also drew attention to parallels between this text and the passion story, but stood the parallel on its head: to him the death and resurrection of Jesus was a secondary development of an earlier account in which an innocent Jesus was imprisoned in the Spring but was later miraculously released.

These different interpretations hinged on the term *ḫursan*. To Zimmern it was the "cosmic mountain" (*Weltberg*) where the realm of the dead was located; therefore its use demonstrated that Bel had gone down to the netherworld from which he was subsequently resurrected. Apparent allusions to "graves" and to "bringing to life" in lines 10–11 seemed to support the "death and resurrection" interpretation, as did line 13 which Zimmern restored as *iḫteliq ina libbi na*[*pšate*], "he disappeared from life." Jensen, on the other hand, suggested that the term *šapte ša ḫuršan*, literally, "'lips' of the *ḫuršan*" had to refer to the edge of river or stream rather than mountain, and therefore referred to the river of the ordeal.

These interpreters regarded this text purely as a religious commentary, as either a major theological composition about a dying and resurrected Marduk or as a kind of "Fastnachtsspiel" (Jensen, 577) which dramatized the god's imprisonment. Doubt about the theological nature of the work was first raised by de Liagre Böhl, who characterized it as a parody emanating from anti-Marduk Assyria at the time of Sennacherib. Nevertheless, de Liagre Böhl believed that the parody underscored Bel's normal imprisonment in the netherworld (*Christus und die Religionen der Erde II*, Franz Köcher, ed., 1951, 477).

The major study of the text has been that of von Soden, who reedited the texts of the composition ("Gibt es ein Zeugnis dafür, dass die Babylonier an die Wiederauferstehung Marduks geglaubt haben?," *ZA* 51, 1955, 130–66) and published an additional fragment of the composition ("Ein neues Bruchstück des assyrischen Kommentars zum Marduk-Ordal," *ZA* 52, 1956, 224–34). He drew attention to two significant differences between this text and other cultic commentaries such as *TuL* 7, 8, and 10. 1) The text is written in the Assyrian dialect, unlike the other commentaries, which, although recovered from Assyria, are written in Babylonian; 2) The colophon involves curses on anyone who fails to spread the knowledge of the composition to others, indicating that this text, like the Erra Epic and Enuma Elish, was intended for wide distribution. The cultic commentary *TuL* 7, on the other hand, specifically enjoins the reader against revealing its secrets to outsiders. Von Soden also argued (as had Jensen) that *šaptu* indicated that Marduk had gone to the ordeal. The intention to give wide distribution to a text in which Bel is punished after a judicial proceeding, and the use of the Assyrian dialect, indicated to von Soden that the Assyrian populace was targeted for propaganda. He suggested that the anti-Babylonian actions of Assyria, specifically at the time of the destruction of Babylon in 689, had to be justified to the Assyrians, who held Marduk in some reverence, and this justification had to be presented in religious rather than political-pragmatic terms.

Von Soden's interpretation has been generally accepted, and the text has been referred to since then as the "Marduk Ordeal Text." Within this political context, subsequent commentators have refocused attention on the form of this text as a cultic commentary. Thus Landsberger states that the text is a "scurrilous creation of the scribal guilds" in which the "Assyrian Party" interprets the cultic events of Babylon, particularly those of the New Year's festival, to refer to the "youthful crime" (*Jugendvergehen*) of Marduk (*BBEA*, 15f. n. 9). To Jacobsen the text is "an Assyrian commentary interpreting events at the New Year's festival in Babylon as phases in a trial of Marduk for treason against Ashur" (Religious Drama in Ancient Mesopotamia," *Unity and Diversity*, Goedicke and Roberts, eds., 1975, 76). However, the anti-Babylonian bias of this text is not clear, and it seems likely that the text justifies and celebrates, not the subjugation of Marduk, but his ultimate vindication after his tribulations. The events that prompted the creation of the text would then be, not the destruction of Babylon in 689, but the return of the statue of Marduk to Babylon in 669.

The fragmentary condition of our exemplars, the linguistic peculiarities and difficult style of the text, the esoteric nature of all cultic commentaries and our lack of knowledge of the cultic events "interpreted" by this text make it difficult to understand precisely what is going on and what happens ot Marduk. The many difficulties are not ameliorated by the fact that there are two different versions of the composition, one from Aššur and the other from Nineveh. The Assyrian version is represented by three exemplars, *KAR* 143 and *KAR* 219 (edited by von Soden, *ZA* 51, 132–53) and *CTN* 2 268 (edited by Postgate, *CTN* 2, 1973, 243–44). This version seems fairly fixed, and there are only minimal differences among the exemplars. The other tradition, the Ninevite, does not seem to have been as rigidly fixed. This is represented by five fragmentary copies: Langdon, *JRAS*, 1931, 111f. (reedited by von Soden, *ZA* 51, 153–7), which includes parts of two distinct tablets; *BM* 134503 (edited by von Soden, *ZA* 52, 224–34); *BM* 134504, which may belong to the same tablet as *BM* 134503 (published by Thompson, *Iraq* VII, 1940 at fig. 16 no. 37 and p. 109; reedited by Postgate, *ZA* 60, 1970, 124–5); and *S* 1903, which may also be a fragment of the same tablet as *BM* 134503 (edited by Postgate, *ZA* 60, 124–7). The two versions of the text have many lines in common, but these lines do not necessarily occur in the same sequence. This may indicate that the order of the lines in this composition was not necessarily determined by the temporal sequence of the ritual, nor was it fixed by the chronology of the political events that underly the composition. The Ninevite version is extremely fragmentary, and cannot be understood without the guidance of the Assyrian text, and for this reason I will follow the sequence in the Assyrian recension.

The text opens with the arrival in Babylon of Nabu and probably Tašmetum from Borsippa (lines 1–11). As the text begins, someone (who is later shown to be Bel) is being held prisoner and is being sought for. The mention of Borsippa and of "his father" in line 8 indicates that it is Nabu who has come looking for his father Bel, who is being held captive. A female is described as praying for Bel's welfare: this is probably Tašmetum, for she is said to have come on Bel's behalf in line 16 (as restored from the Ninevite Text *ZA* 52, 226: 22–23). We would normally expect such an arrival to be part of a ritual like the Akitu festival; here it is described as somehow connected to the captivity of Bel. The text then continues with a digression between the introduction of the searching Nabu and Tašmetum and the explanation of the procession that begins in line 16. These four fragmentary lines (12–16) have been variously restored. They appear to indicate what was found in the search: the place where Bel is being held, and the condition of Bel (or that of the "messenger" who is said to be seeking him in line 4).

The next section, lines 16–29, returns to the procession, beginning with Tašmetum and then discussing those (gods?) "who went with him" (Bel) and "who did not go with him." There is (or has been) a trial of various individuals (gods?) and the text gives the fate of those who did and those who did not "stand with Bel." Since the mention of this "cast of characters" occurs in conjunction with the description of a procession, perhaps the procession is being interpreted in the light of such a trial, mentioned as a flashback. In the parallel section in one of the Nineveh texts (edited in *ZA* 51, 153f), there is no specific mention of a trial. The lines are in a different order, with *ZA* 51, 153 (von Soden text C) line 15 = A 25, 16 = A 22, 17 = A 19, 18 = A 17/18 and 19 = A 9. The mention of "criminals" is interspersed with the description of the procession, thus indicating that the "criminals" are somehow involved in the procession; and the order of the lines in this shorter Nineveh recension indicates that the procession is related to lines 8–11, in which Nabu and Tašmetum search for Bel.

The text goes on to "explain" various ritual items, both those brought in the procession (as apparently the garments in line 30) and possibly those found at the ritual site, and to interpret the various events and objects of the ritual. The composition gives these events a new interpretation by providing them with an application that relates these events to the politico-religious tribulations of Marduk. The exact sequence of the ritual being interpreted by the commentary is not fully known from other sources, and cannot be reconstructed from this text. The mention of the Bit-Akitu in lines 38, 40 and 66; of the month Nisan (month I) in lines 44 and 51, and the reading of the Enuma Elish in lines 34 and 54 all indicate that the events that are being given this new significance by the commentary are parts of the New Year celebration. There is, however, a mention of a footrace of Kislev (month IX) in lines 57f: this may be a "flashback" or may indicate that the commentary does not confine itself to the events of the New Year festival. The ritual "explanation" culminates with the interpretation of the "door of many holes." This is clearly the end of the Assyrian version, for there are approximately 10 lines left uninscribed on the tablet before the colophon begins. There is other material in the Ninevite tradition, but it is too fragmentary to follow.

KAR 143 + 219

[ ]*ka-li*

[ ]*un-ni*

[ ]*ú-še-ṣa-áš-šu*

[ ]x-*da* LÚ A.KIN *ša* EN.MEŠ-*šú man-nu ú-še-ṣa-áš-šu*

5 [ ]*il-lak-u-ni ú-še-ṣa-áš-šu-ni*

[*i-*]*ra-kab-u-ni a-na ḫur-sa-an šu-ú il-lak*

[ ]*il-lak-u-ni* É *šu-ú ina* UGU *šap-te ša ḫur-sa-an ina* ŠÀ *i-ša-a*ʾ*-ú-lu-šú*

[^{d}*Nabu ša* TA *Bár-s*]*íp*^{ki} *il-lak-an-ni a-na šul-me ša* AD-*šú ša ṣa-bit-u-ni šu-ú il-la-ka*

[ ]*ša ina su-qa-qa-a-te i-du-lu-u-ni* ^{d}*Bel ú-ba-a*ʾ*-ma a-a-ka ṣa-bit*

10 [^{d}*Taš-me-tum*$^{?}$]*ša* ŠU^{II}-*šá tar ṣa-a-ni a-na* ^{d}*Sin* ^{d}*Šamaš tu-ṣal-la ma-a* ^{d}*Bel bal-li-*[*s*]*u*

[M]EŠ *ša tal-lak-u-ni* KÁ *qa-bu-re*$^{!}$ *šu-ú tal-lak tu-ba*[*-a*ʾ*-š*]*u*

12 [EN.MEŠ$^{?}$ *ú-*]*ma-a-še ša ia* KÁ *ša* É.SAG.ÍL *i-za-zu-u-ni* LÚ EN.NUN.MEŠ-*šú šu-nu ina* UGU-*šú paq-du i-na*[ ]

[ ]*qu-re*[ ] *e-pi-šu-ni a-ki* DINGIR.MEŠ *e-si-ru-šu-ni iḫ-te-liq ina* ŠÀ-*bi* [ ]

[ ]*ip*$^{?}$*-re ú*[*-pal*$^{!?}$*-*]*láḫ* TA ŠÀ-*bi us-se-ri-du-niš-*[*šu*]

15 [ ]*ša ina* KI.TA-*šú* SÍG$^{?}$ *tar-ri-bu ša lab-bu-šu-ni mi-iḫ-ṣé ša maḫ-ḫu-ṣu-ni šu-nu ina* BE.MEŠ-*šú* [*ṣar-pu*$^{?}$]

16 [^{d}*Taš-me-*]*tum ša is*[*-si-*]*šú kam-mu-sa-tu-ni a-na šul-me-šú ta-ta*[*-lak*]

[*š*]*a is-si-šú la il*[*-la*]*k-u-ni ma-a la* EN *ḫi-iṭ-ṭi a-na-ku ma-a la us-sa-ta-am-maḫ* [ ] (C:18)

[*ina muḫḫ*]*i* ^{d}*Aš-šur de-na-ni ina pa-ni-šú ip-ti-u de-na-ni i-l*[*am*$^{?}$*-mad*$^{?}$]

[*ša is-*]*si-šú la il-lak-u-ni* DUMU ^{d}*Aš-šur šu-u-tú ma-ṣu-ru šu-ú ina muḫ-ḫi-šu pa-qid* URU *ber-tú ina muḫ-ḫi-šú i-n*[*a-aṣ-ṣar*$^{?}$] (C:17)

20 [SAG.DU *š*]*a ina* ^{giš}*tal-li ša* ^{d}*Be-lit-*KÁ.DINGIR.RA^{ki} *e*ʾ*-la-an-ni* SAG.DU *ša* EN *ḫi-iṭ-ṭi ša is-si-šú i-z*[*i-zu-u-ni*]

[*id-d*]*u-ku-šú-ni šu-tú* SAG.DU *ina* ^{UZU}[GÚ$^{?}$] *ša* ^{d}*Be-lit-*KÁ.DINGIR.RA^{ki} *e-ta-a*ʾ[*-lu*]

[^{d}*Nabu ša*] *a-na Bár-sip*^{ki} *i-sa-ḫar-u-ni il-lak-u-ni* ^{giš}*tal*[*-tal-l*]*e ša ina* ŠÀ-*šú is-sa-na-la*[*-a*ʾ] (C:16)

[*ur-ki*] *ša* ^{d}*Bel ina ḫur-sa-an il-lik-u-ni* URU *ina* UGU[*-šu*] *it-ta-bal-kat qa-ra-bu ina* ŠÀ *up*[*-pu-šú*]

[G]I.ÚR.MEŠ *ša* ŠAḪ.MEŠ *ša ina* IGI KASKAL *ša* ^{d}*Nabu ki-i* TA *Bár-sip*^{ki} *il-la-kan*^{an}*-ni i-kar-ra-bu-ni*

25 ^{d}*Nabu ša il-lak-an-ni ina muḫ-ḫi i-za-zu-u-ni im-mar-u-ni* EN *ḫi-iṭ-ṭi ša* TA ^{d}BEL *šu-tú* [ ] (C:15?)

[*a-*]*ki-i ša* TA ^{d}*Bel šu-tú-ni im*[*-mar-*]*šú*

[L]Ú MAŠ.MAŠ.MEŠ *ša ina pa-na-tú il-lak-u-ni ši-ip-tu i-ma-an-nu-ni* ERIM.MEŠ-*šú šu-ni ina pa-na-tú-šú ú-na-bu*[*-u-ni*$^{?}$] (C:22)

LÚ *maḫ-ḫu-u ša ina* IGI ^{d}*Be-lit-*KÁ.DINGIR.RA^{ki} *il-la-ku-u-ni* LÚ *mu-pa-si-ru šu-u a-na* GAB-*šá i-bak*[*-ki*]

[*ú*$^{?}$*-*]*ma-a a-na ḫur-sa-an ub-bu-lu-šú ši-i ta-ta-rad ma-a* ŠEŠ-*u-a* ŠES-*u-a*

30 [x] x *la-bu-su-šu ša a-na* ^{d}GAŠAN-*Uruk*^{ki} *ú-bal-u-ni ku-zip-pe-šú šu-nu it-ta*[*-aṣ-ṣu-ši*]

lu-u KÙ.BABBAR *lu-u* GUŠKÌN *lu-u* NA$_{4}$.MEŠ *ša* TA É.SAG.ÍL *a-na* É.KUR.MEŠ *ú-še-ṣu-ú-ni É-su šu-ú t*[*u*]

^{TÚG}*še-er-i-tu ša la-bu-šu-ni ina ka-dam-me* ⌈*e*⌉*-*[*sip*$^{?}$]

ši-iz-bu ša ina IGI ^{d}Ištar ša URUK^{ki} i-ḫal-li-bu-ni né-mi-il ši-i tu-ra-bu-šú-ni re-e-mu ú-ka-al-lim-⌜ša⌝ [-ni]

e-nu-ma e-liš ša da-bi-ib-u-ni ina IGI ^{d}Bel ina ^{ITU}Nisan i-za-mur-šú-ni ina UGU ša ṣa-bit-u-ni [šu-ú]

35 ṣu-ul-le-e-šú-nu ú-ṣal-la su-ra-re-šú-nu ú-sa-ra-ar

[x x x] šu-tú i-da-bu-ub ma-a dam-qa-a-te ša ^{d}Aššur ši-na e-ta-pa-áš ma-a mi-i-ni ḫi[-iṭ-ṭu-šu$^{?}$]

[ ]ša AN-e i-da-gal-u-ni a-na ^{d}Sin ^{d}Šamaš ú-ṣal-la ma-a bal-li[-ṭa-an-ni$^{?}$]

[ša] qaq-qu-ru i-da-gal-u-ni ḫu-ur-ri$^{!?}$-šú ina UGU[-šú] kar-ru-ni ša TA ŠÀ ḫur-sa-an il[-lik/lak-u-n]i

[t]a ^{d}Bel a-na É a-ki-ti la ú-ṣu-ni x ú ša LÚ ṣa-ab-te i-na-áš-si i-si-šú [-]ib

40 [^{d}Be-lit-K]Á.DINGIR.RA^{ki} ša ina ŠÀ É á-ki-it la il-lak-u-ni MÍ šá-ki-in-tú ša É [ši-i$^{?}$]

[ ]ti É tu-di-i ma-a É uṣ-ri ina ŠU^{II}-ki ú[ ]

[^{d}Be-lit-KÁ.DINGIR.]RA^{ki} ša SÍG GI$_6$ ina ku-tal-li-šá-ni SÍG tab-ri-bu ina pa-ni-š[á-ni lab-šat$^{?}$]

[ ]uš-sá da-mu ša ṣur-ri ša tab-ku-ni

[ ]ki ša U$_4$ 8-kam ša ^{ITU}Nisan ŠAḪ ina pa-ni-šá i-ṭa[-ba-ḫu-ni]

45 [ ] šá É ši-i i-šá-a^{ʾ}-lu-ši ma-a man-nu EN ḫi-iṭ-ṭi ma-a [ ]

[ ] ú-bal-u-ni EN ḫi-iṭ-ṭi i [ ]

[ ] il-lak-u-ni áš (or pa$^{?}$)-ge ša a-ki im-ma[

[ ]ú A.MEŠ ár-ḫiš i-ṣa-am-mu [ ]

[ ]ḫu-ni ú-ṣar-ra-ru-u-ni A.MEŠ da-al-ḫu-tu šú-nu [ ]

50 [ ]ne⌜la/na$^{?}$⌝-ba-ak-te i-kar-ra-ru-ni ša qa-du-ur-ti-šu

[ZÍD.D]A ša ina ŠÀ ^{ITU}Nisan a-na ma-gal ma-a^{ʾ}-du-ni ZÍD.DA ⌜x⌝ ki-i ṣa-bit-u-ni i[-]

A.MEŠ ŠU^{II} ša ú-qar-rab-u-ni bi-it ib-ku-ni šu-ú di-i^{ʾ}-a-t[u] [ina ŠÀ]

TÚG še-er-i^{ʾ}-i-tu ša ina muḫ-ḫi-šú ša$^{!}$ i-qa-bu-u-ni ma-a A.MEŠ[ ]

53* si-li-^{ʾ}a-a-te-ši-na šu-ú ina ŠÀ e-nu-ma e-liš iq[-ta-bi]

ki-i AN-e KI-tim la ib-ba-nu-ni ^{d}Anšar it[-tab-ši]

55 ki-i URU u É ib-šu-u-ni šu-ú it-tab-ši A.MEŠ ša ina UGU ^{d}Anšar [ ]

šu-u-tú$^{?}$ ša ḫi-ṭi-šú ina ŠÀ ka-dam-me šu-tú e-si-ip la A.MEŠ la-biš$^{?}$ ka[ ]

li-is-mu ša ina ^{ITU}Kislim ina IGI ^{d}Bel ù ma-ḫa-za-ni gab-bu i[-lab-bu-u-ni$^{?}$]

ki-i ^{d}Aššur ^{d}Nin-urta ina UGU ka-šá-de ša ^{d}Zi-i iš-pur-u[-ni] ^{d}[

ina IGI ^{d}Aššur iq-ṭí-bi ma-a ^{d}Zu-u ka-ši-id ^{d}Aššur a-na ^{d}[x iq-ti-bi]

60 ma-a a-lik a-na DINGIR.MEŠ-ni gab-bu pa-si-ir ú-pa-sa-ar-šú-ni ina UGU [ ]

da-ba-bu gab-bu ša ina ŠÀ-bi LÚ.GALA.MEŠ [ ]

ša ḫa-ba-a-te ša i-ḫab-ba-tu-šú-ni ša ú-šal-pa-tu-šú-ni šu-ú DINGIR.MEŠ AD.MEŠ-šú šu-nu i[-]

UR.ZÍR ša É-sa-bad ib-bir-an-ni LÚ A.KIN šu-u-tú ^{d}Gu-la ina muḫ-ḫi-šú ta-šap-pa-ra

^{KUŠ}E.SÍR ša ina É ^{d}Be-lit-KÁ.DINGIR.RA^{ki} ub-bal-u-ni it-ḫu-ur šu-u-tú ú-še-bal-áš-ši

65 né-mi-il a-na šá-a-šú la ú-šar-u-šú-ni la ú-ṣu-u-ni

^{giš}GIGGIR ša a-na É a-ki-it tal-lak-u-ni ta-la-kan^{an}-ni EN-šá la-áš-šú ša la EN ta-sa-bu-u^{ʾ}

ù ^{d}Sak-ku-ku-tú ša TA URU ta-lab-ba-an-ni ba(/na$^{?}$)-ki-su ši-i TA URU ta-la-bi-a

^{giš}IG bir-ri ša i-qa-bu-u-ni DINGIR.MEŠ šu-nu i-ta-as-ru-šú ina É e-tar-ba ^{giš}IG ina IGI-šú e-te-di-li

69 šu-nu ḫu-ur-ra-a-te ina ŠÀ ^{giš}IG up-ta-li-šú qa-ra-bu ina ŠÀ-bi up-pu-šú

[*I* THE PROCESSION]

[*1.* *The seeking of Bel*]

[ ]

[ ]

[ ]brought (*or* sent) him out

[ ] the messenger of his lords: who sent him out?

5 [that?] he goes. He sent (*or* brought) him out.

[ ] who (*or* he) rides. That one? goes to the *ḫursan*

[ ] who (*or* he) comes. That house at the edge of the *ḫursan*; in (its) midst they question him.

[Nabu, who comes from Bor]sippa: he comes on behalf of his father who is captive.

[ ] who (*or* he) is roaming the streets: is looking for Bel—where is he held?

10 [Tašmetum] whose hands are outspread: she is praying to Sin (and) Shamash, saying "Grant Bel life."

[ ] that she goes: she is going through the gate of the graveyard looking for him.

[*2. The Condition of Bel*]

12 [The str]ongmen$^?$ who stand in the gate of Esaggil: they are his guards who were appointed over him. They gu[ard him?]
[ ] . . . [ ] they made. When the gods confined him, he disappeared from the midst [ ].
[ ] he f[ea]red$^?$. They brought him down from the midst.
15 [ ] which is beneath him. The red wool with which he is clothed: [it is colored] with his blood$^?$ from the wounds where they beat him

[*3. The Procession of the Gods*]

16 [Tašme]tum, who kneels w[ith] him, had gone on his behalf.
[ ], who does not go with him, saying "I am not a criminal," saying "I do not take part [ ]."
[on beha]lf of ^{d}Aššur they opened the case before him, he h[ears$^?$] the case.
[the one] who does not go with him: he is a "son of ^{d}Aššur," he is the guard appointed over him, he g[uards$^?$] him in a fortress-city.
20 [the head w]hich they hang on the gateposts of the "Mistress of Babylon": that is the head of the criminal who stood with him.
21 [ ] they [k]illed him and hung his head on the [nec]k of the "Mistress of Babylon."
[As Nabu] turns and goes to Borsippa he is sprinkled with p[alm]-stalks in its midst—
[after] Bel went to the *ḫursan*, the city revolted against [him$^?$], they made war in its midst—
(and) the "pig-reeds" that are on the way of Nabu when he comes from Borsippa greet him (i.e. the people greet him with the "pig-reeds"?)
25 When Nabu comes, he stands before him and sees him: he is the criminal who from Bel [ ];
[S]ince he is from Bel he s[ee]s him.
The *mašmašu*-"exorcists" who go before him recite formulas: they are his troops who speak before him.
The *maḫḫu*-priest who goes before the "Mistress of Babylon" is the herald: he cries on her breast,
[s]aying, "They have brought him to the *ḫursan*"; she comes down crying "Oh, my brother, oh my brother."

[*II* RITUAL AND *"EXPLANATION"*]

30 [ ] his clothes, which they take to the Lady of Uruk, are his *kuzippu*-garments—they have [brought them out].
(whatever they are carrying), whether silver gold or (precious) stones: (these are the items) which they brought out from Esaggil to the (various) temples. His house[. . . .]
The (divine) *šeritu*-garment in which he (was$^?$) dressed; in the *kadammu* [it is stored$^?$]
The milk which they milk before *Ištar* of Uruk is because she brought him up and he showed her mercy.

34 Enuma Elish, which is said before Bel in Nisan: he$^?$ sings it because he (Bel) is captive (*or*: before Bel who is captive).
35 He prays their prayers, their supplications he implores.
[ ] he speaks, saying, "For the good of ^{d}Aššur he has done this," saying, "What is [his$^?$] s[in$^?$]?"
[and he$^?$,] while looking at the heavens, prays to Sin and Šamaš saying, "grant [me l]ife."
38 [while] looking at the ground—his hole$^{!?}$ is prepared for him when he c[omes (*or* came)] from the midst of the *ḫursan*.
[ ] Bel did not go out to the Akitu-house . . . of the prisoner he carries, with him [ ] he [ ]

40 [The "Mistress of B]abylon" who does not go out from the midst of the Akitu-house is the "overseer"$^?$ of the house.
[ ] "you know the house," saying, "Guard the house. In your hands [ ]."
[The "Mistress of Baby]lon," who wears black wool on her back, [wears] red wool on [her] front.
her [ ] the blood of the innards which spilled.
[ ] before whom they slau[ghter] a pig on the eight day of Nisan [ ].
45 She is the [ ] of the house; they ques-

tion her, saying, "Who is the criminal," saying, [ ].

[ ] they (*or* he) bring(s) the criminal . . . .

[ ] he (*or* they) come(s) . . . .

[ ] he quickly thirsts for water [ ]

[ ] which they libate: that is the "muddy water" [ ].

50 [ ] which they prepare . . . .

[that flou]r which is exceedingly abundant in Nisan: [ ] flour, since he is captive . . . [ ]

The "hand water" which they bring near to the "house of crying$^{?}$": these are the tears [in the midst . . .]

The (divine) *šeritu*-garment that is before him: (that is the one) of which they spoke, saying "the water. . . ."

*53 The sprinking$^{??}$ (*or* the infection$^{?}$): that which is said (in) Enuma Elish,

When heaven and earth had not been made, Anšar existed. The water before Anšar [ ]

He$^{?}$—because$^{?}$ of his sin he is "gathered" in the *kadammu*, without water, wearing$^{?}$ [ ]

57 The footrace which (takes) place before Bel in Kislev, and they s[urround] all the places [(xx)]

Because Aššur sent Ninurta to capture Zu, the god [ ],

Before Aššur he said, "Zu is captured," and Aššur [said] to the god [ ],

60 "Go and announce to all the gods before [ ].

The whole speech which is in it$^{?}$ the *kalû* priests. . ."

As for the plunder which they plundered, (that) which they ruined—the gods, his fathers, they [(ordered it$^{?}$)].

The dog which crosses Esabad: that is the messenger, Gula has sent (it) before him (*or* because of him).

The sandal which they brought to the house of the "Mistress of Babylon": that is the . . . . , they bring it to her.

65 Because they have not let him free, he has not come out.

The chariot which goes to the Akitu-house comes (back) without its master; it rides without a master.

And the *Sakkukutu* that surround the outside of the city: that is his mourning promenade that goes around outside the city.

The "door of many holes" of which they speak: the gods imprisoned him; he entered the house; the door was locked before him.

69 (Then) they opened holes in the midst of the door; they made war inside.

PHILOLOGICAL NOTES

This edition basically follows that of von Soden in *ZA* 51, 1955. Some philological observations are:

10. [*Tašmetum*] Von Soden's restoration of ^{d}Be-let-Babili^{ki} is possible, but it is more likely that it is Tašmetum who arrives with Nabu.

11. *qa-bu-re*$^{!}$ standard *qubūru*, literally "grave." This phrase was originally read *qu-bu-rat*. Von Soden's reading is based on the photograph of the text; see von Soden, ad line 11. This reading does not resolve the issue as to whether the term should be understood as "cemetary" (like Syriac *qbwrt*ʾ, Jensen) or "grave."

12. *i-na* [ ] Von Soden restores *i-na-ṣ*[*u*$^{?}$*-ru-su*, "they guard him," but this involves emending the text.

13. Zimmern restored at the end *ina* ŠÀ-*bi na*[*pšate*] "(he disappeared) from the midst of li[fe]," in accord with his idea that the text was about death and resurrection. Von Soden reads the line [*ša ina muḫḫi s*]*i-qu-re*[*-te*] *e-pi-šu-ni a-ki ilāni*^{meš} *e-si-ru-šu-ni iḫ-ti-liq ina lìb-bi i*[*k/q* . . . , "Was auf der Temple Hochterasse gemacht wurde, kam, als die Gotter den Bel eingeschlossen hatten, ganz ab; darin . . ." and suggests that this may be a allusion to the destruction of the temples in 689. This is a tempting suggestion.

14. Von Soden restores the beginning as [LÚ *mar ši-*]*ip-re*, "[The messen]ger (was afraid)," but the line may refer to Bel.

15. Von Soden's restoration [*ta-ḫab-šu*] at the beginning of the line makes good sense, "the mat which is under him," but does not exhaust the possibilities.

tar-ri-bu Von Soden emends to *tab*$^{!}$*-ri-bu*, but the sign is clearly *tar*, and this may be a genuine orthographic variant. The term has been discussed by Landsberger, "Über Farben im Sumerisch-Akkadischen," *JCS* 21 (1969), 168, where he posits a Hurrian source for the word. The meaning is clearly a shade of red.

16. [^{d}*Taš-me-*]*tum* The name is restored from the parallel line *ZA* 52, 226:22.

19. The important variant *ina* URU GÚ.DU$_{8}$.A^{KI} "in Kutha" in *ZA* 51, 153:17 is discussed in the body of this article.

21. ^{UZU}[GÚ$^{?}$] This restoration is suggested by von Soden. If it should prove to be correct, it would be a striking equation of the gateposts of the goddess's temple with the neck of the goddess.

22. ^{giš}*tal[-tal-l]e* For a discussion of this as the term for "palm-stalks"$^{?}$ see Landsberger, *The Date Palm and its By-Products According to the Cuneiform Sources* [*AfO* Beiheft 17], 1967, 19, who rejects the identification with Hebrew *taltalim*, "fronds" (19 n. 59).

23. This line seems interposed between lines 22 and 24, with line 22 being the greeting of Nabu going to Borsippa, and line 24 coming back. We might question then whose city rebelled against whom after Bel went to the *ḫursan*. It may not be Babylon rebelling against Marduk, but rather Borsippa abandoning Nabu (perhaps to follow a pro-Assyrian policy). This is admittedly speculative, but the line would be out of place if it referred to a rebellion against Bel.

24. G[I].UR.MEŠ *ša* ŠAH.MEŠ For these "pig reeds" see *CAD* A^{1}, sub *adattu*. Von Soden's "Schweine 'nester'" does not seem justified.

25–26. It is hard to be certain who is seeing whom in these lines, but quite possibly Nabu is the one who sees and the text, having digressed to the modes of greeting Nabu on his way to and from Babylon, has brought us back to Babylon, where Nabu sees the criminal hanging on the gate-posts of Belet-Babili (lines 20–21).

30. *kuzippu* This seems to have been a type of cloak used in ceremonial contexts. The *kuzippu* of the king was particularly important and was used in rituals at the Sargonid court. For references see *CAD K*, s.v. *ú-bal-u-ni* reading with *KAR* 219. *KAR* 143 had *ú-še-bal-u-ni*

32. *kadammu* This has been rendered by von Soden, *AHw* 419 as "Kerker?" and by *CAD K*, s.v. "(a building)." The term occurs elsewhere only in *ABL* 564:12, where slave girls are "gathered" in the *kadammāti* and in line 56 below. It seems therefore to be a word for some sort of place, perhaps a prison or a dungeon. Since the verb used below and in *ABL* 564:12 is *esēpu*, I have restored *e-*[*sip*$^{?}$] here.

33. *re-e-mu ú-ka-al-lim-*⌜*ša*⌝*-*[*ni*$^{?}$]. Von Soden reads *re-e-mu ú-ka-alim-šú*[*-ni*] and has difficulty finding a subject for the verb, translating, "und sie [ihm] Erbarmen gezeigt hatten," which is difficult. *CAD K*, s.v. *kalû* reads *ša . . . re-e-mu ú-ka-al-lim-*<*u*>*-šú-*[*ni*] "those who showed him mercy," but the *ša* in the line governs only *i-ḫal-li-bu-ni*. The *šú* at the end of the line is not entirely clear and might be part of *šá*, which would give the good sense, "he showed her mercy." Alternatively we would have to say that despite the *u* prefix the subject of the verb is still Ištar: she showed him mercy when she nurtured him.

34. *i-za-mur-šú-ni* Von Soden takes *KAR* 143 as his standard text, thus reading *i-za-mur-ú-šu-ni*, "they sing." However, *KAR* 219 (von Soden's text B) has *i-za-mur-šú-ni*, which may be more correct. If so, it would indicate that the subject of this verb is the same as the subject of the singular verbs in line 35. Note, however, that the Nineveh text (*ZA* 51, 154:29) has *i-za-am-mu-ru-ú-šu-ni* in a similar context.

35. *ú-ṣal-la* Again reading as in *KAR* 219, which is better preserved in these lines and therefore is taken here as the standard text. *KAR* 143 (text A) has *ú-ṣal-ṣal-la*. Note that the verb is singular in both texts.

36. Von Soden suggests reading the beginning of the line as AD ^{d}*Šamaš šu-tú i-da-bu-ub*, "Vater Schamasch ist es, er spricht," but although such a reading might fit the small remnants of the initial signs that are visible, it is not really convincing. It is thus also possible that the person who is the subject of lines 34 and 35, who recites Enuma Elish, prays prayers and entreats entreaties, is also the one who speaks here about Bel's innocence. Another possibility is that the subject of this line may be the same as that of lines 37 and 36, i.e. Bel himself; if so, we should restore *ḫi*[*iṭ-ṭi*] at the end. It may also be possible that the subject of all these lines is the same, i.e., a cult functionary who recites the prayers, reads Enuma Elish, and represents Marduk before the gods, speaking of him in the first person.

37. *bal-li*[*-ṭa-a-n*]*i* The verb has been restored in the first person, "Grant [me] life," rather than in the third person (*bal-li-*[*su*]) on the basis of the line *ZA* 51, 154:21 [*a-na* ^{d}*Aššur*] ^{d}*A-nim* ^{d}*Sin* [^{d}*Ša*]*maš* [*ú-ṣal-l*]*a ma-a ba-li-ṭa-a-ni* ^{TÚG}*še-er-at*$^{?}$*-ia*$^{?}$[ ], "He [pray]s [to Aššur], An, Sin, (and) Šamaš, saying 'Grant me life', my *šeritu* . . . ," which seems to be parallel. The context in which this line occurs is not the same as that of line 37, however, so that parallel is not assured.

38. *ḫu-ur-ri*$^{!?}$*-šú* Von Soden reads here *ḫu-ur-sa*$^{!?}$*-šú* and translates "dessen Ordalstätte auf in (oder: seinetwegen?) [. . . (hin)geworfen ist]." This does not seem plausible. In the first place it does not seem to make much sense, but in addition, it would be the only occurrence of *ḫursan*, "ordeal" with a suffix of any kind, (in addition to being the only occurrence of *ḫursan* in the sense of ordeal-site). The reading *ḫurrišu* is suggested by *KAR* 307 rev. 8 *áš-šú* ^{d}*An-šar a-na* ḪABRUD ir-du-du-šú-ma, "because Anšar pursued him (Marduk) into a hole (and closed its door)" in a similar context. This reading has the additional advantage of not requiring too much change in the copy. for *karāru*, "to prepare, lay a foundation," sess *CAD K*, s.v.

42. The meaning of this line seems to be that Belet-Babili (or her representative) is wearing motley garments that are colored red in front and black in back. The meaning of this costume, if explained by the commentary, is lost in the breaks.

43. Landsberger, "Über Farben," *JCS* 21, 168, translates the line "durch Ritzen mit Steinmesser vergossenes Blut" without explanation, but apparently taking *tabkuni* from *tabāku* and *ṣurri* from *ṣurru*, "flint." This conjecture is worth considering, but we cannot reject the possibility that *ṣurri* here are the innards, even though it raises associations of the "wounded heart" and the "sang réal" (Holy Grail). The

question as to whether there was a flagellation rite attached to this ritual must be held in abeyance.

47. Von Soden reads here [ ]*il-lak-u-ni pa-ge-le-ša im-ma-a*[*t-ḫu-u-ni*. . .], ". . . kommt, als ihre *Libationsgefasse aufge*[*hoben* wurden . . .]"; the context is so broken it is difficult to make convincing restorations.

50. Von Soden reads the first half of this line [. . .]*ina muḫ*$^{!?}$*-ḫi*$^{!?}$ *na*$^{!?}$*-at*$^{!?}$*-ba-ak-te* "auf ein *Zubringerkanälchen*." *ZA* 52, 226:110 has [UZ]U KA$^{?}$-NE *la-ba-ak*/*q-te*, which von Soden translates ". . . *Bratfleisch* des . . ." *CAD K*, 209 translates our line as "they place the roasted meat before Bel."

51. *si-li*ʾ*-a*ʾ*-a-te-ši-na*. The word *sili*ʾ*tu* frequently occurs in the sense of "infection," which does not seem to fit the context here. Possibly this noun is from *salā*ʾ*u* in the sense "to sprinkle."

53*–54. The line arrangement here is according to the sense.

56. Von Soden's suggestion to read the beginning of this line *šu-u* U$_4$ *ša ḫi-ṭi-šú*, "Dies ist der Tag der Sünde (oder Strafe?)," is tempting, but it is difficult to see how such a line would fit, and I have therefore opted for a less courageous suggestion. *šu-u-tú* also occurs in line 63 and 64, where *šu-u* U$_4$ is impossible, and seems to mean something like "he" or "that one."

68. The possible significance of this line and the next is discussed in the body of the article. Note that in *CTN* 28, line 68 is given, but line 69 is not, while in *ZA* 52, 226:25 there is a parallel to line 69, not at the end of the text, and apparently not after an equivalent of line 68.

COMMENTARY

The most striking feature of this text is the captivity of Bel. He is said to be "held" or "captive" in lines 8–9, and this is a recurrent motif throughout the composition. Details about his captivity are given: we are told that someone has gone to the *ḫursan* and is being questioned there (lines 6–7); from line 23 it is clear that it is Bel himself who is at the *ḫursan* and that this is connected in some way to his captivity. Bel's *šeritu*-garment is "gathered"$^{?}$ in the *kadammu* (line 32+ *ZA* 52 226:5), and he himself is said to be "gathered" there (line 56); from its only other occurrence (quoted in the textual notes), *kadammu* appears to be a word for some sort of place, perhaps a prison or a dungeon. We are further told that Bel is being guarded: we learn that the [*u*]*maše* who stand in the gate of Esaggil are guardians appointed over him (line 12), and that the person who did not "stand with Bel" and "take part" in the conspiracy with him and thus was not a criminal was appointed his guardian and was guarding him in a fortress (URU *ber-tú*, line 19). In the Ninevite recension of the text, the place in which Bel is guarded is called URU.GÚ.DU$_8$.A, Kutha: this may be a reference to the city of Kutha, which would imply that Kutha did not join in some anti-Assyrian conspiracy; it may also be a name for the netherworld.

The captivity of Bel is connected to the *ḫursan*, to which Marduk is said to have gone. However, despite the opinions of Zimmern, Jensen and von Soden, there is no ordeal in this composition. There is a legal proceeding mentioned (line 18), but it is neither an ordeal, nor even a trial of Marduk. Rather, it metes out punishment and reward for those who either did or did not "stand with Bel" and serve as his accomplices. The text's only connection with an ordeal is the presence of the term *ḫursan*, and even von Soden, who interprets *ḫursan* to indicate an ordeal, does not claim that the text actually talks about this ordeal. Rather, he states: "Bel ist in Haft, wird geschlagen und einem Ordal unterworfen, von dessen Ausgang wir nichts erfahren, und dann wieder eingeschlossen." (*ZA* 51, 161).

The uses of *ḫursan* in this text are:

6. *a-na ḫur-sa-an šu-ú il-lak*, "that one goes to the *ḫursan*"
7. É *šu-ú ina* UGU *šap-te ša ḫur-sa-an ina* ŠÀ *i-ša-a*ʾ*-ú-lu-šú*, "that house at the edge of the *ḫursan*: in (its) midst they question him."
23. [*ur-k*]*i ša* ^{d}*Bel ina ḫur-sa-an il-lik-u-ni*, "[After$^{?}$] Bel went to the *ḫursan* (the city revolted)."
29. [*ú*$^{?}$-]*ma-a a-na ḫur-sa-an ub-bu-lu-šú*, "[S]aying, 'they bring him to the *ḫursan*!'"
38. *ša* TA ŠÀ *ḫur-sa-an il*[*-lik*/*lak-u-n*]*i*, "When he c[omes *or* came] from the midst of the *ḫursan*."

Among these expressions, two might refer to ordeals: the phrase *ana*/*ina ḫursan alāku* is the standard term used for going to the ordeal; and *ana ḫursan ubbulu*, although not otherwise attested, could be a term for bringing someone (perhaps against his will) to an ordeal. However, the phrase TA ŠÀ *ḫursan*, "from the midst of the *ḫursan*," and the term "house on the edge of the *ḫursan*" clearly indicate that the text is using *ḫursan* as the name for a location rather than as a term for a judicial proceeding. It might be possible to argue that the use of *ḫursan* as the name of a place is derived from its meaning of ordeal, with the term secondarily applied to the place where the ordeal is held. Such a use of *ḫursan* is, however, not known. The second theoretical connection is that the use of the term *ḫursan* for a cosmic locale is the reason that the ordeal is called *ḫursan*. Although this second possibility seems plausible,[1] it is irrelevant to this text. In this text *ḫursan* is the name of the place to which Marduk has been taken: he has gone to the *ḫursan* and is being held captive in the "house on the edge of the *ḫursan*." In a similar context in the Nineveh recension (*ZA* 52, 153f) we read [ ] AN *šu-ú il-lak i-na* ŠÀ É *á-k*[*i-ti*] "[. . .] he went into the A[kitu]-house" (line 7). This does not seem to be an allusion to the ritual procession of the Akitu festival, for we are told in the Assyrian recension (line 39) that Bel did not go out to the Akitu house, as we would expect during the period of his captivity. The term É *akitu* in the Nineveh recension, like the term *ḫursan*, is a cosmic/poetic name for the place in which Bel is held captive.

The occurrence of Kutha in the Ninevite version as the name of the place in which Bel is being guarded and the fact that the goddess goes looking for Bel through the gate of the graveyard in line 11 make it likely that the *ḫursan* of this text has something to do with the netherworld, and that this text gives a political "interpretation" of a tale in which Bel went down to the netherworld (and perhaps was trapped there). We have other hints of such a tale. In *TuL* 7 (*KAR* 307), another cultic commentary, we read *dMes-lam-ta-è-a dMarduk šá a-na* KI-*tim* E_{11}-*ú* E_{11} *áš-šú dAn-šar a-na* ḪABRUD *ir-du-du-šú-ma* KÁ-*šú* BAD-*ú*, "Meslamtaea is Marduk who went down to the Netherworld. He went down (*or* went down to the Netherworld and came up) because Anšar pursued him into the hole and closed its door." (rev. 7f). This allusion to the Netherworld is quite explicit and it is clear that this commentary is interpreting an episode in which Anšar made Marduk a captive as an event in which Marduk went down to the Netherworld (or vice versa). Our text may refer to the same or a similar episode: the locale of Marduk's captivity is called the Akitu house Nineveh recension) or the *ḫursan* in our text rather than the ḪABRUD or the "netherworld."

Further light on this association of Bel's captivity with the Akitu-house may be found in the commentary text to the "Address of Marduk to the Demons," edited by Lambert in *AfO* 17, 310f. In the "Address" we read [KIMIN *š*]*á a-šar šil*!*-la*!*-ti la i-qab-bu-u a-na-ku*, "[Ditto (I am Asarluhi)] whom they do not mention in the place of blasphemy?" (line 315).[2] The commentary reads [M]U EN *šá ina á-ki-it ina qa-bal tam-tim áš-bu* "[Concer]ning the Lord who sits in the Akitu in the middle of the sea." This association of Marduk with the Akitu and the sea may also be related to the entry in the "Topography of Babylon" (van der Meer, *Iraq* 5, 61:14) *ti-amat šu-bat dBel šá dBel ina muḫ*!*-ḫi*! *áš-bu* "Tiamat—the dwelling of Bel where Bel dwells in the midst (of Tiamat)."[3] In these two texts it appears that part of the New Year's festival involved/recalled a period before Marduk's victory in which he was considered to be in the power of Tiamat and that this period was related to events at the Akitu house. Our commentary text appears to connect this episode of the New Year's ritual with the captivity of Marduk on which it lays so much stress, indicating this connection by the use of the terms Akitu-house (Nineveh recension) and *ḫursan*. The evidence is too scant to speak with any assurance, but the absence of any ordeal in this text, and the reference in the commentary text *KAR* 307 to an episode in which Marduk descended into the netherworld make it probable that our text also refers to a cosmic location, called *ḫursan*, in which Marduk was held captive.[4]

This does not mean that our text is a tale of Marduk as a "dying and resurrected god." The material in our text (and probably in *KAR* 307) is manifestly political and relates to the enmity between Aššur and Marduk, i.e., between Assyria and Babylonia.[5] Von Soden has suggested that the *raison d'être* of this text was a religious justification of Sennacherib's

[1] There are indications that the river ordeal, or at least the river of the ordeal, was associated with the netherworld. This evidence comes from the use of the term Ilurugu (The Sumerian name for the ordeal river) in contexts that suggest a netherworldly river. For a discussion of this evidence and of the term *ḫursan*, see my forthcoming *Judicial Ordeal in the Ancient Near East.*

[2] Lambert originally read this line [KI.MIN *š*]*á a-šar ḫaṣ-ba-ti la i-qab-bu-u a-na-ku* (*AfO* 17, 315:4), translating "[Ditto wh]o does not speak in the 'Place of the Potsherd' am I" (p. 318). The correction to *šillati* is Lambert's, *AfO* 19:118, but is not entirely convincing.

[3] I have corrected the text according to a suggestion of W. G. Lambert. Van der Meer read *ina* ZUR.QAR, with no translation.

[4] There is no evidence for a *Weltberg*. However, there are indications that *ḫursan* as the name of the river ordeal may ultimately be related to concepts involving the netherworld; see note 2.

[5] For further discussion of politicization, see Jacobsen, in *Unity and Diversity*, 65–97; esp. 76 and 95–97.

destruction of Babylon and of the temple of Marduk there in 689. There do seem to be allusions to the events of 689 but, as von Soden himself realized (*ZA* 51, 164), this interpretation suffers from the fact that the text nowhere makes a clear condemnation of Marduk. On the contrary, in line 36 someone is obviously intervening on behalf of Bel, claiming that everything that he did was done for the benefit of Aššur. Despite the fact that Bel is captive and suffering in this text, the composition cannot be considered anti-Marduk or anti-Babylonian.

The captivity of Bel portrayed in this text does not seem to have been permanent. The final two lines of the Assyrian recension, in which the gods have made holes in the door behind which Marduk is locked, seem to indicate that there was a denouement to the story in which the gods fought to free Marduk. We cannot lay too much stress on the fact that these lines come at the end of the Assyrian recension, for the equivalent to line 69 is found in the midst of the Ninevite composition *ZA* 52 226:25 and is not found at all in the fragmentary text published by Postgate in *CTN* 2 (no. 268). Nevertheless, the presence of the line indicates that at some stage the gods entered the prison of Marduk, most probably to free him. This, together with the absence of any condemnation of Marduk in this text, suggests that the document was written to justify and celebrate, not the subjugation of Marduk, but his ultimate vindication. A further indication that Marduk is not in total disfavor in this text is the colophon in which Bel is listed as one of the gods who guarantees the punishment of whomever either destroys the text or attempts to keep it secret (line 72).

With this in mind, we may suggest that the politico-historical background to the writing of this text is not the subjugation and destruction of Babylon in 689, but rather the events of 669, when the statue of Marduk was returned to Babylon. This statue had been taken by Sennacherib in 689 and held in Assyria. Sennacherib's inscriptions give the impression that he demolished the statues of the Babylonian gods, but it is clear from the inscriptions of Esarhaddon that the gods had escaped destruction by "flying away like birds," and that Esarhaddon renewed and recreated them as part of the *rapprochement* with Babylon and her traditions that also involved rebuilding the temples of Babylon that Sennacherib had destroyed.[6] Finally, in 669, during the accession year of Šamaššumukin, the statue was returned. The Esarhaddon Chronicle relates the event (Grayson, "Chronicle" 14, 127)[7]

31 For eight years (during the reign of Sennacherib) for twelve years (during the reign of) Esarhaddon
twenty years (altogether), Bel stayed [in B]altil (Assur) and the Akitu festival did not take place.
Nabu did not come from B[ors]ippa for the procession of Bel.
In the month of Kislev Aššurbanipal, [his s]on, ascended the throne in Assyria.
35 The accession year of Šamaššumukin: In the month Iyyar Bel and the gods of [Akkad]
went o[u]t from Baltil and on the 25 of Iyyar [they entered] Babylon
Nabu and the gods of Borsippa [went] to Babylon.

This great return of the Babylonian gods to Babylon may be the background of *KAR* 143 + 219. The return of Bel and their previous capture had to be cast into some sort of rational framework. The Babylonians had to understand why their god had been in captivity. Equally important, the Assyrians had to be able to understand and accept the return of Marduk to Babylon without feeling that his initial capture had been a national sin on their part. In order to accomplish this, Marduk's most recent adventure, his captivity, was related to his cultic adventures, particularly to his trials and triumphs recorded and celebrated in the New Year's rituals. This situation may be analogous to that which prompted the writing of Enuma Elish. According to Lambert ("The Reign of Nebuchadnezzar I," *The Seed of Wisdom* [*T. J. Meek AV*], 1964, 3–13), Enuma Elish was written after the statue of Marduk was returned to Babylon during the reign of Nebuchadnezzar I. At that time the New Year's festival was officially reinterpreted to include a battle of Marduk against Tiamat. Much later, the return of the statue of Marduk from Assyria at the beginning of the reigns of Šamaššumukin and Aššurbanipal may have occasioned a similar new interpretation and religious assimilation. The ritual, which already celebrated a triumphant Marduk, was reinterpreted to include the most recent chapter in the story of

[6] For a discussion of the fortunes of the Babylonian gods and temples during the time of Sennacherib and his successors, *Brief eines Bischofs von Esagila an König Asarhaddon*, 1965, 17–27.

[7] There are also parallel passages in the Babylonian Chronicle, Grayson Chronicle I iv (p. 86): 34–36 and the Akitu Chronicle, Grayson "Chronicle 16," 131: 1–8.

Marduk. The commentary text was written to incorporate this historical event into the religious framework and to include a celebration of this event in all future Akitu celebrations.

This explanation cannot be proposed with any finality, for certainty about this text and its political background must wait at least until we have a complete text, without the gaps and damaged lines of our present composite edition. But it should by now be clear that the text is not about an ordeal, that it is not manifestly anti-Marduk and that the title "Marduk Ordeal Text" is misleading and should be dropped.

LITERARY LETTERS FROM DEITIES AND DIVINERS MORE FRAGMENTS[1]

A. KIRK GRAYSON

UNIVERSITY OF TORONTO

THAT LETTERS FORMED PART OF THE SCRIBE'S LITERARY TRADITION IN ANCIENT MESOPOTAMIA has long been known and Professor Samuel Noah Kramer, whom we honour in this volume, has had a major role in recovering the Sumerian works which belong to this genre. The literary letters, which in fact are known both in Sumerian and Akkadian, can be distinguished from everyday letters by their elaborate style; by the content which often concerns matters of state importance; and by the fact that copies were kept in libraries and schools where they could be read by scholars and used as style manuals by teachers.[2]

Epistles between human and divine beings form an important corpus within the category of literary letters, the majority of these being letters to a god from a man.[3] This corpus includes the letters of Assyrian kings to the god Ashur, the most famous of which is the letter of Sargon II reporting on his eighth campaign. The existence of letters addressed in the other direction, from a divine being to a human being, has on the other hand been poorly attested. It is therefore gratifying to be able to add some fragmentary textual material to this little known category.

The purpose of this article, therefore, is to highlight the little known group of literary letters from deities and diviners; to publish a fragment of a previously unknown representative of this genre; and to edit a fragment previously identified with this group but never published. The letters from deities, of which two fragments are now extant, will be presented first and with full edition. This will be followed by a briefer treatment of the letters from diviners.

The two letters from deities are K 2764 (Macmillan, *BA* 5/5, no. XVIII)[4] and BM 38630 (previously unpublished).

I LETTER FROM BELIT-BALATI

The new text, BM 38630 (80-11-12, 514) is published by courtesy of the Trustees of the British Museum. I am grateful to Dr. Edmond Sollberger, Mr. C. B. F. Walker, and Dr. I. Finkel of that museum for their help and co-operation. The tablet, of which less than a third is preserved, is written in the Neo-Babylonian script and probably comes from Babylon. It in turn is a copy, as stated in the colophon, of a text in Borsippa. The most significant feature of the inscription is the beginning of the colophon which states: "Letter which Belit-balati sent to Nusku-taqishu-bullit, son of Etil-pi-Marduk."

The identity of Belit-balati is crucial to an understanding of the nature of this tablet and, while it cannot be definitively demonstrated, I believe that she is almost certainly a goddess rather than a human being. On the obverse the writer of the letter calls herself ^{d}*Ma-nun-gal* and in a bilingual hymn (*LKA* 21) to ^{d}Nungal/^{d}Manungal the deity ^{d}Nin-din-(bàd-é) appears (on Manungal see Sjöberg, *AfO* 24, pp. 26f). Thus both this bilingual and BM 38630 indicate that Belit-balati (^{d}Nin-din) is a manifestation of the deity Manungal. Belit-balati is also known as a star name.[5] The new text associates Belit-balati with the city Borsippa and the cult of Nabu, a fact not known before. That *bēlit balāṭi* "mistress of life" is used here only as an epithet for another divine name is unlikely,

---

[1] This research has been supported by the Social Sciences and Humanities Research Council of Canada.

[2] Regarding Letters as a genre see S. N. Kramer, *ANET*^{3}, 480f.; W. W. Hallo, *Proceedings of the American Academy of Jewish Research*, 46-47 (1979-80), 316-22 and *Proceedings of the Seventh World Congress of Jewish Studies*, 1981, 17-27; and for full bibliography Borger, *HKL* 3, 57f., §59.

[3] Regarding Letters to the God see Borger, *RLA* 3, 575f.

[4] Bibliography of K 2764:
Macmillan, *BA* 5/5, no. XVIII
Nougayrol, *RA* 36 (1939), 33f.
Borger, *RLA* 3, 576b
———, *HKL* 1, 327
Grayson, *Or. N. S.* 49 (1980), 158, n. 88

[5] Cf. Tallquist, *Epitheta*, 271
Gössman, *Planetarium*, nos. 52 and 68

BM 38630 obverse.

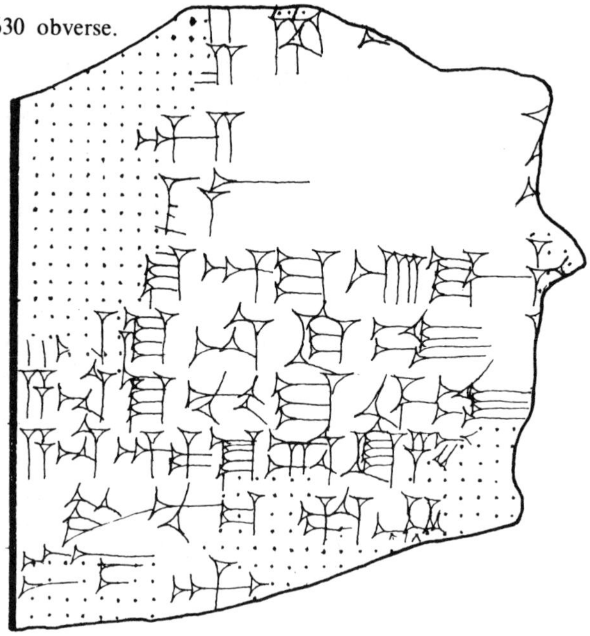

BM 38630 reverse.

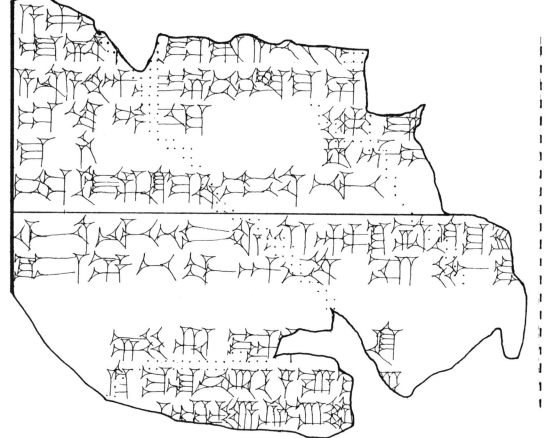

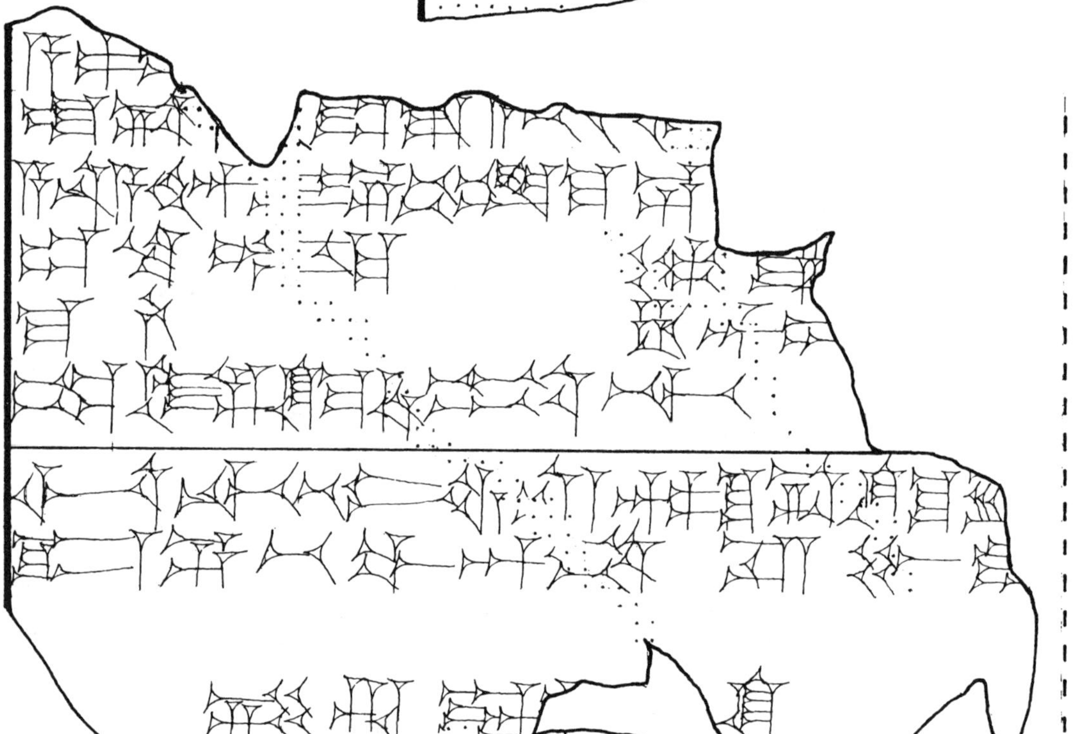

particularly since it is an epithet rarely used (only of the goddesses Damkina, Sahan, and Shuzianna).[6]

There is a remote possibility that Belit-balati is simply a hypocoristicon of the name of a human priestess. The name Belit-balata-erish is known from Kassite times (cf. Clay, *CPN*, 64). Moreover the two words for priestess with which the letter-writer identifies herself, *nadītu* and *kulmašītu*, are only applied to humans, never otherwise to divine beings. On the other hand it is surprising that Belit-balati calls herself the goddess Manungal and that her name was not written out in full at the end of the tablet if she were human. Thus I believe it highly probable that the writer of this letter is a goddess called Belit-balati and Manungal.

The erotic nature of the conclusion of BM 38630 indicates the general area of Belit-balati's activity, love-making and fertility, and this explains the meaning of her name "Mistress-of-Life." While the closing lines are generally reminiscent of Mesopotamian Love Lyrics there is no formal relationship.[7] There is some evidence for the date of BM 38630 for, although it is known only from a Neo-Babylonian copy, the name of the addressee and his title indicate the Middle Babylonian period. Nusku-taqishu-bullit is otherwise known only as the name of a man in the time of Kurigalzu.[8] The title he is given in BM 38630, *laputtû*, was already dying out as a real administrative post by the Middle Babylonian period where it "only occurs in a standard formula in kudurru texts" (*CAD* L, 99). This fact suits the literary nature of the letter. The occurrence of the name Nusku-taqishu-bullit on both obverse and reverse of the fragment indicate that the same letter is involved on each side.[9]

BM 38630 (80–11–12, 514) measures c. 7.5 × 5 cms. and represents a little less than the top third of the original tablet.

TRANSLITERATION

Obverse

[Lacuna]

1′) [x x x] x ḫa x [... ...]

2′) [x x x] x [... ...]

3′) [x x] ^{d}MIN x [... ...]

4′) [x x] x LAL x [... ...]

5′) [*a-na*]-*ku* ^{d}*Ma-nun-gal* x [... ...]

6′) ⸢*a-na*⸣-*ku na-di-tum* x [... ...]

7′) *a-na-ku kul-ma-ši-tum* x [... ...]

8′) *a-na* ^{d}*Nusku*(enšada)-*ta-qí-šá-bu*[*l-liṭ mār Etil-pî-Marduk*]

9′) ^{lú}*laputtû*(nu.⸢bàn(?)⸣.da) ^{d}⸢*Nabû*(a[g])
[... ...]

10′) x x DINGIR x [... ...]

[Lacuna]

Reverse

[Lacuna]

1′) *a-pa*-x [... ...]

2′) *at-ta* ⸢*qa*⸣-[*ar*]-*ra-da-a-ti* ⸢*ù*(?)⸣ [x x x]

3′) *a-na a-ḫi an*-⸢*ni*⸣-*i e-bi-ram-ma e*-[x x x]

4′) *ap-te-tak-ka* *li-biš*-[*ša-ti*]

TRANSLATION

Obverse

[Lacuna]

1′-4′) [Too broken for translation]

5′) ⸢I⸣, divine Manungal [... ...]

6′) I, a *nadītum* [... ...]

7′) I, a *kulmašītum* [... ...]

8′) to Nusku-taqisha-bu[llit, son of Etil-pi-Marduk],

9′) *laputtû* of the god Na[bu ... speak!]

[Lacuna]

Reverse

2′) Thou art the hero and [...]

3′) Cross over to this side to me [...]

4′) I have opened for you [my] vulva;

[6] Cf. Tallquist, *Epitheta*, 57f.

[7] Cf. W. G. Lambert "The Problem of the Love Lyrics," in Goedicke and Roberts (eds.), *Unity and Diversity*, 98–135; *MIO* 12 (1966), 41–56. For further bibliography see Borger, *HKL* 3, 83, §83.

[8] Cf. A. T. Clay, *CPN* 115b.

[9] I wish to thank Dr. Douglas R. Frayne for his comments on BM 38630.

5′) *ma-ḫaṣ* *ḫa-an-du-*[*ut-ti*]
6′) *bi-iṣ-ṣu-ru ki-ma peq-qu-ut-ti* [x x (x)]

7′) *ši-pir-ti Be-lit-balāṭi*(din) *a-na* ^{md}*Nusku*(enšada)*-ta-qi-šu-bul-*[*liṭ*]
8′) *mār*(dumu) ^{m}*E-til-pi-*^{d}*Marduk*(amar.utu) *iš-pu-r*[*a*]
9′) *gabarî*(gaba.ri) *Bár-s*[*ipa*]^{ki}
10′) *ki-ma la-bi-ri-šú šá-ṭir b*[*a-r*]*i*
11′) [*qāt*] ^{md}*Nabû*(ag)*-ēṭir*(kar)*-ir* *ṭupšarri*(dub.sa[r])

5′) Strike [my] clitoris!
6′) The Venus mound like a *pequttu*-plant [...]

7′) Letter which Belit-balāti sent to Nusku-taqishu-bul[lit],
8′) son of Etil-pi-Marduk
9′) Copy from Borsippa.
10′) According to its original written (and) collated
11′) [by the hand of] Nabu-etir, the scribe.

Comments

Obv. 9′) The reading BÀN is not certain from the traces but from the context there is no alternative. A *laputtû* in the Shamash temple is known (see *CAD* L s. v.); in the present text Nusku-taqishu-bullit seems to be a *laputtû* at the Nabu temple at Borsippa.

Rev. 4′-6′) *libištu*, *ḫanduttu* and *biṣṣūru* are listed as synonyms in lexical texts; see *CAD* B, 268 f. sub *biṣṣūru*.

5′) *maḫaṣ*: This seems to be the only plausible reading.

6′) *peqquttu*: plant name; cf. *AHw*, 854b sub *peqqû*.

9′-11′) On this colophon cf. Hunger, *Kolophone*, nos. 124–40.

II LETTER FROM NINURTA

Turning to the second literary letter from a deity, K 2764, we go from love to war for this letter is from Ninurta, the god of war in Assyria. The text is indeed in Assyrian script and preserved on a tablet from the time of Ashurbanipal as attested by the colophon. There is no evidence as to the date of the original composition. But it is formally related to BM 38630 since it too concludes with the statement that it is a letter sent from a deity (*šipirti* ^{d}*Ninurta a*[*na* ...]). This fact necessitates a closer study of K 2764 and I therefore include in this article a new edition of the text based upon personal collation.

It has been generally assumed that K 2764 was a letter addressed by the god to an Assyrian king, an assumption which I share. Nevertheless the fact that BM 38630 is addressed to a non-royal personage shows that these letters are not always to kings. Indeed, the highest title given to the addressee in the extant portion of K 2764 is "governor" (*šakkanakku*) (a title which kings could bear) and the reference to "throne" (*kussû* which can simply be "chair"—see *CAD* K and *AHw*, s.v.) is not proof of his royal character. But this is splitting hairs and I think K 2764 must have been addressed to an Assyrian king, probably of the ninth century B.C.

K 2764 measures c. 7 × 6 cms. and represents less than one third of the original tablet.

TRANSLITERATION

Obverse

1) *bēlu*(en) *rabû*(gal)^{ú} *šar*(lugal) *ilāni*^{meš} ^{d}*Nin-urta iš-pu-ra* [...]
2) *a-na ru-bé-e ti-ri-iṣ qa-ti* [...]
3) *a-na ma-ḫir* ^{giš}*ḫaṭṭi*(gidri)^{ti} ^{giš}*kussê*(gu.za) *ù* x [...]
4) *a-na šakkanakki ša qa-ti-ia* (erasure) *q*[*í-bi-ma*]
5) *um-ma* ^{d}*Nin-urta bēlu*(en) *rabû*(gal)^{ú} *mār*(dumu) ^{d}*En-líl* [...]

TRANSLATION

Obverse

1) The great lord, king of the gods, Ninurta has written [...]:
2) To the prince, the outstretched hand [...]
3) To the receiver of the sceptre, throne and [*crown*]
4) To my appointed governor, [speak]!
5) Thus says Ninurta, the great lord, son of Enlil [...]

6) *uš-šu-šá-ku ra-'i-ba-ku ze-na-ku* [*ana bītiia*]
7) *uš-šu-šá-ku man-nu li-*[...]
8) *ra-'i-ba-ku man-nu li-*[...]
9) *ze-na-ku a-na bīti*(é)*-ia man-nu l*[*i-*...]
10) *a-bar-šá a-na ba-ni-šu* [...]
11) *a-a-in-na ta-mi-tu* [...]
12) *ta-tan-ni-du-ku-ma* [...]
13) *ù ina damē-šá* ⌜*ú*⌝-[...]
14) *at-ta ki-i* x [...]
15) *a-na mār*(dumu) [...]
16) *a-na* x [...]
17) *šá i-*[...]
18) x [...]
[Lacuna]

6) I am upset, I am wroth, I am angry [with my temple].
7) I am upset: who would [...]!
8) I am wroth: who would [...]!
9) I am angry with my temple: who would [...]!
10) Surely for its builder [...]
11) Which is the omen [...]?
12) Thou ... [...]
13) Now in her blood [...]
14) Thou like [...]
15) To the son [...]
[Lacuna]

Reverse

[Lacuna]
1) x x [...]
2) *a-di a-*[...]

---

3) *ši-pir-ti* ^{d}*Nin*$_{5}$*-urta* ⌜*a*(?)⌝-[*na* ...]

---

4) *ekal* ^{m}*Aš-šur-bāni*(dù)*-apli*(a) [*šar māt Aššur*]
5) *ša* ^{d}*Nabû*(ag) *ù* ^{d}*Taš-me-t*[*um uznu rapaštu išrukuš*]
6) *i-ḫu-uz-zu īnā*^{II} *na-mir-*[*tu nisiq ṭupšarrūti*]
7) *ša i-na šarrāni*^{meš} ^{ni}*a-lik maḫ-ri-ia* [*mamma šipru šu'ātu la iḫuzzu*]
8) *né-me-qí* ^{d}*Nabû*(ag) *ti-kip sa-an-tak-k*[*i mala bašmu*]
9) *ina ṭuppāni*^{meš} *áš-ṭur as-niq ab-r*[*e-ma*]
10) *a-na ta-mar-ti ši-ta-as-si-ia qí-rib ekalli-*[*ia ukîn*]

Reverse

3) Letter of Ninurta ⌜*to*⌝ [...]

---

4) Palace of Ashurbanipal, [king of Assyria]
5) To whom Nabu and Tashmetum [granted wisdom],
6) Whose bright eye learned [the best of the scribal craft]
7) which no king before me [had learned],
8) the wisdom of Nabu, cuneiform signs, [as many as there are],
9) I wrote on tablets, I examined, I collated [and]
10) [set] in my palace for me to read.

Comments

r. 4. The two circles in Macmillan's copy are part of the erasure.

r. 3. Borger, in an unpublished copy of Zimmern, read ^{d}NIMIN.DU(?); see *RLA* 3, 576b; *HKL* 1, 327. He also noted that the *-ti* was certain. From my collation the reading is clearly what I have put in the transliteration.

r. 4–10. This is a shortened version of a standard Ashurbanipal colophon. See Hunger, *Kolophone*, no. 319.

III LITERARY LETTERS FROM DIVINERS

Fragments of two literary letters from diviners are known, VAT 9628 (*KAH* 2, 142) and K 14676. Weidner edited VAT 9628 in *AfO* 9 (1933–34), pp. 101–4, where he identified the text as a letter from a god concerning the fifth campaign of Shamshi-Adad V. In his article (102, n. 91) Weidner drew attention to the fragment K 14676, which was briefly described by King, Cat. p. 119 as having several sections introduced by "Concerning that which you wrote [to me]" (*ša tašpur*[*anni*]), and noted that the same phrase introduced the sections in VAT 9628. Subsequently Nougayrol in *RA* 36 (1936), 33, n. 4 suggested that these were not letters from gods *per se* but from diviners. I believe Nougayrol is correct (cf. *Or. n. s.* 49

[1980], 158, n. 88) since the phrase which is crucial to the identity of VAT 9628, "Through the command of my great divinity (it befell)" (*ina pî ilūtiia rabīti*) is precisely the same as the formula in the oracle requests of Esarhaddon published by Klauber (*PRT*) and Knudtzon (*AGS*)—e.g. *AGS* no. 1:15.

These letters from diviners are not the same as the "extispicy reports," on which see most recently I. Starr "Extispicy Reports from the Old Babylonian and Sargonid Periods" in *Essays . . . Finkelstein*, pp. 201–8.

While VAT 9628 has been edited and published by Weidner, K 14676 has never been published in full and so I present an edition in this article.

K 14676 is a fragment (c. 2.5 × 4.5 cms.) from the upper left corner of a tablet; only one side, presumably the reverse, is preserved.

1 *ša taš-[pur* ...]
2 *šarru*(lugal) *ša* [...]

3 *ša taš-pur* [...]
4 *in-nab-[tu* ...]
5 *áš-šú* [...]
6 *šarrāni*(lugal)^{meš} [...]

7 *ša taš-p[ur* ...]
8 *ina* x [...]
9 x [...]

10 x [...]
[Lacuna]

EZEKIEL 17: A HOLISTIC INTERPRETATION

Moshe Greenberg

The Hebrew University of Jerusalem

To have been a student of Samuel Noah Kramer is to have acquired for life a model of independence —based on firsthand control of data painstakingly collected and analyzed, and of scholarly reserve— manifested as a preference for acknowledging ignorance over filling in blanks speculatively. Biblical studies might benefit from both these attributes. The great pioneers joined careful analysis to venturesome speculation which, though they marked it as such, was subsequently dogmatized by their followers as the "assured results of scholarship." The modern critical study of the book of Ezekiel is a sequence of fashions, starting from the nineteenth century view of the book as an integral whole and developing into the disintegrating analyses that are still with us. True, since the Second World War a conservative trend is evident in commentaries, but just what this means may be seen in a table prepared by B. Lang by way of summarizing his review of opinion concerning the authenticity of the material in the book. Out of a total of 1273 verses, the most conservative commentators assign the following numbers, respectively, to the sixth century B.C.E. prophet: 886 (Fohrer, 1955), 808 (Eichrodt, 1970), and 764 (Zimmerli, 1969)—that is, at most only two-thirds of the material presently found in the book of Ezekiel are deemed authentic by "conservatives." To what extreme "radicals" can go is illustrated in the work of J. Garscha, who ascribed to the prophet 21 verses (Garscha, 1974; all the data cited are from Lang, 1981: 18). The assumptions of a critical method that leads to such fluctuations in results call for a fundamental scrutiny. I have argued that the text-critical component of this method is flawed (Greenberg, 1978), and that the analytical-resolving faculty of its practitioners has been developed often to the detriment of the ability to perceive integrating devices and patterns and designs of structure (Greenberg, 1980). Since the latest study of Ezek 17 that has come to my attention (Hossfeld, 1977; see ahead) continues the "radical" trend, I have chosen to present a holistic interpretation of the oracle to the judgment of colleagues, hoping to contribute thereby to redressing the balance between exemplars of the former—so many—and of the latter —so few.

Reserving a detailed analysis of the oracle for later, we must now review its gross features for the sake of discussion. The oracle has two main parts: a poetic allegory (vss. 1–10) and a prosaic interpretation (vss. 11–21)—both threatening doom; these are followed by a brief poetic "coda" describing restoration (vss. 22–4). The allegory is about two eagles and two plants: the first eagle lops off the top of a cedar and transplants it; he then plants a vine that turns to the second eagle; for that, the vine will be uprooted by the eagle and withered by the east wind. The prose first gives a political interpretation: Nebuchadnezzar exiled one king of Jerusalem (Jehoiachin) and appointed another as his sworn vassal (Zedekiah); but, flouting the oath, the Jerusalemite sent to Egypt for help in rebelling against the Babylonian; this will result in his destruction (vss. 16–8)—indeed God swears to destroy the oath-breaking king and his army (vss. 19–21). The short poetic coda relates God's promise to replant the top of the cedar in the land of Israel and make it glorious.

Our representative survey of modern critical treatment of this oracle begins with G. Hölscher's influential *Hesekiel: Der Dichter und das Buch* (1924), whose governing assumption (itself not argued) was that Ezekiel was a poet, and that all the prose in the book is inauthentic (Hölscher credited the prophet with 147 verses). Accordingly, the original oracle ends at vs.9 with a warning (as Hölscher understands it) that the second eagle (=Egypt) will despoil Judah; the rest of the oracle—the prose interpretation depicting Babylon as the destroyer—is a later distortion of the prophet's original message, made in the light of the actual events. L. P. Smith and W. A. Irwin represent the aversion to repetition that characterizes so many modern critics. Smith does away with one of the two eagles (Smith, 1939); Irwin concurs, and eliminates the vine as well (it entered the text through "an error of text or exegesis" (Irwin, 1943: 110–8). Recent commentators are less drastic, on the whole, but several still take offense at the "redundancy" of vss 16–18 alongside vss 19–21 (two oaths by God concerning the destruction of the king; see Fohrer, 1955; Eichrodt, 1970; Wevers, 1969), and it is generally held that the east wind's withering of the vine is an inconsequent, unoriginal addition to the eagle's uprooting it in vs. 9. The coda, full of hope, is regarded by most critics as a discordant later addition to an oracle dealing exclusively with doom. Exemplary analytical subtlety is exhibited by F. Hossfeld (1977), who discerns six strata in our oracle, laid down in this sequence: onto vss. 1–10—the Ezekelian core—the prophet's disciples added 11–15; 19–21; 16–17; 18; and finally 22–24. Hossfeld discerns these strata throughout the book; all belong to the sixth century yet none are to be ascribed to the prophet. Stylistic criteria of incredible refinement are invoked; thus, vss. 16–18 "are strikingly distinguished by their clumsy construction from the style of the preceding context."

The arbitrariness of this critical procedure has resulted in as many Ezekiels as modern scholars studying him. Is there no other way of exercising judgment on the text than to approach it with ready-made notions of what a prophet could say and how he could say it? The following analysis of the structure and content of the oracle offers a glimpse of an alternative; it is based on the endeavor to immerse oneself wholly in the text, activating all possible sensors in order to obtain clues to its means of expression. It is taken from a commentary in progress on the entire book (hence the occasional allusion to matters discussed elsewhere), but I have omitted the detailed textual and philological comments that precede and underpin it in the larger work. Nothing essential to the argument of this analysis depends on them, and it is as an example of a method of critical text analysis that I wish the following pages to be judged. I have elsewhere called this method holistic (Greenberg, 1980), and do here invite judgment of its validity and comparison of it with alternative procedures according to the basic criterion: how successfully does it give an account of the various phenomena present in the text?

* * * * *

The two revelation formulas of this prophecy—one at its start, before the fable (vs. 1) and one in its middle, before the interpretation (vs. 11)—underline the symmetry of fable and interpretation (Rivlin, 1973: 344; somewhat comparable are 12:8; 21:6). The two concluding formulas (vss. 21, 24) round off the main body—a doom prophecy, and the coda—a consolation. Divisions of the oracle are further articulated by the messenger-formula (vss. 1, 19, 22) and oaths (vss. 16, 19) as will emerge in the sequel.

Duality pervades the prophecy: fable and interpretation, two eagles, two plants, two modes of punishment, two planes of agency (earthly and divine), doom and consolation. With this duality agrees the double command with which the oracle opens: "Pose a riddle and tell a fable"—an indication that more is here than meets the eye. As a whole, the bipartition of the oracle —in this case, poetic fable and prose interpretation— with an added coda evoking its beginning (poetic and in terms of the fable)—is a familiar pattern (e.g., chs. 13, 16).

The detail of the structure is as follows:

A. THE FABLE/RIDDLE (vss. 1–10). The revelation formula is followed by a command to tell a fable, introduced by the messenger formula (vss. 1–3a).

A.1 *The offense.* What follows is marked as poetry by its measures (changeable though they are), its parallelisms and repetitions, and its devices (chiasm, assonance; for a suggestive treatment see Rivlin, 1973). A great eagle arrives at a mountain (vs. $3a^{\beta}$–$3b^{\alpha}$, two lines, whose stress-count is a staccato 2:2:2, 2:2:2; *gadol-g^{e}dol*; wings//pinions//feathers; first line has chiastic vowel pattern; each phrase has article). He crops a cedar-top and removes it to a merchant-city (vss. $3b^{\beta}$–4b, two lines, 3:3, 3:3, parallelism, chiasm). He then plants a native seed in optimum conditions (vs. 5, two lines, 3:3, 3:2; *zera^{c}-zara^{c}*), intending it to be a subservient but thriving vine; and it thrives (vs. 6, three lines, 6 [1+5], 3:3, 2:2:2—variations of diminishing length on 6 stresses, ending of episode staccato as beginning, parallelism). Another, less imposing eagle appears, to which the vine, surprisingly, appeals (vs. 7, three lines, 3:3, 3:3, 3:4, but the second and third lines are not segmented; parallelism between them; variation on terms of first eagle's tale—*rab/male*; *pana/kapan*), though it lacked nothing in order to prosper (vs. 8, two lines, 2:2:2, 2:2:3, staccato, climactic repetition of vss. 5, 6c with heightened variants *ṭob*, *š^{e}tula*, *peri*, *$^{\supset}$adderet* [contrast *soraḥat* of vs. 6a]). We note that the first eagle alone is active, and in his tale the plants are passive or supine; the second eagle is merely there, while in his tale, it is the vine that is active—the eagle serving as a temptation the vine cannot resist.

A.2 *The punishment* (vss. 9–10). After an introduction resembling vs. $3a^{\alpha}$, a series of rhetorical questions (*h^{a}lo* amounts to an asseveration) urges the hearers to realize the consequences of the offense. a. The first eagle will uproot the vine so that it withers, and he will need no great force to do so (vs. 9a contains the introductory formula and the rhetorical "Will it prosper?", outside the lines of poetry; the rest of vs. 9 has two lines, 3:3:3 [each segment ending with a verb], 3:3—*šorašeha* frames this section). b. The east wind's touch will wither it (vs. 10, three lines, 3, 2:2:2, 3; repetition of "Will it prosper," *ybš* [cf. vs. 9b]). The poetic measure of the latter part of vss. 9–10 is hard to determine, and it is mainly through the repeated forms of *ybš* that the segments are identified.

B. THE INTERPRETATION (VSS. 11–21). In a new revelation, the prophet is instructed first to ask his audience to consider the meaning of the fable (vss. 11–12a), then to tell it. It unfolds on two planes.

B.1 On the earthly plane (vss. 12b–18), the decipherment of the fable (vss. 12–15) shows its correspondence to the relations of the kings of Judah to the kings of Babylon and Egypt; the offense of the Judahite is exposed (vss. 12b–15a = A.1), and the question put rhetorically, "Will he prosper/escape"? (vs. 15b = 9a). Thus far the plot involves human actors only (as A.1 involved only eagles and plants).

The punishment that the Babylonian king will inflict on the Judahite for his treachery is then described (vss. 16–18); it goes beyond the uprooting (exile) foreshadowed in the fable, to Zedekiah's death in captivity. This is in line with the practice noted in chs. 5, 12 and 15, where the interpretation of a figure advanced beyond the scope of the figure; this need not imply accretion. Although the actors in the punishment passage are still human (Nebuchadnezzar, Zedekiah, and [later] Pharaoh), the whole is framed as an oath of God, ("By my life, declares Lord YHWH") who is therefore involved as guaranteeing the execution of punishment. The passage ends with an affirmation that the violator of the covenant shall not escape (vs. 18), answering the rhetorical questions of vs. 15b (relation to the question is indicated by the inversion of its parts).

B.2 The interpretation then rises to the divine plane: God will vindicate his curse-oath and covenant (vss. 19–21). Just when the meaning of the fable seems to have been exhausted, *laken* (vs. 19) advises us that only now have we arrived at the consequential part of the oracle. A messenger formula announces the new message, which begins with a second oath by God, that he shall requite Zedekiah for violation of his (God's) curse-oath and covenant. Capture, exile and judgment in Babylonia (and here the dispersal of the Judahite army is added as well) are attributed to God. This passage appears to depict the celestial plane of the earthly events predicted in B.1. As the mere agent of God, the Babylonian king has disappeared; God alone is the author of punishment, and when it occurs it will be recognized as his decree (vs. 21b). The two planes of punishment in the interpretation recall the double agency of punishment in the fable: eagle and wind (A.1.a.b.).

C. THE CODA: a prophecy of restoration (vss. 22–24). To the prediction of God's punishment is attached a forecast of his renovation of the kingdom of Judah, without a new revelation formula—and hence as a continuation, yet with a messenger formula—and hence as a discrete message. This passage is again poetic, with all the abovementioned features of poetry; characteristic of the first two verses (22–23) are tristichs whose last stich is resumptive-climactic and one stress longer than the preceding—symbolic of increase. Line structure and imagery draw on the fable for precedent. The coda falls into two parts: C.1 God's new planting of a cedar-shoot (vss. $22a^{\beta}$–$23a^{\alpha}$, 2:3 [omitting *w^enatattî*]:4, 2:3:4, each augmenting tristich framed by *wqtlty ʾny—ʾqtl* emphasizing the activity of God the speaker, parallelism), and its thriving (vs. $23a^{\beta}$-b, 2:2:3, 2:2:3 tristichs of a different augmenting pattern; note the frame *wšknw—tišknh*).
C.2 Universal recognition of God as the reverser of national fortunes (vs. 24, an expanded recognition formula is broken up to frame two sets of antitheses [lower-heighten, wither-bloom], each 3:3). Drawing its imagery from the fable and its theocentrism from the upper plane of the interpretation, the coda serves to bind together all the chief elements of the oracle.

The structure of this prophecy may be diagrammed as a spiraling progress of characters and planes (see fig. 1; movement clockwise, starting from the fable):

Medieval and modern exegetes regard the lesson of this oracle (minus the coda) as unitary: the fatal culpability of Zedekiah in breaking his vassal oath to Nebuchadnezzar. Assessment of the art of the fable is generally confined to the observation that it is overly tailored (not, however, because human actions and motives are ascribed to non-humans; that is the way of fabulists): e.g., eagles are not stationary so that vines can grow under, or twine about, them. This appreciation of the oracle depends on the reflection of vs. 19 in II Chron 36:13: among Zedekiah's offenses the Chronicler counts his rebellion against Nebuchadnezzar, "who made him swear an oath by God." It is likely that the source of that allegation was this oracle since no other allusion to such an oath exists; but the Chronicler's interpretation trivializes the leap from plane to plane in vs. 19 that the unprejudiced reader

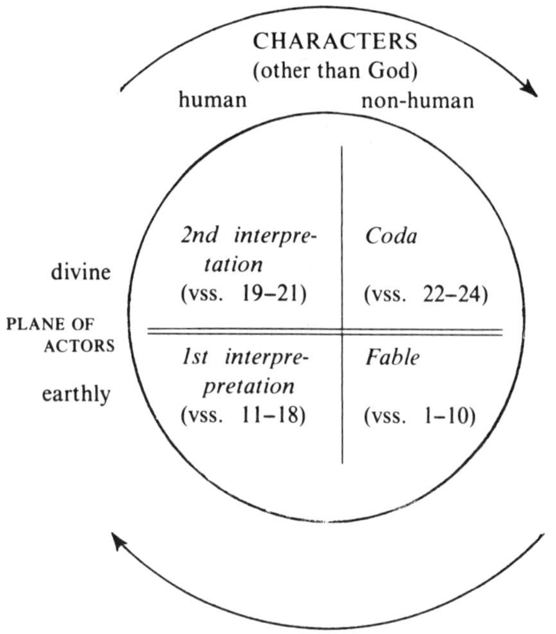

Fig. 1

senses as momentous. Worse, it impedes appreciation of the ambiguity present in the fable, which is exploited in the planar leap.

How would the first hearer of the fable, who did not know its interpretation, decode it on the basis of familiar biblical imagery? He might, of course, anticipate the correct decoding; on the other hand he might light upon alternatives which would almost yield a coherent solution. The grand eagle might be YHWH—as in the figures of Exod 19:4; Deut 32:11; the cedar—Israel (Num 24:6); Canaan—the real land so named; the planting and care of the vine—God's installation of Israel in its land (Ps 80:9–12); the lesser eagle that does not act but only tempts to infidelity—a foreign deity; the vine's appeal to it for sustenance—apostasy; the first eagle's (and the east wind's) destruction of the vine—God's punishment (Isa 5:5f; Ps 80:13f; Hosea 13:15). Such a partial decoding—Lebanon and the double planting of the first eagle remain unaccounted for—would indeed be the one most ready to hand, considering Ezekiel's regular themes. The ambiguity of most of the terms in the fable allows such a misconstruing and justifies its being entitled a riddle as well as a fable; the prophet's challenging "Surely you know what these things mean!" points to the possibility of misunderstanding.

To one who had worked out an interpretation along these lines the true decoding (B.1) would appear as an illumination and a surprise—the former, for it would take account of all the terms of the fable, the latter because for once the prophet had got off his theocentric hobbyhorse and had dealt with human events! The effect would be to drive home a dreadful premonition: Zedekiah's defection from his Babylonian overlord must earn a terrible revenge; Nebuchadnezzar could not possibly allow such a breach of a sworn vassal-treaty to escape unpunished.

And now, just when the hearer was satisfied that he had got the point, *laken* puts him on notice that the chief consequence of the oracle is still to come. According to the accepted view (based on II Chron 36), the climax of the oracle consists of God's identifying the Babylonian king's treaty enforced by oath as his own. M. Tsevat has argued that Nebuchadnezzar made Zedekiah swear allegiance to him by YHWH when he appointed him king; that, furthermore, Ezekiel—uniquely among the prophets—regarded that extorted oath as binding. Tsevat ascribes to Ezekiel the singular doctrine that even such an oath is protected by the absolute injunction to honor one's word found in Lev 5:4 with respect to individuals. "The law . . . has its place in the life of the individual; . . . Ezekiel . . . applies it . . . in the relation between the imperialist state and its captive vassals . . . No longer do two standards prevail" (Tsevat, 1959: 204). Now, that Nebuchadnezzar (or any neo-Babylonian king) imposed on his vassals an oath of allegiance by their own gods is otherwise unknown. The neo-Assyrian evidence cited by Tsevat (supplemented by Frankena, 1965: 131; Cogan, 1974: 47f.) is mostly supplied by conjectural fillings-in of lacunae. There is one clear case of the Assyrian king Esarhaddon including Phoenician gods in the curses sanctioning his treaty with Baal of Tyre (*ANET*, p. 534); but that appears as a special concession (see Cogan). The only evidence for neo-Babylonian practice is II Chron 36—probably based on the Chronicler's understanding of our Ezekiel passage and therefore no independent witness (Mendenhall, cited by Zimmerli, bases himself on nothing else).

But even granting the possibility that Nebuchadnezzar did adjure Zedekiah by YHWH, is the natural sense of vs. 19 that YHWH solemnly makes that oath his own? We understand that the Chronicler, intent on gathering all possible support for his theodicy, should have read this meaning into our verse; we recall how in II Chron 35:22 he explained Josiah's untimely death by the invention of "an oracle of God," defended by Necho, which the Judahite king spurned. But what other compelling reason is there for turning Ezekiel into a zealous partisan of Nebuchadnezzar's interested doctrine of the validity of an extorted oath by YHWH? The natural—indeed the obvious—construction of vs. 19 is to make "my curse-oath . . . and my covenant" in YHWH's speech refer to his covenant with Israel (as in 16:59), which the king was held responsible to maintain.

Indeed, the historian of the book of Kings holds it as established doctrine that the kings are responsible for covenant violations of their kingdoms (I Kings 12:28f; 14:15f); violations of the Torah of Moses are laid at the door of Manasseh (II Kings 21:8–11). Ezekiel so far shares this view as to blame the religious "straying" of Israel on the dereliction of its kings (34:6). As for Zedekiah, II Kings 24:18 judges him "evil in the sight of YHWH," and in Ezekiel 21:30 the prophet brands him a "desecrated, wicked man."

There is, then, warrant for taking vs. 19 according to its natural sense, and seeing in all of B.2 a shift from earthly to divine matters. Both fable and its earthly interpretation are suddenly transposed into an allegory of the relation between God and (the king of) Judah. The earthly suzerain Nebuchadnezzar will not let rebellious Zedekiah get away with his treachery; how much less will the divine sovereign countenance the Judahite's breach of faith with *him*.

By this understanding of the course of the oracle, two turnabouts are assumed in the audience's perception of it. What may vaguely have been thought to be an allegory of apostasy is interpreted as wholly political; but then the political transaction is used as a model from which a theological analogy is drawn. Justice is thus done (1) to the ambiguities of the fable—whose glimmerings of a divine reference are thus affirmed, and whose riddle quality is now realized; (2) to the structure of the oracle, whose consequential *laken* passage now receives its full weight; and (3) to the thought of Ezekiel, which is now freed of the idiosyncratic burden of questionable validity imposed on it by the Chronicler-Tsevat interpretation.

All parts of the prophecy are now mutually illuminated: the fable is truly a riddle (*ḥida*)—solved by identifying its human referents, all on an earthly plane. Then an allegorical cast is thrown on both by the rise to the divine plane of interpretation; that is, all the preceding political transactions are but a "likening" (*mašal*) to the relations between God and the Judahite king. (Note the correspondence between the sequence of *ḥida* and *mašal* in vs 2 and their literary realization [suggested by Lou Levine of Toronto].)

Finer points emerge: the dual agents of punishment in the fable (eagle and wind) presage the earthly and divine planes of the real punishment of Zedekiah. Moreover, the divine oath introducing the earthly interpretation of the fable, and expressing God's guarantee that the human suzerain will vindicate his violated compact, is given a new dimension by the parallel oath introducing the divine plane of events. Events on the two planes are indeed parallel and simultaneous: for his own reasons Nebuchadnezzar will punish the Judahite rebel, but in so doing he will (all unknown to him) be executing the design of the divine architect of history upon the king responsible for violation of his covenant with Judah. This brings us to the coda.

The coda is not only the planar correspondent of the fable (poetic, and with non-human characters), it is the diametric divine counterpart of the earthly arrangements made by the king of Babylon (see figure). Without the coda, God appears only in the character of destroyer, the divine correspondent to the Babylonian king in the role of outraged overlord. To the constructive arrangements of the human no analogue on the higher plane appears. The coda supplies that lack; not only is it a planar analogue of the fable, but it portrays God as undoing and superseding the earthly order, reversing its every effect. The revolutionary character of God's deeds is highlighted by the emphatic pronouns "*I* will take," "*I* will plant," and the antitheses of vs. 24.

This prophecy has thematic and verbal links with the preceding one. The theme of faithlessness to the covenant dominates both; indeed, the proximity of the expression "violate covenant and flout curse-oath" in 16:59 to our oracle provides a clue for our understanding of that expression in vs. 19. Only in these two oracles does this terminology appear. Incidental contacts, common to these two oracles alone (and suggesting they were composed at about the same time), are the terms *riqma* "embroidery" and "Canaan" for Chaldea.

If our surmise is correct concerning the secondary character of "Pharaoh" in vs. 17 and the occasion of its entrance into the text (Greenberg, 1957: 308f.), the body of this oracle will have predated the siege of Jerusalem. The embassy to Egypt (vs. 15) belongs to the very beginning of the rebellion, during the last days of Psammetichus II. The prediction of the rout of Zedekiah's forces, his capture, captivity and death in Babylon echo 12:13–14 and do not necessitate a post-fall date. That the particular horrors of

Zedekiah's fate—the slaughter of his children and his blinding—are not mentioned points to a date of composition before the fall of the city.

Critics are almost unanimous in regarding the coda as a post-fall consolation, of a piece with the visions of chs. 34–48. As in the case of the coda of ch. 16, they question the suitability of a restoration oracle in a doom context. There are two issues: did Ezekiel prophesy consolations before the fall? Is this consolation pre-fall? Lang, 1978: 84ff has pointed to the incidental restoration prophecies in 11:17f; 13:9 as evidence that Ezekiel (like Jeremiah, ch. 24) anticipated a restoration well before the fall. We have argued that the restoration coda of ch. 16 is integrally related to the dooms preceding it. Here it is less obvious that the coda is necessary to the message of the body of the oracle, unless it is maintained that the rise to the divine plane of events entailed the assertion of YHWH's superiority over all earthly kings in the constructive as well as the destructive dealing with kingdoms. But before deciding that the coda is late, we must give due consideration to the fact that in post-fall restoration prophecies, anxiety over the damaged reputation of YHWH appears as a motive of God's healing acts (36:20ff; 39:25ff); that theme is hardly present here. In language and conception the coda suits the body of the oracle, and completes it; there is no ground for doubting its Ezekielian provenience. But whether it was from the first the denouement of the doom oracle, cannot be answered decisively, though its literary fit is perfect.

BIBLIOGRAPHY

Cogan, M.
1974 *Imperialism and Religion: Assyria, Judah and Israel in the Eighth and Seventh Centuries B.C.E.*

Eichrodt, W.
1970 *Ezekiel*, trans. C. Quinn [Old Testament Library]. (orig. *Der Prophet Ezekiel.* 1965–6).

Fohrer, G.
1955 *Ezechiel.* [Handbuch zum alten Testament.]

Frankena, R.
1965 "The Vassal Treaties of Esarhaddon and the Dating of Deuteronomy," *Oudtestamentische Studiën* 14:122–54.

Garscha, J.
1974 *Studien zum Ezechielbuch: Eine redaktionskritische Untersuchung von Ez 1–39.* [Europäische Hochschulschriften XXIII/23.]

Greenberg, M.
1957 "Ezekiel 17 and the Policy of Psammetichus II," *JBL* 76: 304–9.
1978 "The Use of the Ancient Versions for Understanding the Hebrew Text: A Sampling from Ezek II,1–III,11," in *Congress Volume, Göttingen 1977.* [Supplements to Vetus Testamentum 29.] Pp. 131–48.
1980 "The Vision of Jerusalem in Ezekiel 8–11: A Holistic Interpretation," in J. L. Crenshaw and S. Sandmel, eds., *The Divine Helmsman: Studies on God's Control of Human Events, Presented to Lou H. Silberman.* Pp. 146–64.

Hölscher, G.
1924 *Hezekiel, der Dichter und das Buch.* [Beiheft zur Zeitschrift für die altestamentliche Wissenschaft 39.]

Hossfeld, F.
1977 *Untersuchungen zu Komposition und Theologie des Ezechielbuches.* [Forschung zur Bibel.]

Irwin, W. A.
1943 *The Problem of Ezekiel: An Inductive Study.*

Lang, B.
1978 *Kein Aufstand in Jerusalem.* [Stuttgarter Biblische Beiträge.]
1981 *Ezechiel: Der Prophet und Das Buch.* [Erträge der Forschung 153.]

Rivlin, A.
1973 "The Parable of the Eagles, the Cedar and the Vine [Hebrew]," *Beth Mikra* 54: 342–59.

Smith, L. P.
1939 "The eagle(s) of Ezekiel 17," *JBL* 58: 43–50.

Tsevat, M.
1959 "The Neo-Assyrian and Neo-Babylonian Vassal Oaths and the Prophet Ezekiel," *JBL* 78: 199–204.

Wevers, J.
1969 *Ezekiel.* [The Century Bible, n.s.]

Zimmerli, W.
1969 *Ezechiel.* [Biblischer Kommentar altes Testament 13.]

A HURRO-HITTITE HYMN TO ISHTAR

HANS G. GÜTERBOCK
THE UNIVERSITY OF CHICAGO

THE HITTITE TEXT I AM HERE PRESENTING TO MY FRIEND SAMUEL KRAMER has been known for a long time. It takes up the first and part of the second column of a tablet, *Bo* 2024, published in cuneiform copy by A. Walther as *KUB* 24.7 in 1930; the tablet is now kept in the Istanbul Museum. The second part of the tablet contains the well-known tale of "The Sungod, the Cow, and the Fisherman."[1]

In contrast to that tale the hymnic first part of the tablet (*CTH* 717) was for a long time more or less left aside because of the difficulties of understanding it. A. Goetze, in 1933, gave the first translation of col. i 12–32 (*AM* pp. 262f.), in which he correctly brought out the essentials. C. G. von Brandenstein (in the places cited under *CTH* 717) only commented on individual lines. Only recently have editions of the whole text been published. In 1977 there appeared an article by A. Archi, "I poteri della dea Ištar hurrita-ittita," *Oriens Antiquus* 16, 297–311, that contains a full transliteration and translation of the hymn (pp. 305–11). Almost simultaneously Ilse Wegner included individual parts of the text in her dissertation, *Gestalt und Kult der Ištar-Šawuška in Kleinasien.*[2] These editions have become a basis for further study and have been helpful in the preparation of this article.

For some time I wondered whether the hymn was an introduction to the tale of "The Sungod and the Cow." In the beginning of the story the Sungod falls in love with a beautiful cow, and (apparently as a result of their union) the cow gives birth to a human child. Was that the reason for prefacing the tale with a hymn to the goddess of love? I no longer think so. It is more likely that *KUB* 24.7 is simply a *Sammeltafel*, a tablet upon which two separate texts happen to be written. Whether the scribe who thus combined them was thinking of Ištar's role in the adventure of the cow is another question. The main reason for separating the two texts, however, is their form: the tale is told in prose, while the hymn has a clear strophic structure. Another reason may be the following: In *Kumarbi*, 119–22, I included both the Appu story and the tale of the Cow among Hittite texts of Hurrian origin, and both Friedrich (*ZA* 49, 213 ff.) and Hoffner (l.c. in note 1) followed me in this. But Siegelová (*StBoT* 14, 33f.) showed that there is no evidence for Hurrian origin in these two tales, and the repertory of preserved Hurrian mythological fragments published by M. Salvini (*SMEA* 18, 1977, 73–91) does not include a Hurrian text on Appu or the Cow story. The hymn, on the other hand, shows its Hurrian origin clearly in the names of the goddesses who are attendants of Ištar. If thus the two texts have different backgrounds, this is one more reason for keeping them apart.

I shall first present the text in transliteration and translation; this will be followed by a philological commentary and a literary analysis.

---

[1] Abbreviations as in the *Chicago Hittite Dictionary* (*CHD*) and *HW*, *HW*².

CTH, 363; part of it was made available by H. Ehelolf as early as 1926 (*OLZ* 29, 766–69); the standard edition is by J. Friedrich, *ZA* 49 (1950), 224–33. In my *Kumarbi* (1946), 119–22 I gave an outline of the story, connecting it with the tale of Appu (*CTH* 360, ed. by J. Siegelová, *StBoT* 14, 1971, 1–34) for reasons that in my mind are still valid. A new analysis of "The Hurrian Story of the Sungod, the Cow and the Fisherman" was published by H. A. Hoffner in M. A. Morrison and D. I. Owen, eds., *Studies on the Civilization and Culture of Nuzi and the Hurrians in Honor of E. R. Lacheman* (1981), 189–94.

[2] *Hurritologische Studien* III = *AOAT* 36, published 1981, but, according to the preface, completed in 1976.

TRANSLITERATION

Col. i: First six lines lost; line 7 damaged.

§1 7 [. . . . .]-*ma* ⌜*la-aḫ-ḫi*(?) *i-ia*⌝[-*at*/*an-t*]*a-ri*(?)
8 [. . . .] *ku-e-e*[*z-za* o o]MEŠ(?)[3] *na-at ku-ra-ak-ki*
9 [*ma-a-an*?] *a-ša-an-zi šar-ga-u-e-eš-ma ku-e-ez-za*
10 [UR.SAG?].MEŠ *nu za-aḫ-ḫi-ia tar-aḫ-ḫi-iš-kán-zi*
11 [*ku-e-ez*?]-*ma* $^{SAL.MEŠ}$*e-ši-in-zi* $^{SAL.MEŠ}$KAR.KID-*ia* SIG$_5$-*an-te-eš*

TRANSLATION

§1 (about six lines missing)
(7) But [when she] go[es] (or: [they] go) to war,
[. . .] on one side (are) [the . . .]s,
they are [like] pillars;
on the other side (are) the mighty [heroes],
they always win in battle;
and [on another side] (are) the *eši*-women and 'good' (shapely?) prostitutes.

---

§2 12 [*wa-al-l*]*a-aḫ-ḫi-ia-aš ŠA* ^{d}GAŠAN *ḫa-an-te-ez-zi-uš* ^{SAL}SUḪUR.LÁL.ḪI.A
13 [^{d}*Ni-na*]-*at-ta-an* ^{d}*Ku-li-it-ta-an* ^{d}*Ši-en-tal-ir-te-in*
14 [^{d}*Ḫa*]-*am-ra-zu-un-na-an nu-kan* ^{d}*IŠTAR-li* É-*ir ku-it*
15 [*a-aš-ši*]-*ia-at-ta-ri nu a-pu-u-uš a-pé-e-da-ni* É-*ni*
16 [*š*]*u*?-*wa-u-wa-an-zi u-i-ia-az-zi nu* KIN-*an ku-it an-ni-iš-kán-zi*
17 ⌜*na-at*⌝ *ḫal-wa-am-na-az an-ni-iš-kán-zi* É-*ir-ma ku-it*
18 *an-ni-iš-kán-zi na-at du-uš-ka-ra-at-ta-az-za* (erasure)
19 *an-ni-iš-kán-zi ḫa-an-ta-ir-ma* $^{SAL.MEŠ}$É.GE$_4$.A-*uš*
20 *nu* TÚG-*an ša-ri-iš-kán-zi ḫa-an-da-ir-ma* DUMU.MEŠ É-*TI*
21 *nu* A.ŠÀ-*an* IKU-*li ḫar-ši-iš-kán-zi*

§2 (12) I shall praise them, the 'first' lady attendants of Ištar:
Ninatta, Kulitta, Šintal-irti (and) [H]amrazunna.
Whatever household is beloved by Ištar,
she sends these into that house in order to look (after it)(?).
The work which they (the people of the house) perform,
they perform with laughter;
(17) the house for which they care,
they care for it with joy.
The young brides have been in harmony,
and (so) they keep weaving cloth;
and the sons of the house have been in harmony,
and (so) they continue plowing the field by the acre.

---

§3 22 *wa-al-la-aḫ-ḫi-ia-aš ŠA* ^{d}GAŠAN *ap-pé-ez-zi-uš* ^{SAL}SUḪUR.LÁL.ḪI.A
23 ^{d}A-*li-in* ^{d}*Ḫal-za-a-ri-in* ^{d}*Ta-ru-wi*$_5$-*in*
24 ^{d}*Ši-na-an-da-du-kar-ni-in wa-al-la-aḫ-ḫi nu-kán* ^{d}GAŠAN-*li*
25 [*k*]*u-it* É-*ir pu-uk-kán nu a-pu-u-uš a-pé-e-da-ni* É-*ri*
26 *a-ni-ia-u-wa-an-zi* (eras.) *u-i-ia-zi nu* É-*ir tuḫ*[-*ḫi-ma-az-z*]*a*
27 *píd-du-li-ia-az-za e-eš-ša-an-zi nu-kán* ^{SAL}⌜É⌝[GE$_4$.A-*x*]
28 *kap-pí-la-a-ir nu-kán 1-aš 1-an* SAG.DU⌜-*an*⌝
29 *šal-la-an-ni-iš-ki-iz-zi nu nam-ma ḫa-an-t*[*a-an-te-eš*(?) TÚG-*an*]
30 *Ú-UL ša-a-ri-ia-an-zi* LÚ.MEŠ *AT-ḪU-TIM*[-*ma*]
31 ⌜*ku*⌝-*ru-ri*-⌜*ia*⌝-*aḫ-ḫi-ir nu nam-ma* A.ŠÀ-*an* [IKU-*li Ú-UL*]

§3 (22) I shall praise them, the 'last' lady attendants of Ištar:
Ali, Halzari, Taruwi (and) Šinanda-dukarni I shall praise.
Whatever household is hated by Ištar,
she sends those into that house in order to treat it.
They do the housework with gr[oaning] and anguish.
(27) The you[ng brides] were at odds,
and (so) one always pulls the other by the head,
and they no longer weave [cloth] in har[mony].
The brothers have become enemies,
and (so) they [no] longer plow the field [by the acre];

---

[3] Or [o - o-*t*]*e-eš*?

32 ⌜*ḫar*⌝-*ši-ia-a*[*n-z*]*i* *ḫal-lu-wa-nu-e-er-m*[*a-at-za*(?)]
33 *nu nam-ma* [ŠE? *m*]*a-al-lu-u-wa-ar* Ú-U[*L ki-ša-ri*(?)]
34 *nu* UR.GI$_7$ GI[M-*an* ŠA]Ḫ(?) *Ú-UL ḫa-an-ta*[-*iz-zi*(?) . . . (?)]
35 *nu-kán* NINDA.X[o o]x ⌜^{NA_4}⌝*ku-un-ku-nu-uz-zi-i*[*n* . . . .]
36 GIM-*an ú-e-te-ni an-da tar-nir na*[-*at* . . . .]
37 *ar-ḫa ḫar-ni-in-ki-i*[*r*]

they have quarreled,
(33) and (so) grinding [of grain] no longer [takes place].
Just as the dog do[es] not [get] along with the pig(?),
they let [. . .] bread (and?) basalt into the water like [. . .]
and (so) they have destroyed [. . .] completely(?).

---

§4 38 LÚ-*iš-ma-kán* DAM-*ZU-ia ku-i-e-eš a-aš-ši-ia-a*[*n-ta-ri*]
39 *nu-uš-ma-aš-kán a-aš-ši-ia-tar* ZAG[-*aš*]-*ša-an ar*[-*nu-wa-an-zi*]
40 *na-at tu-e*<-*da*>-*az-za* ^{d}*IŠTAR-li-az-za* [*t*]*a-ra-a-an* SAL$^{!}$-*n*[*a*$^{!}$-*an ku-iš*(?)]
41 *pu-pu-wa-la-iz-zi nu-za-kán pu-pu*⌜-*wa-la*⌝-*tar* ZAG-*aš*[-*ša-an*]
42 *ar-nu-uz-zi na-at tu-e-da-za* ^{d}GAŠAN-*li-z*[*a ta-ra-a-an* . . .]
43 Ì.DÙG.GA *na-at wa-aš-ta-ri tu-uk-ma-kán* [*ku-iš* . . .(?)]
44 [*a-aš*]-*ši-ia-at-ta-ri nu-uš-ši zi-ik* URU-*a*[*š an-tu-uḫ-ša-tar*(?)]
45 [*ga*]-*la-ak-ta-ra-ši na-an an-da ka-a*[-*ri-ia-ši*]
46 [*nu-ká*]*n*(?) *tu-e-da-az*$^{!}$-*pát* ^{d}*IŠTAR-li-az a-pé-e* [. . . (?)]
47 [o]-*x ar-ḫa Ú-UL ku-it-ki iš-da*[*m-ma-aš-ša-an-zi*]

§4 (38) A man and his wife who love each other
and carry their love to fulfillment:
that has been decreed by you, Ištar.
[He who] seduces a w[oman]
and carries the seduction to fulfillment:
that [has been decreed] by you, Ištar.
[. . .] (43) sweet-scented oil, and it is pleasing.
For him [who] is beloved [by you]
you make the town['s people] drowsy and cover him,
(so that) thanks to you, Ištar, those [people] do not hear anything.

---

§5 48 [*ma-a-a*]*n* SAL-*TUM-ma A-NA* ^{LÚ}*MU-TI-ŠU pu-u*[*k-kán-za na-an zi-ik*]
49 [^{d}GAŠAN-*iš*(?)] *pu-uq-qa-nu-wa-an ḫar-t*[*i*] *ma-a-an* [LÚ-*iš-ma A-NA* DAM-*ŠU*(?)]
50 [*im-ma*(?)] *pu-uk-kán-za nu-uš*[-*ma-aš*]-*kán* [. . . . . .]
51 [*zi-ik*(?)] ^{d}*IŠTAR-iš iš-ḫu-u-wa*<-*an*> ⌜*ḫar-ti*⌝ [. . . . .]
52 [. . . .]*x na-aš mar-la-tar pu-pu-wa*[*la-tar* . . . . . .]
53 [. . . . .]*x ma-na-at-kán wa-at-ku-an*[-*zi* . . . .]
54 [. . . . . . . T]I-*nu-zi ap-pa-an-zi-ma*[-. . . . . . .]
55 [. . . . .] *e-šu-wa-ar mar-la*[- . . . . . .]

§5 (48) But [if] a woman is ha[ted] by her husband,
[then you, Ištar] have caused [her] to be hated.
[But] if [a man] is [even(?) hated [by his wife],
then [you], Ištar, have heaped up [. . .] for them.
[They/he will . . .]
(52) and he [will commit] a foolish act, (namely) adul[tery].
They might elope,
[but . . .] will not save [them].
They will be seized [. . .];
to be [. . .] is fooli[sh](?).

---

§6 56 [^{d}*IŠTAR-in*(?) *iš-ḫa-m*]*i-iš-ki-mi na-an*[. . . . . .]
57 [. . . . .]*x-in nu-mu* LÚ.*x*[. . . . . . .]
58 (traces)
(gap of about 5 lines)
ii 1 [. . . . . . . *wa-aš*(?)]-*ta-aš-ku-wa-ar zi-ik* ^{d}*IŠ-TAR*[-*iš*]

§6 (56) [Of Ištar] I shall [si]ng and [. . .] her.
(Two lines too fragmentary for translation, then gap of ca. 5 lines)
(ii 1) [. . .] constant [tra]nsgression [did] you, Ištar, [commit]:
you devoured your husbands:

2 [. . . . . .]*x nu-za* LÚ*MU-TI-KA ar-ḫa ka-ri-i[p-ta]*
3 [*ku-in-kán* LÚ-*a*]*n* LÚ.ŠU.GI-*aḫ-ta ku-in-ma-kán* LÚ-*an* ZAG-*na*
4 [*ar-nu-u*]*t*(?) *ku-in-ma-za* LÚ-*an* LÚGURUŠ-*an-pát ḫar-ni-ik-ta*
5 [*nu-z*]*a* LÚ.MEŠ *ḫu-el-pí* GA.RAŠ.SAR *i-wa-ar ar-ḫa ka-ri*[*ip-ta*]
6 [*z*]*i-ik* dIŠTAR-*iš e-ša-ra-ši-la-aš-ma-aš a-ri-ša-an-d*[*a*]
7 GIM-*an du-wa-ar-ni-iš-ki-it na-aš-za-kán* ŠE.LÚ.SAR ⌈GIM-*an*⌉(?)
8 *IT-T*[*I* NUM]UN(?) *ka-ri-ip-ta na-aš-kán ar-ḫa ḫar-ni-ik-ta*
9 TÚG.NÍG.LÁ[M-*aš-ma*(?)]-*aš-za* GIM-*an pár-ku-wa-ia wa-aš-še-eš-ki-ši*
10 *nu ku-in* [*pa*]-*ap-ra-aḫ-ti ku-in-ma-za pár-ku-un-pát ar-ḫa píd-da-la-ši*
11 *ku-in* ⌈*ú-wa-te*⌉-*ši na-an* GIŠAN.ZA.GÀR GIM-*an pár-ga-nu-ši*
12 *ku-in-ma*[-*ká*]*n a-pé-el-pát ú-e-ta-an-da-aš pa-ra-a*
13 *ú-wa-te-š*[*i*] A-*aš-ma* (? *a-aš-ma*?) *ku-wa-pí la-ḫu-uz-zi*
14 *nu wa*⌈*-at-ta-ru*(?)⌉ KÚ-*iz-zi zi-iq-qa-za* dGAŠAN-*iš* LÚ.MEŠ-*uš*
15 *QA-TAM-M*[*A zi*]-*in-ni-iš-ki-ši nu-uš-ši-kán* MÁŠ.TUR.ḪI.A
16 GIM-*an* [*ta-r*]*u-up-pa-an-zi* EGIR-*an-da* GUL-*ki-š*[*i* . . . . . .]*x*(?)
17 GIŠ*kat-ta*⌈*-lu*⌉*-uz-zi-ma-aš* DÙ-*at na-aš-kán* GÌ[R-*it* . . . . . .]

[One man] you made old,
another man you [let attain] fulfillment,
another you destroyed even in his prime:
you devour[ed] men like fresh leek.
(6) You, Ištar, kept breaking them like the . . . of their . . .
and devoured them like coriander with (its) [see]d(?),
and completely destroyed them.
When you put clean festive garments on them,
you soil one,
and another you neglect even though he is clean(!).
(11) Another you bring and make him high like a tower,
still another you lead out to his own . . . ,
but when he pours into the waters (? when he first pours?)
he keeps eating (? drinking?) . . . :
you, Ištar, thus always finish men off.
Afterwards(?) you keep hitting at(?) him(?)
just as one herds kids together.
You have made them into a threshold
and [trample] them [with your] feet.

---

§7 18 ANŠE-*aš-ma-za* GIM-*an pu-un-tar-ri-ia-li-iš z*[*i-ik*]
19 SAL.LUGAL-*aš* dIŠTAR-*iš x-ga-x* (traces)
20 *nu-ut-ta ku-wa-pí* [o] *x* [. . . .
21 UR.MAḪ-*ma-za* GI[M-*an* . . .
22 KALAG.GA-*aš al-p*[*a-aš*(?) . . .
23 LÚ.MEŠGURUŠ-*aš-ma-za* [. . .
24 SAL.MEŠKI.SIKIL-*aš x*[. . .
25 SAL.MEŠ*al-la-wa-an*[- . . .
26 *zi-ik-pát* d*I*[*ŠTAR-iš* . . .

§7 (18) You are stubborn like an ass, O queen Ištar!
[. . .]
And when [. . .] you [. . .]
You are(?) like a lion [. . .
a terrible clo[ud . . .]
To the young men [. . .]
to the maidens [. . .]
the *a.*-women [. . .]
Only you, Ištar [. . .]

[End of hymn lost. Walther estimated the gap between line 26 and the double rule marking the end of the hymn as ca. 17 lines.]

(§§ **8ff.** lost: about 17 lines to the end of the hymn.)

COMMENTARY

i.9: Instead of [GIM-*an*] (Archi) I restore [*ma-a-an*], the same word spelled out, because it fills the space better. Although the text uses GIM-*an* more often, the same tablet (same scribe, although the other text) has UR.MAḪ-*aš* GIM-*an* and *ḫuwanḫueššar ma-a-an* side by side in col. iii 24, 26.

10: [UR.SAG].MEŠ is free restoration based on the context and the space available.

11: $^{\text{SAL.MEŠ}}$*ešinzi*, Luwian nom. pl., not known otherwise.— $^{\text{SAL.MEŠ}}$KAR.KID, Akk. (sg.) *ḫarimtu*, Hitt. reading unknown. In the Hittite Laws (§ 194) the word occurs with its basic meaning "prostitute." The KAR.KID, often in the plural and occasionally with a chief or overseer (GAL, UGULA), plays a role in the cult festivals; for details see H. Otten, *ZA* 53 (1959), 181f. In none of these occurrences do they actually exercise their profession. The only hint is contained in a text which I called "An Initiation Rite for a Hittite Prince," where after much eating and some drinking twelve $^{\text{SAL.MEŠ}}$KAR.KID are brought into the presence of the prince.[4] For a prostitute functioning in the cult the term "hierodule," which is commonly used, is adequate; in our context it may simply be "prostitute."

12 and 22: In contrast, the ^{SAL}SUḪUR.LÁL (also SUḪUR.LAL, i.e., LA_5 and LÁ, respectively) in the Hittite texts is not a hierodule. The definition as a kind of prostitute given for *kezertu* by both the *CAD* and the *AHw* is based on late sources. For the Old Babylonian period, J. J. Finkelstein (*YOS* 13 [1972], 10f.) only considered the possibility that *kezrētu* might have engaged in such activities. B. F. Batto (in 1974)[5] flatly denied it; but M. L. Gallery[6] argues that a certain married woman, among whose activities *ḫarimūtu* "prostitution" is mentioned in one OB document, was a *kezertu*, although she is not explicitly so designated. For the SUḪUR.LÁL in Hittite texts, a perusal of the *Chicago Hittite Dictionary* files[7] resulted in the following picture, supplementing and modifying the observations of J. Friedrich, *SV* 2, 155f., 170f.

(1) The S.L. plays no rôle in the cult.

(2) She belongs to the palace (Huqq. §§ 31, 32; *Dienstanw.* 16; *KUB* 14.4 iii 15). Since she is contrasted to "free" women in the first two occurrences, she must have been unfree. Nevertheless,

(3) a S.L. named Kuwattalla and designated as GEME of the king and queen received a very large estate from Arnuwanda I and Ašmunikal (ca. 1400 B.C.).[8]

(4) A S.L. of the same name, presumably the same person, is the author or co-author of several Luwian purification rituals (references in Laroche, *NH* no. 662.2). In most of the cases she appears together with a certain Šilalluḫi (*NH* no. 1148), a ^{SAL}ŠU.GI, lit. "old woman" but in effect an exorcist.

(5) In some magic rituals the "tongue," i.e., harmful speech, slander *vel sim.*, of the S.L. is exorcised with that of the palace attendant (DUMU.É.GAL), guardsman (*MEŠEDI*), *pašīšu*-priest (^{LÚ}GUDÙ), priest (SANGA) and priestess (AMA.DINGIR); here too she belongs to the personnel of the palace (*KUB* 9.34 i 31–32 and similar texts, cf. *CHD lala-* 4, esp. 4 b 3′).

(6) Deities can have S.L.s. In addition to our text there are these examples: [^{SAL}S]UḪUR.LÁL ^{d}*Ḫé-bat* (*KUB* 10.92 vi 7); the same goddess is kept from falling by her $^{\text{SAL.MEŠ}}$SUḪUR.LÁL (*KUB* 33.106 = *Ull.* III A ii 9). Apart from our hymn Ištar also has them in *KUB* 39.93 obv. 5, a text with recitations in *babilili*, one of which reads: *alikātu ša panīki ali[kātu ša arkiki]* $^{\text{SAL.MEŠ}}$SUḪUR.LÁL-*ki* $^{\text{SAL.MEŠ}}$KAR.KID-*ki* "Those who walk before you and those who wal[k behind you], your S.L.s and your hierodules." There are 2 $^{\text{SAL.MEŠ}}$SUḪUR.LÁL DINGIR-*LIM* "of the deity" in *KUB* 31.67 iv 9, where the deity probably is [Ištar of] Lawazantiya of line 8. In *KUB* 7.54 ii 19, however, the deity meant in the phrase *ŠA* DINGIR-*LIM* $^{\text{SAL.MEŠ}}$SUḪUR.LÁL can only be the male god Yarri (16), most probably the counterpart to Erra.

(7) Rarely does a S.L. act in a magic ritual. In the *Ritual of Tunnawi* (*CTH* 409) ii 65–67 she uses nine combs to cleanse the EN.SISKUR over his whole body while he is bathing, but it is the ^{SAL}ŠU.GI who brings the combs and pronounces the spell. And in *KUB* 27.29 iii 5–7 the S.L. throws water over the EN.SISKUR.

As a result we can state that the S.L. is definitely not a hierodule in Hittite texts. She is an attendant, in the palace (where she is unfree), among gods, and also an attendant of the exorcist. Specifically in this case she is a helper in bathing a person. This function brings to mind the reliefs no. 37 and 36 at Yazılıkaya, where Ninatta carries an ointment horn and Kulitta, a mirror.[8a] There we may call them "lady's maids" (German: *Zofen*), but in general we shall translate S.L. as "attendant woman" or "lady attendant."

12: ^{d}GAŠAN is simply another logogram for Ištar, as shown by the identical phonetic complement *-li-* used with both ^{d}GAŠAN and ^{d}*IŠTAR*. Cf. ^{d}*IŠTAR-li* (14) with ^{d}GAŠAN-*li* (24), both dat. in parallel clauses. Both writings represent the still unknown Hittite name of the goddess; cf. also abl. ^{d}*IŠTAR-li-az(-za)* (i 40, 46) and ^{d}GAŠAN-*li-z[a]* (42), nom. ^{d}*IŠTAR-iš* (i 51,

---

[4] *IBoT* 1.29 rev. 46–56; see Güterbock in D. Sinor, ed., *American Oriental Society Middle West Branch Semicentennial Volume* [*Oriental Studies* 3] 1969, 99–103.

[5] B. F. Batto, *Studies on Women at Mari.* 1974, 114f. (I owe this reference to Jo Ann Scurlock, Chicago.) J. Renger, *ZA* 58 (1967), 188 does not even mention this condition.

[6] M. L. Gallery, "Service Obligations of the *kezertu*-Women," *Or.* 49 (1980), 333–38. (I owe this reference to S. Košak, Chicago.)

[7] Begun by H. A. Hoffner, Jr., continued under a grant from the National Endowment for the Humanities.

[8] *KBo* 5.7, ed. K. K. Riemschneider, *MIO* 6 (1958), 344–55 as LS 1; her name is in rev. 47f.

[8a] Gallery, l.c. (n. 6), 338 with n. 22, cites Finkelstein's suggestion of 1973 that the *kezertu* was a hairdresser. This would fit the reliefs very well and encourages me to interpret the hieroglyph of no. 36, Kulitta (Laroche, *HH*, sign no. 158), as representing curls.

ii 19). The use of the Hittite name of the goddess rather than of her Hurrian name, Šauška, side by side with her Hurrian attendants Ninatta, Kulitta, Šentalirte etc. has a parallel in the Hittite version of the Hurrian Kumarbi cycle; cf. *Kumarbi*, 96. I therefore use the name Ištar rather than Šauška in the translation.

14: Of the two alternative restorations of the first sign of the name as *ḫa* or *na* offered by von Brandenstein, *Bildbeschr.*, 33, I prefer *ḫa*, *Ḫamrazunna*, because of the frequency of the element *ḫamra/i-* in Hurrian; cf. Laroche, *Gloss. hourr.*, 91f.

15: The restoration [*a-aš-ši*]-*ia-at-ta-ri* follows Götze, *AM* p. 262; for *a-aš-*. . . cf. i 38f. For the construction with the dative see Sommer, *HAB*, 185, and *HW*^{2}, 401.

15 end: The sign as copied is *-ni* rather than *-ir*. The text writes É-*ir* (*per*) for the nom/acc. (i 14, 25) and É-*ri* (*peri*) for the dat.-loc. (25), but here É-*ni* (*parni*), the more frequent form of the dat.-loc.; probably a modernization by the copyist.

16: The restoration of the first sign and with it of the verbal stem is uncertain. Goetze refrained from restoring and translating. Wegner's restoration is against the available space and results in a non-existing form. Archi's restoration [*š*]*u-* is preferable, but "to fill" does not yield a satisfactory sense. I think of the verb *šuwaya-* "to look" although its (unattested) infinitive should be **šuwayawanzi* rather than **suwauwanzi*. But given the known mixing of similar verbs by the scribes (cf. Oettinger, *Stammbildung*, 269ff.) our interpretation seems possible.

16: For KIN-*an* = *aniyan* see *HW*^{2}, 88 r.; for the spelling of the simple verb *aniya-* with single *n*, of its iter.-dur. with double *n* see *HW*^{2}, 87 r.; *anniški-* with "house" as object was translated "besorgen" by Goetze (*AM*, 262), a definition which does not appear in *HW*^{2}; presumably it is subsumed there under "behandeln" (p. 87 sub II 2 our passage is not translated). I chose "to care for" as suiting the context best.

17: For *ḫalwamnaz* see Otten apud *HW 3.Erg.*, 13.

19f.: *ḫantair* has been taken in the sense of "vermählen," i.e., "to marry off, give into marriage" by the previous interpreters. But this translation does not really fit the context: why should the sons of the house have to be married in order to till the fields? Also the contrasting statements in lines 27–32 point into a different direction. Decisive for our passage are two catalog entries: *KUB* 30.56 iii 10–11 *mān* UN-*ši* ÌR.MEŠ-*ŠU* GEME.M[EŠ-*ŠU-ya UL*] SI×SÁ-*anzi* (i.e. *ḫandanzi*) *našma* LÚ-*LUM* SAL-*TUM-ya UL ḫandanzi*, which Laroche, *CTH*, 182, translates: "Quand pour une personne ses serviteurs et ses servantes [ne] s'entendent [pas], ou bien qu'un homme et sa femme ne s'accordent pas"; *KUB* 30.45 iii 6–9 with dupl. 44 iii(?) 2–5, *CTH*, 160f. as lines 14–17 of the composite text and the translation "ne sont pas d'accord." Cf. also (I took Puduḫepa for my wife) *nu ḫandawen* Ḫatt. iii 2, which Otten, *StBoT* 24, 17, translates "wir hielten zusammen." This is a good rendering; "we understood each other, were in harmony, had good relations" would also fit. In these passages *ḫandāi-* is intransitive, whereas in line 19 of our text $^{\text{SAL.MEŠ}}$É.GE₄.A-*uš* is the accus. pl. form. Since, however, DUMU.MEŠ É-*TI* (20) and $^{\text{LÚ.MEŠ}}$*ATḪUTIM* (30) can be both nom. and acc., while ^{SAL}⸢É⸣[.GE₄.A...] (27) is incomplete, and since in the plural improper use of the *-ēš* and *-uš* forms is frequent, I follow the examples cited in taking the verb as intransitive with "brides" as subject. This has the advantage of avoiding change of subject.

29: The restoration proposed by Archi, *ḫa-an-t*[*a-an-zi* Ú-*UL nu* TÚG-*an*], which would give a good sense also with our interpretation of the verb, seems to be too long for the available space. I therefore propose a shorter restoration yielding the same sense. The participle *ḫandant-*, attested with meanings like "corresponding to, aligned with" *et sim.*, may also serve as participle to the intrans. use assumed here.

32: For *ḫalluwanuer* see Goetze, *JAOS* 74 (1954), 188 (*HW 1.Erg.*, 3). Still, the causative form here is difficult. In the Gilgamesh Epic (Otten, *Ist. Mitt.* 8, 114, line 15, to be restored after *Madd.*, 82 n. 1) Gilgamesh and Enkidu "incite" Huwawa "to violence"; but in our text we expect the young men to *be* violent, unless, of course, we assume that here the goddesses are the subject. Since the end of the line is broken, one might think of restoring a *-za* for a reciprocal meaning.[9]

33: In [o]x-*al-lu-u-wa-ar* I can only think of restoring [*m*]*a-* which fits the preserved traces. That the neglect of plowing would lead to curtailment of grinding grain fits the context. There is space for one more sign, for which I propose ŠE.

34: The restoration [Š]AḪ rather than [*n*]*ir* as in line 36 is based on the fact that the line seems to contain a simile: "Just as the dog . . ." (With Archi's restoration GIM[*-an tarn*]*ir* I cannot construe the rest of the line). *ḫa-an-ta*[-...] brings to mind the verb discussed above, although here it seems to be transitive, since there is no "and" after ŠAḪ. But since the next lines are so fragmentary and difficult to understand, it is not clear where such a simile would lead.

35: The traces after NINDA do not support Archi's reading NINDA.⸢Ì⸣$^?$-[E.DÉ]⸢.A⸣?; the first sign looks rather like KASKAL; cf. NINDA.KASKAL-*NI KBo* 2.17:2 (*ŠL* 597, 184). I cannot restore the next few signs. With the "basalt" the grindstone could be meant. After *kunkunuzzi*[*n*] there is space for another word. "Let into the water" is used in magical and medical rituals for immersing and thereby dissolving materials in water. This cannot apply to the stone, so the whole

[9] But the form *ḫalluwanut*, *KUB* 24.7 iii 26 (Cow story, same tablet!) must be "lowered" as given in *HW* after Sommer, *HAB* 76. There seem to be two unrelated homonyms.

remains rather enigmatic. Maybe the GIM-*an* of 36 should be taken as the temporal conjunction "when": "When they let (pret.) [the . . . (35)] into the water . . ." After *na*[. . .] in 36 there is more space than for only the enclitic pronoun *-aš* or *-an* or *-at*. If the lost word was the object, then it would have to be *na*[*-at* . . .] "and they . . ." "And they destroyed [. . .] completely."

39 and 41f.: One expects the phrase beginning with ZAG to be the same in both places. I therefore restore ZAG[*-aš*]*-ša-an* in 39 and ZAG*-aš*[*-ša-an*] in 41, as did Wegner; the last sign in 41, as copied by Walther, can only be *aš*, not *na*. Besides, ZAG*-aš-ša-an* occurs *KUB* 31.125:7, followed by a trace that may be the beginning of *ar*, corresponding to *arnu-* in our text. The form is *kunna* (allative) "to the right" plus *-šan*. For the occurrence of this particle in the interior of a sentence see Carruba, *Part.*[10] p. 20. ZAG*-aš-ša-pát KUB* 21.27 ii 32 could be either mistake for ZAG*-aš-ša-an-pát* or contain the possessive pronoun *-ša*, "to his/its right."

ZAG*-na* is used as adverb. The right side being the propitious one, ZAG*-na* designates what is agreeable to someone, suits him, etc. Cf. *nuttakkan kuit* ZAG*-na nu apāt uppi* "send whatever you please" *KBo* 2.11 rev. 14 (*AU* 242); *mān tukma* *UL* ZAG*-na nu ANA* ᵈUTU*-ŠI ḫatrāi* "if it does not suit you write to His Majesty" Kup. § 19 D iv 3f. (*SV* 1 p. 132); "Let them unload (the grain shipments) in Ura or in Laštiš[a] *kuedani* URU*-ri ANA* DUMU*-YA* ZAG*-na*(!, copy *-uš*) [*na*]*n apiya katta i*[*šḫuwandu*] In whichever city it suits you, my son, [let them] un[load] it there" (*Bo* 2810:14–17, H. Klengel, *AOF* 1 [1974], 171–73). In our text, ZAG*-na arnu-* "to bring/carry to the right," with *aššiyatar* "love" as object,[11] would be "carry it to a state where it is pleasing or satisfying"; for the translation of our passages I chose "carry to fulfillment." In line 39 I restored the verb as 3d. pl. pres. in order to make the construction parallel to 41f., with *-šmaš* (39) corresponding to *-za* (41). One could also think of restoring *ar*[*nuši*] "you (Ištar) carry the love for them to fulfillment," but that would weaken the parallelism and be redundant in view of the next clause "that has been decreed by you, Ištar."

41: *pupuwalāi-*, *pupuwalatar*: Wegner, op. cit., p. 142, came close to the right understanding. The basic stem ᴸᵁ́*pupu-* (or *bubu-*) occurs in the Laws, § 198. This is the man with whom a married woman committed adultery in her house. Goetze (*ANET*, 196) translated "adulterer," Friedrich (*HG*, 87) "Buhle." In *KUB* 43.35:12 ᴸᵁ́*pupuš aššuš* occurs in broken context which belongs in the forensic sphere but leaves us to guess what the adjective "good" is doing here. An abstract noun directly derived from this noun is ᴸᵁ́*pupuwatar*, in *HW* 1.Erg., 16, without reference, now *KBo* 9.73 obv. 6, the Old Hittite Ḫabiru treaty (*CTH* 27): [. . . *w*]*aštai nu* ᴸᵁ́*pupuwatar izzi* "sins and commits *p.*," here perhaps "fornication" in general rather than "adultery."

In our passage *pupuwalatar*, abstract noun derived from the verb *pupuwalāi-*, has a positive connotation. I think that the term refers to all kinds of love affairs other than marriage; for translation I chose "to seduce, seduction."[12] In the oracle questions *KUB* 49.94 obv. 2–14, where someone, presumably the king (cf. line 4), "was determined by oracle with regard to the word/affair of *pupuwalatar*" (3) and where someone (again the king?) has to perform a SISKUR *pupuwalannaš* "a ritual of/against *p.*" (11), the connotation is obviously one of reproach, regardless of whether the king had actually had an affair or whether there had only been some gossip of that sort.[13]

40: For the restoration [*t*]*a-ra-a-an* cf. *KUB* 14.4 iii 24, *KBo* 10.7 ii 18, etc.

40 end: My restoration SAL*-n*[*a-an ku-iš*] is based on my understanding of *pupuwalāi-*. The traces given by Walther, while not exactly suggesting the reading SAL*-n*[*a-*...], at least are not excluding it (not collated).

43: Ì.DÙG.GA must have been preceded by a word at the end of 42, after restored [*tarān*]; *waštari* after E. Neu, *StBoT* 5, 192 (:)*waš*(*š*)- "angenehm sein" with n. 3 about our passage.

43 and 45: In restoring [*ku-iš*] and *ka-a*[*-ri-ia-ši*] I follow Archi. This latter restoration together with *UL kuitki iš-d*[*am-*...] (47) seems to mean that Ištar somehow prevents someone—perhaps the townspeople (44)—from noticing the lovers. This leads me to my restoration and understanding of the first word in line 45.

45: [*ga*]*laktaraši*, 2d sg. pres. For the first sign I can only think of *ga*, since I know of no other word continuing with

[10] O. Carruba, *Die satzeinleitenden Partikeln in den indogermanischen Sprachen Anatoliens* [Incunabula Graeca 32], 1969.

[11] Both Archi and Wegner took it as subject, which would result in intransitive use of *arnu-*, not registered in *HW*². I could not find our passage in *HW*² at all.

[12] Archi correctly distinguishes between this paragraph, where the verb has a positive connotation (but where his rendering "adorare, adorazione" is, to my mind, not specific enough) and the next paragraph, where it is negative and where his translation "infedeltà" is appropriate. But I am not sure that this necessitates to restore **pupuwa*[*tar*] instead of *pupuwa*[*latar*].

[13] In the prayer of Hattušili and Puduhepa, *KUB* 21.27 ii 32 (cf. above under ZAG, i 39) cited by Wegner, 142, the restoration of [*pupu*]*walatar* is uncertain because of the trace of a vertical at the end of the gap which is also too long for [*pu-pu-*] alone, while a spelling *[*pu-pu-ú*]-... is not otherwise attested; nor do the traces in the next line fit a form of *arnu-*.

-laktar-.... A noun *galaktar* is known. It designates something that is usually deposited in incantation rituals together with other objects, most frequently with *parḫuena-*. Otten, *ZA* 46, 218, n. 1, defined both words as "angenehme, süsse Produkte pflanzlicher Art." In some instances these substances are expected to have the effect that the deity be *galankanza* (partic. pass.) "pacified, reconciled" *vel sim*. It is assumed that the verb and the plant (product) are connected at least by the magic of the assonance, if not by etymology. There is one passage where *galaktar* is inserted or stuck into some vessel.[14] Thus *g.* itself is a plant, apparently one with a stem. In our passage the verb denominated from *g.* has the result, outlined above, that the lovers are not noticed.

A plant with a stem and having this effect may be the poppy, which is at home in Anatolia. I leave it open whether the Hittites extracted the sap or only used the seeds. It is tempting to connect Hitt. *galaktar* with Greek *gála, gálaktos* etc., Latin *lac, lactis*, but I must leave it to the specialists to judge this connection. The milky sap of the poppy might be the link. However, there is another word for "milk" in Hittite, *pankur* (if this tentative definition of mine is correct; *HW 3.Erg.*, 25).[15] And according to W. Farber[16] there is no evidence for the use of the poppy or of opium in ancient Mesopotamia. Thus I refrain from positing *galaktar* "poppy," but I think that the context allows for the interpretation expressed in the translation.

51: I can only make sense out of the signs following *iš-ḫu-u-wa-* by inserting an omitted *-an* and restoring *ḫar-ti*. The object of the verb is lost.

52: For *marlatar* see *HW 3.Erg.*, 23; for *pu-pu-wa*[-. . .] see above. In view of the bad state of preservation of these lines the translation can only be tentative.

56: Here begins a new paragraph. Given the small size of the gap at the end of col. i it is probable that the beginning of col. ii still belongs to the same. Since Ištar is addressed in col. ii it is assumed here that her name was the object to "I shall sing of" ([*iš-ḫa-m*]*i-iš-ki-mi* with Archi).

ii 1: The restoration [*wa-aš*]*-ta-aš-ku-wa-ar* is based on the fact that according to the *Glossaire inverse* of P. Reichert[17] this is the only verb that fits the preserved syllables, also because the following lines indeed describe the misdeeds of the goddess.

2: The first sign, *aš*, could be the ending of a 2d sg. pret., but I am unable to restore the verb.

3: Beginning of line restored in parallelism to the following *kuinmakan* LÚ*-an*.

3 end: The last sign is *na* rather than anything else, and according to the copy nothing is missing after it. This recalls the phrase ZAG*-na arnu-* of i 39 ff., and [*ar-nu*]-⌈*ut*⌉ fits the space and the trace at the beginning of line 4. It is true that this, in contrast to the list of her misdeeds, would be a positive act of the goddess, but this has a parallel in line 11.

6: The last two words are *hapax legomena*. I would analyze the first as *ešarašilaš+šmaš*, gen. pl. with poss. pron. of 3d. pl.[18]

8 beg.: The traces look like *IT*-⌈*TI*⌉ (thus also Archi), followed by traces which could belong to NUMUN. At least, "coriander with (its) seed(s)" would make sense.

9: . . . [*-aš-ma*]- is the only restoration I can think of that fits the space and the trace and yields some sense. TÚG. NÍG. LÁM must be neuter according to the adj. *parkuwaya*. The restored reading would be neuter plur. ending *-a+šmaš+za*; *-šmaš* would refer to the men, since the following *kuin—kuin* presupposes a plurality.

10: Although *parkun*, strictly speaking, is from *parku-* "high," the context here calls for *parkui-* "clean, pure." Mixing of the two adjectives is easy to assume; it would be the mistake of a scribe who thought of the verb *parganu-* "to make high" of the next line. Archi also has "pure."[19]

12–14: These lines are very difficult. *wetandaš* looks like the participle of *weda-* "to build" or perhaps *wida-* "to bring," but neither of them fits the context. Because of *laḫḫu-* in 13 one thinks of water, but *wetandaš* is not a form of *watar, wetenaš*. However, there is a derived *-ant-* stem attested as *ú-i-te-na-an-za* (nom. sg.)[20] and *ú-i-te-na-an-te-eš*

[14] *KBo* 22.225 ii? 5–7 with dupl. *Bo* 2646 iii 2–4 (Otten, *HTR*, 121 with obsolete translation); cf. *KBo* 22 p.vi.

[15] Not to speak of GA*-uš KUB* 28.70 rev. 12, which could be a mistake for GUD*-uš*.

[16] Walter Farber, "Drogen im alten Mesopotamien—Sumerer und Akkader," in G. Völger, ed., *Rausch und Realität: Drogen im Kulturvergleich* (Materialienband zu einer Ausstellung des . . . Museums für Völkerkunde der Stadt Köln. Cologne, 1981), 270ff., 271; courtesy of the author.

[17] Pierre Reichert, *Glossaire inverse de la langue hittite* =*RHA* 21/73 (1963), 59–143; 108.

[18] For *arišand*[*a*(-) ...] see HW^2, 299 with reference to *areša-*, 259. This cross-reference need not imply morphological or semantic connection.

[19] It has been claimed that *parkui-* originally is the IE feminine in *-ī* from an adjective **parku-* "clean," and that the *-i-* was retained in order to distinguish this adj. from its homonym *parku-* "high." See O. Szemerényi in *Studi linguistici in onore di Vittore Pisani*, vol. 2, 1969, 991f. with references to Holger Pedersen, *Hittitisch und die anderen indoeuropäischen Sprachen*, 1938, 35f., and H. Kronasser, *Etymologie der heth. Sprache*, 1962–66, 107. If this were correct, *parkun* could be an archaic masculine form here, as tentatively suggested by Eric P. Hamp orally.

[20] *KBo* 10.45 ii 24 (Otten, *ZA* 54, 122); cf. ibid. p. 156 ad *KUB* 41.8 iv 37 = p. 139 n. 242, where, however, the

(nom. pl.),[21] and there is a short stem *wit*(*a*)- (*HW*, 255). Thus it is conceivable that an *-ant-* stem existed also from this short stem and that our form was the dat.-loc. pl. of that.

In line 13 one might read A as logogram "water." Since the pronoun *-aš* "he" has to follow *-ma*, not to precede it, the *-aš* here would have to be phonetic complement to A, for *wetenaš* or the hypothetical *wetandaš*. But a reading *a-aš-ma* "first" is not excluded either; cf. *HW*, 36 and *HW*², 425.

14 beg.: Since there is no quoted speech with *-wa*(*r*)- in this whole text, one has to separate *nu* from the following. The traces and the somehow "watery" context lead to a restoration *wa-a*[*t-ta-r*]*u*. The following word must be an iter.-dur. form, regardless of whether it is meant to be KÚ (as written) or rather NAG (with an easy mistake): *azzikizzi* or *akkuškizzi*, not *ezzazzi* or *ekuzi*, respectively.

If all these hypotheses were correct, they would result in something like this: "But another one you lead out to his own waters(?), but when he pours into the waters (or: when he first pours?) he keeps drinking(?) the foun[tain]." And what would be meant by this?

15f.: After the plural LÚ.MEŠ-*uš* of 14 the text here returns to the singular, *-ši* "to him/her." This pronoun probably refers to a man, not to Ištar, who is here addressed in the 2d person: GUL-*ki-š*[*i*] (again iter.-dur., *walḫeškiši*). The first verb in 16 was restored to ⌜*ta-ru*⌝*-up-pa-an-zi* by both Archi and Wegner. Indeed the traces given by Walther point in this direction, and if the verb were only *uppanzi* "they send" I would be unable to explain the traces before it. Since *tarup-* is transitive, MÁŠ.TUR.ḪI.A should be object; the 3d. pers. pl. then stands for the general subject "they" in the sense of German *man*, French *on*. This would result in a translation "When they gather the kids for him, you keep hitting/beating afterwards(? or: from behind?)." EGIR-*anda* (*appanda*) normally means "afterwards, thereafter," but cf. *HW*², pp. 148ff., *appa*³, sections III and VI.—The translation adopted is another attempt to understand the sentence.

18: *puntarriyališ* was translated "ostinato" by Archi, who already referred to the vocabulary entry *KBo* 1.50 + *KUB* 3.99, lines 11–12:[22]

gú.[o o]x a[o?]	= [o o]-*ku*	= *pu-un-tar-ia-u-wa-ar*
gú.e.la.a.e	= [o-o-*ku*] *šá* ANŠE	= ANŠE-*aš pu-un-ta-ri-ia* [*-u-wa-ar*]

"To be stubborn," "the stubbornness of an ass" are obvious translations. Our text has an adj. in *-ali-* derived from it. The clause is a nominal clause with *-za*; it therefore has to be understood with the pronoun of the 2d person as subject.[23]

25: For SAL.MEŠ*al-la-wa-an*[-...] see *HW*², 57. *KUB* 45.43 ii 5–7 cited there has *eḫu* ᵈ*IŠTAR* URUx-x[-...] *IŠTU* É *al-la-wa-an*[-...] *kalmušaza IŠTU* É[...](end of paragraph). "Come, O Ištar, from(?) the town of [...]; from the *a.*-building [...], but from the house [of the king(?) get] the lituus." The word is not listed in Laroche's *Gloss. hourr.*

LITERARY ANALYSIS

It is immediately obvious that the text has a certain structure. "I shall praise the first attendants" (i 12, §2) and "I shall praise the last attendants" (i 22, §3) form a pair, as do "The husband and wife who love each other" i 38, §4) and "If a woman is hated by her husband" (i 48, §5). As is the case with most Hittite literary compositions, the text is written as if it were prose, without attention to poetic 'lines' or stichoi.[24] When I was editing "The Song of Ullikummi" in *JCS* 5–6 (1951–52) the editor, Albrecht Goetze, kindly allowed me to render the text twice, once in the traditional transliteration following the lines of the tablet (i.e., the tablet chosen as main manuscript) and once in 'broad transcription' arranged according to syntactic units (clauses) which could be assumed to coincide with the poetic 'lines' (cf. *JCS* 5, 141f.). In the present case, it seems best still to transliterate the text according to the lines of the original, so as to facilitate comparison with the cuneiform copy and also to give the reader an idea of the space available in broken passages. In contrast, I arrange the translation according to the clauses supposed to be verses. In order not to clutter it I enter only a few of the original line numbers, hoping that they will enable the reader to compare the translation with the text without too much difficulty.

As will be seen from my arrangement of the lines some clauses can be combined with others to form larger units or sentences; in terms of verses, these form distichs or tristichs. In broken passages the arrangement of such units is uncertain, with the result that the distribution chosen here is by necessity arbitrary to a certain extent. Where syntactic units are

---

restoration ⌜*ú-e*⌝[*-te-na-z*]*a*, variant to A-*az*, and the interpretation as nom. sg. are not certain. The central piece of *KUB* 41.8 iv 36–42 is now (1982) missing, so the width of the gap cannot be ascertained.

[21] *KUB* 32.121 ii 28 (Laroche, *RA* 48, 48).

[22] To be published in *MSL* 17 as Erim-ḫuš Bogh. C.

[23] H. A. Hoffner, Jr., "On the Use of Hittite *-za* in Nominal Sentences," *JNES* 28 (1969), 225–30.

[24] One exception is the Hittite version of "The Great Prayer to Ištar" (E. Reiner and H. G. Güterbock, *JCS* 21 [1967], 255–66), *KUB* 31.141, where each written line is a stichos. Note the line numbers of the Hittite version, Hi (1) etc. on pp. 257ff., and cf. p. 265.

very short two of them may have formed a single 'verse.'

As far as the inner structure of the stanzas or strophes (here numbered as §§) is concerned, a fair amount of parallel structure can be observed in the two pairs mentioned above, §§ **2** and **3**, §§ **4** and **5**.

Thus in §§ **2** and **3** the introduction "I shall praise" forms a distich with the list of four divine names. This is followed by another distich, "Whatever household is beloved/hated, she sends these/those into that house." Thereafter, however, the two distichs of §**2** ending with the words "with laughter" and "with joy" are contrasted in §**3** by a single line combining "groaning" and "anguish" in one sentence. Then again §**2** has one distich each for the girls' weaving and the youths' plowing, whereas §**3** devotes a tristich to the girls and two distichs to the youths. After this come the enigmatic lines 34–37 of the text, where both the division into clauses and the translation are problematic; but in any case these lines form an addition over and above the parallel parts—if the term be allowed, a coda.

In the second pair of stanzas (§§ **4** and **5**) the comparison is made difficult by the bad state of preservation of §**5**. Both speak of married couples first, of other relations second. In §**4** the structure is fairly regular: one tristich each for the married couple and the other lovers; then, after an incomplete and unclear line (43), another tristich on Ištar's help for the lovers. In §**5** I wrote the translation in five distichs, but they include a short clause that is lost and other short clauses that may have to be combined with the next one. But while the exact wording and verse structure are problematic, the sequence: married couple—extramarital relations—consequences of the latter, is parallel to that of §**4**.

It is a pity that §§ **1**, **6**, and **7** are incomplete. In §**1** it would seem that five preserved original lines (7–11) and six lost lines preceding them would have formed one, rather than two, stanzas.

Above we proposed to take the entire text from col. i 56 to ii 17 as one stanza (§**6**). But even if this were wrong, i.e., if the end of col. i (three preserved plus five lost lines) were a stanza by itself, the paragraph from ii 1 to 17 would still be longer than any of the others. And of §**7** only the first sentence, or stich, is preserved; otherwise only unconnected words at the beginning of lines; only the length, nine lines on the tablet, is given.

About the inner structure of §**6** I need not say much beyond what is expressed by the arrangement of the translation. The one feature that stands out are the sequences of *kuin—kuinma* "the one—the other" clauses, from time to time interrupted by a general statement. These *kuin—kuinma* chains are comparable to those with *kuez—kuezza* "on one side—on the other side" of §**1**.

Concerning the contents, the structure of the text is clear—as far as preserved. §**1** seems to deal with Ištar the Warrior. If understood correctly it describes those who follow her into battle. In this context the two kinds of women in the last line might be camp-followers (German: *Marketenderinnen*) and prostitutes.

In §§ **2–3** the consequences of Ištar's favor and disfavor is described as it affects whole households; in §§ **4–5**, as it affects individuals. In §§ **4–5** one may say that it is the mutual love, or the lack of it, of a married couple that determines Ištar's attitude. In §§ **2–3**, on the other hand, we do not learn why one household is loved and the other hated by the goddess.

§**6** is the most surprising part of the whole composition. It is a long list of invectives, reminiscent of the sixth tablet of the Gilgamesh Epic, although different in detail. Not every single point is negative, though: we found that probably two statements give credit to the goddess (ii 3–4 ZAG-*na a*[*rnut*] and 11 *parganut*). They would underline the unpredictability of the goddess, also known from Mesopotamia,[25] but the overall tenure of the stanza is to show her cruelty. This cruelty or dangerousness of the Goddess of Love is, of course, an essential part of her nature; in singing about it the poet, in a sense, praises her might.

One would like to know what §**7** really contained. The comparison of the goddess with a stubborn ass at its beginning lets one expect a lighter tone, but nothing is preserved that would hint at such a tone. And after §**7** there must have been at least one more stanza, to judge by Walther's estimate of a minimum of 16 and a maximum of 20 lines missing.

Even in this incomplete form this text is a piece of poetry of high quality. In the form in which it has come down to us it is the work of a Hittite writer. How close he followed a Hurrian original we shall only learn if and when such a Hurrian text is discovered. Ultimately one of course looks for Mesopotamian models. I hope that Sam Kramer, the rediscoverer of Sumerian literature, will be able one time to tell us about that.

---

[25] This side of her character has been illustrated by selections from many sources in the chapter "Inanna = Infinite Variety," by Thorkild Jacobsen in his book *The Treasures of Darkness*, 1976, 135–43.

LUGALBANDA EXCAVATED

William W. Hallo
Yale University

I. Introduction

When he first heard of my call to Yale two decades ago, Professor Kramer immediately urged me to devote myself to the large corpus of Sumerian literary texts in the Yale Babylonian Collection. He was familiar with their riches, having been the first to prepare a systematic catalogue of them based on his own identifications and those of Goetze, Stephens and others. Among them, the large tablet numbered *YBC* 4623 particularly interested him. He asked me to copy it for him so that it could be incorporated in an edition of the full text by him or one of his students. Accordingly I prepared a copy, complete except for dividing lines, and submitted it to him in 1965. Sol Cohen was thus enabled to incorporate the text of the Yale tablet in his preliminary edition of the entire composition, from which I in turn have greatly benefited. But neither his edition nor my copy has been published, and it thus seems appropriate to make at least the latter available in this volume. While there is no intention to anticipate the definitive edition, an attempt will be made to provide an overview of the whole text, and an appreciation of the significance of the central portion of it which the Yale exemplar covers. Duplicates will be taken into account as far as they are published. The reader's indulgence is requested for the imperfections of a copy made before many of these duplicates were available or known to me; a few improvements, plus dividing lines, have been added to the copy by Randall McCormick. The text of the composition was the subject of a seminar in Sumerian Myths and Epics offered in the fall of 1980; the members of that seminar (Mary Rebecca Donian, Jean Svendsen and Marc Van De Mieroop) provided a critical sounding-board for some of the suggestions now offered here.

A word about the name of the composition may be in order first. Its incipit was restored as u$_4$-ul-an-ki-ta by J. Klein, *JAOS* 91 (1971), 297, but as long as the restoration is uncertain, it is risky to employ it as the modern designation. More commonly, it is referred to as "Lugalbanda in (or and) Hurrumkurra," and indeed these elements represent the protagonist and principal scene of the composition. But it is not wholly clear whether the latter term is a toponym or a generic term ("cave of the mountain" or the like; Klein, ib. 296f. n. 7; previously Kramer in *La Poesia Epica*, 1970, 827, n. 9.). Since there can be little doubt of the intimate connection (including verbatim resemblances) between this composition and the so-called Lugalbanda-epic, and since the action of the former clearly precedes that of the latter, it is here proposed to refer to the two compositions as Lugalbanda I and II respectively. (Note that Klein, *Kramer AV*, 1976, 288 *ad* l. 57, seems to do likewise.) For the latter, the edition of C. Wilcke, *Das Lugalbandaepos* (1969; hereafter cited as LE) provides an indispensable guide; Wilcke has also edited much of the first half of Lugalbanda I, as indicated below. Significant portions of the second half were dealt with by Cohen, first in his dissertation, *Enmerkar and the Lord of Aratta* (University of Pennsylvania, 1973), 10–14, and then in his "Studies in Sumerian lexicography," *Kramer Anniversary Volume* [*AOAT* 25] 1976, 99–101.

II. Structure of the Composition

The basic themes and structure of Lugalbanda I have been characterized by B. Alster in *JCS* 26 (1974), 180 n. 9 and in the *Kramer Anniversary Volume* (1976), 15 and may be further refined to yield the following outline (previous treatments in parentheses):

A. Exordium

1–11:	"Prologue in heaven": the separation of heaven and earth
12–18:	Uruk given to Enmerkar the son of the Sun (Utu)
19–39:	Levy and departure of the troops of Enmerkar (Wilcke, LE, 196)
40–56:	The first part of the march to Aratta (LE, 35f.)
57–69:	The seven brothers and friends (LE, 49f.)
70–72:	?
73–82:	Lugalbanda becomes ill (LE, 189f.)
83–136:	The brothers and friends deal with Lugalbanda's illness (LE, 54–60)

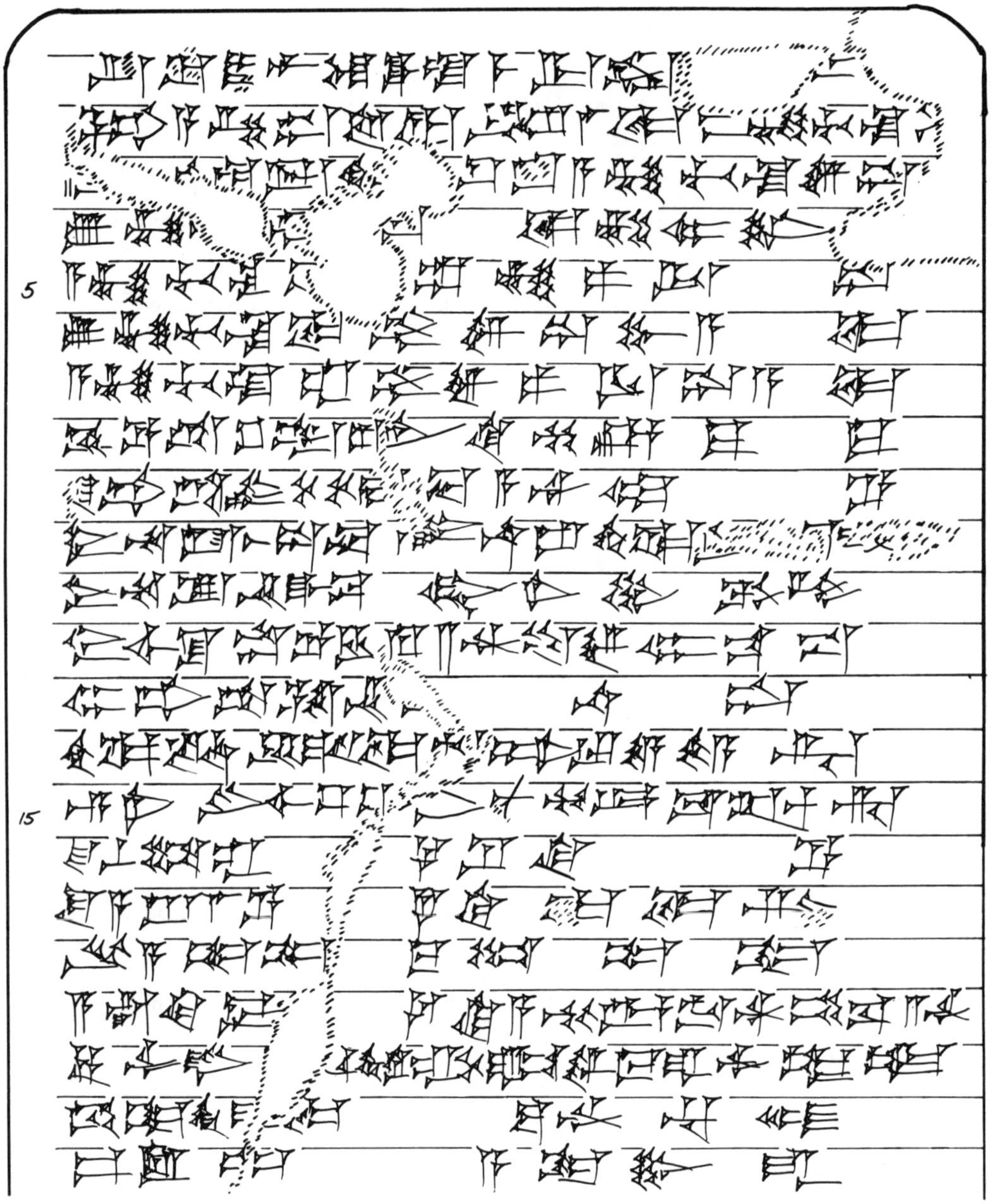

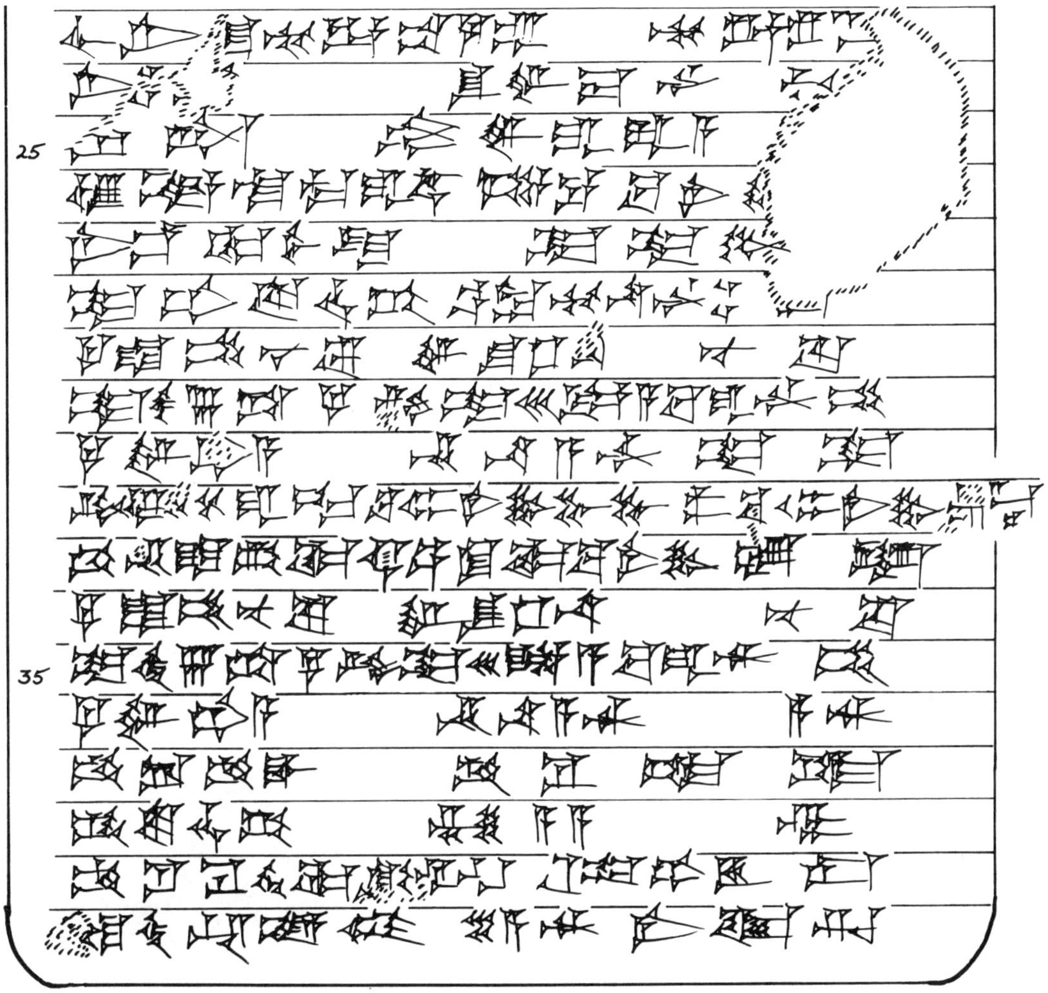

YBC 4623 obv.

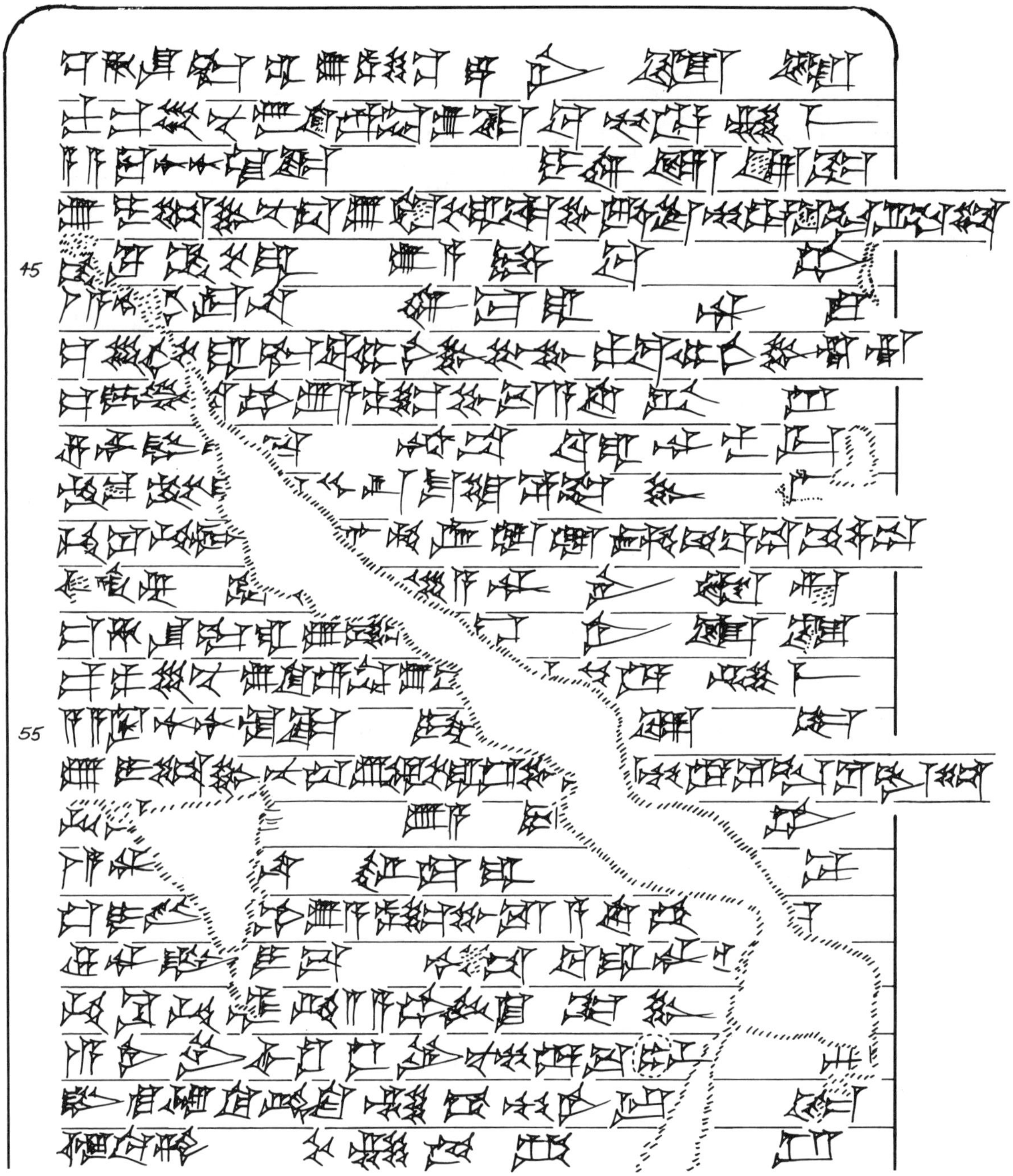

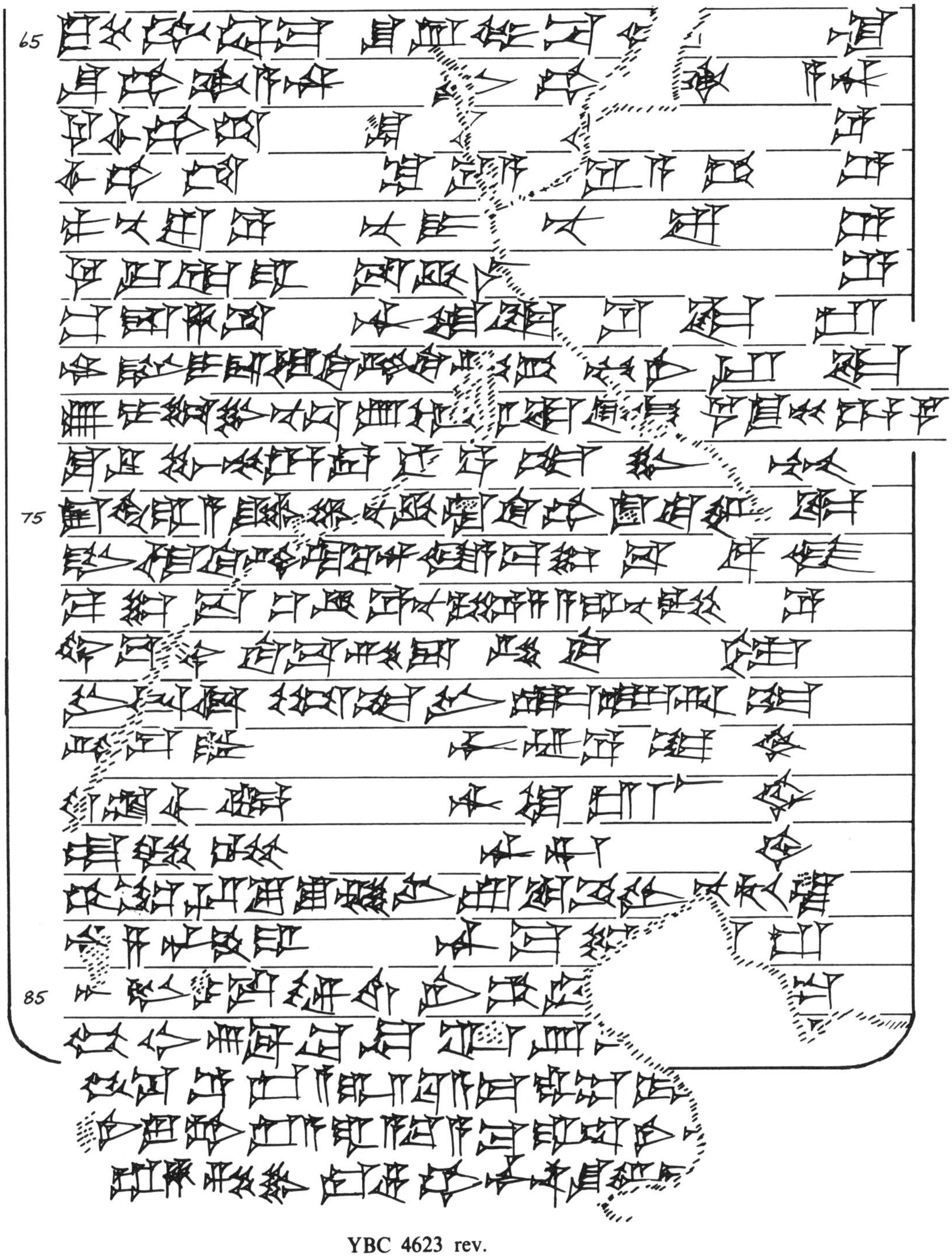

YBC 4623 rev.

B. The Argument—Part I
137–168: Lugalbanda prays to the Sun at dusk (LE, 78–81)
169–195: He prays to the evening-star (Inanna) (LE, 68f.)
169–222: He prays to the moon (Su'en) (LE, 75–7)
223–256: He prays to the Sun at dawn (LE, 81–4)

C. The Argument—Part II
257–276: Lugalbanda leaves the cave
277–291: He lights a fire to bake cakes and bait a trap
292–316: He captures an aurochs and two(?) goats (Cohen, ELA, 10–14; in part: *Kramer* AV, 99–101)
317–338: He lies down to sleep
339–353: Lugalbanda's dream
354–376: The dream fulfilled: the divine repast (*tākultu*)

D. Peroration
377–386: The moon appears
387–445: The powers of darkness arrive from the *apsû*
446–475: Inanna arrives as the morning-star and enters the gate of battle
476–490: The Sun rises and the powers of light and justice fill the universe
(text breaks off)

Assuming that the text as now extant is nearly complete, it thus can be broken down into three "rhetorical" portions (cf. a similar analysis proposed for nin-me-šár-ra by Hallo and van Dijk, *The Exaltation of Inanna*, 1968) and four sections of more or less similar length. The Yale exemplar covers the first 88 lines (out of 120) of the third of these sections (plus the immediately preceding line as a catchline?) and it is this section to which the following brief remarks will be addressed.

III. THE ARGUMENT—PART II

Mythic and epic elements are conspicuously intermingled in Lugalbanda I. We are thus entitled to look behind the plain sense of the narrative even of a seemingly straightforward section like the one under discussion for some more transcendent meaning, perhaps, more particularly, for an aetiology. Aetiology informs many a myth: it is the explanation of a presently observed condition by appeal to an imaginary one-time event in the past or, in other words, the use of the punctual to explain the durative (cf. Hallo, 17 *RAI*, 1970, 117 n. 1; cited with approval by F. R. Kraus, *Vom mesopotamischen Menschen*, 1973, 132). But aetiologies (along with proverbs!) are also found in Sumerian epic, as noted, e.g., by G. Komoróczy ("Zur Ätiologie der Schrifterfindung im *Enmerkar-Epos*," *AoF* 3, 1975, 19–24). And it is possible that there is one here.

Lugalbanda is alone (note the recurrent emphasis on this fact, e.g. in lines 271 and 317; cf. also l. 286 and in Lugalbanda II lines 231f. = 335f.) as befits an epic hero (cf. Alster, *JCS* 26, 1974, 180), and must fend for himself. In so doing, he recapitulates what for the author may have constituted the beginnings of an essential aspect of civilized human life—the consumption of animal meat. Both the practical and the ritual aspects of this process are spelled out in detail. By his own efforts, Lugalbanda traps and tethers the wild animals. He then gets divine approval in a dream for slaughtering them. In repeating the latter action in his waking state, he confirms the divine approval by inviting the four principal deities of the Sumerian pantheon to a ritual meal. These deities are entirely distinct from the three (astral) deities who hear Lugalbanda's four prayers in Section B and who dominate the denouement in Section D, thus underlining the discrete and possibly aetiological character of Section C.

Both aspects of this section—the "practical" and the ritual—are worthy of deeper study than present space permits. Suffice it only to note here that Lugalbanda seems to employ a combination of methods to catch and dispatch his quarry. As interpreted below, he first places a trap (giš-umbin; l. 264) on the ground, then baits it with dainties (l. 288); the aurochs stumbles into the trap (l. 294; not repeated in the goat-passage); both it and the goat(s) are caught in the ambush (restoring [šubtu]m_x-ma-na in ll. 301 and 313) or, more likely, by the snare (restoring [giš-di]m-ma-na) presumably attached to the trap; all are tethered with rope made of rushes (ll. 305–316). In slaughtering the animals, a pit (si-du_{11}-ga) seems to have been of practical or ritual importance, receiving the blood (ll. 349–359) and providing a site for the divine repast (l. 365).

The practical role of pits and pitfalls, and to a lesser degree of traps, has received a great deal of attention in Assyriological circles of late. A brief review of the literature may therefore be in order. The older evidence was summed up in one short paragraph by E. Ebeling, *RLA* 3/1 (1957) 5. My review (*JAOS* 87, 1967, 64) noted, i.a., the contribution by A. K. Grayson, "Ambush and animal pit in Akkadian," in *Studies . . . Oppenheim* (1964) 90–94. Grayson returned to the subject in 1970 with his "New evidence on an Assyrian hunting practice" in J. W. Wevers and D. B. Redford, eds., *Essays on the Ancient Semitic World*, 3–5. In the same year, G. Dossin discussed *ARM* 14:2 in "Une capture de lion au

Habour," *Bulletin de l'Académie Royale de Belgique, Lettres* 27.7.1970, pp. 307–20. M. Held dealt with "Pits and pitfalls in Akkadian and Biblical Hebrew" in the *Gaster Volume* (*JANES* 5:173–90) in 1973. In the same year, A. Salonen devoted a chapter to "Vogelfanggeräte" in his *Vögel und Vogelfang im alten Mesopotamien* (Teil II). In 1976, he followed this with a chapter on "Jagd- und Fanggeräte der Jäger" in his monograph on *Jagd und Jagdtiere im alten Mesopotamien* (Teil II), as well as a briefer article on "Die Fallgruben der sumerischen Jäger," in *Kramer Anniversary Volume* (*AOAT* 25), 399f. Finally, mention may be made of P. Michalowski's "An Old Babylonian literary fragment concerning Kassites," *AION*, Ann. 41 (1981), 389f. and of M. Greenberg's "Two new hunting terms in Psalm 140:12," *Hebrew Annual Review* 1 (1977), 149–53. The wealth of lexical and technical data assembled in these and other studies cannot be exploited here.

The ritual aspect is also extremely intriguing. If indeed the text offers an aetiology of meat-consumption, it is interesting that the highest figures of the pantheon are invoked to render the (original) act acceptable. What this suggests is that the act evoked guilt feelings and that these were assuaged by turning mere consumption into a ritual act, making it sacred, a sacrifice. Comparable notions have been detected in the Old Sumerian archival texts by Y. Rosengarten, *Le Concept sumérien de consommation dans la vie économique et religieuse* (1960), and in the Levitical legislation of the Pentateuch (see my "Leviticus and Ancient Near Eastern literature," in W. G. Plaut, B. J. Bamberger, and W. W. Hallo, *The Torah: a Modern Commentary* (1981), 740–8, and previously J. Milgrom, "A prolegomenon to Leviticus 17:11," *JBL* 90 [1971], 149–56).

IV. THE TEXT

The transliteration is based on the Yale exemplar (A) as far as l. 344, and on *CBS* 7085 (Kramer, *From the Tablets of Sumer*, 1956, 246) thereafter (F). Restorations [in brackets] in the text and variants in the footnotes are cited from published duplicates according to the following sigla:

Siglum	Museum No.	Place of Publication	Lines of Text
A	*YBC* 4623	below	256–344
B	*HS* 1449	*TMH* n.F. 3:8; Wilcke, *Kollationen*, 16	282–308
C	*HS* 1471	*TMH* n.F. 3:9; Wilcke, *Kollationen*, 17	325–342; 387–396
D	*HS* 1479	*TMH* n.F. 3:10; cf. Wilcke, *Kollationen*, 18	1–258
E	*CBS* 10885	*HAV* 4	288–252; 253–274
F	*CBS* 7085	Kramer, *FTS* 246 (obv. only) *History Begins at Sumer*[3] (1981), 242	327–387; 388–441
G	Ni. 9933	*ISET* 1.198	306–310; 325–333
H	Ni. 4405	*ISET* 2:43	307–313 (or 294–301?); 321–329
I	Ni. 4553	*ISET* 2:45	277–302; 336–348
J	Ni. 9913	*ISET* 1:196	308–319; 321–323?
K	Ni. 4441	*ISET* 1:156	351–359; 376–379
L	Ni. 2511	*SRT* 33	357–374
M	3 N–T 917, 368	*SLFN* pl. 8	256–262; 283–285
N	3 N–T 919, 467	*SLFN* pl. 8	345–359
O	3 N–T 902, 74	*SLFN* pl. 7	290–296
Z	6 N–T 638	(Cohen, *ELA*, 10–4; *Kramer AV* 99–101) (Ur III exemplar)	(292–316)

(Note that A has 10-line marks in the left margin.)

Based on the assumption of a text of approximately 495 lines, a tentative typology of the published manuscripts may be offered here along the lines laid down by Hallo and van Dijk, *The Exaltation of Inanna* [*YNER* 3], 1968, 38f. The suggested joins (indicated by +) remain to be tested against the originals.

(1) One-tablet recension in 10 columns of about 50 lines each: *SEM* 20 +(?) *SEM* 111

(2) Two-tablet recension in 11 columns of about 45 lines each:
   a. Tablet I (1–258): D; *ISET* 2:42 Ni. 4291
   b. Tablet II (259–495)

(3) Three-tablet recension in 10 columns of about 50 lines each:
   a. Tablet I (1–200): *ISET* 2:44 Ni. 9677
   b. Tablet II (201–495)

(4) Five-tablet recension in 9 columns of about 55 lines each:
   a. Tablet I (1–109)
   b. Tablet II (110–218)
   c. Tablet III (219–326)
   d. Tablet IV (327–441): F
   e. Tablet V (442–495)

(5) Six-tablet recensions in 11 columns of 40–50 lines each:
   a. Tablet I (1–90) (1–81)
   b. Tablet II (91–179): *ISET* 1:202 Ni. 9959; * (82–162)
   c. Tablet III (180–255) (163–243)
   d. Tablet IV (256–344): A (244–324)
   e. Tablet V (345–430) (325–396): C + K + L
   f. Tablet VI (431–495) (397–495)

(6) Seven-tablet recension in 14 columns of about 35 lines each:
   a. Tablet I (1–69)
   b. Tablet II (70–138)
   c. Tablet III (139–207)
   d. Tablet IV (208–276)
   e. Tablet V (277–348): G + H + I + J
   f. Tablet VI (349–422)
   g. Tablet VII (423–495)

(7) Ten-tablet recension in ±20 columns of about 25 lines each:
   c. Tablet III (87–133): *CT* 42:46
   e. Tablet V (227–274): E
   j. Tablet X (430–487): *TRS* 90

(8) 13-Tablet recension in 25 columns of about 20 lines each:
   c. Tablet III (82–120): *OECT* I pl. xix

(9) Fragments: M, N, O
   ISET 1:138: Ni. 4276; 153 Ni. 4427; 140 Ni. 4237

(10) Exercise tablet: B (note dittography of ll. 282–285)

**TMH* n.F. III 11 + *ISET* 1:128f. Ni. 4012f. + *ISET* 2:44 Ni. 9648

V. TRANSLITERATION

ADEM	256	ur-sag dumu ^{d}nin-gal-la me-téš ḫé^{a}-[i]-⌜i⌝-[ne]
ADEM	257	u$_4$-bi-a zi-du šà-kúš^{a} ^{d}En-líl-lá-ka^{b}
ADM	258	ú$^{!a}$-nam-ti-la ì^{b}-[im-mú]^{c}
AEM	259	⌜i$_7$⌝-[ḫal-ḫ]al-la ama-ḫur-[sag]-gá-ke$_4$ a-nam-ti-la im-túm^{a}
AEM	260	ú-nam-⌜ti⌝-la-⌜ka⌝ KA nam-mi-in-[gub]
AEM	261	a-nam-ti-la-⌜ka⌝ DUB nam^{a}-rig$_7$
AEM	262	ú-nam-ti-la KA ḫé-im-gub-bu-a-ka
AE	263	a-nam-ti-la DUB ḫé-im-rig$_7$-a-ka
AE	264	gú-e-ta $^{giš a}$umbin-diš^{b}-ni ki mu-un-dab$_5$-dab$_5$
AE	265	ki^{a}-bi-ta anše-kur-kur-⌜ra⌝-gim àm-gul-e
AE	266	dùr^{ùr}-AŠ.DU.GIM^{a}-^{d}šakan-na^{b}-ke$_4$ ḫur-sag ì-si-il-(le)
AE	267	dùr^{ùr}-uru$_x$(EN)-gal-gim kušu(U.PIRIG) ì-tag$^{!}$-tag-ge
AE	268	anše-libir^{a} kas$_4$-e kin-gá-àm im-mi-DU.DU
AE	269	gi$_6$-bi-ta u$_4$-te-en-(na-šè?) na-DU
AE	270	ḫur-sag (šà-sig) ^{d}EN.ZU-na^{a}-ka$^{?b}$ ⌜kas$_4$⌝ mi-ni-ib-kar-kar-re
AE	271	aš^{a}-a-ni^{b} lú-igi-nigin lú^{c} nu-mu-un-da^{d}-ab^{e}-bar-re
AE	272	^{kuš}maš-^{a}li-um^{a} níg-si-sá-e
AE	273	^{kuš}a-gá-lá-e níg-sá-du$_{11}$-du$_{11}$-ge^{a}
AE	274	šeš-a-ne-ne ku-li-ne-ne
A	275	a-šed$_7$-gim ninda ki-e mu-un-da-an-du$_8$-uš-àm
A	276	kù-^{d}Lugal-(bàn-d)a ḫur-ru-um-kur-ra-ta im-ma-ra-an-íl-íl
AI	277	gú-izi-ur$_5$-ra-ka$^{?}$ ba-an-sa$_4$
AI	278	^{giš}bugin$_x$-ÚR a bí-in-ra / igi-ni-šè mu-un-ta^{a}-gar-ra mu-un-si-i(l)^{b}
AI	279	na$_4^{!}$-ga$^{?}$ šu im-ma-an-ti
AI	280	⌜téš⌝-bi$^{!}$ ḫé-im-ra-ra-a-t(a)
AI	281	ù-dúb-gùn ma-ra-sig edin-e^{a} ba-ni-i[n-k(u$_4$)?]
ABBI	282	^{na_4}KA-sal-la izi bí-in-(mú)$^{?}$
ABBIM	283	izi-bi šà-sig-ga u$_4$-gim mu^{a}-na-an-⌜è⌝
ABBIM	284	ninda-gúg-du$_8$ nu-zu im-šu-rin-na nu-zu
ABBIM	285	izi-ur$_5$-imin-ta ninda-gi-izi^{a}-eš-^{b}dé-a^{b} ba-ra^{c}-an-du$_8$
ABI	286	ninda ní-bi-a en-na àm-šeg$_6$-šeg$_6$
ABI	287	gi-šul-⌜hi⌝-kur-ra úr-ba mi-in-in-sù-sù pa-ba mi-ni-in-suh-suh
ABI	288	gú^{a}-en-gúg-ga-ka pad babbar-šè KA ba-ni-in-íl-íl
ABI	289	ninda-gúg-du$_8$ nu-zu im-šu-rin-na nu-zu
ABIO	290	izi-ur$_5$-imin-ta ninda-gi-izi-eš-dé-a ba-ra-an-du$_8$
ABIO	291	^{a}ninda ní-bi-a en-na šèg-šèg
ABIO	292	am-síg am-sa$_7$ am-si-^{a}gùr-gùr^{a}
ABIO	293	am-šà-sig-ga nam-a^{a}-a-ak
ABIO	294	am-si-si hur-sag ki-sikil-la umbin-bi kin-gá

ABGHIO	295=307	⌜ù⌝-ur$_{5}$-re šim-gig še-àm ì-tukur$_{2}$-re^{a}
ABGHIJO	296=308	^{giša}ha-šu-úr-ra ^{ú}numun$_{2}$-bur-[g]im^{b} ì-KA×ŠÈ-KA×ŠÈ
ABGHIJ	297=309	pa-^{giša} še-nu ^{ú}KI.KAL-gim ú^{b} ka-ba mu-un-sim^{c}
ABHIJ	298=310	a-i$_{7}$-hal-hal-la-ka^{a} i-im-nag-nag-NE^{b}
AHIJ	299=311	^{ú}i-li-in-^{a}nu-uš^{a} ú-sikil-kur-ra-ke$_{4}$^{b} bu-lu-úh mu-un-si-il-si-il-le
A	312	máš-⌜si$_{4}$⌝ (máš-ù)z ú-a su$_{8}$-[ba]-bi
AI	300	am-si$_{4}$ am-kur-ra ú-a su$_{8}$-ba-bi
AI	301=313	diš-àm (giš-di)m-ma-na im-ma-ra-an-dab$_{5}$
AI	302	^{giš}še-dùg-kur-ra úr-ba mi-ni-in-sù-sù pa-ba mi-ni-in-suh-suh
A	303=314	^{giš}i$^{!}$-ri$_{x}$(LÚ×šeššig)-⌜na⌝-bi ^{ú}A.U$_{4}$.SAKKAR$_{x}$-gíd-da-a-šà-ga-ke$_{4}$
A	304=315	kù-^{d}Lugal-⌜bàn-da⌝ gír-ta ba-ra-an-šab
A	305	am-si$_{4}$ am-kur-ra saman$_{x}$(ÉŠ.SU.NUN.ÉŠ.DU)-e bí-in-lá
AG	306	máš-si$_{4}$$^{!}$ máš-ùz (máš-za)-lá máš-sa-KÉŠ.KÉŠ-sa máš-gú-è-gú-è^{a}
	307=315	[see above]
AJ	316	máš-si$_{4}$ máš-ùz máš-min-a-bi du$_{10}$-gurum éš bí-in-⌜lá⌝
AJ	317	diš-a-ni lú-igi-nigin lú^{a} nu-mu-un-da-ab(erased)-bar-re
AGJ	318	lugal-šè ù-sá-ge sà nam-ga-mu-ni-ib-du$_{11}$$^{?}$
AJ	319	ù-sá-ge kur nam-gú-ga-( )-ke$_{4}$
A	320	KU.KUR-galam-gim-ma šu É-SIG$_{4}$-gim-⌜gul⌝-la
AHJ	321	šu-bi galam-àm gìr-bi galam-àm
AHJ	322	níg igi-bi-ta AD$^{?}$ šú-šú-e
AHJ	323	igi-bi-ta AD$^{?}$ diri-diri-ga-e
AH	324	ugula nu-zu-e nu-banda nu-zu-e
ACGH	325	níg ur-sag-ra á-gál-lá^{a}-e
ACGH	326	^{giša}da-ha-ta ^{d}Nin-ka-si-ka-ke$_{4}$
ACFGH	327	^{d}Lugal-bàn-da ù-sá-ge^{a} sá nam-ga-^{b}mu-ni^{b}-ib-du$_{11}$
ACFGH	328	^{ú}i-li-in-^{a}nu-uš^{a} ú-sikil-kur-ra-ka ki-ná-gar-šè mu-un-gar
ACFGH	329	zulumhi (TÚG.SÍG.SUD) mu-un-dag gad(a)-babbar ^{a}bí-in^{a}-búr
ACFG	330	è-ur$_{5}$-ra a-tu$_{5}$-tu$_{5}$ nu-gál-la ki-bi-šè sá im-du$_{11}$
ACFG	331	lugal ù-sá-ge la-ba-an^{a}-ná-a^{b} ma-mú-da^{c} ba-ná
ACFG	332	ma-mú-da^{a} ^{giš}ig-e nu-gi$_{4}$-e za-a^{b}-ra nu-gi$_{4}$-e
ACFG	333	lul-da ⌜lul⌝-di-da zi-da zi-di-dam
ACF	334	lú-húl-húl^{a}-le-dè lú-šìr-re-dè
ACF	335	^{gi}pisan-kad$_{5}$ dingir-re-e-ne-kam^{a}
ACFI	336	unu$_{6}$-igi-ša$_{6}$ ^{d}Nin-líl-lá-kam^{a}
ACFI	337	ad-gi$_{4}$-gi$_{4}$ ^{d}Inanna-kam
ACFI	338	gu$_{4}$-NE$^{?}$ ur^{a}-dib-dib-nam-lú-ulu$_{3}$^{b}-ka am$^{?!}$ lú nu-ti-la
ACFI	339	An-za-an^{a}-gàr-ra dingir-ma-mú-(d)a-ke$_{4}$
ACFI	340	^{da}Lugal-bàn-da ní-te^{b}-ni gu$_{4}$-gi(m ur$_{5}$ im)-ša$_{4}$
ACFI	341	amar-áb-šilim-ma$^{?a}$-gim gù-nun ì$^{?}$-( )
ACFI	342	amar-si$_{4}$-e gá-a^{a}-ra a-ba-a ma-ra-ab-sa(r)$^{?}$-[e]
ACFI	343	ì^{a}-udu-bi gá-a-ra a-ba-a ma-ra-ab-zal-z(al)$^{?}$-[e]
ACFI	344	^{urudu}ha-zi-in-mà kù-bi an-na šu im-m(a-an-t)i
FIN	345	[gír-ù]r-r–a-mà an-bar-sù-àm im-m[a-da-(sur-re)]
FIN	346	[am]-si$_{4}$ am-k[ur-ra-k]e$_{4}$ lú-gešpu$_{2}$-gim <hé>-im-(ma-ab-gin) (lú)-liru-ma-(gim) (hé)-[im-ma-ši-gam]
FIN	347	lipiš-bi [hé-im-t]a^{a}-zi ^{d}Utu-è-a-ra [ù-mu-na-gur]
FIN	348	máš-si$_{4}$ [máš-ù]z máš-min-a-bi SAG.DU-bi še-gim ^{a}um-ta-an^{a}-dub
FN	349	úš-bi [si]-du$_{11}$-ga um^{a}-ma-ni^{b}-dé-dé
FN	350	ì edin-(na) DU.DU-a-bi
FKN	351	muš-u(l$_{4}$)-kur-⌜ra⌝-ke$_{4}$ si-im hé-im-ši-ak(a)-ne
KN	352	Lugal-bà(n-d)a i-zi-im ma$^{!}$-mú-da im-bu-lu$^{!}$-úh ù-sá-ga-àm
KN	353	igi-(né) šu bí-in-gur$_{10}$ níg-me-gar sù-ga-àm
KN	354	^{urudu}h[a-z]i-in-na-ni kù-bi [an]-na šu im-m-an-ti
KN	355	gír-[ùr]-ra-ka-ni an-bar-sù-àm im-ma-da^{a}-ak
FKN	356	a(m-s)i$_{4}$ am-kur-ra-ke$_{4}$ lú-gešpu$_{2}$^{a}-gim im-ma-ab-gin lú-liru-ma^{b}-gim im-ma-ši-gam
FKLN	357	[lip]iš-bi im-ta-an-zi ^{d}Utu-è-a-ra ^{a}mu-na^{a}-an-gar
FKLN	358	[máš]-si$_{4}$ máš-ùz máš-min-a-bi SAG.DU^{a} še-gim im-ta-an-dub
FKLN	359	[ú]š-bi si-du$_{11}$-ga im-ma-ni-in^{a}-^{b}dé-dé^{b}
FL	360	ì-bi edin-na DU.DU-a-bi
FL	361	muš-ul$_{4}$-kur-ra-ke$_{4}$^{a} si-im im-ši-ak(a)-ne
L	362	^{d}Utu nam-ta-è-a-aš šilam$^{?}$ ( )
L	363	Lugal-bàn-da mu ^{d}En-líl-le zi$^{!}$-( )

FL 364 An ^{d}En-líl$^{a\ b}$ ^{d}En-ki^{b} ^{d}Nin-hur-sag-gá-ke$_{4}$

FL 365 si-du$_{11}$-ta gizbun(KI.KAŠ.GAR)-na im-ma-ni-in-dúr-ru

FL 366 kur-ra ki-gar-ra mu-un-ak^{a}-a

FL 367 gizbun ba-ni-in-gar ^{a}ne-sag^{a} ba-ni-in-dé

FL 368 kaš-gi$_{6}$ kurun zíz-babbar

FL 369 geštin-nag-nag gú-me-zé-du$_{10}$-ga

FL 370 edin-na a-šed$_{x}$(MÙŠ.DI)-šè im-ma-ni-in-dé-dé

FL 371 uzu-máš-si$_{4}$-ke$_{4}$ gír bí-in- ak

FL 372 HAR$^{?}$ ninda-gi$_{6}$ izi im-mi-ni^{a}-in-sìg

FL 373 NA-izi-SI-ga-gim i-bí-[B(A)]-ni bí-in-mú

FL 374 i-gi-in-zu ^{d}Dumu-zi ì(ir)-du$_{10}$-ga ⌜gi$_{4}$-a ku$_{4}$-ra⌝

F 375 níg-šu-du$_{11}$-ga Lugal-bàn-da

FK 376 An ^{d}En-líl ^{d}En-ki ^{d}Nin-hur-sag-gá-ke$_{4}$ du$_{10}$-ga-bi mu-un-kú-uš^{a}

VI. VARIANTS

256 ^{a}D: àm; E: mu.
257 ^{a}D and E add: ù; ^{b}D and M: ke$_{4}$.
258 ^{a}D and M omit; ^{b}D: i; M omits?; ^{c}not a separate line in A.
259 ^{a}M; tùm.
261 ^{a}E and M add: -mi-in.
264 ^{a}E omits; ^{b}E adds: a.
265 ^{a}E: u$_{4}$?
266 ^{a}E: e; ^{b}E: ne.
268 ^{a}E: NITA.ÙR.SAL.LA.
270 ^{a}E omits; ^{b}E omits.
271 ^{a}E: DIŠ; ^{b}E adds: im; ^{c}E omits; ^{d}E: du; ^{e}erased in A; E omits.
272 $^{a\text{-}a}$E: lum-e.
273 ^{a}E: ga.
278 ^{a}I: DU; ^{b}separate lines in A.
281 ^{a}I: na.
283 ^{a}B (once) adds: un.
285 ^{a}B, I and M: zi; $^{b\text{-}b}$B, I and M: ta; ^{c}B (twice) omits.
288 ^{a}I: gi?
290 variants (B and I) as in l. 285.
291 $^{a\text{-}a}$B, I and O: ⌜bar$^{?}$-ba$^{?}$⌝ zú-lum-ma ninda-ku$_{7}$-ku$_{7}$-da hi-li ba-ni-in-du$_{8}$-du$_{8}$.
292 $^{a\text{-}a}$B: gur$_{6}$-gur$_{6}$.
293 ^{a}B: mu; O: me.
295=307 ^{a}B and G: e.
296=308 ^{a}H omits; ^{b}A (l. 296 only) omits.
297=309 ^{a}H omits; ^{b}J omits; ^{c}B: si-im.
298=310 ^{a}J adds: ab-sin; ^{b}B: e.
299=311 $^{a\text{-}a}$J: um?; ^{b}A (l. 299 only): ka.
306 ^{a}G adds: e.
317 ^{a}J omits.
325 ^{a}C: la.
326 ^{a}C and H omit.
327 ^{a}C: ke$_{4}$? $^{b\text{-}b}$C: ri.
328 $^{a\text{-}a}$F: uš; H: um?
329 $^{a\text{-}a}$C: mu-u[n].
331 ^{a}C: omits; ^{b}C: e; ^{c}C, F and G: dè.
332 ^{a}C and G: dè; ^{b}C omits.
334 ^{a}C and F omit.
335 ^{a}F: ke$_{4}$.
336 ^{a}F: ka?
338 ^{a}C: ib?; ^{b}C: u$_{x}$-lu; ^{c}C: gù(KA)
339 ^{a}I omits.
340 ^{a}F and I omit; ^{b}C adds: a.
341 ^{a}C omits.
342 ^{a}F omits.
343 ^{a}C, F and I add: ì?
347 ^{a}N adds: ab.
348 $^{a\text{-}a}$I: hé-im.
349 ^{a}N: ù$^{?}$; ^{b}N adds: in.
355 ^{a}K adds: an.
356 ^{a}K: liru; ^{b}K omits.
357 $^{a\text{-}a}$K: im-ma; N: ù-mu-[na].
358 ^{a}N adds: bi.
359 ^{a}N omits; $^{b\text{-}b}$N: sì-sì?
361 ^{a}L: ka.
362–363 from L; F omits.
364 ^{a}L adds: le; $^{b\text{-}b}$F omits.
366 ^{a}L: LU.
367 $^{a\text{-}a}$L: nesag.
372 ^{a}L omits.
376 ^{a}F: kú?

VII. TRANSLATION

Lugalbanda's departure from the cave (257–276)

(256 Hero, son of Ningal, let them praise you as you deserve.)

257 At that time the righteous one who takes counsel with Enlil

258 Caused the plant of life to grow.

259 The fast flowing stream (or: the Tigris), the mother of the mountain, brought the water of life.

260 The plant of life he verily placed in (his) mouth,

261 The water of life he verily drank (with his) hand(?).

262 In the act of verily placing the plant of life in (his) mouth,
263 In the act of verily drinking the water of life with his hand—
264 From this side he caused his one trap to "seize" the ground (i.e. he set the trap?).
275 From that ground he "tears off" like a horse(?) of the mountain,
266 Like a wild donkey of Šakkan, he runs over the mountains,
267 Like a large powerful donkey he gallops,
268 As the slender donkey, eager to run, he rushes forth.
269 From that night until the (next) day grew cold he verily wandered.
270 The mountains, the wasteland of the moon, he hurries through.
271 Being alone, no one, even with a roving eye, can see him.
272 Things filled into leather pails,
273 Things put into leather bags,
274 By (his) brothers (his) friends—
275 It is they who are able to bake bread on the ground with (like?) cold water
276 Holy Lugalbanda lifts himself out of the cave of the mountain.

Lighting the fire and baking the cakes to bait the trap (277–291)

277 By the side of the embers? he was summoned(?).
278 The bucket/trough he filled(?) with water.
278a That which had been placed in front of him he smashed(?)
279 He took hold of the . . . stones
280 After he repeatedly(?) struck them together,
281 The glowing coals . . ., they entered(?) the open ground,
282 The fine red (flint?)-stone struck a spark (lit. raised a fire).
283 Its fire came forth for him like the sun on the wasteland.
284 Not knowing how to bake a cake, not knowing an oven.
285 With seven coals he baked the gizešta-dough.
286 The bread, (left) by itself until well baked,
287 The *šalalu*-reed of the mountain(?)—its roots he tore out, its tops he took away.
288 The totality of the cakes as a white morsel were lifted into the mouth (of the trap).
289 Not knowing how to bake a cake, not knowing an oven,
290 With seven coals he baked the *gizešta*-dough,
291 On its outside it was decorated with dates and sweet breads.

Capture of the wild oxen and wild goats (292–317)

292 A woolly aurochs, a handsome aurochs, an aurochs tossing (its) horns,
293 An aurochs with weakened insides was reposing,
294 A horned aurochs of the hills, the pure place, having found that trap(?),
295 He (the ox?!) in melancholy languor was chewing *kanaktu*-(seed) as if it were barley,
296 He was grinding up the wood of the *hašurru*-cedar as if it were alfa grass,
297 He was sniffing with open mouth at the foliage of the *šenu*-tree as if it were grass,
298 He was drinking in the water of the fast-flowing stream (or: Tigris),
299 He was crumbling into pieces soapwort, the pure herb of the mountain.
300 While the red aurochs, the aurochs of the mountain, was milling about in the meadow,
301 There being (only) one (trap), with (this) his (one) snare he (Lugalbanda) captured it.
302 The juniper tree of the mountain—its roots he tore out, its top he took away.
303 Its roots which were like the long rushes of the field
304 Holy Lugalbanda cut off from them with a knife.
305 The red aurochs, the aurochs of the mountain, he tethered.
306 A red goat, a goat of a nanny, a diseased(?) goat, a sick goat, a flabby goat,
307–315: see above 295–304
316 The red goat, the goat of a nanny, the goats both of them, he tied to a rope with bended knee.
317 Being alone, no one, even with a roving eye, can see him.

Lugalbanda's First(?) Dream (318–337)

318 To the king (i.e. Lugalbanda) sleep finally overcame him too,
319 Sleep, the land of oppression(?).

320 It is like an extensive flood, a hand destroyed like a brick wall,
321 Whose hand is extensive, whose foot is wide.
322 The thing in front of it covers over the . . .
323 In front of it, it overflows with . . .
324 One who knows no lieutenant, knows no captain,
325 Something which is a commander for the warrior
326 By means of (her) wooden DA.HA, Ninkasi
327 Let sleep finally overcome Lugalbanda too
328 Soapwort, the pure herb of the mountain, she(?) placed as food on (his) bed,
329 She(?) spread out a linen (blanket?), she(?) loosened there the white linen (garment).
330 There being no slave girl or bath-attendant, he "made do" with that place.
331 The king had no sooner laid down to sleep when he laid down to dream.
332 In the dream: a door which does not close, a door-post which does not turn(?).
333 "With the liar it acts the liar, (with) the truthful one it acts truthfully."
334 In order for someone to celebrate joyfully, in order for someone to sing (dirges),
335 It is the *huppu*?-basket of the gods
336 It is the beautiful (connubial) chamber of Ninlil,
337 It is the counselor/consort of Inanna.

Lugalbanda's Second(?) Dream (338–353)

338 The (domesticated) ox, the captive animal of mankind, the (once) wild ox whom man would not allow to live,
339 Anzaqar, the god of dreams,
340 Bellowed (at) Lugalbanda himself like a domesticated ox.
341 Like the bullock of a domesticated cow he roared [and said?]
342 "The red bullock—who will tie it up for me?
343 Who will make its animal fat flow for me?
344 He must be able(?) to take my axe whose metal is meteoric iron(?),
345 He must be able to wield(?) my hip-dagger which is of (terrestrial) iron.
346 The red aurochs, the aurochs of the mountain, like an athlete let him carry it away, like a wrestler let him make it submit,
347 Let its strength leave it when he turns toward the rising sun.
348 The red goat, the goat of a nanny, the goats both of them—when he has heaped up their heads like barley,
349 When he has poured out their blood in the pit
350 —their fat running(?) over the plain—
351 Let the snakes hurrying through the mountains sniff it (the blood and fat)."
352 Lugalbanda awoke—it was a dream. He shivered—it was sleep.
353 He rubbed his eyes, he was terrified.

The divine repast (tākultu) *(354–376)*

354 He took his axe whose metal is meteoric iron,
355 He wielded his hip-dagger which is of (terrestrial) iron.
356 The red aurochs, the aurochs of the mountain, like an athlete he carried it away, like a wrestler he made it submit.
357 Its strength left it, he placed it toward the rising sun,
358 The red goat, the goat of a nanny, the goats both of them, their heads heaped up like barley.
359 He poured out their blood in the pit
360 —Their fat running(?) over the plain—
361 The snakes hurrying through the mountains sniff it.
362 As the sun was rising [. . .]
363 Lugalbanda, [invoking] the name of Enlil,
364 Makes An, Enlil, Enki (and Ninhursag)
365 Sit down to a banquet at the pit.
366 In the mountain, the place which he had prepared,
367 The banquet was set, the libations were poured—
368 Dark beer, mead, and emmer-beer,
369 Wine for drinking, sweet to the taste—
370 On the open ground he poured all of it as a cold water libation.
371 He put the knife to the flesh of the red goat(s),
372 . . . and the black bread he roasted there for them.
373 Like incense placed on the fire, he let the smoke rise to them.
374 As if Dumuzi had brought good fat(?) into the . . .
375 So of the food prepared by Lugalbanda
376 An, Enlil, Enki and Ninhursag consumed the best part.

VIII. NOTES TO SELECTED LINES

257 I.e., Lugalbanda; cf. *LE* 50 n. 158. In Lugalbanda I 40, Enmerkar bears this epithet.

259 Cf. LE p. 162; Moran, *JCS* 31 (1979), 70 n. 16 and below, line 298. The identical phrase in a late *namburbi*-text favors the translation as "Tigris"; cf. R. Caplice, *Or.* 40 (1971), 141: 35′; *idem*, *SANE* 1 (1974), 18f.; W. G. Lambert, *RLA* 6 (1981), 219f. See also *ad* l. 294.

260 Or tooth, reading zú. . .gub with van Dijk, *Or.* 44 (1975), 62 *ad VS* 17:33:6; cf. also Civil, *JNES* 23 (1964), 9 (46).

261 Cf. rig_7 = *šatû* in *MSL* 14:133:16; kišib = *rittu* in *AHw* s.v.

262–263 I.e. no sooner had he eaten and drunk; for the syntax contrast l. 331 below.

264 giš-umbin = *uturtu*; Hh VI 9 and Salonen, *Jagd* 34: "a round, claw-shaped, hair-clasp shaped trap with a string attached to it."

266–268 Same lines in Enmerkar and Ensuhkešdanna (ed. A. Berlin) 45–47. Cf. also Heimpel, *Tierbilder*, 29.2. But si-il-si-il here probably equals, not *duppuru*, "absent oneself" (Berlin *ad.loc.*) but *nutturu*, *šalāṭu* or *šarāṭu*, "split, tear." Cf. the English idiom "to tear along/through" = make haste. Cf. IV *R* 26:3:37f.: kur-kur-ra gal-gal-la mu-un-si-il-si-il = *mu-šat-ti-*<*ir*> *šadi*^{i} *zaq-ru-ú-ti*, emended with Lugale I 11 (for which see Sjöberg, *AS* 16, 1965, 67 n. 3): kur-kur-ra si-il-lá = *mu-šat-tir šadi*^{i}.

267 for kušu . . . tag see Civil, *AS* 20, 135.

270 Cf. LE 77 n. 319; Alster, *Kramer AV*, 14 n. 6: "Suen's horrible mountain"—a stage of the moon? But cf. Hallo, *JNES* 37 (1978), 273 (2) *ad loc.* For ša-sig as "deep (narrow) interior/midst" or as variant of šà-sù-ga = *hurbū, mērênu*, "wasteland, emptiness" see Sjöberg, *TCS* 3, 10.

271 Cf. l. 317, below.

272–274 Cf. Lugalbanda I 96–98 (Wilcke, *LE*, 55).

274 Cf. Alster, *Kramer AV*, 15. For the seven heroes cf. Klein, ibid., 288 *ad* Šulgi 0 57; for seven brothers, cf. also the Cuthean legend of Naram-Sin.

276 Cf. Perhaps Enlilsuduše 37 for x-ta. . .-ra-íl (Gragg, *Infixes*, 95).

277–283 See below, APPENDIX I.

278 The bugin-vessel recurs in Lugalbanda II 22 in connection with Ninkasi (cf. below, line 326) and 402f. in connection with Enmerkar's catching fish for Inanna.

282 For ^{na_4}-zú-sal-la = na_4 *su-ú* see Stol, "The stone called *sûm*," *On Trees, etc.* (1979) 94–96. But cf. also NA_4.KA = *ṣurru*, obsidian or flint.

283 For u_4-gim . . . è cf. Römer *SKIZ*, 232 *ad* Iddin-Dagan *7:70. For ša-sìg-ga cf. l. 270.

284 Cf. line 289. For im-šu-rin-na (etc. etc.) = *tinūru* see Salonen *BM* 3 (1964), 101–3; Civil, *JCS* 25 (1973), 172–5. According to Jerrold Cooper, all the different Sumerian and Akkadian forms of this word go back to Indian tandoor, "oven"; letter to N.Y. Times, 2-8-1977.

285 Cf. line 290 and LE, 152 *ad* l. 53.

287 Cf. line 302.

291 Translation follows B, I, and O. A repeats l. 286 (more or less; reading courtesy M. Civil).

292–316 Cf. S. Cohen, *ELA*, 12f.

292 Cf. S. Cohen, *ELA*, 10ff.; Heimpel, *Tierbilder* 5.1 (differently Civil, Oppenheim *AV*, 79).

293 For šà-sig-ga cf. l. 270; for nam-a-a cf. l. 224 and *CT* 17:22:155 = IV R^2 4 iii 13–15: nam-a-a-ta = *ina nu-uh-hi.*

294 hur-sag = hills or foothills, to distinguish from kur = mountain; cf. T. Jacobsen, *Or.* 42 (1973), 281–6. But cf. l. 17 for umbin kin-kin-ba?

295–299 Cf. S. Cohen, *Kramer AV*, 99–101. Cohen takes Lugalbanda as the subject of these lines, but more likely it is the ox (respectively the goat).

296 For the various orthographies of ^{ú}numun = *elpetu* see most recently Hallo, *ZA* 71 (1981), 49. For ^{ú}numun-búr-(ra), "alfa grass from reed clearings," = *elpet mê purki*, "alfa grass (growing) in stagnant water," see *CAD* E, 109. The term recurs in the Tummal History 6 (Sollberger, *JCS* 16, 42) and in Iddin-Dagan *6:176 (Römer, *SKIZ*, 133); the simile recurs in Inanna and Ebih 142 (Limet, *Or* 40:15) and in the Eridu Lament 5:6 (M. W. Green, *JCS* 30 [1978], 137).

297 For si-im (var. sim) cf. si-im (var. sim)-ak in l. 361 and the references collected by Heimpel, *Tierbilder*, 356, 482f.

298 Cf. l. 259.

299 Cf. LE, 188; Alster, *Or.* 41 (1972), 355.

300 In view of l. 305, I take this ox to be the (single) victim, and the verb therefore iterative not plural.

301 Cohen restores [giš-di]m-ma-na, "snare" and compares *ŠL* 94:20 = *umāšu*! Note that in the equivalent line 313, the Ur III version (though differing) introduces the PN Lugalbanda here. Is it possible to restore instead šubtu(m) = *šubtum*, "ambush"? Cf. *MSL* 3:136:78; 14:191:283f.; B. Alster, *Dumuzi's Dream* (= Mesopotamia 1), 1972, 98f.

303 Cf. Civil, *JCS* 15:125f. for erina/arina/irina = *šuršu*, root.

306 For máš-za-lá = *ibhu*, máš-^{sa}sar-kés-da$^{!}$ =

miqqānu, and máš-gú-è-gú-è = *tahlappanu* see Hh. XIII (*MSL* 8:33), 234–236. The fact that all three occur together in the lexical text lends support to the hypothesis that they, and many other lexical entries, are taken from literary and archival sources (cf. already Hallo, *HUCA* 30 (1959), 136). If correctly translated, the implication is that sick animals were *not* sacrificed.

317 Cf. l. 271.

318 Cf. l. 327. Cf. 2nd Ur Lament (*ANET*^{3}, 614) 176f. for sá-du$_{11}$ in sense of "caught up with (someone/thing)."

319 Cf. nam-gú-(ak-a) = *dullulu, habālu* (*CAD* s.v.v.).

327 Cf. l. 318.

330 Cf. Lugalbanda I 244 (Wilcke, *LE*, 82).

331 Cf. B. Alster, *Dumuzi's Dream* (1972) p. 88; M. Civil, *Kramer AV* (1976), 92 (22). For the syntax, cf. Gordon, *SP*, 2.68 and contrast l. 263.

332 Taking gi$_4$ as *turru* = close (doors) for which see *AHw*, 1335 (16b); Salonen, *Türen*, 145. For za-ra = *ṣerru* cf. *ib.* 66f.; *CAD* Ṣ, s.v.

332–337 See below, APPENDIX II.

338 Or: captive lion (ur-dib = *girru*).

339–341 Cf. Heimpel, *Tierbilder*, 9.1, but restore line 340 in light of ibid., 5.35–5.39.

342–343 Note the ma- prefix with first person dative, as in Gregg, *AOATS* 5, (1973), 83. The -ra- infix is essentially ablative.

343 This is effectively the last line of the Yale tablet, if we may regard 344 as a catch-line to the following tablet. For ì-udu cf. Gordon, *SP*, 1.190 and 5.86.

344 Cf. line 107, translated by Wilcke, *LE*, 58. For the other literary reference to an axe of iron (or tin?) cited there (n. 210) see also Civil, *RA* 63 (1969), 180 (14).

345 Cf. line 110, translated by Wilcke, *LE*, 59. But it is not necessary to follow him (ib., n. 212) for sù = filigree, since an-bar-sù = *parzillu* (*MSL* 13:173). For gír-ùr-ra (var. gìr-ùr-ra) = *patar šibbi* see Wilcke, *LE*, 59 n. 212 and Lipit-Ištar *23:73 (cited below *ad* l. 371). For the restoration of the verb, see line 355.

346 Cf. the translation of this line by Civil, *Oppenheim AV*, 79. For lú-gešpu$_2$ = *ša umāši* and lú-lirum = *ša abāri* see *CAD* A/1, 38 and B. Landsberger, *WZKM* 56 (1960), 113–7; 57 (1961), 22.

347 Alster, *Kramer AV* 15, takes this line as an injunction "to overpower bulls and present them as offerings to the sun." In this he is following Kramer in *La Poesia Epica* (1970), 827. But cf. ll. 362–365 below, where the goats, if not the bulls, are consumed by other gods at sunrise.

348 Cf. ll. 306 and 316.

349 For si-du$_{11}$-ga = *šuttatu* and *huballu* and sidug (LAGAB×DAR) = *haštu* and many other Akkadian equivalents for pit or pitfall, see Salonen, *Jagd und Jagdtiere*, (1976), 36 and 55f. For the alleged TÚL.KA = *hu-ba-al-lum* quoted there and *CAD* H, s.v. read rather si-dug$_4$ with *MSL* 13, 30:385 and A. Sjöberg, *ZA* 63 (1973), 46 n. 15.

351 For the translation, cf. Heimpel, *Tierbilder*, *ad* 81.10 and 84.3. Cf. also si-im-si-im = sniff, said of a dog in Gordon SP, 2.109.

352–353 This literary topos describing the end of a dream recurs with minor variants in Gudea Cylinder A xii 12f.; Gilgameš and Huwawa 72f.; and Dumuzi's Dream, 17f.; cf. Alster, *Dumuzi's Dream*, 88. The second line could also be translated: "before him(?) he bowed down, he was filled with silent acclaim"; cf. *YNER* 3:86 s.v. níg-me-gar.

354–361 Cf. ll. 344–351. For the reading of the verb in l. 355, cf. Römer, *SKIZ* 166: kur-gar-ra urú(!)-na-ka gír nu-ak-a-na. For another alleged occurrence (Jestin and Lambert, *Thesaurus* 2 (1955), 18f.) read rather gír-ùr-ra ù-sar-ak-a-me-en (Lipit-Ištar *23:73; cf. already Sjöberg, *Or.* 35, 293 *ad loc.*).

362–363 These lines occur only in S; they are omitted in F.

364 Read with L and line 376 against F. The four deities head the Sumerian pantheon.

---

[1] Even for a dream, the lines 332–337 appear exceptionally enigmatic, and utterly unrelated to the surrounding narrative. They begin and end, however, with precious clues to their possible significance. The door and its various components are intimately connected and even identified with Inanna in the Akkadian epic of Gilgamesh, and this symbolism has been traced back to its Sumerian sources by J. D. Bing, "On the Sumerian epic of Gilgamesh," *JANES* 7 (1975), 1–11. Moreover, the symbolism strongly alludes to Inanna's sexual aspect and her role as generator of fertility as celebrated in the sacred marriage. If Enmerkar and Lugalbanda were, like Gilgamesh, partners of Inanna in this rite, then line 337 probably alludes to this role; for the double-meaning of ad-gi$_4$-gi$_4$ in this context, cf. Hallo and van Dijk, *YNER* 3 (1968), 53 and note 20. The preceding line similarly suggests the place where the sacred marriage was consummated; for unu$_6$ (usually: dining-hall) as the place where the crown-prince was born of this union cf. A. Sjöberg, *Nanna-Suen*, 94 and Hallo, "Birth of Kings," *Pope Festschrift* (forthcoming). Thus the first dream of Lugalbanda (or the beginning of his single dream) may anticipate the royal role for which Inanna has helped to save him.

365 See above, l. 349 for the pit. For causative dúr with gizbun = *tākultu*, cf. Lugalbanda II 12 and Wilcke's comments *ad loc.*, LE, 136.

366 Translation based on context, and on the assumption that the periphrase with ak has the same sense as would ki . . . gar.

367 Cf. the translation of this line by Römer, *SKIZ* 194. For gar (or gál) with gizbun, cf. Iddin-Dagan *6: 202 (Römer, *SKIZ* 134) and the passages cited by Römer, 197 *ad loc. LE* p. 136. For ne-sag, nisag (= *nisannu*) cf. van Dijk, *JCS* 19 (1965), 18–24; for n. with dé, cf. nin-mul-an-gim 22 (Hallo, 17 *RAI*, 1970, 124 and 131).

368–369 Cf. lines 101f. as translated by Wilcke, *LE* p. 57. gú-me-zé, literally "edge of the chin" or "palate."

371 For the verb, see above, *ad* l. 355.

372 For izi-sìg = *ṣarāpu*, *šamû*, *kamû* see *MSL* 13:157 and Inanna and Ebih 44: giš-tir-ús-sa-bi-šè izi ga-àm-sìg.

373–376 See Wilcke, *JNES* 27 (1968), 235[1]f.

IX. APPENDIX: *The Invention of Fire*

The reading of lines 279–283 owes much to suggestions of M. Civil. We have in this short pericope a veritable aetiology of yet another cultural fundamental: fire-making. The sense seems to be that Lugalbanda arrived at the campfire of his brother-friends (1.277) only to find the last embers dead so that he was thrown on his own resources to restart the fire. He accomplished this by striking a spark with a suitable stone. The operative terms are ne-mur and ù-dúb, both of which are equated with Akkadian *pēmtu* / *pēntu*; see *AHw* s.v. and previously Hallo, *Bi.Or.* 20 (1963), 139f. and 142 (6) s.v. *pêntu*; *YNER* 3 (1968), s.v. izi-ur$_5$. The reading ne-mur seems preferable in view of that reading, now well-attested, in connection with the near-synonym *tumru*, "glowing ash, ember"; see *AHw* s.v. That may indeed be the intended meaning of ne-mur here. For ù-dub = *pēmtu* see now also *MSL* 13: 36(A) 11. The Akkadian word, which is clearly cognate with Hebrew PḤM, "coal" (so already Hallo, *loc. cit.*), was expanded by the addition of the nisbe-ending to form *pentû*, explained as *aban išati*, "firestone, stone for making fire"; cf. *AHw* s.v. *pe/indû*, and *MSL* 10:32:92: na$_4$-izi = *aban i*[*šati*] = [*pindû*]; ib. 35α: na$_4$. ^{d}ŠE.TIR = *pindû* = *aban išat*. This in turn was borrowed into Sumerian as (na$_4$) pí-in-di; cf. *UET* V 292 and 558 as interpreted by W. F. Leemans, *Foreign Trade* (1960) 28 and 30. In our text, however, the stone employed is identified more specifically as flint or silex (line 282; cf. line 279).

Udub also occurs as a logogram, written LAGAB × IZI, i.e. "block (*lagabbu*) with inscribed fire" (Hallo, *Bi.Or.* 20, 140 n. 61) and in late, purely syllabic orthography as u-tu-ba (Salonen, *JEOL* 18, 338). Phonologically, it resembles i-šub / ù-šub, "brickmold" (Salonen, *Bi.Or.* 27, 1970, 176f. and *Ziegeleien*, 1972, 80f., 87–100) and other "cultural" terms ending in -ub. Salonen does not list it among these "substrate" nouns (*ibid.*, 7–14; *Fussbekleidung*, 1969, 97–119, esp. 110f.; *Zum Aufbau der Substrate im Sumerischen* = *St.Or.* 37/3, 1968, 5f.) but its appearance in Lugalbanda I, in the context of an aetiology (?), is suggestive of its antiquity.

X. APPENDIX II: *Remarks by Th. Jacobsen*

After this paper had gone to press, Thorkild Jacobsen kindly agreed to study it. His 13-page critique deserves separate publication; here there is room only to signal his principal divergences from my understanding of the text, particularly as to the technique used by Lugalbanda for catching his prey.

In line 264, Jacobsen understands ^{giš}umbin as *imṭû*, "chisel" (not "trap"), i.e. Lugalbanda got out of "a steep ravine such as is characteristic of mountain streams . . . presumably by cutting footrests" with "a single . . . stone chisel." He then moved "a full day's journey away" (line 269), hence could not have intended to trap his prey there. In lines 277–291, "the idea of baiting a trap for a herbivorous animal like an ox with a cake decorated with dates seems rather odd," hence line 288 should be understood as "with fibers (?) of *šišnu*-grass (gúg for gug$_4$) he tied them together (ka ba-ni-in-sír-sír) for a *šutukku* reed hut (šudug, var. šudug-UD)" and in line 291 the repetition of line 286 is to be preferred over the variant. Line 294 should be understood as "the reddish brown aurochs (am-si-si, phonetic for am-si$_4$-si$_4$ in Z), searching with its hooves (umbin-bi; cf. šu ur$_x$ (ÚR×U)-bi in the copy of Z, against Cohen's reading umbin; i.e. its front and hind-legs) the clean (i.e. 'snow-clad' ?) ground, the foothills" [cf. already my comments ad loc.]. Space considerations suggest an alternate restoration in line 301: "he caused by his approaching ([t]e-gá-na [but collation rules this out!]) the first one to make its way out toward him." In short, "Lugalbanda puts halters on the animals as they graze" rather than trapping them; cf. lines 305 and 316. The more explicit version in Z inserts before one of these lines the following: mu-dar šu bí-gur$_{10}$ saman mu-[dím], "he split them and twisted them (šu-gur$_{10}$ for later šu-gur) and made a halter."

Note also that egar (É.SIG$_4$) in line 320 is probably to be understood not as *igāru*, "brick wall," but as *emūqu*, "strength" [or as *lānu*, *mēlû*, *damtu*, (*pa*)*dattu*, *gattu*, "figure, height"]; for all these equations see PBS 5:106 rev. ii 5′–10′ = Diri V 276–282.

In the (single!) dream of Lugalbanda (lines 332–353), the introductory lines (332–338) all serve as anticipatory descriptions of Za(n)qara (line 339; "loan from Proto-Akkadian *zaqqara* 'to call up mental images,' 'to remember',"): he is "the one not turning back at the door, not turning back at the pivot, who will talk lies with the liars, talk truth with the truthful, who will rejoice one man, have a(nother) man lament, the gods' tablet-box, the one for whom Ninlil has a favoring mouth (u n u$_6$ = *pû*) and eye, Inanna's counsellor, saying to mankind: 'Let me restore!', the border district of men no (longer) alive."

THE EFFECTIVE SIMILE IN BIBLICAL LITERATURE

DELBERT R. HILLERS
THE JOHNS HOPKINS UNIVERSITY

PROF. S. N. KRAMER HAS WRITTEN ABOUT SUMERIAN SIMILES from a literary point of view,[1] an interest to which G. Buccellati has already paid appropriate tribute.[2] It is my intention to investigate certain biblical similes, and their counterparts in Mesopotamian literature, not so much as part of literary production as of "effective" speech, that is, speech intended to produce an effect in the world beyond ordinary discourse. If it were not certain to invite misunderstanding, especially on the biblical side, the paper might have been called "Similes and Magic."

Magical texts and treaties in Akkadian and Hittite abound in similes. At least two types of similes must be distinguished in the magical texts and in the lists of curses in simile form. The first involves manipulation of an object. Thus the benevolent witch-doctor in the Maqlû series, intending to rid a victim of a black-magic spell, makes images of tallow, copper, dough, asphalt, clay, or wax.[3] These figures are identified with the sorcerer or sorceress who has laid the spell on the victim.[4] Then they are burned as the magician recites the spell, containing a simile: "As these figures melt, dissolve, and run down, so may sorcerer and sorceress melt, dissolve, and run down!"[5] A parallel is Sefire I A 36–37 "This *GNB*' and [. . .] (are) Matiʾel; it is his person. Just as this wax is burned by fire, so may Matiʾ[el be burned by fi]re!"[6] Note here the explicit identification of Matiʾel with the wax, and that the identification precedes the simile. Similarly, in the Akkadian treaty between Ashurnirari V of Assyria and Matiʾilu: "This head is not the head of a lamb, it is the head of Matiʾilu, it is the head of his sons, his officials, and the people of his land. If Matiʾilu sins against this treaty, so may, just as the head of this spring lamb is torn off, and its knuckle placed in its mouth, . . . , the head of Matiʾilu be torn off, and his sons . . . , etc."[7] The simile follows, and depends on, a magical identification which is posited. Its intention is perfectly clear. We do not know in all cases of similes in magical texts and curses whether actual objects were manipulated.

Clearly, this sort of simile, accompanying a rite, is not meant to decorate the discourse, or to arouse or give vent to emotions, or to point out a resemblance between two different objects. The spell is meant above all to work, to be effective, to accomplish something in the practical world. The language of the spell is not in the ordinary sense communication, but effective objective action. Furthermore, these similes involve first of all an explicit or implicit identification of two different objects, and comparison comes in only in the second place: what is done to the one object is to have similar effect on the other. Moreover, the relation between the two objects is not so much perceived as it is posited.

In many cases in magical texts or treaty-curses, we are not told any concrete rite accompanied the simile, and it seems practically certain that none did. For example take these similes from an Akkadian "Fire Incantation" (Section II, lines 11–15):[8]

> Depart like a snake from your hole (?)
> Like a partridge (?) from your lair.
> Do not turn back to your prey.

[1] S. N. Kramer, "Sumerian Similes: A Panoramic View of Man's Oldest Literary Images," *JAOS* 89 (1969), 1–10.

[2] Giorgio Buccellati, "Towards a Formal Typology of Akkadian Similes," in *Cuneiform Studies in Honor of Samuel Noah Kramer*. Ed. by B. L. Eichler *et al.* 1976, 59–70.

[3] Gerhard Meier, *Die assyrische Beschwörungssammlung Maqlû* [*AfO* Beiheft 2]. 1937, *passim.*

[4] This is especially clear in I 31–33 and III 17–21.

[5] II 146–47; similar expressions occur elsewhere in the series.

[6] The translation is that of Joseph A. Fitzmyer, *The Aramaic Inscriptions of Sefire* [Biblica et Orientalia, 19]. 1967, 15.

[7] Translated by Erica Reiner, in *The Ancient Near East: Supplementary Texts and Pictures Relating to the Old Testament*. Ed. by James B. Pritchard. 1969, 532–3 (96–97). Hereafter cited as *ANET*³.

[8] W. G. Lambert, "Fire Incantations," *AfO* 23 (1970), 40.

Scatter like fog, disperse like dew,
Like smoke ascend to the heaven of Anu."

Here surely the objects mentioned—at least the fog and dew—are not under the sorcerer's control. Yet the intention of this sort of simile is, it seems to me, essentially the same as that of those where an object is manipulated. The similes are not far-fetched, or private. Instead, as a rule, they appeal to readily observed natural phenomena or the enduring and most obvious qualities of an object: the scattering of fog, the evaporation of dew, the rising of smoke, that doves do fly to their nests, that crows cross the sky, that chaff flies before the wind, that dew falls at night, that rain falls down and does not go back up, that mules do not have offspring, and so on. The sorcerer need not always lay his hand on something and control it, for he can by his words appeal to what is inevitable in nature for the same purpose. These, too, then may be considered "effective" similes. In my opinion, one might propose that these also rest on an implicit identification of the two objects concerned.

Turning now to the Old Testament, I propose that we can find there examples of the "effective" simile, verbal counterparts to the much-discussed "symbolic actions" of the prophets. Two lines of evidence point in this direction. The first is that one can point out verbal resemblances between some Old Testament similes and similes in magic and curse texts. The second, and more important in my opinion, is that one can observe a significant number of cases in which a blessing, curse, or pronouncement of doom in the Old Testament employs one or more similes. That is to say, pronouncements that are meant to be effective often use the simile form as a figure peculiarly apt, by its connection to the concrete, for such utterances.

First, then, some examples of resemblance in content of Old Testament and extra-biblical similes. There are two similes in Ps 68:3. I use W. F. Albright's translation:[9] "Let YHWH arise, May his foes be scattered, And let his enemies flee before him! Like smoke may they be put to flight, Like the melting of wax before the fire! Let the wicked perish before YHWH." This is undoubtedly an old poetic fragment; we must also agree with Albright that "the hymn is an appeal to YHWH, not a mere prediction of what he will do."[10] It can be called a prayer or a curse on the enemies of Yahweh.

Before looking for extra-biblical evidence, let us consider the Old Testament parallels. Is 65:5 and Prv 10:26 use a smoke simile, but with a different point: "smoke gets in your eyes" in Proverbs; "in your nose" in Isaiah. Isaiah 51:6 is closer: "For the heavens will vanish like smoke"; here, however, the simile is descriptive rather than effective in intent. Hos 13:3 is closer in spirit to the strong expression of will which shines through Ps 68:3. "And now they sin more and more, and make for themselves molten images . . . Men kiss calves. Therefore they shall be like the morning mist or like the dew that goes early away, like the chaff that swirls from the threshing floor or like smoke from a window." Note that the prophet means for this to happen, and how he heaps up similes, including that of chaff before the wind, to which we shall return later, and smoke, our present concern.

This same simile, of smoke rising, occurs in numerous passages in Akkadian magical literature. Maqlû I 135–141 is part of a short incantation that begins thus: "Incantation. I raise the torch, I burn the figures of the *utukku*," etc. (other demons are named) "and of all evil which may seize a man. Melt, dissolve, and run down. May your smoke rise up to heaven!" Note that what is burned, we may infer, are tallow figurines; cf. Maqlû II 146–47 and the incantations similar to Maqlû published by W. G. Lambert,[11] to which reference will be made below. In other words, the idea of melting and dispersal as smoke are combined in Maqlû as in Ps 68:3. This simile is very common in Akkadian incantations; for references see *AHw* s.v. *qutru*. It is often joined with another: "Like an uprooted tamarisk, never return to its place." Slightly different is the form it assumes in the "Fire Incantation," already quoted, where it is joined with other similes.[12] Of interest there is occurrence of the smoke simile along with the fog and dew similes, as in Hos 13:3. The smoke simile also occurs in a Hittite treaty (in Akkadian), the treaty of Mattiwaza-Suppiluliumas:[13] "May I, Mattiwaza, together with any second wife I might take, and we Hurri-people, together with our possessions, go up like smoke to the sky." Cf. also the line from a *lipšur* litany; "may my sin rise skyward like smoke." (type II 1 line 7') p. 141[14]

[9] "A Catalogue of Early Hebrew Lyric Poems (Psalm LXVIII)," *HUCA* 23 (1950–51), 36. The textual problems are discussed on p. 17.

[10] Albright, *HUCA*, 17.

[11] W. G. Lambert, "An Incantation of the Maqlû Type," *AfO* 18 (1958), 294.

[12] Lambert, *AfO* 23 (1970), 40.

[13] Ernst F. Weidner, *Politische Dokumente aus Kleinasien* [Boghazköi-Studien, 8], 1923, 55.

[14] Erica Reiner, "Lipšur Litanies," *JNES* 15 (1956), 141.

The second simile in Ps 68:3 is "like the melting of wax before the fire!" This simile is otherwise used in the Old Testament to describe great suffering (Ps 22:15) or of the melting of the mountains in a theophany (Micah 1:4; Ps 97:5). These are descriptive, and do not resemble Ps 68:3 in intent. As extra-biblical parallels we may mention Maqlû II 146–47, which prescribes the making of a figurine of tallow, and concludes with the similes: "As these figures melt, dissolve, and run down, so may sorcerer and sorceress melt, dissolve, and run down." Figurines of wax are mentioned in Maqlû II 159; IV 40; and IX 25, and in texts related to Maqlû published by W. G. Lambert.[15] Another parallel which has already been quoted is in Sefire I A 36–37, an eighth-century Aramaic treaty: ". . . (are) Matiʾel; it is his person. Just as this wax is burned by fire, so may Matiʾ[el be burned by fi]re!"[16] For further parallels and discussion, see the literature cited by Fitzmyer.[17] Noteworthy is the passage in the Hittite Soldier's Oath:[18] "Then he places wax and mutton fat in their hands. He throws them *on a pan* and says: 'Just as this wax melts, and just as this mutton fat dissolves,—whoever breaks these oaths, [shows disrespect to the king] of the Hatti [land,] let [him] melt lik[e wax], let him dissolve like [mutton fat]!'." From the Esarhaddon vassal-treaties comes this simile: "Just as one burns a wax figurine in fire, dissolves a clay one in water, so may they burn your figure in fire, submerge it in water."[19]

Hos 13:3, which was mentioned in the preceding discussion of the smoke simile, also uses a chaff simile: "Therefore they shall be . . . like the chaff that swirls from the threshing floor." This simile, using either the Hebrew word *moṣ* "chaff" or *qaš* "stubble, chaff," with reference to its being carried off by the wind, is very common in the Old Testament. In many cases, as in Hos 13:3, it occurs in contexts where an imprecation is intended, where the simile is, in my terms, effective or creative in intent. Other prophetic passages of similar intent include Is 29:5; 41:15; Jer 13:24; and perhaps Is 17:13.[20] In the Psalms we have 35:5: "Let them be like chaff before the wind, with the angel of the Lord driving them on." Similar is Ps 83:14; note the heaping-up of comparisons beginning at v. 10—the enemies should be like Midian, Sisera and Jabin, Oreb and Zeeb, Zebah and Zalmunna, and after the chaff simile the passage closes with similes of fire and storm (v. 16).

Once again Maqlû offers parallels to the effective use of the simile: "May their sorceries be blown away like chaff" (V. 57). The simile is repeated in varied form at V 11–20; V 32–35; VIII 57–58. Of interest is the fact that there was an accompanying ritual: Maqlû IX (Ritual Tablet) 176–77: "One puts chaff in a slender clay vessel and blows through its opening into a wash-basin." Contenau cites the same simile from Ti'i Tab. IX[21] ". . . may the headache which is in the body of this man be driven off and not be able to return, like the chaff which the wind drives off." The same simile occurs in a Hittite ritual text: "As the wind chases the chaff and carries it far across the sea, so also may it chase away the bloodshed and impurity of their house and carry them far across the sea."[22]

A famous Old Testament simile makes use of the observation that rain and snow fall and do not return, Is 55:10–11 (RSV) "For as the rain and the snow come down from heaven and return not thither, but water the earth, making it bring forth and sprout, giving seed to the sower and bread to the eater, so shall my word be that goes forth from my mouth; it shall not return to me empty, etc." The idea is found also in Akkadian and Hittite texts. From a *lipšur* litany (translated by Erica Reiner) we have (Type II 1 line 20') "May my sin, like falling rain, never return to its origin."[23] From a Hittite conjuration of the underworld: They pour down the rainspout a pot of wine, and say "As the water runs down the [roof] and does [not] return [again] through the [rainspo]ut, so also the evil pollution, etc., of this house be poured out and not return."[24] From an Akkadian prayer of conjuration: "As a rain-shower from heaven does not

---

[15] Lambert, *AfO* 18 (1958), 292.

[16] Fitzmyer, *Sefire*, 15.

[17] Pp. 52–3.

[18] Trans by A. Goetze, *ANET*³, 353.

[19] Lines 608–611, trans. by Erica Reiner, *ANET*³, 540 (104).

[20] Zeph 2:2 is too difficult textually to permit certain interpretation, though it may belong here.

[21] G. Contenau, *La magie chez les Assyriens et les Babyloniens*, 1947, 221, citing R. Campbell Thompson, *The Devils and Evil Spirits of Babylonia*, Vol II. 1904, 68–9.

[22] Translation by Harry A. Hoffner, Jr., *Alimenta Hethaeorum: Food Production in Hittite Asia Minor* [American Oriental Series, 55]. 1974, 32. Hoffner discusses the meaning of Hittite *ezzan* "chaff," which had been in doubt, and use of the product by the Hittites, on pp. 37–8. In the Ullikummi myth, Kumarbi wished that the storm god would be crushed like chaff, p. 33.

[23] *JNES* 15 (1956), 141, Type II 1 line 22'.

[24] Volkert Haas and Gernt Wilhelm, *Hurritische und luwische Riten aus Kizzuwatna* [Hurritologische Studien I; *AOAT* Sonderreihe]. 1974, 27.

return to its place, as the water of a rainspout does not flow back, as water flowing downstream does not flow back upstream, so take (the evil) out of the [body] of NN, son of NN, and take it away. Let it not come back."[25] Haas and Wilhelm cite an analogous simile from the treaty of Suppiluliumas and Kurtiwaza: "As the water of a rainspout does not return to its place, so may we, like the water of a rainspout, not return to our place."[26] The same simile is used in a prayer to Telepinus.[27] Hoffner notes a badly damaged text which apparently has the same idea: "A[s] the water of a [p]ail [is poured out and does not go back] . . ."[28] One may recall in this context the saying of the wise woman to David, 2 Sam 14:14: "We are like water spilt on the ground, which cannot be gathered up again."

In Ps 2:9, the king is told "You shall break them with a rod of iron, and dash them in pieces like a potter's vessel." The simile is paralleled of course, in Jeremiah's famous symbolic action, Jer 19. Compare also Is 30:13 "Its breaking is like that of a potter's vessel . . . ." We find these lines in the *lipšur* litanies (Type II 1 lines 15'–16'): "May my sin, like a potter's broken pot, never return to its former state, may my sin be shattered like a potsherd."[29] Contenau cites an Akkadian text in which the tongue which has charmed the sufferer is threatened: "May one break you in pieces like this goblet."[30] Note also "Smash them like a pot, let their smoke, as from a furnace, cover [the heavens]," in an incantation of the Maqlû type.[31]

This listing of some Old Testament similes with parallels in Near Eastern magic or ritual texts is, of course, incomplete. Even if more parallels could be found, however, we should have to ask if the parallels are at all significant. Certainly they are not sufficient to establish any lineal descent of Old Testament similes from a magical tradition, though one cannot rule that out. But, as was said above, the writers of spells and rituals seem to have drawn their similes from the most obvious, familiar, and inevitable phenomena of their world and idioms of their language, and the Israelite writers, living in essentially the same world, could have created such simple similes quite independently. On the other hand, the parallels are perhaps enough to suggest that the function of some biblical similes was not altogether different.

In Hebrew poetry, (similes in prose will be dealt with in a separate treatment) in prayers and in prophetic oracles, similes are frequently found in contexts where the writer expects or desires some objective effect on his world. Some have already been quoted above. A good example is Ps 83, a prayer against the enemies of God (vss. 9–15): (RSV): "Do to them as thou didst to Midian, as to Sisera and Jabin at the river Kishon, who were destroyed at En-dor, who became dung for the ground. Make their nobles like Zebah and Zalmunna . . . . O my God, make them like whirling dust, like chaff before the wind. As fire consumes the forest, as the flame sets the mountains ablaze, so do thou pursue them . . . ." A good clear example from the prophets is Jeremiah's curse and blessing, 17:5–8; "Thus says the Lord: 'Cursed be the man who trusts in man and makes flesh his arm, whose heart turns away from the Lord. May he be like a shrub in the desert, and not see any good come. May he dwell in the parched places of the wilderness, in an uninhabited salt land. Blessed be the man who trusts in the Lord, whose trust is in the Lord. May he be like a tree planted by water that sends out its roots by the stream, and does not fear when heat comes, for its leaves remain green, and is not anxious in the year of drought, for it does not cease to bear fruit.' " One can discover many more; I count about 20 passages in Isaiah that use what I have called "effective" similes.[32] Similarly, one can find more or less plausible examples in the rest of Old Testament poetic literature.

To sum up, these similes should be drawn into the discussion of the symbolic actions of the prophets. In his monograph on the subject[33] and in a later article on prophecy and magic,[34] G. Fohrer clearly demonstrates the connection of the symbolic actions of the prophets to analogic magic, and notes that a symbolic action is not just a symbol, not a didactic or homiletic tool, but "wirkungsmächtige und ereignisgeladene Tat," —a powerfully effective and actually productive action. I suggest that this insight be extended—as indeed

[25] Ibid., p. 28.

[26] Ibid., 28, citing Weidner, op. cit., 54ff. (KBo I 3 Rs. 31.)

[27] Ibid., 27.

[28] Hoffner, *Alimenta Hethaeorum*, 138.

[29] Reiner, *JNES* 15 (1956), 141, lines 15'–16'.

[30] Contenau, *La magie*, 226.

[31] Lambert, *AfO* 18 (1958), 294, line 75.

[32] 1:30; 5:24; 10:18; 13:12; 13:14; 13:19; 17:5–8; 19:14; 19:16; 24:13; 25:10; 28:4; 29:5–8; 30:13–14; 30:17; 41:15; 42:14–15; 49:26; 50:9 (cf. 51:8); 55:10; 58:11; 65:22.

[33] Georg Fohrer, *Die Symbolischen Handlungen der Propheten* [*AThANT*]. 2nd ed., 1968.

[34] Georg Fohrer, "Prophetie und Magie," *ZAW* 78 (1966), 25–47.

Fohrer does extend it, in a limited way—[35] to some of the verbal symbols, the similes, of the prophets and other Old Testament writers as well. Sayings which use similes, like the divine word in general, are often not so much communication between speaker and hearer as the turning loose of an effective power in the world. If I am right, what we may call magical thought for want of a better term, is more pervasive in the Old Testament than has previously been recognized.

Fohrer says that in prophecy magic is overcome, because success of the symbolic action depends on fellowship with God [36] and the promise of God.[37] But the same holds true of many of the magic and ritual texts which have been cited here. Maqlû begins (I 1): "I have invoked you, O gods of the night" and goes on "Come near, O great gods, hear my complaint!" (I 13). At another spot the magician has an almost prophetic consciousness of his calling (Maqlû 61–64): "I have been sent, I go; I have been commanded, I speak. Against my sorcerer and my sorceress Asariludu, lord of the art of conjuration, has sent me: What is in heaven, pay attention! What is on earth, hear!" If Fohrer wants to call the relation of magic to Israelite religion a "broken" one, then we must say the same for Mesopotamian religion.

---

[35] Op. cit., 35ff.

[36] *Symbolische Handlungen*, 108.

[37] "Prophetie und Magie," 27, 35.

A PRAYER OF MURŠILI II ABOUT HIS STEPMOTHER[1]

Harry A. Hoffner, Jr.
Oriental Institute, Chicago

KBo 4.8 is listed without join or duplicate in *CTH* 71. The measure of its importance as a testimony to matters political, religious and social in Hatti is indicated by the many important studies it has elicited, none of which, however, has constituted a full edition of the text.[2] The historical incident which forms the background to this prayer is the conflict between the widow of Šuppiluliuma, named Tawannanna, and the wife of King Muršili II. Most of the evidence for this incident can be found either in *KBo* 4.8 (*CTH* 71) or *KUB* 14.4 (*CTH* 70), which are prayers of Muršili. F. Cornelius once intended to fully edit these two texts, but a serious illness made this impossible. He could only prepare a partial edition in an article which he entitled "Ein hethitischer Hexenprozess."[3] Meanwhile, using transliterations of unpublished Boğazköy fragments kindly made available to me by H. G. Güterbock, I was able to identify "Izmir 1277" as a join to the main text *KBo* 4.8.[4] On the field transliteration of 1206/u (photocopy in the possession of Güterbock) Otten identified the fragment as a duplicate to *KBo* 4.8. On his copy of the transliteration of 245/w Güterbock wrote "Murs. gegen Taw.?" Subsequently I was able to join these two fragments in Ankara. Since the unpublished join "Izmir 1277" has shown, contrary to all expectation, that Muršili was authorized by the oracle to execute Tawannanna, it is important to publish a complete edition of *CTH* 71. I promised such an edition in *JCS* 29 (1977), 155 and now wish to fulfil that promise. Since the text shows a lofty style and is characterized by an eloquence not always found in Hittite prayers, I present it here to Professor Kramer, who more than anyone has contributed to our understanding and appreciation of ancient Sumerian literary texts.

Exemplar A, which is the principal copy, consists of *KBo* 4.8 + "Izmir 1277". The Izmir piece directly joins the upper right side of column II and the lower right side of column III. This requires assigning a new, cumulative line count to column II. But, because previous studies and citations of this text have used the *KBo* 4.8 line count, these line numbers have also been retained for column II in parentheses.

Exemplar B, consisting of 1206/u + 245/w, is only cited to provide the textual variants. All readings from B have been controlled from photos in the possession of Güterbock, who kindly allowed me the use of both photos and field transliterations.

My join 1206/u + 245/w was initially confirmed by Mr. Cem Karasu of the Ankara Museum. I was able subsequently to verify the join during personal visits to Ankara in 1981 and 1982. I would like to thank Mr. Karasu for his kind assistance.

Exemplar B is preserved only on the reverse. It duplicates A iii 5–18.

TRANSLITERATION

1 [o o o o o o o o o o o o o o o] x x x
2 [o o o o o o o o o o o o o o o] x-*kán ku-en-ta*
3 [o o o o o o o o o o o o o o o]-*ma-mu ku-ri-pa-it*
4 [o o o o o o o o o o o o o o o]⸢*e*⸣-*eš-ši-iš-ta*
(1) 5 [o o o o] x x x *na-a*[*t-m*]*u*? SAG.DU-*aš ḫi-in-kán*

TRANSLATION

[. . . . .] She killed [my wife . . . . .] She bereaved(?) me. [. . .] She . . . -ed [. . .]. And was it a capital crime (lit. death of the person) [for m]e,

[1] Abbreviations peculiar to Hittitology employed in this article follow the *Hittite Dictionary of the Oriental Institute of the Unversity of Chicago* (abbrev. *CHD*) (Chicago, 1980).

[2] See the bibliography given in *CTH* 71 (p. 15).

[3] *RIDA* 22 (1975), 27–45.

[4] Details of the discovery and some points of information about the join piece's wording were given in *JCS* 29 (1977), 155f. with note 22.

(2) 6 ⌜*e*⌝-*eš-ta ma-a-na-aš Ú-UL* BA.ÚŠ *k*[*a-a-š*]*a-za* DINGIR.MEŠ *BE-LU*^{MEŠ}-*IA*
(3) 7 [E]GIR-*pa pu-nu-uš-šu-un na-aš-mu ku-na-an-na* SI×SÁ-*at*
(4) 8 *kat-ta a-ša-an-na-ia-aš-mu* SI×SÁ-*at na-an-kán a-pí-ia-ia*
(5) 9 *Ú-UL ku-e-*≪*nu-*≫*un na-an-kán A-NA* ^{SAL}AMA.DINGIR-*LIM-UT-TIM*
(6) 10 *ar-ḫa ti-it-ta-nu*<*-nu*>*-un na-aš kat-ta a-ša-an-na ku-it* SI×SÁ-*at*
(7) 11 *na-an kat-ta a-ša-aš-ḫu-un nu-uš-ši* É-*er AD-DIN*
(8) 12 *nu-uš-ši-kán* ZI-*ni Ú-UL ku-it-ki wa-aq-qa-a-ri*
(9) 13 NINDA-*aš-ši wa-a-tar nu ḫu-u-ma-an ša-ra-a ar-ta-ri*
(10) 14 *Ú-UL-aš-ši-iš-ša-an ku-it-ki wa-ag-ga-a-ri* TI-*an-za-aš*
(11) 15 *nu* ^{d}UTU *ŠA-ME-E* IGI.ḪI.A-*it uš-ki-iz-zi* NINDA-*an-na-az*
(12) 16 TI-*an-na-aš az-zi-ik-ki-iz-zi am-me-el ka-a-aš-pát*
(13) 17 1-*aš dam-me-eš-ḫa-aš ki-i-ia-an* 1-*an dam-me-eš-ḫa-nu*≪*nu-*≫*un*
(14) 18 *IŠ-TU* É.GAL-*LIM-pát-kán ku-it kat-ta u-i-ia-nu-un*
(15) 19 *A-NA* DINGIR.MEŠ-*ia-an AŠ-ŠUM* ^{SAL}AMA.DINGIR-*LIM-TIM ar-ḫa ti-it-ta-nu-nu-un*
(16) 20 *nu am-me-el ka-a-aš-pát 1-aš dam-me-eš-ḫa-aš nu-za* DINGIR.MEŠ
(17) 21 *ki-i DI-NAM pí-ra-an kat-ta da-a-iš-ten na-at pu-nu-uš-ten*
(18) 22 *ki-nu-na a-pé-el* TI-*tar i-da-la-u-e-eš-ta* TI-*an-za ku-it*
(19) 23 *nu ne-pí-ša-aš* ^{d}UTU-*un* IGI.ḪI.A-*it uš-ki-iz-zi*
(20) 24 TI-*an-na-ša-za* NINDA-*an az-zi-ik-ki-iz-zi nu am-me-el*
(21) 25 *dam-me-eš-ḫa-aš ŠA* DAM-*IA ḫi-in-kán* SIG$_5$-*ia-at-ta-at*
(22) 26 [*k*]*u-en-ta-an-kán ku-it nu-za-kán* TI-*an-na-aš* UD.ḪI.A-*uš*

Col. III

1 [ZI-*IA da-an-k*]*u-i da-ga-an-zi-pí kat-ta-an-da*
2 [*a-pád-da-še-er pa-i*]*š-ki-iz-zi am-mu-uk-ma tal-wa-tal-la-it*
3 [*a-pa-a-aš-ma-m*]*u*$^{?}$ *ku-ri-pa-aḫ-ta*[5] *nu* DINGIR.MEŠ *Ú-UL*
4 [*še-ek-te-e-ni k*]*u-e-el-la-aš dam-me-eš-ḫa-aš*

if she didn't die? Lo! I consulted the gods, my lords. And she (i.e., Tawannanna) was determined by oracle for me to execute. She was also determined by oracle for me for unseating/dethroning. But even then I did not execute her, but I deposed her from the office of *šiwanzanni*-priestess. And because she was determined by oracle for unseating/dethroning, I unseated/dethroned her, and I gave her a house (or: estate). Nothing is lacking to her desire. She has food and drink (lit. bread and water). Everything stands at (her) disposal. Nothing is lacking to her. She is alive. She beholds the sun of heaven with her eyes. And she eats bread as one of life (or: eats the bread of life). Mine is only this one punishment: I punished her with this one thing, that I sent her down from the palace; I deposed her from the gods in the office of *šiwanzanni*-priestess. Mine is only this one punishment. O gods, set this case down before yourselves and investigate it! Has her life now become miserable? Because she is alive, she beholds the sun of heaven with her eyes. As one of life she eats bread (or: She eats the bread of life). My punishment is the death of my wife. Has this gotten any better? Because she killed her, throughout the days of life [my soul] goes down to the dark netherworld [on her account]. For me it has been unbearable(??). She has bereaved(?) me. Don't you gods [recognize] whose is the punishment?

[5] Cf. ii 3 *ku-ri-pa-it*.

5 [o o o o -[6]*š(a-m)]a-aš-ša-an A-NA* ^{SAL}AMA.DINGIR-*LIM-UT-TI ku-it*

6 [o o o *ar-ḫa t(i-it-t)]a-nu-nu-un am-mu-ug-ga*[7] *A-NA* DINGIR.MEŠ

7 [EN.MEŠ-*IA* SISKUR.SISKU(R.ḪI.A E)]GIR-*an ar-ḫa-ḫa-ri nu-za* DINGIR.MEŠ *e-eš-ša-aḫ-ḫi*

8 [*nam-ma*$^{?}$*-ma A-N(A* DINGIR.MEŠ *AŠ)-]ŠUM* ^{SAL}AMA.DINGIR-*LIM-TIM le-e*

9 [*ti-it-ta-nu-ut-te(-ni kap-p)]u-u-wa-at-te-ni-ia-an-za-an le-e*

10 [*ku-it-ki nu k(a-a-aš-m)]a u-wa-aš-šu-ú-ra-ia*[8] *ku-it Ú-UL*

11 [o o o o o (*-ia*$^{?}$*-an-za*)] *e-eš-ta ku-it-ma-na-aš* SAL.LUGAL *e-eš-ta*

12 [*na-aš* DAM-*IA ḫur-za-k(i-i)]t na-an-kán ku-en-ta*

13 [*na-an-ša-ma-aš*$^{??}$ *ku-(w)]a-pí AŠ-ŠUM* ^{SAL}AMA.DINGIR-*LIM-TIM ar-ḫa*

14 [o o o *ti-it-ta-nu-nu-un n]a-an te-ep-nu-nu-un*

15 [SAL.LUGAL-*an-kán IŠ-TU* É.G]AL-LIM *kat-ta u-i-ia-nu-un na-aš ki-nu-un*

16 [^{LÚ}SANGA-*KU-NU* ÌR-*KU-N]U Ú-UL ḫur-za-ki-iz-zi*

17 [o o o o o o o o]x *ku-wa-at-qa na-an ka-ru-ú*

18 [o o o o *ku-it iš-ta]-ma-aš-ten nu ki-nu-un-ma* DINGIR.MEŠ EN.MEŠ-*IA*

19 [o o o o o -*KU-N]U QA-TAM-MA nu* ḪUL-*aš me-mi-an*

20 [o o o o o o o *n]u ka-a-ša am-mu-uk* ^{m}*Mur-ši-li-iš*

21 [LUGAL GAL LUGAL KUR ^{URU}*ḪA-AT-TI*] *pí-ra-an wa-aḫ-nu-nu-un*

22 [*nu-uš-ma-aš ku-e-da-ni me-mi-ni ḫu*$^{?}$*-d]a*$^{!}$*-ak* ⸢*ar*⸣*-wa-nu-un*

23 [*nu-mu iš-ta-ma-na-an pa-ra-a e-ep-ten nu-mu i]š-ta-ma-aš-[t]en*[9]

24 [ ] *ḫur-za-ki-iz-zi*

25 [ ]*-an-na ku-it-ki*

26 [-*N]A* É-*IA*

27 [-]*at-te-ni*

---

28 [ ] DINGIR.MEŠ *BE-LU*^{MEŠ}*-IA*

29 [ḪUL-*wa-aš ud-da-a-a]r ku-it*

30 [*iš-ta-ma-aš-ten*]x

(Breaks off entirely)

Now because I [depo]sed [the queen] from the office of *šiwanzanni*-priestess to you (plural), I will provide for the [offer]ings of the gods and I will regularly worship the gods. Don't [re-inst]all [her] in the office of *šiwanzanni*-priestess for the gods! Don't [take] her [into ac]count! Because she was not . . . -ed for *uwaššuraya*, while she was queen, she kept [curs]ing [my wife] until she had killed her. When I had de[posed her] from the office of *šiwanzanni*-priestess [to the gods], I curtailed her power. I sent [the queen] down [from] the palace. And now does she not continue to curse [your priest and yo]ur [servant]? [. . . . .] somehow. [Because] you (plur.) listened to her once before, is your [will(?) . . .] the same, O gods, my lords? The word of evil [will you hear?] Lo, I Muršili, [the Great King, King of Hatti Land] have come forward. [In what matter] I have [promp]tly(?) presented myself [to you,] [hold forth your ear to me and] hear [me]! She is cursing [. . . . . .] something [. . . . .] in(?) my house. Do[n't . . . . . .]!

[. . . . .], O gods, my lords! Because [you have heard the word]s [of evil . . . . .]

---

[6] Restore perhaps [SAL.LUGAL-*an-na-š(a-m)]a-*.

[7] B 3: *am-mu-uq-qa.*

[8] B 4: *ú-wa-aš-šu-ra-ia.*

[9] Here the Izmir fragment joins with *-t]en* in its first line. The following lines are entirely from the Izmir fragment.

COMMENTS

II 3 *kuripait* is probably synonymous with *kuripahta* (III 3). The translation assumes some connection with *kurimma-* "lonely, orphaned, bereaved." Cf. Hoffner, *JCS* 29:155.

II 5 For the construction *natmu* SAG.DU-*aš ḫinkan* compare *natši mān* SAG.DU-*aš ḫinkan KBo* 18.142:5–6. The question contains irony. Why should Muršili be held guilty of such a grave offence? He didn't take her life, even though he had oracular authorization.

II 6 Against a reading IN[IM-*n*]*a-za* (i.e., *memiyanaza*) is the need of the particle *-za* in this construction (*appa punuš-*): *nu=*[*z*]a pankun EGIR-*pa punuški KUB* 1.16 iii 61 (*HAB*), cf. ibid. iii 70, *ugat=za appa* ^{SAL}ENSI-*ta natta kuššanka punuššun KUB* 30.10 rev. 21. *appa punuš-* occasionally occurs without *-za* where the sentence enclitics at the head of the clause are preserved (*KBo* 13.72 obv. 12, *KUB* 36.55 ii 30), but in these cases the meaning seems to be different from "to consult (someone)." In [. . . LÚ].É.DINGIR LIM=*ya= šmaš* EGIR-*pa punu*[*š*]*šanzi* (*KBo* 13.72 rev. 3) the *=šmaš* with a third person plural verb is the functional equivalent of *-za*.

II 7 The absence of *Ú-UL* on the join piece is contrary to all expectation expressed in earlier restorations. The theory that Muršili was refused permission to execute his stepmother has been accepted by everyone, including those who have commented on the matter most recently: Ünal, *TH* 3 ('74) 40, Cornelius, *RIDA* 22 (1975), 41 and Archi, *Florilegium Anatolicum*, 1979, 39, note 13. Archi translates without indicating the free restoration, "et il fut décidé pour moi de ne pas la tuer mais de l'exiler." As I pointed out in brief remarks in *JCS* 29 (1977), 155 note 22, the new join casts an entirely different light on this incident. Muršili chose to spare her life, although he had a divine permission to take it. This permission, once obtained, gave him a card which he could play any time he chose. There was no time limit on the gods' authorization. His temporary restraint in the matter was politically wise and earned for him propaganda points with the public.

II 8 *katta ašanna* and *katta ašašḫun* (II 11) see Kammenhuber, *MIO* 2:249 and Friedrich, *Heth. Elementarbuch*^{2} paragr. 276c. On the meaning and translation of *katta ašeš-* here see discussion below. *apiya=ya* "even then," i.e., in spite of the permission granted.

II 9 The proper preterite 1 sg. of *kuen-* is *kuenun*, as amply attested (*ku-e-nu-un*, *KUB* 23.21 rev. 30, Hatt. II 40), especially often in the texts of Muršili II (*KBo* 2.5 ii 11, *KBo* 3.4 i 40, *KBo* 14.20 + 4, *KUB* 14.16 ii 19, *KUB* 19.39 ii 6, etc.). It seems unnecessarily cautious, therefore, on the basis of this single example of *ku-e-nu-nu-un* in a text whose scribe repeatedly shows confusion about whether or not to write consecutive *-nu-* signs (cf. II 10 and 17) to seriously propose an alternative form *kuenunun* (Friedrich, *HW*, 113).

II 12 In this construction *-šan* and *-kan* are interchangeable, cf. II 14.

II 14ff. (cf. II 22ff.) TI-*anza=aš* "she is alive" is made more explicit in II 22 TI-*anza kuit* "because she is alive, (she enjoys all these benefits which my dead wife does not)."

II 15 The writing *-az* for the particle *-za* is unusual in New Hittite.

II 15-16 To take the following TI-*annaš* as dependent on NINDA-*an* ("bread of life"), is difficult although possible in view of TI-*annaš=a=za* NINDA-*an* in II 24. An alternative interpretation would be TI-*annaš* "one of life" (allowed to live a full and normal life span), cf. Hatt. I 15, *KBo* 4.14 iii 9. The expression "bread of life" occurs nowhere else in Hittite.

II 17 Note the change of gender from *kaš dammešḫaš* to *ki* "this (one) thing." It is possible with Friedrich, *HW*, to posit on the basis of the hapax *dammešḫanunun* a *nu*-causative verb from the verb *dammešḫai-*, virtually synonymous with the latter. But in view of our scribe's problems with dittography and haplography of *-nu-* (cf. II 9–10) this may be only dittography for *dammešḫanun*. The verb governs two objects in the accusative, *ki* . . 1-*an* "this one thing" and *=an* "her." Cf. Sommer, *AU* 164.

II 22 TI-*anza kuit* "because she (i.e., the Tawannanna) is alive (although deposed)" stands in contrast to *kuenta=an kuit* "because she (i.e., the Tawannanna) killed her (Muršili's wife)" in II 26.

II 26 UD.ḪI.A-*uš* is formally acc. pl. "Throughout the days of life" could be acc. of duration.

III 1–2 On this restoration and the similar phrase in *KBo* 13.62 obv. 10–11 which prompted it, compare Hoffner, *JCS* 29 (1977), 155. In a letter dated January 29, 1979, Professor Jonas Greenfield of Jerusalem called my attention to parallels in Ugaritic (C. H. Gordon, Ugaritic Textbook, text 67, col. VI, 24–25: *ʾaṯr bʿl ʾard bʾarṣ*) and Hebrew (Genesis 37:35). The Genesis passage is particularly interesting. "Surely I will go down to Sheol in mourning for my son." The Hittite clarifies its interpretation, showing that the going down weeping to Sheol was not something anticipated at the end of Jacob's life, but his anticipated daily experience for the rest of his life.

III 2 The hapax verb *talwatallait* probably has an impersonal subject: "It has become . . . to me."

III 3 For the restoration compare II 3.

III 10 *uwaššuraya* only occurs here in the main text and the duplicate.

III 12 The translation "kept cursing my wife until she had killed her" is based on the sequence of *-ške-* verb followed by the non-*ške*-verb. Compare Telepinu Proclamation I 7: *nu utne ḫarninkiškit nu utne arḫa tarranut* "He kept devastating the lands until he had worn the lands out."

III 14 For *tepnu-* "to curtail power, demote" (without *-za*), versus "to belittle (verbally)" (with *-za*), see Hoffner, *JCS* 29 (1977), 152–4.

III 16 Restore either ÌR-*KU-N*]*U* or ^{LÚ}SANGA-*KU-N*]*U* on the basis of Muršili II Plague Prayers *KUB* 14.14 + 19.1 obv. 6, rev. 37, *KUB* 14.10 i 3.

III 21 *piran waḫnu-* is usually intransitive. What is expected therefore in the lacuna following *ammuk* ^{m}*Muršiliš* is a series of titles or epithets. The string proposed here is attested as applied by Muršili II to himself. Cf. H. Gonnet, *Bibliothèque des Cahiers de l'Institut de Linguistique de Louvain*, 15 (Hethitica III), p. 50 number 86a. Strike *KBo* IV 8 iii 20 therefore under the number 82a on page 48.

III 22–23 Restorations based on Fourth Plague Prayer of Muršili II, *KUB* 14.13 i 17–20.

The general significance of this prayer has been understood for quite some time.[10] Muršili II, who in the companion text *CTH* 70 complains of specific abuses of power by his stepmother, the Tawananna, here seeks to defend himself against charges by her that he has sinned against the gods by removing her from her position as *šiwanzanni*-priestess. It was Tawannanna who was first hostile. Repeatedly she asked the gods to take the life of Muršili's wife. Eventually, she succeeded: Muršili's wife died. It was then that Muršili sought the advice of the gods through oracle. This oracle authorized him either to execute Tawannanna or to dethrone her.

Although both options were therefore open to him, in mercy he chose the second option. He furthermore provided her with all amenities befitting her high social position, so that she lacked nothing she might wish for. Vividly he contrasts her condition with that of his deceased wife whom she had killed. This contrast takes on added meaning, now that we know from the join piece that Muršili was authorized to put the Tawannanna to death. Why should she complain of being demoted, when she could have been dead like Muršili's wife? Furthermore, the king contrasts the Tawannanna's present state with his own, as a bereaved husband. He reminds the gods that she made him a widower (*kuripait* II 3, *kuripaḫta* III 3). And in one of the most moving lines of the entire prayer (II 26, III 1–2) he describes his daily agony of bereavement in terms of a series of daily trips to the dark netherworld.

The Tawannanna's complaint against him may also have included the accusation that by his removing her from her office as *šiwanzanni*-priestess he brought about a diminution of the sacrifices and festivals for the gods. It has already been observed by others that the *šiwanzanni*-priestess was not a high position.[11] Each local sanctuary had at least one of them. Considerations of this kind have even led some to translate "I ousted her and made her Siwanzanna-priestess,"[12] but the syntax will not allow this translation.[13] What suggests that the Tawannanna's *šiwanzanni*-priestesssship was something much more exalted is the statement (II 19, III 8) that she had been *šiwanzanni*-priestess "for the gods" (ANA DINGIR.MEŠ), i.e., for all the gods, not just for one temple.[14] Therefore, although our text does not explicitly call her "chief *šiwanzanni*-priestess," something very much like this must have obtained. This office, with its powers of allocating sacrifices, votive offerings, perhaps even temple lands, allowed her considerable control over the assests of the state cult.[15] Doubtless it was for this reason that Muršili could describe her abuses of power in terms which suggest the depletion of the material resources of the royal house in order to bestow goods on her favorites: "Do you gods not see how she has turned the entire house of my father (Šuppiluliuma I) into the 'stone house' (mausoleum) of the god LAMMA (and) the 'stone house' of the god? Some things she brought in from the land of Šanhara. Others in Hatti [. . . .] to the populace she handed over(?). She left nothing. . . . And even that which was not done/made, she handed over to you. My father's house she destroyed." (*KUB* 14.4 ii 3–12) To protect the resources of king and gods, therefore, Muršili removed her from this office which allowed her to dispose of revenues. To counter her claim that this would reduce offerings and services for the gods he points out (III 5–10, 21) that, because he had personally assumed control (*piran waḫnu-*), he would exercise supervision (EGIR-*an arḫaḫari*) of the rites and ceremonies and offerings made to the gods. Thus he urges the gods not to direct that on this ground the Tawannanna be reinstalled in office (III 8–9). He notes that, now that her earlier cursing has brought death to his wife, she has turned her attention

[10] The general bibliography is: E. Forrer, *Forschungen* II (1929), 1f.; E. Laroche & H. G. Güterbock in *Ugaritica* III (1956), 101f.; A. Goetze, *Kleinasien* (2nd ed., 1957), 93 note 2; S. R. Bin-Nun, *The Tawananna in the Hittite Kingdom* (= Text der Hethiter, 5, 1975), 185ff.; F. Cornelius, *RIDA* 22 (1975), 27–45.

[11] Bin-Nun, *TH* 5, 191ff.

[12] Houwink ten Cate, *Numen* 16 (1969), 93; cf. Bin-Nun, *TH* 5, 189, who almost adopted this translation.

[13] Cf. Ünal, *TH* 3 (1974), 40 note 21.

[14] Bin-Nun, 190 note 126; 193.

[15] Bin-Nun, 186–9.

to him, and is now cursing (thus, threatening with death) "[your priest, y]our [servant]" (III 15–16).[16]

Various translations have been employed for the verbs in this text which describe Muršili's actions against the Tawannanna. I shall summarize them here and indicate my own preferences. The verbs in question are *katta ašeš-* (II 11) and its infinitive *katta ašanna* (II 8, 10), *dammešḫa(nu?)-* (II 17), *katta uiya-* (II 18, III 15), *arḫa tittanu-* (II 10, 19, III 13-14), *tepnu-* (without *-za*, III 14). There is little disagreement among those who have treated this passage regarding the translation of *dammešḫa(nu?)-* and *katta uiyu-*. The former indicates punishment,[17] and the latter expresses the removal of the queen from the scene of the royal power on the acropolis ("I sent her down from the palace").[18] For *tepnu-* Friedrich's glossary[19] gave the translations "gering machen, verringern; —demütingen," which includes 1) verbal humiliation, and 2) real diminution of power. In 1977[20] I demonstrated that meaning 1 is regularly indicated by the presence of the particle *-za*. Without *-za*, as in this text, the word always denotes a real curtailment of power of privilege, not just harsh words. *arḫa tittanu-* and its constructions were studied by A. Ünal in 1974.[21] He translated the verb in the construction found in *KBo* 4.8 as "j-en j-em von einer Stellung absetzen." The following chart gives an idea of the various translations proposed for *katta ašeš-* and *arḫa tittanu-*.

	katta ašeš-	*arḫa tittanu-*
1930 Götze[22]	absetzen	
1952 HWb	niedersetzen; verbannen(?)	heruntersetzen
1969 Houwink ten Cate[23]	confine	oust
1974 Ünal[24]	verbannen	absetzen
1975 Cornelius[25]	absetzen, verbannen	absetzen
1975 Bin Nun[26]	depose	depose

It can be noted that Friedrich, Cornelius and Bin-Nun see relatively little difference in meaning between the two verbs. Friedrich, Ünal and Cornelius see the notion of banishment in *katta ašeš-*, while Bin-Nun finds that aspect expressed in *katta uiya-*. Houwink ten Cate alone translates *katta ašeš-* as "to confine." Although I too see minimal difference between *katta ašeš-* and *arḫa tittanu-*, it seems to me that *katta ašeš-* forms the antonym of *ašeš-*, just as *arḫa tittanu-* forms that of *anda tittanu-*. I would be inclined therefore to translate the first pair as "dethrone, unseat" and "enthrone, seat," and the second as "depose" and "install." That the Tawannanna was in fact put under a kind of house arrest or internment seems clear, but I do not see how *katta ašeš-* can be the term to express such a procedure, nor do I find any good reason to suppose with Friedrich (*HW* 35) that *katta ašeš-* is synonymous with *kattan ašeš-* (twice, *KUB* 10.54 v 18 and *KBo* 16.99 vi? 10, both in broken contexts). If it be insisted that *katta* should here mean "down," I would prefer to say that it means to make someone take a lower seat.

[16] Bin-Nun, 186.

[17] Goetze, *Hatt.* (1925), 63, Friedrich, *HW* (1952), 208.

[18] Bin-Nun, *TH* 5, 189 "banished."

[19] Friedrich, *HW* 221.

[20] *JCS* 29 (1977), 152–4.

[21] *TH* 3 (1974), 40.

[22] *Neue Bruchstücke zum grossen Text des Hattušilis*, 30.

[23] *Numen* 16, 93.

[24] *TH* 3, 40f.

[25] *RIDA* 22, 27–45.

[26] *TH* 5, 185ff.

LAD IN THE DESERT

THORKILD JACOBSEN
BRADFORD, N. H.

AMONG SAM KRAMER'S NOW THIRTY-NINE "FIRSTS" one finds the farmer (The First "Farmer's" Almanac) and the orchardman (The First Experiment in Shade-Tree Gardening)[1] but not, as far as I can see, the shepherd. It might be of interest to him, therefore—if only for his amusement—to take a look at an idyllic Sumerian passage dealing with the shepherds' life in the desert in the spring with its manifold urgent tasks. Since the passage clearly antedates both Theocritus' *Idylls* and Vergil's *Bucolics* he could also, if so minded, claim for it status as "The First Pastoral."[2]

The passage in question occurs in a Dumuzi lament published by Zimmern in his *Sumerische Kultlieder aus altbabylonischer Zeit* [Zweite Reihe, *VS* 10], 1913, as no. 123 in obv. col ii′. 1′ - rev. 1.4. What is left of the preceding obv. ii′ contains a lament for the dead Dumuzi spoken by his sister,[3] but when the text resumes in the lower part of obv. iii′ it is his mother who is speaking. She recalls how he drove his flocks into the desert to pasture, and how he sent a message to her to come out and join him there, when the work was getting too much for him. She says:

obv. iii
[ì-ĝen-na-e[a] ì-ĝen-na-e]
[na-ám[b]-e pa bí-in]-⸢e⸣ [pà-bi im-me][c]
ì-⸢ĝen-na-e⸣ ì-ĝen-na-e
na-ám É-dùg[d]-e pa bí-i-è pà-bi im-me

---

[1] See Samuel Noah Kramer, *History Begins at Sumer: Thirty-Nine Firsts in Man's Recorded History*, 3rd revised edition. 1981. See Chapters 11 and 12.

[2] Idyllic in mood is also the attractive picture of Geshtinanna given in *SEM* 90 ii. 5′–10′ with which we have elsewhere dealt under the title "Bucolic" (Jacobsen and Wilson, *Most Ancient Verse*, 1963, 7 and *Toward the Image of Tammuz* ed. by W. L. Moran, 1970, 215). We would now read and translate

nin-a-ni ^{ĝiš}al-ĝar-gù-du$_{10}$-ga-[k]a
ama ^{d}Geshtin-an-na amaš-a mu-un-da-an-tìl
wa-aš-ba-[a]z-zu(!)
u$_8$ ì-gíd-dè sila$_4$ ba-ab-sum-mu
i-ša-da-ad *i-na-di-in*
úz ì- gíd -dè máš ba-ab-sum-mu
šu-zi-da-ni ^{dug}šakir-ra bí-in-ĝar
i-mi-it-ta-ša i-na MIN(!) *ša-⸢ak⸣(!)-na-at*
munus-e gáb-bu-na ^{ĝiš}al-ĝar tigi [bí]-in-ĝar

His sister of the sweet-voiced lyre,
dame Geshtinanna, dwelt in the fold with him,
was milking the ewes and giving to the lambs,
was milking the goats and giving to the kids,
her right hand she placed on the churn
in her left the (young) woman put lyre and harp.

As shown by this passage both Sumerian gíd and Akkadian *šadādu* have—within their general semantic range of "to pull"—also the specific meaning "to milk." See also *AS* 12, 62 lines 361–62 gud-zu tur-bi-a ba-ra-mu-un-gub ià-bi nu-mu-ra-ak-e/e-zé-zu amaš(!)-bi-a ba-ra-mu-un-dúr-ru ga-bi nu-mu-ra-ŠU-BU-e "your oxen no longer stand in their pen, their butter is not made for you, your sheep no longer dwell in their fold, their milk is not milked for you." ŠU-BU with the readings ul, dubul, and dulu (*CAD* E, 86) corresponds to Akkadian *elēpu/ullupu* "to stretch forth," "to stretch," "lengthen," and would seem, like gíd and *šadādu*, to be capable also of the specific meaning "to milk." (The precise sense of ga-ŠU-BU:*šu-un-nu-qu* of *MSL* 13, 165 line 148 escapes us.)

The title ama given Geshtinanna is here a title of respect only, and does not in that use imply motherhood. In the Dumuzi materials Geshtinanna is typically the young unmarried girl whose loyalties are to her brother. In our earlier translation we translated "Maid Geshtinanna," which sounds better, but which undoubtedly underplays the note of respect, and fits badly when the term is used of matrons as e.g. Baba(*SAK*, 86 h iii. 2) or Nintur (e.g. Langdon, *Babylonian Liturgies*, no. 75 (K 6110 rev. 7 or *TuMHnF* 4/2, no 86 obv. 4). We have therefore preferred "Dame" in its sense of "woman of station or authority" (*Webster's Collegiate Dictionary*, 5th ed., 255) which seems to come close.

[3] For a partial translation (col. ii. 10–21) see our *Treasures of Darkness*, 52 and cf. *TIT*, 87.

ià-lum[e] edin-šè ì-g̃en-na-e
ià-la-lum edin-šè ì-g̃en-na-e
na-ám-Ama$_5$[f]-e pa bí-in-è
na-ám-Unu^{ki}ga-ke$_4$ pà-bi im-me
na-ám-^{kul}Kulaba$_x$ (UNU)^{ki}-ke$_4$ pa bí-in-è
na-ám-Ama$_5$ pà-bi im-me
A-ra-li[g] da-ma-al-ba e-zé mu-na-dab-dab-bé[h]
u$_8$-e sila$_4$ ke ba-an-da-ab-tag[i]
/muruš-e[j] edin-na
ud$_x$(UZ)-dè[k] máš ke ba-an-da-ab-tag[l]
/muruš-e edin-na
⌜ga⌝ šà-ba sahar-harub nu-me-a[m]
kiši(Ú-GÍR)-e mu-na-ab-lá
ga a-⌜ú⌝-duru$_5$-bé[n] nu-me-a
a-gár-e mu-na-an-dé
ga i-ti-i[r]-da [o] máš-en-na nu-me-a
ki-in-⌜dar⌝ mu-na-ab-ku$_5$
ga-ara$_3$-didli (TUR-TUR) du$_6$-šè
/du$_6$-šè mu-na-⌜sukud⌝ muruš-e
ga-ara$_3$-gal-gal mudru-šè[p] mu-na-nú
/muruš-e edin-na[q]
ga im-tuku$_4$-dím šu im-ra-ra[r]
/muruš-e edin-na
muruš edin-zé-ba kúm mu-da-ab-ak[s]
mu-di-ni-màr
muruš-e edin-na
ki-bi-a muruš-e ama-u-gù-ni-ir
kin mu-un-da-ra-ši-in-gi$_4$[t]
lú-du ama-g̃u$_{10}$-úr du$_{11}$-ga-na-ab
edin-šè hé-im-ma-du
iv ià mu-da-g̃ál ga mu-da-g̃ál[u]
ga-g̃u$_{10}$ duk-šakir-ra[v] ma-tu$_x$-tu$_x$(TÙM-TÙM)[w]
ga im-tuku$_4$-dím šu im-ra-ra
ga i-ti-ir-da imi-dím ià in-tag$_4$-e
edin-šè hé-em-ma-du

COMMENTARY

a. This and the following lines—in Emesal since spoken by the mother—describe Dumuzi's progress as he drives his flocks out to the pastures in the Arali desert between Bad-tibira and Uruk. The precise route taken by him, while undoubtedly familiar to the ancient listeners, is not clear to us since the precise location of the various landmarks mentioned, except for Uruk, is not known.

We analyze ì-g̃en-na-e as a punctive 3 p.sg. i-g̃en "he went," nominalized with -a as i.g̃en.a (written ì-g̃ena^{na}), "he who went," and given the adessive mark -e to form i.g̃en.a.e "unto him who went." The indefinite "he" of this and the following line is specified as ià-lum and ià-la-lum in lines 3′ and 4′ to form a so-called "particularizing stanza." See *TIT*, 334f.

b. na-ám is standard Emesal orthography for nam. For the meaning "(administrative) district," "prefecture," see Deimel, *ŠL* 79.9 nam:*pîhatum*. Each of the temples mentioned had apparently its own precinct and own separate administrative status.

c. pa-è "to appear" means literally "to put out the top" and refers apparently to the fact that in the desert in Iraq, owing to mirage-effect, the first thing one sees of an approaching person or object is the seemingly free floating top of it.

The prefix bí- of pa bí-in-è indicates occurrence of the action of the verb outside, at some distance from the speaker and listener's place. We therefore translate "loomed up."

The prefix -m- indicates nearness to the speaker's place: hither/here/hence (see *AS* 16, 77f.). We accordingly translate im-me as "came into view"; it implies that the thing appearing is close enough to be seen in its entirety, is in full view. The writing im-me represents i.m.e durative of e/dug$_4$. On the use of this verb as a helping verb see Poebel, *AS* 11, 67–101. pà... e/dug$_4$ has the same meaning as pàd alone.

The -n- of bí-in-è presumably resumes the adessive of ì-g̃en-na-e (cf. *AS* 16, 80 note second col.). In im-me<i.m.(n).e it seems to be assimilated to the preceding -m-.

d. É-dùg is here clearly—on the principle of *pars pro toto*—the name of a Temple. The term, which literally means "sweet house/room," denotes primarily the private quarters in a house, specifically the bedroom. See Gudea, Cyl. B ix 6-14, where the duties of Kinda-zi, who is in charge of it, are listed. They are those of a chambermaid.

e. ià-lum we tentatively take to represent a loan from Akkadian *ialum*/*aialum* "stag" and ià-la-lum in the next line we analyze as ial alum "noble stag." In a-lum, an epithet for sheep later replaced by as-lum "fine," we would see a variant of alim/elum: *kabtu*. The term ià-lum occurs as an epithet of Dumuzi also in *RA* 8, 168. 18 and the parallel *SK* 2.i.16. Whether we are right in all of this may well be questioned. One could consider seeing in ià-lum and ià-la-lum variants of the well known cries alali and e'ellu, the latter of which is a cry used in driving animals (cf. *STVC* 75 rev. ii 6′-7′ dealing with plough-oxen).

Not to be connected with the ià-lum of our passage is the phrase with which Enkidu tries to encourage Gilgamesh in the stories of "Gilgamesh and Huwawa" and of "Gilgamesh and the Bull of Heaven." It reads ià(var. ia$_4$)-lum-lum (var. om) ù(var. ú)-luh-ha-sú-

sú dumu-ge₇ giri$_x$-zal-dingir-re-e(var. om)-ne (*JRAS* 1932, 914–21 iv. 9–14 vars. from *SK* 196 iv. 18–19) "Sprinkler (of) rich oil on the rod, princely child, the gods' delight." To sprinkle oil on the rod means tempering discipline with kindness; the oil soothes the wales left by the rod. The phrase thus praises Gilgamesh as a kind master.

f. Ama$_5$ here, as É-dùg above, clearly serves—*pars pro toto*—as name of a separate temple with its own administrative district around it.

g. Arali was the name of the desert between Bad-Tibira (Medinah) and Uruk (Warka). There, according to the Dumuzi texts from those two cities, Dumuzi pastured his flocks, and there he was killed. Because it figures so constantly in the laments for Dumuzi, it took on, to later generations, unfamiliar with the ancient topography of Uruk, Nether World connotations and became in time a name for the Nether World. Such usage, however, is clearly secondary.

h. A reading of the verb as dab-dab is indicated by the complement -bé. The signs are LAGABxMAŠ. The verbal form we take to be an intransitive durative 3rd nonpersonal in -e, the reduplication of the full root indicating plurality of subject.

i. tag is phonetic writing for tag$_4$ "to leave," "to abandon." Sheep are notoriously bad mothers and the ewes tend to leave their new-born lambs on the ground after they have yeaned. The shepherd must thus go to look for them to take care of them.

j. Apparently the g of g̃uruš is the nasalized one that appears as m in Emesal. See the value mu-ru-uš given in *MSL* 2, 58 344 (= *MSL* 14, 45. 344). The form as it stands, muruš-e, is probably best interpreted as an adessive with directional datival force. This use of the adessive -e is normal with words for non-personals, but occasionally it is found, instead of -ra, also with words denoting persons, as shown by Falkenstein *ZA* 45 (1939), 181f. The examples there discussed, all have -e follow a genitive. Occasionally, though, -e in such use appears also without preceding genitive element. Such cases, apart from the one here discussed, are Scheil, *RA* 8, 161ff. line 72 (cited by Falkenstein and treated by him on p. 176f. of his article) g̃al$_5$-lá-tur-e g̃al$_5$-lá-gal-e gù mu-u[n-na-dé-e] "The little ranger was saying to (-e) the big ranger," and Gudea Cyl. B xvii. 21 arád-dè lugal-e zag mu-da-DU-àm "while the slave walked beside the master." See also Kramer, *Enki and Ninhursag̃* (1945), 14.91, 111 and p. 18. 197 sukkal-a-ni-^{d}Isímu-dè gù mu-na-dé-e.

In the first of these quotations g̃al$_5$-lá is a term for the infernal policemen, "rangers," who are seeking Dumuzi. The term denoted apparently originally a fighter who, like Marduk in Enuma eliš, was armed with a net, a *retiarius*, as may be seen from the entry g̃al$_5$-lá:*sa-ha-šum* *ŠL* 376.77b *AOF* 7, 274, 21 and Lambert *BWL*, pl. 73 *VAT* 10756 line 7. See *AHw*, 1008 s.v. *sahāšu*.

In the passage from Cyl. B the verb written DU should be active transitive with zag as direct object. Perhaps one could read di$_6$ (cf. de$_6$:*babālu* *ŠL* 206.19 as well as zag-DU:*šanānu* ibid. 332.89b and zag-de: *šaninu* ibid 332.115) and assume the construction to reflect "bring up the side at/to with (someone)."

The use of -e to denote movement to external contact, also with words for persons, represents undoubtedly an original usage. However, since movement to external contact with a person would usually tend to affect him also internally, i.e., emotionally, -e tended to yield to -ra, which had that latter implication, so that by historical times -e survives with words for persons only in special cases—especially after genitive element.

Interesting is that when, consonantly with the older construction, adessive -e was resumed by an adessive -ni- in a following verbal form, later usage changed only the -e of the free form to -ra. The -ni- remained frozen as a bound form in the verb and was not changed to -na-. Cf. e.g. É-an-na-túm-ra lú ti mu-ni-ra "a man shot an arrow at Eannatum" *EAN* 1, obv. ix 2–3 ^{d}Nin-g̃ír-zu-ke$_4$ ..... É-an-na-túm-ra ..... mu m[u]-ni-[sa$_4$] "Ningirsu ..... gave Eannatum ..... the name ....." *EAN* 1, obv. iv 13–29; Igi-sa$_6$-ga arád Maš-gu-la-ra ì-bí-la Maš-gu-la-ke$_4$-ne gù in-ni-g̃á-g̃ar^{ar}-eš "The heirs of Mashgula laid claim to Mashgula's slave Igisaga" *ITT* 3/2 5286 Falkenstein *NSGU*, no. 205 2–4 cf. ibid 27–29. As an example of survival of the original construction may serve ^{d}Iš-me-^{d}Da-gan dumu ^{d}En-líl-lá-ke$_4$ ki-sikil ama ^{d}Ba-ba$_6$..... nam-dùg mu-ni-tar ..... "Unto Ishme-Dagan, Enlil's son, did the maiden, dame Baba, determine a good fate." Römer *SKIZ*, 237 29–30. Side by side with it, though, we have ^{d}Iš-me-^{d}Dagan dumu ^{d}En-[líl-lá]-ra nam-tìl ud-sud-rá sag̃-e-[eš] [ri]g$_7$-a-ni-ib "Unto Ishme-Dagan, Enlil's son, grant life of long days as a gift" op. cit., 238.64.

It should be noted that the replacement of adessive -e after a word denoting a person with retaining of adessive infix as bound form in the following verb is not an isolated instance. Similar replacement by -ra of other dimensional case-marks with retention of their corresponding infix in a following verb are frequent.

k. For the reading ud$_x$ of ÙZ see Landsberger *MSL* 8/1, 28 note to line 192a.

l. We assume the signs inscribed in DAG+KISIM to be [Ú]-⌜G̃ÍR⌝ and so read harub. As noted in *CAD* H, 129f the

Ancient Mesopotamians called the fruit of the shôq (camel thorn) harub:*harubu* "Charob." In sahar harub we see an "apposition of substance" (like har-guškin "gold ring") meaning "charob powder." Charob powder was added for flavor.

m. nu-me-a presumably stands for nu.me.a.a "for . . . which was not." Since me expresses "*esse*" "so-sein" only, not also "*existere*," "dasein," a translation "in which there was not" would hardly be right.

As to case, we have tentatively assumed inessive in -a, functioning as *dativus commodi* with non-personals (cf. Falkenstein, *Anal. Or.* 29, 90 104 a 2 and references p. 99 104 e. 2). Possible is also directive of purpose -šè, which after a vowel would become -š not rendered in writing.

n. Sheep normally need no water if they pasture on fresh juicy grass or other verdure. If such verdure is lacking, and if, as a result, they feed on dry grass, they need water, especially if they are to produce sufficient milk. Here the water is furnished, when needed, by the fields with their irrigation canals.

o. iterda is "buttermilk," the milk left in the churn after the butter is made. See below note 20. The buttermilk was used to feed kids and lambs, who got it instead of their mothers' whole milk, which was reserved for human consumption. Note the passage quoted above in note 2; Geshtinanna has her hand on the churn, i.e., is churning, so that the milk she is feeding to lambs and kids may well be buttermilk.

Goats need a certain amount of salt and the present passage suggests that salt was mixed into the buttermilk fed to the prize kids. The source of this salt, readily available to a shepherd in the desert, was apparently the ever-present patches of strongly saline Solonetzic soils with their characteristic gaping cracks in the surface.

p. The phrase mudru-šè mu-na-nú "were laid onto the rod for him" parallels du$_6$-šè mu-na-⌜sukud⌝ "were piled high for him" and so would seem to be connected in some way or other with "stacking" or "piling." The phrase is also used concerning grain. In the "Farmer's Almanac" it constitutes the next to last operation after the grain has been winnowed: še-nir-ra-zu ^{ĝiš}PA-šè nú-bí-ib/ siskur-siskur ud-te-en-ĝe$_6$-ba du$_{11}$-ga-ab/ ud-sa$_9$-a-gim še búr-ra-ab

"Lay your cleaned (i.e. winnowed) grain to the rod/ Say the 'prayer of the cool of even and night'/ Release the grain about midday" (*UET* 6/2, no. 172 iv 9–11). One text, *OECT* I, pl. 32–35, adds še-búr-ra a-ra-ab-túm-t[úm]-e "and the cleaned grain is ready to be carried off for you." The "rod" to which the grain is laid is mentioned also in *ana ittišu* (*MSL* 1, 4 i. 39ff, which lists items to which the renter of a field can lay claim at the division of the produce. After mention of interest on the seed-grain he had provided come ^{ĝiš}PA-àm:^{ĝiš}*haṭṭam*, "the rod itself," and dur-gun-na(?):*ri-ki-is bilti* "the bindings for the yield" (the usual translation "twine of the sheaves" does not fit since the grain is at this point both threshed and winnowed). Lastly the hymn to the grain-goddess *TRS* 29 11–14 lists: gi-gur-mah-zu ^{ĝiš}li-it-ga-zu/ še PA-šè nú-a-zu/ $^{\text{du-ur}}$dúr-bi níĝ-ság-nu-⌜di⌝ / gur-ru-àm silim-àm/ : "Your great reed basket! Your wooden standard measure!/ Your grain laid to the rod!/ Its bindings, things not to be scattered,/ are twisted, are intact." Here the mention of the "rod" in close connection with terms for standards of measuring suggests for it a similar function. It may have been a measuring stick used to measure grain-piles before the grain was loaded in sacks that were then tied up for transport from the threshing-floor. Such measuring, both of grain and, as here, of cheeses, would be a sensible safeguard against pilfering during the transport from the field or from the sheep-fold in the desert.

q. The products of the sheepfold here mentioned occur for the most part, *mutatis mutandis*, in the list of the shepherd's products given by Dumuzi in the tale called "Inanna Prefers the Farmer" (*SRT* 3 ii. 18–iii.11), and in the same order. This is of some interest since the latter list clearly proceeds from the more to the less valuable items. It has "black ewe and white ewe," corresponding roughtly to lambs and kids in *SK* 123. Then follow yellow milk (ga-sig$_7$), clabber or "lebn" (ga ki-⌜si⌝-[im-ma]), whipped cream (?) (ga-bul-a) "grass" milk (ga-ú), and buttermilk (ga i-ti-ir-da).

The term ga-sig$_7$ "yellow milk" is self explanatory. The yellow colour indicates the richness of the milk.

ga-ki-⌜si⌝-[im-ma], which has the ideogram ga-LAGAB, has been interpreted as "stinking milk," due to a reading of the ideogram as ga-hab (*MSL* 11, 109). Such a meaning does not however, accord well with its place here as second most valuable milk product and equated in value with the farmer's "good beer" (kaš-sig$_5$) in *SRT* 3. We accordingly translate the term as "clabber" the *lebn* of the present day Iraq, which resembles yoghurt and is a very popular delicacy.

ga-bul-a we have tentatively rendered "whipping cream" assuming that bul here has the meaning "blow up," "fill with air," "make effervescent" (*napāhu ŠL* 515. 6). The same word, written phonetically, may occur in ga šu-nu-bu-ul:*el-du* (Hh. 24.92, *MSL* 11, 81) "milk that won't whip," "skim milk." The term *eldu*(<*eṣdu*) "mowed," when used of milk, can hardly refer to other than the skimming off of the cream. In the Hh passage cited it parallels [ga zi-i]l-lá and [ga-

ur_4]-ra (restored from *MSL* 11, 122.8 line 16. Note ur_4:*eṣēdu ŠL* 594.2) both rendered as *eldu*. An alternative reading of the sign bul is, of course, $tuku_4$ "to shake," but "shaken," i.e. "churned," milk hardly belongs at this point in the list; it comes in later with ga itirda.

ga-ú "grass milk" is also self explanatory. It is milk from pasturing ewes feeding on grass. Such milk is likely to be light. It is pitted in *SRT* 3 against the Farmer's thin *billatu* beer.

ga-i-ti-ir-da "buttermilk." The reference of this term is made clear by lines iv. 3–4 of *SK* 123 ga im-$tuku_4$-dím šu im-ra-ra/ga i-ti-ir-da imi-dím ià in-tag_4-e ... "She will be beating the milk like a buffeting wind, making the buttermilk leave butter as were it clay (sediment after the flood)." The term seems to be an early loan from Proto-Akkadian with the characteristic ending -a. A variant itirtum (perhaps reflecting a slightly later loan) is also attested. Tentatively we would interpret it as *(w)itirtum* "surplus" i.e. what is poured off as the butter is made.

In ea IV 38 (*MSL* 14, 356) the sign U+GA, perhaps to be read di-im-na, is rendered as *i-tir-tum* in the Akkadian column. The sign in question goes back to a picture of a milk-jug (GA) covered with a pointed lid, for which the Obeid dairy frieze may be consulted. The seated man shown there holds a large vessel thus covered, which he apparently is using to churn with, by rolling it back and forth on the ground.

The line also shows that ià in sheepfold or byre context means "butter" and not "fat," as it is usually rendered due to its Akkadian equivalent šamnu, which must, of course, in such context *also* be rendered "butter" rather than "fat." The rendering of ià as "butter" fits in well with ià-nun "princely ià" i.e. "rendered butter," "ghee." Note also Arabic *samn* "ghee" formed from the same root as *šamnu*. A further passage that helps to clarify this particular meaning of ià is "The Epic of Lugalbanda" line 155ff. Anzu is there offering hé-g̃ál ^{dug}šakir-kù-^{d}Dumu-z[i-d]a-[ka-ka]/ì-bi ki-šár-ra-ke_4 ša-ra-x [. . . . .]/ gára-bi ki-šár-ra-ke_4 ša-ra-x [. . . . . .]/ "The butter of Dumuzi's pure churn's plenty in places of abundance I will give (?) you instead/ its cream in places of abundance I will give (?) you instead." Here very clearly, ià is a product of the churn and so not "fat." (For ki-šár-ra-ke_4 cf. "Enki and the Weltorder" 330 ^{d}Ašnan ninda-šár-ninda-ki-šár-ra-ke_4 "Ashnan who makes bread abundant, bread of myriad places"). See also "Lament for Ur and Sumer" 296 (*UET* 6/2, 131 rev. 40 ià-bi lú-ià-nu-zu-ne ì-im-du_9-du_9-NE, "men who knew not butter were churning its butter." Here too "fat" would not fit. We are pleased to note that A. Berlin in her *Enmerkar and Ensuhkešdanna* also abandons the unsuitable translation of ià as "fat." She prefers "cream" and comes very close to our view in her note 21 on p. 82 with the qualification "cream" (i.e., butterfat).

The ga-ara_3-làl refers apparently to cream-cheese covered with honey as flavoring. With any other kind of cheese a combination with honey would hardly be palatable. It may be noted that cylinder seals picturing life in the sheepfold, the Etana seals, regularly show a rectangular board with circular markings which could be the rims of cylinders seen from above. Frankfort, in his *Cylinder Seals*, 139, interpreted this as a representation of cheeses on a mat. We would prefer to see it as a cheeseform. A very similar cheese-form for a soft variety of cheese to be eaten quite fresh like cream cheese (Gervais) is pictured in *The Encyclopaedia Britannica*, 11th edition, vol. 7, 751, Fig. 9.

ga-ara_3-didli "small cheeses" seems self explanatory. More problematical is the question of what one should understand by ga-ara_3-gal-gal "the big cheeses." Here perhaps, we may be dealing with harder types of cheese, since large soft cheeses seem impractical to handle.

r. šu-ra-ra is "to beat repeatedly with the hand" and refers to the action of churning, which the *Encyclopaedia Britannica* (11th ed., vol. 6, 350) describes as "shaking or beating the cream so as to separate the fatty particles which form the butter from the serous part or buttermilk." The term recurs in line iv 3 below, which deals with milk already in the churn since the direct object of the verb is ga "milk" rather than šakir "churn." It seems probable that the reference is to beating the milk inside the churn with a dasher.

That the ancients may have had the upright churn with dasher is perhaps indicated by the Etana Seal, Frankfort, *Cylinder Seals*, xxiv g, where the vessel shown directly above the seated figure can hardly be otherwise interpreted (cf. op.cit. p. 139). The dasher itself and the lid of the churn through which it passes seems to be pictured in the sign BÚR with the readings dun_x and du_9. The early form of the sign as given in Deimel *LAK* 52 (a still earlier, slightly damaged, example is Falkenstein *Archaische Texte* no. 259) shows a rod passing through a tapering lid (apparently meant to fit the tapered neck of the churn and keeping the milk from slopping over), ending in two slanted appendages, which will represent the bottom plate or flat blades of the dasher. Since the dasher is an implement for "stirring" and "beating" milk it serves well as a symbol for the meanings attributed to its pictogram "to stir," "to churn," "to push," cf. *MSL* 14, 501, 158–161 [d]u-u:

BÚR:*da-a-pu* (i.e. *da*ʾ*āpu* "to push") *du-[u-pu]* (thus rather than *du[-up-pu]* for *du*ʾ*upu*: "to push") *ma-a-ṣum* (!?) "to churn" *na-[a-šu]* "to stir."

Besides churning with upright churn and dasher, other ways of churning were probably in use. Above in note 20, in the discussion of itirda, we suggested rolling a vessel with milk back and forth, as one such. On the so-called Etana seals one or two men are often shown rocking an upright vessel back and forth in the fold, presumably also a way of churning (see e.g. Frankfort *Cylinder Seals*, pl. xxiv g and h and Porada *Mesopotamian Art in Cylinder Seals*, 1947, fig. 36). Lastly, in discussing the myth of Inanna and Bilulu (*JNES* 12 [1935], 166, *TIT*, 57), we have noted a reference to the primitive method of churning by jogging a skin with milk on the knees.

s. kúm mu-da-ab-ak var. mu-di-ni-màr "was made hot with it" var. "heat was established for (lit. "with") him there."

t. kin mu-un-da-ra-ši-in-gi$_4$. It seems to have been customary for shepherds to send for the women of their household to come to the desert to help with the work at the height of the yeaning and milking season. As Dumuzi here sends for his mother, so does his sister Geshtinanna often join him (see note 2 above). Also his bride Inanna, though young and inexperienced, may be called on to help as in *TCL* 16, 97. 4–10. ^{d}Inanna ^{dug}šakir-e gù hé-em-me / ^{dug}šakir nitalam-zu-ur gù hé-em-me ^{d}Inanna<^{dug}šakir gù hé-em-me>/ ^{dug}šakir ^{d}<Dumu-zi-ra gù hé-em-me>/ ^{d}Inanna <^{dug}šakir gù hé-em-me>/ dun$_x$-dun$_x$(BÚR-BÚR) ^{dug}šakir-ra ga-mu-ra-ab-zu (!?)/ ^{d}Inanna ur$_5$-re hé-mu-e-húl-e. "Inanna, may you have the churn give voice!/ may you have the churn give voice for your bridegroom!/ Inanna, may you have the churn give voice/ may you have the churn give voice for Dumuzi!/ Inanna, may you have the churn give voice/ let me teach you the churning of the churn/ and may you, Inanna, have joy in that!" For the reading of the somewhat cramped sign at the end of line 10 as zu cf. the shape of zu in line 17.

Churning seems to have been considered joyful work rather than a chore, and was done to songs or yodel: ilulamma. Cf. "Enki and the World Order" 29–30. [gù un]u$_3$-dè i-lu-lam-ma-na (var. -bi) du$_{10}$-ge-eš im-mi-ib-bé/ [siba-]dè dun$_x$-dun$_x$(BÚR-BÚR) ^{dug}šakir-ra-ka-na (var. om.ka) ud im-di-ni-íb-zal-e/ "The cowherd was giving voice sweetly in his (var. in the manner of) ilulamma (yodel)/ the shepherd was spending the day in his churning of the churn" and "Lament for Ur and Sumer" (*UET* 6/2, 124. 45). ⌜i⌝-lu-lam-ma dun$_x$-dun$_x$(BÚR-BÚR) ^{dug}šakir-ra amaš-a nu-di-dè "that ilulamma and the churning of the churn be not sounded in the fold."

The infix -n.da- "was able to" indicates that by a happy chance a traveller happened to pass by Dumuzi's fold in the desert.

u. ià mu-da-g̃ál ga mu-da-g̃ál "I have butter, I have milk" is here said by the shepherd, and so refers to sheeps' or goats' butter and milk. It can also be said by a cowherd and refers then to cows' butter and milk. Cf. e.g. *SK* 68.10 where the cowherd Nanna sends a message to Ningal beginning: ià mu-da-g̃ál [ga mu-da-g̃ál] "I have butter, I have milk."

Usually however ià "butter" is used as characteristic of the products of the byre—natural, since most butter is from cows' milk—whereas ga "milk" serves to represent the sheepfold. Cf. the Nidaba hymn, Hallo, *Actes de la XVIIe Rencontre*, 1969, 128 line 82: ^{d}Nidaba tùr-ra ià hé-me-en amaš-a ga hé-me-en "Nidaba, in the byre you are verily the butter, in the sheepfold you are verily the milk" and "Lament for Ur" *AS* 12, 62 lines 361–365. gud-zu tùr-bi-a ba-ra-mu-un-gub ià-bi nu-mu-ra-ak-e/ e-zé-zu amaš(!)-bi-a ba-ra-mu-un-dúr-ru ga-bi nu-mu-ra-ŠU-GÍD-e/ ià-g̃ùr-ru-zu tùr-ta nu-mu-ra-dú èn-tukum-šè-SAR/ ga-g̃ùr-ru-zu amaš-ta nu-mu-ra-du èn-tukum-šè-SAR. "Your oxen nowise stand in their byre, their butter is not being made for you./ Your sheep and goats nowise lie in their sheepfold, their milk is not milked for you./ Your butter-carriers come not to you from the byre . . . . / Your milk-carriers come not to you from the sheepfold . . . ."

Characteristic of the byre rather than the sheepfold is apparently also gár:*lišdu* "cream," specifically, one guesses, the thick, firm buffalo cream. The sign for it represents originally a milk jug (GA) with shading of the neck where the cream would accumulate. It figures in the name of the wife of the bull-god Nin-gublaga: ^{d}Nin-é-ià-gár-ka "the lady of the house of butter and cream" i.e., "Lady of the Dairy" (*UET* 1, 10b ii. 4), and Gudea mentions it and butter as products of Eninnu's cowbarn é-gud-bi-ta ià-ku$_4$ gár-ku$_4$ "from its cow-barn butter was coming in, cream was coming in." Cyl. A xxviii 3–4. The dairy goddess is also mentioned in line 205 of "Lament for Ur and Sumer" (*PBS* 10/4, no. 6 rev. 43) and in *TCL* 15, 10. 159 as wife of ^{d}Lugal-hár and in An:*Anum* (*CT* 25. 19.4 and 24. 21.71) as ^{d}Nin-ià-gára and ^{d}Nin-iá$^{ga\text{-}ra}$ga-raš wife of ^{d}Hár, various names of the same bull-god.

In Cyl. B x 3–6 where the goatherd En-lulim is to ià-šár-a-da gár šár-a-da/ úz-kù úz-ga-nag̃ máš-lulim/ ama ^{d}Nin-g̃ír-zu-ka/ ià ga-bi éš É-ninnu-a muš nu-túm-da "to make butter abundant, to make cream abundant, not to allow the butter and milk of the holy goat, the suckling goat, Ningirsu's mother's hind, to cease in the estate Eninnu." (We assume that the writing ^{d}Nin-g̃ír-su-ka in line 5 is short for ^{d}Nin-g̃ír-su-ka-ka which in turn stands for a quadruple genitive) the writing gár for ga in line 3 is probably a mistake, as suggested by the ga of line 6 which would seem to refer back to it.

v. The meaning "churn" for šakir, Akkadian šakiru, is well established by Hg II 70 (*MSL* 7, 110) dug$^{\text{ša-ki-ir}}$ URUxGU:*ša-ki-ru*:*na-ma-ṣu šá šiz-bi* "churning implement for milk" and passages like *SBH*, 130, 12f. umun ^{d}Mu-ul-líl-lá ga nu-du$_9$-du$_9$ ^{dug}šakir-ra i-bi-in-dé:*be-lum* ^{d}MIN *ši-zib la ma-ṣi ina šá-ki-ri ta-aš-pu-uk* "Lord Enlil, after you had poured into the churn milk that would not churn (you were installing over the country a herder who does not sleep" i.e. you are relentlessly driving the country at an impossible task).

The usual sign with which the word is written is šakir:URUxGU but a variant šakír:URUxGA is also attested (see *MSL* 14, 442 43–44). If one may be allowed to assume that šakír originally pictured a churn with sides tapering upwards (cf. the vessel above the seated figure in Frankfort's *Cylinder Seals*, pl. xxiv. g) but was early merged with the URU sign, the inscribed GA "milk" to indicate content would make good sense. More difficult is šakir URUxGU, where the inscribed sign seems to be part of a syllabic combination gu.uru, representing the sign's other value guru$_5$ of quite different meaning. Here again, however, if we may assume that URU originally was a picture of a churn, the inscribed GU probably belongs above it rather than in it, and represents a crude picture of the funnel through which milk was poured into the churn. An early form of šakir such as *LAK* 602, thus modified, would compare not too badly with the representation of the act of filling a churn through a funnel on the dairy frieze from Obeid. For the use of a funnel to fill the churn cf. also *TuMHnF* 4/2 no. 7 iii 90–95 áb tùr-ra um-m[i]-⌜x⌝[. . . .]/ ga šakir-⌜kù-ga⌝ bi(!?)-
iš-tu
za ù-mu-un-[dé]/ ^{d}Šu-ni-du$_7$ kin-g̃á ù-mu-⌜un⌝-
[i-n]a ma-a-ṣi-im
ni-[til]/ lú-ki-sikil amar(!?)-tur-ra-g̃u$_{10}$-šè ga ù-
ši-iz-ba-am
⌜nag̃⌝/ [du]g-a ga luh-[h]a-g̃u$_{10}$ ba-[til-le-en]/
x[. . .]/
^{d}Nin-gal é-zu-šè g̃á- e ga-mu-ra-d[a-du]/ "When I have milked(??) the cows in the byre/ and have poured milk through a funnel into the pure churn/ have made Shunidu finish the work (Akk. "from churning")/ and fed, O maiden, milk to my young calves/ then I shall finish my rinsing the milk off in(side) the jugs/ and, Ningal, I would come to you to your house."

Cleaning out the vessels used for milk is a necessary chore. It may be illustrated on the Obeid dairy frieze, the man with his arm inside the pot is probably cleaning it. Shunidu (as here written means: "His hand is appropriate," more usually the name occurs as šu-ni-du$_{10}$(g) "his hand is good/sweet") is a minor deity listed as a chief herder (unu(ÁB+KU)-mah) of Suen and one of eight sons of ^{d}Gaiu in An:*Anu* (*KAV* 179 ii.11, 172 ii.10). "The Lament for Ur and Sumer" line 335 (*UET* 6/2, with parallel *SET* 403 rev. 8, ^{d}šu-ni-d[u$_7$]) describes him as ^{d}Šu-ni-dùg ià-ga-àr-ra -du$_6$-ul-du$_6$-ul-e ià-ga-àr-ra nu-du$_6$-ul-du$_6$-ul "Shunidu, who wraps up the butter for (cottage) cheese, wrapped not up the butter for (cottage) cheese." We assume that du$_6$-ul stands for dul (for other examples of this singular writing see van Dijk, *SGL* II, 139 to line 7) : *pussumu* "to veil" ŠL 459.11 (the sign there is U+TÚG, not du$_6$) and see the passage as a reference to wrapping up butter and suspending it to drip to make cottage cheese.

w. We read tu$_x$(TÙM)-tu$_x$(TÙM) for tutu.u<tutu.e since a durative is called for by the context and the parallel durative in-tag$_4$-e in iv. 4. Both this and im-ra-ra are "curtailing reduplications" of the roots tum and rah with durative ingressive force. See *AS* 16, 96 and the earlier statement about this kind of reduplication by Poebel *GSG* 446 c-f. For the value of tu$_x$ of TÙM see á viii. 3.13 (*MSL* 14, 506).

As to the meaning of tùm here it may be noted that it is performed on the milk when it is already in the churn, apparently by the use of both hands, as shown by *SRT* 9. 32–34 (variants from *TCL* 15, 21) dealing with Suen. ga-áb-sig$_7$-a (var. ga-edin-za-a) ^{dug}šakir-ra i-ni-in-dé/ šu-zalag-zalag-ge ga na-tu$_8$-t[u$_8$] (var. tu$_x$(TÙM)-t[u$_x$(TÙM)])/ lugal-g̃u$_{10}$ kin-g̃á ti-la-ni. "milk of yellow cows (var. "milk of your desert") he poured in the churn/ was ready to ------ by (using) the pure hands./ When my master had finished from work" etc. The term can thus hardly refer to other than the process of churning, and, as the last line shows, it covers the complete churning operation. Line iv.3 which follows in *SK* 123 "beat the milk like a buffeting wind" must thus parallel and qualify the action. An easy—but probably rather too easy—solution would therefore be to consider tu$_x$-tu$_x$(TÙM-TÙM) a variant orthography for du$_9$-du$_9$ "to churn."

The passage may accordingly be translated in the following manner:

Unto him who walked along, unto him who walked along,
a domain loomed up, came into view;
unto him who walked along, unto him who walked along,
the "Bedroom" prefecture loomed up, came into view;
unto the stag who walked along toward the desert
the Serail prefecture loomed up;
the prefecture of Uruk came into view,
the prefecture of Kullab loomed up,
the Serail prefecture came into view,
and into the vastnesses of the Arali (desert)
the sheep were passing for him.
The ewes left lambs with him on the ground—
for the lad in the desert,
the nanny-goats left kids with him on the ground—
for the lad in the desert.
For milk without carob-powder in it,
the *shôq* bore it for him;
for milk without its (needed) waters of lush pasturage,
the fields made them flow for him;
for what was not the sturdy kids' (salted) buttermilk,
cracks in the ground split open (with salt) for him.
Small cheeses piled up high in heaps for him—
for the lad,
large cheeses were laid onto the rod for him—
for the lad in the desert,
milk was whipped as by buffeting winds.
The lad was made hot (from working)
in the pleasant desert—the lad in the desert—
and the lad managed to send a message
from there to the mother who gave him birth:
"Wayfarer! Speak to my mother, may she come to the desert!
I have butter, I have milk.
She will be churning(?) my milk for me in the churn,
will be beating the milk like a buffeting wind,
making the buttermilk leave butter
as were it clay (sediment after flood).
May she come to the desert to me!"

THE CAPTURE OF AGGA BY GILGAMEŠ (GA 81 and 99)

JACOB KLEIN
BAR-ILAN UNIVERSITY

A CHARACTERISTIC FEATURE OF SUMERIAN EPIC LITERATURE is the frequent repetition of entire strophes, which may represent a vow and its fulfillment, or a message and its report, and so on.[1] A repetition of this kind is attested in the epic of Gilgameš and Agga, where a lengthy direct speech, addressed by Girišḫurdura to Agga (ll. 70–81), is partly and verbatim repeated by the narrator toward the end of the composition (ll. 92–99). The two strophes under discussion read as follows:[2]

A. 70 lú-še lugal-mu in-nu
71 lú-še lugal-mu ḫé-me-a
72 sag-ki-ḫuš-a-ni ḫé-me-a
73 igi-alim-ma-ka-a-ni ḫé-me-a
74 su$_6$-^{na_4}za-gìn-na-ka-a-ni ḫé-me-a
75 šu-si-sa$_6$-ga-ni ḫé-me-a
76 šár-ra la-ba-an-šub-bu-uš šár-ra la-ba-an-zi-ge-eš
77 šár-ra saḫar-ra la-ba-an-da-šár-re-eš
78 kur-kur dù-a-bi la-ba-an-da-šú-a
79 ka-ma-da-ka saḫar-ra la-ba-da-an-si
80 si-^{giš}má-gur$_8$-ra-ka la-ba-ra-an-ku$_5$
81 ag-ga lugal-kiš^{ki}-a šà-erén-na-ka-né šaga (LÚ×GÁNA-*tenû*)-a la-ba-ni-in-ak

B. 92 lú-še lugal-mu ì-me-a
93 bí-in-du$_{11}$-ga-gin$_7$-nam
94 šár-ra ba-an-šub-bu-uš šár-ra ba-an-zi-ge-eš
95 šàr-ra saḫar-ra ba-an-da-šár-re-eš
96 kur-kur dù-a-bi ba-an-da-šú
97 ka-ma-da-ka saḫar-ra ba-da-an-si
98 si-^{giš}má-gur$_8$-ra-ke$_4$ ba-ni-in-ku$_5$
99 ag-ga lugal-kiš^{ki}-a šà-erén-na-ka-né šaga (LÚ×GÁNA-*tenû*)-a ba-ni-in-ak

When in 1949 Kramer published his *editio princeps* of Gilgameš and Agga, relatively little was understood of the above two difficult strophes.[3] The concluding lines in these two parallel passages, which also constitute the climax of the epic, namely ll. 81 and 99, were rendered by Kramer as follows:

81 "Agga, the king of Kish, *restrained* not his *soldierly* heart."
99 "Agga, the king of Kish, *restrained* his *soldierly* heart."

Kramer's translation of these lines, although grammatically defendable, makes little sense contextually, and deprives our epic of a crucial piece of information, without which the dramatic and unconventional end of the story (ll. 100 ff.) is incomprehensible, namely that Agga *was captured* by Gilgameš and his troops. Consequently, the transition to the dialogue between Gilgameš and Agga in ll. 100 ff. becomes abrupt and rather unexpected.[4]

The first substantial contribution to the correct interpretation of these passages was made by Jacobsen, in 1957, who contended that "Gilgamesh and Enkidu make a successful sortie from beleaguered Uruk, penetrate the boat-camp of the attackers and take the leader Agga of Kish captive."[5] Accordingly, Jacobsen read LÚ×GÁNA-*tenû*-a, in l. 99, as šaga$_x$-a, and correctly translated this line as follows:

---

[1] See e.g. A. Berlin, *Enmerkar and Ensuḫkešdanna*, 1979, 24 f.; J. Klein, *Three Šulgi Hymns*, 1981, 55; 62 ff.; G. Komoróczy, *A Sumer Irodalmi Hagyomány*, 1979, 41; C. Wilcke, *AS* 20 (1975), 212 f.

[2] See W. H. Ph. Römer, *Das sumerische Kurzepos* >*Bilgameš und Akka*<, Neukirchen-Vluyn 1980 (=*AOAT* 209/1), pp. 33 ff. Our eclectic transliteration is based primarily on text L.

[3] "Gilgamesh and Agga," *AJA* 53 (1949), 1 ff. (cf. also *ANET*, pp. 44–47).

[4] Kramer, in his edition, already felt that the passages under discussion "are of utmost importance for the understanding of the plot of the tale," and surmised that "in some way Agga has been induced to take a more friendly attitude and probably to lift the siege (ll. 68–99)" (cf. ibid., 6).

[5] *ZA* 52 (1957), 116, n. 55.

"Agga, king of Kish, at his (place in the) center of the army he took captive."[6]

The above rendering cleared the way to the understanding of the end of the plot. As Jacobsen rightly pointed out, Gilgameš, having captured Agga, acted the generous hero, and set him free, as a sign of gratitude for a "previous benefaction," on Agga's part.[7]

The next attempt at an interpretation of the above passages in our epic was again made by Kramer, who in 1963 translated that part of Girišḫurdura's speech, wherein the verbal form ḫé-me-a is constantly repeated (ll. 71–75), as a series of *irrealis*, hypothetical wishes: "Would that that man were my king,/ That it were his strong forehead" and so on.[8] However, Kramer still did not ascribe ll. 76–81 to Girišḫurdura's direct address, and at this time he translated ll. 81 and 99 of our epic as follows:

81 "Agga, the king of Kish, restrained not his troops."
99 "Agga, the king of Kish, restrained his troops."[9]

A major step toward the correct understanding of the above passages was subsequently taken by Falkenstein, who in 1966, pointed out that the recurring ḫé-me-a in ll. 71–75 marks a series of *irrealis* conditional sentences; and that ll. 76–80 of our epic are also part of Girišḫurdura's direct speech, addressed to Agga, to be interpreted as rhetorical questions, anticipating the poet's narration in ll. 89 ff., in a prophetical fashion. Accordingly, Falkenstein translated ll. 70–80 as follows:

" 'Der Mann da ist nicht mein König.
Wäre der Mann da mein König,
so wäre (doch) sein wilder grimmiger Blick,
sein Wisenstier Auge,
sein Lapislazuli-Bart,
sein glückbringender Finger (zu sehen)!
Wurden da nicht (die Gegner) zu Tausenden hinzustürzen, (andere) zu Tausenden (zum Kampfe) aufstehen,
(dann aber ebenfalls) zu Tausenden sich im Staube wälzen?!
Wären dadurch nicht die Länder insgesamt gestürzt,
der Mund des Landes mit Erde gefüllt,
die 'Hörner' (Steven) der Transportschiffe abgerissen?!' "[10]

In spite of the fact that the verbal form la-ba-ni-in-ak, in l. 81; just like the verbal forms in the preceding lines (76–80), is a negative one, prefixed by the morphemes la-ba-, Falkenstein failed to recognize that syntactically line 81 must be *a natural continuation* of the lines preceding it, and hence to be part of Girišḫurdura's direct speech. Consequently, and because of grammatical considerations, he interpreted l. 81, as the narrator's comment, and translated it similarly to Kramer's first rendering in his *editio princeps*, as follows:

"Agga, König von Kiš, unterdrückte nicht seinen Zorn als Krieger."[11]

However, since he understood that ll. 94–98, further on, clearly describe the crushing victory of the troops of Unug over the troops of Kiš, he was forced to assume that the subject of l. 99 is Gilgameš (or Enkidu), rather than Agga, translating the above line quite artificially as follows:

"Gegenüber Agga, dem König von Kiš, unterdrückte er (d. i. Gilgameš) seinem Zorn als Krieger."[12]

Römer, in his revised edition of our epic,[13] reaches the conclusion that Falkenstein's interpretation of šà-

---

[6] Ibid., 117.

[7] Ibid., 117–18. According to Jacobsen's conclusions, the outcome of the political strife between Gilgameš and Agga was that the former reacknowledged the latter as his liegelord (ibid., 118). For our disagreement with this hypothesis see n. 20–21 below.

[8] *The Sumerians*, 189.

[9] Ibid., 189 f. Apparently, Kramer translated šà-erén-na-ka-ni LÚ×GÁNA-*tenû-a* (la-)ba-ni-in-ak literally: "he captured (not) the heart of his soldiers," and understood this as an idiomatic expression for "he restrained (not) his soldiers."

[10] *AfO* 21 (1966), 48.

[11] Ibid., 49. Falkenstein admits that according to his rendering, we would expect here *ag-ga lugal-kiši^{ki}-a-ke$_4$, i.e. a complex ending with an agentive suffix.

[12] Ibid., with n. 24. The supposition that the subject of this line could be Enkidu, is totally incredible, in the light of Enkidu's brutal and cruel behaviour, in the episode of the slaying of Ḫuwawa (see Klein, *AOAT* 25, 290, n. 25).

[13] See *AOAT* 209/1, 40–41; 87 f.

erén-na-ka-ni "wird wohl die einzig sinvolle sein," and accordingly he translates ll. 81 and 99 of the epic as follows:

> 81 "Akka, der König von Kiš, beherrschte nicht seinen Zorn eines Kriegers."
> 99 "Akka, der König von Kiš, beherrschte seinen Zorn eines Kriegers."[13]

Falkenstein rejected Jacobsen's translation of šà-erín-na-ka-ni in l. 99—"at his (place in the) center of the army"—for purely grammatical reasons: He argued that according to Jacobsen's rendering we would expect here a "Genetiv ohne Regens," and a locative /-a/ at the end of the complex.[14] We propose here to revert to Jacobsen's rendering of this line with a slight modification, translating it as follows:

> "Agga, the king of Kiš, was captured at his center-of-the-army."

This proposal may be supported by the following considerations:

a). As Falkenstein himself admitted, the compound verb šaga(LÚ×GÁNA-*tenû*)-a ak never takes šà as its (direct) object.[15] It normally takes a category of human being as a direct object, and it can only be translated "to capture," "to oppress."[16]

b). In view of the absence of a clear acting agent in the preceding lines, the only logical subject of our sentence must be "Agga, the king of Kiš," and the verbal form must be understood in the passive voice.[17]

c). The complex šà-erén-na-ka-né contains an "internal genitive," which normally precedes the possessive pronoun, and seems to end with the locative-terminative suffix /-e/, replacing the expected locative suffix. Consequently, this complex should be translated: "at his center-of-the-troops," i.e. "at his army-center." The same type of "internal genitive" is attested also in ll. 73 (igi-alim-ma-ka-a-ni) and 74 (su$_6$-^{na_4}za-gìn-ha-ka-a-ni).[18]

d). The above rendering of our line provides us with the climactic event of the plot, namely the capture of Agga, which was the natural outcome of the storm-attack, staged by Enkidu and his commando-troops, under the charismatic inspiration of Gilgameš (ll. 84–98). Gilgameš's subsequent gallant address to Agga (ll. 100 ff.) becomes now comprehensible.

If our above rendering of l. 99 is justified, then the meaning of l. 81 becomes now clear: this line is to be considered as a syntactically natural continuation of the lines preceding it, i.e., as a rhetorical question, concluding Girišḫurdura's address to Agga. Accordingly, we propose to translate it as follows:

---

[14] I.e., according to Falkenstein, we would expect *šà-erén-na-ka-ka-na; cf. ibid., 48, with n. 20. Falkenstein admits that an idiomatic combination of šaga-a aka with šà is unknown from elsewhere, and hence its supposition is somewhat doubtful (ibid., 49).

[15] See preceding note.

[16] For šaĝa(-a) ak see now Römer, *AOAT* 209/1, 87 f.; J. Klein, *Three Šulgi Hymns*, 164; J. Krecher, *Festschrift Lubor Matouš* (1978), II, 57.

[17] Thus, in spite of the appearance of the personal infix -n- in the verbal form ba-ni-in-ak! Cf. Römer's translation of ll. 95–98 as passives, although their verbal forms exhibit this element universally. For the -n- infix in such contexts see now M. Yoshikawa, *JCS* 29 (1977), 89 ff.; P. Michalowski, *JCS* 32 (1980), 95 f.

[18] Such "internal genitives" are normally attested in "fossilized" genitive compounds, such as divine names (e.g. ^{d}en-ki), personal names (e.g. ^{d}ur-^{d}nammu), temple names (e.g. é-an-na), and as in the present context, in technical expressions. In such compounds, the genitive may be occasionally omitted (cf. J. Klein, *Three Šulgi Hymns*, 151). Or else, the genitive may appear before the possessive pronoun, and the case marking suffixes. Cf. e.g. Lugalbanda-Ḫurrum. 95 (=*OECT* I pl. 19, obv. 12 = *TMHNF* III 10, 95 = *CT* 42, 46 obv. 9) igi-^{giš}banšur-ra-ka-né (var. omit -né) si ba-ni-in-sá-sá-eš "they set them up at his front-of-the-table" (Cf. Wilcke, *Lugalbanda*, p. 55); Lugalb.-Ḫurrum. 110 (=*TMHNF* III 10, 110 and dupls.) gíri-úr-ra-ka-ni (gloss.: *pa-tar-šu*) "his side-dagger" (cf. Wilcke, ibid., 56); Lugalb.-Ḫurrum. 68 (=*TMHNF* III 10, 68 and dupls.) en-ra ka-kešda-igi-bar-ra-ka(-na) mu-na-su$_8$-su$_8$-ge-eš "To the lord they stepped up with his selected troops" (cf. Wilcke, ibid., 49); *MLM* 12–13 (cf. Civil, *JNES* 23, 2) dingir-sa$_6$-ga-dag-gi$_4$-a-ka-né "the gracious goddess of her (city-) quarter"; *SRT* 13, 32–33 (=ŠV) x-alan(?)-u$_4$-sud-rá-mu-da-ri-ka-na mul-an-né-eš(?) bí-in-gùn(?) "His . . . *statue* of long days and everlasting fame he let *shine* like the heavenly stars." For this "internal genitive" construction in the Gudea inscriptions see Falkenstein, *AnOr* 28, 87, sub h; *AnOr* 29, 56 f., sub paragraph 96; Kärki, *StOr* 35, 230 f. According to Falkenstein and Kärki, the genitive in these constructions normally has an adjectival function. A similar internal genitive seems to underlie the form a-ù-mu-un-zu "your lordly seed" and a-lugal-mu "my royal seed' (lit. "my-seed-of-the-king") in Enlil and Ninlil, ll. 83 ff. et passim (cf. Behrens, *Enlil und Ninlil*, 183 ff.), in spite of the seeming absence of the genitive suffix /-ak/, in these forms.

"Would then Agga, the king of Kiš, not be captured at his center-of-the-army?"

The above interpretation of lines 81 and 99 of the epic seems to clarify Girišḫurdura's role in the battle. Girišḫurdura volunteers to go to Agga and confound him (ll. 55–58). This he indeed accomplishes successfully, by arousing tension in Agga, by undermining his confidence in his own capacity of leadership, and by shaking his trust in the military superiority of his own troops. Alternatively, his task may have been to divert the attention of Agga and his generals from the city-gate, the point from where Enkidu and his commando-troops planned to launch their attack on the army of Kiš.[19] Consequently, the ensuing attack takes the besieging army by surprise, and Agga is *captured* in the midst of his body-guards, at the most protected place of his military camp, and thus Girišḫurdura's "prophecy" comes true.

As to the end of the story, we agree with Falkenstein and Römer[20] that Agga, upon acknowledging Gilgameš's superiority (ll. 107–111), was released and allowed to return to Kiš (ll. 112–113).[21]

In view of the above considerations, we can now translate lines 70–81 and 92–99 of our epic as follows:

A. 70 "That man is not my king.
71 Would that man be my king,
72 Would that be his fierce forehead,
73 Would that be his bison-like face,
74 Would that be his lapis-like beard,
75 Would those be his fine fingers—
76 Would not then multitudes be felled, would not multitudes rise (to attack)?
77 Would not multitudes roll in the dust on account of him?
78 Would not the foreigners, all of them, be overwhelmed by him?
79 Would not the (people of the) countryside bite the dust on account of him?
80 Would not the prow(s) of the magur-boat(s) be cut down?
81 (And) would not Agga, the king of Kiš, be captured at his center-of-the-army?"

B. 92 "That man is indeed my king."
93 No sooner had he said this,
94 Multitudes fell, multitudes rose (to attack),
95 Multitudes rolled in the dust on account of him,
96 The foreigners, all of them, were overwhelmed by him,
97 The (people of the) countryside bit the dust on account of him.
98 The prow(s) of the magur-boat(s) were cut down,[22]
99 (And) Agga, the king of Kiš, was captured at his center-of-the-army!"

[19] One could speculate that Girišḫurdura's speech (ll. 70–81) contained some sort of effective spell or magic, which neutralized Agga and his troops, and brought about the capture of Agga. But such a hypothesis cannot be substantiated by the text, and it would be at variance with the literary nature of the whole epic. For, as G. Komoróczy correctly pointed out (cf. his *A Sumer Irodalmi Hagyomány*, 40 ff.; 54–55), one of the major characteristics of our epic, indicating its great antiquity, is the conspicuous absence of magical or mythological motives from its plot.

[20] *AfO* 21 (1966), 49 f.; *AOAT* 209/1, 41, 97 f.

[21] As I formerly tried to show, in ŠO 60, Gilgameš is praised by Šulgi for having brought the kingship over from Kiš to Unug, *AOAT* 25, 288.

[22] It is not impossible that the epic refers here to only *one* boat, namely to the royal magur-boat, wherein Agga was standing, as the commander-in-chief of his army. This alleged command-ship, must have been located right in the center of the army.

EINE NEUE PROBE AKKADISCHER LITERATUR
BRIEF EINES BITTSTELLERS AN EINE GOTTHEIT

F. R. Kraus

Oegstgeest, The Netherlands

Nippur, in altbabylonischer Zeit die Hochburg der sumerischen Literatur, hat den Ausgräbern auffallend wenig akkadische literarische Texte geliefert, selbst wenn man Tafeln aus allen Perioden zusammennimmt; meist sind es auch noch unbedeutende Fragmente. Der einzige akkadische Beitrag Babyloniens zur Weltliteratur, der nach Inhalt und Ton allgemein menschlich und jedermann unmittelbar verständlich ist, das Schelmenmärchen vom armen Burschen aus Nippur, spielt zwar in Nippur und dürfte auch dort entstanden sein. Aber nicht einmal die uns bekannten Handschriften des Märchens stammen aus Nippur, bis auf den Tafelrest N 4022, s. M. deJ. Ellis, *JCS* 26 (1974), 88f.

So darf das bescheidene Werkchen, das den Gegenstand der folgenden Seiten bildet, mindestens Seltenheitswert für sich beanspruchen. Es scheint gerade für S. N. Kramer, der uns weit über seine Vorläufer Radau, Langdon, Poebel und Chiera hinaus die sumerische Literatur der altbabylonischen Zeit aus Nippur erschlossen hat, eine passende Gabe. Möge sie ihm willkommen sein nicht nur, weil sie aus Nippur kommt, sondern auch besonders als frappantes Beispiel für den breiten und nachhaltigen Einfluss der sumerischen auf die akkadische Literatur. Möge sie ihn nebsther an die längst verflossenen Jahre erinnern, die wir zusammen in Istanbul in der Tontafelsammlung des Museums verbracht haben.

Ni. 13088. Umschrift und Übersetzung

		Umschrift	Übersetzung
Vs.	1.	*[a-na b]ẹ-lí-ia* [......]	Zu meinem Herrn [*Nabûm*],
	2.	*[ša] ta-ar-si-is-s[ụ* ......]	*zu dem zu beten* [..........]
	3.	x UG GU *as-ma-t[im*(?) ......]	.... *des Angemessenen* [......],
	4.	*qí-bí-[ma]*	sprich!
	5.	*ga-am-ma-li a-zi-ri ta-ạ-ạ-[ri]*	Ihn, dem Schonungsvollen, Verzeihenden, Barmherzigen,
	6.	*ša ar-ḫiš na-ap-šu-ru ba-[aš-ta-šu]*	dessen Haupteigenschaft es ist rasch zu vergeben,
	7.	*šu-un-ni-šum-[ma]*	dito!
	8.	*ki-ma šu-mi-šu-ma šu-ma-am ṣi-ra-a[m na-bi]*	Entsprechend seinem Namen ist er mit erhabenem Namen benannt,
	9.	*iš-tu sa-as-su-ri-šu ši-im-tum ṭà-[ạ]b-t[ụ]m*	vom Mutterleibe an ist ein gutes Geschick
	10.	*ši-ma-az-zu šu-ul-[li]s-súm-ma*	sein Geschick, zu ihm abermal!
	11.	*be-lí le-*IA*-um tu-ta-ru*	Mein fähiger Herr, ...,
	12.	nir.gál*-lum ša sì-qar-šu ki-na-tum at-ta-ma*	ein Held, dessen Wort Wahrheit ist, bist du.
	13.	*en-ma* ^{d}EN.ZU*—na-din—šu-mi-im*	Hier (folgt, was ausrichten lässt) Sin-nādin-šumim,
	14.	*ab-du pa-li-ḫu-um*	der ehrfürchtige Knecht,
	15.	*ša a-na qí-bi-ti-ka ma-di-iš i-na-ak-ku-du*	der sich vor deinem Befehl sehr bangt,
	16.	u$_4$*-mi ù mu-ši ma-ḫar* dingir *ù iš-ta-ri*	Tag und Nacht vor Gott und Göttin
	17.	*su-pé-e-ka ṣa-ab-tu*$_4$	in Gebet an dich versunken,
	18.	ìr*-ka-ma*	dein Diener.
	19.	*be-lí a-na ša la i-da-a-ku*	Mein Herr hat sich aus mir unbekanntem Grunde
	20.	*e-li-ia iš-bu-us-ma*	über mich erzürnt und

21. *mu-ḫa-as-si-sa-am ul ar-ši*
22. *i̯-na-an-na be-lí*
23. *ia-ši tu-ši-ip-pa-am-ma*
24. *ma-ar-ṣa-at im-ḫur-an-ni*
25. *a-na be-lí-ia lu-ta-mi*
26. [*i*]*š-tu* u$_4$-*um ṣe-eḫ-re-e-ku*
27. [*a*/*i*]-*na pa-an* ^{p}*ib-ni*—^{d}en.líl[l .....] x
(28.) x *ul* [..........]

Rs. (die ersten zwei Zeilen fehlen, Z. 31–40 unbrauchbare Zeilenenden)

41. [..........] KI *i ba ra* [x]
42. [..........] x *ul i-za-an-nu-nu*
43. [*be-lí ki-ma wa*]-*ar-di-šu pa-ni-šu e-li-ia*
44. x [........] *aḫ-ḫi-ni*
45. x [......] x *e-ṭí-ra-am ul ar-ši*
46. *eš*-[*te*]-*i̯-ma ma-am-ma-an qa-ti ul iṣ-bat*
47. *nu-u̯*[*g-g*]*a-at be-lí-ia lip-šu-ḫa-am-ma*
48. *be-lí* [*š*]*u̯-bar-ra-a-a liš-kun-ma*
49. *a-na sì-qar* [*be-lí-i̯*]*a*
50. [*m*]*a-di-iš l*[*u* ....].

21. ich habe keinen Fürsprecher bekommen.
22. Nun *hast*/*bist* du, mein Herr,
23. mir .... und
24. die Schwierigkeiten, die mir begegnet sind,
25. will ich meinem Herrn erzählen!
26. Seit meiner Jugend
27. *gegenüber* Ibni-Enlil [........]
28. .... [..........]

Rs. (Lücke von zwei Zeilen, dann elf Zeilen unbrauchbar)

42. [..........] versorgen sie nicht.
43. [Mein Herr hat] mir *als* seinem Diener sein Gesicht
44. [Nicht zugewendet. *Unter*] meinen Brüdern
45. habe ich keinen [........ *oder*] Retter bekommen.
46. Ich habe stets gesucht, aber niemand hat mich bei der Hand gefasst.
47. Möge sich der Zorn meines Herrn mir besänftigen und
48. möge mein Herr mich von meiner Last befreien! Dann
49. will ich *für den Namen* meines Herrn
50. viel *beten*!

KOMMENTAR

Die Ergänzungen in der Umschrift sind prinzipiell als hypothetisch zu betrachten, auch wenn sie im Druck nicht eigens als unsicher bezeichnet sind.

Vs. 1. Zur Ergänzung s. zu Z. 8. Schreibung und Form des ergänzten Götternamens sind nicht zu eruieren.

2. Wegen des dem Worte *tarsītu* suffigierten Possessivpronomens Ergänzung zu entweder "zu dem zu beten gut ist" oder "von dem gilt, dass das an ihn gerichtete Gebet erhört wird" wahrscheinlich.

3. Vielleicht darf man an [*g*]*u̯-uq-qù* — freilich nach *AHw.*, 298 rechts, erst j/spB belegt — *as-ma-t*[*i̯m*], "angemessene ......-Opfer," denken, aber ich wüsste das Zeilenende nicht zu ergänzen.

4. *āziru* nach *CAD*, A/2, (1968), 527 links, übersetzt.

7. S. u. zu Z. 10.

8. Erstes Zeichen über Rasur. — In der zweiten Zeilenhälfte kann nach dem Zusammenhange nur etwas wie "er trägt einen erhabenen Namen" gestanden haben, was nach der ersten Zeilenhälfte bereits aus dem Namen der Gottheit hervorgehe. Da etwa dingir-maḫ und ^{d}nin-maḫ, die einem sofort bei "erhaben" einfallen, als Göttinnen hier, wo der Kontext einen männlichen Gott verlangt, ausscheiden, könnte man die Lücken am Ende von Z. 1 und 8 so ausfüllen, dass man sozusagen ausnahmsweise eine Gleichung mit zwei Unbekannten löst, indem man x = y ansetzt. Das ergäbe für Z. 8 [*na-bi*], für Z. 1 [^{d}*na-bi-um*] oder ähnlich. Zwar wäre *nabium*, als "Benannter" verstanden, für uns noch kein "erhabener Name," aber vielleicht darf man sich vorstellen, der Autor des Briefes habe bei "erhabenem Namen" an Nabiums Beinamen mu-dùg.ga-sa$_4$.a, EME.SAL mu-zeb.ba-sa$_4$.a, "Mit-schönem-Namen-Genannter," gedacht, s. Tallqvist, *StOr.* 7 (1938), 380; 376 f. Einigermassen bestätigt wird die Ergänzung ^{d}*na-bi-um* oder ähnlich beim Vergleich der ihm hier zugeschriebenen Eigenschaften mit den sonst erwähnten; mit Z. 2 und 5 f. vgl. Tallqvist, 384 vierter Absatz; mit Z. 11 *ib.* letzter Absatz.

9. Akkadisch "von seinem Mutterleibe," was sich zwar mühelos als "vom Mutterleibe, in dem er gelegen hat" verstehen, aber nicht wörtlich übersetzen lässt.

10. Die Verbalform, offenbar der ältere Typ neben wohl jüngerem *šulliššumma*, folgt der nach Veenhof, *SD* 10 (1972), 90 Anm. 142, nicht allgemeinverbindlichen Regel von Soden, *AnOr.* 33 (1952), § 30 f: *š* (von **ṯl̤ṯ*) + *š* = *ss*. — Bedeutet der dreifache Auftrag an den Boten — oder darf man hier etwa annehmen: an den Brief? — *qibī*[*ma*], Z. 4; *šunnišumma*, Z. 7; *šullissumma*, Z. 10, dass er die erst mit Z. 13 beginnende Mitteilung des Absenders dreimal vortragen soll? Oder darf man bei dem offenkundigen Zusammenhange von

šunnûm mit dem Worte für "2," von *šullušum* mit dem für "3" an die graphischen Wiederholungszeichen KI.MIN, "Platz 2" = "dito," und ki 3 denken (in manchen lexikalischen Listen werden mehrere aufeinanderfolgende Wiederholungszeichen mit (ki) 3, (ki) 4 usw. durchlaufend numeriert)? Dann hätte man in altem Schriftdeutsch etwa "sprich! .... ihm *iterum*! .... zu ihm *tertium*!" zu übersetzen, in modernem vielleicht "sprich! .... dito! .... zu ihm abermal!"

16. Erstes Zeichen über Rasur. Am linken Rande davor ein klein geschriebenes IM, von dem ich nicht weiss, wohin es gehört.

21. Erstes Zeichen über Rasur. *ḫussusum*, "erinnern," findet sich in *ARM* 10 (1978), Nr. 112 Z. 14 in einer Bedeutung "(jemanden) bei jemandem in Erinnerung bringen."

23. *tušippam* sieht wie eine Form des Punktuals D eines Verbums *mediae infirmae* **š p* aus, das ich nicht kenne.

24. Der Autor hat *marṣāt* versehentlich als Singular behandelt.

Rs. 43 f. Vgl. *AHw.*, 819 rechts 15) d), wonach am Anfange von Z. 44 vielleicht *ụ*[*l iš-ku-un*] zu ergänzen. Als sein Subjekt würde [*be-lí*] am Beginn der Z. 43 den Satz zum Pendant des folgenden machen und beide *per merismum* die hier naheliegende Klage "niemand nimmt sich meiner an" ergeben. *bēlī* legt uns dann die weitere Ergänzung [*ki-ma w*]*a-ar-di-šu* nahe.

44 f. Abteilung der Sätze und Annahme, am Beginn der Z. 45 habe ein *ēṭiram* paralleles Wort gestanden, sind nicht sicher.

47. *lipšuḫ* bezeugt eine dritte Vokalklassen-Spielform, von AHw., S. 840, noch nicht verzeichnet und schon deshalb nicht zu datieren.

49 f. Wie viele Bittbriefe schliesst auch dieser mit einem Gelöbnis, welches in Babylonien unsern Dank ersetzt. Da keines der gewöhnlich dazu verwendeten Verben für "preisen" mit *ana* konstruiert wird, denkt man an das ebenfalls viel vorkommende *karābum*, "beten." Ich kenne jedoch keine Parallele zu dem sich hier daraus ergebenden Satz.

Ni. 13088 im Altorientalischen Museum zu Istanbul ist nach seinem Äusseren eine Schultafel, seinem Inhalte nach ein Brief, gehört aber trotzdem nicht zu jenen Texten, die ich in *JEOL* 16 (1964), 16–39, als "Briefschreibübungen" bezeichnet habe. Von ihnen trennt unsern Brief seine auffallendste Eigentümlichkeit, die Adresse. Sie unterscheidet sich durch ihre Länge, Z. 1–18, und Form von allen Adressen sowohl der Briefschreibübungen als auch der wirklichen altbabylonischen Briefe in akkadischer Sprache, entspricht aber den Adressen gewisser kleiner literarischer Werke in sumerischer Sprache, welche die Form eines — oft an eine Gottheit gerichteten — Briefes haben. Eine ausgezeichnete Übersicht über solche "letter-prayers" verdanken wir Hallo, *JAOS* 88 [= *AOS* 53] (1968), 75–80 II.; 88 f. V., der selbst auch zwei von ihnen bearbeitet hat, S. 82–88 IV. und *AOAS* 25 (1976), 214–24, nachdem zuerst Falkenstein, *ZA* 44 (1938), 1–25, eine Probe dieses Genres ediert und ausführlich besprochen hatte. Innerhalb dieser Gruppe ist es Hallos B_{16} (S. 89 links, vgl. S. 76 rechts Ende zweiter Absatz), dessen Adresse sich als genaues Vorbild für die unseres Briefes erweist. Während sonst dreiteilige Adressen vorkommen, ist sie vierteilig. Ihre Verbalformen lauten (1) ù.na.a.dug₄/ù.ne.dug₄, (2) ù.na.dè.daḫ/ù.ne.dè.daḫ, (3) ù.na.dè.ḪA/ù.ne.dè.peš, (4) na.ab.bé.a, s. u.

Das Genre geht auf die Zeit der III. Dynastie von Ur zurück, wie ein solcher an König Šulgi gerichteter Brief zeigt, vgl. Xerox Dissertation F. A. Ali (1967), 53–62 B: 1, und erfreute sich grosser Beliebtheit in den altbabylonischen Schulen von Nippur, Uruk, Ur und anderen Städten, wie man aus der relativ grossen Anzahl der dort gefundenen Textexemplare folgern darf. Darauf deutet auch der Umstand, dass die soeben angeführten Verbformen (1), (2) und (3) der Adresse in lexikalische Listen aufgenommen worden sind, was man *AHw.*, S. 1146 rechts *šalāšum* D Anfang; 1165 rechts D Anfang, entnehmen kann. Bereits altbabylonisch ist "Proto-Izi (Bilingual)" I Section D IV

3. [ù]-⌜na-a⌝-[dug₄] = *qí-bi-šum*
4. [ù-na-dè-da]ḫ = *šu-ni-šum* ≪*um*≫
5. [ù-ne-dè-peš] = *šu-li-su-um*,

MSL 13 (1971), 38, Z. 3 f. ergänzt nach "Proto-Izi I" Z. 487 f., S. 33. Einen ähnlichen Eintrag weist die Serie Antagal auf, s. *Bab.* 7 (1913–1923), Tf. VII Kol. 7–10; er erscheint in fast der gleichen Form noch in der kanonischen Serie lú = *ša* 1 Excerpt II Z. 84–86, *MSL* 12 (1969), 106.

In unserem Zusammenhange ist der Umstand wichtig, dass zwei der "letter-prayers" aus Uruk mit einer interlinearen Teilübersetzung ins Akkadische versehen sind, W 16743 b = Falkenstein, op. cit. Exemplar B; akkadischer Text in den Fussnoten, und W 17259 w, zuletzt Sjøberg, *Nanna-Suen* (1960), 104–7 11. Ob nun auch der Text unseres Briefes aus dem Sumerischen übersetzt oder aber eine akkadische Neuschöpfung nach sumerischem Vorbilde ist, lässt sich nicht feststellen. Soweit ich sehe, gibt es keinen sumerischen literarischen Brief gleichen Inhalts, andererseits kenne ich keine altbabylonischen akkadischen literarischen Briefe dieses Genres.

Altbabylonisch ist übrigens allenfalls die Vorlage unseres Briefes, nicht er selbst. Er hat zwar in Wortformen und Orthographie deutlich altbabylonisches

Gepräge, weist aber Einzelheiten auf, die meines Erachtens nicht altbabylonisch sein können. Freilich sind unsere Kenntnisse und unser Material viel zu gering, als dass wir unseren Brief auf Grund seiner Abweichungen vom Altbabylonischen datieren könnten. Als solche nenne ich

1) *tarsītu*, Z. 2, nach *AHw.*, 1331 rechts I, erst in Synonymen-Listen;
2) *gammalu*, Z. 5, nach *AHw.*, 279 links *gamallu/û* I, erst jB;
3) *āziru*, Z. 5, nach A/2, 527 links, erst SB;
4) LIŠ für *lis* in *šu-ul-*[*li*]*s-súm-ma*, Z. 10, nach *AnOr.* 42[3], Nr. 220 erst "5–8," d.h. mA-spB;
5) *siqar*, Z. 12; 49, nach *AHw.*, 1526 rechts *zikru* I, erst j/spB;
6) SUM für *sì* in *sì-qar*, Z. 12; 49, nach *AnOr.* 42[3], Nr. 115 erst "6–8", d.h. nA-spB;
7) *abdu*, Z. 14, nach *AHw.*, 6 links, jB dichterisch, in Synonymen-Listen und späten Vokabularen, nach *CAD*, A/1, 51 links SB;
8) *supû*, Z. 17, nach *AHw.*, 1060 rechts 2), j/spB; mit *ṣabātum* nach *CAD*, Ṣ, 32, in neubabylonischen Königsinschriften;
9) TUM für *tu*$_4$ in *ṣa-ab-tu*$_4$, Z. 17, nach *AnOr.* 42[3], Nr. 137 seit mB;
10) *idâku*, Z. 19, nach *AHw.*, 188 links A. 6) a), nB.

Wenn man sich auf diese Datierungen im allgemeinen verlassen könnte, wäre unsere Tafel nicht älter als neubabylonisch. Diese Schülerarbeit weist somit noch die Besonderheit auf, dass sie einen altbabylonischen Schriftduktus nachahmt, und zwar nicht ohne Geschick.

Vor eine zusätzliche Frage stellt uns das Wörtchen *enma*, Z. 13. Es ist nämlich schon während der Zeit der III. Dynastie von Ur aus der Adresse echter (alt)akkadischer Briefe verschwunden, vgl. *AHw.*, 218 rechts; 1553 rechts. Dass bereits in einer Zeit, in der *enma* noch üblich war, literarische Briefe wie der unsere geschrieben worden sein sollten, scheint in jeder Hinsicht ausgeschlossen. Der n a c h der neusumerischen Periode tätige Urheber unseres Textes muss sich also mindestens in diesem Punkte einer archaischen Schreibweise befleissigt haben. Wie es damit bei den oben erwähnten interlinearen Teilübersetzungen zweier sumerischer "letter-prayers" steht, können wir nicht mehr erkennen, denn der erste lässt die betreffende Passage unübersetzt, im zweiten ist sie verloren gegangen.

Die Entstehung unseres *specimen eruditionis* könnte ich mir am ehesten in der späteren altbabylonischen Zeit vorstellen, vorausgesetzt, dass ich Nabium richtig als Adressaten ergänzt habe und mein Eindruck mich nicht trügt, Nabium sei erst gegen Ende der Periode beim Publikum zu Beliebtheit gelangt, vgl. Pomponio, *Nabû* [Studi Semitici 51]. 1978, 15–40. Bleibt dann die bange Frage, wie die Kopie Ni. 13088 vielleicht tausend Jahre später hergestellt werden konnte.

Der Inhalt unseres lückenhaften Briefes ist von mässigem Interesse. Als Prosa religiösen Inhalts betrachtet, halten sich Adresse und Einleitung der eigentlichen Mitteilung, Z. 1–20, im Rahmen des beim literarischen Umgang des Babyloniers mit seinen Göttern Üblichen. Sie sind frei von theologischen Anspielungen und prunkvollen Phrasen, einfach gehalten, jedoch ohne dass wörtliche Parallelen mit religiösen Texten anderen Genres aufzuzeigen wären; nir.gál-*lum*, Z. 12, fehlt sogar in unseren Wörterbüchern. Bei dieser flüchtigen Bemerkung muss ich es hier bewenden lassen. Tieferen Einblick in eventuelle Zusammenhänge beonders mit den sumerischen "letter-prayers" würden uns vielleicht systematische Vergleichungen verschaffen; man wird sie aber erst anstellen können, wenn die Texte einmal gesammelt und bearbeitet sind.

Der Absender nennt nur seinen Namen, Sin-nādin-šumim, Z. 13, ohne jegliche weitere Angabe über seinen Zivilstand, hebt aber als Vorbereitung auf seine eigentliche Mitteilung seine fromme Anhänglichkeit an die Gottheit, welcher er schreibt, und die gewissenhafte Erfüllung seiner religiösen Pflichten hervor, Z. 14–18.

Der Übergang zur Mitteilung selbst ist kurz und zielbewusst formuliert: Zorn des Gottes aus unbekanntem Grunde, Z. 19 f., ein bekanntes Motiv, das indirekt die Schuldlosigkeit des Absenders andeuten soll, der, ohne Fürsprecher, Z. 21, seinen Fall der Gottheit vortragen will, Z. 24 f., die sich ihm jetzt versöhnlich gezeigt habe — das vermute ich in Z. 22 f. Die Darlegung seiner schlechten Lage beginnt mit einem anderen bekannten Motiv "seit der Jugend des Bittstellers/Beters," Z. 25; es findet sich z.B. auch noch in einem Gebete des Königs Assurbanipal, *OECT* 6 (1927), Pl. XIII Rs. 8′. Dann wird ein gewisser Ibni-Enlil gennant, Z. 27, aber das Weitere ist bis auf unzusammenhängende Reste verloren, aus denen ich nur ein einziges Wort herauslesen konnte, das mehrdeutige IK-*ta*-ZA-AZ am Ende von Z. 35. Wo der Text wieder verständlich wird, liest man allgemeine Klagen, nirgends winke Hilfe, Z. 42–46. Auffallend kurz und bescheiden ist dann die Bitte, derentwegen der Brief doch geschrieben ist, die Gottheit möge nicht mehr zürnen, Z. 47, und dem Bittsteller "Lastenbefreiung" gewähren, Z. 48, ein Ausdruck, dessen konkreten Inhalt ich nicht kenne, falls er einen hat. Schlicht und wortkarg ist auch der Schluss, ein einfaches Gelöbnis, Z. 49 f., statt des Dankes-im-voraus, mit dem wir Briefe beendigen.

Rückschauend kann man konstatieren, dass der enormen, aber im Ausdruck doch massvollen Adresse, Z. 1–18, eine Mitteilung folgt, die nüchtern und sachlich vorgetragen wird, soweit ihr fast zur Hälfte verlorener Wortlaut zu beurteilen gestattet. Insofern unterscheidet sich unser Brief freilich von vielen sumerischen "letter-prayers" und erinnert eher an die "Briefschreibübungen" des altbabylonischen Schulunterrichts. Vielleicht gehörte die altbabylonische Vorlage unseres Textes also doch zu ihnen und sollte einem praktischen Bedürfnis dienen, das uns wenigstens durch zwei Privatbriefe an Gottheiten bezeugt ist, vgl. mein *RA* 65 (1971), 27–36, besonders S. 35 Mitte f. Trifft das zu, dann hätte der altbabylonische Urheber unseres Textes zu diesem speziellen Zwecke eine literarische Anleihe aufgenommen, nämlich seine Adresse entweder derjenigen der sumerischen "letter-prayers" nachgebildet oder sie deren akkadischem Pendant entnommen, falls es so eine Sammlung gab.

[Nachtrag vom 30. VI. 1982: Inzwischen hat Hallo den in *AOAT* 25, 212, von ihm beschriebenen ersten Brief des Königs Sin-iddinam von Larsa veröffentlicht, übersetzt und kommentiert in "zikir šumim," 1982, 95–109. Die Arbeit, die ich erst am 19. III. 1982, nach Abschluss meines Manuscripts zu Gesicht bekommen habe, ist hier nicht mehr berücksichtigt.]

A NEO-BABYLONIAN TAMMUZ LAMENT

W. G. Lambert

University of Birmingham, England

The impact of the Sumerians on Mesopotamia continued to be felt long after they had disappeared as an ethnic group. In literature this meant both the copying and handing down of traditional Sumerian texts when the language was no longer spoken and the composing of new texts either in the then learned language or in the spoken Babylonian, though based on Sumerian models. The text to be studied here* falls in the latter category and is Babylonian. A common type of Sumerian text is the lament over Tammuz. This is not the place to go into details in such a vast and difficult field. A meeting of the Rencontre Assyriologique Internationale was devoted to Dumuzi/Tammuz,[1] and Professor Kramer has given much attention to the Tammuz myths,[2] while T. Jacobsen has a full corpus of the laments in an advanced state of preparation. The Babylonian text dealt with here survives in a single copy on a Late Babylonian tablet written on September 16 287 B.C. The tablet is oblong, 61 × 76 mm. in size, and the text is a mere twenty-three lines long. There is no formal indication whether this is the complete work or an extract from a larger whole, but the content suggests that the text is complete.

It was first published in 1901, and there are good reasons for taking it up again at the present time. Originally the tablet was partly encrusted with hard salt so that a number of signs have hitherto been misread and even totally omitted. Also there has been no agreement so far on its interpretation. The date of composition of the text has been put either in the late Third Millennium, or at some point earlier or later in the First Millennium! In all cases alleged historical allusions have been the basis for dating. The tablet has been fired and treated in recent times so that its clearly written text is now virtually complete and readable. The transliteration given here has been made directly from the tablet. And major advances in knowledge of the last fifty years allow much greater certainty in interpretation.

T. G. Pinches gave the editio princeps in *PSBA* 23 (1901), 197ff., with copy, transliteration, translation and notes.[3] According to him the text was composed over the destruction in Sumer wrought by the Guti about the time of the decline and fall of the Akkad dynasty. The historical circumstances in the Seleucid period explain why the old text was recopied then. His interpretation was based on an alleged reference to the Guti in ll. 12–15. Jules Oppert promptly republished this text from Pinches's copy in *Académie des Inscriptions et Belles-Lettres, Comptes Rendus*, 1901, 830ff. While here and there he improved on the editio princeps, he concluded, from what is now seen to be a mistranslation of the colophon, that the text had been composed by the scribe's father, and so reflected Seleucid-period events. S. H. Langdon next repeated the text from Pinches's copy, in his *SBP*, 263ff., where he accepted Pinches's opinion of its origin, adding the suggestion that it reflected a Guti invasion under Šar-kāli-šarri, but in an addendum on p. 351 he changed his mind and described the text as follows: "a Semitic composition, probably refers to the Aramean invasion of Babylonia in the time of Erba-Marduk [770 *circa*] mentioned in the Chronicle BM 27859 rev. 10–12 and in Nabuna'id's *Stèle*, cols. III and IV." This was in 1909, but by 1923 Langdon had reverted to Pinches's view, which he expressed in the *Cambridge Ancient History*[1] I, 424, and assent to it was given later by Sidney Smith in *JRAS* 1932, 301ff. and Julius Lewy in *HUCA* 17 (1942/43), 73. If this view is correct, this is a unique Akkadian literary document from about the end of the Akkad dynasty. Any Akkadian scholar with even a modest feel for style may well wonder

---

*The first draft of this article was read and discussed with I. L. Finkel and M. J. Geller, who are thanked for their useful suggestions.

[1] *CRR* 3 (Leiden, 1954).

[2] See his most recent contribution in *PAPS* 124 299ff. and literature there cited.

[3] He gave a slightly corrected translation in his *The Old Testament in the Light of the Historical Records and Legends of Assyria and Babylonia*, 477f.

whether the text is really that old, and it is hardly without significance that C. J. Gadd in the revised *Cambridge Ancient History* of 1963, etc. I/2 pp. 454ff. wrote on the Guti without mentioning this document. Before proceeding further, a revised text and translation should be presented.

Obverse

1	*mar-ṣa-a-tú uruk*^{ki} *mar-ṣa-a-tú* a.ga.dè^{ki} *šu-nu-la-ak*	1	"You are grieved, Uruk, you are grieved, Akkad, that I am prostrate."
2	*aška*(unu)^{ki}*-a-a-i-tu*$_4$ *tab-ku* *šá paṭ-rat gu-zi-lit-su* KI+MIN *šá šaḫ-ṭu*(! tablet: LU) *di-du-šú*	2	The goddess of Uruk wept, whose lady-in-waiting had departed. The goddess of Uruk wept, whose loincloth had been snatched away.
3	*mārat uruk*^{ki} *tab-ku* *mārat a.ga.dè*^{ki} *ta-nam-bi*	3	The daughter of Uruk wept, the daughter of Akkad was lamenting.
4	*šá mārat la*$_7$*-rà-ak*^{ki} *ina* ^{túg}*sissikti*(síg)*-šú kul-lu-lu-ma pānū-šú*	4	The face of the daughter of Larak was enveloped in her garment.
5	*ḫur-sag-kalam-ma*^{ki}*-i-tu*$_4$ *tab-ku* *šá ek-me-tu*$_4$ *mut*(dam)*-su*	5	The goddess of Ḫursagkalamma wept, who was deprived of her spouse.
6	^{uru}*ḫul-ḫu-ud-ḫu-ul-i-tu*$_4$ *tab-ku* *šá taš-qu-pu ḫu-ṭa-áš-tu*$_4$	6	The goddess of Ḫulḫudḫul wept, who had set down her staff.
7	MÁŠ^{ki}*-i-tu*$_4$ *tab-ku* *šá 7 aḫḫū*^{meš}*-šá di-i-ku* *8 ḫa-tan-šú šu-nu-ul-lu*	7	The goddess of MÁŠ wept, whose seven brothers were killed, whose eight brothers-in-law were laid out.
8	a.ga.dè^{ki}*-i-tu*$_4$ *tab-ku* *šá pa-ar-mu sa-as-su* *di-ku bēl la-le-e-šú*	8	The goddess of Akkad wept, whose shoe-soles were in tatters (?), whose beloved lord had been killed.
9	*ke-e-šú-i-tu*$_4$ *tab-ku* *a-ši-bat*(! tablet MAŠ?) *dul-ba-nu* *šá bēl bīti-šú* *ú-qát-tu-ú a-z/ṣa-ḫu*	9	The goddess of Kesh wept, who lived in the passageway, the lord of whose house had been wiped out by . . .
10	*dun-na-a-a-i-tu*$_4$ *tab-ku* *ana man-nu* ^{giš}*eršu* *ana man-nu mu-ṣe-e*	10	The goddess of Dunnu wept, "For whom the bed, for whom the spreads,
11	*ana man-nu itti-ia na-aṣ-ri mu-ṣe-e šu-ḫar-ru-ru-tu*	11	for whom am I keeping the silent spreads?"
12	*mārat nippuri*^{ki} *tab-ku* *ana qu-ti-i ga-ma-ri šá šip-ri*	12	The daughter of Nippur wept, at the total cessation of the rites
13	*su-re-et ap-pi-šú* *ek-me-et mut*(dam) *la-le-e-šú*	13	her face was sore, she was deprived of her beloved spouse.
14	*dēri*(BÀD.AN)^{ki}*-i-tu*$_4$ <*tab-ku*> *ana qu-ti-i ga-ma-ri* <KI+MIN>	14	The goddess of Der <wept>, at the total cessation <of the rites her face was sore, she was deprived of her beloved spouse>,
15	*šá nap-lu āl-šú* *ḫe-pu-ú šul-pu-tu bīt abī-šú*	15	she whose city was demolished, whose ancestral house was shattered and desecrated.
16	*áš-šá uruk*^{ki} *bi-ka-a'* *ki-li-li bal-tum maḫ-rat*	16	"Weep over Uruk: thorns have got my turban,

Reverse

17	*ia-a-ši ina me-ḫe-e* *a-šar ak-*⌈*bu*⌉*-su ul i-di*	17	and as to me, I do not know where I am treading in the tempest.
18	*áš-šá la*$_7$*-rà-*<*ak*>^{ki} *bi-ka-a'* ^{túg}[*lu-ba*]*-ri ḫu-ul-la-nu ek-me-ek*	18	Weep over Larak: I am deprived of my robe and wraps,
19	*īna-a-a la im-mar* d[a]? ku? x [(x)]*-ú-a nu-uk-ku-su šá-tur ummāti*^{meš}	19	my eyes cannot look on my . . . the ripping of the mothers' wombs.

20	*áš-šá nippuri*^{ki} *bi-ka-a'* *ia-a-ši a-šib-tu*$_4$ *qù-ul-tu*$_4$	20	Weep over Nippur: stillness abides with me,
21	*šamû*^{ú} *uk-tat-ti-mu-in-ni* ^{22} ^{giš}*kussî né-met-ti-iá ul-ta-bal-ki-tan-nu*	21	the heavens have covered me, ^{22}my seat has been overturned on me.
23	*ḫa-mi-ru mut*(dam) *la-le-e* *i-te-<ek>-ma-ni* ^{d}*bēl*	23	Bel has deprived me of my consort, my beloved spouse."
24	gim sumun-*šú* sar-*ma* igi.tab *u up-pu-uš*	24	According to its original written, checked and finished.
25	im ^{md}en.numun.giš a *šá* ^{md}en.ad.ùru dumu ^{lú}zadim	25	Tablet of Bēl-zēru-līšir, son of Bēl-aba-uṣur, son of Seal-cutter.
26	šu^{II} ^{md}en.tin-*su* dumu.a.ni *pa-lìḫ* 20 *ina* ki.kal nu giš-*šú*	26	Written by Bēl-uballiṭsu, his son. He who fears Šamaš will not . . . it.
27	e^{ki} iti.kin ud.15.kam mu.25.kam ^{m}*si-lu-ku u* ^{m}*an-ti-ú-ku-su*	27	Babylon, 15th of Elul, 25th year of Seleucus and Antiochus,
28	lugal kur.kur	28	King of the lands.

PHILOLOGICAL COMMENTS

3ff. Smith argued in *JRAS* 1932, 301f. that *mārat uruk*, etc. can only refer to the women of the towns in question, and not to a goddess, but *mārat uri* in *JNES* 33, 224 6 does refer to a goddess, so the issue has to be settled by judgment as to which is appropriate.

7 For the numerical figure of speech, see W. M. W. Roth, "The Numerical Sequence x/x + 1 in the Old Testament," *Vetus Testamentum* 12, 300ff., where some examples from outside the Old Testament are also quoted.

8 The interpretation adopted assumes a root *parāmu*, cognate with the Hebrew *pāram* 'rend (a garment),' Aramaic and Syriac p^e*ram* 'cut, tear,' and the Arabic *farama* 'chop.' Note especially the Syriac *prmyt'* 'torn shoes' (C. Brockelmann, *Lexicon Syriacum*^{2}, 598a). Another example in Akkadian occurs among epithets of Nabû in BM 46082 col. A 19: *pa-ri-im na-piš-tú rag-gu* "who cuts the throat of the wicked."

9 The *u* after *keš-* is strange, and perhaps one should add a wedge to the sign ŠÚ to make it ŠI: *ke-e-ši!-i-tu*$_4$.

10 Cf. *Or.* 39 144 6: giš.ná *u* ^{túg}*mu-ṣe-e* (Namburbi).

12 In the context it is difficult to find any way of making *qu-ti-i* into the Guti. One could take *ana qutî gamāri* alone as "(her face was sore) to destroy the Guti," but there is then no obvious way of fitting in *ša šipri*. Thus it is necessary to take *quttî* and *gamāri* as in apposition, synonyms used together for emphasis.

13 *su-re-et*: from *sêru* II/1 'rub.'

25 Both the sign-form and the reading of ZADIM are matters of debate, see most recently *CAD* sub vocibus *aškapu* and *zadimmu*, also R. Borger, *ABZ* p. 166. An unpublished LB duplicate of *CT* 25 48 14 (DIŠ ni.in.[x x (x)] = ^{d}nin.MUG (one upright) = ^{d}*é-a ša* ^{lú}MUG (three uprights) reads: DIŠ nin.za.dím = ^{d}nin.U+MUG = ^{d}*é-a ša* ^{lú}bur.gul. On this LB evidence it is suggested that the family name ^{lú}U+MUG in LB documents should perhaps be read *pu/arkullu*. Prosopographic studies of LB documents might yield confirmation or otherwise.

26 For the obscure line-ending see J. Oelsner, *ZA* 56, 263^7.

In form the text is a mixture of speech and narrative. The grieving party speaks in line 1, then lines 2–15 are narrative, followed in 16–23 by more direct speech of (presumably) the same lamenter. The grieving party speaks in the first person singular, as also in the fragment of direct speech in lines 10–11 within the narrative. The narrative frequently makes clear that the lamenter is female and singular: either "she of (a named cult centre)" or "daughter of (the same)." A glance at these places leaves no doubt that Ištar is meant: note Uruk, Akkad, Ḫursagkalamma and Nippur. This is confirmed by express statements that she was weeping over her spouse (*mutu*) (ll. 5, 13, 23). Also the "beloved lord" in 8 and "the lord of her house" in 9 clearly allude to the same spouse. Further, lines 10–11 mention the marital bed—silent, due to the absence of this spouse. The text is very clearly a lament by Ištar over the taking away of her beloved Tammuz. The more difficult matter is how Sidney Smith failed to see this. However, this observation of the essential character of the text by no means exhausts its exegesis.

Laments over Tammuz are otherwise a Sumerian genre, so the language itself is a matter of interest. The Sumerian Tammuz myth told how the demons that took away Tammuz created havoc in the dairy.

Thus a Tammuz lament could naturally refer to destruction and chaos at his shrines, but this Akkadian text goes further. The killing of Ištar's seven brothers and eight brothers-in-law (7), the destruction of her city (15), and the ripping up of pregnant women (19) seem to allude to invasion by an enemy army. There was of course a Sumerian genre of laments over the destruction of cities, and this may have inspired these elements. But the most striking thing about this Akkadian text comes like a hammer-blow at the end, in the very last word.[4] The Sumerian laments do not ordinarily assign blame for Tammuz' demise, but in this text Bel, "the Lord" par excellence, city god of Babylon, is pointedly accused of depriving Ištar of her spouse. There is something astonishing in this apparent sectarian strife.

Evidence exists which at least helps to explain this phenomenon. Marduk's defeat of Tiāmat in Enūma Eliš is only one version of a type of myth wherein miscreant gods are sent down to the underworld for their sins. Tammuz occurs in lists of such "defeated" gods alongside such characters as Qingu, Enmešarra and Lugaldukuga (see e.g. *RA* 41, 30). No doubt the underworld associations of Tammuz caused him to be put in such company. Thus by defeating Tammuz and consigning him to the underworld Marduk deprived Ištar of her spouse. The myths of Marduk's victories, however, present his enemies as evil, while the lament under discussion, like Tammuz laments generally, is full of sympathy for Tammuz and so points the accusing finger at Marduk. The mythological perspective in the last phrase, therefore, does not explain everything about this text.

It appears that in the beginning Tammuz was a personification of seasonal forces of fertility observed in nature. His months on earth corresponded with the flourishing of crops and flocks, his months in the underworld with the annual period of decay and inactivity. This text is clearly reinterpreting the old myth as a parable of certain historic events, as its first interpreters correctly understood. Such reinterpretation of traditional mythological motifs is not confined to this text. It has been suspected in some Sumerian myths, though not with absolute certainty. But the Erra Epic, the last great Babylonian myth, uses the traditional concept of Erra, god of plague and destruction, as the basis of a narrative describing a foreign invasion of Babylonia. Here the Tammuz myth is used evidently to describe conflict between Babylon and (apparently) the rest of Babylonia. The text is written from the standpoint of the latter.

The present writer does not have any precise proposal to offer on this subject. Knowledge of history during the most likely times is very scanty and the allusions are much too inexplicit to be used. Cities were being destroyed and pregnant women ripped up, but those were no rare events in antiquity. The best that can be done for the present is to assess the evidence for the date of composition. First, certain words used are not so far attested before Middle Babylonian: *ḫuṭārtu* (6), *dulbānu* (9) and *ḫullānu* (18). The orthography and grammar are consistently those of the First Millennium B.C. Note *ḫu-ṭa-áš-tu*₄ (6), *bi-ka-a'* (16, 18, 20), the third person fem. *tab-ku* (passim), and the regular use of masc. suffixes for fem. Of course an older text could have been adjusted in such matters by a first-millennium scribe, though the consistency does perhaps favour a first-millennium origin. The variants of Ištar can be compared with the older, Sumerian listings as collected by C. Wilcke in *RLA* V, 78. Only four here, Uruk, Akkad, Ḫursagkalamma and Nippur, also occur there. Larak was a cult centre of Ninisinna, and Keš of the mother goddess, though in late theological texts these goddesses do merge with Ištar.[5] The other four are less helpful: Ḫulḫudḫul is apparently unknown elsewhere; both reading and location of MÁŠ are uncertain; there were several places Dunnu, all little known; and while Der's chief goddess, Dērītum or Šarrat-Dēri, is known as spouse of Ištarān,[6] that is all that is known. The use of Bel for Marduk is potentially the most precise evidence for dating. Generally it was not used in the Second Millennium, though it does occur in the literary texts describing events in the reign of Nebuchadnezzar I, texts very probably dating from that king's own reign. They of course are favourable to Marduk, a text hostile to him would only use Bel when it was so well established that its implicit claim was not thought about in current use.

A theory about the place of its composition can be hazarded. Quite appropriately Uruk is the first centre

[4] As a parallel, note how Enūma Eliš IV 123–26 puts Marduk, the subject of five verbs in a long subordinate clause, at the very end of the clause to give him emphasis.

[5] For example, the Ištar god list *CT* 25 30–31, K 2109+ combines the names of Ištar with those of the Mother Goddess, while the Gula hymn last published by C. J. Mullo-Weir in *JRAS* 1929, 9ff. in an unpublished continuation takes in numerous local forms of Ištar as names of Gula.

[6] *RLA* V, 211b.

of Ištar mentioned. And it is known that Uruk in the First Millennium did produce literature favourable to itself and by implication, or even openly, hostile to Babylon. There is another first-millennium text clearly composed in support of Uruk and against Babylon. It is in the form of a prophecy about the rulership of Babylonia. The text is published by H. Hunger in *STU* I 3, and various interpretations have been proposed, all finding allusions to events in the First Millennium. In the present writer's view[7] the surviving, intelligible parts cover Merodach-baladan, four Assyrian kings who either *de facto* or *de jure* ruled Babylonia, and the two kings who built up the Neo-Babylonian empire: Nabopolassar and Nebuchadnezzar. They are said to have their origin in Uruk and to be destined to rule Uruk like gods. This is precisely the standpoint of the lament under consideration, and, despite their very different literary forms, it is very probably to be taken as a piece of political propaganda denouncing Babylon for certain military operations in the course of which Uruk and other cities had been ravaged.

[7] See his *The Background of Jewish Apocalyptic* [Ethel M. Wood Lecture, 1977], 10ff.

AN INSCRIPTION OF AŠŠUR-ETEL-ILANI

Erle Leichty
University of Pennsylvania

The inscription published below was found in the Princeton Theological Seminary collection during the course of cataloguing that collection. The approximately 3,000 tablets in the Seminary's collection were purchased from Yale University in 1915. Yale had purchased them from dealers. The tablets are currently on long-term loan to the University Museum where they are being conserved and catalogued. The collection consists primarily of economic documents from the Ur III and Neo-Babylonian period, but it also contains some Old Babylonian texts and a few extraneous inscriptions. The text published here records a donation of the Assyrian king, Aššur-etel-ilani.

The tablet. The inscription is on a roughly-shaped oval tablet which has been flattened out at the edges. Although the quality of the clay is good, the tablet is very atypical in shape. There is every indication that a previously inscribed tablet was moistened and then flattened out for reuse. Marks from fingers and a cloth can be seen in several places. The tablet is obviously not an archival copy.

The obverse of the tablet has a large and deliberate gap between lines 4 and 5 even though the inscription continues with no break in the context. This gap has a solid line at the bottom. The rest of the obverse contains seven lines.

The reverse begins with an unintelligible line. This line is inserted between lines 11 and 13, but there is no contextual break between lines 11 and 13. After a gap the inscription resumes with line 13. At the end of this section (line 20) the main inscription ends and is followed by an erased line and another gap. The last two lines contain an offering, the name of the donor, and a date.

The lines of the obverse are written all the way from the left edge. The lines of the reverse are indented. In the left margin of the reverse between lines 16 and 17 are traces of what may be two signs. If these are truly signs I would read ⌜*šá nu*⌝.

The tablet contains three major erasures: after line 12, in the middle of line 16 and after line 21.

TRANSLITERATION

[*a-na* ^{d}AMAR.UD] *kab-tu šit-ra-ḫu* ^{d}EN.LÍL DINGIR.MEŠ *šá-qu-ú*

[*e-li* DINGIR].MEŠ *a-šir* DINGIR.MEŠ *ka-la-me mu-kil mar-kas* ^{d}*í-gì-gì*

[*ù* ^{d}*a*]*-nun-na-ki mu-ma-ʾ-ir* DINGIR *ku-na* LUGAL ŠÚ AN-*e ù* KI-*tim*

[*šá a-na*] *zik-ri-šú* DINGIR.MEŠ GAL.MEŠ *pal-ḫiš ú-taq-qu-ú qí-bit-su*

šaḫ-tú la-a-nu ši-i-ḫu šá ina ZU+AB *ir-bu-ú bal-ti šur-ru-ḫu*

me-na-a-ta šu-tu-ru ṣu-ub-bu-ú nab-ni-ti li-ʾ-um

li-ʾ-ú-tu mu-du-ú ka-la-me la-mid ṭè-im ZU+AB

a-ḫi-iz pi-riš-ti làl-gar EN KÁ.DINGIR.RA.KI

a-šib É.SAG.ÍL EN GAL-*ú* EN ŠÚ ^{m}AN.SÁR-*e-til-li-*DINGIR.MEŠ

LUGAL ŠÚ LUGAL KUR AN.ŠÁR.KI GIŠ.BANŠUR GIŠ.MES.MÁ.GAN.NA

iṣ-ṣi da-ru-ú šá ṣa-ri-ri ḪUŠ.A *uḫ-ḫu-zu*

šá nu kát maš ⌜x⌝

[*i*]*-na ši-pir* DUMU.ME *um-ma-nu nak-liš šu-pu-šú a-na si-ma-a-ta*

⌜*ma-ka*⌝*-li-e* KÙ.ME *šu-lu-ku a-na* DIN ZI.MEŠ-*šú še-me-e*

su-pi-e-šú sa-kap LÚ.KÚR.MEŠ-*šú* BA-*eš*

^{d}AMAR.UD EN GAL-*ú* (erasure) GIŠ.BANŠUR *šu-a-ti*

ḫa-diš ina nap-lu-si-ka ^{d}*Šul-pa-è-a* EN GIŠ.BANŠUR

ina ra-kas GIŠ.BANŠUR *šá-rak sur-qin-nu ka-a-a-an la na-par-ka-a*

a-mat SAL.SAG$_5$ ^{m}AN.SÁR-*e-til-li-*DINGIR.ME LUGAL KUR AN.SÁR.KI

NUN *mi-gir lìb-bi-ka lit-tas-qar ma-ḫar-ka*

(line erased)

2 SÌLA 3 *šal-šú* NINDA AMAR×ŠE 1 (PI) 1 (BÁN) GIŠ.PÈŠ ḪÁD.A *ina maš-šar-ti šá* ITI.DU$_6$

^{m}*Na-din* A ^{md}EN-PAP.ME-BA-*šá* ITI.KIN UD.11.KAM MU.3.KAM

Plate 1. PTS 2253

TRANSLATION

To Marduk, venerable, magnificent, Enlil of the gods, highest of the gods, who directs all the gods, who holds the bond of the Igigi and Anunnaki, commander, true god, king of the totality of heaven and earth, at whose mention the great gods fearfully attend his command,

humble (though) gigantic in stature, who was raised in the *apsû*, abounding with dignity, surpassing of form, perfect of features, the able one, the knowledgeable one, he who knows everything, who understands the will of the *apsû*, who comprehends the mystery of the *lalgar*, the lord of Babylon who resides in Esaggila, the great lord, lord of the universe—Aššur-etel-ilani, king of the universe, king of the land of Assyria, presented a table of *musukkannu*-wood, the durable wood, which is mounted with glittering gold,

(unintelligible insert)

manufactured with the skill of clever craftsmen, and made fit for pure food-offerings; for his longevity, the hearing of his prayers (and) the trampling of his enemies. (O) Marduk, great lord, when you look joyfully upon this table, may Šulpae, lord of the table, during the setting of the table (and) the giving of regular unceasing offerings, speak a good word before you for Aššur-etel-ilani, king of the universe, king of the land of Assyria, your favored prince.

Two *sila*, three and one third *ninda* (as) offering; one *pi*, one *ban* of dried figs from the *maššartu*-holdings of the seventh month. Nadin, son of Bel-ahhe-iqiša; sixth month, eleventh day, third year.

The Script. The tablet is written in Neo-Babylonian script. However, in line 5 the *šaḫ* sign is Neo-Assyrian in form. Likewise, in line 8 the KÁ and RA signs are Neo-Assyrian. This unusual mixture of sign forms would seem to indicate that the scribe of this inscription was an Assyrian trying to write Neo-Babylonian sign forms.

Content. The inscription represents the dedication of an offering table to Marduk by the late Assyrian king Aššur-etel-ilani. A text of similar genre was published by A. Goetze in his article "An Inscription of Simbar-Šīḫu," *JCS* 19 (1965), 121ff. That inscription records the dedication of a throne for Ellil. Both texts use similar terminology and are similar in format.

The first nine lines of our text address the recipient, Marduk, and consist of a string of epithets. Most of the epithets are well known and are frequently attested for Marduk. The exception is *šaḫtu* at the beginning of line 5 which is used frequently as an epithet of kings, but is so far not attested for gods. [But, cf. ^{d}*Anunnaki ašriš šuḫarruru nazuzzu šá-aḫ-tiš* (Hinke, *Kudurru* i 8), in a different context.]

The donor, Aššur-etel-ilani, is introduced at the end of line 9. The description of the gift, an offering table, begins in line 10 and ends in line 14. The vocabulary is similar to the Simbar-Šīḫu inscription. This is followed by the motive for the gift.

Finally, lines 16 through 20 contain a prayer to Marduk invoking Šulpae, the lord of the table, to bless the donor Aššur-etel-ilani whenever the table is used. [The epithet "lord of the table" is discussed by Falkenstein in *ZA* 55, 17ff.] The last two lines contain an offering, the name of the scribe and a date.

Purpose. The purpose of the tablet itself is not immediately apparent, but we can speculate in order to suggest a possible use. That the tablet is ill-shaped, that it is written hurriedly with several erasures, and that it has no colophon preclude its identification as an archival tablet recording the donation. It was also not copied from an inscription on the table itself; if it had been, there would certainly be a colophon. Also, I would expect a much finer copy. Once the table was entered in Esaggila, only a small number of functionaries could have had access to it and I doubt that anyone so highly placed would have made such an imperfect copy.

I believe that the inscription is a manuscript for the inscription to be carved or painted on an offering table, before its placement in the temple. I would therefore like to suggest the following scenario: Nadin was an Assyrian official (note the use of three Neo-Assyrian signs) stationed in Babylon during the reign of Aššur-etel-ilani. He was ordered by the king to construct and dedicate an offering table for Esaggila, the main temple in Babylon. When the craftsmen finished the table they asked Nadin what he wished to have inscribed on the table. Nadin may have been in an office where writing was not normally done, but where tablets were kept or were passed through. In fact, he may have been in the craftsmen's shop. Not having fresh clay, he reused an older tablet and wrote out the inscription for the craftsmen. The cursory nature of the inscription would indicate that the craftsman in charge or the wood-worker himself was literate.

I assume that the last two lines of the inscription were not to be carved on the table. The amounts of the offering listed are much too small to be regular offerings to Marduk. In addition, the prescribed offerings in the inscription are called *surqinnu* while the listed offering is called AMAR×ŠE. I believe that the offering listed on line 21 was to be presented with the table when it was delivered to Esaggila. The offering was to be made in the name of Nadin as composer of the inscription. Thus, the last two lines serve as an 'order' to the chief craftsman and require Nadin's signature and a date. Note that part of the offering was to be drawn from *maššartu*-holdings which would presumably require authorization.

The Marginalia. Line 12 and the two signs in the margin between lines 16 and 17 are a mystery to me. However, I would like to suggest that they, as well as the blank spaces on the tablet, have to do with the placing of the inscription on the table. Since we do not have the table, it is very difficult to be sure. Perhaps these notes refer to decoration on the table in which case we should probably read NU as *ṣalam* 'relief, drawing.'

Historical Implications. The text published here may have important historical implications which go well beyond the date of the tablet.[1] If the Oates chronology is correct,[2] then the third year of Aššur-etel-ilani is the same as the second year of Nabopolassar. According to Chronicle 2,[3] during the first year of Nabopolassar the Assyrians and Babylonians fought to an inconclusive end and Nabopolassar withdrew, presumably to Babylon. In Nabopolassar's second year we are told that the Assyrians went to Babylonia and encamped at the Banitu-canal at the beginning of Ululu. They then again fought what appears to be an inconclusive battle. The donation recorded on our tablet is dated to the eleventh day of Ululu. Could this table be part of some sort of peace settlement? The timing would be good, and it would explain why the Assyrian king was dedicating a precious object to a Babylonian god in Babylon. Both Nabopolassar and Aššur-etel-ilani were under tremendous pressure at this time and they might well have sought peace from each other—even on a hurried or short-term basis.

Once again, if Oates is correct,[4] is it a coincidence that Adda-guppi moves from Harran to Babylon in the same year, presumably to marry Nabu-balassu-iqbi? These questions cannot be settled on the basis of the presently published evidence, but they must certainly be kept in mind when evaluating the historical sources for this fascinating period.

---

[1] The chronology of the last Assyrian kings is still somewhat problematical. Attempts at solutions have been offered by, among others, Borger, *JCS* 19 (1965), 59ff., J. Oates, *Iraq* 27 (1965), 135ff., von Soden, *ZA* 58 (1967), 241ff., and Reade, *JCS* 23 (1970-71), 1ff. There is a great deal of unpublished evidence in the "Sippar" collection of the British Museum and when the "Sippar" catalogue is completed the whole problem will have to be restudied.

[2] I believe that the Oates chronology will probably turn out to be the correct one, but final judgement must await the rest of the evidence.

[3] Grayson, *Chronicles*, 87ff.

[4] Oates has suggested that Adda-guppi left Harran in the third year of Aššur-etel-ilani and therefore ascribes him only three years of reign. The rest of his reign would be subsumed under the regnal years of the king of her new residence, Nabopolassar. I find this suggestion to be most intriguing and probably correct.

REST AND VIOLENCE IN THE POEM OF ERRA

Peter Machinist

University of Arizona

The poem[1] about the god Erra must clearly be reckoned one of the major texts of Mesopotamian religious literature, whether gauged by its content and literary artistry or by the evidence of its ancient popularity. Not less than thirty-six copies were recovered from at least five sites of the first millennium B.C.—a larger number, as L. Cagni points out, than even the copies known to the Gilgameš Epic from the same period.[2] Despite its importance, the Erra poem has generally been neglected in modern writing about Mesopotamian religion and the religions of the ancient Near East. Part of the reason has been its textual condition, for although work on the poem has proceeded for over one hundred years, ever since George Smith published portions of it in 1875,[3] only in the last decade or so have enough lines been recovered for intelligible editions to appear in Italian, French, and English.[4]

But another part of the reason for Erra's forlorn status has been its critical evaluation, for much of the debate over this poem has been rather narrowly invested either in particular philological skirmishes or in the issue of date and historical setting. The latter, to be sure, commands no little attention, since the poem, perhaps unique among the major works of Mesopotamian religious literature, appears to be a transparent "mythologization" of a specific historical event or period. This point is nowhere better illustrated than in Tablet IV:3, where, to describe how Erra caused a civil war and destruction in Babylon, the poet claims: *i-lu-ut-ka tu-šá-an-ni-ma tam-ta-šal a-me-liš*, "You changed out of your divinity and made yourself like a man."[5]

Unfortunately, all the efforts to find a date and setting have not created a full consensus.[6] Most are agreed that the Erra poem is of first millennium B.C. origin and probably the work of a Babylonian. But the historical episode or period underlying has yet to be settled on.[7] Some see it as a rather specific event: thus, von Soden, who looks to certain disturbances in Uruk in 765–763 B.C.[8] Others, like Lambert and Bottéro, tend toward a broader and longer process, particularly the Aramaean and Sutean incursions into Mesopotamia around the beginning of the millennium.[9]

Abbreviations follow W. von Soden, *Akkadisches Handwörterbuch*, 1965–81 (= *AHw*) and/or R. Borger, *Handbuch der Keilschriftliteratur*, I–III, 1967–75.

[1] Tentatively, I prefer to use the general term "poem" for this composition rather than something more specific, because while it is possible to agree on the text as poetry, it is difficult to identify it fully by such foreign labels as "myth" or, worse, "epic," as have been urged in the past. Cf. L. Cagni's similar position in his recent *The Poem of Erra* [*SANE*, 1/3], 1977, 13 and my review in *JAOS* 101 (1981), 402–3. Some thoughts on literary connections are offered at the end of the present study.

[2] Cagni, *Poem* (n.1), 5. The five sites are Assur, Babylon, Nineveh, Sultantepe, and Ur; but there may be others, as the provenance of all the tablets is not known. For a listing of the extant sources of the poem, see L. Cagni, *L'Epopea di Erra* [Studi Semitici 34], 1969, 13–23, 50–4, and B. Hruška, *ArOr*. 42 (1974), 355–8.

[3] George Smith, *The Chaldean Account of Genesis*, 1875, 123–36, where it is entitled "The Exploits of Lubara." For bibliography and a history of research on the poem, see Cagni, *Epopea* (n.2), 9–10, 13–23, and *idem, Poem* (n.1), 5–6.

[4] *Italian*: Cagni, *Epopea* (n.2); *French*: R. Labat, in R. Labat, *et al., Les religions du Proche-Orient asiatique*, 1970, 114–37, and J. Bottéro, *Annuaire de l'École pratique des hautes études, IV. section*, 110 (1977–78), 107–64; *English*: Cagni, *Poem* (n.1).

[5] Cagni, *Epopea* (n.2), 104. Cf. also the broken IIB 27 on p. 84. In the remainder of this study, the text of the poem is quoted and numbered according to the edition in Cagni's *Epopea*.

[6] For a survey of opinions, see Cagni, *Epopea* (n.2), 37–45; *idem, Poem* (n.1), 20–1, to which should be added Bottéro, *Annuaire* (n.4), 140–7.

[7] The confuson over this is reflected in Cagni's recent *Poem* (n.1). See my review in *JAOS* 101 (1981), 402.

[8] W. von Soden, *UF* 3 (1971), 253–63.

[9] W. G. Lambert, *AfO* 18 (1957–58), 396–8, 400; Bottéro, *Annuaire* (n.4), 140–7.

Whatever the case, it would seem obvious that the question of date and setting must not eclipse—as in fact it often has—a prior issue, the understanding of the poem on its own terms: how it is structured, what are its leading motifs, and what purpose(s) it is to serve. It is this internal analysis on which the present paper will center.

We begin with the content and character of the Erra poem as a whole. The text is in five tablets, of which I, IV, and V are essentially complete, while II and III are largely broken, surviving, respectively, in three and four fragments each. These tablets contain 642 lines of text, about 532 of which are well preserved or restorable. As for the original length of the complete poem, if we assume that Tablets II and III were designed to approximate the lengths of I (192) and IV (151)—V being much shorter (61), but since it is the last tablet, it may not be indicative of the lengths of the others—then the original number of lines was in the range of 750, as Cagni has supposed.[10] Thus, at present roughly 70% of the composition—532 of 750 lines—is available in a full or nearly full form.

Together these lines yield a reasonably detailed story. After an invocation, we are introduced to the god Erra, who, sleeping wearily in his chamber with his consort Mami, is aroused by his counselor, Išum, and his sidekicks, the personified weapons known as the Sibitti, and urged to go to war, and so to exercise that ability for which he is famous (*I 1-91*). A dialogue follows between Erra and Išum, in which the latter, seeing how violent Erra has suddenly become, tries to hold him back, but to no avail (*I 92-123*). For Erra plans war and destruction on a global scale, and to accomplish that, he must get his superior, Marduk, out of his way. He does this by reminding Marduk that the latter's insignia and attire of office need cleaning and refurbishing, a task for which Marduk will need to vacate his throne of authority. Marduk agrees to this and to the further suggestion of Erra that Erra occupy the throne in Marduk's absence, since, as Erra claims ironically, without someone in the seat, the cosmic order will dissolve back into chaos (*I 124–191).*

Once Marduk has gone and despite apparent objections by other gods (*IIA 1–10, IIB 1–55*), Erra resolves on war. Tablets II and III are taken up with a further long dialogue between our hero and Išum, in which the former expounds his plans, with ever-increasing vehemence, and the latter tries, again unsuccessfully, to dissuade him (*IIC 1–47, IIIA 1–35, IIIB, IIIC 1–74*). Išum concedes the debate at the end of Tablet III by affirming that Erra now holds the top position in heaven (*IIID 1–15*).

The result is that Erra finally goes to battle. The arena for this battle, as Išum describes it in another long speech, is Babylonia and its major cities, Babylon, Sippar, Uruk, Dūr-Kurigalzu, and Dēr. So destructive is the work that the whole society is turned topsy-turvy, and, as Išum accuses, righteous and unrighteous are killed alike. Indeed, the destruction reaches to heaven itself, with Erra voicing his desire to hold on permanently to Marduk's supreme seat (*IV 1–127*).

The conclusion of Išum's speech ends this part of the war, and Erra seems at least partially appeased. He himself now begins to speak, ordering Išum to complete the war by destroying Babylonia's enemies, especially those (= the Suteans) around Mt. Ḫeḫe; and this Išum carries out (*IV 128–150*).

With this act, full appeasement now settles on Erra. He certifies his change of mood and mind by a personal confession of his unrestrained rage before an assembly of all the gods, to which Išum responds (*V 1–19*). Erra then leaves Marduk's seat to return to his own in Emeslam, commanding that Babylon be restored (*V 20–38*). The text concludes with praise of the protagonists and details of the poem's authorship and transmission, as well as of its importance to gods and men (*V 39–61*).

The preceding summary should make clear that the central issue of our poem is the nature of the god Erra. On the one hand, he appears as a warrior, gone berserk in his rage and destruction. On the other, he is someone overcome by sleep, content to do nothing else but loll in his bedchamber, with the most strenuous efforts required to arouse him. This contrast is highlighted already in the introduction (*I 1–22*), in the complex relationship presented there between Erra and Išum. Indeed, so intertwined are their personalities that modern commentators have had great difficulty identifying the lines of the introduction belonging to each.[11] A close look, however, suggests that Išum is the addressee of the hymnic invocation in I 1–5, principally because he is named explicitly as the subject of lines 4–5 and thus must also govern lines 1–3, since 1–4 constitute a substitution parallelism familiar from

[10] Cagni, *Epopea* (n.2), 26; *idem, Poem* (n.1), 5.

[11] Cf. a representative sampling of opinions in Cagni, *Epopea* (n.2), 135 ff. to which one could add, *inter alia*, B. Hruška, *BiOr*. 30 (1973), 5 and C. Wilcke, *ZA* 67 (1977), 191–8.

hymnic invocations going back to third millennium B.C. Sumerian literature.[12] Likewise, as Hruška has supposed,[13] Išum should be the third person subject of I 6–14, and Erra the second person addressee there (I 9–14), whom Išum encourages to battle as he does the Sibitti (I 7–8). For when Erra himself is identified as subject in the following I 15–18, his intent is exactly the opposite of the subject of I 6–14, namely to *discourage* the Sibitti and others from battle. In I 19–20 Išum returns as the addressee, this time of the poet, and he remains as such in I 21–22. I 21–22, in fact, being a sequence of invocatory epithets, parallels the opening lines I 1–5, where Išum, as we have seen, is also the poet's addressee; and the two thus form an *inclusio* to the entire introduction.

Once the lines of the introduction are assigned in this way, the contrasts become clear. Erra, although we are told that he is supposed to be warlike (I 13–14, 19)—and he becomes so later—here appears slothful and unresponsive to the call for war. His weariness, in fact, is so great that he cannot even sleep properly (I 15); and he is so negligent in watching over his surroundings that, as a following section informs us (I 83–86), the land falls prey to depredation and disaster. Išum, on the other hand, although portions of the *inclusio* describe him as caring and peaceful (I 3, 21–22)—qualities that will predominate later in the poem, with the seeming exception of the campaign in IV 139–150—is largely pictured as bellicose, goading Erra and the Sibitti to war (I 4–14). The two protagonists, thus, appear in the introduction as exactly the reverse of each other and of what they are each to become; and this double reversal is underscored by the fact that in I 10–11, Išum addresses Erra by the very epithets with which he himself is otherwise labelled or associated (*dipāru* in I 10: cf. I 21–22 for Išum;[14] *ṭābiḫ[u]* in I 12: cf. I 4 for Išum; *ālik maḫrimma* in I 11: cf. I 99, 105, 108; IIIC [11], 15, 39, 54; IV 137; V 13, 46 for Išum, though note for Erra again in IV 15).[15]

The rest of the poem continues to explore the Erra-Išum relationship. Thus, Erra, initially in a state of ineffectual weariness, becomes increasingly violent until, beyond control, he is portrayed destroying Babylonia, after which he is calmed by the restoration of the country. In this respect, he is only expanding on a similar pattern evidenced, not coincidentally, by the same Marduk whom he tries to supplant (cf. I 130–178). Conversely, Išum, having first called for violence, increasingly urges calm to offset Erra's growing violence. Ironically, to do this, his own speech must become more and more impassioned, culminating in his own campaign of violence, at Erra's behest, against Babylonia's enemies. Once the campaign is over, however, the way is clear for Išum's return to peaceful calm, matching that of Erra. We observe, then, in the poem two intersecting cycles for Erra and Išum, built on the tension of rest and violence. At the beginning, both gods are apart: Erra in rest and Išum in violence, but with intimations of the reverse. Subsequently, they crisscross: Erra moves to violence, Išum to calm tinged by violence. At the end of the poem, they meet in harmony, in a new state of rest, as signified by their mention together in the concluding section of praise (V 39–41). The effect of all this is to emphasize the intertwined nature of their personalities—something apparent even from the etymologies of their names[16]—or more precisely, it is to show the

---

[12] Cf. Cagni, *Poem* (n.1), 27:n.1. In addition, the use of Ḫendursag̃a as an epithet for the addressee in I 2 makes good sense if the latter is Išum: see the discussion in Cagni, *Epopea* (n.2), 138–40.

[13] Hruška, *BiOr.* 30 (1973), 5.

[14] See Cagni, *Epopea* (n.2), 136, 142; Hruška *BiOr.* 30 (1973), 5 and n. 24.

[15] One may also note that in the very first lines where Erra and Išum are juxtaposed, I 4–5, they are sharply contrasted, the bellicosity of Išum discomfiting the weary Erra:

> ^{D}*I-šum ṭa-bi-ḫu na-a*ʾ*-du šá ana*
> ⌜*na-še-e*^{GIŠ}*kakkē*^{MEŠ}⌝*-šú ez-zu-ti*
> *qātā*^{II}*-šú as-ma*
> *ù ana šub-ruq ul-me-šú še-ru-ti*
> ^{D}*Èr-ra qar-rad ilāni*^{MEŠ}*i-nu-šú*
> *ina šub-ti*
>
> Išum, famed slaughterer, whose
> hands are fit to wield his fierce weapons
> And to make his sharp lances flash like
> lightning—Erra, the hero of the gods (in the process)
> being shaken up in (his) dwelling.

Here, as Cagni has seen (*Epopea* [n.2], 59, 141 *ad* 5), *qātā*^{II} *-šú as-ma* is a pivot phrase (cf. W. G. E. Watson, *ZAW* 88 [1976], 239–53), governing the parallel expressions *ana* . . . *ez-zu-ti* and *ana* . . . *še-ru-ti*. Significantly, there is no smooth connection to the following clause, which introduces Erra, ^{D}*Èr-ra* . . . *šub-ti*. The connection is, rather, abrupt, almost anacoluthic, thus emphasizing the contrast between the two gods.

[16] That is, if we follow J. J. M. Roberts, *JCS* 24 (1971), 11–6 and *The Earliest Semitic Pantheon* 1972, 21–9, 84:

importance of Išum in defining the range of Erra's behavior.

The cycles of rest and violence we have been discussing in overview are elaborated at a more detailed level by the treatment of several key word clusters.[17] On the "violence" side are the words for (1) "anger" or "fury" (*agāgu* and its derivatives *aggu* and *uggatu*; *ezēzu* and its derivative *ezzu*; *galātu*; *râbu*[18]; *sabāsu*); (2) "noise" (*ḫubūru; ikkillu; rigmu*); (3) "arousal" (*dekû*; *tebû*);[19] and (4) "destruction" or "punishment" (various words, particularly *šipṭu*). Opposing these are the "rest" group: (1) "rest" (*nâḫu* in G) or "appeasement" (*nâḫu* in D); (2) "utter silence" (*šaḫrartu*); (3) "sleep" (*dalpu; salālu; šittu*) or "weariness" (*anḫu*); and (4) "justice" or "governing order" (*šipṭu*).

Within each group alone the interaction of the words is evident at a number of points. Thus, for "rest," we find Erra beset by "weariness," yet not able fully to "sleep" (I 15–16). Or there are the Anunnaki gods, who love "utter silence" and the "sleep" that goes with it (I 81–82). In the "violence" category, when Erra or another character "arises" or is "aroused," it is regularly to carry out "destruction" of some kind (I 13, 132, 170–173; IV 62, 64, 136). Note, for example, the pun in I 45–46, where the Sibitti, whose weapons are already "raised" (*te-bu-ú*) for battle, cry to Erra to "arise" (*te-bi*) and join them. "Arousal," in turn, is accompanied by or creates "anger" (I 45–46, 123, 132; IIIC 50–51; IV 61–62), which leads directly to war and "destruction" (I 132; IIC 10; IIIA 16, C 23; IV 23, 61–62; V 7, 40, 57–58; cf. also the *kakkū ezzūtu* in I 4, 35, 44, 98, 186; IIIC 26). And "arousal" itself can be brought on by talk of "destruction" (I 13–14) or by the "noise" of humans, who then have to be "destroyed" (I 41–42, 73; IIC 45; IIIA 17–18; IV 68).

The two word groups also, of course, are set in opposition to each other in the poem. So Išum is praised as the one who "appeased" Erra of the "wrath" that had caused "destruction" (IIC 5–6 (?);[20] V 19, 40–41). It is the "noise" of men which prevents the Anunnaki from their "utter silence" and "sleep" (I 81–82). When Marduk "rose" from his seat of authority, the "governing order" dissolved or threatened to do so into chaotic "devastation" (I 136, 170–171). And Erra, being "weary" and fitfully "sleepful," does not know whether to "arise" (I 15–16), until Išum and the Sibitti come to "arouse" him (I 19, 45–46).

Finally, the poem contains a number of instances where the words jump groups, so to speak, to play ironically against one another. Thus, at one moment, Išum can be found telling Erra that despite all the "killing" and "devastation" you have wrought, *ù na-ḫa-am-ma ul ta-nu-uḫ* "You could find no rest at all!" (IV 112; cf. IV 87–111).[21] "Destructive fury," in other words, does not simply oppose "rest," it can also bring it about, by the cleansing exhaustion it creates. And while at the moment of Išum's remarks, this has not yet worked for Erra, by the end of the poem, we know that it has. The relationship of "rest" to "destruction" is played on in several other ironic ways as well. We learn of the citizens of Dūr-Kurigalzu who did not "rest" in their lamentation over their temple, which an enemy, "aroused" by Erra, had "destroyed" (IV 63–64). And there is the man who built a house to "sleep" in daily and to "sleep" in when dead—a death unexpectedly hastened by the "devastation" of Erra (IV 99–103). "Noise" also is the subject of ironic play. Thus, the Sibitti urge Erra to go on the warpath and:

> . . . *tu-ruk*$^{[\text{GIŠ}]}$*kakkē*^{MEŠ}-*[k]a*
> *ri-gim-ka dun-nin-ma* . . .
> . . . .
> *nišī*^{MEŠ}*lip-la-ḫa-ma lit-qu-na ḫu-bur-ši[n]*
> . . . Make your weapons resound,
> Raise a loud noise . . .
> . . . .
> (That) people may be afraid,
> and their noise be tamed.
> (I 60–61, 73)[22]

In short, the "noise" of Erra's "destructiveness" aims to control the "noise" of men (cf. IIC 45; IIIA 17–18).[23] Lastly, there is the "*šipṭu* (= "governing order")

---

n.157, Erra means "scorched earth," while Išum means "fire." This, of course, disregards the "midrashic" play on the etymology of Išum in the poem as "famed slaughterer" (I 4; cf. Lambert, *AfO* 18 [1957–58], 400).

[17] For the occurrences of these words in the poem, see the glossary in Cagni, *Epopea* (n.2), 261 ff., to which must be added (1) *agāgu*-IIC 5 (restored: cf. Cagni, *Poem* [n.1], 40, 41:n.73), and (2) *dalpu*-I 15. *dekû* is given by Cagni, incorrectly for the occurrences cited, as *dakû*.

[18] Of the occurrences in the poem, that in I 134 seems irrelevant here.

[19] Only the occurrences in G and Š, not in D, seem relevant.

[20] See Cagni, *Poem* (n.1), 40, 41:nn. 73–74.

[21] Cagni, *Epopea* (n.2), 112–6.

[22] *Ibid.*, 64.

[23] The play here is found in other Mesopotamian religious literature as well. For example, in the Old Babylonian edition

of heaven and earth," which, as we have observed, dissolves if Marduk leaves his seat (I 132, 170). So when Erra promises, in taking Marduk's place, that he will keep this *šipṭu* strong (I 182), we are treated to the patent irony that Erra does indeed maintain *šipṭu*—but the *šipṭu* of "destruction," as is made explicit later (IV 76–77; V 53,58).

In sum, the interplay of the two groups of words we have been examining reflects the interplay of the rest and violence they represent. The point is that rest and violence are not discrete concepts or forces; they interpenetrate. Where, the poem is saying, there is rest among the gods or on earth, there will also or soon be violence, the two revolving together in a ceaseless cycle. But the matter does not stop here. For rest and violence are only part of the larger tension between inactivity and activity in the universe. In itself that tension is morally neutral, or more properly, it can exhibit, at least to men, both beneficial and deleterious sides. Thus, activity is necessary for the universe to function. But too much activity brings on violence and potential chaos. Likewise, a certain inactivity, if understood as peacefulness and calm, helps to insure a balanced and just order. But too much inactivity is the equivalent of paralysis and death, and invites violent activity to fill the void it has left.

In various ways our poem is aware of this duality. "Noise," for example, can refer to the normal activity that undergirds human life (IIC 45; IIIA 17–18; IV 68); but it also can describe Erra's destructive wrath that aims to wipe this noise and life out (I 73; cf. IIC 45; IIIA 17–18; IV 68).[24] "Weariness," as we have seen, is the paralyzing inactivity that afflicts Erra at the beginning (I 15–20), encouraging depredation in the land which he should be guarding (I 83–91). But "rest" at the end is a positive state, signaling the exhaustion of Erra's fury and a new sense of order and human concern that the god had earlier lacked (V 6–15). Finally, there is the destructive activity of Erra, which once engaged loses all proportion as it breaks the established (Babylonian) world, both of gods and of men (IV 104–127; V 6–15). Balancing this, however, is Išum's campaign, against the very enemies Erra had used in Babylonia's destruction (IV 139–150). What is significant here is that though Išum leads that attack, it is Erra who decides to order it (IV 137–138). The campaign thus marks the necessary step before a full return to order and appeasement of Erra, which in the poem follows immediately (V 1–38).

If, then, activity and inactivity have their "bad" and "good" sides, as it were, and if these not only alternate separately, but revolve together in a cycle, the problem for men is how to deal with this. Or in terms of Erra, upon whom the problem focuses in the poem, how is the god "appeased" when he reveals his "violent" side, and how is he then enlisted on behalf of human beings? If once he has reached a state of beneficial "rest," as he has at the end of the poem, is there any guarantee that activity will not resume, and when it does, that it will not be his violent activity, which not only devastates human beings, but cracks the very boundaries of the cosmos?

The poem, it would appear, is designed to deal with this problem; and it does so in the first instance by laying out, as we have discussed, the contours of Erra's character, that is, the parameters of his cycle, and the involvement in it of others, particularly Išum. What is important about this explication is that it is done primarily through speeches, not third person descriptions. Speeches, in fact, occupy over three-quarters of the extant text,[25] and usually appear as dialogues between Erra and another character: Išum especially, but also the Sibitti and Marduk. Thus, less time is spent describing Erra's actual destructions than expounding, in a long series of dialogues in tablets I, II, and III, his plans for destruction and the attempt to turn these back. And even when the destruction is presented, it is in a long speech by Išum in tablet IV, which creates the impression that the action is taking place off stage, so to speak. Finally, Erra himself only comes completely to "rest" when he confirms this in a *mea culpa* at the beginning of tablet V (1–15), with a response by Išum (16–19). The

of Atraḫasīs, the flood Enlil sends against humans to stop their "noise" (*rigmu*/*ḫubūru*) is itself called *rigmu* (III iii 20 [?], 23 and cf. III ii 50, iii 15, in W. G. Lambert and A. R. Millard, *Atra-ḫasīs: The Babylonian Story of the Flood*, 1969. Cf. W. L. Moran, *Biblica* 52 (1971), 57:n.3; 58).

[24] Examples like these undermine the old attempt, codified in G. Pettinato, *Or.* NS 37 (1968), 165–200, to interpret "noise," especially when it pertains to humans, as meaning "sin," viz., sins against the gods. "Noise" stands, rather, for "activity" whether of humans or of gods, and can be beneficial or excessive depending on the practioners and the audience. Any connotation of "sin," therefore, is secondary, not primary. Further discussion, which would take in also analogous usages of "noise" in such texts as Enūma Eliš and Atraḫasīs (see n.23), must await another occasion.

[25] Based on the fact that of the 642 lines of the poem preserved in one form or another, about 505 are connected with speeches.

speeches, thus, lend the poem a certain introspective quality, entirely appropriate to the goal of "appeasing" the violent Erra.

Indeed, it is the power of language itself which is the constitutive element of the Erra poem, and the conscious emphasis on this reaches its most explicit expression in the conclusion (V 39–61). There the focus is no longer either the divine protagonists or even the human compiler of the text (*ka-ṣir kam-mì-šú* in V 42), it is the text itself. And it is upon this text that the burden of stopping and transmuting the rest/violence cycle is thrown. As the final lines proclaim, the very remembering and reciting of the "song" (*zamāru* in V 49, 59)[26]—not merely by men, but by the gods as well—is what will provide the needed defense against a repetition of Erra's violent behavior (V 49–61).

The poem of Erra, thus, may be understood, in conception and execution, as a kind of incantation—that form of literature where, one might argue, the power of language is most explicitly recognized and celebrated, and put to use, as here, both to expose a problem of potentially cosmic dimensions to its source and to offer a means for its resolution or neutralization.[27] Consequently, we should not be surprised that at least one copy of the complete text of our poem and several copies of tablet V alone have come to us in *amulet* form.[28] The physical form of the amulet, however, is only an outward sign of the deeper, fundamental character of the poem itself,[29] and it is that which we have tried here to discern.[30]

[26] This word may have generic significance here and in other texts, but precise conclusions must await a comprehensive study of its usage.

[27] One recalls a text like "The Worm and the Toothache"—hardly so exceptional as sometimes thought—where the "myth," "incantation," and "ritual" sections all work together to explain and "solve" the problem at hand.

[28] The tablet with the complete text is *KAR* 169. For a brief survey of the evidence, see Hruška, *ArOr*. 42 (1974), 356–7.

[29] See also Hruška, *ArOr*. 42 (1974), 357.

[30] It should be emphasized that the purpose of this paper has not been to cover all aspects of the Erra poem, but to focus on one thematic complex of central importance in it. Thus, other themes like the making of the divine image have been ignored. Equally, the presence of our theme in other Mesopotamian texts has not been systematically noted. That, hopefully, will come on another occasion.

CHARLES OLSON AND THE POETIC USES OF MESOPOTAMIAN SCHOLARSHIP

JOHN R. MAIER
STATE UNIVERSITY OF NEW YORK, BROCKPORT

> Once, as best I can recall, we were discussing heroes, and I tried to get him to discuss the concept of hero, from the individual-as-hero of the Greeks through the society-oriented hero of the Romans, mentioning several well-known scholars, but he refused even to consider it. "You're too much influenced by Greek and Latin already; too much of our literature and concepts are traced there already. Go beyond that, to the Sumerians, and before. Break the hold time has on you; get outside it."

THE CURIOUS REMINISCENCE BELONGS TO O. J. FORD, who was recalling an exchange with his teacher, the American poet Charles Olson (1910–1970).[1] Olson came to poetry rather late in his life. His impact as a poet on American poetry was felt after World War II. He was a poet and a teacher of poets, an intellectual who distrusted intellect, a man driven to read deeply the scholarship on the Ancient Near East who yet rejected ordinary scholarship. Nothing is more characteristic of Charles Olson than his rejection of the Western tradition in favor of Hittite, Akkadian, and especially Sumerian literature. Olson's poetry and his writings about poetry are filled with his attempt to get back to the "origins," and that attempt meant at least a rejection of the Judeo-Christian and Greco-Roman ways of looking at the world. Not since Gustave Courbet grew an Assyrian beard has any Western artist attempted such a sweeping rejection of the roots of Western civilization and identified with the Ancient Near East "beyond" Homer and "beyond" the Bible. For him the Sumerians were crucial to the attempt. Sumer was at the "center," at the point of "origin." Although he was not and did not consider himself a scholar, Charles Olson was guided in his attempts by Ancient Near Eastern scholarship, most notably by the work of Samuel Noah Kramer. The two men never met, but they corresponded briefly. This essay traces the influence of Sumerian scholarship on Charles Olson, an influence that is in large measure the impact of Samuel Noah Kramer.

As a student in American Studies under the direction of F. O. Matthiessen, Olson produced an important critical study of Herman Melville, *Call Me Ishmael* (1947). Less than a decade later he was applying for a Fulbright lectureship, hoping that a program in Baghdad would open up. He wrote in 1951 that,

> I have found it increasingly important to push my studies of American civilization back to origin points on this continent and this, in turn, has involved me increasingly in questions and in the development of methods to investigate the origins of civilization generally. . . . My desire is to go to IRAQ to steep myself, on the ground, in all aspects of SUMERIAN civilization (its apparent origins in the surrounding plateaus of the central valley, the valley-city sites themselves, and the works of them, especially the architecture and the people's cuneiform texts. . . . The point of a year of such work at the sites and in collections is a double one: (1), to lock up translations from the clay tablets, conspicuously the poems and myths (these translations and transpositions have been in progress for four years); and (2), to fasten—by the live sense that only the actual ground gives—the text of a book, one half of which is SUMER.[2]

To prepare himself for such a task, Olson had begun to collect books and articles on Ancient Near Eastern

[1] O. J. Ford, "Regaining the Primordial (Charles Olson as Teacher)," *Athanor*, 1 (1971), 52. Material for this essay was gathered in part under a grant from The Research Foundation of State University of New York. George Butterick, Curator of the Olson Archives, University of Connecticut, has been very helpful in my research, as have been Douglas Calhoun, editor of *Athanor*, and my research assistant, Parvin Ghassemi.

[2] *Alcheringa* 5 (1973), 11–12. He had applied for Turkey and Iran, but was allowed to switch his application when a program in Iraq did indeed open up; but the disposition of the application is not known.

history, archaeology, myth, and literature, and he continued to do so until his death.[3] His prose and poetry reflect this drive to Sumer.[4] *The Special View of History*, a series of lectures given at Black Mountain College, where Olson was rector,[5] takes off from a saying of Heraclitus, "Man is estranged from that with which he is most familiar," and leads Olson to this principle.

[3] George Butterick has been publishing lists of Olson's reading in *Olson*, the journal of the Olson Archives. Many of the books and articles gathered by Olson and now in the Olson Archives have been annotated by Olson. These notes and extensive files have not as yet been published. While Olson was rector of Black Mountain, he invited scholars like Robert Braidwood to speak about the Ancient Near East. He corresponded with Samuel Noah Kramer about the possibility of convening a seminar in "Pre-Homeric Literature," and Kramer was quite receptive to the idea. Kramer in turn suggested that Olson contact Cyrus Gordon and Hans Güterbock, and they, too, were interested in the seminar. But the school folded before the meeting could take place. Olson had hoped to run the seminar in 1955–1956. When, in 1959, a symposium was held in Mexico City that eventually became *Mythologies of the Ancient World*, 1961, Black Mountain was only a memory; but Olson would use *Mythologies*, a book that comes as close to his idea of the seminar as anything produced, in his classes at other schools. It was a suggestion of Kramer that led Olson to purchase *Ancient Near Eastern Texts*, the second edition of which is heavily annotated by Olson. See Kramer's letters in the Olson Archives for 5/24/52, 1/23/57, and 11/18/59. According to George Butterick, Olson's Ancient Near Eastern materials amounted to well over one hundred books and articles, from *BASOR* (1941–1947) and the *American Journal of Archaeology* (1942, 1943, 1948) through works by Alexander Heidel, N. K. Sandars, W. G. Albright, Cyrus Gordon, Hans Güterbock and others. The most heavily annotated are the second edition of *ANET* and three of Kramer's works: *From the Tablets of Sumer* (1956), *Sumerian Mythology* (revised edition, 1961), and *Mythologies of the Ancient World* (1961). Two works by L. A. Waddell, *The Aryan Origin of the Alphabet* (1927) and *The Indo-Sumerian Seals Deciphered* (1925) are in the Olson Archives and made an impact on Olson, but the copies are not marked. Olson was clearly offended by Waddell's racist views. In "Mayan Letters" (1953), in *Selected Writings* (ed. Robert Creeley), 1966, 97–98, he wrote to Creeley:

> until we have completely cleaned ourselves of the biases of westernism, of greekism, until we have squared away at historical time in such a manner that we are able to see Sumer as a point from which *all* "races" (speaking of them culturally, not, biologically) egressed, we do not have permission to weigh the scale one way or another (for example, Jakeman, leaves, so far as I have read him, the invention of maize to the Mongoloids, as well as the arts of ceramics, weaving, and baskets! And, *contra* (contra all these prejudiced Nordics, among whom I include Hooton, who has sd, from skull-measurements, that it is true, there were Caucasians here), there remains China, ancient and modern China. Until the lads can verify that the Chinese, as well as the people of India, came off from the Tigris-Euphrates complex, they better lie low with their jumps to conclude that only the Caucasian type was the civilizing type of man). ((As you know, this whole modern intellectual demarche, has, at its roots, a negative impulse, deeper, even, than the anti-Asia colonialism of Europe: at root, the search is, to unload, to disburden themselves, of Judaism, of Semitism.))

[4] Allusions are quite frequent in his work, from an Uruk tablet in "Logography," *Additional Prose* (ed. George Butterick), 1974, 26. He acknowledges his debt to I. J. Gelb in that essay. In *Causal Mythology*, 1969, 13, he refers to Enki, seeing in the Sumerian god a similarity to Prometheus, and he expresses his admiration for the Gilgamesh stories. In *Letters for Origin, 1950–1956* (ed. Albert Glover), 1970, 57, he observed that the ancients exactly reversed our modern metaphors (e.g., the phallus), an observation which led to a discussion of Sumer. He wrote to Creeley about the Sumerian logogram, *a*, *Selected Writings*, 96. In his poetry, too, he refers often to Sumerian and Akkadian motifs: to Inanna and the world-tree in "for my friend," for example, *Archaeologist of Morning*, 1970, n.p.; to Mesopotamian ziggurats in *Maximus, The Maximus Poems, Volume Three,* ed. Charles Boer and George F. Butterick (NY: Grossman, 1975), pp. 77, 84, 119; to Tiamat in an unpublished poem, "she is the sea . . . ," in *Olson* 9 (1978), 19; to the plant given Gilgamesh by Utnapishtim in one work, *Olson* 9 (1978), 20; to the *kishkanu* tree in "The four quarters," to Inanna before Ereshkigal in "like two spiders," and to Humbaba in "Dogtown the Dog Bitch," *Olson* 9 (1978), 38, 39, 46. See also in the same issue, "A Norm for my love in her NOMOS, or. . . ." In "Watered Rock . . ." he alludes, by way of "Bigmans," to Gilgamesh, *Olson* 9 (1978), 37.

[5] *The Special View of History* (ed. Ann Charters), 1970, 1. For Olson at Black Mountain, see Martin Duberman, *Black Mountain, an Experiment in Community,* 1972, 368–385, and Sherman Paul, *Olson's Push,* 1978, 67–114.

> I am persuaded that at this point of the 20th century it might be possible for man to cease to be estranged, as Heraclitus said he was in 500 B.C., from that with which he is most familiar. At least I take Heraclitus' dictum as the epigraph of this book. For all this I know increased my impression that man lost something just about 500 B.C. and only got it back just about 1905 A.D.[6]

Olson was one of many grappled with the idea of a "pre-rational" or "pre-logical" or "mythic" thought, still available in Homer and especially Hesiod and the Pre-Socratic philosophers, but covered over by the Classical Period.[7] The distinction between *logos* and *muthos* directed Olson to the "orality" of literature.[8] Again, Olson was but one of many to turn to "oral literature," but what is more surprising is his belief that his period in the 20th Century offers the possibility of overcoming the "estrangement" that has dominated our thinking since the Classical Period. He proclaimed a "new localism, a polis to replace the one which was lost in various stages all over the world from 490 B.C. on."[9] The "falsest estrangement of all," which he called "contemplation," was brought in with logic and classification in the 5th Century B.C.[10] Since it was myth that was displaced, and "all myth is projective, and thus has to be seen in its root or etymology,"[11] only a return to myth would overcome the grasp of the rational. Olson was one of those who call themselves "post-modern" thinkers, and "post-modern" man aims at recovering "the Pleistocene"[12] and thus overcoming the split between *logos* and *muthos*.

Between the estrangement brought about by Greek philosophy and the Pleistocene lay Sumer. In the Sumerians Olson found a "will to cohere" that was lost through the expansion of thought westward and the exhaustion of Mesopotamian thought.[13] Post-modern, post-humanist, and "post-historic" man is engaged in the process of recovering mythic thought. Olson felt he was a moving force in the movement, and he challenged traditional ways of writing, arguing, persuading, and expressing himself poetically through the use of unusual prose styles, poetic devices, and even in his style of teaching.

Sumer even appears in an Olson attack on American education.

> What I am kicking around is this notion: that KNOWLEDGE either goes for the CENTER or it's inevitably a State Whore—which American and Western education generally is, has been, since its beginning. (I am flatly taking Socrates as the progenitor, his methodology still the RULE: "I'll stick my logic up, and classify, boy, classify you right out of existence.")[14]

The "center" turns out to be Sumer. One may be jolted by the combination of Olson's three scholars:

> Which brings us home. To Porada, & S. N. Kramer's translations of the city poems, add one L. A. Waddell. What Waddell gives me is this chronology: that, from 3378 B.C. (date man's 1st city, name and face of creator also known) in unbroken series first at Uruk, then from the seaport Lagash out into colonies in the Indus Valley and, circa 2500, the Nile, until date 1200 B.C. or thereabouts, civilization had ONE CENTER, Sumer, in all directions . . . that a city was a coherence which, for the first time since the ice, gave man the chance to join knowledge to culture and, with this weapon, shape dignities of economics and value sufficient to make daily life itself a dignity and a sufficiency.[15]

Whatever one may think of this as history (or as geography!), it is this schema that drives Olson's idea of "the Sumer thrust."[16] The "will to cohere" leads Olson to meditate on Sargon of Agade, "GUDA, King of the port Lagash" and the subtle tale of Gilgamesh, who "was sent the rude fellow Enkidu to correct him because he, even Gilgamesh, had become a burden, in his lust, to his city's people."[17] The conclusion to this rather misty (or mystified) historical excursus, though, makes a telling point:

---

[6] *The Special View of History*, 15.

[7] Surprisingly, he did not seem to know Thorkild Jacobsen's work in *The Intellectual Adventure of Ancient Man* (now *Before Philosophy*), 1946.

[8] *The Special View*, 20.

[9] *The Special View*, 25.

[10] *The Special View*, 25.

[11] *The Special View*, 30.

[12] *The Special View*, 37.

[13] *The Special View*, 51; *Additional Prose*, 26–32, 40. See also "Notes for the Proposition: Man is Prospective," *boundary 2* 2 (1973/1974), 1–6.

[14] "The Gate and the Center," in *Human Universe and Other Essays* (ed. Donald Allen), 1967, 17–23.

[15] "The Gate and the Center," 19.

[16] "The Gate and the Center," 20.

[17] "The Gate and the Center," 22–3.

> it is an incredibly accurate myth of what happens to the best of men when they lose touch with the primordial & phallic energies & methodologies which, said this predecessor people of ours, make it possible for man, that participant thing, to take up, straight, nature's, live nature's force.[18]

No wonder Olson once lamented that "The trouble is, it is very difficult to be both a poet and, an historian."[19] History tends to become swallowed up in myth when Olson deals with Mesopotamia. On the other hand, it is post-modern (and "post-historic") man that most excites him, and Olson's most singular and most important formulation of things Mesopotamian is, not surprisingly, a very brief allusion in a letter about the project for poetry. The "Letter to Elaine Feinstein" (1959) is usually paired with "Projective Verse" as Olson most impressive statement on the contemporary project of poetry.[20] In the "Letter" Olson sounds a by now familiar note:

> I am talking from a new "double axis": the replacement of the Classical-representational by the *primitive-abstract* ((if this all sounds bloody German, excuse the weather, it's from the east today, and wet)). I mean of course not at all primitive in that stupid use of it as opposed to civilized. One means it now as "primary," as how one finds anything, pick it up as one does new—fresh/first. Thus one is equal across history forward and back, and it's all levy, as present is, but sd that way, one states . . . a different space-time. Content, in other words, is also shifted—at least from humanism, as we've had it since the Indo-Europeans got their fid in there (circum 1500 B.C.) ((Note: I'm for 'em on the muse level, and agin 'em on the content or "Psyche" side.[21]

This sets up the mother/father, Tiamat/Zeus contrast in Olson's notion of the "image":

> Image, therefore, is vector. It carries the trinity via the double to the single form which one makes onself able, if so, to issue from the "content" (multiplicity: originally, and repetitively, chaos—Tiamat: wot the Hindo-Europeans knocked out by giving the Old Man (Juice himself) all the lightning.
>
> The Double, then, (the "home"/heartland/of the post-Mesopotamians AND the post-Hindo Ees:
> At the moment is comes out the Muse ("world")
>
> the Psyche (the "life")[22]

What does this shift from "Classical-representational" to "primitive-abstract" mean for Olson's own poetry? He wrote to Robert Creeley in July of 1952 that:

> and i take it, a Sumer poem or Maya glyph is more pertinent to our purposes than anything else, because each of these people & their workers had forms which unfolded directly from content (sd content itself a disposition toward reality which understood man as only force in field of force containing multiple other expressions[23]

To that end, Olson worked on what he called "transpositions"[24] of ancient poems. Two such "transpositions" that derive ultimately from "Gilgamesh, Enkidu and the Nether World" were produced by Olson, the first, "La Chute," appearing in 1951,[25] and the second, "La Chute (II)," appearing posthumously in 1973.

"La Chute" is a re-working of the opening lines of the Twelfth Tablet of *The Epic of Gilgamesh*, which Olson knew from E. A. Speiser's translation in *ANET*. Olson's version expands what is basically two lines in the original:

> "Lo, [who will bring up] the *Dr*[*um* from the nether world]?
> [Who will bring up] the *Drumstick* [from the nether world]?"[26]

[18] "The Gate and the Center," 23.

[19] "Mayan Letters," 130.

[20] "Letter to Elaine Feinstein," in *Selected Writings*, 27–30.

[21] "Letter to Elaine Feinstein," 28.

[22] "Letter to Elaine Feinstein," 29.

[23] "Mayan Letters," 113.

[24] See *Alcheringa* 5 (1973), 5–11, for a sampling of Olson's "transpositions." Following upon Kramer's attempts in *Sumerian Mythology*, pp. 39–41 and again in pp. 73–75, to find a more or less consistent structure in the very heterogeneous Sumerian "myths of origin" and to describe that structure in a "rational" and then a "theological" way, Olson tried his hand at a Sumerian "creation myth" that linked the various elements together. The result is a poem, first called "FABLE OF CREATION" and revised to "a sumer fable." The poem was not published in Olson's lifetime. In *Alcheringa* 5, 5, the original typed copy and Olson's handwritten revisions of the text have been reproduced.

[25] Reprinted in *Archaeologist of Morning*, n.p.

[26] *ANET*, 97.

The *pukku* and *mekkû*, whose nature are still being debated today, Olson takes as "drum" and "lute."

La Chute

my drum, hollowed out thru the thin slit,
carved from the cedar wood, the base I took
when the tree was felled

o my lute, wrought from the tree's crown

my drum, whose lustiness
was not to be resisted

my lute,
from whose pulsations
not one could turn away

They
are where the dead are, my drum fell
where the dead are, who
will bring it up, my lute
who will bring it up where it fell in the face of them
where they are, where my lute and drum have fallen?

Conspicuous, of course, is the violation of the Akkadian poetic line; Olson's version in its broken typography and white spaces adds emphases where the Akkadian (in translation) does not. The first three lines, which are bundled together (and should be read aloud together), were suggested, not by the Twelfth Tablet itself, but by Speiser's introductory comment, which sets the Sumerian background of the piece. By setting this apart from the single line 4, which in a sense completes it, a powerful emphasis is placed on the working of the wood to produce the drum and lute. The drum is "hollowed out" and "carved," while the lute is "wrought." Olson preserves the noteworthy feature of Sumero-Akkadian poetry in the repetition of the simple sequence: drum/lute, drum/lute. First the working of the drum and lute, and then the force of drum and lute: the "lustiness" of the drum is "not to be resisted" and the "pulsations" of the lute are so tempting that "not one could turn away." This elemental force of the musical instruments owes its power to the source in nature from which it is taken and transformed.

Very likely, Olson saw in the seductive force of drum and lute not merely a connection with the Sumerian story, which binds the tree to the fascinating Inanna, at whose request Gilgamesh and Enkidu fell the tree; but also to the opening of Tablet One of *The Epic of Gilgamesh,* where, according to one interpretation, Gilgamesh tyrannized the citizens by the drum that "aroused his companions" and caused the people to cry out for relief.[27] The drum is power and is also heavily erotic ("lustiness"), the drum of battle and the summons to the first-night privileges of the lord. The "pulsations" of the lute further emphasize the powerful sway and erotic fascination of "my lute." Gilgamesh speaks here in such a way to underscore the power in his hands to use the (sacred) instrument; the others could not resist.

The felling of the tree, also by the hands of Gilgamesh, is picked up in the last five lines, another bundle, where the fallen drum is assimilated to the fallen dead. If the earlier part of the poem tied the drum to Gilgamesh's earlier arrogance, the final part of the poem is a touching lament that spreads death over all. Olson's diction in the poem (except for the archaic "wrought" and "lustiness" and rather stilted "pulsations") is simple, clean. The elemental fact of death is everywhere glimpsed in the "life" and "death" of the drum itself. Olson picks up a chunk of Akkadian poetry, and his "transposition" of it does not contain a hint of consolation that the lamented "death" will somehow be overcome.

"La Chute (II)" exists in two versions, one published in *Alcheringa*, and an earlier draft in the Olson Archives.[28] It picks up where "La Chute" left off, in the sense that it contains Gilgamesh's advice to Enkidu on the way to enter the land of the dead. While Olson had worked with the Akkadian in *ANET,* "La Chute (II)" shows evidence of reworking in the light of Kramer's translation of the same passage in *Sumerian Mythology.*[29] (That Olson knew the passage in *The Epic of Gilgamesh*, Tablet XII, was itself a translation

---

[27] See *ANET,* 73–4. Olson had marked his copy of the second edition concerning the *pukku* and *mekkû* in *The Epic of Gilgamesh.*

[28] *Alcheringa* 5 (1973), 7–8. The draft is in folder 1260–2 of the Olson Archives. There are over twenty variations between the drafts, almost all of them in the accidentals of capitalization and punctuation. Of the more meaningful changes, the lines about striking and embracing the sons at first contained the injunction, "do not embrace the beloved son," and "the hated" for the hated son, instead of the phrase, "his brother," that replaced it. The breasts of the mother were at first merely "bared," and they were bared "to the dead" instead of lying open to "the judges." The final line of the poem has been improved greatly by removing the "have fallen" (for the drum and lute), and adding instead the stark "are."

[29] *Sumerian Mythology*, 35.

of a Sumerian original, is clear from his markings in Kramer's *From the Tablets of Sumer*, p. 222, which Olson possessed from January, 1957.)

La Chute (II)

If you would go down to the dead
to retrieve my drum and lute
a word for you, take my word
I offer you directions

Do not wear a clean garment
they below will dirty you
they will mark you
as if you were a stranger

Nor rub yourself with oil
the finest oil from the cruse.
The smell of it will provoke them
they will walk round and round
alongside you

Carry no stick. At least
do not raise it,
or the shades of men will tremble,
will hover before you

Pick up nothing to throw, no matter the urging.
They against whom you hurl it will crowd you,
will fly thick on you.

Go barefoot. Make no sound.
And when you meet the wife you loved
do not kiss her
nor strike the wife you hated.
Likewise your sons. Give the beloved one no kiss,
do not spit on his brother

Behave, lest the outcry shall seize you
seize you for what you have done
for her who, there, lies naked
the mother
whose body in that place is uncovered
whose breasts lie open to you and the judges

in that place
where my drum and lute are

Olson's poem does not, at first glance, seem to offer much of a departure from either Akkadian or Sumerian original. The sequence of clothes, oil, throw-stick, sandals, kissing and striking wives and sons in the instructions Gilgamesh gives Enkidu is retained. (Olson nowhere indicates the source, however, and does not make it evident at all that the speaker is Gilgamesh or the listener is Enkidu.) The grouping of lines is not as striking as in "La Chute;" indeed, it mainly follows Kramer's stanzaic translation (Speiser's is not sectioned into stanzas). Olson has taken pains to remove the trappings of traditional rhetoric thought appropriate to "epic" poetry (or derived from Biblical translations of the Renaissance). Consider Olson's ll.21-26, with its direct and colloquial English, against either Speiser's:

> Sandals to thy feet thou shalt not fasten,
> A sound against the nether world thou shalt not make,
> Thy wife whom thou lovest thou shalt not kiss,
> Thy wife whom thou hatest thou shalt not strike,
> The son whom thou lovest thou shalt not kiss,
> Thy son whom thou hatest thou shalt not strike![30]

or Kramer's:

> Do not put sandals on thy feet,
> In the nether world make no cry;
> Kiss not thy beloved wife,
> Kiss not thy beloved son,
> Strike not thy hated wife,
> Strike not thy hated son.[31]

Gone in Olson are the "thy's" and "thou shalt not's" and the correct but ponderous "whom thou lovest's" of Speiser's (and to a lesser degree, Kramer's) versions. "Go barefoot" and "Make no sound" are direct and forceful. On the other hand the "sound" which is "in" or "against" the nether world is largely, though not entirely dropped by Olson's colloquial rendering. Olson retains something of the rigid symmetry of the original—but only a hint. And "do not spit on his brother" for the "Strike not thy hated son" may simply miss the mark of the original. In general, though, Olson's is a looser but more vigorous "transposition" of the scholarly treatments.

In two respects, though, Olson has modified the original in striking ways. He has introduced the "drum and lute" where the originals do not specify them at all. That Olson introduces them at the beginning and then again at the end shows that he saw the descent into the nether world as a shamanic journey, and that he thought the poetic closure gave the piece a unity it

[30] *ANET*, 97.

[31] *Sumerian Mythology*, 35.

may not originally have had. Even more striking is his treatment of the goddess, Ereshkigal. He avoids the specification, "mother of the god Ninazu," and thus reduces the goddess to elemental "mother." There is some question why Ereshkigal should be described the way the Sumerian and Akkadian originals portray her, but Olson's interpretation makes it clear that *he* thinks the mother lying naked, her body uncovered, her breasts exposed to "you and the judges" is an image of erotic seduction—more like Inanna than her sister. Finally, Olson downplays the "outcry" of the nether world, with all its magical properties, and plays up instead an ambiguity in the original. Is Enkidu really to be seized "for what you have done/ for her"? The statement, never clarified, suggests a descent to the mother/mistress, a life/death goddess because of an action for/against her. The possibilities open up in the Olson version, and no attempt is made to reduce the ambiguities in his "transposition."

Whatever else Olson was doing in his "transpositions" of Sumerian poetry, he was listening for the utterance of man at the "origin," listening for a word of the earliest known poets and myth-makers, a word not yet split into *logos* and *muthos*. The transpositions are likely to strike the scholar and the critic as a little too close to the scholarly translations to be independent compositions, a little less flamboyant than the usual Olson offering. The perception is true, but the judgment is false to Olson's careful listening. Olson's poetry is for the most part highly idiosyncratic—not, indeed, an unusual case among contemporary poets. For Olson, though, the "subjectivism" of Western poetry from the Greeks to at least the beginning of the 20th Century was a major problem, and he proposed instead, "objectism."

> Objectism is the getting rid of the lyrical interfence of the individual as ego, of the "subject" and his soul, that peculiar presumption by which western man has interposed himself between what he is as a creature of nature (with certain instructions to carry out) and those other creations of nature which we may, with no derogation, call objects.[32]

The very fidelity with which Olson keeps close to the Sumerian is evidence of his listening closely, his avoidance of "the lyrical interference of the individual as ego."

Charles Olson's reputation depends, for the most part, on his essay, "Projective Verse," and his long poem, *The Maximus Poems*. Sumerian and Akkadian allusions are many and important to these works, but they are not, of course, the only ancient and non-Western concerns in his works. Olson had a deep interest in Mayan culture, for example, and the Mayan materials were more accessible to him than Sumero-Akkadian materials. Because he does not speak of these matters with immediate reference to his personal life and to the political issues of the day, it is difficult to say how much personal and political causes help sustain the ancient, mythic images in his writing. Olson declined a political occupation after World War II. Certainly he believed that America in the post-war era had certain connections with a very ancient Sumerian civilization. Beyond the overcoming of the Greek "estrangement" by going beyond the Judeo-Christian and the Greco-Roman traditions, though, very specific causes are difficult to discern. It may come as a surprise, though, that the prototype of Maximus, the poet-hero of Olson's complex "long" poem, was Olson's "Bigmans." And the early "Bigmans" is a transposition of what Olson knew of that most sturdy of Sumero-Akkadian heroes, Gilgamesh.[33]

[32] "Projective Verse," *Selected Writings*, 24.

[33] The Olson Archives files 566–79, "Bigmans," contain "Bigmans" I, II, and III. "Bigmans" (I) is an invocation, not directly from *The Epic of Gilgamesh*. Another "Bigmans" (on the verso of the typed sheet, "Bigmans II") is a transposition of the opening of the Akkadian epic. "Bigmans III"—otherwise known as "III The Brother"—is a transposition in different versions of Gilgamesh on the hunter and Enkidu, as the harlot is picked to seduce the wild man. The piece was left unfinished and is, in any case, pretty poor stuff. Olson's partly handwritten, partly typed notes to "Bigmans III" are more interesting. The manuscript is signed and dated August 24, 1950. As is usual with Olson's prose, the notes are difficult and digressive, but they make a point of the "single" and the "double" involved in the complex relationships of Gilgamesh, Enkidu, and the harlot.

APPENDIX

Musical Settings for Cuneiform Literature: A Discography.
J. M. Sasson

Dr. Maier's paper has focused on the effect that a recovered cuneiform literature had on a specific modern poet. To be sure other poets (e.g. A. R. Ammons, "Gilgamesh Was Very Lascivious," "Sumerian," etc.) and novelists (e.g. R. Lehrman, *Call Me Ishtar*) participated in this reshaping of ancient materials into contemporary visions. But it may not be amiss, in this context, to briefly append a listing of musical works, *available on disks*, wherein nineteenth- and twentieth-century composers imaginatively distilled the contents of Mesopotamian myths and epics and presented them either as extended compositions which fused words to music or as shorter, purely instrumental, pieces. This brief survey is but a sampling, and it does not interpret or assess the various attempts. Additionally, I have avoided speculating on the contexts which quickened musical interest in ancient literature. I have, however, included one or two bibliographical citations for those who would like to pursue the topic further. Compositions which depended on classical or biblical formulations regarding Assyria and Babylon (e.g. Handel's *Belshazzar* etc. . . .) are not included. The discography is American; but European equivalent is available. I would like here to thank Dr. Maier for permitting me to usurp a bit of space for this enterprise.

ISHTAR

Vincent D'Indy (1851–1931). D'Indy visited the British Museum in 1887 and was struck by Assyriological monuments that were then displayed: "Quel bel art et quel flagrant délit de vie et de vérité dans ces tableaux d'une civilisation qui valait bien la nôtre! . . . J'éprouve une impression bien plus grande et plus réellement artistique devant l'art assyrien du VIIIe siècle avant J.-C. que devant celui de Périclès. . . ." He composed *Ishtar, variations symphoniques, Op. 42* nine years later. This very complex series of variations purports to duplicate Ishtar's progressive stripping of clothings and ornaments as she reaches her sister's inner sanctum. D'Indy's work, about fifteen minutes in length, reverses the usual approach to thematic variations, and actually presents the melody in its fullest form only when Ishtar is totally naked and defenseless (a musical technique which was later much favored by Sibelius).

Recording: EMI C 069-14043. Orchestre Philharmonique des Pays de la Loire; Pierre Dervaux, Cond.

Bibliography: L. Vallas, *Vincent D'Indy, II: La Maturité; la vieillesse (1886–1931).* 1950. 236–41. [Quotation is from 238, n. 1.]

Bohuslav Martinů. (1890–1954). The Czech composer wrote *Istar* (H. 130) in Prague during 1918–21 and added "The Dance of Priestesses" while in Paris in 1923. The ballet, in three acts and five scenes, was inspired by the Sumerian accounts regarding Dumuzi and Inanna, freely expanded to include materials drawn from *Ishtar's Descent*, from *Gilgamesh's* 6th tablet, and from Julius Zeyer's mystical imagination. The first act told of Tammuz's capture by Irkalla, the evil (sic) goddess of the Underworld; the second of Ishtar's arrival before her sister and her recovery of her dead lover. The last act finds Ishtar and Tammuz emerging into a world which progressively warms up and regains happiness. The gods, in their joy, eternalize the pair and they ascend to the highest heaven. The score, about two hours in duration, is for a very large orchestra, but Martinů, then strongly under French musical influence, often achieves impressionistic settings. The added 'Dance of Priestesses' includes a woman's chorus that is reminiscent of Ravel's *Daphnis and Chloe.*

Recording: (Selections) Supraphon 1 10 1634. Brno State Philharmonic Orchestra; Jiří Waldhans, Cond.

N. B. Orchestral suites based on *Istar* (arranged by B. Bartoš) are sometimes individually recorded.

Bibliography: H. Heilbreich, *Bohuslav Martinů.* 1968. 324–6. B. Large, *Martinů.* 1975. 26–7.

GILGAMESH

Bohuslav Martinů. In 1954 Martinů was in Nice. By the end of the year, upon finishing a cantata about Christ's passion, *Mount of Three Lights,* he immediately turned to composing the Oratorio, *The Epic of Gilgamesh* (H. 351) and used Campbell Thompson's translation. With a German libretto by A. H. Eichmann, *Gilgamesh* lasts about an hour and is scored for largish orchestra, chorus, soloists, narrator, and speaker. Part I, derived from Tablet 1 and 2, introduces Gilgamesh, a lonely king for whose benefits the gods produce Enkidu. After his own *éducation sentimentale*, Enkidu challenges and befriends Gilgamesh. Part II focuses on Gilgamesh's reaction to Enkidu's death (Tablets 7, 8, 10) and on his awareness of human mortality. Part III, loosely based on tablet 12, contains Gilgamesh's 'invocation,' his meeting with Enkidu's ghost, and his multiple inquiries which are met by detached responses. The oratorio ends with Gilgamesh never quite learning anything beyond what he already knew; a rather startling philosophical development from Martinů's previous involvement with Near Eastern literature (see above). It is worth noting, perhaps, that Martinů's imagination invests the 12th tablet with more legitimacy than does the Assyriologist's.

Recording: Supraphon 1 12 1808. (Sung in Czech). Czech Philharmonic Chorus; Prague Symphony Orchestra, Jiří Bělohlávek, cond.

Bibliography: Halbreich ibid., 279–82; Large, ibid., 110–1. See also the informative remarks added to the recording.

Augustyn Bloch (1929– Grudziądz, Poland). Written in 1968, the ballet-pantomine *Gilgamesz* has been recorded only in its concert version, and that is what I report on. The piece, about twenty-five minutes long, is inspired by the Akkadian epic. The author contends that its sections rejoice over happiness, exult over power, and lament over death. A chorus punctuates the orchestral music with quasi-Gregorian chants. The score, however, is often striking since it eschews violins, oboes and horns, in favor of saxophones and percussion.

Recording: Musa SX 1208. Warsaw National Philharmonic Orchestra and Choir, Andrzej Markowski, cons.
Bibliography. *The New Grove Dictionary of Music and Musicians.* (s.v.)

Per Nørgård (1932–, Gentofte, Denmark). *Gilgamesh, Opera in Six Days and Seven Nights* was composed in 1971–72. As of this writing, the release of this opera had just been announced, and I have not had access to it. Nørgård's interest in Mesopotamian culture goes back at least to 1966 when his oratorio, *Babel* (for clown, rock singer, cabaret singer, chorus and small orchestra) was produced.
Recording: Denmark-DMA 025-6. Members of the Swedish Radio Orchestra, Tamás Vetö, cond.
Bibliography: *The New Grove Dictionary* . . . , s.v. [The Swedish journal, *Nutida musik* 17 (1973–4), 5ff. has devoted a whole issue to *Gilgamesh*].

THE SEVEN (EVIL) GODS

Sergei Prokofiev (1891–1953). Having just completed his *Classical Symphony*, Prokofiev decided to compose "something cosmic" to parallel the momentous events of the summer of 1917: "The revolutionary events that were shaking Russia penetrated my subconscious and clamored for expression. I did not know how to do this, and my mind, paradoxically, turned to ancient themes. The fact that thoughts and emotions of those remote times had survived for many thousands of years staggered my imagination."

Once more (cf., *Songs*, Op. 9, 23), Prokofiev turned to the poetry of the "Decadent Symbolist" K. D. Bal'mont (1867–1943), and chose the last's resetting of a "Chaldean Invocation engraved in ancient Assyro-Babylonian cuneiform on the walls of an Akkadian temple" ("In the deep abyss/Their number is seven;/ In the Azure sky,/Seven, they are seven . . . ." From *Voices of Antiquity*. 1908.) Prokofiev shortened the poem, harped on the number seven, and added a quatrain which was certainly meant to comment on contemporary events, although it is still a matter of debate whether Prokofiev sought thusly to exorcize the Russian Revolution or the German advances toward Petrograd.

The score is for a piece that, pointedly enough, lasts seven minutes. It has a highly expressionistic series of thunderous *tutti* alternating with deafening silences. Shrill piccolos, shrieking choruses, beating drums, and bleatting woodwinds evoke slaughter and plead laments. Greeted as an example of bourgeois decadence, it was not performed in Russia until the late '60s.
Recording: Quintessence PMC 7196. Moscow Radio Symphony Orchestra, Gennady Rozhdestvensky, cond.
Bibliography: I. V. Nestyev, *Prokofiev*. 1960. 149–54. [Quotation from 151, note.] On Bal'mont, E. Lo Gatto, *Histoire de la littérature Russe*, 1965. 629–32.

ENUMA ELISH

Vladimir Ussachevsky (1911- Manchuria; US citizen). Ussachevsky works in two areas of music, choral, where he is influenced by Russian liturgical music, and electronic, where he displays a predeliction for transforming pre-existing material. In 1959 he took part in the founding of "Columbia-Princeton Electronic Music Center." *Creation-Prologue*, composed in 1960–61, is an eight minute piece recorded at a concert where other compositions, each remarkably different in texture and invention, found first presentation. I quote from the record's jacket:

> The work begins in Akkadian, the language of Babylon, implying the chaotic state but giving no description of it. The composer says: "I felt a need of interpolating some such description from another ancient source, and thus the opening lines of [Ovid's] *Metamorphoses*, rendered in Latin, are inserted, or musically speaking superimposed on *Enuma Elish*. I sought to exploit the contrast between the archaic quality of Akkadian and the sound of classical Latin . . . the antiphonal manner of the performance assists in sharpening this contrast." The composition is written for four full choruses and may be performed in various combinations of live performers and pre-recorded chorus, or simply as an entirely recorded work from two or four tape tracks. Antiphonal treatment of the material is frequently employed, and in several instances a dense dissonant texture is achieved by the use of multi-choral polyphony.

Recording: Columbia MS 6566. [I know of this recording thanks to A. Hurowitz and, especially, to Sh. Paul.] An apparently more elaborate version of this composition is listed in the *International Electronic Music discography*, 1979, under the composer's name as *Three Scenes from the Creation* (CRI, SD 297, a record not available to me).
Bibliography: *The New Grove Dictionary* . . . , s.v.; E. Schwartz, *Electronic Music: A Listener's Guide*, 1973, 55ff.

HISTORY AS CHARTER
SOME OBSERVATIONS ON THE SUMERIAN KING LIST

Piotr Michalowski

University of Michigan, Ann Arbor

The text which we know as the Sumerian King List has been with us for quite some time.[1] Seventy-one years ago V. Scheil published the first manuscript of the composition but the text truly made its imprint on the field of Assyriology due to the pioneering efforts of A. Poebel and, most importantly, those of T. Jacobsen, who published his now classic treatment of the "List" in 1939.[2] Since that time the King List has been dissected and commented upon there has been, surprisingly, little critical literature on the subject. Most studies of early Mesopotamian history have in one way or another made use of this text and while one often encounters isolated comments on the "tendentious" nature of the composition, to this day we lack any comprehensive modern study of the non-philological aspects of the King List.

In the comments that follow I would like to make a preliminary attempt at a reevaluation of the Sumerian King List. I cannot pretend to solve most of the questions which I feel should be raised concerning this composition; I would, however, like to discuss a number of issues which arise from the study of this rather peculiar text. I use the word peculiar not because of the fact that like most of us I often feel frustrated and lost when confronting any ancient text, but because I am becoming convinced that the King List is unique in many ways and that it contains certain features which it shares with no other Sumerian text.

Most discussions of the King List have centered around the historical value of the text. Some have perceived this composition as a historical source, albeit a skewed one, or as a form of meta-commentary, classified under the heading of "historiography." Terms such as "history" and "historiography," however, are semantically loaded and such concepts only acquire meaning within particular ideologies. The ontological status of "historical facts" and "sources" has been debated by countless philosophers and historians.[3] In recent years discussions of these problems have once again become focal points in the works of numerous historians, mainly due to the influence of Hayden White.[4] The positivistic heritage of Assyriology, however, has largely served to discourage debate on such theoretical issues.[5] In this article I should like to invoke some of these problems in the context of the study of the Sumerian King List.

The study of textual sources is, by its very nature, part of the larger problematic of narrative. Thus, in a radical vein, one could very well posit that there is no such thing as history or histories but that there are only texts: ancient or modern. This point of view requires that we view the problem of historical sources in the same manner as we would approach any other text. The major corollary of this point of view is the simple fact that the question of realism cannot be invoked in order to single out certain texts as historical, and therefore, somehow "real" in opposition to those

---

[1] Old Babylonian royal inscriptions are cited according to the system found in I. Karki, *Die sumerischen und akkadischen Königsinschriften der altbabylonischen Zeit: I. Isin, Larsa, Uruk*, 1980.

[2] T. Jacobsen, *The Sumerian King List* [Assyriological Studies 11], 1939.

[3] As a good example from American historiography one may cite C. L. Becker, "What are Historical Facts?" *Western Political Quarterly* 8 (1955), 327–40 (often reprinted). A highly instructive essay on some of these matters by an ancient historian is to be found in P. Veyne, *L'inventaire des differences*, 1976.

[4] See H. White, *Metahistory: The Historical Imagination in Nineteenth-Century Europe*, 1973; idem., *Tropics of Discourse: Essays in Cultural Criticism*, 1978.

[5] For a recent critical account of the ideological underpinnings of the main trends of reconstruction of the history of the Ancient Near East, concentrating primarily on "Biblical History," see J. M. Sasson, "On Choosing Models for Recreating Israelite Pre-Monarchic History," *JSOT* 21 (1981), 3–24.

which one could, conceivably, label as "fictions."[6] Texts are stories, or narratives, or whatever one may wish to call them, but there is no way in which any verbal artifact can be said to be ultimately more true than any other. In a more cautious and less radical vein H. White has written:

> It is sometimes said that the aim of the historian is to explain the past by "finding," "identifying," or "uncovering" the "stories" which lie buried in chronicles; and that the difference between "history" and "fiction" resides in the fact that the fiction writer "invents" his. This conception of the historian's task, however, obscures the extent to which "invention" also plays a part in the historian's operations. The same event can serve as a different kind of element of many different historical stories, depending on the role it is assigned in a specific motific characterization of the set to which it belongs.[7]

These comments can be brought to bear not only upon the work of the modern historian but also equally well applied to the analysis of any ancient work which we suspect to be "historical."

Historical sources are thus narrative. This form of narrative, however, often has its own particular features. R. Barthes has suggested that historical texts are characterized by what he terms "*l'effet du réel*" in which the signified (i.e. the mental image of the sign) is confused and fused with the referent, that is the perceived reality which the sign points to in a given communicative act.[8] The complex confusion between referent and signified is found in all texts which aspire to the realm of "realism" and thus the historian is confronted with the unending task of unraveling these chains of meaning in "source" narratives as well as in his own meta-commentary on these "events." These observations hold true for highly developed prose narratives but they are equally applicable to a text such as the Sumerian King List.

Viewed as a narrative form the King List exhibits a structure which is difficult to define. It is in many ways a list but, although it is constructed by means of an unrelenting repetition of formulas, it cannot be easily classified as a chronicle, as an annal, or as any of the other of the traditionally designated forms of elementary historical narratives. Thus studies of simple historical narratives from other cultures, let us say those of Medieval Europe, are of little value to our efforts. More close to home, moreover, the very status of this particular text within the set of other known Sumerian literary compositions of the Old Babylonian period is equally difficult to define. Briefly stated, the sources of the King List belong to a class of tablets which cannot be easily classified within the bounds of our present knowledge of Sumerian literary tablets. Of the fifteen sources known at this time more than half, specifically nine texts, derive from Nippur.[9] As far as I am able to discern, all of the Nippur sources contained the entire composition of the List in its "Nippur recension," that is without the section enumerating the antediluvian kings.[10] None of these texts represents any of the typical Nippur student tablets; no extracts are known. It should also be noted that no copy of the King List was found in the third post-war season of excavations at Nippur in the private houses in the well-known TA area of Tablet Hill which yielded a large group of practice tablets which represent a cross-section of the school curriculum of this city during the time of Samsu-iluna.[11] In light of these facts it is difficult to designate the King List as a school text in the same manner in which we view the majority of Old Babylonian literary works from Nippur and, perhaps, from Ur. Compositions which were written solely on large tablets are difficult to place in the curriculum; perhaps they were the exercises of highly advanced students. The only problem with this hypothesis is the fact that often the large tablets of other compositions contain an unusually high percentage of errors in comparison with the extract texts.[12] The place of the King List in the tradition is

[6] For a radical criticism of these concepts see D. Nye, *The Semiotics of Biography: The Lives and Deeds of Thomas Edison* [Toronto Semiotic Circle. Monographs, Working Papers and Prepublications], 1981.

[7] H. White, *Metahistory*, 6–7.

[8] R. Barthes, "Le discours de l'histoire," *Social Science Information / Information sur les sciences sociales* 6 (1967), 65–75.

[9] For the most recent list of manuscripts of this text see D. O. Edzard, "Königslisten und Chroniken. A. Sumerisch," *RlA* 6 (1980), 77–8.

[10] See W. W. Hallo, "Beginning and End of the Sumerian King List in the Nippur Recension," *JCS* 17 (1963), 52–7.

[11] Most of these texts were published by J. W. Heimerdinger, *Sumerian Literary Fragments from Nippur*, 1979. The significance of this group of texts has been discussed briefly by M. Civil, *MSL* 14, 8.

[12] See, for example, the remarks by J. Klein, *Three Šulgi Hymns: Sumerian Royal Hymns Glorifying King Šulgi of Ur*, 1981, 170–1.

therefore difficult to define. It is so particularly in light of the observation that the repetitive nature of the composition, combined with the fact that it consists mainly of personal names, would have made it a useful tool for the learning of cuneiform signs at an early state of instruction.[13]

Given this state of affairs little can be said of the place of the King List in the set of other Old Babylonian literary compositions, a matter further complicated by the fact that there is, at present, considerable disagreement on the date of composition of this document.[14] These matters are of great importance for any understanding of this, or, for that matter, any text since meaning is never hermetically sealed within a text but resides, in the words of Harold Bloom, "between texts."[15]

Any discussion of the King List can only begin to unravel the levels of meanings which circulate within, around and next to this composition. While uncertainties abound and the semantic space of the text may be difficult to grasp, the sources of the compiler can, most probably, be better perceived. The likeliest sources for the sections containing information from the Old Akkadian period to the time of the Isin dynasty are the date-lists. Such date-lists exist and, for the most part, it is not difficult to reconcile the data of the King List with information which can be independently gleaned from these sources.[16] The earliest year-dates go back to the time of Enšakušana, but the consistent use of this type of dating began with the Akkad dynasty.[17] It is, therefore, no coincidence that the fewest manuscript problems and variant readings are found in those portions of the List which concern historical periods when year-dates were in use. For other periods some of the possible sources are votive and triumphal inscriptions which were still available during the Old Babylonian period. The ever-growing corpus of Old Babylonian copies of pre-Sargonic, Sargonic and Ur III royal inscriptions testifies well to this fact. Nippur, in particular, must have been a good source of older texts. It is now quite evident that triumphal inscriptions were set up in the Ekur and possibly in other shrines of Enlil in that city; this is apparent from the subscripts in the well-known compilations of Sargonic inscriptions from Nippur.[18] A recently published text of similar contents contains a concluding note specifying that the inscriptions copied on the tablet were found in the courtyard of the Ekur.[19] The Old Babylonian tablet of the inscriptions of the Ur III ruler Šū-Sîn likewise was copied from texts from temples of Enlil and Ninlil in Nippur.[20] Individual inscriptions do not, however, necessarily provide the name of a given ruler's father and therefore are difficult to seriate in a list. I suspect that this may be the source of the large variation in the order of kings in the early sections of the king list. It must be said, however, that of the sixty or so names of rulers in the pre-Sargonic sections of the list, only approximately six are presently attested in contemporary texts.[21] Moreover, as J. Cooper reminds me, the unstable manuscript tradition for these sections is also a function of the transmission history of the text and thus one must look for other reasons to explain why certain parts of the list were less subject to change than others.

---

[13] Lists of personal names as well as primers based on names were utilized in Old Babylonian schools at early levels of instruction. See E. Sollberger, "A Three-Column Silbenvokabular A," *AS* 16 (1965), 21–8; M. Çiğ and H. Kızılyay, "Additions to Series B and C of Personal Names from Old Babylonian Nippur," *AS* 16 (1965), 41–56.

[14] For a recent survey of various opinions on the subject see D. O. Edzard, *RlA* 6 (1980), 80–1.

[15] "An empirical thinker, confronted by a text, seeks a meaning. Something in him says: 'If this is a complete and independent text, then it has a meaning.' It saddens me to say that this apparently commonsensical assumption is not true. Texts don't have meanings, except in their relations to other texts, so that there is something uneasily dialectical about literary meaning. A single text has only part of a meaning; it is itself a synecdoche for a larger whole including other texts. A text is a relational event, and not a substance to be analyzed," H. Bloom, *Kabbalah and Criticism*, 1975, 166.

[16] See R. Borger, *HKL* III, 37 par. 19.

[17] A. Westenholz, "Early Nippur Year Dates and the Sumerian King List," *JCS* 26 (1974), 154–6.

[18] See H. Hirsch, "Die Inschriften der Könige von Agade," *AFO* 20 (1963), 72.

[19] P. Michalowski, "New Sources Concerning the Reign of Naram-Sin," *JCS* 32 (1980), 239.

[20] See for the possibilities of restoring the subscript, see M. Civil, "Šū-Sîn's Historical Inscriptions: Collection B," *JCS* 21 (1967), 37.

[21] See T. Maeda, "'King of Kish' in Pre-Sargonic Sumer," *Orient* 17 (1981), 2 and J. Cooper, *Reconstructing History from Ancient Inscriptions: The Lagash-Umma Conflict*, 1982, in press. The actual number depends on how many restorations one accepts in broken passages in the King List as well as in original Early Dynastic inscriptions.

The variations of entries in these early sections may have originated in a variety of ideological and perceptual influences which cannot presently be recovered. Whatever these may have been, one thing is clear; there is absolutely no reason to trust the data contained in the King List. The unreliable nature of the early sections of the text may be most dramatically demonstrated in the case of the Dynasty of Gutium. It is well-known that almost everything we know of that "dynasty" comes from the King List. This matter has been discussed recently by W. W. Hallo and I shall not repeat his arguments here.[22] Suffice it to say that of the four known manuscripts which preserve this section, no two agree on the names, order, regnal years, or number of the Gutian Kings. An unpublished tablet from Nippur, edited below, preserves the names of five of these rulers, among them two who do not appear in any other text of the List. In light of these facts I would venture to state that one cannot privilege any particular manuscript of the King List and that it is at present impossible to produce a composite text of this composition which would reflect any historical "reality."

Let me now turn briefly to a discussion of the ideological context of the King List. It has often been stated that this text contains a fiction, a notion that Sumer and Akkad were always ruled by one dynasty at a time. A word commonly encountered in discussions of the composition is the adjective "tendentious."[23] What this tendentious slant may have been, however, is less often spelled out with any detail in the literature on the subject. The most detailed account of the propagandistic nature of the King List was offered by J. J. Finkelstein who, building on previous statements by T. Jacobsen and F. R. Kraus, interpreted this composition as an expression of the idea of centralization of power in the hands of one dynasty, ruling from one city, an idea which found its roots in the period directly following the "expulsion of the Gutians" and which was ultimately realized as a legitimation of the Isin dynasty.[24] In the discussion which follows I should like to develop this idea further and to suggest an ideological context which may help to explain one aspect of the conceptual basis of the King List.

After the fall of the Third Dynasty of Ur, Mesopotamia was ruled by a variety of competing kingdoms which were unable to achieve unity until the brief period of hegemony by Hammurabi and Samsu-iluna of Babylon. It is commonly accepted that the petty kingdoms of Babylonia during this period were in the hands of rulers who were of Amorite origin. The very nature of these Amorite origins, however, is a matter which is difficult to gauge and it is clear that a purely inductive analytical stance cannot cope with such problems; comparative studies and the use of models are necessary if the historian is to make any sense of the meager, selective and highly biased ancient sources available. In the paragraphs that follow I shall attempt to provide one model for the interpretation of certain aspects of Old Babylonian royal ideology.

However one may view the ethnic makeup of the local rulers of Babylonian during this period, one thing stands out: with very few exceptions these dynasties somehow stressed the fact that their ancestors were Amorite. The most dramatic evidence for this is the well-known "Genealogy of the Hammurabi Dynasty" and the related list of Shamshi-Adad's ancestors embedded in the Assyrian King List.[25] Hammurabi calls himself the ruler of all the Amorites but other kings, I would suggest, also proclaimed their connection with some aspect of "Amorite ideology." Thus Zabaja and Abi-sarē of Larsa, as well as Sîn-gāmil of Diniktum, are described in royal inscriptions as *rabiān amurrim* "Amorite chieftains."[26] The

[22] W. W. Hallo, "Gutium" *RlA* 3 (1971), 711.

[23] See, for example, D. O. Edzard, *RlA* 6 (1980), 77.

[24] J. J. Finkelstein, "Early Mesopotamia, 2500–1000 B.C.," in H. D. Lasswell, D. Lerner and H. Spier (eds), *Propaganda and Communication in World History. Volume I: The Symbolic Instrument in Early Times*, 1979, 60–3. See M. Civil's observation, "*La finalité de la liste royale sumérienne, par example, semble être la légitimation des revendications territoriales de la faible dynastie d'Isin,*" in *L'archéologie de l'Iraq du début de l'époque néolithique à 333 avant notre ère. Perspectives et limites de l'interpretation anthropologique des documents*, 1981, 230. A similar interpretation was expressed by J. Krecher, "Sumerische Literatur," in W. Röllig (ed.), *Neues Handbuch der Literaturwissenschaft. Altorientalische Literaturen*, 1978, 138–9.

[25] See J. J. Finkelstein, "The Genealogy of the Hammurapi Dynasty," *JCS* 20 (1966), 95–118.

[26] For references see M. Stol, *Studies in Old Babylonian History*, 1976, 87–8. A new inscription of an Old Babylonian ruler who bears the title *rabiān amurrim* was recently excavated at Tell Hadad in the Hamrin basin. Dr. Rashid al-Arwi, who is preparing the text for publication, was kind enough to allow me to see his copy of the inscription and generously allowed me to quote it. The text commemorates

case of the early kings of Larsa is an interesting one in this context. The true power of this dynasty dates from the time of Gungunum, traditionally the fifth ruler of that line. No year-dates are preserved from the period prior to this king's reign. A date-list as well as a king list, however, provide us with the names and lengths of reign of four of Gungunum's predecessors.[27] It is clear, nevertheless, that the power of these early rulers—if indeed all of them actually reigned at Larsa itself—could not have extended far beyond the immediate environs of the city. In recent years new information has been published which sheds light on the reigns of two of Gungunum's predecessors. The first piece of evidence is found in an inscription of Gungunum himself; the opening lines read as follows:[28]

1. *gu-un-gu-nu-um*
2. lugal arar.ki-ma
3. lugal ki-en-gi ki-uri
4. ibila kala-ga
5. *sa-mi-um*

Gungunum, king of Larsa, king of Sumer and Akkad, rightful heir of Samium.

Note that while Gungunum dresses himself in the Mesopotamian titular trappings of power, calling himself "King of Larsa," "King of Sumer and Akkad," the name of Samium is not followed by a title. The recent excavations at Larsa have brought to light a monumental text of Zabaja, the brother of Gungunum who preceeded him on the throne of Larsa. The full text of this inscription reads:[29]

1. *za-ba-a-a*
2. *ra-bí-an* MAR.TU
3. DUMU *sa-mi-um*
4. É.BABBAR.RA
5. *i-pu-uš*

Zabaja, the *rabiān amurrim*, son of Samium, (re)built the Ebabbar.

Abi-sarē, the king who followed Gungunum on the throne of Larsa, likewise used this title in one of the few inscriptions which are presently available from his reign.[30] His family relationship with the preceeding rulers of Larsa is not known, however. The full implications of the use of this title are impossible to ascertain. One could, of course, claim that these "Amorite titles" were meant to refer to the tribes which lived within the scope of rule of these kings. I would like to suggest, however, that another explanation is in order. It appears that the best interpretation of these titles is to assume that legitimacy in this period was not only a function of the traditional Mesopotamian trappings of power, as well as of power itself, but was also related to the status of a given ruler within the kinship structure of the Amorite tribes. In other words, I am suggesting that these titles provide a form of "genealogical charter" for the legitimization of kingship; it was not enough to be king, one had to claim descent from the proper lineage within the Amorite tribes.[31] Indirect evidence in support of this hypothesis may be found in the inscriptions of the Old Babylonian dynasty of Uruk. The first ruler of this dynasty, Sîn-kāshid, claimed as one of his titles the designation "King of the Amnanum (Tribe)" (lugal *am-na-nu-um*).[32] The same title was held by Sîn-gāmil, most probably his grandson.[33] When, however, the throne of Uruk passed into the hands of Anam, a *homo novus* who had served as a high official under Sîn-gāmil, we find this title conspicuously absent in the inscriptions of the new king. In the light of our hypothesis we may claim that the reason why Anam could not claim the title "King of the Amnanum" was that he was not descended from the royal lineage within that tribe. If we were to assume that the title simply referred to the fact that the Amnanum were an important component in the domain of Uruk under Sîn-kāshid and his successors,

---

the (re)building of the wall of ME.TUR.AN^{ki} by *a-ri-im-li-im* / dumu *i-ba-a-a* / *ra-bí-an* MAR.T[U] (lines 1–3).

[27] The *Larsa King List* (*YOS* I, 32), edited most recently by A. K. Grayson, "Königslisten und Chroniken," *RlA* 6 (1980), 89–90, and the *Larsa Date List*, see A. Ungnad, "Datenlisten," *RlA* 2 (1938), 149–59. Both texts list the four predecessors of Gungunum but the date list only begins the enumeration of actual year formulae starting with that king.

[28] Gungunum 1.

[29] Zabaja 1. See now also the fragmentary Old Babylonian letter from Girsu which includes the lines: (10′) *uš-tu za-ba-a-a be-lí* (11′) *i-na* giš.gu.za-*im uš-bu-ma*, D. Arnaud, "Texts relatifs a l'histoire de Larsa: I," *RA* 71 (1977), 4.

[30] Abi-sare 4: I, 27.

[31] For this concept see L. and P. Bohannan, "A Genealogical Charter," *Africa* 22 (1952), 301–15.

[32] D. O. Edzard, *Die "zweite Zwischenzeit" Babyloniens*, 1957, 106.

[33] Sîn-gamil 3: 7.

we would be at a loss to explain its absence in the inscriptions of Anam since contemporary evidence clearly indicates that this tribal group played an important role in the politics and economics of Uruk during the reign of Anam.[34]

If, for the sake of the argument, one assumes that this form of genealogical charter was an important component of the ideology of royal legitimization during the Old Babylonian period, one is immediately struck by the lack of any evidence of any such elements in the propaganda of the rulers of Isin. The explanation for this is not hard to find, for the founder of the dynasty, Ishbi-Erra, was either not an Amorite or, more probably, was from the wrong lineage within his own tribe, having attained high status and, eventually, control of Isin only through his service to the kings of Ur. Briefly stated, I should like to propose that the Isin kings, from the wrong side of the tracks, so to speak, had no right to claim this particular form of legitimization. Theirs was a different claim, a claim which was, I would suggest, the central issue of the Sumerian King List. The fiction that each city of Mesopotamia in turn held the bala, the turn of office, not only provided them with an alternative to the genealogical charter which was not available to them, but it also served to bolster their claims of hegemony over all the territories which had once been under the rule of the Ur III dynasty. In this sense the King List complements the evidence of the lists which enumerate the Ur and Isin kings as if they constituted one unbroken chain of rulers,[35] the liturgical composition which lists the kings of these dynasties as incarnations of the god Damu,[36] as well as the perpetuation of particular forms of "royal hymns" by the Isin kings.[37] This conscious attempt to link the Isin dynasty with the Ur III kings was most dramatically realized in a literary text which exploited the fall of Ur. The "Lament over the Destruction of Sumer and Ur," clearly an Old Babylonian composition, contains, in effect a full articulation of Isin ideology.[38] Towards the end of the composition Nanna, the god of Ur, goes before Enlil and weeps over the destruction of his city. The answer of Enlil reads as follows:[39]

di til-la inim pu-úḫ-ru-um-ma-ka šu gi_4-gi_4 nu-gál
inim du_{11}-ga en ^{d}en-líl-lá-ka šu bal-e nu-zu
urí.ki-ma nam-lugal ha-ba-sum bala da-rí la-ba-an-sum
u_4 ul kalam ki gar-ra-ta zag un lu-a-šè
bala nam-lugal-la sag-bi-šè è a-ba-a igi im-mi-in-du_8-a

The verdict of the assembly cannot be turned back, the word commanded by Enlil knows no overturning. Ur was granted kingship, it was not granted an eternal reign. Since the days of old when the land was founded until (now) when the people have multiplied, who has (ever) seen a reign of kingship that is everlasting?

The "Lament" and the King List both reflect the same ideology; Isin is in line to hegemony and that is simply the way things are. The explanation of the King List as a form of charter naturally explains the absence of the Larsa rulers from the text. The other major omission, that of the Early Dynastic kings of Lagash may, in effect, be linked to the absence of the Larsean kings. The last rulers of Larsa continually stressed their tribal connections with Jamutbal and with the region of Lagash.[40] Rīm-Sîn mentions his connections with Girsu and Lagash in his inscriptions. In connection with these facts W. W. Hallo has suggested that it was during this time that certain Lagash literary traditions were incorporated in the Nippur literary corpus since such texts as Lugal-e and the Nanshe Hymn clearly reflect Lagashite motifs and stylistic features.[41]

The narrative form of the King List, that of a repetitive list, is perfectly suited for the purpose of the

[34] See the letter between An-am and Sîn-muballiṭ published by A. Falkenstein, "Zu den Inschriftfunden der Grabung in Uruk-Warka 1960–1961," *Baghdader Mitteilungen* 2 (1963), 56–71. The "epistolary" nature of this text has been discussed by F. R. Kraus, *BiOr* 22 (1965), 289–90.

[35] E. Sollberger, "New Lists of the Kings of Ur and Isin," *JCS* 8 (1954), 109.

[36] *TCL* 15, no. 18.

[37] On these matters see already W. W. Hallo, "The Last Years of the Kings of Isin," *JNES* 18 (1959), 57.

[38] The published sources of this composition have been listed by D. O. Edzard, *AfO* 23 (1970), 92 and a translation by S. N. Kramer is available in *ANET*³, 611–9. I am preparing a full edition of this text which will include all known unpublished duplicates.

[39] *STVC* 25 obv. 18–22 = *UET* 6, 132: 71–11.

[40] M. Stol, *Studies . . .*, 63–72.

[41] W. W. Hallo, "Choice in Sumerian," *JANES* 5 (1973), 110.

text—to serve as a historical charter for the Dynasty of Isin. The meaning of the text is not revealed by any narrative episodes but through the cumulative effect of the structure of the composition. The ending of the text is simply the present—the Isin kings. It is therefore not surprising that the order of certain dynasties, the names and even the presence or absence of some groups of rulers are minor details from the point of view of the function of the List. In this instance structure is meaning and therefore the details are of little importance. The result of this state of affairs is that there is no "correct" form of the composition, that is one which would be more true to reality and reflect more precisely the actual chronology of early Mesopotamian history. The vagaries of textual transmission as well as the functional and structural properties of this text are such that we cannot, by any means, privilege any particular manuscript of the King List. I do not want to enter here into a discussion on the comparative merits of different ways of editing cuneiform documents; in the case of the King List, however, we must avoid attempting to reconstruct any ideal manuscript. Given the state of our knowledge we can only assume that there are as many King Lists as there are manuscripts.

Since the King List is not a reflection of real events but is, rather, a depiction of an *idea* of reality, the text should forever be banished from reconstruction of early Mesopotamian history. Others have come to similar, if not as radical conclusions. Thus, T. Jacobsen, who has worked on this text more than anyone else, recently concluded that he had at one time overestimated the chronological value of the King List.[42]

In this article I have reconstructed and contrasted two styles of political legitimation in Old Babylonian Mesopotamia: the ideology of the King List and related documents and the historical charter of genealogical thought. Before concluding this essay I should like to dedicate a few final paragraphs to the ideological and social contexts of these concepts. The central problems which come to mind in any discussion of tribes and genealogies are those of social and economic organization. Traditionally there has been a tendency to associate tribal structure and strong extended kinship ties with pastoralism and nomadism, often collapsing the last two concepts together. This view of the Mesopotamian social landscape has been questioned to good effect in recent studies and there is no reason to confuse these various factors in historical research.[43] It is clear that nomadism can have many forms and that the spectrum between fully settled urban life and total nomadism is a broad one, one which cannot be demarked by simple typologies.[44] Moreover, it is also quite clear that urban settlement does not preclude the perpetuation of kinship ties.[45] When I suggest that Old Babylonian rulers utilized genealogies as charters I do not necessarily wish to claim any particular way of life as a determining factor in the background of these kings. The recognition of their Amorite past, or even present, does not mean that I envision, as has often been done in the past, hordes of semi-nomadic Amorite-speaking tribes descending upon the rich cities of the Mesopotamian plain from Syria through the Jezira. The linguistic situation I leave aside as unsolvable, most likely involving numerous dialects and languages, of which we shall never know, trade languages and various forms of bilingualism. The subsistence pattern of "Amorites" probably differed from place to place and from time to time, depending very much on environmental and political pressures. Finally, the entry point for most "Amorite" groups, or rather the strongest point of contact and interaction, was not the route down the Euphrates from western Syria but through Northern Mesopotamia, the Ǧabal Ḥamrīn and down the Diyāla. Thus Sippar and its environs was probably a crucial place of cultural exchange.[46] Who these "Amorites" were is another matter. In order to even begin to approach such a question we must go back in time and investigate certain aspects of the problem already evident in Ur III times.

R. M. Adams and H. Nissen have drawn attention to the model developed by Owen Lattimore which explained the relationships between Mongolian nomads

---

[42] T. Jacobsen, cited by J. A. Brinkman, "Chronologies of the Near East, 3500–2000 B.C.: The Sixtieth Anniversary Symposium of the Oriental Institute," *The Oriental Institute. Annual Report 1979–80*, 60.

[43] See K. A. Kamp and N. Yoffee, "Ethnicity in Ancient Western Asia During the Early Second Millennium B.C.: Archaeological Assessments and Ethnoarchaeological Perspectives," *BASOR* 237 (1980), 85–104.

[44] See P. C. Salzman, "Introduction: Processes of Sedentarization as Adaption and Response," in P. C. Salzman (ed.), *When Nomads Settle*, 1980, 1–19.

[45] K. A. Kamp and N. Yoffee, *BASOR* 237 (1980), 93.

[46] See P. Michalowski, *The Royal Correspondence of Ur* [Unpublished Yale University doctoral dissertation], 1976, chapter 4. Hereafter cited as *RCU*.

and Chinese authorities during the Han dynasty.[47] Reacting against Chinese narratives concerning the interrelationship between the central government and the frontier areas, Lattimore was able to demonstrate that the political formations on the Chinese borders were as much a consequence of imperial government policy as a function of subsistence patterns in these areas. Imperial control provided the environment for contact and intermingling of peripheral groups from the center as well as pastoral nomads from the steppes. Not surprisingly, in time, the peripheral members of the state began to identify more closely with the other inhabitants of the area who, in turn, adapted certain features from them. Without stretching the analogy it is certainly reasonable to assume, on the basis of the extant data, that a similar situation existed in the border areas of Mesopotamian military control. The best example of the autonomous nature of the *limes* during the Ur III period is found in the literary correspondence between king Šulgi and Arad-mu, the chief military officer of the "empire."[48] In two well known letters Arad-mu complains to the king that Apillaša, the appointed governor of Subartu, has insulted the office of the representative of the crown and has established a virtually independent kingdom in the area. The answer of Šulgi is quite telling; he orders Arad-mu to come to terms with Apillaša and to disregard the latter's insulting behaviour. A similar situation is found in the correspondence between a later king, Šū-Sîn, and his official Šarrum-bāni, an officer sent to oversee the building of the fortifications against the "Amorites" in the north-east.[49] The king actually deposes Šarrum-bāni from his post and replaces him with a more trustworthy official, his uncle Babati.[50] The reason for this action is that Šarrum-bāni has exceeded his orders by engaging in military activity against the Amorites, actions which were specifically forbidden by the king. Šū-sîn makes references to the fact that the military activities as well as his high-handed attitude towards the local leaders, have upset the delicate balance of power and stability in the area. The term used to describe this state of affairs is dím-ma ma-da, the equivalent of Akkadian *ṭēm mātim*.[51] The Sumerian expression is not common but the Akkadian version is well attested, particularly in the omen literature.[52] It is difficult to provide a modern "translation" of this expression but the contexts in which it appears suggest something akin to "the balance of power," and "political *status-quo.*" In the case of the peripheral areas of the Ur III state this situation encompasses not only "hostile" Amorite elements but also the colonists sent there from the core area and a variety of other peoples and social groups which inhabited the border regions; individuals and organizations which interacted in a variety of ways with the central government. It is clear from the Ur letters that the crown recognized the political reality of the tenuous nature of the military and economic control over these areas and adjusted its policy to practical contingencies. The fluid nature of social organization in the regions where we suspect the Amorites lived most probably resulted in a continuous shifting of the status of various elements of the population. As a number of researchers on the subject have stressed, sedentarization and restructuring of nomadic groups can manifest itself in an almost infinite variety of ways and it is impossible to construct a model which would predict the situation in the past in a definite manner.[53] It is reasonably clear, however, that throughout early Mesopotamian history we are dealing not with successive waves of nomadic groups from some putative ultimate homeland, but with differing modes of interaction with population groups which consisted of a variety of elements, some settled, some in various nomadic patternings, some newly arrived and some which had lived in the area for generations. Moreover, one must posit that the varieties of social and economic forms under which these

[47] R. McC. Adams, "The Mesopotamian Social Landscape: A View from the Frontier," in C. B. Moore (ed.), *Reconstructing Complex Societies* [Supplement to the Bulletin of the American Schools of Oriental Research no. 20], 1974, 1–20; H. J. Nissen, "The Mobility Between Settled and Non-Settled in Early Babylonia: Theory and Evidence," *L'Archéologie de l'Iraq . . .*, 285–90.

[48] *RCU*, 135–59.

[49] *RCU*, 224–42.

[50] On Babati see also R. M. Whiting, "Tiš-Atal of Nineveh and Babati, Uncle of Šu-Sin," *JCS* 28 (1976), 173–82.

[51] The expression occurs a number of times in the Šū-Sîn correspondence. See for example, the instructions given to Šarrum-bāni and Babati by the king: ma-da dím-ma-bi nu-kúr-ru-dè nam-ba-sum-mu-[en]-zé-en, "I have instructed you both not to change the political climate of the territory!" (Šū-Sîn—Šarrum-bāni 39–40: *RCU*, 236).

[52] See J. Bottéro, "Le pouvoir royal et ses limitations d'après les textes divinatoires," in A. Finet (ed.), *La voix de l'opposition en Mesopotamie*, 1974, 119–64.

[53] K. A. Kamp and N. Yoffee, *BASOR* 237 (1980), 85–104.

people lived provided the occasion for successive forms of intermingling between those who were from the periphery and those who had arrived from the center. The view of those who wrote documents, the scribes and bureaucrats of Mesopotamia, may not have been the same as those who lived in these areas and thus the variety of tribal names and appellatives does not, necessarily, reflect accurately the native designations for the same concepts. Moreover, these designations may have changed over time. The Mari records, for the most part covering only one generation or so, provide some evidence for a larger "confederation" which encompassed groups which were designated as Amnanum, Ubrabum, Jarihum, Jahrurum, and Rabbaium.[54] Some of the "tribal names" known from Mari also occur in texts from Babylonia.[55] Most intriguing among these are a small number of references to double names;[56] among these the most conspicuous is Amnan-Jahrurum. This designation occurs for the first time in a letter from An-am of Uruk to Sîn-muballiṭ of Babylon where men of this grouping are allies of the ruling houses of these two cities.[57] Two generations later, during the reign of Samsu-iluna, the Amnan-Jahrurum are enemies of Babylon.[58] We have no way of knowing, however, whether these references in fact refer to the same political and military entitites and, most important of all, whether the Amnan-Jahrurum have anything to do with the separate entities Amananum and Jahrurum, both of which were part of the Jaminites encountered in the Mari records.[59] Thus one would be hard pressed to attempt to define or recognize pure Amorite tribes in the extant documentation. Tribal groupings, recognized for particular purposes, must have been quite fluid and the genealogical information within these groupings was probably adjusted to accomodate new situations. Kinship is, in many ways, a fiction, and there is ample documentation for the manipulability of genealogies to serve different ends.[60] Thus one should not expect the various manifestations of genealogical charters, as described above, to be identical from situation to situation. In a survey of recent work on the representation of social reality S. F. Moore has written:

> Established rules, customs, and symbolic frameworks exist, but they operate in the presence of areas of uncertainty, of ambiguity, of uncertainty and manipulability. Order never fully takes over, nor could it. The cultural, contractual, and technical imperatives always leave gaps, require adjustments and interpretations to be applicable to particular situations, and are themselves full of ambiguities, inconsistencies, and often contradictions.[61]

For these reasons any attempt at ascertaining the "original" form of Amorite royal genealogy has been and will always remain, a failure. The differences between the textual remains must be explained in terms of indeterminacy and manipulation. Social groups often require periodic reinforcements of ethnic or other identities, of the fictions which help to bend them together. It is therefore of little surprise that two of the three main ancient royal genealogies, the tablet with the "Genealogy of the Hammurabi Dynasty," as well as the royal ancestor lists from Ugarit, are encountered within the context of ritual offerings to deceased ancestors.[62] These factors also allow us to explain the relative scarcity of genealogical material from Mesopotamia for these are precisely the type of reinforcements which function on a practical level in

---

[54] J. T. Luke, *Pastoralism and Politics in the Mari Period* [Unpublished University of Michigan doctoral dissertation], 1965, 61.

[55] See D. O. Edzard, *Die "zweite Zwischenzeit"*, 104–08.

[56] M. Stol, *Studies . . .*, 86.

[57] A. Falkenstein, *Baghdader Mitteilungen* 2 (1963), 56–71, see note 33 above.

[58] CBS 1627, an unpublished tablet of uncertain contents, mentions Samsu-iluna and, in lines 8 and 9, ù šà mu l-a-ka 6 ugnim ma-da *am-na-an-ia-aḫ-ru-rum*. ki-ma-ke$_4$. The text is very poorly preserved and requires further study. I hope to provide a publication of this tablet in the near future.

[59] In Babylonia these two groupings gave their names to the separate settlements of Sippar-Amnanum and Sippar-Jahrurum. See D. O. Edzard, *Altbabylonische Rechts und Wirtschaftsurkunden aus Tell ed-Dēr im Iraq Museum, Baghdad*, 1970, 19–22.

[60] See, for example, C. Humphrey, "The Uses of Genealogy: A Historical Study of the Nomadic and Sedentarised Buryat," in *Pastoral Production and Society*, 1979, 235–60.

[61] S. F. Moore, "Epilogue: Uncertainties in Situations, Indeterminacies in Culture," in S. F. Moore and B. G. Myerhoff (eds.), *Symbol and Politics in Communal Ideology*, 1975, 220.

[62] J. C. De Moor, "Rapi'uma—Rephaim," *ZAW* 88 (1976), 323–45; K. A. Kitchen, "The King List of Ugarit," *Ugarit-Forschungen* 9 (1977), 131–42.

the society and not necessarily in the selective world of the scribes. Our data are, and will remain, incomplete not only because the available texts constitute the tip of an iceberg, but because they represent the top of only one small iceberg among many, the minute aspects of the society which were committed to writing.

APPENDIX

A New Fragment of the King List and the Problem of the Dynasty of Gutium

UM 29-15-199 is an upper right-hand fragment of a tablet which originally contained the whole text of the King List, most probably without the antediluvian section. The tablet was excavated in Nippur and is currently in the University Museum of the University of Pennsylvania in Philadelphia. The text, which was brought to my attention by Miguel Civil, is published by kind permission of Åke Sjöberg, curator of the Babylonian Section of the Museum.

The preserved portions of UM 29-15-199 contain the remnants of sections containing the Dynasty of Agade (i′) the Third Dynasty of Uruk (ii′), the Gutian Dynasty (iii′) and the Dynasty of Isin (rev. i). As far as I have been able to discern, this tablet does not join any of the presently known Nippur exemplars of the King List. In the edition which follows the numbers in parentheses refer to the line numbering of Jacobsen's standard edition; the section containing the Gutian kings is discussed separately below.

UM 29-15-199

Obverse
i′
1. [rí-m]u-⸢uš⸣ } (vi 37)
2. [dumu šar-r]u-GI
3. [9$^{?}$ mu] ⸢ì-ak⸣ (vi 38)
4. traces
Rest of column broken.

ii′
1. unug.ki-ga } (vii 15)
2. ur-nigin$_{3}$ lugal-àm
3. [x] mu ì-ak (vii 16)
4. [ur-giš.gigir d]umu ur-nigin$_{3}$-ke$_{4}$ (vii 17)
5. [x mu] ⸢ì-ak⸣ (vii 18)
6. traces
Rest of column broken.

iii′
1. si-lu-lu-e
2. 6 mu ì-ak
3. du$_{10}$-ga 6 mu ì-ak
4. i-lu-DINGIR mu 3 ì-ak
5. ia-ar-la-ga-ab
6. 5 mu ì-ak
7. [ku-r]u-um 3 mu ì-ak
8. [x x] x-um
9. [x x x mu ì]-ak
Rest of column broken.

Reverse
i
1′. i-si-in.[ki-šè ba-túm] (viii 22)
2′. i-si-in.ki-[na] } (viii 23)
3′. ^{d}iš-bi-è[r-ra]
4′. lugal-àm
5′. 33 mu ì-ak (viii 24)
6′. ^{d}šu-ì-lí-šu / dumu iš-bi-èr-ra-ke$_{4}$ (viii 25)
7′. 10 mu ì-ak (viii 26)
8′. ^{d}i-din-^{d}da-gan / dumu ^{d}šu-ì-lí-šu-ke$_{4}$ (viii 27)
9′. 21 mu ì-a[k] (viii 28)
10′. ^{d}iš-me-^{d}da-gan / dumu ^{d}i-din-^{d}da-gan (viii 29)
11′. 18 mu ì-ak (viii 30)
End of Column

From the fact that the remains of a vertical column separating two more columns are visible on the bottom of the reverse it is obvious that the text continued in the next column.

It is quite difficult to estimate the number of lines missing in columns ii′ and iii′. One can conservatively assume that each column had approximately thirty lines of text. The lines on the UM tablet are rather short and it is therefore hard to judge exactly how many names must be restored in the Gutian section since columns iii′ and i must have contained not only an unspecified number of Gutian rulers but also the reign of Utu-hegal, the Ur III kings, the beginning of the First Dynasty of Isin, as well as the formulas for each change of dynasty.

The new piece once again draws our attention to the impossibly complicated matter of the "Gutian Dynasty."[63] The only manuscript which contains a complete list of rulers of this dynasty is WB.[64] The other exemplars which have

[63] See W. W. Hallo, "Gutium" *RlA* 3 (1971), 707–20.

[64] The designations for the various manuscripts follow the usage of T. Jacobsen, *The Sumerian King List*, 1939; updated by D. O. Edzard, *RlA* 6 (1980), 77–8.

UM 29–15–199 obv.

UM 29–15–199 rev.

UM 29–15–199 right edge

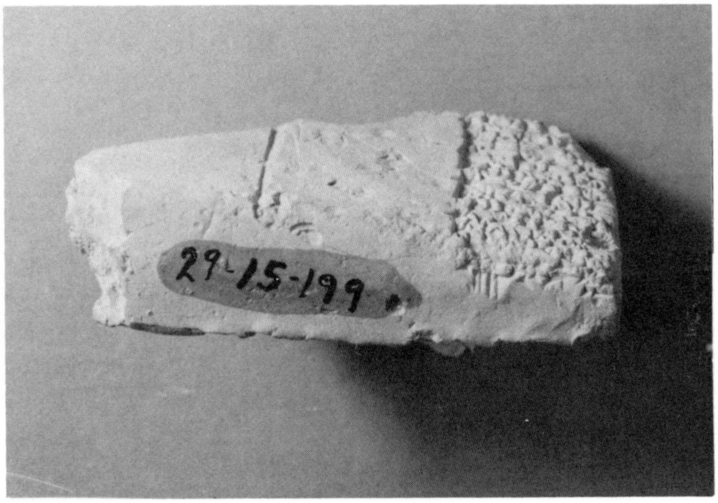

UM 29–15–199 lower edge

partially preserved fragments of this section do not agree with the names, their order, or length of reign, which are attested in WB. Moreover, the summaries preserved on some of the Nippur tablets of the King List indicate that the actual number of kings was different in each text.[65] The new piece edited above only adds to the confusion. The first preserved king, si-lu-lu in iii′ 1, is known only from WB, where he is the third ruler of the dynasty.[66] The next two kings of UM 29-15-199, du_{10}-ga and *i-lu*-DINGIR, are otherwise unattested. The next ruler, ia-ar-la-ga-ab, is to be identified with ia-ar-la-ga-ba, the second king in L_1 and ia-ar-la-gab, the seventh Gutian name in WB. *Ku-ru-um* is the tenth ruler of WB and the final traces of a name in the next line of the new text could represent any of the four kings of WB whose names end in /*um*/.

[65] These summaries have been edited by W. W. Hallo, *JCS* 17 (1963), 55–6.

[66] WB vii 33. The name of this king was formerly read as e-lu-lu. This text was collated by W. W. Hallo, who was kind enough to provide me with the results of his work, as well as by myself on the basis of an excellent photograph which I owe to the courtesy of M. Civil.

THE GRADUATED *ḤAṬṬĀʾT* OF LEVITICUS 5:1–13

JACOB MILGROM

UNIVERSITY OF CALIFORNIA, BERKELEY

THE *ḥaṭṭāʾt* SACRIFICE DESCRIBED IN GENERAL TERMS IN LEV. CH. 4 is also prescribed for the four specific cases of 5:1–13,[1] but with one major distinction: in ch. 4 the sacrifice is scaled according to the socio-religious status of the offender and in 5:1–13, according to his means. In addition to the commoner's standard offering of a female of the flock (i.e., goat or sheep; cf. 5:6 with 4:28, 32), second and third alternatives are allowed: birds (two turtledoves or two pigeons, 5:8) or choice flour (a tenth of an ephah, 5:11). A graduated *ḥaṭṭāʾt* is also prescribed upon recovery from leprosy[2] (14:10, 21–22), though here the flour option is eliminated.[3] There can be no question that all these instances represent an alleviation of the fixed *ḥaṭṭāʾt* ritual; birds and flour relative to livestock are cheap.[4] Why has the *ḥaṭṭāʾt* been mitigated in these cases?

Modern critics tend to regard 5:1–13 as the "poor man's" offering,[5] the option given to the offender of 4:27–35 who cannot afford the prescribed flock animal.[6] This interpretation, however, is beset with stylistic and contextual difficulties:

(1) *wĕnepeš kî* which begins ch. 5 does not continue 4:27–35, where *wĕʾim* is twice used (vv 27, 32), but introduces a new case, thus corresponding to the general introduction to the *ḥaṭṭāʾt*, 4:2aβ,b.[7]

(2) A key condition of the *ḥaṭṭāʾt* is missing: the violation of a prohibitive commandment (4:2, 13, 22, 27, 32).[8]

(3) The sacrifice of ch. 5 is called *ʾāšām*, "reparation" (5:6,7)[9] and confession is required (5:5), terms not used in ch. 4 at all.

(4) Most decisively, the antecedents of *ʾaḥat mēʾēlleh* "any of these matters" (5:13; cf. vv 4b, 5a)[10] can only be the specific and discrete cases of vv 1–4 and not ch. 4 which deals only with one general case.

(5) The ideological objections are equally as strong. In 5:1–4 the requirement of inadvertence (root *šgg*), indispensable to the *ḥaṭṭāʾt*,[11] is absent. In vv 2–4, for example, it makes no difference whether the impurity contracted or the oath uttered was deliberate or not, and v 1, which speaks of the deliberate witholding of evidence, allows for no inadvertence at all. Furthermore, the *ḥaṭṭāʾt* is limited to violations of prohibitive commandments (*miṣwōt YHWH ʾăšer lōʾ tēʿāśênâ*, 4:2, 13, 22, 27). No such violation, however, occurs here. Contracting impurity is not prohibited and the requirement to cleanse oneself of impurity, even when it stipulates sanctions, (e.g., Num 19:13, 20), is not a

---

[1] Because the preponderance of biblical citations are from the book of Leviticus, they will appear henceforth just by chapter and verse.

[2] The translation "leprosy" for *ṣāraʿat* is only a convenient handle to indicate a variety of skin diseases. Cf. R. K. Harrison, *IDB*, s.v. Leprosy.

[3] The parturient is allowed a scaled *ʿōlâ* offering (12:8; cf. *m. Ker.* 2:4; *b. Ker.* 10b [*bar.*]).

[4] It is not known exactly when pigeons were domesticated; our sources stem from the second Temple. But the occurrence of the dove in both the biblical and Babylonian flood story and its frequent presence as a cult object in Canaanite Palestine, e.g., Nahariya, Beth Shean, Gezer, Tell Beth-Mirṣim make its early domestication and, hence, availability a plausible surmise.

[5] Cf. the most recent treatments: R. Rendtorff, *Studien zur Geschichte des Opfers im alten Israel*, 1967, 207–10. K. Elliger, *Leviticus*, 1966, 74f.; M. Noth, *Leviticus*, 1965, 45; R. de Vaux, *Ancient Israel*, 419–21, and *Studies in Old Testament Sacrifice*, 1964, 92; N. H. Snaith, "The Sin-Offering and the Guilt-Offering," *VT* 15 (1965), 73–80.

[6] The rite arose out of "die armseligen Verhältnisse der proletarisierten und verstäderten nachexilischen Gemeinde" according to Elliger, ad loc.

[7] So *inter alia* in chs. 1–5; 1:2b; 2:1; 5:15, 21.

[8] Correctly noted in *b Hor.* 8b.

[9] For the meaning, see J. Milgrom, *Cult and Conscience*, 1976, 6.

[10] Probably 4bβ is to be deleted as a dittography of 5aβ.

[11] See J. Milgrom, "The Cultic *šegāgâ* and its Influence in Psalms and Job," *JQR* 58 (1967), 115–25.

prohibitive but a performative commandment, thus falling out of the purview of the *ḥaṭṭā᾿t*. Clearly this solution will not do.

Later rabbinic tradition takes a different direction. It distinguishes between the sacrifices of ch. 4 and 5:1–13. It never even refers to the latter as *ḥaṭṭā᾿t* but by an entirely separate title, *ᶜôleh wĕyôrēd*, "a scaled offering" (lit. "ascending and descending") which ignores its *ḥaṭṭā᾿t* status and concentrates on its graduated nature. The rabbis, however, interpolate the condition of *ṭûm᾿at miqdāš wĕqādāšāyw*, to wit: having forgotten his state of impurity, the offender enters the sanctuary or comes into contact with sancta.[12] While this rabbinic thesis correctly identifies the graduated *ḥaṭṭā᾿t* as a discrete sacrificial category, its additional qualification that it is brought for "the defilement of the sanctuary and its sancta" cannot be accepted as a critical solution, for the following reasons: (1) The direct contact of impurity with holiness is explicitly banned elsewhere (e.g., 7:20–21; 12:4; 22:3–7) and the punishment is altogether different: excision.[13] (2) 5:3 speaks solely of those who are secondarily infected "when a person touches," implying that those who are primary sources (e.g., the gonorrheic and leper) are excluded;[14] however, contact with sancta suffers no such distinction (cf. 7:20–21). (3) The condition of "the defilement of the sanctuary and its sancta" through contact is plainly eisegesis; it is nowhere expressed.

My own hypothesis is herewith submitted: The graduated *ḥaṭṭā᾿t* is a distinct sacrificial category. It is enjoined for failure or inability to cleanse impurity upon its incurrence. Thus "the sin of which he is guilty" (5:6, 10, 13) is not the contraction of impurity but its *prolongation*. This study will concentrate on 5:2–3, cases of impurity by contact; vv 1 and 4 concerning impurity arising from oaths will be treated on another occasion. The relevant verses, with explanatory comment in parentheses, read as follows:

[2]Or when a person touches any impure thing—be it the carcass of an impure beast (11:27) or the carcass of impure cattle (11:26) or the carcass of an impure swarming thing (either fish, reptile or insect, 11:10, 20, 29–31 respectively)—and, though he has become impure,[15] the fact escapes him but (thereafter) he feels guilt;[16]

[3]Or when he touches human impurity—any such impurity whereby one becomes impure (chs. 12–15; Num. 19)—and, though he has known it,[15] the fact escapes him but (thereafter) he feels guilt;[16]

My hypothesis predicates a redefinition of the term *ḥaṭṭā᾿t*. It cannot and should not be translated "sin offering."[17] Considering the range of its usage, it has nothing to do with sin (the examples already cited specify *recovery* from gonorrhea, childbirth, leprosy). Its meaning is adumbrated by the phrase "waters of *ḥaṭṭā᾿t*" in Num. 8:7 which can only refer to a purifying function. It is a *piel* denominative with "un sens privatif"[18] and can only mean: decontaminate, remove a sin, cleanse (e.g., 8:14–15). "Purification offering" is, therefore, the more accurate rendering.[19]

Our semasiological observation produces an immediate dividend. The *ḥaṭṭā᾿t*, now understood as a purification ritual, immediately invokes the cultic world of the ancient Near East in which purifications play a ubiquitous and obsessive role. The ancients had reason to fear impurity; it was for them the realm of divine evil and alive with malignant power. Moreover,

---

[12] Cf. *m. Šebu.* 1:4–6; *m. Ker.* 2:4; Philo, *Laws* III, §205 (Loeb VII, 603) where this interpretation is implied.

[13] *Kārēt*. For our purposes S. R. Driver's definition will suffice: "death through divine agency, not punishment inflicted at the hands of the community," *Leviticus*, 1898, 69 on 7:21. So indeed, 15:31b and 20:4f., but cf. D. W. Zimmerli, "Die Eigenart der prophetischen Rede des Ezechiel," *ZAW* 66 (1954), 1–26, esp. pp. 9–19.

[14] Since the original carrier of impurity (e.g., the gonorrheic or leper) has the flux, he is always conscious of it and cannot plead temporary amnesia (see below).

[15] *ṭāmē᾿* and in v 3 *yādaᶜ* are perfects between waw consecutives, thrusting this action into the past, correctly rendered by *Tg. Ps.-Jon.*; cf. M. Greenberg, *Introduction to Hebrew*, 1965, §16:2 (p. 75). Further, the addition of the personal pronoun only emphasizes that herein is the critical point: he had knowingly become impure and should have cleansed himself.

[16] cf. n. 9.

[17] So all the versions and all other translations, old and new, we have examined: e.g., *NEB*, *JB* (Jerusalem Bible), *KJV*, *ERV*, *ASV*, *RSV*, *JPS*, *NJPS*, *SB* (La Sainte Bible), *ATD* (Das Alte Testament Deutsch), *HAT*, *HKAT*.

[18] Cf. P. Joüon, *Grammaire de l'Hébreu Biblique*, 1965, §52:d, (p. 118); *Gesenius-Kautzch-Cowley*, 1910, §52:h, (p. 142).

[19] Note the striking passage 14:18–20 where of all the sacrifices listed only the purification offering explicitly purges impurity. Other proofs and implications are discussed in J. Milgrom, "Sin-Offering or Purification-Offering?" *VT* 21 (1971), 149–56.

its force was so powerful and pervasive it could even threaten the gods[20] and penetrate their sanctuaries, necessitating that the latter be purified regularly.[21]

The Priestly source is still anchored in this cultic framework even though the polytheistic elements have been expunged. Impurity is always a threat to God's holiness, especially to His earthly presence within His shrine. Thus Molech worship is forbidden for it defiles "My sanctuary" (20:3); the corpse-defiled who fails to purify himself "has defiled the Lord's sanctuary" (Num 19:20, also v 13); similarly, those with discharges, "lest they die in their impurity by defiling My tabernacle which is among them" (15:31); and the latter two and the leper are banished, according to Num 5:2–3, "that they do not defile the camp of those in whose midst I dwell."

The verses cited above regarding the leper, corpse-defiled, gonorrheic and Molech worshipper, whose mere existence defiles the camp and the sanctuary, should suffice to demonstrate that the sanctuary can be defiled even when impurity is not brought "into contact" with it and that the devitalization of impurity, even in the Priestly source, is not complete. The restriction of dangerous and, hence, punishable impurity to cases of contact with sancta, as we shall see, is the goal of P and not its accomplishment.

It is an earlier stage, I submit, that forms the backdrop of 5:2–3. Here, however, it is no longer sinful to contract impurity, be its source animal (5:2, cf. ch. 11) or human (5:3 and above). Cadavers and fluxes are baneful not because their impurity is imparted to an Israelite but only if it remains on his person. Unless he purifies himself at once, he jeopardizes the welfare of the sanctuary (or camp, see below).[22]

For the willful neglect of purification, the explicit penalty for the corpse-defiled is *kārēt* (Num 19:13, 20)[23] and for the carcass-defiled is *wĕnāśāʾ ʿăwōnô* (17:15–16) which can be shown to mean the same.[24] The implication is clear: punishment is incurred only when the impurity remains uncleansed but not initially when it is contracted. This precisely is the supposition of our verses, 5:2–3.

The more lenient requirement of the graduated purification offering can now readily be explained. Incurring impurity is not a punishable misdemeanor. But delay in purification is dangerous and severely punishable. Our cases, therefore, postulate accidental neglect: "the fact escaped him." Nonetheless, the impurity which he contracted has built up sufficient force to contaminate the sanctuary. It is no longer enough to purify himself by washing. He must assume the responsibility of purifying the sanctuary. However, since the impurity did not arise from the violation of a prohibition (which would require a fixed animal, ch. 4), any *ḥaṭṭāʾt* will do—whatever the offender can afford.

The remaining peculiarities of the graduated purification offering, raised at the beginning of our dis-

---

[20] Examples selected from *ANET*: *Egyptian*—The Repulsing of the Dragon and the Creation, 6f.; The Repulsing of the Dragon, 12; The God and His Unknown Name of Power, 12–4; Curses and Threat, 327 (section b); Religious drama in Egypt, 229f; also see H. H. Nelson "Certain Reliefs at Karnak and Medinet Habu," *JNES* 8 (1949) 201–32, 310–45. *Hittite*—Ritual for the Purification of God and Man, 346; Evocatio, 351–3. *Mesopotamian*—The New Year's Ritual, 331–4, esp. ll. 381f.; Temple Kettle-Drum, 334–8, ll. 14–16; Enuma Elish, 60–72: I, 61–64; IV, 61f., 91; VII, 32f.; Ishtar's Descent to the Nether World, 107: 9: obv. 33–36; 54f. Also cf. R. C. Thompson, *The Devils and Evil Spirits of Babylonia,* I, 1903, 3:65ff., 180ff.; B:46ff.; esp. K:45–49, 60–69, etc.

[21] Examples from *ANET*: *Egyptian*—The Daily Ritual in the Temple, 325, III; Religious Drama in Egypt, 329f. Egyptian temples had protector images and their gods had personal bodyguards. See also A. Moret, *Le Rituel du Culte Divin Journalier en Égypte,* 1902, 95–7; H. H. Nelson (n.20), esp. Episode 30 and figs. 22 and 23. *Hittite*—346; 351–3; 357f. *Mesopotamian*—331–4; 334–8: l. 16; 338f.; Thompson, *The Devils,* II, 3:71; H. W. F. Saggs, *The Greatness That was Babylon,* 1962, 302f., 313–6. *Israel*—Lev 16; Ezek 43:18–27; for Num 28–29, see no. 6, below.

[22] The theology of this dynamic, areal impurity which pollutes the sanctuary regardless of where in the camp it is present is detailed in J. Milgrom, "Israel's Sanctuary: The Priestly 'Picture of Dorian Gray'," *RB* 83 (1976), 390–9. That the prolongation of impurity was considered dangerous even in rabbinic times is clear from *Jos. Ant. 3:267; m. ʿErub,* 10:15a.

[23] Cf. n. 13.

[24] The difference between the two cases is only one of time. 5:2–3 realizes the warning of 17:15–16: the impurity has accidentally been prolonged. 17:15–16 speaks of eating and omits touching (as 5:2–3) because of the context of the chapter whose main theme is the eating of flesh and blood; cf. J. Milgrom, "A Prolegomenon to Leviticus 17:11," *JBL* 90 (1971), 149–56. For *wĕnāśāʾ ʿăwōnô* (cf. 5:1) as equivalent to *kārēt*, see Zimmerli (n. 13), 9–19; Elliger (n. 5), 73.

cussion, are also given a simple explanation. (1) It is now obvious why 5:2–3 says nothing about inadvertence; since no prohibition was violated, it makes absolutely no difference whether the impurity was contracted deliberately or inadvertently. (2) The reason that only the secondarily infected ("he who touches") is allowed a graduated purification offering but not the primary carrier of human impurity (e.g., the gonorrheic) is that the latter cannot plead temporary amnesia, i.e., "the fact escapes him"; he is the bearer of the flux and is surely conscious of it. (3) That 5:2–3 was drawn up for non-prohibited occurrences of impurity is underscored by the use of the term *ʾāšām* (5:6), in its non-sacrificial, civil connotation of "penalty" or "fine"; it could never be used in ch. 4 where the violation of a prohibition has given rise to severe impurity. (4) Confession is required because the impurity may have been contracted deliberately[25] in contrast to the impurity created by the cases given in ch. 4 which are all inadvertences. (5) Finally, the two other instances where the graduated offerings are prescribed, the leper and the new mother upon their recovery, also turn out to be cases where the onset of impurity is not prohibited and its prolongation cannot be prevented. This is the reason, that despite the severity of the impurity involved,[26] a less costly purification procedure is allowed.[27]

Having noted that the Rabbis postulated the graduated purification offering as a distinct sacrificial category, it is well to ask how they could have insisted with equal unanimity that it was restricted to cases of direct contact with sancta, a condition, we have seen, is legislated by P in an entirely different manner. Our way out of this dilemma necessitates first a diachronic reordering of our materials on impurity, albeit in sketchy form. Three stages are reflected:

A. In the pre-biblical stage all sancta communicate holiness to persons, the inner sancta directly by sight and indirectly by touch (e.g. Num 4:15, 18–20). This contagion is lethal even if the contact is accidental. The early biblical narratives exemplify the deadly power of the sancta in the Ark (1 Sam 6:19; 2 Sam 6:6–8),[28] Mt. Sinai (Exod 19:13) and the divine fire (10:1–5). True, there are no biblical texts which attribute an equivalent power to impurity. However, one must reckon with the possibility that there was a time when holiness and impurity were both polaric and interchangeable; note that the bones of the dead defile but those of Elisha resurrect the dead (2 Kgs 13:21).[29]

B. In the Bible, impurity has been thoroughly eviscerated of any mythological or demonic content. Contracting impurity can bring no harm, *per se*; but it dare not be brought into contact with sancta[30] nor, as I have demonstrated, be allowed to persist in the community. P's material, however, is not of the same hue. Two sub-stages come into view when we examine three primary causes of human defilement: leprosy, pathological flux, and the corpse.

(1) The earlier stratum is reflected in Num 5:2–3 which calls for their banishment (also the corpse-defiled in Num 31:19, 24). Here God's presence is co-extensive with the entire camp.[31] This statute is in full accord with the deuteronomic imperative "let your camp be holy" (Deut 23:10–15).

---

[25] Indeed, all deliberate sins against God which are repented require confession for their expiation, *Cult and Conscience* (n. 9), pp. 106–21.

[26] Indicated by such criteria as length and elaborateness of purification rite, e.g., 40 or 80 days for the new mother and four different kinds of offerings for the leper.

[27] As for the remaining impurity cases: the gonorrheic brings birds—the cheapest animal; the corpse-defiled brings no sacrifice at all but is sprinkled with purificatory waters; those secondarily infected by touch, portage, consumption—simple lustration. Again, for all the aforementioned, there is no prohibition against contracting the impurity and no economic amelioration is needed since little or no expense is involved.

[28] Holiness also undergoes diachronic reduction, see J. Milgrom, "Sancta Contagion and Altar/City Asylum," *SVT* 32 (1981), 278–310.

[29] From the plethora of instances we will focus on the example of violating (lit. "eating") taboo: *Shurpu* (ed. E. Reiner [Graz, 1958]) II, 5, 69, 95, 102f.; IV, 4; *Lipshur Litanies* (E. Reiner, *JNES* 15 [1956], 3:129–40) I, 83, 86–88; Prayer to Every God, *ANET*, 400f., ll. 14, 16.

[30] Naturally, the most grievous and terrifying impurity in the ancient Near Eastern world is direct contamination of sancta, e.g., *CT* 32:2 "an unclean person has come near the sacrifice"; Omen text: "if a snake regularly lies across the entrance of the temple gate, an unclean person will enter the temple," *KAR* 384:10 (*CAD ellu* A, 106).

[31] In second Temple days only the leper was put out of the community. The corpse-defiled and gonorrheic were allowed to remain but they were distinguished in regard to their access to the Temple mount; thus the Rabbis were forced to interpret Num 5:2–3 as referring to 3 distinct camps; *b. Pesaḥ* 67a.

(2) The remaining legislation dealing with these three human impurity carriers reveals a later stratum. Banishment is decreed only for the leper. The gonorrheic and corpse-defiled, though they still jeopardize the community (15:31; Num 19:13, 20), are no longer excluded during their defilement.[32] The stringent demands of holiness for the entire camp[33] are now confined to the sanctuary. Significantly, it is precisely the gonorrheic and corpse-defiled, now permitted to remain in the community, who are warned about their danger to the sanctuary (15:31; Num 19:13, 20). Lev 17:15–16 holds out punishment for the one who neglects to purify himself after he eats of what has died or has been torn by beasts. This law is unique to P and the Bible.[34] It is the counterpart of 5:2 and also reflects the fear that procrastination in cleansing impurity may lead to its spread.[35]

C. The third and final reduction in the power of impurity is the rabbinic stage which limits its evil effects to actual contact with sancta. Otherwise there is no longer any sin in remaining impure. This stage is post-biblical but it is clearly adumbrated by the following direction signs within the Priestly source itself:

(1) As we have seen, the corpse-defiled and gonnorrheic have been permitted to stay at home.

(2) There is no longer any penalty for failing to undergo purification after eating or touching impure food.[36] Indeed, in the case of touching the cadavers of permitted animals there is no prohibition either (11:39–40).[37]

(3) The distinction between the sanctuary precinct and the rest of the camp is clearly made in 12:2–3. A second period of purification is enjoined for the new mother wherein contact with sancta alone is proscribed.

(4) Nonetheless, as implied by the preceding and 7:20–21; 22:3, dire consequences follow in the wake of contact between the holy and the impure.

Normative Judaism reflected in tannaitic legislation completes the skein:

(5) The last traces of air-borne impurity now require contact and, moreover, are punishable only if there is contact with sancta.[38] This has already been observed in the rabbinic interpretation of (a) the corpse-defiled (Num 19:13, 20) despite the clear statement of the text to the contrary, and (b) the cadaver-defiled (17:15–16) where there is no mention whatsoever of sancta. Thus,

---

[32] Num 19:18 implies quarantine within the home until the week of purification is complete; see J. Milgrom "The Paradox of the Red Cow," *VT* 21 (1981), 62–72; so also 15:13, esp. 26a "while her discharge lasts." CD 12:1f. and Jos. *Wars* V, 5:6 state that the gonorrheic was excluded from the city of Jerusalem not just from the Temple mount, as taught by rabbinic Judaism (*m. Kel.* 1:8). According to C. Rabin, *The Zadokite Documents,* 1954, 59 n. 2, the stricter rule applied only to pilgrims as a "fence" regulation. However, the Temple Scroll shows that all impurity bearers were barred from Jerusalem (11QTemple 45–47).

[33] Continence, at times, was added to the demands, Exod 19:14–15; Josh 3:15, especially in times of war, 1 Sam 21:6; 2 Sam 11:11 (David's more lenient attitude conforms with Deut 23:10–12).

[34] Contact with animal impurities (eating, touching and carrying) is prohibited by ch. 11 (but not with carcasses of permitted animals!) but penalties are nowhere prescribed. Cf. below and n. 37.

[35] The two sub-stages in human defilement, shown above, have their counterpart in animal impurities. 17:15–16 seems a later stage since it no longer distinguishes between the cadavers of pure and impure animals as do 5:2 and 7:21; it can be shown that 11:39–40 is an appendix to the diet laws.

[36] Contrast Mesopotamian and Hittite religions, n. 29. The Rabbis even follow up the implications of 7:19 that no sin is committed if impure sacrificial flesh is consumed by one who is pure (cf. *Zebaḥ.* 13:2). Thus the elimination of dangerous impurity in the animal kingdom is complete. Impure carrion can never require sacrificial expiation or incur severe penalties. Only the reverse, impure men must beware of contact with sancta.

[37] This is only reasonable. The cadavers are probably of one's own flock and herd and if their owner will not handle them, who else will? The eight species of "swarming things" are similarly exempt (cf. 11:31), for they are household pests and most likely to fall into kitchen utensils. But contact with the cadavers of all other impure animals is explicitly prohibited (11:8, 11, 41–42).

[38] *t. Šebu.* 1:5. Communicability of impurity without contact still remains the property of the human corpse through "overshadowing," based on Num 19:14. But its cases are severely restricted (*m. Ohol.* 3:2, 6). Num 19:15, in turn, is confined to earthenware which if closed protects itself and its contents (*Sipra*, Shemini, Par. 7:6). Moreover, impurity transmitted directly by vessels (11:32) is restricted to priestly (excluding levitical) dues (*Sipra*, Shemini, end of ch. 8; *b. Yeb.* 75a). Yet the fear of impurity prolongation and spread still survives (e.g. *m. Erub.* 10:15). Josephus actually cites a ruling (unknown from any source) which postulates it: a corpse-contaminated person who neglects to purify himself during the ensuing week must bring the sacrificial expiation required of a gonorrheic (*Ant.* III, 11:3 [Loeb IV, 445]).

we find the graduated purification offering of 5:2–3 enjoined for both cases (a) and (b) despite the contradictions we have noted.[39]

One last step. There is complete agreement among the Rabbis that the basic purpose of all festival purification offerings is to expiate for "the defilement of the sanctuary and its sancta" (*m. Šebu.* 1:3–5).[40] Herein lies corroboration that the common ground for all impurity taboos is the fear that impurity may impinge upon the realm of the holy. The Sages, however, by their exegesis have even further reduced the functional area of the public *ḥaṭṭāʾt* to sancta contamination by direct contact.

Thus, the analysis of ritual impurity presupposed by the graduated purification offering allows us to trace the development of a major religious concept over the entire life-span of ancient Israel. The biblical and rabbinic ages are shown to be a single historical continuum in which the progressive reduction of the force of impurity leaves its traces at every stage. The tannaitic legislation is only the end product of a process already at work in biblical days.

The motivating force behind this historical development is not difficult to discern. It is the working of the monotheistic idea. For the pagan, impurity is the domain of supernal evil that threatens the deities as well as man. But under the rule of one God, independent evil cannot exist. Pagan notions of impurity have to go. The baneful still inheres in things but it spreads only under special conditions, e.g., carrion when consumed and discharges when contracted. These, however, are called impurities and are not confused with evils.[41] But as long as impurity is conceived as miasma and allowed to spread invisibly, from afar as well as by touch, it is but a small step to its personification and autonomy. The danger ever persists that notions of demonic evil—affirmed by the surrounding religions during the same millennium—will be retained or reassimilated. The activity of impurity is then restricted to cases of contact,[42] and the cases where purification has been neglected (and a graduated purification sacrifice rather than ablution is enjoined) are further restricted to those in which contact with sancta has occurred.

Finally, the evolution of the graduated purification offering allows us to suggest an answer to the paradox of the Rabbis' exegesis which we initially raised: they recognized the graduated purification offering as a distinct sacrificial category and, on the other hand, they qualified it by the criterion of "the defilement of the sanctuary and its sancta." Of course, the Rabbis did not create the paradox; they only inherited it. The limitation of the concept of active impurity to cases of contact with sancta had taken place long before. It did not come about by the innovation of a reformer. It had no single originator nor did it need one. It was the logical and irrevocable terminus of the monotheistic process and it became oral tradition at an early age.[43]

---

[39] The graduated purification offering requires knowledge of the defilement before and after the onset of forgetfulness, according to the Rabbis (and the plain sense of 5:2–3). But, they add, if there is no awareness at the beginning, i.e., if the offender has both contracted and borne the impurity unknowingly, only the Day of Atonement can expiate his wrong (*m. Šebu.* 1:3). In my opinion, the tradition is correct; the underlying assumption is that the damage is done, the sanctuary has been defiled and must be purged before the unconscious wrong can be expiated.

[40] This is the uncontested opinion of Rabbis Simeon b. Yohai, Meir, Simeon b. Judah, and the school of R. Ishmael, cf. *m. Šebu.* 1:4–5; *t. Šebu.* 9a. The Day of Atonement offerings are also included, following 16:16, 19, "of the impurities," but the scapegoat is excepted, *m. Šebu.* 1:6–7, and in keeping with 16:21, "all the iniquities."

[41] Deuteronomy alone uses the term evil (23:10; cf. 15:21; 17:1) but the original meaning has been transformed. Elsewhere the Deuteronomist uses the term *dābār raʿ* figuratively (e.g., Deut 13:12; 17:5; 19:20). Elsewhere in the ancient Near East, impurities are indistinguishable from evil. Examples from the Assyrian *Bît Rimki* ritual will suffice, Cf. J. Laessøe, *Studies in the Assyrian Ritual and Series bît rimki,* 1955, 40: 51–52 (*w*)*aršu* // *HUL* (=limnu cf. ll. 32, 33); 58:90, 92 *lilanni* // *lumni litbal.* Thus, "evil" // "impurity" and "purify me" // "remove my evil." For stylistic and contextual parallelism with the *Maqlû* texts, cf. p. 47, n. 115.

[42] For the exception of the human corpse see n. 38.

[43] This is certainly attested by the pseudepigraphal and Dead Sea literature. Compare *CD* 5:6–7 with *Pss. Sol.* 8:12–13 (ed. H. E. Ryle and M. R. James, [1891], 78f.), where both passages deal with the violation of 15:31–32. If "the sanctuary" does not actually refer to sacred things rather than the temple building (as seems probable in the *Psalms*, cf. 1:8, 2:3), it reflects the rabbinic exegesis of 15:31, i.e., defiling the sanctuary by entering it; cf. *CD* 11:20.

NOTES ON THE HYMN TO MARDUK IN *LUDLUL BĒL NĒMEQI*

WILLIAM L. MORAN
HARVARD UNIVERSITY

The business of him that republishes an ancient book is, to correct what is corrupt, and to explain what is obscure. Samuel Johnson

TO ANOTHER SAMUEL, DEAN OF THOSE ENGAGED IN THE BUSINESS OF REPUBLISHING the most ancient literature of the world, these few notes of correction and explanation are gratefully presented.

With the publication of ND 5485 by D. J. Wiseman virtually the entire hymn to Marduk with which *Ludlul bēl nēmeqi* begins, is now recovered.[1] It turns out to contain forty lines, which are divided into three parts, each introduced by a first person precative form of the verb: *ludlul*, "I will praise" (1); *lušāpi*, "I will proclaim" (37); *lušalmid*, "I will have (someone) learn" (39).[2] The first and by far the longest part might be called objective, for it hymns the wrath and mercy of Marduk without specific reference to the speaker (1–36). Then, in a single couplet, we hear of the speaker's own experience of this wrath and mercy (37–38). And, finally, the speaker announces his intention to provide the people with instruction in the worship of Marduk (39–40).

The hymn is an eloquent and, in many ways, remarkable document of the Marduk religion of the late second millennium, and we must be grateful to Wiseman for having made it available. There remain, however, a number of problems of reading and interpretation that must be considered before the larger issues of the bearing of the hymn on the interpretation of the work as a whole and of the religious context of the work can be securely discussed. These problems are the subject of these notes.

I 2//4 There are three mss. for these lines: A = K 9810 (*BA* 5, 389–390; *BWL*, pl. 74) + K 9392 (photo; join by W. G. Lambert); B = VAT 10522 (*LKA* 24); C = ND 5485.

A 2	[*e*]-*ziz mu-ši*	*mu-pa-šîr*	[*urru*]
B	[ ] *mu-ši*	*mu-pa-áš-š*[*ir*	*urru*]
C	[ ]	*mu-up-pa-šîr*	[*urru*]
A 4	[*e*⌉-*ziz mu-ši*	*mu-pa-šîr*	[*urru*]
B	[*e-z*]*i-iz mu-ši*	*mu-pa-áš-šir*	*ur-r*[*u*]
C	[ ]	*mu-up-pa-šìr*	*ur-r*[*u*/*ri*]

Enraged in the night, in the daylight calming.[3]

Two readings of the beginning of the lines have been proposed: A [*mu-ṣa*]-bít // [*mu-ṣ*]*a*-bít (var. B, [*mu-ṣa-bi*]-tu), "who lays hold on the night" (*BWL*, 343; also *ANET*, 596); or A [*mu-šá*]-*ziz* // [*mu*]-*šá-ziz* (var. B, [*mu-šá-z*]*i-iz*), "der die Nacht grimmig . . . macht" (R. Borger, *JCS* 18 [1964], 51; also R. Labat, *Les religions du Proche-Orient* [Paris, 1970], 329; *AHw*, 1555, sub *ezēzu*).

Against both are considerations of space. In A, there is certainly not enough room for *mu*-. This is

---

[1] *AnSt* 30 (1980), 102–7.

[2] Cf. the first three strophes of Tablet II where, as recognized by Erica Reiner, *Altorientalische Literaturen* [Neues Handbuch der Literaturwissenschaft Band I], 1978, 196, each begins with a first singular preterite form of the verb (*asḫur-ma*, 2; *āmur-ma*, 11; *aḫsus-ma*, 23). I would suggest, however, that the third strophe is not 26 lines (23–48), but 13, followed by another strophe of 13. Strophe IV (36–48), 36 *ayyû . . . qereb šamê ilammad*, 48 *ana . . . qerebšina lā altamda*; cf. Strophe II (11–22) 11 *āmur-ma*, 22 (last words) *anāku amrāk*.

[3] The translation exploits the ambiguity of English "to calm" (transitive and intransitive), and therefore covers both *mupaššir* and *muppašir* (see below). It is both gratifying and reassuring to note the version of J. Bottéro, which, as he kindly informs me, he came to, not from a new reading, but from a sense of the demands of context: "Qui s'irrite la nuit, mais se calme le jour venu" (*Recherches et Documents du Centre Thomas More*, Document 77/7, 11).

clear from the copies of both Hehn and Lambert (cf. the position of *mu* at the beginning of line 8) and is confirmed by collation.[4] In B, Dr. Liane Jakob-Rost, whose collations I gratefully acknowledge, says of the space before *z*]*i-iz*, "Nach der Tafelkrümmung zu urteilen, kann kaum mehr als ein Zeichen fehlen."

Read [*e*]-*ziz* // [*e*⌉-*ziz*, var. [*e-z*]*i-iz*. Remarks: 1. Hehn's *šá* may be safely disregarded, as there is no other evidence of the tablet's having suffered damage since his time, and he almost certainly saw no more than Lambert did (see copy). 2. The possibility of a preceding *mu* removed, *šá* leads nowhere. 3. The bound-form *eziz* is comparable to the "strong" forms that appear in the predicate state of adjectives with reduplicated final radical (*GAG*, §101 d). 4. If, as seems very probable, I 1//3 ends *ilu muštālu*, cf. especially *En.el.* VI 137 where Marduk as ᵈMir-šà-kúš-ù is *eziz u muštāl sabus u tayyār*, "he is angry but judicious, wroth but forgiving." 5. The contrast in 2//4 (ʾ*zz-pšr*) has a number of parallels:

a. "Merciful Marduk" is *ēzi u pašir*, "is angry but (then) calm" (*Šurpu* VIII 3, text B; also Hehn, *BA* 5, 391:10, cited by Erica Reiner, *AfO, Beiheft* 11, 59). Reiner also cites the MB personal name ᵐēz-u-p̌asir-ana-ardi-ᵈmarduk (*BE* 14, 151:17), and the later name, ᵐēz(i/u-u)-pašir (for references see Reiner, and add *Bagh. Mitt.* 5, 225, n. 40, and *AHw*, 1555, sub *ezû*), which is borne by several people.[5]

b. The well-known šu-ila to Marduk begins: ¹ *qarrādu* ᵈ*marduk ša ezēssu abūbu* ² *napšuršu abu rēmēnû*, "Warrior Marduk, whose anger is a deluge, whose calming (forgiving) is (that of) a merciful father" (Ebeling, *Handerhebung*, 72:1–2, also cited by Reiner; on the citation in *ABL*, 719 rev. 25–26, in which *naplussu* replaces *napšuršu*, see W. von Soden, *Iraq* 31 [1969], 83).

c. In two reports on the activity of Marduk as Jupiter: *apkallu igigallu* ᵈ*bēl rēmēnû qarrād* ᵈ*marduk ina mūši īzuz* (var. *īziz*)-*ma ina šēri ittapšar*, "The sage, sapient one, merciful Bel, warrior Marduk, became angry in the night and then at dawn has calmed" (Thompson *Rep.* 170:4-rev. 1 = Weidener, *OLZ* 1913, 205:1–5).[6] Here, besides the *ezēzu-napšuru* contrast, also paralleling I 2//4 is the assignment of Marduk's wrath and mercy to their respective times in the day. We should add that Dr. Jakob-Rost's collation confirmed the accuracy of the copy in *LKA* 24 of the end of line 4, also kindly providing her own copy, which is even clearer than that of *LKA* 24. Read, therefore, *ur-r*[*u*], not *ur-p*[*í*] (*AHw*, 843; 1432).

d. That Marduk's wrath, almost certainly by night, yields to his calming by day is also found in *bēlu* // ᵈ*marduk uggugka k*[*i-ma . . . ina mūši*], *urra napšurka še-z*[*u . . .*], "Lord // Marduk, your fury is like . . . in the night, In the daylight your calming . . ." (Lambert, *AfO* 19, 64:80ff.).[7]

In I 2//4, it will have been noted, the ʾ*zz-pšr* contrast appears in two forms: *mupaššir* (B) and *muppašir* (C), besides A's ambiguous *mu-pa-šìr*. Both readings can be explained as departures from norms to achieve greater expressiveness. As an active form *mupaššir* departs from the normal N medio-passive in the established *ezēzu-napšuru* contrast.[8] It compels attention, and by leaving us to supply the object it also creates a rich ambiguity. The indefiniteness allows us to think not only of Marduk's wrath but of the "loosening" of other things as well—the sins that provoke wrath, the clutch of demon, disease and pain, the tangle of troubling dreams. Or does *mupaššir urru* depart even further from expectations and make *urru*, not, as the parallelism with adverbial *mūši* leads one to expect, also adverbial, but object, the day cleared and the cloudless a symbol of Marduk's mercy (see below)?

A truly radical departure from the norm is *muppašir*, which presents us with the normal and expected conjugation in a very abnormal and most unexpected form. The participle of medio-passive *napšuru* should

[4] From photo. C. B. F. Walker, to whom I am indebted for much help, also collated the line, and he concurs in excluding *mu-*. W. G. Lambert also checked the tablet and agrees on the possibility of reading simply *e-ziz*, raising, however, questions of interpretation.

[5] On *ēzi*, see Borger, *BiOr* 30 (1973), 175a, confirmed by *TIM* 9 72: 5 *e-zi* = *UET* 6 399:5 *e-ez*; *ēzû* in names < *ēzi u* (otherwise *AHw* 1555 sub *ezû*).

[6] The first text goes on to interpret the shifting moods of the king as evidence of his likeness to Marduk: "King of the universe, you are the image of Marduk. When you raged against your servants, we suffered the rage of the king, our lord, but (then) we (also) experienced the king's reconciliation" (*šar kiššati ṣalam* ᵈ*marduk attā—ana libbi ardānīka kī tar*ʾ*ubu ru*ʾ*ubti ša šarri niltadad u sulummû ša šarri nītamar*).

[7] Whether the distinction reflects simply the common identification of the night as the time of the demonic or something more (allusion to a myth) is not clear; cf. the biblical "help in the morning" (see J. Ziegler, *Festschrift Nötscher* [Bonner Biblische Beiträge 1], 1950, 281–8).

[8] See also Bauer, *Assurbanipal* I 80 rev. 21 (cf. *AHw*, 269) and von Soden, *AfO* 25 (1974–1977), 62:75.

of course be *pašru*, as in the parallels cited above.[9] But here *napšuru* is no longer medio-passive, but active or intransitive. It seems to me the more difficult and therefore probably the original reading. It also fits the context and the parallels better.

I would digress briefly to show how some of the implications of I 2//4 are worked out in the rest of the poem. The succession of night and day suggests a sudden shift of moods, and the suddenness with which mercy dispels wrath is emphasized in the rest of the hymn. In the objective part, "He is moved to mercy, and suddenly *the god is like* a mother, Hastening to treat his loved one tenderly, And behind, like a cow with her calf, back and forth, round about he goes" (^{18} *ik-kar-r*[*iṭ-m*]*a zamar ma*-šil DINGIR? *ālittuš* ^{19} *iddud-ma rīmašu ukanni* ^{20}*ù kī araḫ būri ittanasḫara arkīšu*). Then, in the couplet in which the speaker sums up his own experience, he notes again as integral to the experience the suddenness of the manifestation of Marduk's mercy: "He took pity on me and suddenly how he gave me life" (*īnunam-ma zamar kī ú-bal-l* [*i-ṭ*]*a*-[*an-ni*]); cf. III 49 (*BWL*, 50), "My sickness was quickly (*arḫiš*) finished." Marduk's mood changes, and in an instant one goes from death to life. This is his power and his mystery.

Defined as the times of Marduk's wrath and mercy, night and day, together with the associated images of darkness and light, have a potential symbolism that seems to be drawn on throughout the poem. It is present in the similes of the immediately following lines 5–6, the darkness of the storm and the light at dawn: "Whose fury like a storm-blast is a wasteland (*namû*, all mss.; see already *AHw*, 771b), Whose breath is, like the dawn-wind, pleasing" (*manīt*(*i*) *eš-re-ti* in C; A, *še-re-e-ti*).

The symbolism recurs at a critical juncture, the very end of Tablet I. Despite tears and fears, the sufferer seems to assure himself that his sufferings are at an end: "*There's a festival*, on the morrow good fortune will come my way, The new-moon will *be sight<ed>*, my Sun will shine on me."[10] Good fortune is associated with light: it will come *ina urri*, on the morrow, in the morning light; the darkness of the night sky at the end of the month will be relieved by the appearance of the new-moon (?); and on the sufferer the sun will shine (*namāru*).

The false hope at the end of Tablet I becomes, by the end of Tablet II, despair and certainty of death. At this time the faces of the sufferer's enemies began to shine (*namāru*) and their spirits glow (*neperdû*, 117–118)—an inversion of the symbol, light on his enemies' faces being for him still a time of darkness, i.e., Marduk's wrath—whereas "The day grew dim for all my family, For my neighbors and friends their Sun grew dark." The allusion to, and contrast with, I 119–120 is evident.[11]

Unfortunately, the endings of Tablets III and IV remain uncertain, but we should probably assume a recurrence in some form of the symbolism marking the junctures at I/II and II/III.[12] In the latter case it seems to be extended into the narrative that immediately follows. The very last couplet describing the speaker's sufferings begins *urra u mūšu*, "Day and night alike I was groaning," and then, in chiastic order, further specifying the times, "In dream and

[9] In poetic language, *napšuru* would also be possible. The only real parallel I can find to *muppašru* is *munnaḫzu*; on *muzzakru*, see *CAD* M/2, 323.

[10] ND 5485: ^{119} HÚL? (*ḫidūtu*) GAR-*at* (*šaknat*) *ina urri iššira damiqtu*^{120} *arḫu in-nam-ma*-<ar> *inammera* ^{d}*šamšī*. In 120, it is difficult to see what object might be understood of *enû*, "to change" (transitive), and <-*ar*> would yield a common usage of N *amāru* (and note the sequence *innammar inammera*). In 119, if *ḫidūtu šaknat* is right, the sufferer seems to appeal to some popular belief. The identity of the festival is not clear. It perhaps took place at the beginning of the month, and it would be the "term" referred to in II 1, "This year and the next the term went by." If II 1 is to be understood of the calendar year, then we should think of the New Year's feast. Another possibility: ^{118} [a-di] *ātamû nabrâku nāpalūʾa*, "*until* I said, '*nabrâku* (I was born on the *nabrû*-feast) is my *answer*'"???

[11] See already J. Cooper, *JCS* 27 (1976), 249. I follow Moshe Held, who at the 1981 meeting of the AOS argued convincingly in favor of *īkil* in II 120 as the original reading. I would suggest that the scribe who gave us the variant *i-ri-im* was thinking of Marduk as the subject, for Marduk is referred to in the very next line (III 1, "Heavy was his hand . . ."). He was perhaps also thinking of *En. el.* VII 119, where Marduk is given the name Addu, "May he cover (*lirim*) the universe of the sky."

[12] *BWL*, 54 k *dūtu ummultu ittaperdi*, "(My) dimmed power grew bright (once more)," is a candidate for III 120. It would bring us back by allusion to I 47 (*inneṭir baltī dūtī ūtammil*), the beginning, it seems, of the first visible effects of abandonment by the personal gods and the anger of Marduk. This would leave Tablet IV for public reconciliation with the gods, reversing I 41–46. If *BWL*, 60:50 is actually IV 120 (see M. Vogelzang, *RA* 73 [1979], 180), then note ŠÚ ŠÚ ŠÚ—*itenerrup*(*ū*)-*šú*, ". . . will get darker and darker for him"?

early waking moments (*šuttu u munattu*) I was equally in great pain" (III 7–8). In line 9 the story of deliverance begins, with a succession of purifying and consoling dreams.[13] Finally, Marduk sends his message of deliverance, and it comes *ina munatti*, "in early waking moments," at the edge of night and day.

The opening quatrain is the essence of the entire poem: Marduk, with the power to heal (*bēl nēmeqi*) and the mind to heal (*ilu muštālu*),[14] a god of darkness and wrath, but a god, too, of light and a sudden and matching mercy.

I 14 *e-nu-uš-šú ina karašê ušatbi maqtu*: the parallelism with the previous line, *ina libbāti-*[*šu u*]*ptattâ qabrātu*, "In (the time of) his wrath graves must be opened," argues for *ennu*, "grace, mercy" (otherwise, not after OB), or possibly *e-*<*ne*>*-nu-uš-šú*, the corresponding infinitive. I 15–16 The sequence of *lamassu u šēdu* is noteworthy; correct? End of 16, [*i*]*s-saḫ-ḫar-šú*, N (pres.), as regularly.

I 23–25: ^{23} *iqabbī-ma gíl-la-ta uš-raš-ši* ^{24} *ina ūm išartīsu uptaṭṭarū iʾiltu u annu* ^{25} *šū-ma* TUK.TUK (*irtanašši*) *ka-ša* <di>*-i-na ušarši*, "He speaks and makes (one) give offence. On his day of redress absolved are guilt and sin. It is he who is ever helping, provides that a <*c*>*ase* be heard." Line 23, in the copy fourth sign more like GIŠ; cf. the magical power reported in the following: DU_{11}.GA-*ma bēl amatīya gillatu liršī-ma iraššì*, "If he also says, 'May my adversary become (the) guilty (one),' then he will" (*LKA* 146:20; see Lambert, *AnSt* 30 [1980], 70). This seems to be the first attestation of ŠD *rašû*. The uncommon language befits the uncommon and startlingly bald statement of Marduk's responsibility for sin.

Line 25, I take *kâša rašû* as periphrastic for *kâšu*, "to help, to rescue." To the occurrences of the latter in the dictionaries I would add *Ludlul* I 96–97: ^{96} *ana ša iqbû ahulapī ḫamussu mūtu* ^{97} *ša la kâšim-ma īteme ba-laṭ-su šēdu*[*s*] (ND 5485; for variants and restorations, see *BWL*, and add 79.7–8.225, identified by Lambert: [. . .] *ba-la-*x [. . .]),[15] "For the one who said 'Pity' for me, death was swift. The one against help—his life became life-force itself." After the publication of ND 5485 there is little point in reviewing the previous interpretations of this line: *īteme* can only be from *ewû*, and *šēduš* is to be taken as the late equivalent of *šēdiš*. The sense is clear: the man who took pity and intervened on the sufferer's behalf was soon dead; the man who opposed intervention had his vital forces turned into a *šēdu*, the very fulness of life.

The verb *kâšu* also appears in the D, once in an OB letter,[16] and again in *Ludlul* I 10//12: "Whose soft palm rescues the man about to die (*ukaššu mīta*)." Both *AHw*, 463a and *CAD* K, 295b derive *ukaššu* from *kâšu*, "to tarry," but not only does the claim for Marduk's power that it delays the death of a man, with the unavoidable connotations of simply putting off the inevitable, sound flat and clinically rational rather than lyrical and uncritically celebratory (the hand that the heavens themselves cannot bear can only delay death?), but šu-bar-zi = *kâšu*, and šu-bar-zi belongs to the topos of the rescue *in extremis*; cf. ka-garaš$_2$-a-ka šu-bar-zi, "rescue from the mouth of the grave," as Enki as personal god is petitioned to grant (W. W. Hallo, *JAOS* 88 [1968], 84:52); cf. also the sequence *kiʾāšum bull*[*uṭum*] (*CT* 44 21 ii 8).

For *dīna šuršû*, cf. *šurši dīnī*, addressed to Marduk as Šazu (Ebeling *Handerhebung*, 86:28). After the "day of redress" of the previous line, the appearance of Marduk as the champion of the helpless that

---

[13] Line 11 mentions *munattu* in a still obscure line. The Sumerian equivalents, ma-mú (*šuttu*) and gìr-babbar-ra (*munattu*), are also contrasted; see the comments of M. Civil, *AOAT* 25, 92, n. 35, and, of a different opinion, A. Berlin, *Enmerkar and Ensuḫkešdanna: A Sumerian Narrative Poem* [Occasional Publications of the Babylonian Fund, 2], 1979, 67. Does GIL *bi-rum mu-nat-tum* (*MSL* 14, 328:54) make of the latter a time between night and day (*bīru* C, *CAD* B, 266b)?

[14] "Judicious," usually said of rulers (gods and kings; to PNs add *Sabium-muštāl*, *YOS* 14, 147:24), pertaining to governance often as prudence, in control of anger, not permitting it to be, to the disadvantage of the ruler himself, utterly destructive, and hence its association with mercy; cf. *En. el.* VI 137 cited above ("Angry but judicious, wroth but forgiving"); (Marduk) *nāṣir napšāti ilu muštālu*, "guardian of life, judicious god" (*AfO* 19, 56:26, etc.; cited *CAD* M/2, 284a); (Nabu) *rēmēnû muštālu*, "merciful, judicious" (I*R* 35 No. 2:4, cited *CAD* M/2, 284a).

[15] 79.7–8.225, from photo, cited with the kind permission of the Trustees of the British Museum.

[16] Walker, *JCS* 30 (1978), 240:12–14 (*awīlam ša ukaššū-ma ilikšu ittanaššû lā udabbab*), where *kuššu* is taken as part of an hendiadys ("who continues to perform the *ilku*-duty profitably"). One would like to know more about the individual and the circumstances before ruling out the notion of helpful intervention.

intervenes on their behalf and secures them justice seems appropriate.[17]

I 26 *ip-pa-ru*, dupl. 79.7–8.225: [. . . *ip*]*-pa-ru šu-ru-u*[*p* . . .] This seems to be N of *pâru*, "By your holy spell are shivers and chills sought out (reached and dispelled?)." Or should we assume an error in the earlier tradition, *ip-pa-*<*ša*/*ṭa*>*-ru*?

I 27–28: 27 *muš-niš ṭi-ra-ti* ^{d}IM *meḫiṣti* ^{d}*erra* (dupl. 79.7–8.225: *t*]*i* ^{d}IM u *me-ḫi-iṣ-ti* ^{d}*è*[*r-ra*]) 28 *mu-sal-lim* DINGIR [*ù* ^{d} *iš*]*-ta-ri šabbāsūti* (dupl. 79.7–8.225: [. . .]*ù* ^{d}XV *šab-ba-s*[*u-ti*]), "Healer of Adad's strokes, of Erra's blow, Reconciler of god and goddess sorely wroth." Cf. *En. el.* VI 151, where Asalluhi is given thc name dingir-nam-ti-la, *ilu mušniššu*. The parallelism argues for deriving D*i-ra-ti* from *ṭerû*, "to beat," perhaps *ṭīru*.

I 29//31: *be-lu*$_4$ *ṣ*[*i-i-ru lì*]*b-bi* DINGIR.MEŠ *ibarri* (dupl. 79.7–8.225: [. . .] x (ru?) *lìb-bi* DINGIR.MEŠ *i-*[*bar-ri*]) // ^{d}*marduk ṣ*⌜*i-i*⌝*-ru lìb-bi*. etc., "The *exalted* lord//Marduk sees into the heart of the gods." Marduk as ^{d}Šà-zu; cf. *En. el.* VII 35.

I 30 *ma*-te-*ma* D[INGIR$^{?}$ . . . , "*Never* does a god know his way."

I 33–34: 33 *ana kī kabtat qāssu libbašu rēmēni* 34 *ana kī gaṣṣū kakkēšu kabattašu mušniššat*, "As heavy as is his hand, so merciful is his heart.[18] As savage as are his weapons, so healing is his spirit." The style and more abstract diction endow this couplet, as the objective part of the hymn draws to a conclusion, with a particular solemnity. Note especially the use of anaphora, the balance of clauses (33: 7–6 syllables; 34: 8–7), the alliteration (33: k-k-q; 34: k-g-k-k; cf. also *qāssu-gaṣṣū*, *kabtat-kabattašu*), the frequency of double consonants (33: ss, bb; 34: ṣṣ, kk, tt, šš), and the syntactic repetition (conjunction—predicate adjective—subject + pronominal suffix, subject + pronominal suffix—predicate adjective). Note, too, that in this proclamation, where the perfect correspondence of mercy to wrath is given final, formal expression, there is a collocation of *tremendum* and *fascinans* on the same line, something that does not occur in lines 5–33, and we are brought back to the opening quatrain and to "Enraged in the night, in the daylight calming."

I 35–36: 35*ša la libbīšu mannu meḫiṣtašu lišap*[*šiḫ*] 36 *ela kabtatīšu ayyû liqallil* ⌜*ṭi*⌝*-*[*ra-ti-šú*], "Against his will, who could cure his blow? Would he not, which one assuage *his strokes*?" *qullulu*, only here with some sort of malady as object, but cf. *qalālu* (vs. *kabātu*) said of the restored function of organs and limbs. For the restoration, assuming *meḫiṣtu*//*ṭīrātu*, cf. the reverse order in line 27 (see above). Marduk's power is unique: he can cure the affliction of any god (line 27), but would he not, no one can cure his.

I 40, end of line, perhaps [*māta lušāḫiz*], matching *lušalmid nišē* at the beginning of 39. However, the usual sequence is *mātu-nišē* (see *CAD* M/1, 418; N/2, 287).

A concluding note on the beginning of the narrative:

ND 5485	41*ul-tu* U$_4$.DA$^{?}$ ^{d}EN [iš-ku]-*nu* [ana mūši]
STT 32	[*i*]*š-tú u*$_4$*-ma be-lu*$_4$ [iškunu ana mūši]
ND 5485	42*ù* UR.SAG ^{d}*marduk is*$^{!}$*-b*[*u*$^{!}$*-su eli*/*itti-ia*]
STT 32	*ù qar-ra-du* ^{d}EN [*i*]*s-bu-su* U[GU/KI$^{?}$*-ia*]

After Bel (var. the Lord) *changed the* day *into night*,
And warrior Marduk (var. Bel) became angry with me,

In *STT* 32:42, *isbusu* seems certain, and the subjunctive establishes that *ištu* (*ultu*) is a conjunction. In ND 5485—the surface is damaged—I emend the KU x of the copy. In ND 5485:41, a damaged DA could end up looking like what has been copied (like GUR), and the variant *ūma* lends some support to *urra*. Cf. kukku zalág-šè gar-ra = (*ekletu*) *ana nu-ri* GAR-*nu* (*CT* 51 168 ii 11); ám-u$_4$-zal-la-ke$_4$ gi$_6$-gar-ra-zu : *ša urri ana mūši taškunu*, "you who changed day into night" (*SBH*, 77:18f). Against U$_4$.DA may be urged the fact that in context-passages *urru* is not written logographically.

---

[17] It seems likely that Marduk intervening on behalf of the sufferer and proving his enemies in the wrong was described in Tablet IV.

[18] This line is alluded to in III 1, "Heavy was his hand, I could not bear it" (*kabtat qāssu ul aleʾʾi našâša*), which also has echoes of I 9//11, "(Marduk) the . . . of whose hands the heavens cannot bear" ((^{d}*marduk*) *ša na*G*-be*/*bi qātīšu lā inaššû šamāʾī*). The reason that Marduk is not mentioned explicitly in III 1, it is now clear, is not to avoid associating the god with the sufferings of the victim—this association is not only admitted right from the beginning (I 41–42), it is gloried in (I 37, *lušāpi uggassu*, "I will proclaim his fury")—but rather, it seems, to force us back to the last reference to Marduk (I 41–42, 45–46) and the context of I 33 and I 9//11. We are thus made to recall that besides the heavy hand there is the merciful heart, and besides the hands that the heavens cannot bear, there is the soft palm of the healing god, and we sense that the peripateia, which begins eight lines below, cannot be far off. (III 3, [*en*]*-nes-su ezzeta*, "his furious punishment.")

"After Bel turned day into night"—echoing the opening quatrain, this would be a powerful introduction to the narrative, *si vera lectio.*[19]

ADDENDUM. Since submitting my manuscript I have read B. R. Foster's remarks on ND 5485 in *RA* 75 (1981), 189, and a few further comments seem necessary. Foster on lines **19–20**: "He charges forward(?) like a wild bull (*ri-ma-niš*!?) and imposes (unalterably), but like a cow keeps turning back to the calf behind him." Comments: 1. though the use of G (*iddud-ma*) rather than D (*uddid*, only OB) in hendiadys is otherwise unparalleled ([*i*/*id*]-*du-ud mūtu īterim pānīya*, "Death *quickly* covered my face"? *BWL*, 42:81), it has some support in usage, whereas *edēdu* as *verbum movendi* does not. 2. Though overhanging *i* is well attested with hollow verbs, *kunnu* does not make good sense in context (what is the unexpressed object?), whereas *kunnû*, "to treat tenderly" seems obvious. With the sequence of *kunnû-itasḫuru* in lines 19–20, cf. *CT* 44 27:3–4: u$_8$ sila$_4$-bé mí-zu mu-un-ni-in-du$_{11}$ // ùz máš-bi im-ma-an-nigin-e, "The ewe treated her lamb with true tenderness, The goat was circling round its kid" (cf. J. van Dijk, *HSAO*, 259); mí-(zi)-du$_{11}$ = *kunnû*, nigin = *saḫāru*. 3. There is no reason to emend *ri-ma-šú*; *rīmu*, "Geliebte," though confined to personal names (not so *rīmtu*), seems obvious as the object of *kunnû*. 4. The translation of line 20 is grammatically impossible; *kī araḫ būri* is not *kī arḫi ana būri*, and adnominal prepositional phrase probably could not be separated from its noun, even in poetry.

Line **23**: Foster recognizes *gíl-la-ta*, but allows for ŠD of either *kašû* or *rašû*, and translates, "sin is incurred." Comments: *kašû*, in what meaning? How can *ušarši* be passive?

Line **25**: Foster retains Wiseman's reading, *šu-ú-ma tuk-tuk-ka ša-i-la ú-šar-ši*, and ingeniously proposes that *tuk-tukku* is a loanword, perhaps of the poet's own coinage, from Sum. tuk$_4$-tuk$_4$. He translates, "He it is that sets petitioner to trembling," and he sees this as parallel to line 26, *ina têšu elli ip-pa-ru šuruppû* (*šu-ru-up-pu-u* or *šu-ru-up-pu u*?) *ḫurbāšu*, which he renders, "By his sacral spell both ice and frost are broken up." Comments: 1. Aside from the fact that *šāʾila* would probably have been written *ša-ʾi-(i)-la* (in this ms. cf. *ša-ma-ʾi-i*, I 4, *ú-za-ʾi-i-zu*, I 99; V$_1$-V$_2$ = V'V, only 1 sg. pro. suff., *su-pu-ú-a* I 116, *na-pa-lu-ú-a* I 118, *z*[*i*]-*m*[*u*]-⸢*u-a*⸣ I 112; cf. also *ša-ʾi-i-li* I 52, *ša-ʾi-li* II 82), if the copy is at all accurate, the third sign is certainly not *la* but either *na* or *ba*. As copied it looks a little more like the latter, but I could make no sense out of the reading, and so read *na* (cf. *na* as copied in line 5). 2. There is nothing about ice—*šuruppû* is not *šurīpu*—and frost in line 26, for surely a spell is directed against *šuruppû* and *ḫurbāšu* as diseases or symptoms of disease (see commentary *BWL*, 291), and it is *šuruppû* that afflicts the sufferer and, when he is cured, is dispelled (*BWL*, 42:56; 52:9). 3. Though antithetic parallelism prevails in the hymn, there are many exceptions (1–4, 19–20 [see above], 27–28 [see below], 33–34, 35–36, 39–40), and so 25–26 need not reflect some contrast in Marduk's character. Moreover, though couplets and quatrains dominate, we may not exclude tercets (see Reiner, *Altorientalische Literaturen*, 197 [n. 2]), and I would propose as tercets 23–25 and 26–28. 4. *ip-pa-ru*, "are broken up," I do not understand.

Lines **27–28**: "Who dwarfs the storms *ra*-[*a*?]-*ṭi*) of Adad and the stroke of Erra, Who renders harmless the raging of the plague." Comments: 1. Foster seems to follow Wiseman's *muš-man-ṭi*. I rejected this reading because, whatever the first object of the participle may be, the second, *meḫiṣti Erra*, is certainly some malady (cf. Marduk's *meḫiṣtu* in line 35, and *miḫiṣtu dannat*, *BWL*, 44:99, and the cure, *upaššiḫ meḫiṣtašū-ma*, *BWL*, 52:21), and nowhere is *maṭû* used in connection with disease. Besides, a god worthy of the name should not lessen or mitigate a disease or affliction, he should get rid of it, cure it—hence my preference for *mušnīš* and the consequent necessity of reading *ṭi-ra-ti*, the derivation of which (*ṭerû*, "to beat") accords well with the parallel *meḫiṣti*. Foster avoids this difficulty by his "dwarfs," which is to imply, I suppose, that Marduk makes Adad's storms and Erra's blow seem puny by comparison with his own, but such an interpretation requires parallels. 2. 79.7–8.225 establishes the correct reading of line 28.

Lines **33–34**: "How heavy is his hand and compassionate his heart, How cruel his weapons, tender his feelings". Comments: 1. The closest parallel to *ana kī* is *ana kīma* (OB), which is used only as a preposition or conjunction. 2. Foster's "tender" is like Wiseman's "soft"; the latter reads *muš-ni-lat*, presumably from *šunūlu*. These translations seem to me inaccurate paraphrases; cf. *ušnillū* in II 69 (*BWL*, 42), where the demons lay the sufferer flat like a bulrush.

[19] Note that, as is now clear, Marduk is the subject of *islit* and *iprud* in lines 45–46: "He cut off Life-force at my side, Lady Fortune frightened off to look for someone else."

A PAGANIZED VERSION OF PSALM 20:2–6 FROM THE ARAMAIC TEXT IN DEMOTIC SCRIPT

CHARLES F. NIMS
ORIENTAL INSTITUTE, UNIVERSITY OF CHICAGO
RICHARD C. STEINER[1]
REVEL GRADUATE SCHOOL, YESHIVA UNIVERSITY

INTRODUCTION

IN 1944, RAYMOND BOWMAN ANNOUNCED HIS DISCOVERY that the mystery papyrus of the Pierpont Morgan Library's Amherst collection, a demotic papyrus unintelligible to demoticists, was "An Aramaic Religious Text in Demotic Script." At the time, Bowman could not have been aware that precisely the same conclusion had been reached in 1932 by Noël Aimé-Giron in a letter to Herbert Thompson. In the same article, Bowman published his decipherment of a small part (four lines) of the text (a passage deciphered in part by Aimé-Giron in the above-mentioned letter), based on a transliteration and other materials supplied by C. F. Nims, and spoke of completing the task "some years hence perhaps" (Bowman, 1944:231). Since then, however, nothing more of this extraordinary text has been published, a fact bemoaned by at least one scholar (Kitchen, 1965:54).

About a year after Bowman's death in October 1979, C. F. Nims resumed work on the text, and in March 1981, R. C. Steiner joined him.[2] Since that time, they have been working together to prepare the text for publication. The present article is the first fruit of this collaboration. The opportunity to publish it in a volume honoring our distinguished colleague Samuel N. Kramer is indeed a welcome one.

Before presenting the new and rather startling passage which is the subject of this article, it may be worthwhile to supplement and correct some of the information about the papyrus as a whole contained in Bowman, 1944. It is now known that the papyrus is no. 63 of the Amherst collection, and that it is one of the nineteen papyri "found together in an earthern jar near Thebes," several of which bear dates ranging from 139 to 112 BCE (Newberry, 1899:55).[3] Similarly, one of the rare parallels to the peculiarly shaped ꜣ of this text () comes from Thebes in 98 BCE. It is likely, therefore, that our papyrus is from the late second century BCE—not the Achaemenid period as earlier believed (Bowman, 1944:219, 223, 230).

---

[1] The authors are listed in alphabetical order. C. F. Nims did the Egyptological work, and R. C. Steiner did the Semitic work and the actual writing of this article. Mention should also be made of the many scholars who answered questions or commented on drafts of this article: Zvi Abusch, Klaus Baer, Moshe Bar-Asher, Joshua Blau, H. Z. Dimitrovsky, Zvi Erenyi, Louis Feldman, H. L. Ginsberg, Moshe Greenberg, Jonas Greenfield, Carleton Hodge, George Hughes, Janet Johnson, Shmuel Klein, Leo Landman, Sid Leiman, Baruch Levine, Yochanan Muffs, Bezalel Porten, and Morton Smith. Their generous help is gratefully acknowledged.

[2] We are indebted to Mr. Peter Daniels for making this collaboration possible. R. C. Steiner would also like to express his personal gratitude to Professors Gene Gragg, Carolyn Killean, and Erica Reiner for inviting him to come to Chicago, and to Professor Joshua Blau for giving him his first introduction to the papyrus.

[3] Newberry's description of Nos. "XLVI–LXVI" reads as follows:

> The following twenty papyri, several of which are dated to the second and first century B.C., were found together in an earthern jar near Thebes. One of them is written in Greek uncials and three others in Demotic with Greek dockets: the remaining sixteen in Demotic only. The demotic texts have not yet been examined . . .

There are a number of confusions in these sentences. The Pierpoint Morgan Library does not have any Papyrus Amherst LXVI, and if there were only twenty papyri, as

The papyrus is 350–60 cm. long and 30 cm. high, with 22 or 23 columns of varying width covering all of the recto and sixty percent of the verso. The number of lines per column (not counting two short columns) ranges from 17 to 24. All in all, there are about 290 well-preserved lines and about 132 poorly preserved ones, a total of 422 preserved lines. (These figures are based on excellent nineteenth-century photographs in our possession. The papyrus itself, only recently remounted in glass, has suffered losses since 1921, when Herbert Thompson made the hand-copy and transliteration which he later sent to Aimé-Giron.) The average number of words in the complete lines (assuming word divisions where a contemporary Aramaic scribe would have put them) varies from column to column. The lines in the passage below contain 7.1 words on the average, whereas the lines in col. XX contain 9.8. (In contrast, the Job Targum has around 338 preserved lines, the complete ones containing an average of 7.7 words; the Genesis Apocryphon has around 178 preserved lines, the complete ones containing an average of 16.7 words; and the Palmyra Tariff has 161 preserved lines, the complete ones containing an average of 7.8 words.) These figures suggest that pAmh 63 is the longest ancient copy of an Aramaic text ever found, but it must be admitted that the Genesis Apocryphon is such a close second that certainty is impossible.

The papyrus is a collection of cultic texts, mainly prayers, with a story at the end. With the exception of a few words here and there, the language of the entire papyrus is Aramaic. The script is a peculiar variety of demotic, many signs having a form met with rarely, if at all, outside of our text. The Aramaic values of many non-alphabetic signs (i.e. signs which in normal demotic texts do not represent single consonants) are still unknown.

It goes without saying that this script fails to express many of the contrasts expressed by the traditional Aramaic script (with the exception of the contrast between *ḥ* and *ḫ*, where the opposite is true![4]). Thus, dem. *t* stands for Aram. *t*, *d*, *ṭ*; dem. *k*, *ḳ* for Aram. *k*, *g*, *ḳ*; dem. *s* for Aram. *s*, *z*; dem. *y* for Aram. *y*, ʾ; dem. *r* for Aram. *r*, *l*—to mention only the clearest cases of polyphony. Since, in addition, vowels are generally unindicated (pace Bowman, 1944:223) and glottal stops are frequently elided, the renderings are highly ambiguous, some forms having dozens of possible interpretations.

Even when the scribe attempted to eliminate the ambiguity of his renderings, he did not always succeed. There are good reasons for believing that the scribe intended *r̄* (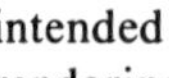),unlike *r* (/), to be an unambiguous rendering of Aram. *r* (cf. Bowman, 1944:222): (1) The sign is very complex (eight strokes vs. one stroke for *r*) and would hardly have been used by a scribe taking dictation[5] unless it had some advantage over *r*. (2) The value of the sign in Egyptian is *r*ꜣ "mouth", yielding Coptic reflexes with *r* in all dialects except Fayyumic[6] (in which *r* > *l*), in contrast to *r*, which is an alphabetic sign with two values (/r/ and /l/) in demotic Egyptian. And, in fact, in the overwhelming majority of cases, dem. *r̄* renders Aram. *r*. The problem is that in a small minority of cases (so far, around ten in all—two in our passage below), dem. *r̄* seems to render Aram. *l*. These should probably be considered mistakes; however, since almost all of them involve a final radical, it may turn out that we are dealing with a conditioned sound change within Ptolemaic Egyptian Aramaic.

Comparison of the parallel (i.e. repeated) passages in the papyrus reveals that the scribe not infrequently omits letters (especially ʿ and *r*) or misplaces determinatives (i.e. word-dividers)[7] in one of the passages. The parallels in question are quite close together, often in the same column. The mistakes (especially the falsely divided words) and the use of determinatives show that the scribe frequently did not understand what he was writing and thus that he was not the author. The inconsistencies show that he was unable to recognize repetitions and hence that he was not writing from memory. The deviations from normal Aramaic orthographical practice show that he was not transliterating a written Aramaic text. It seems likely, therefore, that the scribe who first reduced this text to writing did so from dictation.

The peculiarity of the script mentioned above is matched by the peculiarity of the transliteration system adopted here. Several of the standard symbols have been modified with the aim of making this brain-

Newberry states, there cannot ever have been one with that number. Indeed, the Pierpoint Morgan does not have any Papyrus Amherst LXV either. Moreover, the dates on the Greek dockets are 139, 114, and 112 BCE, and the date on the Greek uncial papyrus is 112 BCE. Since these are the only dates which had been read, the statement about first-century papyri must also be erroneous.

[4] See below.

[5] See below.

[6] We are indebted to Prof. Carleton Hodge for pointing out this exception.

[7] For a similar phenomenon in a *medieval* Semitic text in Egyptian transcription, cf. Blau 1979:217–18.

teasing text more transparent to the Semitist: (1) *ỷ* is used instead of plain *y* to transliterate  , in deference to the use of this sign to write both Aram. *y* and the Aram. glottal stop; (2) *ẻ* is used instead of plain *e* to transliterate  , in deference to the use of this sign to write the Aram. glottal stop; and (3) . is used instead of the overly prominent and distracting ȝ to transliterate the ubiquitous—but (pace Bowman, 1944:223) almost meaningless—.

An overline is used to indicate signs not used alphabetically in demotic texts. Demotic determinatives (used mainly as word-dividers in this text) are indicated by raised letters. The ones in our passage are:

- ^{m}—"man-with-his-hand-to-his-mouth," used in Middle Egyptian after words indicating speech (as well as thought, emotion, silence, eating, etc.) but in our papyrus after almost *any* word, apparently because the word is the basic unit of speech (Bowman, 1944:220). Thus, in our papyrus, this sign has changed from a determinative of the signified into a determinative of the signifier.
- ^{g}—"god."
- ^{w}—"seated woman," a determinative whose use is not yet understood.

The linguistic contributions of the papyrus as a whole, which are enormous, will hopefully be dealt with in a separate article. For the purposes of the present article, it suffices to note that

(1) the Proto-Semitic contrast of *ḥ* with *ḫ* is perfectly preserved (cf. now Blau, 1982 for this contrast in the Ptolemaic Egyptian pronunciation of *Hebrew* as reflected in the LXX).
(2) Aram. *k* (rendered by *k*, never *ḫ*) and *p* (rendered by *p*, never *f*) have no spirantal allophones. The same is presumably true of *b*, *g*, *d*, *t* as well, but the dem. sound system lacks the phones needed to prove this directly, viz. *v*, *γ*, ð, *θ*.
(3) Aram. *ṣ* (rendered by *t* + *s*) is an affricate (cf. Steiner, 1982:57–9).
(4) The Aram. glottal stop (rendered by *ẻ* and, less frequently, by *ỷ*) has vanished almost without a trace in medial and (of course) final position; in initial position, it is frequently elided as well, apparently via a sandhi rule.

Of the considerable number of passages in the papyrus which we have to some extent succeeded in deciphering during the past year, we have chosen to present here a seven-line passage from column XI, stretching from the section marker (dem. *sp* "remainder") in the middle of line 11 to the section marker at the end of line 19 (a short line at the end of the column). The reason for publishing this passage first is the unusual degree of certainty about its meaning afforded by the discovery that it bears a striking resemblance to Ps 20:2–6. It is reasonable to expect that conclusions reached on the basis of this passage will constitute a firm foundation for future work on the papyrus.

TEXT

Papyrus Amherst Egyptian 63, Col. XI, lines 11–19		Psalm 20
Transliteration of Demotic Script	*Semitic Interpretation*	
(11)ỷ.ʿn.n.^{m} .Ḥ̅r̅^{g} b.m.tsw$\bar{r}$ỷn.^{m}	yʿnn Ḥr bmṣ(w)ryn	(2)yʿnk YYY bywm ṣrh
(12)ỷ.ʿ.n.n.^{m} ẻ.t.nỷ^{m} b.mtsw$\bar{r}$ỷn^{m}	yʿnn ʾdny bmṣ(w)ryn	yśgbk šm ʾlhy Yʿḳb
h.ỷ.kš.t^{m} b.š.mỷn^{g} (13)s.h$\bar{r}$.^{m}	hy-ḳšt bšmyn Śhr	
š.r.ḥ.^{m} $\bar{t}$sỷ.$\bar{r}$.k^{m} m̅n̅nk.r^{m} ẻ.$\bar{r}$.š.^{w}	šlḥ ṣyrk mn-ʾgr ʾrš	(3)yšlḥ ʿzrk mḳdš
w.m̅n̅$\bar{t}$sp.n.^{m} (14).Ḥ̅r̅^{g} ỷ.s.ʿt.n.^{m}	wmn-Ṣpn Ḥr ysʿdn	wmṢywn ysʿdk
		(4)yzkr kl mnḥtyk
		wʿwltk ydšnh slh
ỷ.m.t.nẻ.r.n.^{m} .Ḥ̅r̅^{g} k.br.b.n.^{m}	yntn-ʾln Ḥr kblbn	(5)ytn lk klbbk
ỷ.mt.n.^{m} (15)ẻ.r.n.^{m} mr^{m} k.br.b.n.^{m}	yntn ʾln Mr kblbn	
ḳr^{m} ỷ.ʿts.t.^{m} .Ḥ̅r̅^{m} ỷh.m.rỷ^{m}	kl yʿṣt<n> Ḥr yhmlʾ	wkl ʿṣtk ymlʾ
		(6)nrnnh byšwʿtk
		wbšm ʾlhynw ndgl
ỷh.mrỷ.Ḥ̅r̅^{g} rỷḫ.^{m} (16)s.$\bar{r}$.^{m} ẻ.t.nỷ^{m}	yhmlʾ Ḥr lʾ-yḥsr^{8} ʾdny	ymlʾ YYY
ḳr^{m} m.šẻ.r.b.n.^{m}	kl mšʾl-lbn	kl mšʾlwtyk

.rb.kšt^{m} .rb.ḥ.nt.^{m} .r̄	lbḳšt lb-bḥnt ʾl	
(17)ẻ.nḥ.n.^{m} mṛ^{m} ỷ.rh̄.n^{w} .H̄r̄^{g} ỷh^{g}	ʾnḥn Mr ʾlhn Ḥr YH	
.r̄.n.^{m} ʿỷp̓.n.^{m}	ʾln ʿypn	
ỷ.ʿ.n..n^{m} (18)m.ḫr̄r.bỷt.r^{m}	yʿnn mḥr̄ ʾl-Byt-ʾl	
bʿr^{g} šmỷn^{g} mr^{m} ỷb.r.ḳ.^{m}	Bʿl šmyn Mr ybrk	
r.ḥ.sỷ.t^{m} (19)tỷk.^{m} b[.]r.k.t.k.^{m}	lḥsydyk brktk	
		(7)ʿth ydʿty ky hwšyʿ YYY mšyḥw . . .

TRANSLATION

Papyrus Amherst Egyptian 63, Col. XI, lines 11–19	Psalm 20
(11) May Horus answer us in [9-]our troubles[-9] (12) May Adonay answer us in [9-]our troubles[-9]	(2) May the Lord answer you in time of trouble. May the name of the God of Jacob keep you out of harm's reach
O Bow in Heaven, (13) Sahar. Send your emissary from the temple of Arash,	(3) May He send you(r) help from the Sanctuary
and from Zephon (14) may Horus sustain us.	and from Zion may He sustain you.
	(4) May He accept the reminders of your meal offerings and accept the fatness of your burnt offerings.
May Horus [10-]grant us[-10] our heart's desire May (15) Mar [10-]grant us[-10] our heart's desire	(5) May he grant you your heart's desire
May Horus fulfill (our) every plan	and may He fulfill your every plan
	(6) May we shout for joy at your victory and in the name of our God raise our banners.
[11-]May Horus fulfill—may (16) Adonay not withhold (even) in part[-11]—every request of our hearts, the request of hearts which you, O El, have tested.	May the Lord fulfill all of your requests.
(17) We—O Mar, our god, Horus, YH, our god—are faint.	
May (18) El Bethel answer us tomorrow. May Baal of Heaven, Mar, bless. Upon your pious (19) ones are your blessings.	
	(7) Now I know that the Lord will give victory to His annointed . . .

[8] Or: *ʾl(y) ʾḫ(y) śr(y)*

[9] Or: Egypt

[10] Or: our god grant

[11] Or: May Horus, (my) god, (my) brother, (my) prince, Adonay fulfill

PHILOLOGICAL COMMENTARY

(11). *ỷ.ᶜn.n.*^{m} = *yᶜnn* "may he answer us," corresponding to Ps 20 *yᶜnk* "may He answer you" with a *second*-person *singular* suffixed pronoun. Other examples of this difference are found in lines 14, 15, and 16. For its significance, see Discussion.

.*Ḥ̄r*^{g} = *Ḥr* "Horus." This seems to be the only logogram in the papyrus which is used in its Egyptian meaning.

b.m.tswr̄ỷn.^{m} = *bmṣ(w)ryn* "in Egypt" or "in our troubles," corresponding to Ps 20 *bywm ṣrh* "in time of trouble." In view of the parallel from Ps 20 and parallels from other psalms, the latter alternative is clearly superior, although the former would have made good sense had the appeal for help been addressed to a god *outside* of Egypt rather than to Horus, especially in light of the reference in line 13 to sending an emissary. The *w* is in parentheses because a demotic sign identical to *w* is apparently used as a determinative in the papyrus. If it is a determinative here, then this is one of the many falsely divided words in our text. If it is a *w*, then this word is, as Prof. J. Blau has pointed out (personal communication), from the root *ṣwr*, attested as a by-form of *ṣrr* in Hebrew (unless, of course, the meaning is really "in Egypt," in which case this form is related to poetic Hebrew *Mṣwr* "Egypt"). The etymologically distinct *ṣwr* which means "besiege," attested in Old Aramaic *mṣr* "siege," would not be appropriate here even if Dahood (1966:127) were right in taking *ṣrh* in Ps 20:2 to mean "siege" (ignoring the several allusions in that verse to Gen 35:3 which have been recognized by amoraic *daršanim* and modern scholars alike). Note that *mṣr* "trouble," unlike *mṣr* "siege," can only be Hebrew, for the reasons to be mentioned in the Discussion.

(12). *ẻ.t.nỷ*^{m} = *ᵓdny* "Adonay," despite the absence of the god determinative. Its appearance in the middle of a series of first-person *plural* pronouns shows that it is used here in the absolute sense of "Lord," not in the sense of "my lord" (cf. Fitzmyer, 1979:135 and the literature cited there). A vocalization *ᵓădōnî* "my lord" is likewise excluded by the neighboring pronouns and by the *consistent* spelling of the word (8x in cols. XI and XII) with dem. *ỷ* at the end, the vowel *î* being only sporadically rendered by dem. *ỷ* (e.g. *ı̄sỷ.r̄.k* = *ṣîrǝ̌kā* in line 13 but *ẻḫ.* = *ᵓāḥî* "my brother" in XIX/15 and XX/4).

h.ỷ. = *hy* "O." This word is obviously the same as the one spelled *hwỷ* in XIII/1 and (alongside *hw*) in XVI/16, whose distribution (both times after *ᵓnt* "you" and before the name of a deity) confirm that it is a vocative particle. The fuller spellings show that it is also identical to Hebrew *hwy*, thus confirming the view of R. Saadia Gaon (1896:110–111) in his commentary to Is 18:1 that *hwy*, though normally scornful or mournful, is also attested as a purely vocative particle with no emotive connotations. Such connotations presumably were a function of intonation rather than inherent in the meaning of the word.—The absence of a determinative here suggests that this word may sometimes have been proclitic, which for a grammatical morpheme would hardly be surprising.

kš.t^{m} *b.š.mỷn*^{g} = *ḳšt bšmyn* "Bow in Heaven," cf. *kšt.k*^{m} *b.šmỷn*^{g} = *ḳštk bšmyn* "your bow is in heaven" in XV/14. The next word shows that, in our passage at least, this is an epithet of the crescent moon.—The final *n* of *šmyn* probably marks this word as Aramaic rather than Hebrew, since the irregular Mishnaic Hebrew shift of final *m* to *n* is attested neither with this word (even in good manuscripts, according to Prof. M. Bar-Asher) nor at this period (judging from the silence of Qimron, 1976:281 and passim). The consistent use of the god determinative with this word in the papyrus (about 10 times) may have some connection with the Jewish use of "Heaven" as an appellation of God, e.g. Dan 4:23, I Macc 3:18–9, and throughout the Mishnah.

(13). *s.hr̄.*^{m} = *Śhr* "Sahar," the moon-god mentioned in Aramaic inscriptions and occurring as a formant of NA, NB, and LB names (Fales, 1978:95).

š.r.ḥ.^{m} = *šlḥ* "send," corresponding to Ps 20 *yšlḥ* "may He send." The proto-root contains a pharyngeal *ḥ* (cf. Ug. *šlḥ* "send"), and that is precisely what the demotic rendering has, here and in the other renderings of this root in the papyrus.

tsỷ.r̄.k^{m} = *ṣyrk* "your emissary," corresponding to Ps 20 *ᶜzrk* but certainly different from it, not so much because ᶜ is missing (there are at least two certain cases of that in the papyrus) as because Aram. *z* is rendered by dem. *s* in this papyrus, not by *ts*.—In Hebrew, *ṣyr* is a poetic synonym of *mlᵓk*, and, like the latter, it can be an emissary of God or man. (The fact that five of the six Biblical instances of this word co-occur with the verb *šlḥ* "send"—the same verb that we have here—supports our identification.) Akk. *ṣīru* belongs here as well, although its connection with Heb. *ṣyr* is not noted (and in fact is obscured) by *AHw* (which renders "Ass. militärischer Führer, Potentat") and *CAD* (which renders "[foreign] chieftain"). Ms. J. Scurlock has pointed out (personal communication) that, according to Postgate (1974: 124), the *ṣīrāni* are "usually mentioned as bringers of tribute" and "could when needed act as ambassadors on other matters as well." Thus, the meaning "emissary" appears to be appropriate in Akkadian as well. In any event, both the meaning of the word and its late attestation (NA and NB) indicate that it is a borrowing, presumably from Northwest Semitic.—The correspondence between *-k* "you, your" and Ps 20's *-k* is at first glance surprising. Elsewhere in this passage we find *-n* "us, our" corresponding to Ps 20 *-k*, and we would therefore expect to find *šlḥ ṣyrn* here. But what would this phrase mean? "Send our emissary" does not make much sense. "Send us an emissary" might have been possible in an earlier period if, as is generally assumed (cf. Joüon, 1923:389), the language had a transformation which attached dative pronouns to the object of a verb rather than the verb itself (e.g. *yšlḥ ʿzrk*, generally taken to mean "may He send you help" rather than "may He send your help"). But this transformation must have been obsolete by the Hellenistic period; even in earlier periods, it may have been restricted to object-nouns derived from verbs, e.g. *ʿzr* but not *ṣyr*. It seems, therefore, that *šlḥ ṣyrn* was avoided because it made no sense.

m̄n̄nk.r^{m} = *mn-ʾgr* "from the temple," corresponding to Ps 20 *mḳdš* "from the Sanctuary." The *n* following the demotic negative *m̄n̄* (⟵ etymological *b̄n̄*) is one of the many phonetic complements in the papyrus. The absence of a determinative after *m̄n̄* is also normal for this text and is reminiscent of the absence of a space after two instances of *mn* in the Ashur ostracon (Gibson, 1975:100) and the presence of *maḳḳef* after almost all of the instances of *mn* in Masoretic Aramaic and Hebrew. Egyptian Aramaic *ʾgr* "temple," like Targumic *ʾygwr* "pagan altar" and Mandaic *ʿkwrʾ* "pagan temple," is a borrowing of Akk. *ekurru* (Kaufman, 1974:48). Its initial glottal stop is one of the many deleted (or, at least, unrepresented) glottal stops in this text.

ẻ.r̄.š.^{w} = *ʾ*rš* "Arash," by far the most common toponym in this text but so far unidentified. It is the place where Mar's temple is located (VII/2), the place out of which Mar comes or has come (X/16). It goes without saying that this problem cannot be separated from the problem of *š.wr̄* (Shur? Ashur?), the place where Mar's consort's temple is located (VII/2). Alašiya in Cyprus, Biblical *ʾlyšh*, is ruled out by the spelling with *r̄*, for, as noted in the Introduction, it is likely that the scribe intended it to be an unambiguous rendering of Aram. *r*. Nor can this spelling of the name with *r̄* be a mistake, because it is the usual one, occurring at least ten times. The Ps 20 correspondence points to Jerusalem as a possibility, but that is even more difficult from the phonetic point of view. The Nabatean and Syriac form *ʾwršlm* does not go far enough toward alleviating this difficulty.—Since this is definitely a toponym, the Phoenician deity Aresh is also ruled out.

w.m̄n̄t̄sp.n.^{m} = *wmn-Ṣpn* "and from Zephon," corresponding to Ps 20 *wmṢywn* "and from Zion." That *t̄sp.n.*^{m} is a rendering of *Ṣpn* "Zephon" is clear from its association with *bʿr*^{g} = *Bʿl* "Baal" in VII/2 (Bowman, 1944:227fn) and XII/15, which parallels the association of Zephon with Baal in a wide variety of sources from Egypt, Israel, Ugarit, and Assyria (Eissfeldt, 1932; Albright, 1950). The initial *t* of *t̄sp.n.*^{m}, which Bowman (op. cit.) considered a problem, is now known to be a common feature of renderings of *ṣ* in this papyrus (cf. the examples in lines 11, 12, 13, and 15) and is only one of many pieces of evidence showing that the affricated realization of *ṣ* is much older than generally realized (Steiner, 1982).—It is entirely possible that the Zephon referred to here is not the original North-Syrian one but an Egyptian copy (Biblical Baal-Zephon and/or Hellenistic Kasion) located on the Mediterranean coast of either Sinai (Eissfeldt, 1932:39ff) or Egypt proper (Albright, 1950:12–3). The correspondence between *Ṣpn* in our passage and *Ṣywn* in Ps 20 is reminiscent of the use of the former as an appellation of the latter in Ps 48:3 (cf. Eissfeldt, 1932:15–6; Lauha, 1943:44; Clifford, 1972:142–3) and may have some element of phonetic word-play in it.

(14). *.Ḥ̄r̄*^{g} = *Ḥr* "Horus." As pointed out in the Discussion, the association of Horus with Zephon here is quite unexpected and hence quite significant. The only parallel is of dubious validity: In Pelusium, the statue of Zeus Kasios—the Greek equivalent of Baal Zephon—was actually an image of Harpocrates (Eissfeldt, 1932:41–2).

ỷ.s.ʿt.n.^{m} = *ysʿdn* "may he sustain us," corresponding to Ps 20 *ysʿdk* "may He sustain you." The stem may be either *ḳal* as in the Hebrew parallel or *pael* as in Biblical Aramaic. The imperative form *sʿdny* "sustain me" in line 19 of the Behistun inscription contributes nothing to the resolution of this question.

ỷ.m.t.n = *ymṭʾn* "may he cause to reach us" or *yntn* "may he grant," corresponding to Ps 20 *ytn* "may He grant." The phonetic problem inherent in the latter alternative is greatly diminished by the existence of two clear instances of *m* for *n* in the papyrus, both before a dental stop: *m̄n̄mt.ḥ.t*^{m} = *mn-tḥt* "beneath" in VI/10 and *t.k.m.*^{m} *t̄ẻ.b.*^{m} = *dḳn dʾbʾ* "the beard of my father" in XI/5 alongside *t.k.n*^{m} *ẻ.b.*^{m} = *dḳn ʾbʾ* "id." in XI/4 and other occurrences of *dḳn* "beard" in XI/1,2,3. The contrast between the two was probably neutralized before dental stops in this dialect of demotic, and so for our scribe *mt* had the same realization as *nt*. The absence of a determinative after *ỷ.m.t.n* (cf. *ỷ.mt.n.*^{m} at the end of the line) suggests that *ỷ.m.t.nẻ.r.n.*^{m}, *like ytn-lk* in the Ps 20 parallel, was one stress unit (cf. also *hwšrln* "send us" in the Ashur ostracon, according to Gibson, 1975:100).

ẻ.r.n.^{m} = *ʾln* "our god" or "to us," corresponding to Ps 20 *lk* "to you." Only the former alternative is possible if *ỷ.m.t.n* means "may he cause to reach us." For the latter alternative, one would have expected (if not *r.n.*^{m} = *ln*, then) *ẻ.r.y.n.*^{m} = *ʾlyn*, since diphthongs are never reduced in this text, but the fact is that in XII/2 we find *ẻ.r.k.*^{m} = *ʾlk* with the meaning "to you" (not "your god"). These *y*-less suffixed forms are presumably due to analogy with (a) *ʾl*, the *y*-less allomorph used when no suffix is present, and (b) *l*, the synonymous preposition which is *y*-less even when a suffix is present. It should also be noted that ᵓ*lhm* "to them," written without *y*, occurs very frequently (113x) in the Masoretic text of the Bible.

k.br.b.n.^{m} = *kblbn* "according to [what is] in our heart = our heart's desire," corresponding to Ps 20 *klbbk* "according to [what is in] your heart = your heart's desire." The preposition *b* "in" of *kblbn* is present in the underlying structure of *klbbk*. This is shown by parallels like *k(kl)* ᵓ*šr blbby* "according to (all of) that which is in my heart" (I Sam 2:35, II K 10:30), where the *b* is not transformationally deleted because it is not attached to the same word as *k* "according to" is. It *is* transformationally deleted in *klbbk* (and in the very common *kymy-* "as [in] the days of") because of a constraint on the co-occurrence of prefixed prepositions. This constraint breaks down in Rabbinic Hebrew, and, as Prof. M. Greenberg reminds me, is by no means absolute in Biblical Hebrew either, cf. *kbr*ᵓ*šnh* "as in the beginning" (Ju 20:32, I K 13:6, Is 1:26, Jer 33:7, 11) alongside *kr*ᵓ*šnh* "as [in] the beginning" (Deut 9:18).—The use of *lb* here, rather than *lbb*, may be due to the late date of our passage (a possibility suggested by Prof. M. Greenberg), but only if that usage is a purely Aramaic one, free of any Hebrew influence (e.g. from a Hebrew *Vorlage*). In most Aramaic dialects of the Roman and Byzantine periods (all Jewish and Christian varieties beginning with the Genesis Apocryphon and Onkelos, and Samaritan, cf. Tal 1980–81 passim), *lb* is the predominant form, *lbb* being rare or non-existent (Sokoloff, 1974:109). In earlier periods (Old Aramaic, Egyptian Aramaic, and Biblical Aramaic—Daniel), on the other hand, exactly the opposite is the case: *lbb* is frequently attested whereas *lb* is rare or non-existent (loc. cit.). Our passage, with four occurrences of *lb* but none of *lbb*, clearly belongs with the later material—unless there is some Hebrew influence here. In that unlikely event, *lb* would not be a sign of lateness (despite the fact that it is the only form attested in Mishnaic Hebrew), since *lb* is well-attested (alongside *lbb*) in all periods of Biblical Hebrew. It is interesting to note that the Job Targum, which is either contemporary with or later than our papyrus, exhibits a more archaic pattern, with one case of *lb* and one or two of *lbb* (Sokoloff 1974:109). This is not the only respect in which the Job Targum gives the *appearance* of being more archaic than our text. Could it be that we are getting a glimpse of the linguistic difference between *oral* Aramaic literature and *written* Aramaic literature? If so, we may soon be in a position to put an end to the debate concerning the date of the Palestinian targums.

(15). *ỷ.*ᶜ*ts.t.*^{m} = *y*ᶜ*ṣt* "plan(s)," corresponding to Ps 20 ᶜ*ṣtk* "your plan." Since "*our* plan(s)" is what the context requires, we must assume that the scribe has omitted final *n* or (as Prof. J. Blau suggests) that the final *n* of *kblbn* is a double-duty suffix. The *beginning* of the form is also puzzling. The word for "advice, plan" in Hebrew is ᶜ*ṣh*, not *y*ᶜ*ṣh*. It is true that the *root* begins with *y*, but initial-*y* roots do not normally retain their *y* in verbal nouns formed with the feminine ending, the only Biblical exception being *ybšt* "drying out." And even in Mishnaic Hebrew, where this rule does not apply (cf. *yrydh* "descent", *yṣy*ᵓ*h* "departure", *yšybh* "academy", etc.), there is no *y*ᶜ*yṣh*. Nor is anything similar known in Aramaic. Could it be that the *ỷ* is misplaced and that it renders the *e* or *i* which *follows* ᶜ? Note that this form can only be Hebrew because dem. *ts* is not attested as a rendering of Sem. *ṯ*, which is what the Aram. cognate (ᶜ*ṭt*, attested in V/3) contains; see also Discussion. Note also that ᶜ*yṣ*ᵓ (<Heb. ᶜ*ṣh*) is attested with the meaning "plan" in Onkelos (not only in places where the *Vorlage* contains ᶜ*ṣh*, cf. Nu 31:16) and, as Prof. J. Blau informs us (personal communication), with the meaning "council" in the Syro-palestinian version of the NT. At present, there does not seem to be any reason to posit a connection between these loanwords and the Hebraism in our text.

ỷh.m.rỷ^{m} = *yhml*ᵓ "may he fulfill," corresponding to Ps 20 *yml*ᵓ "may He fulfill." The stem can only be *hafel*, despite the fact that the *hafel* of *ml*ᵓ "be full" is rare in Aramaic. The demotic final *ỷ* represents not historical ᵓ (certainly quiescent by now, cf. Segert, 1975:294–5, esp. the form *tmly*) but rather final long *ē*.

rỷḫ.^{m} *s.r̄.*^{m} = ᵓ*l(y)* ᵓ*ḥ(y) śr(y)* "(my) god, (my) brother, (my) prince" or *l*ᵓ*-yḥsr* "may he not withhold (even) in part." The former alternative is supported by the determinative after *rỷḫ.* and by the following parallels (if the interpretations suggested here are correct): *rỷẻ.ḫỷ*^{m} = ᵓ*ly* ᵓ*ḥy* "my god, my brother" in XIII/8 (but *ly* ᵓ*ḥy* "for myself, my brother" fits the context just as well) and *m̄n̄s.r̄.ḫ.*^{m} = *mn-śr(y)-*ᵓ*ḥy* "from (my) prince, my brother" in IX/8. Note also that *Śr* is attested as a divine epithet in Palmyrene Aramaic, in Phoenician, and elsewhere in our papyrus (VII/7 and in the names of the main characters in the story). The latter alternative takes this to be one of the many falsely divided words in the papyrus: a D-stem of *ḥsr* "be lacking" (with parallels in Jewish Aramaic, Syriac, and Biblical and Mishnaic Hebrew) plus proclitic *l*ᵓ "not" (as in early inscriptions and, at times, in the Masoretic vocalization). This interpretation is supported by the existence of a close semantic relationship—antonymy—between *ml*ᵓ and *ḥsr* (cf. the relationship between *ntn* "give" and *mn*ᶜ "withhold" in Apocryphal Psalm 155, lines 3–4: *wtn ly* ᵓ*t š*ᵓ*lty, wbḳšty* ᵓ*l tmn*ᶜ *mmny* "and grant me my petition, and my request do not withhold from me," Sanders 1964:67). The use of the negated antonym for emphasis is common—not rare—in Hebrew, as pointed out already by the medieval philosopher Joseph Ibn Kaspi (1906:66) in his commentary to Gen 24:16 (cf. the examples cited there plus Apocryphal Psalm 155, line 11: *zkwrny w*ᵓ*l tškḥny* "remember me and do not forget me,"

Sanders, 1964:68).—The proto-form of *ḥsr* "be lacking" contains a velar *ḫ* (cf. Ug. *ḫsr* "id.," Arab. *ḫasira* "incur a loss"); so does the proto-form of *ʾḥ* "brother" (cf. Ug. and Arab. *ʾaḫ* "id."). Accordingly, the demotic rendering with velar *ḫ* is etymologically justified no matter which of the interpretations given above is correct.

(**16**). *m.še̓.r.b.n.*^{m} = *mšʾl-lbn* "the request of our heart(s)," corresponding to Ps 20 *mšʾlwtyk* "your requests," cf. also Ps 37:4 *wytn-lk mšʾlt lbk* "and may he grant you the requests of your heart." Demotic *r* stands here for a geminate Semitic *l*.

.rb.kšt^{m} = *lbḳšt* "the request" with *l* as accusative marker. For the parallelism between *bḳšh* and *mšʾl*, cf. the parallelism between *bḳšh* and *šʾlh* in Est 5:6,7,8; 7:2,3; 9:12 (all but two of the Biblical occurrences) and Apocryphal Psalm 155, lines 3–4, quoted above. Note that *bḳšh* (more specifically, its root) can only be Hebrew, for the reasons mentioned in the Discussion. And, though the ROOT *bḳš* is old, the NOUN *bḳšh* (combining the Hebrew root with an Aramaic verbal-noun pattern) is late, first attested in Ezra and Esther (Hurvitz, 1965:226–7, 1972:59–60[12]) which suggests that this stich was added in the Persian or Hellenistic periods.

.rb.ḥ.nt.^{m} = *lb-ḥnt* "a heart to which you have shown favor" or *lb-bḥnt* "a heart which you have tested." The latter alternative is far more idiomatic, for *bḥn* "test" is used with *lb(b)* "heart" a full six times in the Bible (Jer 11:20, 12:3; Ps 7:10, 17:3; Pr 17:3; I Chr 29:17; cf. also War Scroll 16:13; Yadin, 1957:352). It seems, therefore, that dem. *b* stands here for a geminate Sem. *b*.—The proto-form of *bḥn* "test" contains a pharyngeal *ḥ* (cf. Arab. *maḥana* "id."); so does the proto-form of *ḥnn* "show favor to" (cf. Ug. *ḥnn* "id.," Akk. *enēnu* "id.," Arab. *ḥanna* "sympathize, pity"). Accordingly, the dem. rendering with pharyngeal *ḥ* is etymologically justified no matter which of the interpretations given above is correct.—It should be noted that both interpretations make *lb* the head of an asyndetic relative clause. (One could, of course, eliminate this construction here by construing *lbḳšt lb bḥnt* as "you tested a heart's request," as Prof. J. Blau suggests, but this would be a rather exceptional use of *bḥn*.) This syntactic construction is quite common in Biblical poetry (cf. Peretz, 1967:80–84 and now Sappan 1981:162–5), but it is not to be found in post-Biblical literature (personal communication from Prof. M. Bar-Asher). Indeed, it was so foreign to the copyists of 1QIs[a] that they occasionally misunderstood it (Kutscher, 1959:33–4). It seems likely, therefore, that this stich was added before the Hellenistic period. Since we have already seen that the word *bḳšh* is post-exilic, we may conclude that the phrase *lbḳšt lb-bḥnt* was added to this prayer during the Persian period.

.r̄ = *ʾl* "El." For the problem caused by the *r̄* in this form, see Introduction. Note also the absence of a determinative here. With rare exceptions (in IX/2 and XI/8), words ending in *r̄* do not take a determinative in the papyrus, apparently because *r̄* has its own internal determinative.

(**17**). *e̓.nḥ.n.*^{m} = *ʾnḥn* "we." Elsewhere in the papyrus (XVI/4), the form *e̓.nḥ.n.n*^{m} = *ʾnḥnn* is used. Perhaps the shorter form used here is to be viewed as a Hebraism rather than an archaism. The proto-form contains a pharyngeal *ḥ* (cf. Arab. *naḥnu* "id.," Akk. *nīnu* "id."), and that is precisely what the demotic rendering has, here and in XVI/4.

y̓.rh̄.n^{w} = *ʾlhn* "our god." For the use of dem. *y̓* to render the Aram. glottal stop, see Introduction.

y̓h^{g} = *Yh* "Lord," probably the *doubly* apocopated form of the tetragram, although it is not really certain that the absence of . at the end of this form is a reliable indicator of the absence of a vowel. At Elephantine, only the singly apocopated form (spelled *Yhw* in papyri and *Yhh* in ostraca) is attested. In magical papyri of the third and fourth centuries CE, the singly apocopated form (written Ιαω in Greek and *Yʿh-ʿo* in demotic) predominates, but the doubly apocopated form (written Ια in Greek and *Yʿḫ* in demotic) is also found. The sequence of Horus plus YH in our passage is reminiscent of the sequence Horus-the-falcon (Αρβαχ or Αρβηχ) plus Ιαω (with one word intervening) in a magical text called the "Diadem of Moses" (Preisendanz, 1931:28).

.r̄.n.^{m} = *ʾln* "our god." For the problem caused by the *r̄* in this form, see Introduction.

ʿy̓p̣n.^{m} = *ʿypn* "faint, weary," more likely a plural adjective or participle than a 1st person plural perfect. We can only guess at the reason for this faintness/weariness. It might be due to hunger and thirst (see Discussion), the lateness of the hour (see Commentary to *m.ḫr̄* immediately below) or the troubles mentioned in lines 11–12.

(**18**). *m.ḫr̄* = *mḥr* "tomorrow." This interpretation was suggested by Prof. M. Greenberg. From the phonetic point of view it is excellent. The velar *ḫ* of the demotic rendering is in place whether *mḥr* is to be derived from an original **mʾḫr* "afterwards" (cf. Ug. *ʾaḫr* "after", Arabic *ʾaḫīr* "last") or to be connected with Akk. *maḫ(a)rû* "first, previous" from the root *mḫr* (cf. *KBHK* s.v.). Furthermore, the spelling with demotic *r̄* (rather than *r*) supports this interpretation in two ways: (1) dem. *r̄* normally represents Aram. *r*, not *l*, in the papyrus (see Introduction), and (2) words ending in *r̄* do not normally take a determinative in the papyrus (see Commentary to *.r̄* in line **16**). On the psychological level, however, this interpretation raises a difficult question: Why would someone in distress ask to be answered "tomorrow"? Admittedly, no one but a magician would have the *chutzpah* to demand results "right now, quick, quick, in this hour and on

---

[12] We are indebted to Prof. Y. Muffs for reminding us of this discussion.

this day" (Preisendanz, 1931:201, cf. also passim), but what possible objection could there be to something on the order of "May He answer . . . this day (*hywm hzh*)" (M Taʿanit 2:4) or "Answer us at this time and juncture (*bʿt wbʿwnh hzʾt*)" (TJ Taʿanit chap. 2, hal. 2, 65c mid)? As Prof. Greenberg points out, the same question was asked about Pharaoh's *lmḥr* "tomorrow" in Ex 8:6 by R. Samuel b. Ḥofni (apud Ibn Ezra, 1976:55): *ʾyn mnhg hʾdm lbḳš rḳ šyswr hmkh mmnw myd* "The usual practice is for a person to request that an affliction be removed from him immediately."

In the case of our passage, a possible answer is that the prayer was recited at night, in which case the beginning of *mḥr*—dawn—would have been only a few hours away. There is independent evidence for a nocturnal setting in lines 12–13 (see Discussion). And, as Prof. Y. Muffs points out (personal communication), there are several references to matinal salvation in Psalms (e.g. 30:6 and 46:6). In any event, Prof. Greenberg's interpretation is supported by the similarity between the proposed *yʿnn mḥr* "may he answer us tomorrow" and the last words of Ps 20: *yʿnnw bywm ḳrʾnw* "may He answer us on the day we call," a similarity pointed out to us by Prof. H. L. Ginsberg.

r.by̓t.r^{m} = *ʾl-Byt-ʾl* "El-Bethel." That the initial dem. *r* is a rendering of Aram. *l* is suggested by the fact that it comes immediately after *r̄* (which normally renders Aram. *r*) and thus seems to have been purposely chosen to contrast with it. The god Bethel, known from Elephantine and elsewhere (Eissfeldt, 1962; Kraeling, 1953:88–91; Porten, 1968:167–70, 328–30, and the literature cited there), occurs eight more times in the papyrus. The combination El Bethel, perhaps with a different meaning, is attested in Gen 35:7 and 31:13.

bʿr^{g} *šmy̓n*^{g} = *Bʿl šmyn* "Baal of Heaven," mentioned also in XVI/17 and XVII/3. See also Commentary to *b.š.my̓n*^{g} in line **12**.

y̓b.r.ḳ.^{m} = *ybrk* "may he bless." This verb can hardly govern *lḥsydyk* "YOUR pious ones"; like *ybrk* in XII/16, it must be absolute.

r.ḥ.sy̓.t^{m} *ty̓k.*^{m} = *lḥsydyk* "to your pious ones." This is one of the many falsely divided words in the papyrus. In this instance, however, the scribe seems to have suspected something was wrong. He originally wrote *r.ḥ.sy̓.*^{m} *ty̓k.*^{m} = *lḥsy dyk*. Later, he corrected this by superimposing a second *t* on the . at the end of *r.ḥ.sy̓.*^{m}, producing *r.ḥ.sy̓t*^{m} *ty̓k.*^{m} = *lḥsyd dyk*. The proto-root seems to contain a pharyngeal *ḥ* (cf. Ασιδαῖοι rather than **Χασιδαῖοι in I & II Macc[13]; the only Arab. cognates which have been proposed are *ḥašada* "mobilize (troops)" and *ḥasada* "envy") and that is precisely what the demotic rendering has.

r.ḥ.sy̓t^{m} *ty̓k.*^{m} *b*[.]*r.k.t.k.*^{m} = *lḥsydyk brktk* "upon your pious ones are your blessings," cf. Ps 3:9 *ʿl ʿmk brktk* "upon your people are your blessings" and Deut 33:8 *tmyk wʾwryk lʾyš ḥsydyk* "your Thummim and Urim belong to your pious ones." It is possible that some or all of these should be taken as jussives.

DISCUSSION

The striking similarity between this passage—embedded in a collection of pagan cultic texts—and Ps 20:2–6 raises the question of who borrowed from whom: Is our passage a pagan adaption of (a prayer based on) Ps 20 and hence of Jewish origin (ultimately, at least), or is Ps 20 a Jewish adaption of this pagan prayer or some earlier version of it?

That the former alternative is correct is shown by both onomastic and linguistic evidence. The most obvious Jewish elements in this prayer are the names YH and Adonay (not Adoni or Adon as in Phoenician). It is true that these Jewish names of God occur in third and fourth century CE magical texts which even Goodenough (1953:206–7) admits are pagan, e.g., the demotic magical papyrus of London and Leiden (Griffith and Thompson, 1921: passim). It is also true, as Prof. Jonas Greenfield notes (personal communication), that "YH . . . may very well occur in Ugarit and elsewhere" in the ancient Near East. But these parallels carry little weight. Even if they are not to be disqualified on chronological grounds, they are rendered irrelevant by an examination of the distribution of the divine names in question within the papyrus. The name YH occurs nowhere in the papyrus outside of our passage, and the name Adonay is limited to our passage and the column (XII) which follows it—a column which has Jewish material as well. In other words, divine names used by Jews occur

---

[13] Since I Macc is earlier than or contemporary with texts which distinguish *ḫ* from *ḥ* (our papyrus and those books of the Bible translated into Greek in the second century BCE, cf. now Blau, 1982), it is not surprising that it too distinguishes *ḫ* from *ḥ*. Velar *ḫ* is rendered by χ in Ιεριχω (9:50), Χαλφι (12:70) and presumably Χεβρων (6:65). Pharyngeal *ḥ* is rendered by Ø in Βαιθωρων (9:50), Αμμαους (3:40, 9:50), Αμαθ- (12:25), Ασωρ (11:67), Ιωαννης (16:1,9), Ονιας (12:7), Φινεες (2:26). (For the etymology of these names, see Blau 1982 and *KBHK*. A dearth of names with *ḫ* makes it impossible to determine whether the author of II Macc made this distinction as well.) Thus, the form Ασιδαῖοι shows that *ḥsyd* had a pharyngeal *ḥ*.

in and around a prayer strikingly similar to one used by Jews and are absent everywhere else. Can this coinciding of Jewish-sounding material be dismissed as a coincidence? Certainly, it is possible to explain away each Jewish-sounding feature in isolation; but the data have to be viewed as a whole and provided with a unified explanation. It remains to be seen whether any theory of pagan origin can meet that requirement.

Linguistic evidence points in the same direction. Alongside grammatical features and lexical items which, in the context of Northwest Semitic in the second century BCE, are symptomatic of Aramaic (e.g. the failure to assimilate *n* in *yntn*, the failure to delete *h* in *yhml*$^{\supset}$, the *-n* ending of *šmyn* and ^{c}*ypn*, the words $^{\supset}$*gr* and *śhr* or *Śhr*), we find lexical items which are unattested in Aramaic and/or exhibit non-Aramaic reflexes of Proto-Semitic phonemes: *mṣ(w)r* "trouble" < **ṣrr* (> Aram. ^{c}*rr*), (*y*)^{c}*ṣh* "plan" < **w*^{c}*ṯ* (> Aram. *y*^{c}*ṭ*), *bḳšh* "request" < **bḳṯ* (> Aram. ***bḳṭ*). Of these, the first two (and the word *ḥsyd* "pious one," as well) are attested poorly, if at all, in Phoenician, but are very common in Hebrew. Thus, the language of our passage (and col. XII, but not the rest of the papyrus) contains a distinct Hebrew component— another sign of Jewish origin.

It is clear, then, that what we have here is a paganized Jewish text embedded in a collection of pagan prayers. There is nothing terribly surprising about this conclusion. At least since the publication of Goodenough's *Jewish Symbols* (1953:190–207), it has been well known that there are quite a few syncretistic Jewish-pagan texts preserved in collections of charms made by pagans (cf. also Gager, 1972:135–6). An even closer parallel is the Aramaic translation of Ps 114:3–6 and Ps 29:5, 9 found with additional Jewish material in two Mandaic religious works (Greenfield, 1981).[14] Thus, the only thing remarkable about the pagan borrowing of Jewish (or syncretistic) material manifested by the Amherst papyrus is its pre-Christian date.

There can be little doubt, then, that the first half of Ps 20 (with deletions and additions, at least one of which[15] can be dated to the Persian period) was recited as a prayer by Egyptian Jews in the Hellenistic period. This is a finding of great interest since there is no other unambiguous evidence for the liturgical use of Psalms outside of Judea in this period (personal communication from Prof. L. Landman).[16] We can even assert with reasonable confidence that already before this prayer left Jewish hands, it was used in public worship, for the original "you, your" of the psalm have been replaced here, wherever possible, by "us, our,"[17] thus converting it from a priestly blessing into a communal prayer (cf. Heinemann, 1977:104–11, esp. fn. 9 on Mishnaic *y*^{c}*nh* $^{\supset}$*tkm* "may He answer you" > Gaonic *y*^{c}*nnw* "may He answer us" in the prayers for public fast-days). Since line 17 contains an instance of "we" which cannot easily be derived from an earlier "you," it is clear that the change to "us, our" must have preceded (or been simultaneous with) the addition of that line. And since that line contains a form of the tetragram, it must have been added while the prayer was still in Jewish hands. Hence, the change to "us, our" must also have been made while the prayer was still in Jewish hands.

On what occasion(s) was this prayer recited? Nothing remotely resembling a definitive answer can be given at this early stage; indeed, in view of the likelihood that we are dealing with diffusion from one group to another, it is not even clear that a single answer will suffice. Nevertheless, the content of the prayer and its immediate context provide some hints which may turn out to be of significance. Thus, in line 12, the crescent moon—vividly described as a "bow in heaven"—is addressed in the second person with a vocative particle and an imperative. This imperative (*šlḥ* "send") stands in marked contrast to the third-person jussives which precede and follow it and to the third-person jussive (*yšlḥ* "may He send") which corresponds to it in Ps 20. One gets the impression that the prayer was recited at night, with the crescent moon visible. (If this invocation of the moon were less isolated, one would be tempted to talk of a New Moon ritual.) We have already pointed out that line

[14] We are indebted to Prof. Jeffrey Tigay for this reference.

[15] See Commentary to *.rb.kšt*^{m} and *.rb.ḥ.nt.*^{m} in line 16.

[16] The hymns sung by the Therapeutae according to Philo in *De Vita Contemplativa* §§80, 84 (cf. also §25 dealing with non-liturgical use) are not necessarily from Psalms (personal communication from Profs. L. Feldman and S. Leiman).

[17] Prof. H. L. Ginsberg points out that this change may have been triggered by the presence of *y*^{c}*nn mḥr* "may he answer us tomorrow" in lines 17–18, corresponding to Ps 20 *y*^{c}*nnw bywm ḳr*$^{\supset}$*nw* "may He answer us on the day we call." In other words, the change was designed to eliminate the difference between *y*^{c}*nk* "may He answer you" at the beginning of Ps 20 and *y*^{c}*nnw* "may He answer us" at the end.

18 (if it contains the word *mḥr* "tomorrow") may also hint at a nocturnal setting.[18]

A second hint about the *Sitz im Leben* of our prayer is provided by the passage which immediately precedes it. That passage seems to be a lament for a drought-stricken city. Despite the section divider separating these two passages (which, judging from other examples, need not indicate a sharp break), one gets the impression that the troubles mentioned at the beginning of the prayer are the ones mentioned in the preceding section. Now, we know from the Mishnah (Taʿanit 1:5–3:3) that during times of drought,. public fast-days were proclaimed, and special benedictions were added to the Amidah. Each of these benedictions contains the phrase *hwʾ yʿnh ʾtkm* "may He answer you" (M Taʿanit 2:4)—a phrase reminiscent of the beginning of Ps 20. In one of the benedictions, that phrase is followed by *brwk ʾth YYY hʿwnh bʿt ṣrh* "Blessed art thou O Lord who answers in time of trouble" (loc. cit.), whose resemblance to Ps 20:2 is even more striking (although not quite as striking as its resemblance to Gen 35:3). Also reminiscent of Ps 20:2 is the quotation from Ps 120:1 at the beginning of another one of the benedictions: *ʾl YYY bṣrth ly ḳrʾty wyʿnny* "to the Lord, in my trouble, I called, and He answered me" (ibid., 2:3).

Ps 20 itself is not mentioned in M Taʿanit, but it *is* mentioned in TJ Taʿanit (chap. 2, hal. 2, 65c top):

> *wlmh šmwnh ʿśrh? ʾmr Rby Yhwšʿ bn Lwy: kngd šmwnh ʿśrh mzmwrwt šktwb mrʾšw šl tylym ʿd yʿnk YY bywm ṣrh. ʾm yʾmr lk ʾdm tšʿh ʿśr hn, ʾmwr lw lmh rgšw lyt hyʾ mnwn. mykn ʾmrw: hmtpll wʾynw nʿnh ṣryk tʿnyt.*
>
> And why eighteen [benedictions in the Amidah]? R. Joshua b. Levi said: The correspond to the eighteen psalms from the beginning of the Psalter until "May the Lord answer you in a day of trouble." If someone tells you there are nineteen, tell him that "Why do the nations rage" is not one of them (i.e. not a separate psalm). From here they said: He who prays and is not answered needs to fast.

This passage, taken together with the Mishnaic passages discussed above, suggests that there may have been a connection between Ps 20 and the public fast-days proclaimed in times of drought. Such a connection would support the idea that in pAmh 63, the prayer derived from Ps 20 is connected with the lament for a drought-stricken city which precedes it.

This connection may even be hinted at in line 17 of the prayer: *ʾnḥn* . . . *ʿypn* "We . . . are faint." Most occurrences of the word *ʿyp* "faint" in the Bible are associated with hunger and thirst. In our passage, hunger and thirst might be a result of the drought itself or a result of fasting—a response to drought mentioned already in Jer 14:12.

Which Jewish community transmitted Ps 20 to the redactors of pAmh 63? Since the papyrus was found near Thebes (presumably in or near a tomb in the Theban necropolis), in the same jar as a demotic papyrus (dated 115–114 BCE) recording the sale of land in Djēme (Medinet Habu, at the southern end of the Theban necropolis), and since one of the rare parallels to its peculiarly-shaped 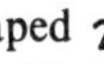 comes from Thebes (in 98 BCE), it is logical to think first of the Theban Jewish community, known from Greek ostraca of the second century BCE (Tcherikover and Fuks, 1957:3).

A second possibility is raised by the frequent mention (15x) of the Egyptian god Horus in our passage and col. XII (which, as mentioned above, is almost certainly also of Jewish origin). This fact is particularly significant because Horus is mentioned only two or three times in the rest of the papyrus (twenty or twenty-one columns) and because the other native Egyptian gods are apparently not to be found anywhere in it.

The infatuation with Horus displayed in these Jewish passages goes even further. It was accepted practice in Egypt, from the New Kingdom to Roman times, to identify Canaanite Baal with Egyptian Seth (Stadelmann, 1967:32–47[19]) and even to write *Bʿr Ḏpn* "Baal Zephon" with the Seth determinative (Eissfeldt, 1963:40; Albright, 1950:7, 8); but in our passage (lines 13–14), the sacred precincts of Zephon—the home of Baal in Canaanite mythology and in our papyrus (VII/3 in Bowman 1944:227, and XII/15 immediately below)—are occupied not by Seth but by his arch-rival Horus. This fact and the appositional phrase (?) *Bʿr*^{g} *m̅n̅t̅sp.n*^{m} *.Ḥ̅r̅*^{g} = *Bʿl mn Ṣpn Ḥr* "Baal from Zephon, Horus" in XII/15–16 seem to point to an identification of Baal with Horus, against the above-mentioned norm.

Where in the vicinity of Thebes did such fervent devotion to Horus survive into the Ptolemaic period? And where in the vicinity of Thebes did Aramaic

[18] See Commentary to *m.ḥr̄* in line 18.

[19] We are indebted to Prof. Yochanan Muffs for this reference.

speech survive into the Ptolemaic period? The answer to these two questions is the same: Edfu. Located sixty miles southeast of Thebes, Edfu was a leading center of Horus worship in ancient Egypt, whose influence increased during the Ptolemaic period (Alliot, 1949:833). Scenes and texts covering the walls of the great sandstone temple of Horus at Edfu show that the cult of the falcon-god was very vigorous there from the third century to the first century BCE (ibid., 834).

Edfu is also our leading source of Egyptian Aramaic documents from the Ptolemaic period. Aimé-Giron's list of such documents (1939:61) is now known to consist mainly of Edfu material (cf. Kraeling, 1953:14), and at least half of the samples of late fourth and early third century BCE Aramaic cursive given by Cross (1955:149fn) are from Edfu. Indeed, there seems to be a presumption, on the part of one specialist at least,[20] that late Egyptian Aramaic documents of unknown provenience come from Edfu.

Finally, Edfu was the home of an important Jewish community in antiquity, a community from which we have nine Aramaic tombstones of the Persian period (Kornfeld, 1973 and 1979; Degen, 1978b) and over 250 Greek tax-receipts of the Roman period (Tcherikover and Fuks, 1960:108–77; Kasher, 1978:151–4).

From the period which concerns us, the Ptolemaic period, we have about a dozen documents in Aramaic and Greek containing Jewish names (Degen, 1978b:60; Kornfeld, 1979; cf. Kraeling, 1953:14 and Cross 1955:149fn; Tcherikover and Fuks, 1957:210–11, 223, 254–5). A few facts about Jewish life in Edfu have been gleaned from these documents (Kasher, 1978:150), but whether or not there was a specifically Jewish quarter in Edfu during the Ptolemaic period comparable to the Jewish "delta quarter" there in Roman times remains controversial (ibid., 152).

Were the Jews of Edfu as polytheistic or syncretistic in their beliefs as those of Patros had been in the Babylonian period (cf. Jer 44:15–29) and as those of Elephantine had been in the Persian period (cf. Dupont-Sommer, 1945; Kraeling, 1953:84–8; Porten, 1968:173–9)? Did they themselves replace the psalm's references to the God of Israel with references to the Egyptian god Horus, possibly as the result of a syncretistic fusion of the two? Or was the substitution made after the prayer left their hands, by Aramean pagans who wished to adapt the prayer for use in the cult of Horus (cf. Tigay 1976:376–7)? These are questions for which we have no answer at the moment.

Our final question is one that relates to the papyrus as a whole. Why was this collection of Aramaic prayers reduced to writing in demotic—rather than Aramaic—script? Indeed, why was it reduced to writing at all? Certainly, a major factor must have been the precarious situation of Aramaic in Egypt at the time. Bearing in mind that our papyrus is about a century and a half later than the latest Egyptian Aramaic documents in Aramaic script, according to Cross' dating of the latter (1955:149fn, 151), we may hypothesize that it was written for a priest whose Aramaic was so poor that he was able neither to memorize the liturgy nor to read it in Aramaic script. Like many American Jews today, he needed a phonetic transliteration into a familiar script. Thus, it hardly matters that our text may have been partially unintelligible even to native speakers of Aramaic with a good knowledge of demotic script. It was never meant to be intelligible. It was meant to enable an Egyptianized Aramean to continue the tradition of reciting prayers in Aramaic despite his ignorance of that language.

[20] Cf. Degen's judgment that three late ostraca in the Austrian National Library "gehören vermutlich nach Edfu" (1978a:33) and his assignment of Cowley no. 81 to Edfu despite the fact that it was "bought . . . from a dealer at Luxor who believed [it] to have come from Ḳus" (Cowley, 1923:190) and the fact that it seems to speak of sending merchandise *to* Edfu (Grelot, 1972:13).

LIST OF REFERENCES

Aimé-Giron, Noël.

1939: "Adversaria Semitica," *Bulletin de l'Institut français du Caire*, 38:1–63.

Albright, William F.

1950: "Baal-Zephon," in *Festschrift Alfred Bertholet zum 80. Geburtstag gewidmet.* 1–14.

Alliot, Maurice.

1949: *Le culte d'Horus à Edfou au temps des Ptolémées.*

Blau, Joshua.

1979: "Some Observations on a Middle Arabic Egyptian Text in Coptic Characters," in *Jerusalem Studies in Arabic and Islam*, 215–62.

1982: *On Polyphony in Biblical Hebrew* [Proceedings of the Israel Academy of Sciences and Humanities, VI/2].

Bowman, Raymond.

1944: "An Aramaic Religious Text in Demotic Script," *JNES* 3:219–31.

Clifford, Richard.

1972: *The Cosmic Mountain in Canaan and the Old Testament.*

Cowley, A.
1923: *Aramaic Papyri of the Fifth Century* B.C.
Cross, Frank.
1955: "The Oldest Manuscripts from Qumran," *JBL* 74:147–72.
Dahood, Mitchell.
1966: *Psalms I* [*The Anchor Bible*].
Degen, Rainer.
1978a: "Die aramäischen Ostraka in der Papyrus-Sammlung der Österreichischen Nationalbibliothek," in *Neue Ephemeris für Semitische Epigraphik*, 3:33–57.
1978b: "Zu den aramäischen Texten aus Edfu," *Neue Ephemeris für Semitische Epigraphik* 3:59–66.
Dupont-Sommer, A.
1945: "Le syncrétisme religieux des Juifs d'Éléphantine d'après un ostracon araméen inédit," *Revue de l'Histoire des Religions* 130:17–28.
Eissfeldt, Otto.
1932: *Baal Zaphon, Zeus Kasios und der Durchzug der Israeliten durchs Meer.*
1962: "Der Gott Bethel," *Kleine Schriften* 1:206–33. [Reprinted from *ARW* 28 (1930):1–30.]
1963: "Der Gott des Tabor und seine Verbreitung," *Kleine Schriften*, 2:29–54. [Reprinted from *ARW* 31 (1934): 14–41.]
Fales, Frederick.
1978: "A Cuneiform Correspondence to Alphabetic ש in West Semitic Names of the I Millennium B.C.," *Orientalia* 47:91–8.
Fitzmyer, Joseph.
1979: *A Wandering Aramean* [*SBL* Monograph Series, 25].
Gager, John.
1972: *Moses in Greco-Roman Paganism* [*SBL* Monograph Series, 16].
Gibson, John.
1975: *Textbook of Syrian Semitic Inscriptions*, 2.
Goodenough, Erwin.
1953: *Jewish Symbols in the Greco-Roman Period*, 2.
Greenfield, Jonas.
1981: "A Mandaic 'Targum' of Psalm 114," in *Studies in Aggadah, Targum and Jewish Liturgy in Memory of Joseph Heinemann*, 23–31.
Grelot, Pierre.
1972: *Documents araméens d'Égypte.*
Griffith, F. Ll., and Herbert Thompson.
1921: *The Demotic Magical Papyrus of London and Leiden.*
Heinemann, Joseph.
1977: *Prayer in the Talmud* [*Studia Judaica*, 9].
Hurvitz, Avi.
1965: "Observations on the Language of the Third Apocryphal Psalm from Qumran," *Revue de Qumran* 18:225–32.
1972: *Ben lašon le-lašon.*
Ibn Ezra, Abraham.
1976: *Peruše Torah*, 2.
Ibn Kaspi, Joseph.
1906: *Mišneh Kesef*, 2.
Joüon, Paul.
1923: *Grammaire de l'hébreu biblique.*
Kasher, Aryeh.
1978: *The Jews in Hellenistic and Roman Egypt* (in Hebrew).
Kaufman, Stephen.
1974: *The Akkadian Influences on Aramaic.*
KBHK = Koehler, Ludwig, et. al.
1967–. *Hebräisches und aramäisches Lexikon zum Alten Testament.* 3rd. ed.
Kitchen, K. A.
1965: "The Aramaic of Daniel," in *Notes on Some Problems in the Book of Daniel*, 31–79.
Kornfeld, Walter.
1973: "Jüdisch-Aramäische Grabinschriften aus Edfu," *Anzeiger der phil.-hist. Klasse der Österreichischen Akademie der Wissenschaften* 110:123–37.
1979: "Zu den aramäischen Inschriften aus Edfu," *WZKM* 71:49–52.
Kraeling, Emil.
1953: *The Brooklyn Museum Aramaic Papyri.*
Kutscher, E. Y.
1959: *The Language and Linguistic Background of the Isaiah Scroll* (in Hebrew).
Lauha, Aarre.
1943: *Zaphon: Der Norden und die Nordvölker im Alten Testament.*
Newberry, Percy.
1899: *The Amherst Papyri.*
Peretz, Y.
1967: *The Relative Clause* (in Hebrew).
Porten, Bezalel.
1968: *Archives from Elephantine.*
Postgate, J. N.
1974: *Taxation and Conscription in the Assyrian Empire.*
Preisendanz, Karl.
1931: *Papyri Graecae Magicae*, 2. 2nd ed.
Qimron, Elisha.
1976: "A Grammar of the Hebrew Language of the Dead Sea Scrolls (in Hebrew)," Unpublished Hebrew University Doctoral Dissertation. Jerusalem.
Saadia Gaon ben Joseph.
1896: *Tafsīr Sefer Yešaᶜyahu* (J. Derenbourg, ed.).
Sachau, Eduard.
1911: *Aramäische Papyrus und Ostraka aus einer jüdischen Militärkolonie zu Elephantine*, 1.

Sanders, J. A.
1964: "Two Non-Canonical Psalms in llQPs[a]," *ZAW* 76:57–75.
Sappan, Raphael.
1981: *The Typical Features of the Syntax of Biblical Poetry* (in Hebrew).
Segert, Stanislav.
1975: *Altaramäische Grammatik.*
Sokoloff, Michael.
1974: *The Targum to Job from Qumran Cave XI.*
Stadelmann, Rainer.
1967: *Syrisch-Palästinensische Gottheiten in Ägypten* [*Probleme der Ägyptologie*, 5].
Steiner, Richard.
1982: *Affricated Ṣade in the Semitic Languages.* [*AAJR Monograph Series*, 3].
Tal, Abraham.
1980–81: *The Samaritan Targum of the Pentateuch.* 2 vols.
Tcherikover, Avigdor, and Alexander Fuks.
1957–60: *Corpus Papyrorum Judaicarum.* 2 vols.
Tigay, Jeffrey.
1976: "On Some Aspects of Prayer in the Bible," *AJSR* 1:363–78.
TJ = *Talmud Yerušalmi.* 1523. Venice: Daniel Bomberg.
Yadin, Yigael.
1957. *The Scroll of the War of the Sons of Light Against the Sons of Darkness.*

THE SLAVE AND THE SCOUNDREL

CBS 10467, A Sumerian Morality Tale?

Martha T. Roth

Oriental Institute

CBS 10467 was first published in *PBS* 8/1 100, where it was catalogued as an undated contract.[1] Due to the poor state of preservation of the tablet at the time E. Chiera copied it for the *PBS* 8 volume, the nature of the text recorded in the tablet has escaped notice.[2] The tablet has since been baked and cleaned at the University Museum, Philadelphia, and nearly all of the tablet can now be read with certainty. As a result, it appears that the inclusion of *CBS* 10467 in *PBS* 8, a volume of "Legal and Administrative Documents from Nippur," was inappropriate, for the tablet is not a legal document at all. Rather, *CBS* 10467 might be better characterized as a comic morality tale, which—perhaps consciously—draws upon and echoes elements of literary and of legal genres.

Included in this article are a photograph, transliteration, and translation of *CBS* 10467, together with brief philological notes. Although the tablet is still imperfectly understood, it is hoped that its publication here will serve to bring attention to an example of a heretofore unrecognized type of Sumerian composition.

		CBS 10467		TRANSLATION
obv.	1.	1 sag-munus ḫa-la-^{d}ba-ú mu-n[i-im]	1.	(Concerning) one female slave, Ḫala-Bau by name,
	2.	sag ⸢ama⸣-ar-gi$_4$-bi gar-r[a]	2.	a manumitted slave:
	3.	ká-⸢dingir-ra^{ki}-ta⸣ ká-dingir-ra^{k}[^{i}-šè]	3.	From Babylon and back,
	4.	erin$_2$-⸢ta bu-ra-àm⸣ ugnim(! text: KI.SU.KU.LU.GAR)-[ta x-àm]	4.	she has been expelled from the camp-followers, [rejected from] the troops,
	5.	un-⸢ta suḫ-àm⸣ ga-ab-šám-d[i-dam]	5.	shunned by the people. She is a huckster,
	6.	$^{bu-bu-àm}$bú-bú-⸢àm zé(?)-zé(?)⸣-àm	6.	she is flighty, she is an exile(?).
	7.	ga-⸢an-za-za-àm du$_{14}$-mú-mú-àm⸣	7.	She is a nymphomaniac, she is quarrelsome,
	8.	ka-⸢lul-la-bal-bal-àm⸣ inim-⸢sig-kú-kú⸣-àm	8.	she is a liar, a slanderer.
	9.	bí-in-⸢dug$_4$⸣ ba-da-⸢gur⸣	9.	She is a double-dealer.
	10.	nu-mu-un-na-kal dumu-munus nin-⸢úr-ra-ni⸣	10.	She is worthless, (this) daughter of Nin-urrani.
	11.	^{I}nin-úr-ra-ni ama-ni	11.	Nin-urrani, her mother,

[1] Many colleagues have discussed this text with me. In particular, I wish to thank Profs. Miguel Civil and Åke W. Sjöberg for their numerous comments and criticisms, and assistance in reading difficult passages. The tablet is published here with the permission of Prof. Sjöberg, Curator of the Babylonian Section, University Museum, Philadelphia. The photographs were kindly taken by Prof. Civil. The unpublished passages from Dialogues were supplied by Prof. Civil, who also graciously allowed me access to his extensive lexical files.

[2] Greengus, in his article discussing the model court record involving an adultery case (*HUCA* 40–41 [1969–70], 43 n. 31) suggested that the tablet belongs to the small group of texts called "literary legal decisions," and characterized *CBS* 10467 as "a dispute of heirs over a slave girl"; see further below, Appendix.

12.	ud-⌈bi-ta NI.BULUG⌉ [K]A (or [S]AG) in-TAR	12.	from that day on, . . .
13.	MUNUS KUR BU(?) ⌈É(?) x-maḫ⌉-ta	13.	....
14.	^{ld}nanna-il[du$_2$-mu] lú ⌈dingir⌉ nu-un-tuku	14.	Nanna-ildu$_2$-mu, the unlucky fellow,
15.	^{giš}si-gar-gal-⌈gin$_7$ ugu-na⌉ bí-in-gili$_x$(GILIM)-ib	15.	secured her as (if he had locked her) with a large bolt.
16.	nam-⌈x⌉-tur-ra ⌈é-a bí-in⌉-ku$_4$	16.	He brought her into his household in the status of . . .
17.	1 sag-arad dingir-da-⌈nu-me-a mu-ni⌉-im	17.	One male slave, Dingirda-numea by name,
18.	1 sag-munus nin-sa$_6$-[ga mu-ni]-im	18.	One female slave, Nin-šaga by name,
19.	5 túg$^{ḫi-a}$ 1 ⌈^{giš}⌉má ⌈10+(x)⌉ gur	19.	Five garments, one boat of ten(?) gur capacity,
20.	$\frac{2}{3}$ ma-na 5 gín [kù]-babbar	20.	Forty-five shekels of silver —
21.	ḫa-la é-[ad]-da-na-⌈ka in⌉-ḫa-la-a	21.	(all this is) her patrimonial inheritance portion which had been divided —
22.	é-a-ni-šè i[n-n]a-⌈ni-in⌉-ku$_4$	22.	he had brought into his own household.
23.	dumu-munus-a-ni UL$_4$.UL$_4$-tum mu-ni-im	23.	His daughter, UL$_4$.UL$_4$-tum by name,
rev. 24.	ke-zé-er in-ak GIŠ.DI.TAR in-ba	24.	acted like a courtesan, . . .
25.	ad in-sa$_6$ lú-e-ne-di dug$_4$-dug$_4$-dam	25.	she sang sweet songs and played games.
26.	^{ld}nanna-ildu$_2$-mu	26.	(Meanwhile,) Nanna-ildu$_2$-mu
27.	ud-šú-uš tigi$_2$ za-am-za-am [tag-tag]-e-da	27-8.	spent all day every day [playing] the tigi and zamzam instruments.
28.	ud mi-ni-ib-zal-zal-e		
29.	itu 6 ud 15-àm zal-la-a	29.	(But) when six months and fifteen days had elapsed,
30.	ú-gin$_7$ mu-un-bu	30.	he was plucked out like reeds,
31.	^{ú}numun$_2$-gin$_7$ mu-un-zé	31.	he was torn out like rushes.
32.	sur-ra šà-⌈gal⌉-la-na e-sír e-sír-ra gú mu-un-gíd-gíd-dè	32.	. . . was his (only) sustenance. He (now) wanders about in the streets.
33.	^{ld}nanna-ildu$_2$-mu	33.	Nanna-ildu$_2$-mu
34.	sila-dagal bàd-zi-ab-ba^{ki}-ka	34-5.	drifts aimlessly through the wide street(s) of Borsippa.
35.	šu mu-un-dag-dag-ge		

TEXTUAL COMMENTS

5. For ga-ab-šám, cf. Izi V 113–115:

ga-ab-šàm = *kap-su-ú*
ga-ab-šàm = *ša-a-a-ma-⌈nu⌉*
ga-ab-šàm-šàm = *na-as-si-ḫ[u]*

The three Akkadian lexical equivalents have been translated in the dictionaries (*AHw.*, *CAD*, s.vv.) as "buyer," based on the context of the Izi passage. ga-ab-šàm = *šajjamānu* clearly is derived from šàm = *šâmu* "to buy," while *nassiḫu* and *kapsû* are attested only here and in a commentary, *UET* 4 208:11 (commentary to Nabnitu XVIII). The context in *CBS* 10467 suggests a pejorative connotation which is not readily apparent from the lexical equations. This connotation is also supported by the following passages from Dialogues 1 and 5 (courtesy M. Civil):

Dial. 1:85f.: ga-ab-šám (var. ga-ab-šám-šám) ganba lú-še-sa-sa-a lú-ní-su-ub-ba-gin$_7$ igi-zu-ta ab-ta-kar-re-dè-eš "(even) the g., (all) the marketplace, the roast barley merchants, flee before you as (from) a maniac" (*SEM* 65 r. 14f. and duplicates, var. from *TuM NF* 3 43 ii 11f.).[3]

Dial. 5:128f.: gáb-šám-ma (var. ga-ab-šám-[ ) ⌈ba⌉-gub-gub-⌈bé⌉ KA na-ám-mu-lu-lu$_7$ bún-dug$_4$-dug$_4$ guruš uru-ka lul-sì-sì-ke ki-sikil-tur dag-gi$_4$-a ti-la ù nu-mu-un-na-ku-ku "always standing as a g., distorting (?) everyone's words, deceiving the young men of the town, the young girls of the district cannot sleep because of you" (unpub. sources).

The gabšam, clearly associated with buying and selling, seems to be a disreputable merchant, a "wheeler-dealer."

6. For bú(-bú) = *našarbūṭ/ṣu*, see Proto-Ea Secondary Branch No. 7 i 23 (*MSL* 14 119): bu-ú BU = *na-ša-ar-bu-ṣum*; Ea I 273 (*MSL* 14 190) and *A* I/6 41 (*MSL* 14 226): bu-ú KASKAL = *na-šar-bu-ṭu* (see further the refs. cited *AHw.*, *CAD* s.vv. *našarbūṭu*, *muttašrabbiṭu*).

The gloss bu-bu-àm is inscribed in small script on the left edge of the tablet, followed by a small horizontal wedge "pointing" to KASKAL-KASKAL-àm (gloss not copied in PBS 8). See the observations of W. W. Hallo on such scribal practices, "Haplographic Marginalia," in *Finkelstein Mem. Vol.*, 101–3. The examples noted by Hallo are all corrections to the texts, in which a line accidentally omitted from the tablet was generally written down the left edge of the tablet (i.e., at right angles to the main text) and a short horizontal line placed at its point of insertion. (Hallo also noted one example of the inserted line written up the left edge, and one in which it was written on the right edge.) The practice of thus inserting additional lines on a tablet is not, however, limited to Sumerian literary compositions. In Sag Bil. A (*YBC* 9896, see *MSL SS1*, forthcoming), about sixteen supplementary entries are inscribed on col. vi, and nine more on the right edge of the tablet. These additions are indicated by the formula egir A B; i.e., after entry A (in the main text) insert entry B. Similarly, in *MLC* 2626 (*BRM* 4 No. 33, Group Voc. C, see *MSL* 18, forthcoming), col. iii is concluded with a double horizontal line, after which there is the entry egir-bi SUD^{ud} = *ru-⌈ú⌉-[qu]*; i.e., "after it"—after an entry indicated by a short horizontal line or other marker which appeared in the broken upper portion of col. iii—the entry SUD^{ud} = *rūqu* was accidentally omitted and is to be inserted. Note also *PBS* 5 140 (*OBGT* XII) 28.

The gloss to KASKAL-KASKAL-àm in our text is similar to the above in that it is an addition to the main text. It differs, however, not only in that it was written horizontally on the left edge, but in that it is a gloss and not an accidentally omitted line. As a gloss, its function was to elucidate an otherwise ambiguous clause.

The traces of the reduplicated grapheme of the second phrase of the line are unclear, but appear to be AB.AB, AD.AD, ZÉ.ZÉ, or the like. Only reading zé-zé, understanding a form related to Akk. *nasāḫu*, yields any sense in the context.

7. For ga-an-za-za, see Izi V 141–144 (*MSL* 13 165):

⌈ga⌉-an-za-za = *ba-ri-r[i-tu]*
[ga]-an-za-za = *mu-ut-ti-k[um]*
[g]a-an-za-za = *mu-ut-ta-ti-k[um]*
[g]a-an-za-za = ŠU-*ú*

and Nabnitu VI ii 16′ (= D b 4): ga-an-z[a-za] = [*ba-ri-ri-tum*]. Note also *KUB* 26 11 No. 38 i 4′f.: *mu-ti-⌈ku-ki⌉*, *mu-ti-ti-ku-ki*, the Sumerian correspondence for which might be restored ga-an-za-za.

8. For ka-lul-la-bal-bal See Å. W. Sjöberg, *ZA* 64 (1974), 154 n. 56; cf. Sag A 31 (*MSL SS1*, forthcoming), and Kagal D Bil. Section 3:13′ (*MSL* 13 244) with Kagal D Section A 14 (*MSL* 13 251).

The reading inim for KA in KA-sig-kú-kú (*karṣa akālu*) is secured by the eme-sal reading in Dial. 5:6, e-ne-èm-sig-zu-um ì-kú. Cf. also Sag A 48 and Kagal D Bil. Section 11:6 (MSL 13 249).

9. The translation of bí-in-dug$_4$ ba-da-gur, literally "she has declared, she has turned away from it (her word)" was suggested to me by Prof. Kramer (personal communication). The phrase implies one who states one thing and then retracts it or ignores it, suggesting a generally unreliable and untrustworthy individual.

10. nu-mu-un-na-kal "she is worthless" (literally, "she is of no value to him/her") is to be compared with lú-kal-la = *wa-aq-rum* in OB Lu B v 20 (*MSL* 12 184 and see OB Lu A 148), and Proto-Izi II 184 RS Recension nu-kal-la = ⌈*la wa*⌉-*aq-rum* (note Proto-Izi II 184 nu-mu-na-kal, *MSL* 13 46); see nu-mu-na-kal-la (var. nu-kal-la) in Ninninšagurra 86 (Sjöberg, *ZA* 65 [1975], 186). Note the use of this expression in the Nippur Homicide Trial (Jacobsen, *AnBi* 12 [1959], 137 = *The Image of Tammuz*, 200) line 36: munus dam-a-ni nu-un-kal-la "a woman who does not value her husband."

12–13. The reading and interpretation of these lines are unclear. I expect line 12 to describe the reaction of Nin-urrani (Ḫala-Bau's mother) to her daughter's conduct; but NI.BULUG in the middle of line 12 remains unexplained.

---

[3] Note that the lú-še-sa-sa, with whom the ga-ab-šám is here associated, appears in a disparaging context in Dial. 2:170ff.: ama-zu ninda-du$_8$-du$_8$ muḫaldim uru^{ki}-ka ad-da-zu é-dam-gàr-ra-ka kir$_4$ zal-šè gub-ba-àm šeš-zu-ne dun-dug$_4$-dug$_4$ lú-uru-a nu-tuš-ù-me-eš nin$_9$-zu-ne lú-še-sa-da-me-eš "your mother is a baker, the cook of the town, your father is an object of derision in the merchant's house, your brothers are . . . they cannot live in town, your sisters are roast barley dealers" (*UET* 6 153, r. 26ff. and dupls.).

BULUG (the shape of the sign rules out MUŠ) is not known as a verb, thus not allowing a reading ì-BULUG ... in-TAR. Further, it is possible to see ud-bi-ta as a frozen form which could take the suffix -ni; note munus ud-bi-ta-ke$_4$-ne in Uruinimgina 6 (Oval Plaque) iii 20 (Sollberger *Corpus* 54 = "Reforms of Urukagina").

14. For the designation of an individual as lú dingir nu-un-tuku, see OB Lu A 62 and B ii 21 (*MSL* 12 159 and 179) lú dingir nu-tuku = *ša i-lam la i-šu-ú* "one who has no god," or "one who has no good fortune." It is unclear whether Nanna-ildu$_2$-mu is here characterized as a "man without a (protective) deity" in the sense of one with no conscience, morals, or scruples, or one who is simply unlucky. (Correct *CAD, I/J*, 101 s.v. *ilu* mng. 5 where this phrase in our text was cited as a personal name.)

15. For si-gar (*šīgaru*) see most comprehensively E. I. Gordon, *Sumer* 12 (1956), 80ff.

16. Although the problematic reading of the second sign does not allow this line to be securely read, I expect it in some way to describe the relationship by which Nanna-ildu$_2$-mu brought Ḫala-Bau into his household. The traces of the second sign look like:

17. For the personal name Dingir-da-nu-me-a, cf. Limet, *Anthroponymie*, 91 and 279, where the name DN (^{d}Bau, ^{d}Amar-Suʾen, ^{d}Ninnu)-da-nu-me-a is cited.

19. The number indicating the boat capacity is no longer preserved on the tablet; 10+(x) follows the copy.

23. The personal name UL$_4$.UL$_4$-tum is unclear. The entire line is written over an erasure. At the end of the line there is an extra -im, partially obliterated by the end of -dam of line 25 on the reverse. This suggests that the scribe rewrote this line only after beginning the reverse.

24. The line is clearly inscribed and there is no doubt about the readings of the signs; however, GIŠ.DI.TAR in-ba remains problematic. No interpretation involving "judge" or "judgment" is warranted by the context. In 24–25, three actions are described: ... in-ak, ... in-ba, ... in-sa$_6$. Perhaps a type of musical instrument is indicated by GIŠ.DI.TAR, thus "she acted the courtesan, played an x-instrument, (and) made sweet songs."

ke-zé-er is known to me in only one other Sumerian composition (and note ke-zé-er-mu in Ugumu 33 [*MSL* 9 53]). In the adultery trial *IM* 28051 published by van Dijk, *Sumer* 15 (1959), pl. 9 (see also *ZA* 55 [1962], 70–77, Greengus, *HUCA* 40–41 [1969–70], 33–34) read line 21 ⌜ke-zé-er ak(?) (or ù?)⌝ sur-ra gal$_4$-la-[ne].

25. For ad as a type of song, see Ea IV 195 (*MSL* 14 363) ad AD = *ri-ig-[mu]*, Nabnitu B 208 ad = *ri-ig-mu šá ir-ti*. See *CAD, I/J*, 188 s.v. *irtu* mng. 4.

30–31. Cf. Lugale XIII 8–9 ^{ú}num[un$_2$-gin$_7$] mu-e-sìg-ge-en-zé-en ^{ú}numun$_2$-gin$_7$ mu-e-bu-re-[en-z]é-en : *ki-ma šup-pa-ti tan-na-as-ḫa-a-ni ki-ma el-pi-ti tab-baq-ma-a-ni* "you (stones) have been torn out like rushes, plucked like reeds." See also the phrase as a literary quotation in a lexical commentary, A III/1 Comm. A 40–41 (*MSL* 14 324).

32. sur-ra in sur-ra šà-gal-la-na remains unclear. Note sur-ra in the adultery trial IM 28051:21 (see note to line 24) ⌜ke-zé-er ak(?)⌝ sur-ra gal$_4$-la-a-[ne].

For e-sír e-sír-ra gú mu-un-gíd-gíd-dè, cf. for example B. Alster, *The Instructions of Šuruppak*, 46:233; Lugalbanda and Ḫurrum (L 1) 402 (=*SEM* 20 "rev. i" 4′ and dupls.); *BRM* 4 9:41 (NB balag); 5N-T52 (=A 30594) ii 3 (Ur III incant.).

34–35. For šu dag-dag, cf. Wilcke, *Lugalbanda*, 207, Innin-šagurra 78 (Å. W. Sjöberg, *ZA* 65 [1975], 184).

The narrative may be summarized: Just as in a manumission or a contract involving a former slave, the tablet begins by introducing Ḫala-Bau, a manumitted slave woman. Although "a manumitted slave" is not generally associated with anything reprehensible, the designation here takes on suspicious connotations by what follows: in and out of Babylon, she has been expelled from the camp followers, rejected by the troops and by the population in general; she is an outcast. In lines 10ff., Ḫalu-Bau's mother is introduced. The interpretation of these lines is unclear, but they may indicate that even her own mother can find no good in her.

We then meet Nanna-ildu$_2$-mu (lines 14ff.). He is immediately described as a lú dingir nu-un-tuku, literally "a man without a god," in this context apparently implying that he is a scoundrel. In some manner, Nanna-ildu$_2$-mu gains control over Ḫala-Bau—she is in his power as surely as if he had locked her up. Along with Ḫala-Bau, Nanna-ildu$_2$-mu gains control of her rich inheritance portion, consisting of slaves, garments, boats, and silver. With this newly acquired wealth, Nanna-ildu$_2$-mu begins to lead the life of the idle rich. His daughter acts like a courtesan (*kezertu* here clearly involving entertainment and not necessarily sexual favors). While she sings and dances, Nanna-ildu$_2$-mu spends all his time idly playing the tigi and zamzam instruments.

The frivolity continues for six months and fifteen days, at which time his luck (and wealth) seems to have run out. After leading the dissipated gay life, Nanna-ildu$_2$-mu is "plucked out like reeds, torn out like rushes." He has no means of support left him, and drifts through the streets destitute. We finally leave Nanna-ildu$_2$-mu wandering aimlessly through the wide streets of Borsippa.

The composition is a curious mixture of styles and genres. Although many of the details we would wish expressly stated to understand the "narrative" or "plot" of the piece are absent,[4] the scribe included such seemingly superfluous details as a gloss in line 6. The vivid descriptions of the slave woman Ḫala-Bau and of the pastimes of Nanna-ildu$_2$-mu and the detailed itemized list of the inheritance are in marked contrast to the silence of the composition on any action or interrelations of the characters.

The use of legal formulae is a disarming literary device. The opening two lines, which deceive the reader (or audience) by beginning in the style of a dry legal document, are immediately followed by a vivid account of the slave woman's outrageous behavior. The reader is later lulled again by the bald, technical listing of the inheritance items, only to be abruptly jarred by the description of the lifestyles of Nanna-ildu$_2$-mu and his daughter.

This juxtaposition of the common with the unexpected is evident not only in style, but also in the choice of phraseology. As opposed to several rare (to the modern scholar at least) lexical items in the description of Ḫala-Bau and Nanna-ildu$_2$-mu, the piece is concluded with what appear to be stock literary phrases. And note that a preponderance of the less common lexical items are to be found particularly in one section of one lexical text, Izi V.

This unevenness of the composition—the combinations of rare lexical items with stock literary phrases, vivid descriptions of characters with dry legal formulations—suggests an unusual interpretation of the origin and function of the text. While it is possible that all these apparently contradictory elements are intentional, that the composition is tongue-in-cheek and consciously mimics aspects of a legal document, it is also possible that we are dealing with no more than the exercise of a clever student scribe. Having recently studied the lexical text Izi, slave and inheritance documents, and such literary compositions as Lugale, Innin-šagurra, perhaps the Dialogues, the student sat down and incorporated elements of these recently-learned texts in his own attempt at an original composition.[5]

APPENDIX

This text first drew my attention because of the possibility that it belonged to the genre of model court records.[6] Study of the text subsequently showed that it does not belong to that genre. Nonetheless, because our picture of the model court records has been skewed by the vagaries of publication, a few general remarks on these texts may be offered here.

To date, three documents have been published which are model court records—i.e., sample court settlements used to train the scribe in the form of the functional court records. The three published model court records are all particularly vivid accounts of dramatic cases, which would accord well with their ultimate function as didactic tools—that which is unusual is interesting, and makes excellent teaching material. However, two more model court records are known to me, both of which are rather mundane in subject matter, thus considerably altering the tenor of the genre as represented by the three published cases. The five cases may be summarized as follows.[7]

(1) A homicide trial (3N-T273+ i–ii, in Jacobsen, *AnBi* 12 [1959], 130–50 = *The Image of Tammuz*, 193–214) begins with a statement of the facts of the case, formulated from the perspective of the final verdict, as is usual in a court case: three men murdered a fourth, Lu-Inanna. The three informed Nin-Dada, wife of the deceased, of their deed, but she remained silent. The case was taken to Isin, where king Ur-Ninurta referred the trial to the Assembly of Nippur (puḫrum Nibru^{ki}-ka). The Assembly pronounced the guilt of the three men and of Nin-Dada, ordering the execution of all four. A minority voice then questioned the applicability of the death penalty for the woman, but was overruled. All four defendants were sentenced to death. The record concludes di-dab$_5$-ba pu-úḫ-ru-um Nibru^{ki}-ka "case accepted for trial in the Assembly of Nippur."

[4] E.g., what became of the slave woman Ḫala-Bau, described so vividly at the beginning of the composition? What was the role of her mother, Nin-urrani? What is the significance of the six months and fifteen days? Why is Babylon mentioned at the beginning, and Borsippa at the end of the text? Because of the limitations of the text itself to convey to the modern reader all the information available to its intended audience, we might never arrive at satisfactory answers to such simple questions; see the remarks of M. Civil, "Les limites de l'information textuelle," in *L'archéologie de l'Iraq* (Colloques internationaux du *C.N.R.S.* No. 580), 225–32.

[5] A similar phenomenon is found in the Middle Ages, when poems may have been composed to demonstrate the poet's erudition and knowledge of rare lexical items; see Ernst Curtius, *Europäische Literatur und lateinisches Mittelalter*, 1948, 143 (who uses the term "versifizierte Lexikographie"). I owe this reference to Prof. E. Reiner.

[6] See S. Greengus, *HUCA* 40–41 (1969–1970), 43 n. 31.

[7] Stephen J. Lieberman plans to include detailed treatments of the model court records with his forthcoming edition of the model contracts.

CBS 10467 obv.

CBS 10467 left edge

CBS 10467 rev.

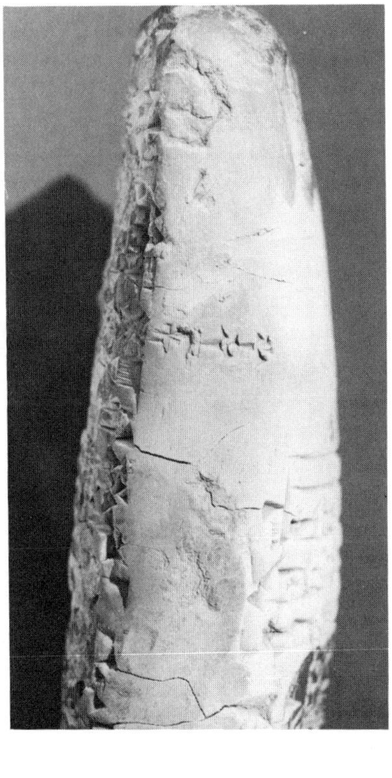

CBS 10467 right edge

(2) On the same Sammeltafel as the homicide trial, there is recorded a dispute over possession of prebends (3N-T273+ iii–iv 1, unpub.). This dispute is taken directly to the Assembly of Nippur by one of the plaintiffs, Paḫaḫum, son of Lugal-a-ma-⸢ni⸣, who charges that Mašqu, son of Nanna-Mansum, has illegally seized two family prebends (nam-má-SUḪUŠ-GAL kar-ra Nibru^{ki}-ka ù bur-šu-ma giš-má ^{d}nin-urta DÙ(or PAP)-Ù-NE [im]-ri-a-bi nam-garza ad-da-mu [^{l}ma-á]š-qu dumu ^{d}nanna-ma-an-sum [i]n-na-dab$_5$ bí-in-dug$_4$ lines iii 4–7). Mašqu's response to the charge is lost in the succeeding broken lines. When the text resumes, the puḫrum has awarded possession of one prebend each to the two parties. Each agrees not to dispute the other's ownership. The final broken lines contain a mutual renunciation clause, and the case concludes [(di-dab$_5$-ba) pu-úḫ-r]u-um Nibru^{ki}-ka "(case accepted by) the Assembly of Nippur."

(3) The trial concerning rape of a slave woman (Finkelstein, *JAOS* 86 [1966], 359) is the third case on the Sammeltafel (3N–T273+ iv 2ff.). Like the homicide trial, it begins with a summary of the facts: Lugal-melam seized and raped the slave woman of one Kuguzana. The charge is brought before the Assembly of Nippur by Kuguzana, and denied by Lugal-melam. Witnesses are called who confirm Kuguzana's testimony, and the Assembly of Nippur imposes a penalty of one-half mina of silver upon Lugal-melam—mu geme$_2$ lugal-da nu-me-a a bí-in-gi$_4$ "because he deflowered the slave woman without her owner's (prior) consent." The case concludes with the subscript [pu]-uḫ-ru-um-e di-d[ab$_5$] [d]i mi-in-dab$_5$-bé-eš "the Assembly decided the case for them."

(4) In an adultery trial (van Dijk, *Sumer* 15 [1959], 12–14, also *ZA* 55 (1963), 70–77; Greengus, *HUCA* 40–41 [1969–70], 33–44) Ištar-ummī is accused by her husband before the Assembly (*pu-úḫ-ru-um*) of three charges: she burglarized his storeroom, secretly stole from his oil jar, and finally was compromisingly caught with another man. The Assembly granted a divorce and ordered certain punishments to be inflicted upon the woman, including making her a prostitute (see the note to *CBS* 10467:24 above), shaving her pudenda, boring her nose with an arrow, and parading her about the city streets. The case concludes [di-dab$_5$-b]a lugal-la-kam ^{d}Išme-Dagan-zīmu maškim-bi-im "it is a decision of the king, in which Išme-Dagan-zīmu was bailiff."

(5) On a Sammeltafel including model contracts (*CBS* 11324 i 26 - ii 31 unpub.) is found the fifth model court record. This case, which is largely broken, records a suit brought by Suen-maḫḫa before Išme-Dagan, in which Suen-maḫḫa charges his father's brother with misappropriating(?) the house and field of his inheritance (PA.AN é-a-šà-ga-bi ḫa-[la] šeš-ad-da-mu nam-⸢gú⸣ mu-un-ak-ma lines ii 1–3). The case is referred to the Assembly of Nippur (pu-úḫ-ru-um Nibru^{ki}-ka), which is said to meet in the ub-šu-ukkin-na.

The single unifying factor in these records is the puḫrum of Nippur. The cases recorded were doubtless actual cases, which were adapted and incorporated into the law curriculum of the Nippur eduba. It is not surprising to find that cases adjudicated by the local assembly might be used in the schools for didactic purposes, in order to teach the student scribes the forms of a court record.

(6) One more text, F. A. Ali, *Sumerian Letters*, B:12 (= *Sumer* 20 [1964], 66ff.), may be mentioned here. In that text, a seal has been lost, and that loss is officially announced, accompanied by the sounding of the herald's horn. After the blowing of the horn, the legal validity of any document found bearing that seal is voided: (line 4) lú-na-me níg-na-me ugu-na li-bí-in-tuku "no one may have any claim against him (= the owner of the lost seal)."[8] Like the above-cited texts, this text is basically a "legal" document, which found its way into the scribal curriculum. It is not, however, strictly speaking, an example of the discussed genre—conspicuously absent is the puḫrum of Nippur.

---

[8] Piotr Steinkeller, in *Seals and Sealing in the Ancient Near East* (= *BM* 6), McGuire Gibson and Robert D. Biggs, eds., 48, suggested that this text might belong with the "literary legal decisions."

MARI DREAMS

Jack M. Sasson
The University of North Carolina, Chapel Hill

. . . Present Fears
Are less than horrible imaginings.
Macbeth, I/iii

The oneiric imagination, sometimes luxuriant and phantasmagorical, feeds upon the personal knowledge and experience of the dreamer. In ancient times, however, the interpretation of dreams was usually assigned to individuals other than the dreamer; for the analytic imagination was not one which could be nurtured without extensive and formal preparations. In literary works, of course, this bifurcation of roles need not have occurred, and the dreams embedded therein were shaped by a poet's omniscient eye, one capable of crafting dreams to suit predicted or known endings. It is not surprising therefore, that when A. Leo Oppenheim chose to take up the problem of dream interpretation in the ancient world,[1] his material was overwhelmingly scientific and literary. At his disposal was but a handful of non-literary examples. Of those he collected from the OB period, only one had come from Mari.[2] Since then, the corpus of epistolary documentation which mentions or reports dreams has increased. One of these letters, *AbB* V:10, mentions dreams in a sharp retort.[3] The remainder was recovered at Mari.[4]

It is probably due to an accident of discovery that the Mari archives have not, as yet, provided us with letters which testify to the critical ability of an expert Mari dream interpreter, to his powers for decoding the signs and symbols of a night's revelation and for converting them into meaningful acts.[5] What we do find among the documents are letters which articulate the dreamer's memory of a nocturnal vision. Occasionally, the reaction of the dreamer, or that of the letter's dispatcher, is lightly and perfunctorily registered. My paper, therefore, will only incidentally interpret a particular dream and will only occasionally try to establish a context for its manifestation. Rather, I will focus on the language and the structure of the Mari dream, and try to analyze the manner in which dream sequences are fitted within the mundane information that is usually communicated in letters. For convenience's sake, I will concentrate on three documents from the dossier of a highly placed lady, Addu-dūri. Since these texts report dreams that are fairly representative of oneiric experiences available from Mari, I shall reserve for an appendix brief remarks on the remaining examples.

---

[1] Oppenheim, 1956. See also his supplementary texts, 1969, and his reassessments, 1966a and 1966b. Further Assyriological discussions on the interpretation of dreams can be found in Falkenstein, 1966 and Bottéro, 1974.

[2] *PBS* VII/1, #17 (discussed in Oppenheim, 1956:229) and *TCL* I:53 (cf. p. 226). The Mari example (A. 15) discussed by Oppenheim, p. 195, will be broached in Appendix *A*. It has been frequently translated and widely discussed. For bibliography, see Noort, 1977:202 (sub. No. 8); Ellermeier, 1968:24–8. The most easily accessible translation is by Moran, 1969b:623. Oppenheim did not treat *TCL* XVIII:100: "Tell Sin-uṣelli, Šērim-ili says: "This day is dark. I walk a mile and stay worried, and yet you don't resolve my problem. While I dream of you constantly, you (act) as if we have never met or as if I don't exist. And you don't resolve my problem . . .'" The problem, as the text clarifies, is most mundane.

[3] In a response to stern message from a lady, a man urges that she dream her own dream, *šunat ramnīki attīma taṭṭulī*. This may be taken sarcastically, see Westenholz, 1974:411–2.

[4] A. 15 (Dossin, 1948:128/130); A. 222 (Dossin, 1975:28); *ARM(T)* X: 10 (?), 50, 51, 94, 100, 117, XIII:112, 113.

[5] Because of the haphazardous archival techniques obtaining at Mari, I seriously question the potential for officials to retrieve letters with oneiric examples either for consultation or in order to match subsequent activities to the guidelines suggested by a dream (Sasson, 1972). I state this despite the fact that all but one letters with dream sequences (X:117) lay in room 115.

Addu-dūri's exact position in the Mari hierarchy and the nature of her kinship, if any, with the royal family are yet to be determined.[6] Batto, 1974:64–72, charts her activities within the Mari palace but can only speculate that she may have been a widow of an ally (a certain Ḫatni-Addu) or that she may have come from Aleppo to accompany Šibtu, the queen. Subsequent information, published by Rouault in *ARMT* XVIII, 234–5, has not appreciably clarified the issue, while Finet's romantic view, 1972:69, that she replaced Šibtu on Zimri-Lim's couch, is far-fetched. She may have been one of Zimri-Lim's sisters. But all this uncertainty in no way alters the obvious fact that Addu-dūri had the king's attention and that she did move easily among Mari's top administrators. She was, therefore, not reticent about conveying her opinions, and she may have felt that her messages and reports of oracular and divinatory activities would elicit appropriate royal response.[7]

Our investigation opens with a fragmentary document, X:117, a letter to Addu-dūri, which was one of three documents (the others being X:105 and 134) recovered from the palace's courtyard (Parrot, 1958: 36–37). Its author, Timlû, is nowhere else attested in the archives. The recoverable passage (11: 4–10) reads as follows:

> It was indeed a sign[8] that when [. . .] Yarʾip-Abba made me leave Kasapā,[9] I came to you and addressed you as follows: 'I saw a dream *in your behalf*, and in this dream of mine. . .'.

Timlû's dream, by which her sign was confirmed, is not extant, with lines of narrative continuity found only at the end of the letter wherein Addu-dūri is asked: "Send me the scarf of your head; may I smell the fragrance of my lady and may my heart, having died, revive (thereby)."[10]

That Timlû is socially dependent on Addu-dūri is clear from her address where she labels the latter "my lady," and from the homage she planned to pay (cf. Dossin, 1938–40:70:2–3). Kasapā, the town which Timlû has left, is in Kurda's territory. But we need not be concerned here with the circumstances which found Timlû so far from Mari and with her relationship to Yarʾip-Abba. What is interesting is the phrase *šuttam āmurakkim*. While the accusative of *šuttum* is often associated with the verb *amārum* (or *naṭālum*), when speaking of dream manifestations, suffixing a dative (with ventive) to *amārum* is rare. The few examples I have collected suggest that *ARMT* X's rendering, "j'ai vu pour toi un rêve," is closer to the mark than, say, Moran's (1969:45) "I had a dream concerning you."[11] And if this understanding is correct, X:117 implies that Addu-dūri, or anyone for that matter, can commission certain individuals to receive dreams on their behalf.[12]

---

[6] See listings of references in *ARMT* XVI/1:50. The reading Hatni-Addu in Addu-dūri's seal is confirmed by Durand's collations, 1981b.

Addu-dūri's dossier was recovered from a number of rooms. 1. *Correspondence*: *a. To* Zimri-Lim, Rm 115 (II:124; X:50–60); to Mukannišum, Rm 135 (X:61). *b. From* Zimri-Lim, Rm 110 (X:142–143; 147–150); Rm 135 (X:146); from Timlû, Rm 51 (X:117). 2. Allusion to Addu-dūri are made in economic and bureaucratic documents recovered from Rms 5 (in *ARM* XII), 110 (in *ARM* VII), 115 (in *ARM* XI and XIII), and 135 (in *ARM* XVIII). For specific entry, see the listings in XVI/1:50. This wide scattering of documentation only accentuates the feeling I reported in n. 5. [Addu-dūri's activities are also charted in texts in rooms 134 and 160 (*ARM* XXI).]

[7] As it apparently did, e.g., in X:143.

[8] Frankena, 1974:32 restores *ina bīt* for the end of l. 5 and translates: "May it be a sign that when ᵐ[ ] in Kasapā brought me out of Yarʾip-Abba's house . . ." While this restoration is plausible, there does not seem to be enough space to accommodate it. Frankena's article collects references for the occurrence of *lū ittum(-ma)* with (*ša*) *inūma*. Of these, only VI:76:5–8 offers a close parallel to our passage. See also *OBTR* 153:5–8. I have adopted *ARMT* X's asseverative use of *lū*.

[9] For this GN see *TAVO* 3:145–6; *ARMT* XVI/1:19, and the entry in *RlA*.

[10] Moran, 1980:188.

[11] Moran, 1969a:45. The evidence for noun in accus. + *amārum* + ventive + dative suffix is as follows:

> (G prec.) *AbB* II:56:8—(timber) *līmurūnikkum-ma*
> (G. imperf.) *AbB* II:175:15—(straw) *ammarakkunūšim*
> (Gtn. imper.) *AbB* VI:199:37—(ox) *atammaram-ma*.

[12] Thorkild Jacobsen has written me as follows: "For what it may be worth I suggest that when Timlû was driven out of Kasapâ she sought refuge with Addu-duri and used a dream favorable to the latter, as a means to get access to her. The dative in [*šu-ut-t*]*a-am a-mu-ra-ki-i*[*m-ma*] 'I saw a dream for you' I would understand along the lines of English: 'I have news for you!'. In the present letter she uses this dream, which presumably was known only to the two of them, as a

What is intriguing about this hypothesis is that Mari's archives include two other letters in which Addu-dūri reports dreams. In *ARM* X:51, Addu-dūri communicates a dream reported to her by Idin-ili, a *šangûm*-priest of Itūr-Mer. In doing so, Addu-dūri involves herself rather lightly; for, as she concludes the dream report, she perfunctorily restates the divine advice delivered within the message. Therefore, Addu-dūri's role in this instance is not too dissimilar from ones in which she communicates the results of extispicies (X:54–55), of an inquest (X:58), of an investigation (X:59), etc. It is not clear whether special significance is to be attached to having a priest of Itūr-Mer channeling Bēlet-bīri's message;[13] if this be fluidity in cultic allegiance, it would not be unusual for Mari. But here two points can be made. *1.* X:10 makes it plain that incubation at Itūr-Mer's temple in Mari quickens the reception of dreams (verb: *amāru*), and *2.* As far as present documentation indicates, Bēlet-bīri, "Lady of Divination," did not have a temple either at Mari or at its environs.[14]

The dream itself is dramatically unimpressive. While it is possible that it is Addu-dūri herself, if not her scribe, who chose to shape its contents in such a rigidly static manner, Idin-ili's own memory assigns no active role for the dreamer. We are told nothing about Idin-ili's whereabouts when Bēlet-bīri manifested herself to him; nothing about the locale, the time, the circumstance; we are given no hints regarding his mental state at any point during the vision.[15] Only a touch of movement in his tableau is suggested by the dative suffix in *izzizzam-ma* (l. 19). But because of the paucity of similar constructions, it is hard to judge the kineticity of that particular act, and the ending may merely convey a ventive dimension that is hard to assess. Moran's (1969b:631) "DN stepped up to me," seems too intense while *ARMT* X's "se tenait (devant moi)" would be more plausible were an imperfect used here. However, whatever the motion implied by the suffix, it is counterbalanced by the preterit conjugation, which freezes the whole scene into a precise moment in the past. The message of Bēlet-bīri, despite the potentially contradictory tenor of its two distinct sections, is meant to assure the king of the goddess's solicitude.[16] It ends abruptly; and

---

'password' (CAD I p. 308. 3a.) to prove that the letter actually comes from her."

Two fragmentary letters which Kibri-Dagan, governor of the Terqa district, dispatched to the king show that even non-commissioned dreams must be delivered to those most affected by their portents. Of interest to us are ll. 16–18 of XIII:113: "This man recounted that dream and he placed the onus on me (*arnam elīya utēr-ma*) with the following words: 'Write to the king!'." The idiom *arnam* [*eli x*] *turrum* occurs in III:12:23 (exchanged by the same correspondents!) and there it likewise implies fulfilling the transmission of a message: (Formerly the Benjaminites used to roam at will; the king went on a campaign giving strong orders to the officials) "I placed the onus on them, so that, as it used to be, no one from among the troublemakers can now come from the Upper Region to his settlement." Note however that *AHw*, 1335 (D. 15dB) still maintains that the idiom in III:12 is *uznam turrum*.

XIII:112, also from the same writer, reveals the price paid by those who fail to communicate a dream to the proper authorities. When a man saw a dream in which a god [read in l. 1′: AN*lum*-*ma*, as in 8′] delivers an ukase, then fails to transmit it, the same dream is repeated the next night [but slightly accented on the active role to be played by the message's ultimate recipients, [compare *bītum šū inneppiš-ma* of l. 3′ with l. 10′ *teppešāšu-ma*], the man was stricken ill. See also *OBTR* 65.

XIII:112, 113 will be discussed in Appendix A.

[13] This Idin-ili may be identified with the *kumrum*-priest of VIII:1:37 ['Assyrian' period]. *ARM* XXI:333:43 mentions an Ea-lamassi *mu-hu-ú* of Itūr-Mer

---

[14] With *AHw*, 118 and 130 and contra *CAD* B. 265 ("Lady of [Erum—a GN]"). While Bēlet-bīri's name became that of Mari's 10th month, as yet no personal names from Mari incorporate the goddess's. See now XXI:34:4–5, 10: "4 UDU {UDU} NITAH, *a-na* dNIN-be-ri . . . *i-na ma-ri*(KI)."

[15] I use the term 'vision' here purposefully since I share the opinion that a distinction between 'dream' and 'vision' cannot be substantiated either through the analysis of vocabulary or through dissecting the forms and structure of the phenomena. On this point see Oppenheim, 1956:188, 190, 192, 205–6, 225–7; Ehrlich, 1953:8–12; Hanson, 1978: 1408–9 (with bibliography).

[16] Von Soden, 1980:210 reads *šar*!-*ru-tum* at l. 12 and prefers to restore *na-am-la-a*[*k-t*]*i*!? at its end: "Das Königtum ist meine Domäne." However Mari's two other attestations of *namlaktum* are applicable to human realms (Finet, 1966:19:12; XIII:143:13). Translate, therefore, : "Kingship is his [. . . ?] and the dynasty his permanent state. Why, (therefore,) is he constantly climbing siege towers? He ought to be protecting himself." Thus, in assuring the king of the stability of his reign and the permanence of his line, the goddess chides him for his reliance on warfare. [See collations below.]

with it ends the dreamer's participation. Only Addu-dūri retains space to deliver her own anxiety about the king's welfare.[17]

This anxiety is most immediately recognized in a dream which Addu-dūri herself experienced (X:50). While two other Mari texts, X:94 and 100 (see APPENDIX), contain dreams reported by their experiencers, Addu-dūri's is certainly the most remarkable manifestation of oneiric imagination yet available. To sustain the interest of the reader through the ensuing analysis which may become too intricate, I have resorted to a convention by which I distinguish between two Addu-dūris: the one who is reporting the dream will be given in ordinary roman letterings, while the one whose movement are charted within the dream will be in small caps (ADDU-DŪRI). The translation given below will be refined as the investigation progresses.

1–2	Tell my lord: Addu-dūri, your maidservant, says:
3–7	Since the *šulum* of your father's house, I have never had a dream (such as) this. Previous portents of mine (were as) this pair (?).
8–12	In my dream,[18] I entered Bēlet-ekallim's chapel; but Bēlet-ekallim was not in residence. Moreover, the statues before her were not there. Upon seeing this, I broke into uncontrollable weeping.
13	This dream of mine occurred during the night's first phase (lit. during the evening watch).
14–20	I *resumed* (*dreaming*), and Dada, priest of Ištar-pišra, was standing at the door of Bēlet-ekallim('s chapel), but a hostile voice kept on uttering: "*tūra dagan, tūra dagan.*"
20–21	This is what it kept on uttering . . .

It is the descriptive power of Addu-dūri, rarely equalled in non-literary documents, as well as her choice of vocabulary, that infuses the message with its uncanny quality. From the outset, she presents the king with her judgment on what is to follow, for she admits that what is to unfold presently had never been matched since major events overtook the king's ancestors. Between this assessment and the detailing of the dream, Addu-dūri inserts a statement that is not easily evaluated: *ittātūya ša pānānum annittān.* While the meaning 'portent' for *ittum* is available to Mari, such a rendering may harm the logic of the full statement. Since Addu-dūri has just disclosed the unprecedented nature of the dream's contents, it may be best to understand this declaration contrastively. Therefore, Addu-dūri is informing Zimri-Lim that the dream is but a reproduction, a reenactment, of an episode drawn from actual experience; the dream partakes of experience that is just a shade removed from reality.[19]

While it is probable that Addu-dūri meant to be explicit about the tenor and significance of *šulmum* of l. 3, one cannot be certain how Zimri-Lim reacted to its usage; for whatever its pristine connotation *šulmum* permutated equivocally and, by the OB period, it had come to mean either 'restoration' or 'destruction' of a royal line. In our case, modern authorities have ranged themselves quite evenly behind each definition.[20] Therefore, however innocent Addu-dūri's choice of words may be, from Zimri-Lim's perspective (as well as from ours), the antonymic potential within *šulmum* invests this letter with a dimension rarely available to epistolary texts. For even as it foreshadows the ambiguity that will remain constant throughout the letter—at least through l. 21a—it also forces the reader of the missive to enter into a sustained dialogue with its author regarding her own understanding of her dream. Additionally, because the use of *šulmum* bodes ill to those who would trust a letter to clearly deliver its conclusions (termed as requests, warnings, factual presentations, etc . . .), it encourages them to gauge nuances for every term, to *interpret* every passage, in order to decode the letter's ultimate message.

In narrating her dream, Addu-dūri is naturally selecting and sequencing memories to suit an understanding that is meaningful to herself, for dreams narrated are, after all, dreams interpreted. Although

[17] On other dreams reported by third parties, see Appendix A.

[18] Craghan, 1974:43–5 argues that *ina šuttiya* is a West Semitic idiom.

[19] On nightmares which result from objective experience, see Hadfield, 1954:180–1.

[20] *AHw*, 1269 (B, 1); Borger, *EAK*, 9:1:5 (cf. Grayson, *ARI*, I, §140 and n. 72). Earlier literature is cited in Römer, 1971:26, n. 5. For antonymic amphibolism, see English "to cleave" which may mean "to split" as well as "to join." Derivatives of the German *aufheben* can sometimes display this tendency. Note also the D-stem of Hebrew *bārak* "to bless," which can also mean "to curse" as in Ps 10:3; Prov 27:14.

she sees herself as entering the goddess's temple, her role as an actor within the dream is at first totally passive. From then on, the ADDU-DŪRI of the dream loses her identity completely, and it is only the voice of the interpreter, that of Addu-dūri of the flesh, which can be heard. What she has to say is given in easily decodable symbols: Bēlet-ekallim, a deity with special attachment to females in the Mari palace, was not in her shrine and the statues ordinarily assembled around her or in front of her had left their places. Note how the interpreter's voice easily slips over the statues in order to first attend to the goddess's disappearance. ADDU-DŪRI may not have had such a spectral reach, but Addu-dūri needed to alert Zimri-Lim to a specific sequence: Bēlet-ekallim's disappearance was not a casual occurrence, but it was a voluntary abandonment of the shrine, an abandonment which was quickly duplicated by the images of other gods, of (deceased) ancestors, perhaps even of living worshippers.

The report insists that it was the goddess, but not necessarily her statue, that was no longer in residence, and this is emphasized by using the *wašābum* (in the G-stem), a verb that is attached to the presence of deities and not normally to their *ṣalmū*. While this observation may not ultimately bear practical distinctions,[21] it does permit the dream reporter to force attention not on the cultic aspect of the goddess's presence, but on the theological import of her disappearance. For, if, as other Mari materials suggest (e.g. X:4:31–34; 8:12–18), Bēlet-ekallim was one of those deities (the others being Dagan, Addu, and Itūr-Mer) charged with protecting the king during his military ventures, then her voluntary exit could only portend evil days ahead.[22]

It is also not clear how Addu-dūri expected her king to understand the statement she makes next. She writes: *u āmur-ma arṭup bakâm* (1. 12). The line is divisible into two brief segments, each with its own emphasis. The first has a conjunction; the second ends with a word (too?) precise in its full writing of the last syllable (*ba-ka-a-am*).[23] But the nuances yet escape us: Is the conjunction to be understood as consecutive, explicative, consequential, digressive? Is *-ma* to be judged as merely coordinative or as an emphatic particle (Finet, *ALM*:§100c, p.280)? Is the plene writing of the last word to be regarded as pausal (Finet, *ALM*:§101–2, pp.282–5)? *amārum* can, of course, regulate both the word for dream (*šuttum*) or the oneiric scene which unfolded in ADDU-DŪRI's temple. Were one to follow the first of these two possibilities ("And when I saw [this dream], I broke into uncontrollable weeping") it would indicate that Addu-dūri awakened from her sleep and, instantly understanding its meaning, lulled herself weeping into another dream sequence. This interpretation would allow for Addu-dūri's precise annotation that the sinister vision occurred during the night's first third (*šuttī annītum ša barartim*—ll. 13–24) and would permit her to inaugurate a second dream (1. 14—*atūr-ma*) which, consequently, must have occurred during the second third of the night.

But it might just be possible that the subject of *āmur* of l. 12 is the ADDU-DŪRI of the dreamworld. In this case, we are permitted to recreate the following scenario: ADDU-DŪRI enters the temple, observes the alarming scene, and begins to shed tears without restraint. For reasons that will be suggested presently, the wakened Addu-dūri inserts l. 13 as an aside because Zimri-Lim must recognize that what will follow happened during the night's *second* watch.

Those who have commented on our text have regarded *atūr* of l. 14 as construed in hendiadys with an *āmur* that, since it occurs in l. 12, must be *sous-entendu*. However, in XIII:112:7′–8′ a full version of the construction obtains: *itūr šuttam iṭṭul*, and on the basis of material cited in *AHw*, 1333 G6, one may question whether the same construction necessarily obtains in X:50:14. One may proceed, therefore, with the hypothesis that *atūr* of l. 14 introduces a narrative

[21] "It makes no difference whether we see [in dreams] the goddess herself as we have imagined her to be or a statue of her. For whether gods appear in the flesh or as statues fashioned out of some material, they have the same meaning. But when the gods have been seen in person, it signifies that the good and bad fulfillments will take place more quickly than they would have if statues of them had been seen." Artemidorous, [1975]:114. On the statues of the gods, see most recently Renger's treatment in *RlA* 3/4: 307–14.

[22] Moran, 1969b:630, n. 82 suggests that the goddess was a patron of the Lim dynasty. It is not possible to ascertain whether "Lady of the palace" was but an epithet of a goddess whose worship was widespread in Mesopotamia. Bibliography on this goddess is in Noort, 1977:55 and n. 2 of p. 55. Her Mari (?) temple is mentioned in IX:14 and in Finet, 1974–7: 126 and n. 35–7. A number of *ARM* XXI texts speak of sacrifices before this deity.

[23] Compare II:32:14 where *bakâm*, in a similar phrase, is given as *ba-ka-am* ("Like a child he broke into continuous weeping, saying . . .").

section which allows the reader to hover within the realms of dream on the one hand, and that of awakened reality on the other. Addu-dūri herself makes no attempt at guiding the king to the precise level of imagination required to fully comprehend the meaning of the lines following. And when that portion of her dream description ends in the midst of l. 21, Addu-dūri does not even clarify her own perspective on the matter, for she fails to add lines which would establish boundaries of that particular scene, lines such as those found in A. 15 (Dossin, 1948:130:40) or variations thereof (e.g. X:94:9′; XIII:112:5′ff; 113:16–17). On the contrary, Addu-dūri immediately moves to yet another realm of perception, that of prophetic ecstasy (ll. 21b–26)—albeit not her own—before lamely summing up with her own response to all the preceding events (ll. 27–28). *Atūr*, therefore, might be understood in its primary meaning, "I returned," perhaps even "I turned back." Referring to ADDU-DŪRI of the dream world, *atūr* resumes the oneiric experience as seen by a woman who has never really awakened from her sleep. Because of the ambiguity in its usage, *atūr* of l. 14 may permit the listener, in this case Zimri-Lim, to imagine his trusted maidservant as walking back toward the entrance of Bēlet-ekallim's shrine when she suddenly meets Dada, the priest of Ištar-pišra.[24] Whether this Dada was alive or (recently) deceased is, as we shall soon note, of interest.[25] That Addu-dūri needed to supply the king with Dada's title and affiliation *may* indicate either that Zimri-Lim was not immediately familiar with this man or that Addu-dūri was underscoring the supernatural nature of the meeting. But the main reason for the elaboration on Dada may have been only to prepare Zimri-Lim for the role that the priest was to presently play.

Depending on how one reads the cuneiform of l. 17, two differing scenes can be reconstructed. Von Soden has recently reiterated his preference for (*izzaz-ma*) KAŠ *ú-na-aq-qa*!. Dada, therefore, would have libated beer (or—as von Soden suggests following an emendation—offered a sacrifice) before proceeding with his invocations of ll.19–21.[26] To my mind, however, *ARMT* X's reading of l. 17 is not only syntactically and grammatically more elegant, but it is also contextually more pregnant. As an alarmed and tearful ADDU-DŪRI turned towards the shrine's exit, a scene crystallized in a frightful state of frigidity, Dada was standing at the entrance, blocking ADDU-DŪRI's path. His face was motionless, but a cry, hostile and harping, emanated from him: *tūra dagan*; *tūra dagan*! Addu-dūri is extremely parsimonious in this account; she does not squander words on preparing the scene or on ushering her character; she does not waste vocabulary in concluding it. Entrance and exit are abrupt, disjunctive, tense; yet conclusive and final. Moreover, because she draws a scene that is integral and complete within itself, Addu-dūri needs neither background nor denouement to fully realize her dream. And, unlike the dream sequence which had just preceded—one in which ADDU-DŪRI's activities were given by means of verbs which affirm human involvement (*erēbum, amārum,* [*raṭāpum*] *bakâm, târum*)—this tableau contains verbs in forms which focus the attention upon the subject, Dada, and the peculiarity of the act: Dada is standing (G imperfect but connoting the stative), *but* (*-ma*, used contrastively) a voice kept on uttering (Gtn imperf.) as follows: *tūra* (imper. with ventive) *dagan*.

The voice's plaint is obviously the message upon which the scene focuses. Not only is it introduced by a verb in an iterative stem, but Addu-dūri twice records it, and frames the whole within repetitions of *kīam ištanassi*. The use of *târum* and the reliance on an iterative form suggests a tenuous parallelism with the

[24] The significance of time in oneirocritical literature is a debated issue, see Oppenheim, 1956:240–1; Hanson, 1978: 2406–7, with n. 46, for bibliography.

[25] In 1980a: 133 I was uncautious about Dada's status. I had reasoned on the basis of an equation between Dada of our text and a Dada who was a well-known money-lender at Šamaš's temple (see listing in *ARMT* XVI/1: 83 sub 2°, to which probably join those sub 3° and 5°). On this score, it can be noted that other lenders (e.g. Asqudum and Habduma-Dagan) similarly functioned on two levels. Other lenders, such as Ibbi-Šahan and Šamaš-rabi, were prominent bureaucrats.

My equation faces the fact that the dated texts mentioning Dada the moneylender (all in *ARM* VIII) are attributable to Zimri-Lim's last years: "Babylon", #22–23; "Dagan/Šamaš," #26; and "IInd Ašlakka," #74. Texts from as yet unsequenced formulae: "Habur," #24; "Yamhad," #25, 30, 79; "Addu of Appan, II," #28. If Dada's ghost was manifesting itself to Addu-dūri, then X:50 was penned while Hammurabi was masterminding Mari's fall. On the chronology and its sequence, see, conveniently, Sasson: 1980b:6–7.

[26] Von Soden, 1980:210 (cf. his 1969:198, followed by Römer, 1971:27 and n. 6). Von Soden also considers emending KAŠ to SISKUR.

previous scene which likewise refers to the same verb (1. 14) and implies a continuous act (*arṭup bakâm*, 1. 12). But it remained to Zimri-Lim to decode the meaning behind the message itself. And at this stage the ambiguity which was instilled at the outset by the use of *šulmum* in 1.3 gains new space and gathers momentum.

Tūra dagan can be analyzed as a full sentence containing an imperative (with a non-mimmated ventive) and means something like "O Dagan, return (here) / come back / reconsider."[27] However, it can be regarded as a proper name. Indeed, Kupper (1971: 118 n. 3) has made a case for connecting it with the name of a Mari ruler who reigned a hundred or so years before Zimri-Lim. Our dilemma was doubtlessly shared by Zimri-Lim. One can readily appreciate the advantage and the implication of opting for the first of these two possibilities. ADDU-DŪRI's horrifying initial vision in which the deity and her attendants had left their shrine, can now be counterbalanced by a summon for Dagan to return to the aid of his beloved, Zimri-Lim.[28] And *if* it were but the ghost of the departed whom ADDU-DŪRI faced, *it might just be possible* that a lore, perhaps available to Mari's citizenry, gave further comfort to Zimri-Lim even as it provides us with a tentative explanation for Addu-dūri's aside of 1. 14: "If a ghost appears in a man's house and it cries during the evening watch, the man will not live long; If it appears in the night watch: fulfillment of wish; (peaceful) ending of one's days" (*CT* 38:26:35–37). Therefore, Zimri-Lim would have been comforted to know that Dada did not make his appearance until *after* the conclusion of the evening watch (*šuttī annītum ša barartim*)!

But it might also occur to the king that Dada was not pleading for Dagan to protect Mari, but was invoking the memory of a previous ruler. We do not have to suppose, as did Kupper, that Zimri-Lim's own ancestors extinguished Tūra-Dagan's line, to realize why Zimri-Lim would have felt discomfort at the mention of this name. For a king who had to be prompted in his duties toward the *eṭemmu* of his own father (III:40—and contrast the piety of Šamši-Adad, I:65), it could not have augured well, at best, to be reminded of yet one more neglect of duty or, at worse, to become haunted by the sins of the ancestors (cf. 1:3).[29]

By choosing to share her dream with the king, Addu-dūri is, of course, but fulfilling the wishes of the gods. But she is also staking a clear claim for herself as worthy of divine notice, and hence capable of channeling information crucial to the future welfare of Mari. Her own perception of the dream's implication can be plausibly assessed. For rather than admitting to physical (cf. XIII:12) or emotional (cf. A.15) derangements which could be provoked by subconscious anxiety, Addu-dūri immediately turns to a differing account concerning divine revelation, and introduces it simply by *šanītam*. This adverb allows her to suggest that she was remaining within the same subject even as she broaches a seemingly new one.[30] She reports that a female ecstatic (*muhhūtum*) rose to warn the king against travelling abroad (11. 22–26). Thereafter, Addu-dūri gives her own advice (27–28) and informs the king of her dispatch of hair and garment fringes (29–33). With this last act, however, Addu-dūri betrays the fact that she remained worried about the negative tenor of her dreams.[31]

ARM X:50 ends, therefore, on an apprehensive note. Foreboding and prickly dread, conveyed by Addu-dūri through an exceptionally vivid recollection of one night's dreams, have now become Zimri-Lim's. At a time when he was receiving contradictory messages—some comforting; others of dire warnings—from the gods and streams of advice from his subjects, Zimri-Lim may well have dismissed this particular manifestation. That it was ambiguous in its allusions may have drained him of any will to act purposefully. But we, who are in a position to predict Mari's fate more clearly than could Zimri-Lim or his advisors, might wish that he had learnt to react better to trustworthy presentiments.

---

[27] Cf. *ARMT* X, p. 262; *AHw*, 1333a. This name also occurs from the Sūmu-Yamam period (cf. XVI/1, s.v.) and from that of Zimri-Lim where it is borne by a tribal chieftain (e.g. XXI:9:2).

[28] See Zimri-Lim's seal impression at VII:259. For this and other Zimri-Lim seals, see, conveniently, *IRSA* IV:F:76c, d. There Zimri-Lim is also labelled as Dagan's *šaknum*.

[29] Kupper's study of the chronology of the *šakkanakku* period, 1971, will have to be amended due to Durand's recent collations of the seal inscriptions, 1981.

See the two studies of Birot and Bottéro in the XXVIe *RAI* volume, 1980, and especially paragraphs 28–35 of the latter's work.

[30] Finet, *ALM* § 47f; conta Koch, 1972:56.

[31] Heintz *apud* Ramlot in *Supplement*, *Dictionnaire de la Bible*, 889.

APPENDIX

I have divided the treatment of the remaining dreams from Mari into two sections, one which considers dreams reported by parties other than the dreamers, the second studies dreams communicated by those who experienced them.

A. The dreams that are reported by intermediaries include **XIII:112** and **113**, both of which were mentioned above. Except for the repetition of the god's message in **XIII:112**—a repetition necessary to fully explain the dreamer's illness and, hence, to underscore persistence of the message—this text seems little inclined to dramatize the dream or to establish contexts for the dreamer's involvement.

It is unfortunate that **XIII:113** is so badly preserved in precisely the lines which report a dream. What is clear is that the dream was quite brief (lines 9–15[?]) and that it recreates soldiers at the ready in fortified cities. Movement within the dream seem to be minimal. Kibri-Dagan, who reported the dream to his king, fails in this instance (as he may well have in **XIII:112**) to even name the dreamer. **X:10** contains yet another dream (?), transmitted by the queen. Unhurried, Šibtu takes time to report first that all is well at home before she turns to a vision of Kakkalide (verb: *amārum*) received while sleeping in the temple of Itūr-Mer. The dream/vision appears to be very favorable to Zimri-Lim and relies on the use of the stative and the imperfect to convey timelessness and permanence, with the stative describing the positions of the actors and the condition of inert objects while the imperfect characterizing the human speech.[32]

By every measure, **A.15**, often studied and translated,[33] contains the most elaborate dream reports within this category. The text was written late in Zimri-Lim's reign since its dispatcher, Itūr-Asdu, succeeded Bahdi-Lim in administering the Mari palace.[34] The dreamer, Malik-Dagan, lived in a village in the Saggaratum district. The dream is narrated in the full style that is better attested in literary documentation. While it is obvious that the core of the dream is the divine message addressing Zimri-Lim, its reporter—or, rather, its first interpreter, Malik-Dagan—is quite resourceful in enhancing the message's import by recourse to detailed setting, vivid similes, richly subtle vocabulary, and, as I will try to show, sarcasm.

At the outset, Malik-Dagan establishes a central place for himself within the dream by furnishing all sorts of information which does not seem to be immediately relevant to the ensuing message. He tells us that a companion, nameless and ultimately futureless, was with him as he left Saggaratum for Mari. He specifies that he meant to traverse the Upper District. But, finding himself, instead, in Terqa (i.e., having taken the river road[35]), he instantaneously (*kīma erēbiya-ma*) enters the temple of Dagan and bows before the god. The whole passage (ll. 13–15) in which verbal forms of *erēbum* are thrice repeated within two lines, highlights the almost unexpected—perhaps even unvoluntary—turn which overtook an innocent voyage. It therefore underscores the urgency with which the god's will summons Malik-Dagan to its presence.

Likewise occurring simultaneously is Dagan's first speech which coincides with Malik-Dagan's genuflection (*ina šukêniya*—l. 15). This notice is made for at least two reasons: it permits the report to stress Malik-Dagan's awareness of the religious meaning of the setting and it indicates his position vis-à-vis the deity, the last measure being a common feature to oneiric accounting (Hanson, 1978:1410). The vocabulary employed to introduce Dagan's communication (*Dagan pīšu ipte-ma kīam iqbê-m*) is usually reserved for literary documents, and is not attested in Mari's epistolary archives. My own reading of Dagan's speech is that it is highly sarcastic,[36] for Dagan, who seems particularly sensitive to neglect (e.g. III:8, 17, 40; X:62), *knows* that Zimri-Lim had *not* come to terms with the Benjaminites! The main point that Dagan wants to make, however, is not found in another dream

---

[32] Two large rafts are blocking (*parkū*—stative) the river, with the king and the soldiers riding (*rakib*—stative). Those on the right were shouting (*išassū*—imperf.) to those on the left. They said: 'Kingship, scepter and throne are (?) stable (*qâmat*—stative)' (and) 'The Country, Upper and Lower, is given (*nadnat*—stative) to Zimri-Lim.' And the soldiers, as one body, shared the refrain (*ippal*—imperf.): 'To Zimri-Lim only are they given (*nadnat*—stative).' These rafts were docked? ([*raksū*]-*ma* [but cf. *ina kār* GN *arkus* in Dossin, 1956:65:22–23]) at the palace's gate and . . ."

It is very likely that the dream was inspired by actual observation, however long in the past, of a royal (re)installation ceremony. On this last topic, see Grayson, 1975:78–86; Tadmor, 1958:28 and n. 52.

[33] Fullest bibliography in Ellermeier, 1968:24.

[34] Birot, 1972:137–9; contra, Kupper, 1982:46 n. 18.

[35] For the two routes between Saggaratum and Mari, see II:120:14–27: "(Atamrum answered me [Buqaqum] as follows:) 'We shall go as far as Saggaratum. In Saggaratum, we shall deliberate and we shall write with certainty whether we shall go to Mari (directly) or detour through the steppe.' While in Saggaratum, I [Buqaqum] will write my lord as to which way, through the steppe or by way of the river, he will proceed."

For the difficult *ina pānīya* of l. 13, see Moran's discussion, 1969b:623, n. 1.

[36] Contra: Gadd, 1966:23 : ". . . a god talking in a strain of curious *naïveté* to a quite ordinary man."

sequence which might have immediately followed on the first (as we find in X:50) nor in one which is repeated almost verbatim the next night (as is learned from XIII:112), but is prompted by Malik-Dagan's unsatisfactory reaction and by his obviously false assumptions about the end of the interview.

Dagan's second speech is a tirade which is given as a twofold statement. The first, (ll. 24b–31) is pungent, chiding, and is couched mostly in rhetorical formulations: Why had Zimri-Lim not consulted Dagan regularly? Were he to have done otherwise, Dagan would surely have delivered the Benjaminites in his hands so that, by now, they would have been suing for peace! The second statement (ll. 32–39) delivers the message which Malik-Dagan is to present to the king.[37] It is much more direct in its demands yet, interestingly enough, it is given in hyperbolic similes whose language is made tangible by the starkness of its colors and the aroma of its vocabulary. While much philological ink has already been spilled to ascertain the precise meaning of lines 37–38's highly picturesque language, its intent is clear and the overall thrust of Dagan's second speech is manifest.[38] It was left to Zimri-Lim to dare ignore such powerful warnings.[39]

For lack of a better slot in which to evaluate it, I place here the dream report (**A.222**) published in Dossin, 1975:28. Dossin's own opinion is that the text displays orthographic features which ought to date it to the Yahdun-Lim period.[40] If this is the case, then this text will stand as the earliest example to contain dream reports in non-literary documents. The document itself is a memorandum which appends a note to authenticate the dreamers veracity, but requests that the veracity of the dream be tested. We never learn the names of the correspondents.

Ayala, in her dream, saw (verb: *naṭālum*) as follows:

> A Šehru-woman and a Mari woman quarreled at the gate of Annunītum's (shrine), beyond town.[41] The one from Šehru said to the one from Mari: 'Return my utensils. Either, you, sit! or, I myself shall sit.'[42]

The translation of the crucial lines is very tentative, and it differs from that of Dossin. We have very little information with which to penetrate this dream. Šehrum was a locality within Mari's immediate district,[43] and it may well be that the struggle between the two ladies was but allegorical, if not parabolic, of Šehrum's claim for a residence in which to house the goddess. In time, we know, the goddess did enter the city.[44] This is sheer speculation and one should be content for now to observe how the static quality of a dream that is witnessed by an omnipresent eye is defeated by recourse to verbs which evoke bodily movement and human contact (Gt of *ṣâlum*, D of *târum*, and *wašābum*).

B. Two other dreams are reported by the dreamers themselves. In **X:94**, Šimatum, daughter of Zimri-Lim and wife of his vassal, reports a dream which is remarkably laconic. A question arose about the presence of a certain girl who belongs (?) to a temple functionary. Šimatum dreams of an official (?) who communicates a positive response. The king is to investigate the authenticity of the dream and to act accordingly.[45]

---

[37] For whatever it is worth as a comment to biblical scholars, one could notice how two versions of the same message may be found in the same text and how both developed from the same context.

[38] For lines 37–38, see the discussion of Moran, 1969b:623, notes 6 and 7; Heintz, 1971:544; Finet, 1974: 41, n. 5; Craghan, 1974:51, n. 5.

[39] One cannot assess here precisely why Itūr-Asdu did not send Dagan-Malik, preoccupied with offering sacrifices, or why he did not dispatch hair and garment fringe samplings.

[40] It might be noted that the legal documentation from the Yahdun-Lim period does not reflect the same orthographical peculiarity in the shaping of the *ú* sign (cf. VIII:55:10; 61:1′; 70:3; 75:16).

[41] *kawītum* is attributive to the temple of Annunītum, and hence the building is distinguished from another within Mari (cf. X:8:5: *ina bit Annunītima ša libbi ālim*).

[42] Dossin, 1975: 28 renders lines 11–13 as follows: "Rends-moi ma fonction de grande prêtresse,/ ou bien, toi, siège/ ou bien que ce soit moi qui siège." See also his comments on p. 30. However, *enūtum* with such a meaning is attested only in SB and NB. Furthermore, the idea that the priesthood is disposable at will—even in dreams—seems to me unproven. Finally, I could not find evidence for a "seat" for priestesses.

Von Soden's *AHw*, 1481 (2,c,) cites this usage of *wašābum* under "being (in GN)." I rather think that the locale is one where legal disputes are resolved, cf. *CAD* B, 19–20 and *BIN* I:42 (NB) which is mentioned there; Kienast, *ABUK*, 93.

On the use of the correlative conjunction *ūlū(ma)* . . . *ūlūma* with imperative in the first segment, see *AbB* VI:63:7–9.

[43] Most recently, Wilcke, 1979:48 (s.v.). According to XXI:17 and 49 sacrifices were made at Šehrum.

[44] *Studia Mariana*, 57, #22. Note, however, that as late as the year "Dagan," this goddess was still not attached to Šehrum, Dossin, 1975:25:6–7. My hypothesis depends on acceptance of a theory which regards many of Zimri-Lim's date years as paralleling better attested ones; see Sasson, 1980b: § 3.2.6.5 (p. 7).

[45] Von Soden's reading for l. 13′, 1980:211, is not convincing. Maybe read <*li*->*ṭe*[!]-*em-ma*, "may my lord look after the girl and may she be called here."

Perhaps even more starkly self-serving is Yanana's dream recorded in **X:100**. This particular dream is interesting because it is interrupted by a long historical insert. Yanana (otherwise unknown) has a servant (daughter?) who had been pressed into palace duty and whose release does not seem to be forthcoming. Dagan's presence may have been felt in a dream or in a vision, but the precise vocabulary employed here is still not clear.[46] Yanana, for some reason, thought it necessary to add that no one touched her while she was having her séance with the god. Dagan's own question to Yanana, "Are you travelling North or South," makes sense when it is remembered that Yanana's hometown, Ganibatum, lay to Mari's north. By responding that she was heading toward Mari but had yet to secure her servant's release (ll. 11–13), Yanana gives occasion for Dagan's categorical statement which, however, does not find space until lines 23–25. Dagan's message to Zimri-Lim is quite flattering to the king since it indicates that only Zimri-Lim can resolve Yanana's problem (i.e., not even the god himself can resolve it). Yanana does not rely entirely on Dagan's soothing words to regain her servant, but sandwiches background information meant to clarify the contexts which finds her frustrated, yet justified in her search: "When my lord went to Andariq [cf. II:32–18–19] the *zimzimu* [obscure] of my 'girl' contested (?) it with Sammetar [a powerful official]. I went to him; he consented, reconsidered, and, turning against me, he did not give me my 'girl'" (ll. 14–21). Yanana's own plea (ll. 26–27), that the king mind the god's message, concludes a letter which reads, if not like a legal brief, certainly like an opportunistic petition.

---

[46] Discussion in *ARMT* X, 271.

I am happy to record here my debt to Thorkild Jacobsen for his close reading of my paper. J.-M. Durand kindly placed *ARM* XXI at my early disposal. In a letter dated 3/11/1982 he offered the following collations:

ARM X:50:

l. 5 : (. . .) *it-ta-tu-{TU}-ia* ; toute la ligne 6 est écrite sur érasures.

l. 9 : *e*-ru-ub-ma* (. . .)

l. 15 : Dans ARMT XXI, j'ai proposé une lecture *Eštar bi-iš-ra* "Eštar Bišréenne"; Le culte de la déesse semble indiquer la région du mont Bišri.

ll. 27–28 : si incroyable que cela puisse paraître, il faut lire les deux lignes en les inversant, malgré la transcription *et* la copie !!

a-na pa-ag-ri-šu na-ṣa-ri-im
be-lí a-ah-šu la i-na-ad-di

l. 31 : *a*-[na-ku] ak-nu-ka-am-ma* ; il faut abandonner l'idée de MÍ !

ARM X:51:

l. 12 : *šar*-ru-tum na-x-x-at-sú.* Le *šar* "archaïque" de Mari, soit HI+IṢ; j'ai collecté beaucoup d'examples. "*di-ru-tum*" est donc à oublier définitivement.

BIBLIOGRAPHY

Artemidorus of Daldis [ca. 2nd century].
[1975]: *Oneirocritica.* Cited from R. J. White, *The Interpretation of Dreams.* [Noyes Classical Studies].

Batto, B. F.
1974: *Studies on Women at Mari.*

Birot, M.
1972: "Simahlânê, roi de Kurda," *RA* 66:131–9.
1980: "Fragment de rituel de Mari relatif au *kispum*," in *Death in Mesopotamia* [XXVIe *RAI*]. 139–50.

Bottéro, J.
1974: "Symptômes, signes, écritures en Mésopotamie ancienne," in *Divination et Rationalité.* 70–197.
1980: "La Mythologie de la mort en Mésopotamie ancienne," in *Death in Mesopotamia* [XXVIe *RAI*]. 25–52.

Castellino, G.
1955: "Rituals and Prayers Against Appearing Ghosts," *Orientalia* 24:240–74.

Craghan, J. F.
1974: "The ARM X 'Prophetic' Texts . . . ," *JANES* 6:39–57.

Dossin, G.
1948: "Une Révelation du dieu Dagan à Terqa," *RA* 42:125–34. [Text A. 15.]
1956: "Une lettre de Iarîm-Lim, roi d'Alep . . . ," *Syria* 33:63–9.
1975: "Tablettes de Mari," *RA* 69:23–30. [Text A.222.]

Durand, J.-M.
1980: (with J. Margueron) "La Question du harem royal . . . ," *Journal d. Savants* Oct.–Dec.: 253–80.
1981a: "À Propos des légendes des empreintes de sceaux . . . ," *RA* 75:180–1.
1981b: "Note brève (#5)," *RA* 75:188.

Ehrlich, E. L.
1953: *Der Traum im Alten Testament.*

Ellermeier, F.
1968: *Prophetie in Mari and Israel* [Th. Or. Arb., 1].

Falkenstein, A.
1966: "'Wahrsagung' in der sumerischen Überlieferung," in *La Divination en Mésopotamie Ancienne* [XIVe *RAI*]. 43–68.

Finet, A.
1966: "Adalšenni, roi de Burundum," *RA* 60:17–28.

1970: "Les Symboles de cheveu . . . ," in *Eschatologie et Cosmologie* [*CER* Annales, 3]. 101–30.

1972: "Le *ṣuḫārum* à Mari," in *Gesellschaftsklassen im Alten Zweistromland* [XVIIIe *RAI*, 1970.] 65–72.

1974: "Citations littéraires dans la correspondance de Mari," *RA* 68:36–47.

1974–7: "Le Vin à Mari," *AfO* 24:122–31.

Frankena, R.

1974: "Dit Zij U Een Teken," in *Vruchten van de Uithof* [Festschrift H. A. Brongers]. 28–36.

Gadd, C.

1966: "Some Babylonian Divinatory Methods . . . ," in *La Divination en Mésopotamie ancienne* [XIVe *RAI*]. 21–34.

Grayson, A. K.

1975 *Babylonian Historical-Literary Texts.*

Hadfield, J. A.

1954: *Dreams and Nightmares.*

Hanson, J. S.

1978: "Dreams and Visions in the Graeco-Roman World . . . ," in *Aufstieg und Niedergang der Römischen Welt*, II, 23/2: 1395–427.

Heintz, J.-G.

1971: Review of Ellermeier, 1968, in *Biblica* 52:543–55.

Koch, K.

1972: 'Die Briefe 'Prophetischen' Inhalts aus Mari . . . ," *UF* 4:53–77.

Kupper, J.-R.

1971: "La Date des *Šakkanakku* de Mari," *RA* 65:113–8.

1982: "Les Pouvoirs locaux dans le royaume de Mari," in *Les Pouvoirs locaux en Mésopotamie . . .* [*IHEB*]. 43–53.

Moran, W. L.

1969a: "New Evidence from Mari on the History of Prophecy," *Biblica* 50:15–56.

1969b: "Akkadian Letters," in *ANET*, 3rd edition, 623–32.

1980: Review of *ARMT* X, in *JAOS* 100:186–9.

Noort, E.

1977: *Untersuchungen zum Gottesbescheid in Mari* [*AOAT*, 202].

Oppenheim, A. L.

1956: *The Interpretation of Dreams in the Ancient Near East* [*APS*, Transactions, 46/3].

1966a: "Perspectives on Mesopotamian Divination," in *La Divination en Mésopotamie Ancienne* [XIVe *RAI*]. 35–43.

1966b: "Mantic Dreams in the Ancient Near East," in *The Dream and Human Society*, ed. by G. E. Von Grunenbaum and R. Caillois. 341–50.

1969: "New Fragments of the Assyrian Dream-Book," *Iraq* 31:153–65.

Parrot, A.

1958: *Mission Archéologique de Mari, II, Le Palais. Vol. I: Architecture.*

1959: *Mission Archéologique de Mari, II, Le Palais. Vol. 3: Documents et Monuments.*

Römer, W. P. Ph.

1971: *Frauenbriefe über Religion, Politik und Privatleben in Mari . . .* [*AOAT*, 12].

Sasson, J. M.

1972: "Some Comments on Archive Keeping at Mari," *Iraq* 34:55–67.

1980a: "Two Recent Works on Mari," *AfO* 27:127–35.

1980b: *Dated Texts from Mari: A Tabulation* [*ARTANES*, 4].

Von Soden, W.

1969: "Einige Bemerkungen zu den von Fr. Ellermeier . . . [1968]," *UF* 1:198–9.

1980: Review of *ARMT* X, in *Orientalia* 49:208–12.

Tadmor, H.

1958: "The Campaigns of Sargon II of Aššur . . . ," *JCS* 12:22–40; 77–100.

Talon, Ph.

1978: "Les Offrandes funéraires à Mari," *AIPHOS* 22:53–75.

Westenholz, J. G.

1974: Review of *AbB* V, in *JNES* 33:409–14.

Wilcke, Cl.

1979: "Truppen von Mari in Kurda," *RA* 73:37–50.

PARALLELISM IN UGARITIC POETRY

STANISLAV SEGERT

UNIVERSITY OF CALIFORNIA, LOS ANGELES

CONTENTS

1. UGARITIC POETRY

No other Semitic literature of the Ancient Near East provides more convenient opportunity to study the parallelistic poetic structure than the poems from the ruins of the ancient city of Ugarit. Only about forty cuneiform alphabetic tablets survive, nearly all of them in fragmentary condition. They were written in the 14/13th century B.C., but they may contain poetic traditions going generations back. The language of these poetic texts found since 1929 on the excavations of Ras Shamra in Northern Syria can be characterized as an ancient Northern Canaanite dialect.

Due to the intensive work of many scholars, the language and the content of Ugaritic poetry are sufficiently known for analysis of poetic structures. The Ugaritic alphabetic writing renders the consonantal phonemes exactly. A fortuitous inconsistency of this system, the introduction of three letters indicating basic vowels *a, i, u,* if they are preceded—or perhaps also followed—by the glottal stop (*ʾaleph*) allows the reconstruction of some vocalic elements of the words. Ugaritic words are also preserved in syllabic cuneiform writing: many proper names in Akkadian documents and considerable number of other words in quadrilingual vocabularies make it possible to reconstruct forms of Ugaritic words with a greater exactness than is possible for Hebrew of the Biblical period.

The meaning of many Ugaritic words has been determined according to their similarity with words known from the Hebrew Bible. Other comparative material from Phoenician, Aramaic languages, Arabic, Akkadian and Ethiopic have provided additional help. Even if the meaning of some words still eludes the efforts of Ugaritologists, their function in the sentence, also important for the analysis of the poetic structure, can be determined with sufficient probability.

One feature of Ugaritic poetry has proved to be especially helpful: many passages are repeated, either without change or with predictable variations. With help of these parallel passages many gaps in fragmentary texts could be filled and some limits of variations determined.[1]

1.1. Parallelistic structure.[2] With the help of poetic structures known from the Hebrew Bible, the basic structure of Ugaritic poetry was recognized

[1] F. Rosenthal, "Die Parallelstellen in den Texten von Ugarit," *Orientalia* 8 (1939), 213–237.

[2] R. Lowth, *De sacra poesi Hebraeorum Praelectiones* (Oxford, 1753; ed. I. D. Michaelis, 2nd ed., Göttingen, 1770), Prael. XIX., 242/371. 249/378, 258/388, cf. 392; id., *Isaiah, A New Translation* (London, 1778, 2nd ed. 1779), x-xi; cf. Jakobson, 399–400. *MLC*, 32–36, 58–62; cf. also *YGC*, 4–10.

D. Pardee, "A Philological and Prosodic Analysis of the Ugaritic Serpent Incantation, *UT* 607," *Journal of the ANE Society* 10 (1978), 73–108; id., "Ugaritic and Hebrew Metrics," *UIR*, 113–30, esp. 128–30. Cf. also in *UIR*: J. M. Sasson, 93–5; P. C. Craigie, 105–10.

Surveys of parallelistic features in the Ugaritic poetry: *UT*, §13.107–170, 14.3–4, pp. 131–46; cf. also *BGUL*, §71.3.—

relatively early after the first publication of the major poetic texts. *Parallelismus*, a term introduced in the middle of the 18th century by Robert Lowth, has also been applied to Ugaritic poems.

From the rich literature on this subject, only the most recent synthetic treatments are mentioned below. The translations preserve the semantic features and most of the syntactic features of the original; they can give an idea about the parallelistic structure of the Ugaritic poetry.

2. APPROACHES AND TERMS[3]

There are many limitations in this outline of Ugaritic parallelism. The fragmentary condition of nearly all the poetic tablets makes any attempt at quantitative assessment difficult. Since the stereotyped passages can be reconstructed with relative certainty, their proportion is much larger when compared to less certain, non-stereotyped, singular verses. The space limitation for this article forces concentration on the more frequent features which can be determined with sufficient certainty. This study of Ugaritic parallelism focuses, then, on the phenomena evident in the bicola and also in some types of monocola. The tricola and combinations of four or more cola mostly go back to binary structural relationships; they are only summarily mentioned. Verses which are not structured according to the parallelistic rules deserve also attention: the contrast may contribute to better understanding of the parallelistic system. This study is strictly limited to Ugaritic poetry; no comparison with other literatures and no general conclusions are attempted. Samples are taken from a representative selection from Ugaritic poems.

2.1. Terminology.[4] More or less commonly accepted terms are used. Only a few new terms have been

---

Some examples on the following pages are taken from the manuscript of *Reference Grammar of the Ugaritic Language.*

Lists of Ugaritic and Hebrew word pairs compiled by M. Dahood: *RSP*, I, 71–382; II, 1–39; III, 1–206; cf. esp. I, 73–84.

Translations: classic English translations: C. H. Gordon, *Ugaritic Literature.* 1949; H. L. Ginsberg, "Ugaritic Myths. Epics and Legends," in: *Ancient Near Eastern Texts Relating to the Old Testament.* ed. J. B. Pritchard, 1950; 2nd ed., 1955, 129–55; Th. H. Gaster, *Thespis.* 1950; 1966; G. R. Driver, *Canaanite Myths and Legends.* 1956.

Recent translations: *English*: *CML*, 35–129, with Ugaritic text; *Spanish*, *MLC*, 81–502, with Ugaritic text and ample references to previous interpretations; *French*: *TOu*, 101–574, with discussions of difficult passages.

General studies on parallelism: *SBP*:1–135, by L. Newman; *SBP*, 435–552, by W. Popper; Jakobson, cf. esp. 399–401, 425–6; J. J. Fox, "Roman Jakobson and the Comparative Study of Parallelism," in: *Roman Jakobson: Echoes of his Scholarship*, eds. D. Armstrong and C. H. van Schooneveld, 1977, 59–90.

[3] This study is based on the edition of Ugaritic cuneiform alphabetic texts by O. Loretz, M. Dietrich and J. Sanmartín—*KTU.* Its quotation system is adopted here. Ugaritic words are transliterated in italics, missing and uncertain letters are supplied from parallel passages. The words are divided by spaces, but word dividers are not indicated. — The present author uses his own arrangement into cola, bicola and tricola, prepared in 1979, with the numbering of cola adapted for this synoptic arrangement.

The samples, whose number is very limited, are mostly taken from complete analysis of a selection of Ugaritic poetic texts in which the main types are represented: complete epic poems (1.17–19; 1.23; 1.24; 1.100; 1.114) and parts of Baal (1.1 and 1.12) and of the Keret epics (1.14). Parallelistic features of remaining major poetic texts (1.2–6; 1.15–16) are also taken into consideration. Texts too fragmentary or too uncertain for interpretation as well as liturgical texts with some parallelistic features (1.110; 1.119; 1.161) are not included. A more complete presentation of parallelistic features with detailed documentation and discussion is being prepared. The translations are intended to reflect the parallelistic features.

[4] *YGC*, 6, n. 15. - The term "hemistich" - "halfverse" is not convenient for indicating a part of a tricolon.—For *kōlon* cf. L-S 1017a.—For *membrum* cf. Ch. T. Lewis and Ch. Short, *A Latin Dictionary*, 1879/1975, 1129c.—There is a slight inconsistency in the accepted terminology: Greek word for the combination of two cola is *dikōlos*, cf. L-S 431a. The commonly used term "bicolon" combines the Latin element *bi-* with the Greek *kōlon*. The Romans themselves, however, used such hybrid words, e.g. *biclinium* for a couch for two persons, cf. Lewis-Short, 236ab.—Cf. *trikōlon*, L-S 1820a; *tricolum*, Lewis-Short, 1898b. Cf. *monokōlos*, L-S 1144b. The term "monocolon" was used by Lowth, *Praelectiones* (v. note 2), 257/388 for Psalm 2:6, an example for his synthetic parallelism. He hypothetically supplied the verbal predicate from the first colon, whose end is marked by *ʾātnaḥ* in the beginning of the second colon and so restituted a bicolon. This verse can be characterized as a bicolon containing one clause only; subject, predicate and object in the first colon,

introduced reluctantly; some of them were rediscovered in older publications, though sometimes with slightly different meanings.

For verse and its parts, the basic terminology introduced by William F. Albright is used here. The basic unit, consisting mostly of three full words is called a "colon"; this Greek term is an equivalent of Latin "membrum." A combination of two cola is called a "bicolon," while "tricolon" is used for a combination of three cola. It seems useful to introduce a new term, "monocolon," for isolated colon.

A bicolon, a tricolon or a monocolon represents a higher unit, termed "verse." The term "line" should be limited only to graphic features of the cuneiform tablet.

The parallelism of cola and members in Ugaritic poetry is mostly positive; it can be called "thetic," in opposition to the "antithetic" parallelism represented only by a few verses. Perhaps a category of "contrastive" parallelistic features for those which do not belong clearly to any of these mentioned here can be introduced. Within the instances of "thetic" parallelism, those of synonymous and complementary kind can be distinguished.

2.2. Verse structure and syntax. Ugaritic prosodic units coincide—with very few exceptions—with syntactic units. Therefore, syntactic analysis of prosodic units, cola and verses, provides a reliable basis for their delimitation and characterization.

---

adverbial modifier in the second colon.—Cf. *versus*, Lewis-Short, 1977a.—Cf. *thetikos*, L-S 796a.

Lowth's "synthetic parallelism" is that in which clauses mutually correspond neither by iteration of matters nor by opposition of diverse elements, but only by the syntactic form, cf. *Praelectiones*, 252–3/ 382–383.

Both complementary and synonymous bicola express parallelity in positive direction; the term "thetic" covers both these categories. The term "complements" was used by W. Popper, *SBP*, 450, for pairs such as "father—son," "heaven—earth," "from now—and unto eternity."

The term "contrast" and its derivatives is used here for oppositions which indicate the same kind, within certain limits. A contrastive parallelism is often used for fuller description. Contrastive items appear more frequently in parallel passages longer than one verse: 1.19:IV:46/47,—47/48 "at sunrise"—"at sunset"; 9/10—20/21 "enter"—"depart".

For a proposal of a notation system cf. S. Segert, "Vorarbeiten zur hebräischen Metrik, "*Archiv Orientální* 21 (1953), 481–542, esp. 485–92.

In Ugaritic poetry, parallelism can be characterized by syntactic and semantic relations of words in the cola. The first colon is usually a self-contained clause. The second colon is often a clause, parallel both syntactically and semantically to the clause of the first colon. The second colon is often used to provide additional information of lower syntactic rank, while the higher syntactic features are referred back to the first colon. Relatively rare are non-parallelistic bicola in which the second colon does not include any syntactic parallel to the first colon. Sentences transcending the limit of a verse are rather rare. Among those conditional sentences or other sentences with subordinate clauses can be easily defined. The same is true of series of short clauses or their parts remarkable for their stereotyped or repetitive character.

The syntactic relationships can be determined by applying traditional syntactic approaches, especially that of dependency.

3. SYNTACTIC STRUCTURES WITHIN ONE COLON

The categories and samples can be taken both from isolated monocola and from cola which form part of bicola or tricola. Those cola which contain an independent clause are considered here first; the other cola have to be categorized as parts of bicola or longer combinations.

The most common clause within one colon is that with one verbal predicate and one subject: 1.17:VI:20 *wy*^{c}*n aqht ǵzr* "and Aqhat the hero answered"; 1.17: V:16 *šm*^{c} *mṯt dnty* "hear, o Lady Danatiya," with subject contained in the personal marker of the finite verb.

A construction with an infinitive forms only a part of the clause: 1.17:V:9 *bnši* ^{c}*nh wyphn* "in lifting his eyes and he perceived." Clauses with two subjects and one predicate are rare, e.g. 1.4:IV:49 *yṣḥ aṯrt wbnh* "there shouted Athira and her sons."

From strictly a formal viewpoint the cola with two verbal predicates can be considered to contain two clauses. Such types of cola are very frequent in the standard introductory formulae of direct speech, e.g. 1.17:II:11/12 *yšu gh wyṣḥ* "he lifted his voice and shouted."

The length of a colon permits the inclusion of two full clauses: coordinate—asyndetic or syndetic—or even subordinate. A coordinate clause can be parallel: 1.6:VI:17: *mt* ^{c}*z b*^{c}*l* ^{c}*z* "Mot is strong, Baal is strong." Two clauses which are not parallel appear in the colon 1.4:IV:33 *b*^{c}*l ṯpṭn win d*^{c}*lnh* "Baal is our ruler and there is none above him." Even if no subordinating conjunctions are used, the following two samples have to be considered as each containing a sentence consisting of a main and a subordinate clause: 1.19:III:32 *ltbrkn alk brktm* "may you bless me that I go blessed"; 1.100:72a *ptḥ bt wuba* "open the house that I may enter."

Even a relative dependent clause can be accomodated within one colon: 1.3:III:23 *abn brq dltd*ᶜ *šmm* "I understand the thunder which the heavens do not know"; 1.23:64b *y att itrḫ* "O my wife whom I married!" The isolated appearance of three obviously parallel words in 1.3:III:18 *ḥšk* ᶜ*ṣk* ᶜ*bṣk* can be interpreted as a series of infinitives with a suffixed pronoun of the second person singular feminine; their meaning is obviously also parallel: an appeal to hurry.

Within the short space of one colon, consisting of three or four full words, it is possible to develop an internal parallelism: perfect, with two syntactically and semantically parallel clauses; or relaxed, with clauses of similar content but not parallel in structure, or with an additional verbal predicate. A tendency to attach monocola to preceding or following cola or verses can be observed in Ugaritic poetry; some monocola cannot be connected with immediately following or preceding verses into bicola and tricola, while their functional connection with more distant verses can be established. E.g. the formulae introducing the direct speech cannot be used alone, without the following speech.[5]

4. SYNTACTIC FEATURES IN BICOLA

4.1. Bicola with complete clauses. The bicola in which each colon contains at least one complete clause, independent or dependent, have to be described first.

There are no simple repetitions of cola in the Ugaritic poetry. One case can be dismissed as scribal error, dittography: The clause 1.14:II:20 is repeated in the following line with the conjunction *w*- "and." This wording has a close correspondence to 1.14:IV:2–3, while the preceding verse does not and thus may be deleted as an error.

Nearly identical are two cola in 1.15:III:20+21: *wtqrb wld bn lh* "and she conceived and bore (one) son to him"; the following colon differs only in *bnm* "(two/more) sons." An emendation creating a pair of complementary terms, *bnm!—bnt!* "sons"—"daughters" has been considered.

4.1.1. *Thetic parallelism* 4.1.1.1. Synonymous parallelism. The most frequent type of parallel bicola in which both cola form a complete clause are synonymous bicola. Each word of the first colon is parallelized by a word in the second colon. Some bicola exhibit the same word order in both clauses. The strict symmetry is relaxed—perhaps to avoid monotony—through the use of affixes, *-m, -n,* or particles, *w-, l-*.

The sequence of synonymous cola is fixed by the hierarchy of word pairs. Words which appear in the first colon are called A-words, those in the second colon B-words. Cf. 1.19:II:8+9:

bkm tmdln ᶜ*r*	weeping she saddled a donkey,
bkm tṣmd pḥl	weeping she harnessed the foal/ he-ass.

Exceptionally the sequence of synonymous, interchangeable words is reversed, cf. 1.14:III:27/28+28/29:

wng mlk lbty	and depart, king, from my house,
rḥq krt lḥẓry	keep far, Keret, from my court!

In 1.14:VI:14+15 the sequence of the imperatives is reversed: *wrḥq—ng*. Also the sequence of the vocatives in both these samples is unusual: the name appears as B-word in the second colon, the title "king" in the first one.

4.1.1.2. Complementary parallelism. The complementary bicola are determined by complementary relationship of relevant word pairs. The syntactic structure and even the word order of the second colon correspond often to those of the first colon.

In the complementary bicola there is at least one complementary pair, in 1.17:V:7/8+8 the end words:

[5] The term "relaxed" seems to be preferable to terms "imperfect" or "defective" if the parallelism is complete. In SBP 462–5, 475–543, abnormal verses which had to be emended are characterized as "defective"; for "incomplete" parallelism cf. 388–440. For pervasive tendency to avoid isolated cola cf. Jakobson, 428–429. For space limitations, the connections of bicola and monocola to the preceding and following verses are not discussed here.

ydn dn almnt	he judges the judgment of the widow,
yṯpṭ ṯpṭ yṯm	he adjudicates the cause of the orphan.

All words can belong to complementary pairs, e.g. 1.4.IV:35/36+36/37:

lḥm bṯlḥnt lḥm	eat bread from the table,
šty bkrpnm yn	drink wine from the goblets!

4.1.1.3. Relaxed parallelistic structures. Thetic parallelism can be expressed even if the syntactic and semantic ties are relaxed. Syntactic relaxation with strong semantic ties can be observed in 1.17:VI: 28/29+29:

ašsprk ^{c}*m b*^{c}*l šnt*	I shall make you count years with Baal,
^{c}*m bn il tspr yrḫm*	with the son of Il you will count months.

Both syntactic and semantic connections are relaxed in the following quotation, but the parallel is preserved by the general sense and supported by the double name of the Moon Goddess, although it appears as grammatical object in the first colon and as subject in the second colon, in 1.24:17/18+18/19:

tn nkl yrḫ ytrḫ	give Nikkal so (that) Yarikh acquires/marries (her),
ib t^{c}*rbm bbhth*	Ibb will (may) enter his palace.

Such loose parallelistic bicola are very rare in Ugaritic poetry.

A considerable number of bicola exhibit syntactic parallelity between the action described in the second colon which is a continuation of the action of the first colon and not merely its paraphrasis. The coherence of this type of bicola is provided mostly by the verbal predicates in the same person; the subject is usually not expressed in either colon.

Continuous bicola appear frequently in a longer sequence of action. More than one action can be presented in one colon: 1.17:II:10+11:

yprq lṣb wyṣḥq	he opened (his) mouth and laughed,
p^{c}*n lhdm yṯpd*	he put (his) foot on the footstool.

Such a bicolon appears also in direct speech 1.18:IV:21+21/22, (followed by the action in 31+32/33):

bn nšrm arḫp ank	among the eagles I will soar,
^{c}*l aqht* ^{c}*dbk*	upon Aqhat I shall direct you.

Because of the pervasive tendency to parallelize originally isolated monocola, even bicola with looser connection can be constructed, connected by syntactically different reference to an actant, e.g. 1.23:70b+71a:

wprṣ b^{c}*dhm*	and he opened (a breach) for them,
w^{c}*rb hm*	and they entered.

A similar relationship may be established between a direct question and its answer: e.g. 1.23:53a+53b:

mh ylt	What did they bear?
yldy šḥr wšlm	My (two) sons, Dawn and Dusk.

4.1.2. Contrastive parallelism. Contrasting actions or concepts usually are expressed by a strictly parallel structure which enhances the effectiveness of semantic distinctions. Word pairs indicate concepts often quoted together because of their contrast. In some instances the contrasting words can be understood as limits, with the elements between them not listed. A clear contrast appears in 1.23:32a+33b *hlh tšpl hlh trm* "behold they go down, behold they go up." Similar contrastive parallelism appears in the same text: 61/62+62 *špt larṣ špt lšmm* "(one) lip to the earth, (one/another) lip to heavens."

At the end of the text 1.12 the consequences of Baal's death are depicted in two bicola, II:58+59, 60+61:

štk mlk dn	ceased the king judging,
štk šibt ^{c}*n*	ceased women drawing (from the) well,
štk qr bt il	ceased noise of the house of god
wmṣlt bt ḥrš	and pounding of the house of the craftsman/smith.

In the first bicolon the highest person in the kingdom is contrasted to those of the lowest rank, in the second the lofty cult of the temple with the commonplace noises of a workshop.

4.1.3. *Disjunctive parallelistic structures.*[6] Since the disjunctive bicolon is used for expressing questions and commands, it can be considered a transformation of thetic complementary construction. The second colon is introduced by *hm* "or" in 1.4:IV:33+34: *rǵb rǵbt . . . hm ǵmu ǵmit* "are you very hungry? . . . or are you very thirsty?" Cf. also the volitive disjunctive sentence within one colon, 1.4:IV:35: *lḥm hm štym* "eat or drink!"

4.1.4. *Antithetic parallelism.* Antithetic parallelism is expressed by antonyms, or by use of negative particles. In the epics, it may indicate a forthcoming change. There are very few antithetic bicola in Ugaritic poetry as the presentation of action is positive, expressed by thetic parallelistic structures.

A probable antithetic parallelism can be found in 1.3:IV:33, perhaps within one colon: *atm bštm wan šnt* "you remain/delay, and/but I leave."

Antithesis between two bicola is not expressed by antonymous words but by the negation particle in 1.114:6/7+7/8:

il dyd^{c}*nn* *y*^{c}*db lḥm*dmṣd*lh* *wdlyd*^{c}*nn ylmn** *bqr*^{c}**ḫṭm tḥt ṯlḥn*	Il to whom he knows presents food of the banquet, and/but whom he does not know (he) strikes with the stick (of) scepter under the table.

A relative object clause with negation stands in thetic parallelism with positive grammatical object in 1.14:III:38+39:

pd in bbty ttn	but what is not in my house give me,
tn ly mṯt ḥry	give me the maiden Ḥurray!

A relaxed parallelistic structure with negation appears in 1:23:63/64+64a:

y^{c}*db uymn ušmal*	they place (food), or from right or from left,
bphm wltšb^{c}*n*	into their mouth, and/but they are not satiated.

The semantic contrast between strong men and weak women in 1.17:VI:39/40+40 is expressed within a relaxed parallelism; a negative answer is expected for the rhetorical question in the second colon:

qštm [ ] *mhrm*	a bow is [a weapon] of warriors,
ht tṣdn ṯintt	now, should womankind hunt (with it)?

4.2. Non-parallel bicola. 4.2.1. *Main and subordinated clauses.* Among the non parallel bicola, whose proportion is relatively low, the most frequent are those formed by one sentence consisting of two clauses: a main clause and a subordinate clause.

In the causal sentences the main clause is in the first colon; the subordinate clause follows: e.g. 1.17:VI: 34+34/35:

al tšrgn ybtltm	do not deceive me, o Virgin,
dm lǵzr šrgk ḫḫm	because to a hero your deceit is rubbish.

In the conditional sentence the protasis precedes the apodosis, e.g. 1.23:71b+71/72:

hm [*iṯ l*]*ḥm*	if there is food/bread
wtn wnlḥm	so give, and we shall eat.

The subordinated indirect question follows the main introductory clause, e.g. 1.19:III:31/33+33/34:

ibq^{c} *kbdh waḥd*	I shall split her liver and I shall look,
hm iṯ šmt iṯ ^{c}*ẓm*	whether there is fat, (whether) there is bone.

Another type of non-parallelistic bicola is that consisting of only one clause which is developed in two cola. In some structures of this type the subject is in the first colon, the predicate in the second. Another kind of non-parallelistic bicolon contains a clause in

---

[6] Disjunctive constructions with double *u- u-* "or-or" appear as part of a clause, or in units longer than a bicolon; e.g. *umlk ublmk* 1.4:VII:43 "(n)either king (n)or non-king," also 1.23:63/64, quoted below. The interpretation of bicola introduced by *u-* in 1.16:I:18/19 and 22 is still difficult; cf. *MLC*, 310, 523; *TOu*, 549, 550, 552; *CML*, 94-5.

the first colon and a supplement to it, an adverbial modifier, in the second colon.

Subject and verbal predicate appear in 1.19:I: 38/39+39/40:

apnk dnil mt rpi	afterwards Daniel the man of Rapiʾu
yṣly ʿrpt bḥm un	prayed to the clouds in oppressive heat.

A sentence with subject qualified by a relative clause appears in 1.19:IV:58/59+59:

yd mḫṣt aqht ǵzr	the hand which has slain Aqhat the hero
tmḫṣ alpm ib št	will slay thousands of enemies of the Lady.

Verbal predicate precedes the coordinate subjects in 1.23:62+62/63:

wyʿrb bphm	and there enter in their mouths
ʿṣr šmm wdg bym	birds of heavens and fishes in/from the sea.

Verbal clause with the adverbial modifier in the second bicolon appears often in the formulae about the journey to a goal, e.g. 1:14:VI:36/37+37/38:

idk pnm lytn	afterwards he certainly directed the face
ʿmm pbl mlk	toward Pabil the king.

The second colon varies according to the goal of the journey, cf. 1.14:V:31 *ʿm krt mswn* "toward Keret to the camp."

4.3. Cola containing dependent clause components. A brief mention of cola which do not form a complete independent clause may be added now, since they are used in combination with the full clauses in the most frequent type of parallelism. These syntactic combinations appear usually in the second cola and are dependent on the full clause expressed by the first colon. It would be possible to present them as clauses from which a constituent was omitted or deleted, but a rather positive approach based on dependency syntax is more convenient for determining the parallelistic structure: The parts of the second colon can be related both to their parallel expressions in the first colon and to the constituents on which they are dependent.

If a subject expressed in the first colon appears only in the first colon but a verbal predicate related to it is repeated in the second colon, this colon alone can be considered a complete clause. Cf. e.g. 1.19:I:34+35. If the clause in the first colon is nominal, the absence of the subject in the second colon makes its nominal predicate dependent on the subject of the first colon: 1.14:III:31+31/32:

udm ytnt il	Udum is a gift of Il
wušn ab adm	and a present of the father of mankind.

A verbal predicate in the first colon governs also the adverbial components in the second colon, and is related to the subject related there. Cf. e.g. 1.9:III:7a+7b:

bph rgm lyṣa	from his mouth the word did not go out,
bšpth hwth	from his lips his utterance.

The subject may be present in both cola, while the nominal predicate appears only in the first colon, 1.17:I:20+20/21:

bl iṯ bn lh km aḫh	may there be a son for him like (that of) his brothers
wšrš km aryh	and descendant like (that of) his relatives.

The subject of the first colon is in the second colon repeated or perhaps rather provided with an apposition; cf. 1.17:II:26+26/27:

ʿrb bbth kṯrt	there entered his house Kotharat,
bnt hll snnt	daughters of Halfmoon, Swallows.

Two parallel objects depend on the verbal predicate of the first colon, e.g. 1.14:III:29/30+30:

ytt nḫšm mhrk	I gave you snakes as your bride price,
bn bṯn ytnnk	sons of serpents as your gift.

Also adverbial modifiers depend on the verbal predicate expressed once in the first colon, e.g. 1.18:IV:17+18:

aštk km nšr bḥbšy	I shall put you like an eagle into my sheath,
km diy btᶜrty	like a kite in my pouch.

Even in some of these samples here above additional clause components appear in the second colon which have no direct counterpart in the first colon. Most of them are on syntactically lower level, as attributes to the higher constituents or components. These "ballast-variants" help to establish or present the quantitative balance between cola. Cf. above *bn bṯn* "sons of serpents" for parallel to one word *nḥšm* "snakes" in 1.100:75+75/76. Many such "ballast-variants" function as epithets.

More rarely than genitival attributes, additional adjectival attributes appear in the second colon, e.g. 1.100:4+4/5:

mnt nṯk nḥš	incantation against bite of snake,
šmrr nḥš ᶜqšr	against poisoning of/by a scaly snake.

5. COMBINATIONS OF MORE THAN TWO COLA

While in the preceding sections the basic binary relationship in Ugaritic parallelistic structures were presented as they appear in bicola and monocola, at least a short mention about their use in larger combinations of cola should be made.

Most of the tricola in Ugaritic poetry can be characterized as parallelistic bicola to which a third colon had been added, usually related to the second colon. (Cf. e.g. 1.18:IV:27+28/29.) In many tricola the first colon is followed by two mutually connected cola (e.g. 1.4:IV:20+21+22). The introductory colon is often proleptic; its elements are taken from and repeated in the immediately following colon. (Cf. e.g. 1.17:VI:26+27+27/28.) There are very few instances of tricola in which the first and third colon correspond to each other, with the middle colon loosely related to them. (Cf. perhaps 1.14:II:32 +33+34.) In all these types of tricola there are various types of mutual relationships between the cola which deserve a further, more detailed study. There is a limited number of tricola in which all three cola are mutually parallel in their syntactic and semantic structure. (Cf. e.g. 1.100:70a+70b+71a.)

It is possible to observe sequences of two bicola each forming a complete sentence exhibiting syntactic semantic relationships between the first and second colon in the ABAB pattern. (Cf. e.g. 1.22:II:58+59 and 60+61.) In other combinations of two bicola, there is only one sentence. The parallel subjects of the first bicolon have their verbal predicates only in the second bicolon (cf. e.g. 1.17:I:0/1+1/2 and 2+3), or a double parallelistic protasis of a conditional sentence is followed by a double apodosis, each of them in a bicolon (e.g. 1.14:IV:40/41+41/42 and 42/43+43). Such combinations of four cola forming a sentence can be graphically symbolized as AABB. Very few combinations of parallelistic cola are arranged in the symmetrical pattern, ABBA; the first colon has a parallel in the fourth colon. (Cf. e.g. 1.19:IV:43/44+44/45+45+46.)

In the Ugaritic poetry there are even longer series of cola or bicola connected by common syntactic structure and semantic characteristics. In most of them a regular pattern is repeated (e.g. 1.4:VI:47–54; 1.17:I:26–33). In isolated instances, longer combinations of cola, less symmetric or less homogeneous, do appear (cf. e.g. 1.14:III:22–25).

6. WORD PAIRS[7]

The semantic character of parallelistic bicola and other parallelistic combinations, in monocola, tricola and longer structures, is determined by the relationship of the word pairs. The functional relationship within the poetic parallelistic structure is more important for their determination than the lexical definition based on extratextual evidence. Because of the high proportion of poetry among our sources for Ugaritic language, many words are attested only in poetic texts and their general function is unknown.

This functional approach necessitates the recognition of many word pairs as synonymous, since they relate to the same poetic or perhaps real referent. Some of these relationships can be labeled as common poetic devices, such as metonymy or synecdoche. A special category of synonymous pairs includes epithets which serve as a parallel to the names of gods and

[7] Various relationships of words in pairs are treated here from the viewpoint of their function in the parallelistic poetic structures. For Hebrew poetry cf. W. Popper, *SBP*, 380–3; J. F. A. Sawyer, *Semantics in Biblical Research*, 1972, 77, with reference to J. Lyons, *Introduction to Theoretical Linguistics*, 1968, 424–6; cf. also Lyons, *Semantics, I*, 1977, 177–97. For general semantic viewpoints cf. Lyons, *Semantics, I*, 197–206, 270–335; A. Leech, *Semantics*, 1974, 95–125; cf. also 43–6, 114–5.

humans, and frequently are parallel to each other. There are many complementary word pairs whose meaning can be traced to a common denominator. Some of these pairs indicate members standing on the opposite limits of a semantic group; their use can be considered an effective poetic device. There are hardly any antonym word pairs in Ugaritic poetry; antithetic relationships are expressed with the help of negative particles.

6.1. Identical word repeated. For various reasons identical words do appear in both cola, in spite of pervasive tendency either to distinguish identical concepts by synonyms or to use complementary words. Some of these occurrences may be explained by the lack of an appropriate synonym, some are probably caused by the requirements of poetic style and can be considered poetic figures.

Quite rarely the same name is repeated in both cola, e.g. *dnil* "Daniel" in 1.17:II:24+25. For some nouns there probably were not any appropriate synonyms available in Ugaritic lexicon. Cf. e.g. *mznm* "balance" in 1.24:33/34+34/35, or *amt* "female servant" 1.12:II:14/15+16/17. Some identical words serve as governing nouns for a synonymous or complementary attribute, genitival or adjectival: 1.14:III:4/5+5 *udm rbt—udm ṯrrt* "Udum the great"—"Udum the well watered"; 1.12:II:60+61 *bt il—bt ḥrš* "house (temple) of Il/god"—"house (workshop) of a craftsman/blacksmith." It may be expected that the category of attributes is the same. Thus both attributes of *mt* "men" in 1.17:I:16/17+17/18 should be genitival, *rpi* and *hrnmy* "of Rapiʾu"—"of the Harnamite," taken as epithet of Rapiʾu.

For poetic effect identical word or words appear at the beginning of each colon—(ep)anaphora—or, very rarely, at the end of each colon—epiphora. In chainlike manner the end of the first colon can be connected to the beginning of the second colon by identical words. Appeals are made more urgent by repetition at the beginning of cola: 1.17:VI:26+27 *irš ḥym* "ask life!"; 1.17:VI:42+42/43 *ṯb ly* "return to me!" Other samples of (ep)anaphora: 1.23:61/62+62a *špt* "(one) lip"; 1.12.II:58+59 *štk* "it ceased," also 60. Among the few occurrences of identical words at the end of each part of a bicolon, *amt* "I shall die," 1.17:VI:38a+38b, may be considered as an emphatic statement.

Chainlike connections of two cola appear in the wish of Daniel, in 1.19:III:1/2+2 etc.: *bʿl yṯbr* "may Baal break." The repetition of *aṯt il* "(two) wives of Il" in 1.23:42a+42b was probably caused by requirements of poetic structure, but similar repetition of *mtqtm* "sweet (du. fem)" also occurs in 50a+50b.[8]

Very rarely are words repeated within a colon; cf. short vocatives and imperatives: 1.23:33a *um um* "my mother, my mother!"; 1.3:IV:32: *lk lk* "go, go!"

6.2. Synonymous word pairs. The synonymous word pairs in Ugaritic poetry refer to one person, object, action or quality. Their function is based on their general semantic relationship. From the viewpoint of semantics, there may be no real synonyms; in poetry their function in forming the parallelistic structure is dominant over their semantic characteristics.

A hierarchy of A-words—those appearing in the first colon—and B-words—those providing parallels to them in the second colon—can be clearly observed.

Some relationships between A-words and B-words are of semantic character, some may be determined by their length.

Semantic relationships:

- general—special: *yd—ymn* "hand"—"right (hand)," 1.14:II:13+14, cf. III:55/56;
- common—rare: *tḥm—hwt* both for "message" 1.14:VI:40+41; *ybk—ydmʿ* "he wept"—"he shed tears" 1.19:IV:15/16+16/17;
- autochthonous—foreign: *bt—hkl* (ultimately from Sumerian) "house"—"big house, palace" 1.100:72a +72b;
- short word—long word: *dn—ṯpṭ* both for "judgment" or "(cause)" 1.16:VI:45/46+46/47; *ks—krpn* "cup"—"goblet" 1.15:II:16/17+17/18;
- simple word—compound: *ḥym—blmt* "life"—"immortality" 1.17:VI:27+27/28;
- basic—derived: *hlk* (G)—*yštql* (Št) "he arrived"—he reached" 1.100:67+67/68;
- one word—compound epithet: *bʿl—bn dgn* or *rkb ʿrpt* "Baal"—"son of Dagan" or "rider on the clouds" 1.12:I:38+39; 1.19:I:42/43+43/44; cf. double names of gods split into two cola, e.g. *nkl—ib* "Nikkal—Ibb" 1.14:17/18+18/19;

---

[8] The term "chain" has been used by the present writer, cf. "Semitic Poetic Structures in the New Testament," in: *Aufstieg und Niedergang der römischen Welt*, vol. 25/2, ed. W. Haase (Berlin, to appear in 1983). The same term was used in the same meaning by N. Turner, *Style* (Vol. IV of J. H. Moulton, *A Grammar of New Testament Greek*), 1976, 65, 116.

noun—pronoun: *ilm—hmt* (both in accusative) "gods"—"them" 1.17:V:19/20+20.

6.2.1. *Paired non-identical numbers.* The synonymous character of bicola and word pairs appears clearly in those with numbers; in contrast to prosaic arithmetic, the poetic function of different numbers does not indicate different quantities, but rather enhances the synonymous character of the bicolon. The functional interpretation of paired numbers is to be preferred to strict lexical understanding; even different numbers can refer to the same poetic entity.

The numbers "1,000" and "10,000" refer poetically to a large amount of precious metal or to a large dimension: 1.24:20/21+21/22: *alp ksp wrbt ḫrṣ* "a thousand (shekels) silver and myriad (shekels) gold"; 1.17:V:9/10+10: *balp šd rbt kmn* "on thousand spaces, (on) ten thousand tracts."

This poetic character of numbers appears even more clearly in pairs of type x—x+1 or x—x+10 or 11: 1.23:66/67+67a *šbᶜ šnt—ṯmn nqpt* "seven years"—"eight turns/revolutions." Cf. for 77 and 88: 1.12:II:48+49. This is true also for the difference between "one" and "two": 1.1:III:9+10: *byd—bklat yd* "in (one) hand"—"in both hands."

The functional, poetic synonymity of different numbers applies also to ordinal numerals used in parallelism—but not in sequence (e.g. 1.14:III:2–3) — and helps to determine related word pairs as functional synonyms: 1.14:II:30+31 *ḫmš—ṯdṯ* "fifth"—"sixth", thus: *lḥm—mǵd* "bread/food"—"a kind of food."

6.2.2. *Epithets.*[9] Epithets have several functions: they provide parallel expressions in the second colon, often they also extend it; and possibly they contribute towards cohesion of cola and bicola on phoneme level.

A very frequent type of epithet is the patronym: *bᶜl—bn dgn* "Baal"—"son of Dagan" 1.12:I:38–39; *aqht— bn dnil* "Aqhat"—"son of Daniel" 1.18:I:18/19+19. Similar is the epithet for the god Il, "father of mankind," *il—ab adm* 1.14:I:35/36+36/37.

Some epithets consist of one word only, giving the general denotation of person or deity, e.g. *aṯrt—ilt* "Athira"—"goddess" 1.14:IV:35/36+36/37; *ḥry—ǵlmt* "Ḥurray"—"young lady" 1.14:IV:40/41+41/42. Rarely, a name is used as a B-word and title or epithet as A-word: *mlk—krt* "king"—"Keret/Kirta" 1.14:VI:14+15. Some epithets are placed before the name, e.g. *ṯr il* "Bull Il" 1.17:I:24; *bn ilm mt* "son of Il/god Mot" 1.5:I:12. Other epithets or titles follow the name, e.g. *pbl mlk* "Pabil the king" 1.14:III:15/16; *ḫrḫb mlk qẓ* "Ḫirḫib king of summer" 1.24:2. The epithets often appear in both the first and the parallel second colon: 1.4:IV:31+32 *rbt aṯrt ym—qnyt ilm* "Lady Athira of the Sea"—"Creatress of gods": cf. also 1.17:I:16/17+17/18.

6.3. Complementary word pairs. In complementary word pairs the A-words denote basic, common, more readily apparent entities, while the B-words are usually more specific and less frequent:

large—small: *arḫ—ṯat* "cow"—"ewe" 1.6:II:28–29;
near—distant: *aplb—bmt* "breast"—"back"—1.5:VI:21-22;
common—rare: *ksp—ḫrṣ* "silver"—"gold" 1.24:20/21.

The position of words in the word pairs is determined by their hierarchy; thus it is relative. Some words appear exclusively as A-words or as B-words, some can appear in either position.

The general short word for "house" *bt* serves only as an A-word, while the corresponding B-words are either the foreign word *hkl* "big house, palace" 1.17:I:44 or the less frequent *ḥẓr* "court." But *hkl* appears as A-word paired to the B-word *ḥẓr* in 1.19:III:9/10+10/11. The word for "honey" *nbt* appears as B-word following the A-word for "oil" *šmn* in 1.6:III:12+13, and also after the A-word for "wine" *yn* in 1.14:IV:1+2. But the word for oil *šmn* functions itself as B-word connected to "dew" *ṭl* in 1.3:II:39. (In a non-literary text, "honey" *nbt* precedes "oil" *šmn*, 4.14:2,7,15.)

A short word used alone precedes a long word—*ks* "cup" and *krpn* "goblet", in 1.15:II:16/17+17/18—, but follows it if provided with an attribute: *krpnm—ks ḫrṣ* "goblets"—"cups of gold, golden cups" 1.4:IV:36/37+37/38 (cf. VI: 58+59).

---

9 Cf. A. Cooper and M. H. Pope, "Divine Names and Epithets in the Ugaritic Texts," *RSP*, III, 333–469.

7. REDUNDANCY

If the concept of redundancy or "Functional Sentence Perspective"[10] approach is applied to Ugaritic parallelistic poetry, the more regular structures exhibit more redundancy. If in a parallelistic bicolon all parts correspond neatly, both in syntactic categories and synonymous meanings, no new information is given in the second colon. New information is provided by addition of new components, not contained in the first colon, or by adding further details to the concepts of the first colon. Many of the additional attributes give only slight or no new data, especially the ballast-variants and stereotyped epithets of divine and human actants.

Cola and their parts, whose relationship can be understood as complementary, can be evaluated from the viewpoint of redundancy according to the semantic distance between them: the greater it is, the more new information is provided. Some redundant words can be considered as kinds of "fillers." If more than three basic elements had to be presented in a bicolon, only three of them could be accomodated in the first colon. In order to preserve the balance—usually 3 + 3—between the cola, one or two elements from the first colon had to be repeated, without adding new information. From the viewpoint of redundancy, the non-parallelistic verses are less redundant, with sentences consisting of one main and one subordinate clause or of one clause going through both cola without parallelistic addition.

8. PHONEMIC FEATURES IN UGARITIC VERSES[11]

There is one feature of Ugaritic poetry which deserves more attention than it has received hitherto. Since the vocalic structure of Ugaritic words is known with sufficient certainty, the relationship of certain phonemes to the parallelistic framework should be investigated. Some phonological features accompany the syntactic parallelity, some were perhaps used intentionally to provide tighter cohesion.

In the narrative passages of Ugaritic poetry most words end with the vowel /-u/. This vowel is the marker of the nominative case; it appears at the end of the subject nouns in the singular, masculine and femine. The same vowel /-u/ is the marker of the indicative mood of the imperfect in the third person. The imperfect is by far the most frequent narrative tense in Ugaritic epics. In a clause that contains a subject in the singular and its verbal predicate in imperfect, there are at least two words ending with the same vowel, /-u/. Cf. e.g. 1.12:I:12/13:

/*ᵓilu yiẓḥaqu bima libbi*/ Il laughed in (his) heart.

Another relatively frequent element ending with /-u/ is the suffixed pronoun of the third person singular masculine, /-hu/; cf. e.g. 1.14:III:53:

/*yirḥaṣu yadahu ᶜammatah*/ he washed his hand to the elbow.

But neither of these/-u/ end vowels appears in the variant of this colon in 1.14:II:10, with the imperative and with the suffixed pronoun of the second person masculine.

The frequency of end vowel /-u/ in a colon is enhanced by additional elements, an appositional or adjectival epithet or a coordinated verbal predicate:

1.16:VI:39 /*yitbaᶜu yaṣṣubu ǵalmu*/ Yassub the lad departed;

1.16:VI:40/41 /*yiššaᵓu gahu wa-yaṣūḥu*/ he lifted his voice and he shouted.

Various morphemes ending with /-i/ can appear in the same colon, e.g. 1.18:I:16:

/*yadaᶜtuki bittī kī ᵓaništi*/ I know, my daughter, that you are kind.

Also cola with a great frequency of /-a/at the end of the words can be cited, e.g. 1.16:VI:48/49+49/50:

/*lē panīka lā tašalḥimu yatuma*/ at your face you do not feed the orphan.

/*baᶜda kaslika ᵓalmanata*/ behind your neck the widow.

A repetition of identical or similar nominal and verbal morphemes consisting of several phonemes also can be considered an enhancement of the cohesion on phoneme level; cf. the frequent use of the feminine marker /-at-/ or the morpheme consisting of /ū/, a nasal /m/ or /n/ and /a/: 1.4:IV:31:

/*ᵓēka maǵayat rabbatu ᵓaṯiratu yammi*/ why did the lady Attira of the Sea arrive?;

1.18:IV:19/20: /*naš(a)rūma tirḫapūna*/ the eagles soar.

Assonances based on phonemic similarity between morphemes of different origin and function can be observed, e.g. 1.17:VI:34+34/35:

---

[10] For "Functional Sentence Perspective" cf. S. Segert, "Prague Structuralism in American Biblical Scholarship. Performance and Potential," in *The Word of the Lord Shall Go Forth: Essays in Honor of D. N. Freedman*, 1983.

[11] Within slashes, phonological reconstruction of Ugaritic phonemes and words is presented, cf. *BGUL*, T 3. Examples of reconstructed poetry: Pardee, *UIR*, 119; Segert, *BGUL*, 85. 1–2.

/*yā batūlatum(m)a*/ — /*ḫaḫūma*/ o Virgin!—rubbish.

In some instances, the ends of both cola, due to the categorial identity or similarity of their final words even provide grammatical rhymes: /*naharēmi*/ — /*tahāmatēmi*/ "of two rivers"—"of two floods" 1.4:IV:21+22.

The syntactic parallelity of two synonymous or complementary cola provides enough correspondences on phoneme level between them, e.g. 1.17:V:7/7+8:

/*yadīnu dīna ʾalmanati*/ he was judging the judgment of the widow,

/*yaṯpuṭu ṯapṭa yatumi*/ he was adjudicating the cause of the orphan.

All the accumulations of identical phonemes and their combinations quoted here above result from the uniformity of Ugaritic morphology and from the regularity of Ugaritic parallelistic verse structure. They enhance the structural cohesion, but probably they were not used for this purpose intentionally.

Pervasive parallelism on syntactic and semantic levels provides cohesion to verse structure of Ugaritic poetry. The usually equal number of words in the cola with the corresponding number of word stresses contributes to the regularity of rhythm, while the homogeneity of word patterns and inflectional morphemes adds more corresponding and parallel elements on the sound level.

All these interconnected levels on which parallelistic structures are expressed and enhanced may provide sufficient explanation of the principles of Ugaritic poetry without recurrence to other prosodical patterns, rules or systems.

Abbreviations

BGUL — S. Segert, *Basic Grammar of the Ugaritic Language*. 1983.

CML — J. C. L. Gibson, *Canaanite Myths and Legends*. 1978.

Jakobson — R. Jakobson, "Grammatical Parallelism and its Russian Facet," *Language* 42 (1966), 399–429.

KTU — M. Dietrich-O. Loretz-J. Sanmartín, *Die keilalphabetischen Texte aus Ugarit. Teil 1*. 1976.

L-S — H. G. Liddell and R. Scott, *A Greek-English Lexicon*, 1940/1968.

MLC — G. Del Olmo Lete, *Mitos y leyendas de Canaan según la tradición de Ugarit*. 1981.

RSP — *Ras Shamra Parallels: The Texts from Ugarit and the Hebrew Bible*, I–III, eds. L. R. Fisher, S. Rummel. 1972, 1975, 1981.

SBP — *Studies in Biblical Parallelism. Part I. Parallelism in Amos*, by Louis I. Newman; *Parts II–III. Parallelism in Isaiah*, by William Popper. 1918; 1923.

TOu — A. Caquot, M. Sznycer, A. Herdner, *Textes ougaritiques*, I, *Mythes et légendes*. 1974.

UIR — *Ugarit in Retrospect: Fifty Years of Ugarit and Ugaritic*. ed. G. D. Young. 1981.

UT — C. H. Gordon, *Ugaritic Textbook*. 1965.

YGC — W. F. Albright, *Yahweh and the Gods of Canaan*. 1968.

GILGAMESH, THE CEDAR FOREST AND MESOPOTAMIAN HISTORY

Aaron Shaffer
Hebrew University

Samuel Noah Kramer was a pioneer in the study of Sumerian epics concerning Gilgamesh and it is due to his work that the first inkling of what took place in the cedar forest became known.[1] I propose to discuss here some aspects of the denouement of *Gilgamesh and the Cedar Forest*. It is a pleasure to dedicate this effort to him.

Gilgamesh and the Cedar Forest, like its noble successor the Akkadian *Epic of Gilgamesh*, is an expression of man's struggle against the oblivion of death. Gilgamesh, a king of Uruk, seeks to surmount human mortality by establishing a name for himself in the cedar forest and by setting up his monument there.[2] It later transpires that this will involve overcoming and then murdering the divinely appointed guardian of the cedars. Thus will Gilgamesh, like later Mesopotamian kings who boast of it, cut cedars in the holy grove; he will be a king of the woods.[3]

The sun god Utu whose domain is the cedar forest agrees and appoints seven genies to help him on his journey.[4] Reaching the forest, Gilgamesh is over-

---

[1] Primarily by his editing of Edward Chiera's copies in *Sumerian Epics and Myths*, and with the first edition of Gilgamesh and the Cedar Forest (called by him "Gilgamesh and the Land of Living") in *JCS* 1 1947, 3ff. I hope to complete my edition very soon.

[2] Lines 7f.

kur-ra ga-an-ku$_4$ mu-mu ga-an-gar
ki-mu-gub-bu-ba-àm mu-mu ga-bí-ib-gub
ki-mu-nu-gub-bu-ba-àm mu-dingir-mu (var. mu-dingir-re-e-ne) ga-bí-ib-gub
"I would enter the land, I would make a name for myself
Where there are already mounuments, I will set up my name
Where there are no monuments, I will set up my god's name (var. the name of the gods)"

This mythic stone monument (NA$_4$.RÚ.A/*narû*) is referred to in the later prologue to the *Epic of Gilgamesh*, tablet I i 8: *iḫruṣ ina narê kalu mānaḫti* "he inscribed all his ordeal on a stone stele." This stele is presumably a source for the epic as recounted on the lapis lazuli tablet which the audience is invited to read, tablet I i 25–26 (*Iraq* 37, 161)

. . . tuppi zaginni šitassi
[kî š]ū Gilgameš ittallak kalu marṣāti
". . . read the lapis tablet,
how he, Gilgamesh, went through all the hardships"

For the author of Gilgamesh, this stele is the bridge between history and myth.

[3] The cedar forest motif is retained in Mesopotamian historical literature in the form of the ritual claim of kings, from the old Akkadian period on, to have gone to the cedar mountain and to have cut cedars there (cf. A. Malamat, *AS* 16, 365f). It also occurs in *Isaiah* 37:24 where Sennacherib is quoted as boasting of cutting the cedars, and in *Isaiah* 14 the marvellous mock elegy over the death of the king of Babylon where the trees themselves express relief that the king is dead, vs 8 "now that you have lain down, no one comes up to fell us."

[4] These demons are brothers, terrifying in their description. In one version of this epic they are clearly astral:

e-ne-ne an-na mul-la-me-eš
ki-a ḫar-ra-an zu-me-eš
an-na mul-dé-da íl-la-me-eš
ki-a kaskal-ki-aratta z[u-me-eš]
dam-gàr-ra-gin$_7$ giri$_3$-bal zu-me-[eš]
tu.mušen-gin$_7$ ab-[làl]-kur-ra zu-[me-eš]
má-ùr-má-ùr-hur-sag-gá-ka hu-mu-e-ni-túm-túm-mu-ne
They, then, shine in the sky,
On earth they know the roads,

whelmed with joy and without taking counsel with his servant Enkidu or the Uruk kinsmen who accompany them, cuts down a cedar. In the drama of "The King of the Wood" (immortalized by Sir James George Frazer in the opening of the *Golden Bough*) the plucking of the bough initiates a monomachia between the intruder and the priest of the forest sanctuary which results in death and, perhaps, in a new *rex nemorensis*. So here, Gilgamesh's hasty cutting of the cedar rouses the forest guardian Huwawa from his lair,[5]

> Huwawa felt a shudder in his chamber,
> Put on his garment sheen against him.[6]

In another version, this is given as:

> Then, as warrior approached warrior
> He twirled his divine sheen on his head like a turban.[7]

Gilgamesh is no match for this supernatural armour. He is overcome and sits in a daze, dreaming. Only after much shouting and prodding is he roused from reveries, in which he had nightmares about Huwawa. In one version, which takes a heroic view of Gilgamesh, the description of these terrors is transferred to Enkidu who tries to dissuade Gilgamesh from persisting. In the other version where a more human Gilgamesh is portrayed, Gilgamesh himself describes these horrific dreams while Enkidu urges him on, quoting, it would seem, advice from "your protective deity," Enki-Nudimmud. The latter may also have provided Gilgamesh with a ruse without which Gilgamesh and the Urukeans clearly have no chance against Huwawa's supernatural aura.[8]

The traditions of the versions, which differ in several respects, diverge sharply at this point. In one version Gilgamesh tricks Huwawa into giving up his protection by offering him his sisters.[9] A second tradition has Gilgamesh offer Huwawa costly gifts for every one of his seven coats. The text is not complete, nor are all the gifts clear, but they include food fit for the gods and costly stones.[10] In all versions Gilgamesh affects a desire to become part of Huwawa's folk.

By these devices Gilgamesh disarms Huwawa. When the seventh and the last coat of divine sheen is removed and the corresponding cedar lumbered away,[11] Huwawa is powerless. He is betrayed, puts up

---

> Stars blazing in the sky,
> On earth they know the road to the land of Aratta,
> They know to change paths like merchants,
> Like swallows they know the cracks of the earth,
> They would guide him through the many mountain passes.

[5] Perhaps it is really his slave/companion Enkidu who plays the role. In the *rex nemorensis* it is a fugitive slave who breaks the bough and offers the challenge. In the Sumerian epic here, it is actually Enkidu who kills the guardian of the forest. Many aspects of this Gilgamesh story which match elements of Frazer's tale—the divine grove, the 'ghastly priest,' the plucking of the bough, the *monomachia*—invite comparison. For a recent and stimulating re-evaluation of the "King of the Woods" see the discussion by Joseph Fontenrose in *The Ritual Theory of Myth*, 36ff. A more sceptical view is taken by David E. Bynum in *The Daemon in the Wood*, 147ff.

[6] ^{d}ḫu-wa-wa ki-ná-a-ni im-ma-ḫu-luḫ-ḫa ní-te-a-ni mu-na-ra-an-lá (var. [gú m]u-ra-è-a).

[7] u$_4$-bi-a ur-sag ur-sag-ra ù-mu-un-na-te me-l[ám-ma-ni sag-gá-na] šu-gur-gin$_7$ i-in-b[úr].

[8] "Your god, the divine protective standard, Enki-Nudimmud has divulged a secret to you," dingir-zu d.urì-gal-^{d}en-ki-^{d}nu-dím-mud-e inim-zu mu-e-ni-è.

[9] Basing himself upon my manuscript, T. Jacobsen, *The Treasures of Darkness*, 200 has already divulged the denouement.

[10] "Fine meal, food fit for the great gods, skins of cold water, dušia-stone, nir-stone, lapis lazuli," zì-esa níg-kú-dingir-gal-gal-e-ne ^{kuš}umun a-šed$_{17}$ ^{na_4}du$_8$-si-a ^{na_4}nir$_7$ ^{na_4}za-gìn-na, *FLP* 1053 obv. 6 and rev. 15 (tablet identified by A. Sjöberg as belonging to *Gilgamesh and the Cedar Forest*).

[11] The relationship between the cedars and Huwawa's powers is not clear. On the one hand these powers emanate from what he wears and at the same time they are embodied in the cedars. As Huwawa gives up his ní-te/me-lám to Gilgamesh the act is translated to the cutting, trimming and lumbering of the cedars. Furthermore, in the Old Babylonian Akkadian Bauer fragment, the cutting of these cedars is termed *nêr* GIŠ.ERIN "murdering the cedars," *JNES* 16, 256: rev. 23, cf. 11, 12, 16: also in the Middle Babylonian Megiddo version, cf. *RA* 62, 121:8, while the *melammū* aura is described as a fallout of luminous particles gradually growing dim: *melammū iḫalliqū namrīrū īrupū*, "the divine auras will be lost, now that the radiance has dimmed," *JNES* 16, 256 obv. 12. For a comprehensive treatment of the subject, see Elena Cassin, *La splendeur divine*, and especially the 5th chapter; cf. also Neil Forsyth, *Acta Sumerologica* 3, 13f.

a fight, pulling hair, biting flesh, but in the end is shackled like a beast.

> When he had extinguished for him his 7th coat of divine aura,
> It grew dark in his chamber (or: he approached his chamber)
> Like a . . . snake he slithered to his dwelling but instead of giving him a kiss, he struck him a blow on the cheek
> Huwawa tore at his flesh, plucked the hair on his forehead.[12]

Gilgamesh took pity on Huwawa, comparing him to a snared bird or a captured warrior, and would have given him his freedom. One version especially develops this noble side of Gilgamesh's character, and has him say to Enkidu,

> "Let us extend a freeing hand to the warrior, let him be our friend,
> he will show us the lay of the paths, let him be our friend,
> Let him be my associate, let him carry my pack."[13]

Enkidu, a sober realist, opposes this suggestion and in an ensuing argument kills Huwawa. Here Gilgamesh has no part in the killing although in one of the Old Babylonian Akkadian versions it is he who strikes the first blow.[14] Huwawa's severed head is put in a sack and, with gross miscalculation and insensitivity, brought before Enlil (and Ninlil) for appreciation.

> "Why have you acted so?," asks the god,
> "Why, by what is done his name is destroyed from the earth!
> You should have seated him before you,
> You should have given him food from your food,
> You should have given him drink from your drink."[15]

The heroes fade away, and one version at least ends with an aetiological coda where Enlil distributes the auras of Huwawa, to the fields, rivers, canebrakes, lions, forests, mountains and roads.[16]

Gilgamesh's pitch to Huwawa is formulaic and nearly structurally identical in both versions. The version which has only the sister motif is of interest here. The text reads as follows:

166 zi-ama-ugu-mu-^{d}nin-sún-ka a-a-mu-kù-^{d}lugal-bàn-da
167 kur-ra tuš-a-zu ba-ra-zu kur-ra tuš-a-zu hè-zu-àm
168 en-me-bára-ge-si nin$_9$-gal-mu nam-dam-šè kur-ra hu-mu-ra-ni-ku$_4$-ra
169 mìn-kam-ma-šè in-ga-na-mu-na-ab-bé
170 zi-ama-ugu-mu-d.nin-sún-ka a-a-mu-kù-d.lugal-bàn-da

---

[12] 199 ní-te-ni-7-kam-ma mu-na-til(var. ti)-la-ta da-ga-na(var. ni) ba-te
200 mùs-kàr-geštin-na igar$_x$-na šu im-ta-du-du
201 ne mu-un-su-ub-ba-gin$_7$ te-na tibir-ra bi-in-ra
202 ḫu-wa-wa zú ba-da-an-bír sag-ki ba-da-gur$_5$-uš.

[13] Version B,
179 gá-nam-ma ur-sag-ra su ga-àm-bar-re-en-dè-en lú-zu-me ḫé-a
180 dúr-kaskal-la igi me-eb-du$_8$-dè-a lú-zu-meḫé-a
181 [e-ne lú-t]ab-ba-mu ḫé-a nigin-mu ḫé-em-mi-íl-íl.

[14] *JNES* 16, 256 rev. 1f.
1 *[iš]me Gilgameš zikir rā'ešu*
2 *ilqi ḫaṣṣinnam ina qatišu*
3 *išlup namṣaram ina šibbišu*
4 *Gilgameš inēršu kišādam*
Gilgamesh listened to his companion's words,
took an axe in his hand,
drew the dagger from his belt,
Then Gilgamesh pierced him in the neck.

[15] *TLB* 2, 4 cf. J. J. van Dijk apud P. Garelli, *Gilgameš et sa légende*, 71 (collated)
105 a-na-àm ur$_5$-gin$_7$ ì-ak-en-zé-en
106 ba-du$_{11}$-ga-ke$_4$-eš mu-ni ki-ta ḫa-lam-ke$_4$-eš
107 igi-zu-ne-ne ḫé-bí-íb-tuš
108 ninda-kú-zu-ne-a ḫé-bí-íb-kú
109 a-nag-zu-ne-a ḫé-bí-íb-nag.

[16] Here again the versions show substantial differences. In one version Huwawa prays to Utu for help, solicites Gilgamesh's mercy but is opposed by Enkidu. In the other version, Huwawa first appeals to Gilgamesh, is opposed by Enkidu, then in desperation prays to Utu. At this point Gilgamesh begins a second speech to Huwawa, but the text breaks off. One can estimate that only 8 lines or so are left, which makes it rather unlikely that this version had the same ending as the other.

171 kur-ra tuš-a-zu ba-ra-zu kur-ra tuš-a-zu ḫé-zu-àm
172 pèš-tur nin$_9$-bàn-da-mu nam-lukur-šè ḫu-mu-ra-ni-ku$_4$-ra-àm[17]
173 ní-zu ba-àm-ma-ra su-za[18] ga-an-ku$_4$
174 ní-te-ni-1-àm mu-na-ra-an-ba etc.

"By the life of my mother who bore me, divine Ninsun, and my father, divine, holy Lugalbanda,
The land where you dwell has never been known, let the land where you dwell be known!
I promise to bring my elder sister Enmebaragesi into the land for you as a wife"
Once again he goes on to say,
"By the life of my mother who bore me, divine Ninsun, and my father, divine, holy Lugalbanda,
The land where you dwell has never been known, let the land where you dwell be known!
I promise to bring my younger sister Peshtur into the land for you as a concubine![19]
But do diminish for me (or: make me a gift of) your divine sheen, let me enter your folk!"
He then diminished for him (or: made a gift to him of) his first divine sheen, etc...

Some literary aspects of this denouement, in which Gilgamesh displays characteristics of deceivers and tricksters, will be discussed elsewhere. Of interest here are social and legal background of Gilgamesh's ruse, onomastic features, and possible historical consequences.

For the Old Babylonian scribe who studied (and perhaps even modified) *Gilgamesh and the Cedar Forest* and left us the exercises upon which we base our reconstructions, Gilgamesh's ruse was based upon social and legal norms obtaining in his times. Sororate marriages, where two sisters marry the same man, are documented from the Old Babylonian period. Indeed, such marriage contracts are extant.[20] Alternatively, a subsystem of sisterhood adoption, wherein the first wife adopts the husband's concubine as sister, is even more widely documented in the second millennium.[21] Furthermore, there are points of contact with fratriarchal practices whereby brothers gave sisters in marriage.[22] This is the practice which Gilgamesh is following in his act of trickery. But while there is reason to suppose that to the Old Babylonian student of Sumerian literature the practice upon which Gilgamesh's trick depended was familiar and acceptable, extrapolating backwards to the putative time of Gilgamesh is more difficult. For the earlier periods, and especially for the period of the historical Gilgamesh (presumably the first half of the third millennium), virtually nothing can be adduced for such a social custom;[23] indeed, the available evidence points to the basically monogamous character of early Sumerian society.[24]

However, at least one detail in Gilgamesh's offer harks back to an earlier age. In his proposal Gilgamesh offers his older sister as a wife (nam.dam) and his younger one as a lukur. This lukur can have nothing in common with the lukur of the Old Babylonian age, the *nadītum*, a cloistered priestess.[25] Except for the *nadītum* of Marduk,[26] a *nadītum* could not marry, let alone be offered in matrimony of sorts in junior status, to judge from what can be learned of her social position in the Old Babylonian period.[27] The lukur offered by Gilgamesh to Huwawa, therefore, refers to the lukurs of the third millennium, and especially the lukurs of the Ur III kings who were much beloved, non-cloistered courtesans.[28] The position of Gilgamesh's younger sister as lukur in Gilgamesh's offer parallels that of the younger sister

---

17 Var. ḫu-mu-ra-ni-túm-en.

18 Var. su-za-a, su-zu-a.

19 The other version adds:
su-zu-àm nu-mu-ra-te-gá-dè-en
"As for your folk, I would not approach them against your will."

20 Cf. R. Harris, *JNES* 33, 369 and S. Greengus, *HUCA* 46, 13ff.

21 R. Harris, *JNES* 33, 363ff., S. Greengus, *HUCA* 46, 3f. for a comprehensive discussion.

22 P. Koschaker, *ZA* 41, 1ff., E. A. Speiser, in *Biblical and other Studies*, 15ff., S. Greengus's survey cf. n. 21: see also the summary by T. L. Thompson, *The Historicity of the Patriarchal Narratives*, 249ff.

23 Greengus claims a reference to 'sisterhood' in the Ur III period (late third millennium), cf. op. cit., n. 21.

24 Cf. A. Falkenstein, *NG* 1, 98. The reference to polyandry in Urukagina (*SAKI* 54 iii 20ff.) is unique. The case of two sisters marrying the same person is illustrated by the daughters of Zimri-Lim of Mari (cf. J. M. Sasson, *JCS* 25, 68ff.). This (Amorite?) custom, which seems to be limited to the second millennium B.C., may have some bearing on dating the traditions regarding Jacob in Genesis.

25 Cf. R. Harris, *Studies Oppenheim*, 106ff., *JESHO* 6, 122.

26 Cf. R. Harris, *Sippar*, 315.

27 Ibid., 305ff.

28 Cf. J. Renger, *ZA* 58, 149ff. and 179 n. 478, S. T. Kang, *Sumerian Economic Texts from the Drehem Archive*, 261.

in the later sororate marriages of the Old Babylonian period mentioned above. In this arrangement the younger sister is a *šugītum*, "usually the sister, presumably the younger sister of the *nadītu*, who married the husband of the *nadītu* of Marduk in order to bear children for the family. . . . a concubine to the husband."[29]

The Old Babylonian term *šugītum* is written either syllabically or ^{mí}šu.gi.[30] However, the lexical series Lú=*ša* preserves an entry equating *šugītu* with lukur, an echo of her more ancient role.[31] Thus Gilgamesh's older sister Enmebaragesi, in this scheme will have been a priestess of high rank, perhaps an *entum* or *ugbabtum*; her name, compounded with en, fits such a role. Such women were usually forbidden to have children. Thus, when given in marriage, Gilgamesh's elder sister would be joined by a second wife whose function is to bear children. In our case, this second wife was Enmebaragesi's younger sister Peštur.

The name of Gilgamesh's younger sister, pèš-tur, ("little fig") is unremarkable; it falls into a common pattern of Sumerian names.[32] However, the name of the elder sister, Enmebaragesi, is more interesting, for it immediately evokes the name of the ruler of Kish, Enmebaragesi, a contemporary of Gilgamesh.[33] Furthermore, the textual evidence for the name is decisive so that we are obliged to consider the name as certain.[34]

Even if the sisters of Gilgamesh are only used as a device supplied by the scribe from his second millennium milieu, a possibility suggested above,[35] Enmebaragesi's name can be based on an authentic tradition. The daughters and sisters of early Mesopotamian rulers were often en priestesses[36] and, as such, assumed names compounded with en-.[37] The scribe may have, of course, fished out a suitably impressive en- name from the hoary past; indeed, the name is associated with Gilgamesh through *Gilgamesh and Agga*, a historical romance which tells of a conflict between Gilgamesh and Agga, "the son of Enmebaragesi."[38] Names compounded with en- are of common gender (even names compounded with lú ["man"] can be feminine[39]), so that the form of the name "Enmebaragesi" is not unequivocal.

Now, it is quite possible that Gilgamesh did indeed have a sister called Enmebaragesi, with no connection to Enmebaragesi of Kish, a sister who simply bore a name of the times. On the other hand, one ought to consider the possibilty of identity. The name "Enmebaragesi" occurs in the following contexts:

1 *Sumerian King List*

> en-me-bára-ge-si lú ma-da-elam^{ki}-ma giš.
> tukal-bi íb-ta-an-gúr
> lugal-àm mu-900 ì-ak
> ak-kà dumu-en-me-bara$_2$-ge-si-ke$_4$ etc.
> Enmebaragesi, the one who crushed the land of Elam together with its armed might, became ruler, ruled 900 years, Akka the son of Enmebaragesi, etc.[40]

---

[29] R. Harris, op. cit., 321.

[30] Seemingly an abbreviated sumerogram.

[31] *MSL* XII 129, 24 [SAL].ME(=lukur)=*šu-gi-tu*. Note that the older *Proto-Lú* (ibid., 42) preserves two sets of lukur 257–260 lukur, lukur-^{d}nin-urta, ama-lukur-ra and then after a separation of 2 lines (261 munus, 262 ^{nu}nunus, "woman"), three lines of lukur, 263–265, glossed by *nadītum*, *qadištum* and *batultum* respectively: cf. B. Landsberger, *AfO* 10 146–149, and especially the structural parallel drawn between dam= *aššatu* ("wife")/dam.kaskal.la= *šeʾītu* ("concubine") and lukur/lukur.kaskal.la, ibid., 149 n. 43.

[32] Cf. simply E. Huber, *AB* 21, 184ff. s.v. tur, banda. She is mentioned in *Gilgamesh, Enkidu and the Netherworld*, 174 in Gilgamesh's lament over the fall into the underworld of his ball and rod which were used in the ritual ball game at Uruk.

[33] For inscriptions of the historical (En)mebaragesi cf. D. O. Edzard, *ZA* 53 9ff.

[34] Variants:

> en-me-bára-ge-si,
> en-me-[x$^{?}$]-ge$_4$-e-si,
> [x-x-bá]rag-ge$_4$-e-si,
> [x-x-bá]rag-ge$_4$-e-si,
> [ ]-e-si

Cf. the biographical note A. K. Grayson, *TCS* V, 215ff. with similar spellings from other sources.

[35] Cf. above.

[36] Cf. E. Sollberger, *AfO* 17, 23ff. and J. Renger, op. cit., above n. 28.

[37] Note that the few occurrences of Enmebaragesi's name in the inscriptions cited above in n. 33, are without en.

[38] S. N. Kramer, *AJA*, 53, 1ff., W. D. H. Römer, *AOAT* 209/1. The battle is mentioned in Šulgi "O," 56ff. (*AOAT* 25, 278) where, however, Enmebaragesi, not Agga, is the combatant.

[39] For example, the incidentally apt lú-ḫu-wa-wa geme$_2$ . . . , "Lu-huwawa, the slave girl," *NG* 126, 2. Note also such logograms as lú-ki-sikil=*ardatum* 'maiden.'

[40] T. Jacobsen, *AS* 11, ii 35ff.

2 *Tummal Inscription*

en-me-bára-ge_4-si lugal-e uru-na-nam
é-^{d}enlil-lá in-dù
ak-kà dumu-en-me-bára-ge_4-si-ke_4 etc.
Enmebaragesi, the ruler, built The City, the temple of Enlil, Akka the son etc.[41]

3 *Šulgi "O"*

[lugal kiš]i^{ki} en-me-$bara_2$-ge_4-e-si
[muš-gin_7 sa]g-gá-na gìri mu-na-ni-ús
You (Gilgamesh) placed your foot there on the head of Enmebaragesi, ruler of Kish, as if it were a snake's.[42]

4 *Gilgamesh and the Cedar Forest* (quoted above)

5 *Gilgamesh and Akka* 1, 49

Ak-kà dumu-en-me-bára-ge_4-(e-)si-ke_4[43]
Akka, the son of Enmebaragesi.

6 *Weidner Chronicle*

^{m}Ak-ka mār ^{m}En-me-bár-a-ge-si ... (broken)[44]

There is nothing in these references which would lead one to suppose that Enmebaragesi of Kish was not a man. On the other hand, one can note that lú (nominally "man") in (1) is simply a relative clause antecedent,[45] and that lugal, usually "king," can also be "queen," in the sense of "reigning monarch." This is clear from the Sumerian King List where the founder of later dynasty of Kish, a woman Kù-Ba-ba_6 is said to have been ruler, lugal-àm.[46] Kubaba is the only obvious queen in the Sumerian King List[47] and her presence is perhaps an echo of a nearly forgotten Kish tradition.[48]

Furthermore, Kish was a city with a tutelary male deity, Zababa, so that ministering to him would be a female en priestess.[49] Was Enmebaragesi an en priestess of Zababa, and at the same time ruler of Kish, while her brother Gilgamesh was ruler of Uruk and en priest of its female tutelary deity Inanna?[50]

It must be admitted that were it not for the name of Gilgamesh's elder sister here it would never occur to anyone to tamper with the sex of Enmebaragesi. This ruler was *sui generis* and not a royal offspring so that the Sumerian King List does not list him as dumu-X, "son of X," or dumu-mí X, "daughter of X." Nor does the List use gender name determinatives, so that even the name of queen Kubaba, also *sui generis*, would have remained unmarked for gender, were it not for the possibly remarkable fact that she began her career as a barmaid.[51] Later tradition seems to be completely ignorant of Enmebaragesi as queen of Kish. In the *Weidner Chronicle*, for example, Enmebaragesi's name is prefaced by DIŠ (transliterated above by ^{m}), which usually, but not always, is found before male names, while "Kubaba" is clearly rendered as a female name.[52] On the other hand, an unpublished manuscript of the Sumerian King List from Ur does not mark "Kubaba" as a female name.[53] Is this simply a scribal error (omission of mí) or does this strand of tradition no longer remember that Kubaba was a woman?

Tradition is certainly not always unequivocal or unambiguous. Take the case of Gilgamesh. Here two different traditions co-exist, and occasionally even

[41] *JCS* 16, 42.

[42] *AOAT* 25, 279.

[43] W. H. Ph. Römer, *AOAT* 209/1 23 ff.

[44] A. K. Grayson, *TCS* V, 147.

[45] A. Poebel, *GSG* sec. 271.

[46] Cf. *Sumerian King List*, V 36ff. (cf. n. 40 above)
kiši^{ki} kù-^{d}ba-ba_6
^{mí}lú.kurun-na
suḫuš-kiši^{ki} mu-un-gi-na
lugal-àm mu-100 ì-ak
In Kish Kubaba, a bar-maid,
who founded a dynasty in Kish,
became ruler, reigned 100 years.
For the original meaning of lugal cf. Jacobsen, *ZA* 52, 103ff.

[47] Omen traditions recall something irregular in Kubaba's ascent to the throne, she is said to have 'seized the throne' (*ša šarrūtam iṣbatu*), *RA* 38, 84 r 29; cf. the biographical note in A. K. Grayson, *TCS* V 223 with bibliography.

[48] The traditions of Kish are special in many ways, cf. I. J. Gelb, *La Lingua di Ebla*, 9ff.

[49] Cf. J. Renger, *ZA* 58, 115ff.

[50] Gilgamesh is called en ("lord" but also "en-priest") throughout the epic literature. His title is en-kul-aba_4, i.e. of Kullab, a sacred precinct of Uruk, but he can be addressed as lugal.

[51] ^{mí}lú-kurun-na cf. above, n. 45.

[52] Cf. A. K. Grayson, *TCS* V, 147, 31 and 148, 42: cf. J. Krecher's remarks on the "Personenkeil," *ZA* 63, 161f.

[53] To be published in *UET* 6/3. The scribe writes kù-ba-ba_6 lú-ku[run-na].

merge. The *Sumerian King List*, on the one hand, records the following:

> ^{d}gilgameš ab-ba-ni líl-lá en-kul-ab-ba-ke$_4$ etc.
> Gilgamesh, his father was a 'demon,' the high priest of Kullab etc.[54]

The epic tradition, on the other hand, considers Gilgamesh as the offspring of divine Ninsun and divine Lugalbanda.[55] One wonders whether in our case the epic tradition has perhaps remembered something which historical memory has not.

Whether or not Gilgamesh did actually use his sisters as pawns in a struggle with an otherwise unbeatable opponent is ultimately as much a question of folklore as it is of history. However, the analysis presented above might provide information for the solution of another Gilgamesh puzzle: the actual *casus belli* for the war described in the story of *Gilgamesh and Akka.* May it not be that behind the enigmatic, laconic riddle in the ditty of the "wells"—which ostensibly contains the incomprehensible challenge—there lay the memory of a dynastic struggle involving Gilgamesh and (according to the hypothesis presented here) his nephew Akka, the son of his sister Enmebaragesi, the ruler of Kish?[56]

In this connection, note the unique way that Kish is referred to when the struggle between Gilgamesh and Enmebaragesi is mentioned in literature, é-Kiš^{ki}, "the *House* of Kish," rather than simply Kiš^{ki}, as expected; cf. *Šulgi "O,"* 56,

> é-[Ki]š^{ki}-šè ^{giš}tukul-zu ba-ta-a-è[57]
> "You (Gilgamesh) went to war against the House of Kish with your armed might"

and *Gilgamesh and Akka* 8, 14, 23, 29,

> é-Kiš^{ki}-šè gú nam-ba-an-gar-re-en-dè-en[58]
> "Do we then submit to the House of Kish?" (Gilgamesh speaking to the council of Uruk).

Thus, to Gilgamesh and Uruk, Kish is not simply another city state against which they wage war: it is the dynastically related royal House of Kish. In the same spirit, a later ruler of Uruk can write to Sinmuballiṭ of Babylon, *anna Uruk u Babili bītum ištēnma*, "Indeed, Uruk and Babylon are one royal House."[59]

---

[54] *Sumerian King List*, III, 17f.

[55] Cf. for example, the proof text quoted above.

[56] Compare, in passing, the inverted parallelism between the story of Gilgamesh and Huwawa and that of Jacob and Laban. In both stories sisters are used for/against a close relative/relative-to-be in trickery. In *Gilgamesh and the Cedar Forest* two sisters are "offered" in marriage by a brother/trickster (Gilgamesh) to deprive an adversary (Huwawa) of a divine power (ní-te/me-lám). In *Genesis*, one of two sisters (Rachel) married to a trickster (Jacob) deprives the adversary father (Laban) of a divine power (*terāfîm*).

[57] *AOAT* 25 278.

[58] W. H. Ph. Römer, *AOAT* 209/1 23 ff.

[59] *Bagh. Mitt.* 2 58 ii 1 ff., cf. *CAD* B 293 ff. for similar references from this letter and other Akkadian parallels.

THE FIRST PUSHKIN MUSEUM ELEGY AND NEW TEXTS

ÅKE W. SJÖBERG

UNIVERSITY MUSEUM, PHILADELPHIA

IN 1960, PROFESSOR SAMUEL NOAH KRAMER, to whom this article is dedicated as a token of my affection and friendship, published two elegies written on one single tablet which is housed in Moscow's Pushkin Museum. Kramer described the text, probably originating in Nippur, on page 48ff of *Two Elegies on a Pushkin Museum Tablet: A New Sumerian Literary Genre*, and identified as a duplicate one lentile schooltext in the University Museum in Philadelphia (UM 55-21-68, see *Two Elegies* pl. III photograph, = line 20).

Since publication of the Pushkin Museum tablet, more duplicates have been identified: (1) CBS 14063 (*SEM* 113, identified independently also by J. van Dijk); N 4205 (identified by M. Civil) is now joined to CBS 14063 (see photograph); (2) UM 29-16-19 (identified by me) (see photograph); (3) N 3285 (identified by M. Civil (see photograph); (4) Ni. 9771: *ISET* 1, pl. 124). As a result, I can now present the following code for the various manuscripts:

A = the Pushkin Museum Tablet, obv. and rev. = 1–112 (the first elegy), 113–178 (the second elegy);
B = CBS 14063 + N 4205, obv. and rev. = 1–26;
C = UM 55-21-68 (lentil schooltext) = 20;
D = UM 29-16-19, obv. and rev. = 91–112;
E = N 3285, obv. = 93–103, rev. = 109–112;
F = Ni.9771, obv. 109–112.

In the following transliteration, I have transcribed only those lines of the first elegy which are duplicated in the new texts, i.e., lines 1–16 and lines 91–112.

1. ⌜ab⌝-ba ki-ri[1]-a-šè dumu-ni-ir[2] kin bí-in-gi$_4$
dumu ki-bad-du gin-na-ri u$_4$-ba[1] ba-ra-an-BAD[2]
ab-ba uru$_2$^{ki}-a[1] tuš-a-ra[2] tu-ra gaba ba-ri[3]
sud-ág-kal-la[1] kur-sù-da[2] pà-da tu-ra gaba ba-ri[3]
5. KA[1]-dìm sa$_6$-sa$_6$[2] lú inim zíl-zíl-le[3] tu-ra gaba ba-ri[4]
alan-sù[1]-tuku sag-du tuku téš-bi tu-ra gaba ba-ri[2]
gal-zu-giš-ḫur-ra me-te-ukkin-na tu-ra gaba ba-ri[1]
lú-gi-na ní-te-gá-dingir-bi tu-ra gaba ba-ri[1]
tu-ra ú nu-kú gaba ba-ri[2] tu-ra ba-an-dab$_5$
10. ka ù-ba-e-šu[1] ninda nu-mu[2]-un-šú-šú šà-sù[3]-ga ba-an-ná[4]
dub-gin$_7$ bar-gin$_7$[1] ni[2]-gál-la-ri íb-gurud-da mu-un-lá[3]
ur-sag gaba ur$_4$-ur$_4$ gìri nu-mu-u[n-da]-bad-dè[1]
KA-tu-ra-a-ni-ta[1] nam-dumu-ni i-si-i[š (x)] ì-kú[2]
šà-sìg-sìg-ge i-si-iš SI.A x̣[1]
15. dub-zu nibru^{ki}-a ki-lul-la ba-an-ug$_5$[1]
inim-bi kaskal-sù-rá-šè[1] dumu-ni-ir ba-[an]-na-te[2]
dumu ad-da-a-ni-ta nu-ub-da-lá-a-gin$_7$[1]
TÚG in-ši-ge$_4$-en-nam nu-ub-da-gur$^{?}$-ra$^{?}$-àm[1]
dumu ír in-pà saḫar-ta ma-ra-da-šub šìr-nam-nar mu-un-na-ab-e[1]
20. ^{I}lú-dingir-ra šà-NE-NE-a-ni-ta[1] i-lu[2] ab-sar-re
ab-ba ki-lul-la ba-an-ug$_5$-ga-ta[1]
^{Id}nanna-a[1] šà-ḫul-dím-ma-ni-ta[2] kur-šè ba-ab-DU-a[3]
dam-zu nì-u$_4$-bi-ta[1] nitalam-a-ni[2] na-nam[3] me-da[4] nu-mu-un-su-a
im-dal-ḫa-mun-gin$_7$ u$_4$ DI ma-ra-ab-kaš$_4$-kaš$_4$-e u$_{18}$-lu ma-ab-sìg-ge[1]
25. á-è-gin$_7$[1] za-e ma-ra-ab-ak-e[2] dím-ma-ni in-kúr[3]
al-lib mu-na-gar[1] i-gi$_4$-in-zu i-im-ši-TU-TU-dè[2]

91. ^{d}nergal[1] ^{d}en-líl-kur-ra-ke$_4$[2] igi-bi-a[3] sa$_6$-ni
ki-TAR kú[1] mu-zu ḫé-pà-dè ú[2]-du$_{10}$ ḫé-ri-ib-kú-e
ÉŠ bar-ra nin-kur-ra ḫé-me-en arḫuš ḫu-mu-ra-an-du$_{12}$-du$_{12}$
ki-nag[1] a-du$_{10}$-ga é-zu ḫé-ni-ib-ús-x̣[2]
95. é-a NIM-ta ḫé-bí-in-KU-x / en ^{d}nin-giš-zi-d[a]
kala-ga ^{d}bìl-ga-mèš silim ḫa-ra-a[n-...][1]
^{I}ne-du$_8$ ù e-ta-na[1] á-daḫ-zu [x x]
dingir-kur-ra-ke$_4$ šùd[1]-zu ḫé-em-DU [x][2]

CBS 14063 + N 4205 obv.

CBS 14063 + N 4205 rev.

obv. UM 29–16–19 Text D The first Elegy rev.

obv. N 3285 Text E rev.

mùš-àm[1] dingir-zu ḫé-em-me nam-zu[2] [x x x]
dingir-uru^{ki}-za-a-kam[1] šà-šu-nigin$_{2}$[2] ḫa-ra-⸢x⸣
šà-ka-kéš šul-a-lum ḫa-ra-⸢du$_{8}$⸣[1]
nam-tag-ga-é-e-ke$_{4}$[1] šid-bi[2] ḫé-en-gaz[3]
nì-ḫul-dím-ma-zu ....[1]
egir-zu[1] ḫé-sa$_{6}$ x̣[x]x x-zu / [.........]x
.... TÚG$^{?}$ ḫé-díb[1]
^{d}udug ^{d}lama ... NÍG-zu ḫé-..(?)[1]
dumu-ù-tu-ud-da-zu[1] [na]m$^{?}$-sag-šè ḫé-ni-sar$^{?}$[2]
dumu-munus-zu dingir ḫé-du$_{12}$-du$_{12}$[1]
dam-zu ḫé-ti im-ri-a-zu ḫé-dagal
ḫé-gál sag-sa$_{6}$-ga[1] u$_{4}$-šú-uš-e[2] ḫé-ni-gùr-ru[3]
a-pa$_{4}$-za kurun nì-du$_{10}$-ga[1] múš nam-ba-an-túm-mu
tu$_{6}$[1]-é-e-ke$_{4}$[2] tu$_{6}$[3] -dingir-za-kam[4] du-rí-šè ḫé-a[5]

1. *1*: B has -ri- written over erasure.
   2: -ir omitted in B.
2. *1*: B has u$_{4}$-bi. *2*: both A and B have -BAD.
3. *1*: A uru$_{2}^{ki}$-a (Kramer; -a omitted in his transcr.); B: uru-a. *2*: B has tuš-a-ri. *3*: B: ba-an-ri.
4. *1*: B: [su]d-DU-ág-kal-la. *2*: so A; B has kur-sur-ta. *3*: B has ba-an-ri.
5. *1*: so also B. *2*: B has dìm-sà-sà(ZA-ZA) instead of dìm-sa$_{6}$-sa$_{6}$ in A. *3*: A: KA zíl-z[í]l-le; B: KA zíl-zíl-i. *4*: B: ba-an-ri.
6. *1*: -GÍD- in B; A seems to have a different sign; cf. comm. *2*: B: ba-an-ri.
7. *1*: B: ba-an-ri.
8. *1*: B: ba-an-ri.
9. *1*: both A and B have ú; ù in Kramer's edition is a misprint.
   2: B: ba-an-ri.
10. *1*: so also B. *2*: B has dìm-sà-sà(ZA-ZA) instead of dìm-damaged in A; B seems to have -sù-. *4*: B has mu-un-ná.
11. *1*: B bar-gin$_{7}$; Kramer reads maš-gin$_{7}$ (text A), but probably bar-. *2*: so A; B has PIRIG- = nè-. *3*: A í-x[x]mu-lá; B: íb-gurud(NUN.KI)-da mu-un-lá.
12. *1*: so A; B: nu-un-da-bad-dè.
13. *1*: B probably [x]KA-tu-ra-ni-šè$^{?}$. *2*: B seems to have ị-sị-iš [x]ịn-ga-àm and seems to have a gloss beneath -àm.
14. *1*: A has i-si-iš[(x)]x-a (Kramer's transl.); B: ⸢i-si⸣-iš SI.A x.
15. *1*: last sign in text B epigraphically uncertain.
16. *1*: B: -GÍD-rá-šè or -sù-rá-šè. *2*: B: ba-na-an-ab-te$^{!}$ for ba-an-na-ab-te.
17. *1*: B has nu-ub-da-lá-a$^{!}$-ke$_{4}$-eš.
18. *1*: traces in text B.
19. *1*: B has [...]⸢x x x⸣-an-ŠÁR[......]x-ma-ab-e; erasure between -ab- and -e; B two lines.
20. *1*: B: šà-NE-NE-a-na; text C (UM 55-21-68) has šà-NE-NE-b[i$^{?}$]. *2*: A has i-KU (error) for i-lu in B and C.
21. *1*: B: ba-an-ug$_{5}$-ga-mu.
22. *1*: B: + -mu. *2*: B omits -ta. *3*: B: kur-šè ba-ab-DU-a.
23. *1*: B omits -ta. *2*: A: MUNUS.UŠ.DAM(nitalam)-a-ni; B: MUNUS.ỤŠ$^{!}$.DẠṂ-ma-ni. *3*: B has me instead of na-nam. *4*: B has a-da-al nu-mu-un-su-a (-da- written over erasure).
24. *1*: B: dal-ḫa$^{!}$(A)-mun-da UŠ x̣[x(x)]x-
25. *1*: B: á-è-gin$_{7}$; A epigraphically uncertain. *2*: B: zà m[a-ra-ab]-ạk-e. *3*: B: dím-ma-ni kúr$^{!}$ LU-àm (scribal error).
26. *1*: A: [x x] mu-ni-in-gar. *2*: B: IM:I-TU-TU-dè; A: i-im-ši-TU-TU-dè.

91. *1*: ^{d}GÌR.UNU-gal. *2*: D has -ka instead of -ke$_{4}$ in A. *3*: so D; A uncertain on photo (Kramer: igi-bi-šè$^{?!}$).
92. *1*: A (Kramer) šul(?) ninda-kú-ù-ne (mu-zu ...) (-u-ne is a misprint); ki-TAR kú in D. *2*: ù- in Kramer's edition (text A) is a misprint, read ú-.
94. *1*: also A seems to have ki-nag. *2*: line read according to D.
96. *1*: D: DI ḫa-ra-a[n-.
97. *1*: D and E have ^{d}ne-ti ^{d}e-da-na.
98. *1*: KA×ŠU. *2*: ḫé-em-DU[x] in text D; A has šùd-dè mu-ra-[ab$^{?}$-bé$^{?}$].
99. *1*: D, E have múš-àm-zu. *2*: so A (Kramer); D: nam$^{!}$-.
100. *1*: D, E: dingir-uru-za-ke$_{4}$. *2*: šà-šu-nigin$_{2}$ in A (collated on photo); D: šà-šu-nigin$_{2}$; E: šà-šu-nigi[n$_{2}$.
101. *1*: verb only preserved in D.
102. *1*: D, E: n[am-t]ag-é-e-zu. *2*: -bi in D; A seems to have šid-da. *3*: verb preserved only in text B.
103. *1*: Kramer, text A: nì-ḫul-dím-ma-zu .... NI [ḫé]- .... ; D: nì-ḫul$^{??}$-⸢dím⸣-zu SAL$^{?}$ kur-ta$^{?}$ gi-in-na-bi. Line seems to have an interlinear Akk. translation.
104. *1*: egir-zu in A; D has a somewhat different shape of the sign.
105. *1*: so Kramer, text A; D seems to omit this line.
106. *1*: so Kramer, text A; D: ^{d}lama [x x x x] sag-za-x ^{d}a-x [x x x]x nì-za-x (two lines).
107. *1*: D: [d]umu-tu-d[a- . *2*: D: ḫé-sa[r(x)].
108. *1*: also A has dingir ḫé-du$_{12}$-du$_{12}$.
110. *1*: E and F has sag-sì-g[a], F: -[ga]. *2*: -e omitted in E and F. *3*: A has ḫé-ni-gùr-ru, D: ḫu-x[...].
111. *1*: nì-du$_{10}$-ga omitted in D.
112. *1*: so A; D has KA, E seems also to have KA instead of tu$_{6}$. *2*: D and E have -é-e-zu. F needs collation. *3*: D and F (copy) have KA. *4*: D: -dingir-za-ka, F: -dingir-za-x. *5*: ⸢ḫé⸣-gál.

AKKADIAN INTERLINEAR TRANSLATIONS IN TEXT A

4. *ša i-na tu-qá-ar ša-di-i* to kur-sù-da (A); B has kur-sur-ta.
6. *la-na ša*-x-*da-ḫa i-šu-ú* to alan-dìm$^?$-tuku (A); B has alan-sù-tuku.
10. *ú-ul il-te-em* to nu-mu-un-šú-šú.
12. *mu-ut-tap-ri-rum* to ur$_4$-ur$_4$ (or gaba ur$_4$-ur$_4$).
15. *i-na ša-ga-aš-ti* to ki-lul-la.
24. *ki-ma a-ša-am-šu-ti ša-..-si i-na me-ḫi-e i-..-sa-šu* to im-dal-ḫa-mun-gin$_7$ u$_4$ DI ma-ra-ab-KAŠ$_4$-e u$_{18}$-lu ma-ra-ab-sìg-ge.
25. *ki-ma* (rest uncertain).
26. I was not able to read the Akk. translation.

96. On the lower edge of the tablet immediately beneath his line is a full-line gloss which seems to be read *i-na da-na-ti ša-la-mu* ...
100. Illegible translation beneath šà-šu-nigin$_2$.
103. Illegible transl. following nì-ḫul-dím-ma-zu.
104. Illegible transl. following ḫé-sa$_6$.
107. *tu-wa-li-du* to ù-tu-ud-da-zu.
110. .. *du-um-qá-am* to sag-sa$_6$-ga.

TEXTUAL COMMENTS

1. See J. Krecher, ZA 57, 17. u$_4$-ba ba-ra-an-BAD is difficult; perhaps u$_4$-ba ba-ra-an-bad "on that day he was very far away (from his father)." If this interpretation proves correct, u$_4$-bi in text B is a scribal error.

4. Text A has kur-sù-da with Akk. interlinear translation *i-na tu-qá-ar ša-di-i*; text B has kur-sur-ta. *tu-qá-rù* corresponds to Sum. sur in 5R 16, 73 g (cf. Brünnow, 2993; ŠL 101, 39); written *tu-qa-a-ru* = *iš*-[x(x)] in *CT* 18, 5 K.3906+ rev. 13 where I am inclined to restore *iš*-[*du*] "base, foundation, bottom." For etymology cf., perhaps, Aram.-Syr. *jagrā* "heap of stones," Eth. *w g r* "tumulus, collis" (Dillman) (Dr. S. Cohen drew my attention to this root in Semitics). Cf. úr-ḫur-sag-gá "the foot (lit., foundation, bottom) of the mountain."

5. KA-dìm occurs also in the Second Elegy line 162 KA-x-la$^?$ KA-dìm KA-sa$_6$ me-àm. There might be a connection between KA-dìm and Kagal D, Sect. 3, 14′ (see also line 15′, *MSL* 13, 245) ka-dim-rú-a = *pu-um ša i-na* ⌜x x x⌝[x x]; note, however, that *MSL* 13 reads -dìm- but original (collated) has a clear DIM. For an alternation between dim and dìm cf. giš-dìm(var. DÌM+ME) = *ma-ku-tu*$_4$ "pole" Ḫḫ VI 159 and di-im = dim = *ma-ku-tú* S^b Voc. II 333, also Recip. Ea D 4′. zíl-zíl = *dummuqu* (v.), cf. *JCS* 26, 169 where some refs. have been collected. inim zíl-zíl would correspond to *amata dummuqu* "to make (one's) word pleasing."

6. alan-sù (reading -sù instead of -GÍD almost certain in text B) would correspond to Akk. *lānu šīḫu* "tall figure." S. N. Kramer reads text A as alam-dìm(?)-tuku but second sign seems to be different from dìm in line 5. Text A has the Akk. interlinear translation *la-na ša*-x-*da-ḫa i-šu-ú* "who has a ... figure (body)." I was not able to read the sign following *ša*-. With sag-du tuku compare sag-du nu-tuku = *la i-ša-nu* "powerless" Nabn. IV 23.

10. šú, šu-šú = *lêmu, lemû* "eat (and drink)"; A translates nu-mu-un-šú-šú as *ú-ul il-te-em*. ka ù-ba-e-šú (var. ù-bí-in-šú) is ambiguous: (1) "with mouth(?) shut tight(?)" (Kramer; šú = *katāmu*). (2) "(his) mouth being able (earlier) to eat and drink." For šà-sù-ga "empty, hungry, starving" see Cl. Wilcke, *Das Lugalbandaepos*, 168f.

11. ní gál "to instill fear, to frighten." Note var. nè in B instead of ní in text A. nè with var. ní (and ne) as corresponding to Akk. *emūqu* "strength" is common in Sumerian texts but nè gál "to instill fear" is, as far as I know, attested only in this line, but cf. ní-gal (Akk. *namrirrū*) ši-im-du$_8$-du$_8$ *UET* 6/1, 118 i 27 with var. nè (PIRIG)-gal in CBS 10512, 1′ (unpubl.). gurud = *nadû* (v.).

12. gaba ur$_4$-ur$_4$ has, in text A, the Akk. interlinear translation *mu-ut-tap-ri-rum* (not read in Kramer's edition), cf. *CAD* M/2, 308 *sub muttaprirrum* "roaming around"; see also ga-ba-ur$_4$-ur$_4$ = *mut-tap-ri-r*[*u*] Izi V 131, *MSL* 13, 164, in a group with cohort. preformative ga- (ga-, ga-an-, ga-ba-) + verb which are frozen verbal forms used as active participles. Note gaba in our text. Our line is read gaba kin-kin in *CAD* M/2, 308 but text B has ur$_4$-ur$_4$; *MSL* 13, 164 reads Izi V 131 as -UR$_4$-UR$_4$. gìri bad, lit., "to open one's foot," "to move" does not seem to be attested elsewhere.

13. nam-dumu (Akk. *mārūtu*) refers here to the children of the dying man.

15. dub-zu, lit., "who knows the tablet" (Kramer: the scholar) seems to be attested only in our text. Kramer translates ki-lul-la ba-an-ug$_5$ (see also line 31) as "died . . . (of wounds received) in an attack(?)." This translation does not seem to agree with lines 3ff. tu-ra gaba ba(-an)-ri "he was stricken with illness" since tu-ra (dú-ra, Akk. *murṣu*) as referring to wounds received in a battle seems highly improbable. The problem how to interpret ki-lul-la remains to be solved.

19. saḫar-ta ma-ra-da-šub (Kramer: threw himself to the dust) is grammatically difficult: the scribe might have confused saḫar-ra šub "to throw oneself to the dust" and saḫar-ta (saḫar-da) šár (infix -ta- or -da-), for the last-mentioned expression see most recently W. Ph. Römer, *Bilgameš und Akka*, 82ff. Prefix ma- is an error. - šìr-nam-nar is attested only in our text.

20. The reading of šà-NE-NE is uncertain: (1) šà-bar$_7$-bar$_7$ (or šà-bir$_9$-bir$_9$): bar$_7$ = *napāḫu*, cf. *libbašu napiḫ* HS 1883 rev. 10, (2) ša-kúm-kúm, kúm = *emmu* "hot."

23. Note that text B has a-da-al "now" instead of me-da "where?" in text A.

24. Interpretation of this line remains difficult. 25–26. These two lines have been translated by Wilcke in *JNES* 27, 234 as "Als hätte sie dich grossgezogen, ist ihr Verstand verstört. Sie ist deprimiert, als gebäre sie." al-lib = *šittu* "sleep" 5R 16, 24gh, cf. lib = *kâru* "to be depressed," see *CAD* K, 240 *kâru* B v.; = *kūru* "daze, depression" Šurpu V–VI 3/4. al-lib mu-na-gar would correspond to Akk. *šittu* (*kūru*) *ittaškanši*(*m*). For al-lib see Wilcke, *JNES* 27, 234 n. 19.

91. igi-bi-šè? (A) and igi-bi-a (B) refers to Utu, Nanna (lines 88 and 90), and Nergal.

92. Reading di-ku$_5$ (beginning, as an epithet of Nergal) is excluded since text D has ki-TAR.

93. Text B: ÉŠ bar-ra, text A is epigraphically uncertain. Translation remains uncertain.

94. This line implies that the household of the dead man should always pour water into his grave.

95. Translation?

96. kala-ga has been translated (text A) as *i-na da-na-ti* (cf. *CAD* D 87 *dannatu*) but I doubt it is accurate. "the strong one, Bilgameš . . ." (epithet of Gilgameš)?

97. Etana is nu-banda$_3$-kur-ra-ke$_4$ "the 'steward' of the 'Land' (=the netherworld)" in *ZA* 67, 14, 78 (Utu Hymn) where he is in charge of the gate (line 79).

98. Is dingir-kur-ra an individual deity in the netherworld? Kramer: "The gods of the Nether World."

101. References for šà-ka-kéš(kešda) are found in *ZA* 65, 226 with n. 19; see further šà-ka-kéš-da-zu in *TCL* 15, 37, 33. According to P. Michalowski, *Royal Correspondence of Ur* (Diss. Yale Univ. 1976), 159 šà-ka-kéš would correspond to Akk. *kiṣir libbi* "anger, wrath" (cf. *CAD* K, 429f. *sub kiṣru* 5.). šà-ka-kéš du$_8$ would then be Akk. *kiṣir libbi paṭāru*, see for that expression *CAD* K, 429f.

107. nam-sag is further attested in *UET* 6/1, 95, 4 nam-sag-zu an-né ^{d}en-líl-lá sag-gi$_6$-eš rig$_7$-zu; *JCS* 12, 71 SP Coll. 5.122 nam-sag-gá al-ak-e (in difficult context) which E. I. Gordon translated as "is treated with privilege(?)." *AfO* 14, 150, 195ff. imin-bi-e-ne á-mušen-na ḫuš-a alan-^{d}nergal nam-sag-gá-zu-ne-ne gub-ba-zu (var. omits -gá-) = *si-bit-ti-šú-nu šu-ut kap-pi ez-zu-ti ṣa-lam* ^{d}*nergal ina re-ši-šú-nu ul-ziz* ^{d}nuska nam-sag-gá-zu-ne-ne ki-izi gar-ra-àm = ^{d}MIN *ina re-ši-šú-nu ina ki-nu-ni aš-kun* is highly obscure since *ina rēšišunu* would correspond to Sum. sag-gá-ne-ne.

111. For a-pa$_4$ = *arūtu* "(clay) pipe" (through which libations to the dead are made) see Sjöberg, *AS* 20, 63f.; also *TCS* 3, 87f.; see further a-pa$_4$-kur-ra-ke$_4$ gál ša-mu-ra-ab-tag$_4$ "(. . .) opened for you the pipe (leading down) into the netherworld" Ninegalla Hymn 70 (CBS 14187, 70 = Ni.4334 ii 19′ = UM 55-21-308 ii 15′ = *SEM* 89 + CBS 13669 ii); a-pa$_4$-a-ne a na-an-dé-e (referring to the pipe leading down into the netherworld) G. Castellino, Incantation to Utu 24, A rev. 23 and dupl. CBS 1686 rev. ii 14′; a-pa$_4$, a-pa$_4$, a-ru-tum, a-pa$_4$-AN Proto-Kagal 426–428 (*MSL* 13, 79); a-gidim-m[a], a-pa$_4$, a-pa$_4$-AN Kagal III 226–228 (*MSL* 13, 233).

TWO OLD TESTAMENT STORIES AND THEIR HITTITE ANALOGUES

MATITIAHU TSEVAT
HEBREW UNION COLLEGE-CINCINNATI

I. *Jacob's Nocturnal Bout and a Hittite King's Challenge to a Deity.* The story of Jacob's struggle with a mysterious stranger (Gen 32:23–32) has invited interpretations which adduce analogous elements from folklore explored by anthropologists. The "man" who contended or fought with Jacob is seen as a numen, perhaps a demon, perhaps the personification of the Jabbok River itself or the guardian of the ford who seeks either to prevent Jacob from crossing over or perhaps even from invading his domain by stepping foot into the river.[1] Westermann urges the acceptance of this interpretation, citing the plethora of analogies and its exegetical good sense.[2] Despite this, such an interpretation of the story is by no means universal, and with good reason. There is little in the core of the narrative (vs. 25–30[–32]) that has parallels in the citations from folklore.

There is, however, one observation in the anthropological literature which merits quotation: "... the struggle [with the spirit] was purposely sought by Jacob for the sake of obtaining his blessing." These words of J. G. Frazer[3] are the more worthy of note since there is not much in the vast amount of folkloristic material, marshalled on ten pages, on which he could base his remark.[4] Yet that judgment may now be supported by advancing a Hittite text.

The text has been published by H. Otten, who copied, transliterated, translated, and commented on it. He also, without going into detail, cited Gen 32:23ff.[5] The passage, the translation of which follows, is part of a description of, or prescription for, a festival in honor of Teshub and Khebat, celebrated in the city of Lawazantiya in northeastern Kizzuwatna, classical Cataonia.[6] It deals with the transportation of divine statues to various locations in a sacred precinct.

> *I:59*... Then one takes Khebat, *60*and as one brings her into the building, *61*one locks the door. Thereupon the priest says, "The goddess (says) to the king as follows: *62*(Illegible in the Vorlage of the original[7])." The king (answers), "Come back!" The goddess (says) as follows, *63*"If I come back, will you in whatever manner[8]—(such as) with horses and chariots—*64*(strive to) prevail over me?" The king (says) as follows, "I shall (strive to) prevail over you." The goddess (says) as follows, *65*["Make (then) a wish."[9]] The king (says) as follows, "Give me life, health, *II:1*sons (and) daughters in the future, *2*[(strong weapons(?)[10])], and put my enemies under my feet." Thereupon one opens the door and takes Khebat out.

---

[1] As representatives of *Genesis* interpretation I mention, H. Gunkel, (1901, third edition) 1910, 359–65 and C. Westermann, vol. 2 (the fascicle is dated 1981), 624–35 (it contains ample literature). Earlier it was thought that the numen tried to bar Jacob's passage into Canaan (B. Studer, 1875; from A. Dillmann's commentary of 1892, 365).

[2] Id., 629.

[3] *Folk-lore in the Old Testament*, vol. 2, 1919, 412; abridged edition, 1923, 252.

[4] Pp. 413–23; abridged edition, 252–8. Closer come the few examples from Greek myths, 413 f. (252 f.). The great majority of stories and descriptions of rites collected there lead away from, rather than lead to, his proposal.

[5] KBo 21, 34:I:59–II:3; *Baghdader Mitteilungen* 7 (1974; Fs. A. Moortgat), 139–42. This is *CTH* 699 plus fragment Bo 6871, here utilized where it is significant.

[6] The whole text, which records the ceremonies of the fourth (fifth?) day of the festival, has been transliterated, translated, and provided with a short introduction and notes by R. Lebrun, *Hethitica 2* (1977), 116–42.

[7] This is indicated by several flattened St. Andrew crosses (Forrer, no. 330). For the sign, however, see also A. Ünal, *Ein Orakeltext über die Intrigen am hethitischen Hof* (*KUB* 22.70), 1978, 23.

[8] Although not otherwise known to me, I take simple *kuēz* as an indefinite pronoun, instead of the full forms found in J. Friedrich, *Hethitisches Elementarbuch* I^2, §120a, 124, 126, in order to avoid the coincidence of a question (*kuēz*) with its answer (ANŠE KUR.RA.MEŠ, etc.) in the same clause.

[9] *ú-e-ek-wa-za* from Bo 6871.

[10] [*ta*]*r-ḫu-i-li-in-na* GIŠTUKUL, as apparently (Otten) Bo 6871 adds.

The features common to the two texts are the following (B standing for Bible and H for Hittite ritual): 1) A fight of a human with a deity or a numen,[11] actual (B) or envisaged (H). 2) The deity is physically detained (B and H). 3) The deity asks to be released (B explicitly, H inferentially in the illegible passage at the beginning of line 62). 4) The request is granted on condition (B and H). 5) The condition is divine blessing (B and H). 6) The blessing is given (B, H not explicit but a narrative necessity flowing from the granting of the release).

The principal importance of this listing is not the identity of the several narrative components, the "features," in the two texts corresponding to one another, but rather the number of the corresponding elements appearing in two texts so brief and the virtual identity of their sequence in both of them.[12] What makes this the important consideration is the exceedingly small probability that the presence of the elements and their common sequential order in both texts is the result of chance; that is to say, coincidence rather than the result of a genetic process such as, for example, that both narratives ultimately derive from one and the same source. Given the virtual identity of structure and similarity of content, together with the highly probable hypothesis of a genetic relationship, we have the strong likelihood that the intent is the same in the two narratives. The Hittite king would from the beginning be seeking to obtain a blessing, to which end he is ready to fight the deity; similarly, Jacob in his fight with the numen would have been motivated by the same purpose.

In short, the foregoing is a vindication of Frazer's speculation. This is not to say that I regard the support that he adduces for his interpretation as at all sufficient or impressive. He gives us in a long paragraph a highly romantic description of the gorge through which the Jabbok flows, which description, he suggests, "may help us to understand the strange adventure which befell Jacob at the passage of the river."[13] This reed of hope provides more amusement than the citation of some travellers' portrayal of the gorge provides enlightenment. But these signs of weakness of method and insufficiency of standards render his perception of the sense of the narrative all the more remarkable. The contribution of anthropology and folklore to the interpretation of Gen 32:23–32 is limited to accident and decorations; none of it bears upon the essence of the text. That essence does emerge, however, at least in part, from the study of the Hittite text whose context, by contrast with the wilderness gorge, is civilization and an established shrine.

One important difference between the texts must be noted. The content of the Hittite text constitutes an isolated event, integrated in a ritual, whereas the Genesis text is an episode in the continuing history of the patriarchs and, as part of that history, retrojects the origin and explanation of the name of Israel to a time anteceding its emergence as a people. The bestowal of the name actually prefigures the existence of the people. This difference points, in turn, to the reason for another important difference between the texts, namely, the different nature of the blessing, a difference so clear as to require no elaboration here.

Against the understanding that it is Jacob who initiated the fight one might cite the wording of the biblical text. After telling us that Jacob remained alone, the text continues: "A man (then) fought with him" (*wayyēʾābēq ʾîš ʿimmo*, vs. 25). The argument would be that, had Jacob sought and started the struggle, the normal and more precise formulation would have been: "*Jacob remained alone and (then) fought with a man" (**wayyiwwātēr yaʿaqōb lᵉbaddô wayyēʾābēq ʿim ʾîš*). But the price of normality and precision would have been dull narration and flabby cadence. How, by contrast, lively narration is accomplished, a quotation from Reichel in König's *Stilistik* says: "Je unbekannter . . . [ein Satzteil] ist, desto weiter rückt er nach vorn."[14] This rule, combined with the stylistic felicity achieved in introducing a protagonist by making him the subject of the sentence, shows us why the sentence is built the way it is.

II. *The Biblical Minor Judges, Their Children, and the Royal Children of Kanish.* From 1950 to 1982 there has been a spate of special studies on the minor

[11] Genesis calls him *ʾîš* and *ʾelōhîm*, Hosea *ʾelōhîm* and *malʾāk* (12:4 f.).

[12] In the Hittite text the detention precedes the fight because of the staging of the plot, a circumstance which results from the integration of the narrative in the ritual.

[13] Frazer (supra, n.3), 410 f. (abridged ed. 252).

[14] E. König, *Stilistik, Rhetorik, Poetik in Bezug auf die biblische Literatur*, 1900, 152. Cf. very unusual positions of words at the beginning of a sentence for the sake of emphasis in Isa 7:25 (*wekol hehārîm . . .*); 34:12 (*xorēhā*); 66:18 (*weʾanōkî*). None of these is a casus pendens!

judges of early Israel.[15] The interest of almost all of those who have contributed to the discussion is sociological or historical, the latter occasionally to include the history of biblical literature and its chronology (a sample question is, Did the listing of the kings of Israel and Judah in Kings antecede and influence that of the minor judges or has the section of the minor judges historical priority?). Gottwald summed up three decades of research with these words: ". . . a scholarly consensus on the sociopolitical structural position of these leaders [the minor judges] seems farther from attainment than ever."[16]

I agree with most workers that there is probably some historical reality behind the report on the minor judges, but I shall not add answers to questions of history, geography, society, institutions, religion, or history of literature. Rather, I shall deal with what has been left out of almost all considerations: the elaborations of the Bible on the many sons, asses, and towns of some of the judges and their families.[17]

As to the text of the section of the minor judges, there is far-going, though not full, agreement that it is a unit comprising Ju 10:1–5 and 12:7–15. The unit is broken apart because one man, Jephthah, figures both among the major and the minor judges, with the stories about Jephthah the major judge coming first (11:1–12:6).[18] The author of the book conjoined the materials about both roles of Jephthah, and at the joins both kinds of material sustained losses. There are six minor judges: I Tola (10:1–2), II Jair (10:3–5), III Jephthah (12:7), IV Ibzan (12:8–10), V Elon (12:11–12), and VI Abdon (12:13–15). There is rhythm to the list. Two verses comment on each of the odd-numbered judges and three on the even-numbered, except that apocopated Jephthah, amply compensated in 11:1–12:6 outside the list, has only one verse to his name within the list.

The pattern, common to all members of the group except Jephthah, is this: (a) the name of the judge with his geographical or societal connections; (b) his activity, in which he followed a predecessor (the pattern is so strong that even the member who opens the list, Tola, is given a predecessor, Abimelech, although the latter is not a member of the list); (c) the duration of his office; (d) his death; (e) his burial; (f) the location of his grave. With the even-numbered judges the pattern is expanded in the following manner (hence the three verses to each of them): II Jair: "He had thirty sons who rode thirty asses (*^{c}ayārîm*); they had thirty towns (*^{c}ayārîm*[19]) in the land of Gilead,

---

[15] M. Noth, "Das Amt des Richters Israels," *Fs. A. Bertholet*, 1950, 407–17 (reprinted in his *Gesammelte Studien zum A.T.*, II, 1969.71–85). A brief observation in a similar vein was made earlier by A. Alt, *Die Ursprünge des israelitischen Rechts*, 1934, 31 f. (reprinted in his *Kleine Schriften I*, 1953.300 f.). A combination of the following bibliographies makes for a very ample representation of the recent literature: R. de Vaux, *Histoire ancienne d'Israël* [II], 1973, 68–74, nn.3–30; N. K. Gottwald, *The Tribes of Yahweh*, 1979, 749 f., n.254; E. T. Mullen, "The 'Minor Judges': Some Literary and Historical Considerations," *CBQ* 44 (1982), 185–201.

[16] Ibid., 750.

[17] J. A. Soggin, "Das Amt der 'kleinen Richter' in Israel," *VT* 30 (1980), 245–7, addresses himself to this point. He says that the section of the minor judges is a fragment of an eponym list drawn up for a chronological purpose: the expansions are mnemonic devices. This is unconvincing: The expansions are similar to the point of being almost repetitive; thus they tend to blur and confuse instead of single out and profile the entries said to be remembered.

[18] A. J. Hauser, "The 'Minor Judges'—a Re-evaluation." *JBL* 94 (1975), 190–200, and, in part, Mullen (supra, n.15) deny at the end of their articles that there is an essential difference between the major and the minor judges. I do not accept their position.

[19] The Hebrew text (Received Text, RT) of this passage has come under attack by Boling in a lengthy note and must be defended (R. G. Boling, *VT* 16 (1966), 295 f.; condensed in his *AB* commentary on Judges, 1975, 188). The following observations are limited to the points that pertain to the present study.

Comparing the Received Text with the Septuagint (G), Boling avers that, according to RT, Jair's sons "possessed thirty ^{c}*ayārîm*," continuing: "For the latter, LXX read towns (^{c}*ārîm*)." This he annotates: "Unless ^{c}*ayārîm* be taken here as diminutive." To begin with this comment, Boling leaves it to the reader to discover the rule that ties together the noun form (^{c}*ayārîm*) with the semantic function (diminutive); I have been unsuccessful. (What H. Ewald says, *Ausführliches Lehrbuch der hebräischen Sprache*, 1870, 435, n.1, is fantastic. At any event, his only example, *n^{e}bāyôt*, is an Arabic name, possibly taken from Assyrian, see E. C. Broome, *JSS* 18 (1973), 1–16; it is not a Hebrew word.) Speculative semantics aside, Boling presupposes that the plural ^{c}*ayārîm* "towns" was unknown to the Greek translators. Now these men were active between the times of attested biblical and mishnaic Hebrew; they should, therefore, not be denied out of hand acquaintance with the plural stem of ^{c}*îr* that is common in

which to this day are called Havvoth-jair" (10:4). IV Ibzan: "He had thirty sons; thirty daughters (*bānôt*) he gave away in marriage outside his clan,[20] and thirty daughters-in-law (*bānôt*) he brought for his sons from outside his clan" (12:9). VI Abdon: "He had forty sons (*bānîm*) and thirty grandsons (*bᵉnē bānîm*) who rode seventy asses" (12:14). These three are men of note.

Regarding the expansions we observe: (1) Each expansion has a phonetic unit of word length which occurs twice in the section—*ᶜayārîm, bānôt, bānîm.* (2) The number "30." Its importance is brought out by its sevenfold occurrence describing the aggregate of the sons (twice), grandsons, daughters, daughters-in-law, towns, and asses. Its dominance is highlighted by the fact that it replaces the traditional "60" of the number of the Havvoth-jair although the larger number is well established, occurring, as it does, in three passages of literary mutual independence (Jos 13:30; 1 Ki 14:13; 1 Chr 2:23). (3) The numbers "7" and "70." Not as important as "30," they should not be missed. (a) The featured "30" is mentioned seven times, as noted, and is thereby emphasized. (b) There are six judges, yet the list has seven names if Abimelech (10:1) is counted, as he ought to be, because his name appears in the formula "And after [PN] arose/judged (Israel) . . ." (c) There are seventy asses owned by the descendants of Abdon. The features (1)–(3) are present almost everywhere in the group of judges II, IV, and VI and afford a measure of control of the Received Text; emendations, such as Boling's,[21] partly destroy the three-faceted order.

From the formal details to the content and the meaning: There is the "30." As a number for people, 30 (more generally, 3×10^n) is exceedingly rare in Old Testament stories except for military affairs. What Ju 10:1 ff.; 12:7 ff. tells about the sons of Jair (II), Ibzan (IV), and Abdon (VI) has nothing to do with the military. The sons and grandsons are numerically matched with the 30 guests of Samuel (1 Sam 9:22[22]) and perhaps the 30,000 men of Solomon's corvée (1 Ki 5:27), if with this paramilitary organization the emphasis is more on para than on military.[23] Then

the latter, namely *ᶜayārôt*. So much for the basis of the Greek translation.

As to biblical Hebrew, a few one-syllable nouns with a long /u/ or /o/ form plurals with /w/: *šôr—šᵉwārîm, šûq—šᵉwāqîm, dûd—dūdîm* and *dᵉwādîm* (different meanings?). There are, besides the noun *ᶜîr* under discussion, no such nouns with a long /î/ that behave similarly, but the existence of the pattern with /w/ stakes out a place for a pattern with /y/. As to the different plural endings *-îm* and *-ôt* of the same word or stem, there is a talmudic observation about the biblical versus Middle Hebrew distribution of these endings, shown in the case of rᵉxēlîm—rᵉxēlôt "lambs" (b.Xullin 137b to Gen 32:15).

Then there is the difference between the numbers of the sons, asses and towns—"thirty" in RT, Targum, Peshitta, Vulgate, and Josephus versus "thirty-two" in G (not in "each of the versions," Boling). He remarks (295, n.3) that the difference "may be due to haplography" (apparently in combination with the end of vs. 3 "[twenty-]two"). This application of the concept of haplography is confusingly loose. Ours is a case of two (minimal) similar segments of text, A and B, with A having a word or a phrase that B lacks. The critic who is to determine whether this is a case of haplography or dittography must decide first and on independent grounds which of the segments represents the correct, at the very least the better, reading. If it is A, the minus of B is declared a haplography; if it is B, the plus of A is explained as a dittography. Boling makes no explicit decision and, of course, gives no independent reason for the preference of "thirty-two." He only says—correctly—that the assumption of a scribal mistake (haplography) here requires the further assumption that "it had to be levelled through at three points," which requirement makes it more difficult to accept the "thirty-two" (Ockham's razor). I am leaving the conflict "thirty"/"thirty-two" aside as unsolvable at this point but will later support "thirty" as part of a numerical scheme.

In general, Boling "has done nothing to insure confidence" in his critical operation. Referring to other biblical books he states: "when Jair 'renames' the towns, the idiom is *yiprāᵓ ᵓôtām* (Deut iii 14) or *yiprāᵓ ᵓethen* (Num xxxii 41)"; it is not *lāhem* as in Ju 10:4, which text is therefore suspect. What he fails to tell his readers is that the very next verse of the Numbers passage just quoted reports that Nobah, too, renamed a town and its environs, and that the expression is *wayyiqrāᵓ lāh* (G: *autas*). Suspicion dismissed.

[20] *Haxûcā*, as in Deut 25:5.

[21] See n. 19.

[22] G "70," here and repeatedly in Samuel, for "30" of RT.

[23] This is an overview of the numbers 3×10^n (n running from 1 through 5), referring to people, which occur in Old Testament narrative texts outside the minor-judges section. The list, containing actual numbers and scriptural references, does not include occurrences from 1 Ch 11; 12; 27 repeating or reflecting occurrences in Samuel-Kings. (a) 3,000 (Ex 32:28). (b) 3,000 (Jos 7:4). (c) 30,000 (8:3). (d) 300 (Ju 7:6, 7, 8, 16; 8:4). (e) 30 (14:11). (f) 30 (14:19). (g) 3,000 (15:11). (h) 3,000 (16:27). (i) 30 (20:31). (j) 30 (20:39). (k) 30,000 (1 Sa

there are the asses. The ass is the common riding animal of the age, therefore we wonder why this lean text tells twice that young men have asses. Finally, the only happening told, the only narrative feature in the strict sense of the word, is that the sons are kept home, the daughters are sent away to be married elsewhere, and from elsewhere wives are imported for the sons.

All these features can be accommodated for by introducing one text, the opening twenty lines of the Old Hittite narrative about the city of Zalpa/Zalpuwa. The text was published and, separately, edited by H. Otten.[24] The section of our concern is fairly well preserved, but uncertainties remain, particularly at the end.

> The queen of Kanish[25] gave birth to thirty sons in a single year. She (said) as follows, *2*"What is this? I have born a gang."[26] She filled containers with excrement(?), *3*put her sons in them and turned them over to the river. The river *4*scarried them to the sea (on the way to) the land of Zalpuwa. The [gods], however, took the sons *5*out of the sea and reared them. *6*In the meantime, as the years went by, the q[ueen] gave birth again, (this time) to thirty daughters. *7*Those she reared herself. (Then) the sons went[27] back(?) to Nesha. *8*They drove an ass/asses, and when they arrived at (the city of) Tamar[mara], they said, *9*"Here you have heated the room, and an ass/asses mate(s) (?)."[28] *10*This is what the men of the city (said), "Whereever we have come (?),[29] an ass/asses mate(s) (?) [. . .]." *11*This is what the sons (said), "Wherever we have come, a woman [bea]rs a child [only once a year]; *12*us, however, she bore (all) at once one time." This is what the men of the city (said), "Once o[ur quee]n of Kanish *13*bore thirty daughters, (all) at one time, but the sons have disappeared."

4:10). (l) 30 (9:22). (m) 300,000 (11:8). (n) 30,000 (11:8). (o) 3,000 (13:2). (p) 3,000 (24:3). (q) 3,000 (26:2). (r) 30,000 (2 Sa 6:1). (s) 30 (23:13, [18, 19, 22], 23, 24). (t) 300 (23:18). (u) 30,000 (1 Ki 5:27). (v) 300 (11:3). (w) 30 (Jer 38:10). (x) 300 (Est 9:15). (y) 300,000 (2 Ch 14:7). (z) 300,000 (17:14). (aa) 300,000 (25:5). (bb) 3,000 (25:13).

The overwhelming majority of these passages deal plainly with military affairs (organization, tactics, fighting, fatalities). The following remarks apply to the minority. (a) A military, *xerem*-like operation (cf. Deut 13:7–16). (e), (f), (h) The 30 of Judges chs. 10 and 12 may be a numerical device for linking the Samson cycle (chs. 13–16) with its surrounding texts and thus anchoring it better in the book. The link with ch. 17 stands out: 1,100 (shekels of) silver in 16:7 (Samson) and 17:2,3 (Micah); the expression is unique in the Bible. (r) Whether the 30,000 Israelites were picked for the transportation of the ark (2 Sa 6:2ff.) cannot be made out. If they were, the reason may be the military connotation inherent in the object or the act; see H. P. Smith, *A Critical and Exegetical Commentary on . . . Samuel*, 1899, 291. (s) The text is uncertain in places; emendations, in brackets, after *BH*[3]. (u) The task of Solomon's conscript laborers is peaceful, their organization paramilitary. (v) The 700 wives ("princesses") and the 300 concubines of Solomon combine to form another numerical pattern; cf. Job 1:2,3; 42:13. (w) Commentators are not aware of the military aspect of the happening and they often emend "30" to '3', the argument being that three men are enough to pull one man out of the pit—as if this were the issue! The issue is that the king first handed Jeremiah over to hostile officers (Jer 38:5), then, listening to Ebed-melech and recognizing the danger to the life of the prophet (38:8f.) or for other reasons, changed his mind and decided to save his life. He sent a military detachment to back up his decision and protect Jeremiah if necessary. The only clearly independent nonmilitary passage outside of the minor-judges section is (l), telling about Samuel and his 30 invited guests at the *bama*. Hence the "thirty" is not a "designation of a circumscribed body of public functionaries . . . known from the Bible" (thus S. Talmon, *BASOR* 176 (1964), 33; Boling, *Judges*, 231); the alleged known body occurs nowhere else in the Bible, and also to Egypt it cannot be traced (Talmon and Boling; refuted by B. Mazar, *Knaᶜan wyiśrael*, 1974, 183f., n.2).

[24] *KBo* 22, 2 (1974) and *Studien zu den Boğazköy-Texten* 17, 1973.

[25] The name of the city is written Kanis (Kaniš) here and in line 12, Nesa (Neša) in lines 7, 15, 15. This difference is maintained in the article, although Kammenhuber says, probably correctly, that Kaniš is a logographic spelling for Nesa ([J. Friedrich-] A. Kammenhuber, *Hethitisches Wörterbuch*[2] [fasc. 4, 1979], 301a). For the city, see Otten, ibid., 57 f.; for the city of Zalpa/Zalpuwa, id., 58–61, and J. G. Macqueen, *Anat. Stud.* 30 (1981), 179.

[26] H. A. Hoffner, *Or. N.S.* 49 (1980), 290.

[27] *yanzi*. Otten: "machen sich auf den Weg," a German idiom, for which he finds support in KASKAL-*an iyat* (supra [n.24], 25). Perhaps the word is a scribal mistake for *(i)yanniyanzi*.

[28] Otten leaves it open (ibid., 29 f.). Kammenhuber (supra, n.25), 301b.

[29] *a-ru(?)-me-en*; see Otten, ibid., p. 29, n.50, p. 30. Kammenhuber, ibid., 209a: *a-ú-me-en* "we have looked."

> Thereupon the sons said *14*before their heart,[30] "Whom are we seeking (yet)? We have found our mother. *15*Come, let us go to Nesha!" As they were travelling to Nesha, *16*the gods made (implanted in) them another heart (i.e., changed their personality?[31]); their mother *17*[. . .] did not recognize the, and she gave her daughters to her sons. *18*[The fi]rst ones did not recognize their sisters, the last one, however, *19*[said], "Let us [not] take our sisters. Do not commit an abomination!" *20*[. . .] right(?). And s[lept] w[ith t]hem(?). [Large lacuna.]

To return to the biblical text, when its peculiar features are taken together and compared with the group of similar features of the Hittite text, the probability is very small (although not to a degree as overwhelming as in the case of Gen 32:23–32) that the biblical text or a forerunner of it was composed, in Israel or outside of it, independent of the Hittite text. That is to say, Judges depends directly or indirectly on the story about Zalpa, or else both texts owe a debt to a common source. When the narrative expansions of the text of the minor judges II, Iv, and VI were composed, the Hittite story or a descendant or a cousin of it must have been fairly well intact and known in Israel. Without the narrative bond that makes the text an integrated whole, the details of the Hittite story would not have held together and could not have been so preserved in the Old Testament. Only after their absorption in their new literary environment could their original matrix have disappeared in Palestine.

[30] I.e., "to themselves" or "excitedly." See Otten's comment, ibid., p. 32.

[31] The similarity of this expression with 1 Sa 10:9 is interesting.

The following aspect perhaps points to another, if minor link between the Hebrew and Hittite texts. Israelite society, as it appears in Judges, is tribal; Hittite society is not. Of the six minor judges, numbers I and V[32] have tribal identifications, numbers II, IV, and VI, the judges of the expanded passages which contain the features common to the Hebrew and the Hittite texts, are identified by geography (territoiries or towns), the kind of identification encountered in the Zalpa story.[33]

The foregoing provides the explanation of the peculiar elements of the Old Testament text in which we are interested. Their presence in Israelite literature is the result of their migration from their foreign moorings. The next question follows: What was their attraction for the Israelite author who integrated them into his text? The answer to this question is informed by considerations of intention and literary composition and is of the order of an interpretation rather than an explanation. The story of Zalpa vividly depicts the danger of incest, however unintended. Once upon a time thirty young men slept with their sisters. And there is a moral to the story. The pater-familias who want to protect himself and his house against such a horrible thing and avoid misalliances of all sorts keeps his sons home, handpicks his daughters-in-law (and marries his daughters off to distant places); this is what Abraham did for Isaac and Hagar for Ishmael. If this is not possible, he directs his sons to particular places or clans; this is what Isaac and Rebeccah did for Esau and Jacob. And this is also what Ibzan, one of the three notable minor judges, did. A boy from a good family must not be footloose and fancy-free.

[32] The information on number III, Jephthah, is cut away; see supra, p. 323.

[33] This would not be true if Gilead, identifying judge II, is meant to designate the tribe rather than the territory.

HEROES OF AKKAD

JOAN GOODNICK WESTENHOLZ

ASSYRIOLOGICAL INSTITUTE, COPENHAGEN

ALL STUDENTS OF NEAR EASTERN LITERATURE OWE AN INCALCULABLE DEBT TO SAMUEL NOAH KRAMER for his lifetime of work in Sumerian literature. One of his many and varied insights in this field was the introduction of the concept of the Sumerian Heroic Age with its epic literature on the basis of such parallels as Greek, Indian and Teutonic Heroic Ages.[1] This concept has been the basis of many studies.[2] The present contribution in his honor will compare the Sumerian epic literature to the Akkadian and discuss their similarities and divergences.

While no one has seriously questioned the applicability of the term "epic" or "heroic epic" to the various Sumerian texts dealing with the exploits of the ancient heroes of Uruk,[3] the corresponding Akkadian literary works have been the subject of an extensive, even futile terminological debate. There are two main definitions of the term "epic" which I would term the maximal theory and the minimal theory. According to the first, the term includes all narrative poetry. This is the common Assyriological convention used by Hecker in his *Untersuchungen zur akkadischen Epik*[4] and by many others.[5] According to the minimal definition, "epic" is limited to the heroic narrative poems. Nougayrol has worked with this definition: "en ce qui touche à l'épopée, je pense qu'il est utile de délimiter d'abord le *fonds heroïque* dont elle est née."[6] It is the minimal theory which guided the selection of the Sumerian tales mentioned above and which is espoused in the discussion offered below.

Unfortunately, certain pieces of heroic narrative have never been included in epic literature—by neither the maximal nor the minimal definition. These are variously termed 'autobiographies,' 'pseudo-autobiographies,' and '*narû*-literature.'[7] These texts are ex-

---

[1] Samuel Noah Kramer, "Heroes of Sumer," *Proceedings of the American Philosophical Society*, 90 (1946), 120–30; "Epic Literature: Man's First Heroic Age," *History Begins at Sumer*, 1956, 200–11; *The Sumerians: Their History, Culture, and Character*, 1963, 183–205.

[2] e.g., I. J. Gelb, "Sumerians and Akkadians in their ethno-linguistic Relationship," *Aspects du Contact Suméro-Akkadien* (*CRRAI*, *Genava*, n.s., 8), 1960, 262.

[3] At present, we can ascribe to this literature nine epics varying in length from one hundred to more than six hundred lines: Enmerkar and the Lord of Aratta, Enmerkar and Ensuhkešdanna, Lugalbanda and Enmerkar, Lugalbanda and Mount Hurrumm, Gilgamesh and Agga of Kish, Gilgamesh and the Land of the Living, Gilgamesh and the Bull of Heaven, Gilgamesh, Enkidu, and the Netherworld, The Death of Gilgamesh. For references, see M. Lambert, "La littérature sumériènne à propos d'ouvrages récents," *RA* 55 (1961), 181–4. To be added to that bibliography are: S. Cohen, *Enmerkar and the Lord of Aratta* (Ph.D. diss., University of Pennsylvania), 1973; Adele Berlin, *Enmerkar and Ensuhkešdanna* ("Occasional Publications of the Babylonian Fund," 2), 1979; C. Wilcke, *Das Lugalbandaepos* 1969; A. Falkenstein, "Gilgameš," *RLA* 3, 357–63.

[4] *AOATS*, 8, 1974.

[5] W. G. Lambert and A. R. Millard, *Atra-ḫasīs*, 1969, 7. They have been taken to task undeservedly by J. Renger, *JNES* 32 (1973), 342 for not using the term "myth" as a description of Atra-ḫasīs.

[6] Jean Nougayrol, "L'épopée babylonienne," *La poesia epica e la sua formazione*, 1970, 854.

[7] Güterbock introduced the term '*narû*-literature' in his fundamental work "Die historische Tradition und ihre literatische Gestaltung bei Babyloniern und Hethitern bis 1200," *ZA* 42 (1934), 19 to designate the "Sargon Birth Legend," *BRM* 4 4, the Boissier text of the "Great Revolt Against Naram-Sin," and the various known pieces of the Cuthean Legend of Naram-Sin. In place of '*narû*-literature,' 'poetic autobiographies' was introduced as the common term for this genre, which included poetic narratives of historical events told in the first person by a king (Grayson and Lambert, "Akkadian Prophecies," *JCS* 18 (1964), 8). This term was changed to 'pseudo-autobiographies' by Grayson in his *Babylonian Historical-Literary Texts* ("Toronto Semitic Texts and Studies," 3), 1975, 7. Most recently, Erica Reiner has used the term 'autobiography' to include the Sargon

cluded because they have a moralistic message or because they are in the first person.[8] In the opinion of this author, that is not sufficient reason to separate these texts from the other heroic narrative epics and thus they will also be included in the following considerations.

It is not the aim of this article to propose yet another set of terminology. However, I feel that of the various terms in use, the designation '*narû*-literature,' first coined by Güterbock and recently fallen into undeserved disuse, gives a much clearer definition of the contents of the texts in question, whereas '(pseudo)-autobiography' puts too much stress on the use of the first person, or on the fictional character. In the following, I shall therefore use the term '*narû*-literature' to describe any text that purports to be a copy of an authentic royal inscription.

Another general assumption in this study is that the legends concerning the heroes of Akkad were handed down orally before some were written down in the form we have them today. Thus, these legends developed shortly after the events, to which additions and subtractions, anachronistic shifts and confusion of events were made as in any other body of heroic poetry.

To this Akkadian heroic narrative literature belong the tales of the kings of the third, second, and first millennia. Of these, the texts dealing with the kings of the Akkadian dynasty were certainly far more important and influential than the later sagas. As long as the Akkadian literary tradition was alive, the fortunes of this dynasty were seen as paradigmatic for any later ruler or dynasty.[9]

At present we can ascribe to this literature fragments of six texts and the incipit of yet another to Sargon, and six texts to Naram-Sin. Since the texts are in fragments, it is difficult to decide when one fragment is a part of the same text as another, a different version of the same text, or an entirely different text. Thus, the following numbers and descriptions are only tentative. From the known fragments, we can conclude that we are dealing with texts of similar length to their Sumerian counterparts. Moreover, in the following, an attempt has been made to give these fragments titles comparable to the Sumerian ones.

THE TEXTS

A. Sargon

1. *The Rise of Sargon.*[10] This composition written in Sumerian was found in Warka and dated according to the script to the Old Babylonian period. It is a corner of a four-column composition. The beginning of the text is lost, and after some obscure lines we find ourselves in Kish where Ur-Zababa reigns in joy until An and Enlil decide to terminate his kingship. Then the focus shifts to Sargon, whose pedigree or humble origins of city and parents are mentioned. Then, it is probable that a birth story (mu im-ta-tu-ud-da-[...], i 13) or a story of early precociousness (Šarrukin šà-du$_{10}$-ga mu-[...], i 12) follows. Unfortunately, here is where our fragment breaks off. It might have contained a life story of Sargon. When the text resumes on the reverse, there is a typical Sumerian exchange of messengers between Sargon and Lugalzagesi, apparently because of the violation of Lugalzagesi's wife by Sargon. Lugalzagesi is very upset, sitting on the ground lamenting his fate. The messenger brings a demand from Sargon for submission. The rest of the text is broken, the fragmentary nature of the whole does not allow an opinion as to whether this tradition was friendly or unfriendly to Sargon. [See the article of Cooper and Heimpel in this issue.]

2. *Sargon, the Conquering Hero.*[11] This is the only complete text we have but is in such a sad state of preservation that much cannot be read. It is an Akkadian composition of 123 lines, Old Babylonian script, and of unknown provenience. This very difficult text begins probably with an introduction by a raconteur. The story itself begins with a speech perhaps by Ilaba to Sargon announcing a battle on the morn and instructions to the vizier to encourage the reluctant army.[12] Then follows a glowing description of soldiers

---

Birth Legend and *BRM* 4 4 which begin *anāku Šarrukīn* and the term '*narû*-literature' to include poetic narratives of historical events concerned with a famous past king which have a moral message to the future kings as a conclusion; "Die akkadische Literatur," *Altorientalische Literaturen*, Wolfgang Röllig, ed., 1978, 176–80.

[8] See the references collected above, as well as Hecker, *Epik* 37, n. 1.

[9] J. J. Finkelstein, "Mesopotamian Historiography," *PAPS* 107 (1963), 466.

[10] V. Scheil, "Nouveaux renseignements sur Šarrukin d'après un texte sumérien," *RA* 13 (1916), 175–9.

[11] Jean Nougavrol, "Un chef d'oeuvre inédit de la littérature babylonienne," *RA* 45 (1951), 169–83.

[12] Based on a possible reading of line 10: *i-nu-ma ìl-a-ba$_4$ a-ša-re-du-um* ... and of line 32f.: *ta-ak-li-ma-tim li-im-ḫu-u*[*r*] *šu-kal-l*[*um*].

—probably but not certainly the enemies. Sargon attacks the far-off land and here occurs the celebrated darkness when the sun darkened and the stars came out. Then we have the results of the razzia—the booty returned to Akkade and the destruction of cities—followed by about 20 lines too damaged to read. When the text again becomes legible Sargon is extolling his conquests—nine are mentioned and the text ends on Sargon's challenge to the future—any king who will rival me should go where I have gone.

3. *Sargon in the Lands Beyond the Cedar Forest.*[13] This text was found somewhere in Harmal and thus dated to the early Old Babylonian period. There is one large fragment with parts of four columns and six small pieces. Although several passages resemble the preceding text, relating both of them to other texts about Sargon,[14] there is little other connection. It bears the marks of being an unaccustomed attempt at writing down an orally transmitted epic. The verse lines do not match the line division of text. It has a unique poetic structure of repeating one line twice followed by a third line: AAB, CCD, EEF but apparently this poetic structure only occurs in col. i. In this ballad section, Sargon crosses the rivers Irnina and Zubi and the Amanus range, the dwelling of the cedar. At that point, he seeks omens,[15] puts down his weapons, pours libations, humbles himself and prays. His prayer is answered by Irnina bidding him to conquer the land of Maldaban. In col. ii, we seem to have a description of a land which is said to be not like Amurru. Col. iii mentions Simurrum and appears to be an abbreviated duplicate of text 2, lines 30–67. Here we have the speech of encouragement to the soldiers, the glowing description of martial armor, and the bringing of booty to the land of Akkad. The fourth column is badly damaged but contains the legend of the darkening of the sun in the forest.

4. *I, Sargon.*[16] This Old Babylonian piece of unknown provenience contains the first nine lines of a first-person narrative. Thus, it is a piece of *narû*-literature. In the form of epithets, this fragment points to Ishtar's love for Sargon and his wanderings to the corners of the world—two elements that occur elsewhere in the Sargon literature. The real content of the story is entirely lost.

5. *Sargon and the lord of Purušḫanda.*[17] Although the story was known in Old Babylonian times,[18] we have textual witnesses only from the Middle Babylonian and later periods. However, it has been claimed[19] that both or either of 'Sargon, the Conquering Hero,' and 'Sargon in the Lands beyond the Cedar Forest' are Old Babylonian versions of this story but as yet there is little evidence for such an attribution. What we have is three Middle Babylonian pieces from Amarna, labeled the first tablet of *šar tamḫāri*, "finished", plus two Neo-Assyrian pieces from Assur and Nineveh and five pieces from Boghazköy in Hittite. This is a text which concentrates on dialogues and only deals with the fighting in summary fashion. In the preserved text, the merchants residing in Purušḫanda persuade Sargon to come to their aid despite the warnings of his soldiers that the way is long and hazardous. Meanwhile, Nur-daggal, the lord of Purušḫanda, 'the favorite of Enlil,' speaks with his warriors of their security, but before he is finished speaking, Sargon attacks. A dialogue between the two ensues and the tablet ends with Sargon staying for three years in Purušḫanda.

6. *The Sargon Autobiography.*[20] This is a conglomerate text which may, like the Marduk Autobiog-

[13] First published by J. van Dijk, "Textes du Musée de Baghdad," *Sumer* 13 (1957), 66, pls. 16–19 and republished in *TIM* IX 48.

[14] It has been suggested that both of these texts are Old Babylonian versions of "Sargon and the lord of Purušḫanda."

[15] In line 12′, it might be possible to read: *bi-ri ib*(!?)-*ri*(?). This reading is based on similar passages elsewhere (see *CAD* sub *bīru*) and contextual meaning. For a discussion of rituals performed before and after battle, see J. van Dijk, "Un rituel de purification des armes et de l'armée," *Symbolae Biblicae et Mesopotamicae . . . de Liagre Böhl dedicatae*, M. A. Beek *et al.*, ed., 1973, 107–17.

[16] *BRM* 4 4.

[17] For the Amarna pieces, see A. F. Rainey, *El-Amarna Tablets 359–379* (AOAT, 8), 1970, 6–11 and for the later pieces see *KAV* 138 and W. G. Lambert, "A New Fragment of the King of Battle," *AfO* 20 (1963), 161–2. For the Hittite pieces see E. Laroche, *Catalogue des Textes Hittites*, 1971, 53 no. 310.

[18] Cf. *UET* 7 73 i 1–16 which is the beginning of a fictive letter from Sargon, the great king, to 8 individuals concerning conquering Purušḫanda (*ana Purušḫanda ṣabātim*). For discussions of this text, see Kraus, "Der Brief des Gilgameš," *An.St.* 30 (1980), 115.

[19] e.g., Hecker, *Epik* 36 and most recently A. K. Grayson, "Histories and Historians of the Ancient Near East: Assyria and Babylonia," *Or.* 49 (1980), 185.

[20] Brian Lewis, *The Sargon Legend*, 1980.

raphy,[21] be a prophecy or a wisdom text.[22] The composite text comes to us in three Neo-Assyrian pieces from at least two copies from Nineveh and one piece from a Neo-Babylonian library. The Sargon autobiography makes up the beginning of the text, forming a frame story for the real message of the text, now largely lost. In this story, we have the well-known folktale about the abandoned child brought up by a gardener and raised to kingship by Ishtar, and a list of the king's exploits which any rival king of the future should try to emulate (cf. no. 2 above).

7. *"Šarrukīn, šūpû."* This incipit is listed together with the incipit of no. 6 in two Neo-Assyrian catalogues, one of which is definitely from Assurbanipal's library.[23] Therefore, we know that this library contained two distinct Sargon narratives.

B. Naram-Sin

1. *Naram-Sin and the Enemy Hordes.*[24] This was the most popular of all the legends, according to our written evidence. Of this composition, there is one Old Babylonian version, two versions in Akkadian from Boghazköy, and a late version found in four copies from Nineveh and one from Sultantepe, in addition to possibly three Hittite versions from Boghazköy. The story tells about a catastrophical invasion of Babylonia by some barbarian hordes. These hordes are described as led by the 6 (or 7) brothers (sons of Anubanini) coming down from the mountains to devastate the whole Near East. On their devastating march, they are joined by 17 more kings. Having made sure that these hordes are human beings rather than demons and evil spirits, Naram-Sin decides to attack them and asks the gods for an oracle. The oracle is negative, but Naram-Sin in his *hubris* decides to ignore the answer and proceeds with his attack. Year after year, his forces are annihilated so that "not one came back alive." Deeply depressed and seriously doubting whether he is at all fit to be king, Naram-Sin again seeks counsel of the gods through oracles. Apparently, the answer is now positive since Naram-Sin suceeds in battle. However, he is not allowed to pursue his victory and exterminate the enemy since Enlil will do that for him in his own good time. This text has a moral mesage attached to it at the end—it is one of pacifism—not to go forth against an enemy no matter what he does to your land but to be meek and humble, responding to their wickedness with kindness. According to both the introduction and the closing section, the text purports to be a stele, a *narû*, to be read aloud, and is thus a piece of *narû*-literature par excellence.

2. *The Great Revolt Against Naram-Sin.* This legend is extant in three very different Old Babylonian versions.[25] There seems also to have been a Hittite version with much Anatolian overlay.[26] This Hittite version offers a list of 17 rebellious kings, echoing 'Naram-Sin and the Enemy Hordes,' but that may be a confusion. The Old Babylonian versions differ in the number of rebel leaders, one giving 11 kings, the other giving x+20.

One of the Old Babylonian versions, which is available in two manuscripts, has been shown to be an adaptation from an authentic stele of Naram-Sin.[27] The main difference is that the Old Babylonian version is told in the first person and, of course, in Old Babylonian dialect. The first person style is in agreement with the preference for first person in the royal inscriptions of the Old Babylonian period. The two other Old Babylonian versions of the story are likewise in the first person but very fragmentary. Common to these versions are a catalogue of enemy kings, a detailing of their ungrateful behavior, a mention of the nine battles in which Naram-Sin overcame them,

[21] R. Borger, "Gott Marduk und Gott-König Šulgi als Propheten, Zwei prophetische Texte," *BiOr* 28 (1971), 3–24.

[22] For the discussion of this claim, see my review of Lewis's book, forthcoming in *JNES*.

[23] C. Bezold, *Catalogue of the Cuneiform Tablets in the Kouyunjik Collection*, Vol. IV, 1896, 1627 Rm 618; lines 4 and 21; and W. G. Lambert, "A Late Assyrian Catalogue of Literary and Scholarly Texts," *Kramer Anniversary Volume* (*AOAT*, 25), 1976, 314 K 13684:6–7.

[24] See the references collected by A. K. Grayson, "Assyria and Babylonia," *Or.* 49 (1980) 188 n. 216. For the two versions in Akkadian from Boghazköy, see the discussion by Harry A. Hoffner, "Histories and Historians of the Ancient Near East: The Hittites," *Or.* 49 (1980), 319 § 14.2 and for the Hittite material, ibid., § 14.3.

[25] The three different versions are: (1) The version found in the Boissier (Genève) piece and Mari piece are published in A. K. Grayson and E. Sollberger, "L'insurrection générale contre *Narām-Suen*," *RA* 70 (1976), 103–28; (2) the version found in the London fragment published in the same place; and (3) *VAS* XVII 42.

[26] Güterbock, "Die historische Tradition," 66–80.

[27] Piotr Michalowski, "New Sources Concerning the Reign of Naram-Sin," *JCS* 32 (1980), 233–46.

and, contrary to historical fact, the attribution of Sargon as Naram-Sin's father.

A miserable Old Akkadian exercise tablet[28] shows that this story was already transformed into saga within one generation of the event itself.

3. *Naram-Sin and the Lord of Apišal.*[29] This text exists in a Pinches copy of an unknown original from the now dispersed Amherst collection. Pinches has two columns on the obverse and one column on the reverse, but it is impossible to see what is missing. This text differs from the above two in being a third-person narrative in Old Babylonian hymno-epic style. The part of the text which has a narrative rather than panegyric concerns the officer of Naram-Sin giving a reply from the Lord of Apišal.

4. *Erra and Naram-Sin.*[30] This composition is found on one almost complete single column tablet. This unusual composition deals with the obtaining of weapons of victory by Naram-Sin, then a return promise to build a temple for Erra. Thereafter, the two warriors, Erra and Naram-Sin, set out for battle. After the successful conclusion of the military campaign, the king builds the temple. The text ends with a blessing on Naram-Sin, the wise one who takes pleasure in justice. The language is poetic and in the Old Babylonian hymno-epic dialect. Nevertheless, the placing of a *narû* in Cutha brings to mind the Cuthean Legend, "Naram-Sin and the Enemy Hordes."

5. "*narû dialoguée.*"[31] This text was found in Larsa recently and is still unpublished. It is listed in the catalogue of texts with no description.

GENERAL CONSIDERATIONS

Considering the body of this literature as a whole, the most striking feature is one of extreme fluidity and a most confusing lack of textual stability. Except for the manuscripts from Assurbanipal's Library, which of course belong to canonized written editions, there are almost as many tales as there are tablets, with each tale witnessed by one manuscript only. This situation differs sharply from that of the contemporary Sumerian literature, where the textual variability rarely goes beyond the exact form of verbal infixes and the like. The natural conclusion to draw from these facts is that while the Sumerian literary tradition in Old Babylonian times was basically a written one, most of the contemporary Akkadian literary texts should be regarded as either exercise compositions made once and for all by the student on the basis of the ancient stories, or adaptations by the scribes of the stories for some contemporary purpose, all based on an essentially oral tradition. Only in exceptional cases may we have straight transcripts of the oral tradition itself. This means that it may be pointless to ask whether, for instance, the Old Babylonian fragment of "Naram-Sin and the Enemy Hordes" is a "forerunner" of the Cuthean Legend or not, or whether it is the Old Babylonian manuscript of "Sargon, the Conquering Hero" or "Sargon in the Lands beyond the Cedar Forest" that is somehow ancestral to *šar tamḫāri*. The truth of the matter is probably that there were a number of stories about the Akkadian kings, each of them current in several variants. One such story was how Sargon rescued the merchants of Purušḫanda, another how he went to the farthest corners of the world, or how he encountered darkness or enemy soldiers of iron. These elements might be combined in almost any fashion. Likewise, a number of stories were told about the great rebellion against Naram-Sin. This event must have impressed the Mesopotamians deeply, both in Naram-Sin's own time and later,[32] and it formed the basis of the only story about Naram-Sin that was accepted into the written canon, namely "Naram-Sin and the Enemy Hordes." As mentioned above, however, this is more likely to be an Old Babylonian scribe's adaption of the orally transmitted story rather than the story itself, so that, already from the beginning, this text had a different status. The only exception among the Old Babylonian texts to the rule that no duplicate manuscripts are found occurs in the Genève and Mari tablets of "The Great Revolt against Naram-Sin." However, as already said, this text bears a much closer relationship to an authentic inscription by Naram-Sin than any of the other compositions.

---

28 *MAD* I 172 (TA 1931–729).

29 H. G. Güterbock, "Bruchstück eines altbabylonischen Naram-Sin-Epos," *AfO* 13 (1939/40), 46–9.

30 W. G. Lambert, "Studies in Nergal," *BiOr* 30 (1973), 357–63.

31 D. Arnaud, "Larsa. Catalogue des Textes et des objets inscrits trouvés au cours de la sixième campagne," *Syria* 53 (1976), 77.

32 See T. Jacobsen, "Ipḫur-Kīshi and His Times," *AfO* 26 (1978/9), 1–14.

Although these compositions are difficult to harmonize in an analysis of the Heroes of Akkad, we shall try to evaluate the character of the protagonists, the motifs, and the literary styles found in the above compositions.

THE PROTAGONISTS

The Heroes of Akkad show their uniqueness and superiority in their outstanding abilities in the clash of arms:

ajû šarru ušannan kāša gērûka ul ibbašši
nākiršunu gašru attu qāmu libbi nākirūka
What king can rival you? Your adversaries do not exist.
Their mighty opponent are you, the consumer of the heart of your opponents.
"Sargon and the lord of Purušḫanda," *EA* 359 rev. 21–22, also *KAV* 138:7′–9′

Naram-Sin šarrum dannum šar Akkade
šar kibrāt arbaʾi ...
mušēṣi dunni GIŠ.TUKUL(!) *ana kala šarri*
Naram-Sin, the strong king, King of Akkade
King of the Four Quarters of the World
Who extends the strength of weapons against all kings
"The Great Revolt Against Naram-Sin," *RA* 70, 111 G 2–9

The heroes' lust for battle can turn into a superhuman fury and frenzy and as such they are often compared to wild animals or to some irresistible power of nature:

birbirrūka girri rigimka addum
kīma nēšimmi nāʾirim tabašši
bašmummi pīka anzûm ṣuprāka
Your luminosity is fire, your voice is that of the thunderstorm
You become like a raging lion,
Your mouth is a horned snake, your nails are (those of) the A.-bird
"Naram-Sin and the lord of Apišal," *AfO* 13, 46 rev. ii 1–3

Not only in the feats of arms but also in unusual feats of prowess which no man has done before, do the Heroes of Akkad display their heroism:

[*šad*]*ê dannūti ina akkullāte ša erê lu ar*[*ḫiṣ*]
[*lu*] *ētelli šadî el*[*ūti*]
[*lu*] *attatablakkata šadî šapl*[*ūti*]
[*ma*(?)]-*ti tiāmat lu alma* [*3*]-*šu*
Difficult mountains I passed through using copper picks
The upper ranges I climbed again and again.
The lower ranges I jumped over again and again.
The sea-land(?) I circumnavigated three times.
"Sargon Autobiography," i 15–18

In the heroic tales, there are always assumptions about honor. The enemies may be treated with sympathy and respect or may be despised as inferior beings. Both are apparent in the character of the Heroes of Akkad. Both the unnamed lord of Apišal and Nur-Dagan, the lord of Purušḫanda are treated as equals. Amnesty is given the Gutian king in the "Revolt Against Naram-Sin" (L ii 16) and nine times did Naram-Sin free the rebels after they revolted (*VAS* XVII 42). However, the enemy hordes are treated as demonic creatures who must be tested as to their humanity. They are described as monstrous creatures.

The heroes are usually described as possessing feelings of great personal worth and honor. In "Naram-Sin and the Enemy Hordes" this quality is indeed present to such excess that it takes on a negative appearance:

ajû nēšu bīri ibri
ajû barbaru išʾal šāʾiltu
lullik kī mār ḫabbāti ina migir libbija
u luddi ša ilimma jāti luṣbat
What lion (ever) observed oracles?
What wolf (ever) consulted a dream priestess?
I will go like a robber according to my own inclination,
and I will cast aside that of the god, I will take charge of myself.
"Naram-Sin and the Enemy Hordes," *An.St.* 5, 102:80–83

Of course, Naram-Sin had to pay dearly for this.

This episode and its disastrous consequences formed the basis for the well-known characterization of Naram-Sin as an *Unheilsherrscher*.[33] By his impiety,

[33] Güterbock, "Die historische Tradition," p. 75; O. Gurney, "The Cuthean Legend of Naram-Sin," *An.St.* 5 (1955), 96; J. J. Finkelstein, "The So-called Old Babylonian Kutha Legend," *JCS* 11 (1957), 88; J. J. Finkelstein, "Mesopotamian Historiography," *PAPS* 107 (1963), 467–70; Piotr Michalowski, "Amar-Su'ena and the Historical Tradition,"

Naram-Sin brings destruction upon his own people; when he in his pride refuses to accept the answer of the oracles, he makes the disastrous mistake of an *Unheilsherrscher*. However, the epilogue is a lecture given by Naram-Sin on the virtues of humility and turning the other cheek, a very anti-heroic attitude. Naram-Sin brings destruction, not because he is the "ill-fated ruler," but because he is a hero, too much of one at that. There is no sharp distinction between Sargon and Naram-Sin as *Heil* and *Unheil*; both are heroes if in different measure. Furthermore, we should not forget that this characterization of Naram-Sin is limited to the one text "Naram-Sin and the Enemy Hordes";[34] otherwise the victorious king was remembered more favorably. We may therefore in "Naram-Sin and the Enemy Hordes" have a philosophic tract on the values of anti-heroism rather than a tradition about the destructive reign of Naram-Sin.

THEMES

The poetry of every people develops its own special qualities and reflects the society which produces it. The Akkadian *Volksgeist* reveals itself in the themes which filter through these compositions. However, over the millennia the society changed from a more military aristocratic structure to a bureaucratic traditional society. Thus, there are layers of motifs in these compositions.

The first motif, known also from royal inscriptions, is exploration into the unknown—to go where no man has gone before. It is epitomized in the frequent usage of the verb *alāku*, especially in the Gtn (*atalluku*):

> *šarrum ša išannananni*
> *ša anāku attallaku šū littallak*
> let the king who would equal me
> go everywhere where I ever went
> "Sargon, The Conquering Hero," *RA* 45, 176:121–123

> *ali ilišu uštālik*
> wherever his god causes (him) to go
> "Sargon in the Lands Beyond the Cedar Forest," *TIM* IX 48 iii 8′

> *muttallik kibrāt erbettin*
> who roams the four quarters of the world
> "I, Sargon," *BRM* 4 4:3–4

> *ina alāk [urḫi] u ašābi mīnu Šarrukīn irdê*
> Who can follow Sargon in traversing the road and stopping?
> "Sargon and the lord of Purušḫanda," *EA* 359 rev. 26f.

This motif was an important part of the Sargon cycle of stories and it was employed even in the first millennium compositions—the World Map (*CT* 22 48:10) and the description of the Empire of Sargon of Akkade.[35]

Naram-Sin is also known from his royal inscriptions and date formulas to have gone to faraway places. However, only one of the literary texts, "Naram-Sin and the lord of Apišal," makes such a mention:

> *Naram-Sin urḫašu illak*
> Naram-Sin shall go on a journey
> *AfO* 13, 46 obv. ii 2

The religious outlook was imposed on this unbridled self-aggrandizement in "Naram-Sin and the Enemy Hordes." In this composition the gods do not allow Naram-Sin permission to go afar. Not only is the wandering not allowed, it is equated with foolishness:

> *nam[zaq] ilāni rabûti ana alākija u zaqīqija ul iddinamma*
> ... of the great gods do not give permission for my going and my foolishness
> *An.St.* 5, 102:78

This religious overlay is more apparent in "Naram-Sin and the Enemy Hordes" than in any other text.

The second motif is valor in battle and the honor which one receives from it. This is clearly shown in the Sargon cycle which often mentions soldiers in addition to the central figure of Sargon. In the Naram-Sin texts, Naram-Sin is hardly out of the limelight. The winning of glory in battle is proclaimed by the marshall to the troops in both "Sargon, the Conquering Hero" and "Sargon in the Lands beyond the Cedar Forest" in the same words:

Ancient Near Eastern Studies in Memory of J. J. Finkelstein, 1977, 156–7; A. K. Grayson, "Assyria and Babylonia" *Or.* 49 (1980), 189.

[34] Disregarding the Weidner Chronicle, which takes a negative view of everybody, and the Curse over Akkade, which clearly was based upon a Sumerian tradition only.

[35] See A. K. Grayson, "The Empire of Sargon of Akkad," *AfO* 25 (1974/77), 56–64.

kīma urram tuštarraḫu ina qereb ekalli ...
kakki nakiri muḫur ze-ru-ni nassu
attaḫdakkumma šarrum ālilī lišēpīka
ṣalamka lišziz ina maḫar ṣalmišu
If tomorrow you will be praised in the palace,
meet the weapons of the enemy, the fiend will be discomfited
I will praise you and may the king acclaim you as 'my warrior'
may he erect your statue in front of his own statue
RA 45, 172:30–39; *TIM* IX 48 iii 3′–6′

This heroism can be shared by man and his god as a companion according to the composition "Erra and Naram-Sin." They share the glory in the following:

ilum Erra u Naram-Sin
puḫriš illiku ruʾšu u šū
tattakpiš mātam qabalšu
itnallak ištašu qurādum Erra
The god Erra and Naram-Sin
Went together, his companion and he,
His battle overwhelmed(?) the land
As the warrior Erra went with him
BiOr 30, 361:33–36

Another motif which goes through all the compositions is the religious piety of the hero. Heroes pray to the gods and take oracles from the sacrifices before battle and give thanks for their victory afterwards. When Sargon has reached the Cedar Forest, he prays for instructions:

ittaqqi niqišu ilbin appašu te-li-ša-am iskur ellūtim
He poured libations, he humbled himself, he pronounced the holy words syllable by syllable (?)
TIM IX 48 i 13′–14′

After one battle and before another battle, Naram-Sin also prays and makes a libation of beer:

ašar parakki ilija Šullat u [*Ḫaniš*...]
askuru telītam Eštar umm[*ī* ...][36]
udeššû sirāš ú-ga-[...]
at the place of the throne of my god, Šullat and [Haniš]
I invoked puissant Eštar my mother ...
I made abundant the beer, I ...
"The Great Revolt Against Naram-Sin,"
RA 70, 115 L ii 9′–11′

This piety towards the gods and their wishes is a basic trait in Akkadian culture. When Naram-Sin defies the will of the gods, he must suffer for it. He acknowledges his fatal error in the following passage of "Naram-Sin and the Enemy Hordes":

anāku essiḫi enniši
akâd ānaḫ āšuš amṭīma
umma anākuma ilum ana palēja mīnam ublam
anāku šarrum la mušallim mātišu
u rēʾûm la mušallim nišīšu
jāši palê mīnam ublam
I became confused, I was bewildered,
I despaired, I groaned, I grieved, I grew faint
Thus I thought: "What has God brought upon my reign?
I am a king who has not kept his land prosperous
And a shepherd who has not kept his people
Upon myself and my reign, what have I brought?'
JCS 11, 85 iii 8–13

This passage in the Old Babylonian version shows a revelation of character if we assume that the question: 'What has God brought upon my reign?' is answered by 'What have I brought upon myself and my reign?' It is not in the stars but in ourselves that the tragic fault lies, is what Naram-Sin may be saying in this paragraph.

LITERARY STYLE

There are three basic literary styles found in these compositions: a prose style, a normal Old Babylonian poetic style, and a highly evolved Old Babylonian hymno-epic style. The prose style is found in those compositions of *narû*-literature that are closest to a real *narû*. These would be: "I, Sargon" and "The Great Revolt Against Naram-Sin." These contain the stylized language and particular structural features of royal triumphal inscriptions.

The normal Old Babylonian poetic style has basically a simple structure: the basic unit is the line which is a unit of sense and is usually divisible into four metric units or two half lines. At present, there

[36] Whatever *te-li-ša-am* may mean (von Soden, *AHw têlišam*, suggests "Silbe für Silbe"), the similarity in sound between the two passages quoted here is noteworthy. Another instance of similar-sounding passages with quite different meanings was noted in "Help for Rejected Suitors," *Or.* 46 (1977), 214f. and n. 31.

are still many unsolved problems concerning Akkadian meter, and the nature of the line with its ability to vary greatly its number of syllables. The verse is short, word order is different from normal prose syntax and to a certain degree influenced by metric considerations. This style is found in the late Old Babylonian texts from Sippar such as Atra-hasīs and is found among the heroic narratives in "Sargon, the Conquering Hero" and "Naram-Sin and the Enemy Hordes" as well as in "The Sargon Autobiography" although this is not Old Babylonian.

The highly evolved Old Babylonian hymno-epic style is most frequently found in the Old Babylonian narrative hymns. This style is characterized by its archaisms, convoluted syntax, rare words, and abstruse epithets.[37] Moreover, there is some use of assonance and alliteration.[38] Consequently, there is the beginning of the development of the stanza.[39] The compositions are: "Sargon in the Lands Beyond the Cedar Forest," "Naram-Sin and the Lord of Apišal," and "Erra and Naram-Sin."

The one composition not listed above is "Sargon and the lord of Purušḫanda," since its literary style is not Old Babylonian. The verse line, which is only barely discernible in a few passages, does not correspond to the line division of the main manuscript from Amarna[40]—the fragments from Assyria are too small to be of any use.

A comparison between the Sumerian and Akkadian heroic epics reveals a number of differences, both in outlook and in form. Like his Akkadian counterpart, the Sumerian hero is an outstanding individual, richly endowed with superior abilities; but it does not follow that he must make them manifest in action. In "Gilgamesh and Agga," the mere appearance of Gilgamesh on the wall of Uruk so overwhelmed the besieging host of Kish that they fled precipitously. The Sumerian heroic epics are full of competition, boasts and contests between the hero and his opponent, with displays of enormous pride and vanity on both sides. Both the hero and his opponent are presented as more or less equal. The Sumerian heroic epics also tell us of supporting characters: Lugalbanda, the champion of Enmerkar, and Enkidu, the servant of Gilgamesh, or the heroes of Kullab, Birhurturre and Zabardibunugga. A very noteworthy trait of the Sumerian hero is that he often engages in contests, not of armed force, but of intellect and magic power and knowledge, as well as of charisma and divine favor.

On the whole, the Sumerian heroes partake far more of the divine realm than the Akkadian. They are scions of the gods and, as kings, mediate between gods and men. This feature goes back to ancient Sumerian concepts of kingship.[41]

The Akkadian heroic ideal is one of manhood and honor. The hero must pass through ordeals to prove his worth, and these almost always involve some kind of violent action. Fearful obstacles and disasters which await the great are more apparent in the Akkadian epics than in the Sumerian. In the Akkadian, the catastrophic hour is the occasion for the hero to make his greatest effort and to achieve victory in the throes of defeat. He fights against human foes and wins over them, not by help from above but by his own strength. He goes up against obstacles—both human and natural—almost singlehandedly. As yet, we know only the names of their opponents but not of a single

---

[37] Examples are: (a) archaisms—the use of *išti* instead of *itti* (e.g., *AfO* 13, ii 3, rev. ii 4), the use of *-iš* instead of *ana* (e.g., ibid. rev. ii 13), the use of the dual (e.g., *BiOr* 30, rev. 49), the use of nunation (e.g., *AfO* 13, ii 5); the lack of contraction of *u* and *i* (e.g., *ša-du-ú-i* ibid. i 3); (b) free syntax: Obj.-Verb—Verb-Obj. *[Ḫa]manam uštētiq uštētiq ramanšu Ḫam[anam]* *TIM* IX 48 i 11′, Subject-Verb-Prepositional Phrase *il mātim illaku ištišu AfO* 13, ii 3, Prepositional Phrase-Verb-Subject *immaḫra illaka pālil urḫim*, ibid. 4, Subject-Prepositional Phrase-Verb *Irnina ištišu illak* ibid. rev. ii 4; (c) rare words: *ši-in-ši-ri-iš* 'twelve times' *TIM* IX 48 i 10′, *te-li-ša-am* ibid. 14′f. and many others; (d) abstruse epithets: *immaḫra illaka pālil urḫim iwwarka Zababa e-da-ta-am qarnīn* (von Soden *JNES* 19, 164 reads *eddam qarnīn* "mit spitzen Hornen") 'in front goes the guardian of the way, behind goes Zababa, the sharp-horned one,' *AfO* 13, ii 4f.

[38] Examples of assonance in subsequent lines with *u* in the first line followed by *i* in the second and *a* in the third: *raksu turrušu tukkušu u-x [...-a]m, ina šigarim muribbim bābim ka[wī]m šakna bašmān sipara retitān daltān*, *BiOr* 30, rev. 47ff. Examples of alliteration with *l*, *š*, *k* are: *lušārik elīk lušarpiš kikunnâk lušalbiš warqam* ibid. 28f.

[39] For a discussion of the stanza in 'Sargon in the Lands Beyond the Cedar Forest' see above.

[40] See Hecker, *Epik*, 200f.

[41] Aage Westenholz, "The Old Akkadian Empire in Contemporary Opinion," *Power and Propaganda: Symposium on Empires in the Ancient World*, ed. M. T. Larsen (*Mesopotamia*, 7), 1979, 109 and Åke Sjöberg, "Die göttliche Abstammung der sumerisch-babylonischen Herrscher," *Orientalia Suecana* 21 (1972), 87–112.

supporting character like Lugalbanda or Enkidu. The element of competition with the foe is not much in evidence; Nur-Dagan is no match for Sargon (though it is not so clear about Naram-Sin and the lord of Apišal).

It may finally be noted that the Akkadian epics clearly seem to contain a much larger element of historicity, despite poetic liberties. The catalogue of rebel kings in "The Great Revolt Against Naram-Sin" resembles similar catalogues in other heroic poetry, such as the Catalogue of Ships in the *Iliad*, or the Catalogue of Kings in *Widsith*, which are usually accorded a high historical value.

There are also differences in literary pattern and structure between the Sumerian and Akkadian epics. The Sumerian poems frequently begin with an introduction. The story is set in a background of time or place—either "in days of yore," "when . . . ," or in radiant Uruk. These introductions are missing in Akkadian epics as we have them. If there is an introduction in the Akkadian epic, it is that of the raconteur "I will sing . . . ," followed by a paean to the hero.

The action of the poem is also treated differently. Instead of the leisurely unhurried style of the Sumerian epics, the Akkadian epics proceed at such a rapid pace that even small gaps in the texts make it impossible for the modern reader to follow the story. The Sumerian poet concentrates on dramatic speeches to the detriment of the action of the story. Not only is the action glossed over in one line as when Gilgamesh defeats Huwawa but also the opportunities to describe battles are missed as in the conquest of Aratta in Lugalbanda and Enmerkar.

In Sumerian, parallelism and other types of repetition are the means for achieving the basic poetic structure. There is apparently no meter or fixed number of syllables to a verse line. On the other hand, the Akkadian Old Babylonian epics normally use little parallelism and repetition though they are found in the compositions written in the hymno-epic style. Even when they are used, they are much shorter than their Sumerian counterparts. The feeling for phonetics may be stronger in the Akkadian—although the Sumerian uses rhyme, alliteration and assonance within the line and rarely in longer strophes,[42] the Akkadian uses them more commonly. Neither the Sumerian nor Akkadian uses them as basic building methods of poetry. Both Sumerian and Akkadian literature have static epithets and fixed formulas. Nevertheless, the Akkadian heroic epics scarcely employ the fixed formulas apart from the introduction of direct speech.

This short overview demonstrates the heterogeneity of the Akkadian heroic narrative material in relationship to the Sumerian. The problem with defining and evaluating the Akkadian literary tales has been confused by terminological discussions and the lack of literary analysis. It is hoped that by assembling all tales—both prose and poetry—story and song—concerning the heroes of Akkad together, we can begin to understand the heroic and non-heroic outlook of Akkadian literature.

---

[42] Claus Wilcke, "Formale Gesichtspunkte in der sumerischen Literatur," *Sumerological Studies in Honor of Thorkild Jacobsen* (Assyriological Studies, 20), 1975, 217f.

IN SEARCH OF SUMER
A PERSONAL ACCOUNT OF THE EARLY YEARS

SAMUEL NOAH KRAMER

PHILADELPHIA

[*On p. 452 of the* Kramer Anniversary Volume *(AOAT, 25),* Gods, Heroes, Kings, and Sages: A Scholar's Journey into Time and Space *is listed as "In Preparation." This volume never saw publication, and this is why.*

Back in the middle 60's the publishing house of Charles Scribner's Sons developed a series wherein invited contributors were asked to weave within an autobiographical background accounts of their own research, the hurdles which they surmounted, the discoveries they made, and the impact they had on their field of specialization. The whole was to be within modest proportions and to address an interested, but not necessarily academic, audience. Among those who were commissioned were the Nobel Laureate (1950) E. C. Kendall, the astronomer H. Shapley, the pharmacologist W. Weaver, the Egyptologist J. A. Wilson, and Samuel Kramer. Sam finished a 328 page manuscript and submitted it in the early 70's. It was edited and waited publication. But after the publication of four volumes, by the above mentioned authors, the series was terminated in 1972 and Sam's volume was left stranded.

In these pages, I offer samplings from that manuscript. Rather than gleaning choice morsels from here and there, I have opted for presenting more or less in extenso *the first quarter of the volume. However, I have occasionally pared down information which either depended on the non-published portions of the ms in order to acquire full meaning or contained illustrations which are well known from Sam's other writings. But I could not resist selecting a segment from the ms's last pages since I think it conveys Sam's hopes for the future of cuneiform studies in one of the areas of the world where Ancient Near Eastern literature originated.*

I do recognize that this method of honoring a scholar, by presenting him with a dais from which to address an audience, is uncommon nowadays. Nevertheless, I am hoping that Sam's own words regarding his first steps in Sumerology will be found interesting and, I dare say, inspiring. They should, at the very least, give us insight into the creative effort which has convinced many that history does indeed begin in Sumer. The Editor]

1. *From the Talmud to Cuneiform* (*Zashkov and Philadelphia 1897–1929*)

I was born on September 28, 1897, in Zashkov, a ghetto *shtedtle* in the district of Kiev in the Ukraine. The week of my birth happened to coincide that year with *Simchath Torah*, the annual Jewish festival commemorating the reading in the synagogue of the concluding portion of the Torah, the Five Books of Moses. This coincidence of birth and feast inspired my father to name me Simcha, "Joy." The *ch* in this Hebrew word, which represents a harsh Semitic guttural, later proved to be a thorn in the throats of my Philadelphia teachers when they tried to Anglicize my name. To make matters worse, the week in which I was circumcised coincided with the reading in the synagogue of the weekly portion of the Pentateuch that tells the story of the patriarch Noach (Noah in the English Bible), and this concurrence of *brith* and Flood-hero, prompted my father to give me the middle name Noach. So there I was, beginning life in the Czar's Zashkov with the "begutturaled" name Simcha Noach Kramer.

The last name, Kramer, "storekeeper," must have been acquired by the family in a German-speaking community long before my father's day. For my father was no merchant, big or little, wholesale or retail. He was a *Gemoorah-rebbi*, that is, a teacher of the Talmud. His pupils were boys aged nine to thirteen who had finished their earlier elementary studies in the Pentateuch and the Prayer book and were now ready to tackle the more difficult, complex, and deeply revered Talmud, which consists of numerous compendia of legal lore and legends (traditional). Our town had no Yeshivah (rabbinical college), and the pupils who completed their Talmudic studies with my father and wished to delve deeper into Talmudic and kabbalistic lore would wander off to some larger town renowned as a center of learning.

The number of pupils in my father's school, which was located in our home, was about a dozen, and the remuneration he received from the parents was, as I recollect, about ten rubles per student per year. This annual income of approximately 120 rubles barely sufficed for our family of five—I had an older brother and sister—and there was little danger of our suffering from overeating and surfeit. Many a meal consisted of cabbage soup and tea with a piece of hard sugar to bite on. But our little house with plastered walls and a straw roof was our own, and there was a goat to provide us with milk and cheese. And then there was the Sabbath, glorious and holy, that lit up our home once a week and turned it into a palace. On Friday night we gorged ourselves on fish and meat, and *kugel* and *tzimes*, and sang our hearts out to God and praised his goodness.

On my fourth birthday, my older brother brought me to the *dardeki rebbi* (elementary teacher) in our town to begin my studies in Bible and prayer. I was not a bad student, and by the time I was eight, I had covered the reading and translating into Yiddish of a good part of the Bible, including the commentary of the venerated medieval French-Jewish scholar Rashi, printed in small type below the Biblical passages. The teaching was by rote, and there was many a Biblical sentence whose meaning I knew only superficially. But it imbued me with profound faith in Yahweh's love for his suffering people, and I had no doubt that one day the Messiah would appear and turn things around, so that the mistreated and oppressed Jews would be "sitting pretty," while the *goyyim* looked on in envy.

My special heroes were Judah, son of Jacob, who dared talk back to Joseph whom he took to be second only to Pharaoh in power and station; Moses, the man of God and leader of his people; the brave Joshua who made the sun stand still until "the people had avenged themselves upon their enemies"; David, the valiant, generous singer of psalms; and Solomon the wisest of men. King Solomon was a favorite in our house since, as every believing Jew knew, he was the author of the *Song of Songs*, a book that my father cherished and loved. So much so, that from time to time, when in a happy mood, he would seat me on his knee, and ecstatically intone voluptuous words which were redolent with lust and desire. For its two ardent lovers, he assured me, were none other than Yahweh and the people of Israel, and their rapturous speeches were but avowals of their tender love and yearning. Little did I dream that one day, with innocence gone and faith departed, I would write a learned monograph to demonstrate that the *Song of Songs* echoed the pagan fertility rite of a sacred marriage between a ravishing goddess of sexual love and her blissful royal acolyte.

Heroes were certainly needed in those dark, bitter days in the early part of the twentieth century, when both the Czarist court and the Russian church were inciting the populace to organize pogroms and massacre Jews. No pogrom had yet actually violated our *shtedtel,* but neighboring towns had been pillaged and ravaged, and terror was at our doors. A number of the more daring and enterprising Zashkovites had now departed for America, the land of liberty and opportunity. Some of them had settled in Philadelphia and were doing well as storekeepers and merchants. There was plenty to eat and drink and much material comfort, but they were deeply worried about their children who were being well educated in the public schools but learning nothing of Hebrew lore and tradition. From time to time those who had studied in Zashkov wrote to my father, urging him to leave pogrom-ridden Russia and come to Philadelphia to teach their young the Bible and the Hebrew prayer book. In 1905, though in his fifties, he decided to hearken to their plea. Since there was not enough money to take along the entire family, he traveled alone in order to prepare the way. The very next year, with savings from his earnings as a Hebrew teacher, he sent us *Schiffskarten* (travel tickets) to bring us from Zashkov to Philadelphia, and we were off to America, fearful and hopeful.

We almost did not make it. We, like most other Jewish emigrants, were leaving Russia without official permission and therefore had to "steal the border," to translate literally the Yiddish idiom. This was a clandestine procedure carried out in the dark of night, when an agent of the travel agency from which our tickets had been bought would lead a batch of emigrants across the border, after having bribed both the guards and the customs officials. Usually this was a smooth operation, carried out without difficulty or mishap. But our group ran into trouble; we were caught and arrested on the Austrian side of the border. We were not mistreated, however, and after an anxious, frightening night, and some additional bribes no doubt, we were permitted to board the train for Rotterdam and the steamer that would take us to New York. Our journey continued without further misadventure, and after landing at Ellis Island, we left immediately by train for Philadelphia, where my father installed us in a small but not uncomfortable "tenement" apartment on Bainbridge Street, in a section of the city inhabited largely by immigrant Jews and Italians. As I learned in later years, it was not far from Independence Square and the home of the American Philosophical Society that was one day to be a pillar of support to me and my researches, but of this I had no inkling at the time. Here, then, in the month of June, 1906, in a South Philadelphia tenement, began the acting out and realization of one version of the American dream, though somewhat Jewish tinted and tainted.

July and August were school vacation months. But in early September I was taken to the Meredith elementary school, not far from home, and was matriculated in the first grade. Then and there began my first confrontation with the Anglo-Saxon world and the loss of some of my native identity. My first grade teacher, Miss Nellie, a lovely, buxom lady whom I remember with no little affection, helped with my matriculation, and when she saw in cold black ink the given names Simcha Noach, she became alarmed—these were hardly words fit for the English tongue. Simcha was changed there and then to the more commonplace Samuel, and Noach to the less exotic Nathan. And so I became Samuel Nathan Kramer and continued to be so called throughout my school and college years. These are also the names on my naturalization papers, my passport, and my earliest publications. Only when my publications increased in number and weight did I become more daring and defiant, and while hesitating to tamper with Samuel, I changed the middle name to Noah (for Noach), so that all my later publications, including this one, are signed Samuel Noah Kramer. And, though this is perhaps a hallucination, the change from Nathan to Noah seemed to have had some effect on my academic colleagues; they began to read my lucubrations more respectfully and attentively.

Still this name transformation had its darker consequences. Librarians tend to look upon me as an enemy, since every time they catalogue Kramer, Samuel Noah, they have to add "See also Kramer, Samuel Nathan." And whenever in my many travels I show my passport with its "Samuel Nathan Kramer," I do so with some trepidation, since my suitcases bear the inscription Samuel Noah Kramer," and I might be taken to be some kind of imposter. So much for what the lovable Miss Nellie did to my identity.

I was eight years old on entering the first grade, while most of my classmates had begun their school career at six. But as I was still a good student, I was moved to a more advanced grade several times, so that when I reached the last grade in the elementary school I was fourteen which was the average age of elementary school graduates at the time. I remember these early school days with much pleasure, for my teachers were dedicated and devoted and did their best to give us of their knowledge and learning, however limited these may have been. In fact, throughout my school experience, elementary and advanced, I found most of them sympathetic and sensitive in their attitude to the immigrant "greenhorn" pupils, whom they endeavored to make part and parcel of the American scene—they believed truly and fervently in the American melting-pot and at no time denigrated the mores and customs of the diverse ethnic groups with whom they came in contact. In the present era of rampant "ethnicity," it may not be amiss to help keep the record straight with some mitigating memories of former days.

The Philadelphia public schools were not the sole source of my education. My father, who remained an observant orthodox Jew to the end of his days and who absorbed and assimilated very little of the English language and the American culture, was deeply concerned about my Jewish religious education. At that time there was a Yeshivah in Philadelphia, and he had me matriculated in it not long after our arrival. The hours were from about four in the afternoon to seven in the evening, and there were also sessions on Sunday morning. This, admittedly, did not leave as much time for play. Nevertheless, we Yeshivah students did manage to find time for baseball and other games during recesses and holidays; and our bodies were not neglected altogether, though the educational emphasis was almost entirely on the intellect.

Virtually the sole discipline in the Yeshivah consisted of the study of the Talmud, together with the commentaries composed by medieval scholars. Having a rather logical, analytic mind, I did not find the Talmudic type of close chain reasoning from given, unquestioned, premises, difficult to follow, and I rather enjoyed my Talmudic experience. The pedagogy, to be sure, was at times rather bizarre: the volume on divorce, for example, was taught before the one on marriage, not to mention the fact that neither theme was very close to the hearts of youngsters barely in their teens. Nevertheless, my mental processes were stimulated no little by the Talmudic dialectics and argumentation. It was then, too, that I made a rather interesting psychological observation of the scholarly mentality, one that was corroborated in later life by my academic experience.

Even in those early years I perceived that there were two main types of scholars. There were those whom the Yeshivah professors designated as *genarniks*, a Yiddish word for the students who "fooled" themselves by reciting glibly and smoothly the assigned Talmudic passage no matter how involved and convoluted, without understanding the underlying postulates and reasoning. On the other hand, there were students who tended to hesitate, and even stutter and sputter in their recitation, because they felt the need to make sure of the validity of their data and logical inferences, prior to stating their conclusions. Not infrequently, too, the glib type of student was the possessor of an unerrring memory and could pride himself on remembering the exact page on which any given Talmudic quotation was to be found, a quality that was not characteristic of the sharp analyst. Again, not surprisingly, it was the former who tended to favor the fanciful, mythic, and mystic portions of the Talmud, while the latter felt more comfortable with the rational, realistic, legal sections. As I learned many years later, a similar dichotomy of attitude and predilection characterizes the academic world and is responsible for no little controversy and contention among professors, including those in my chosen discipline, the Ancient Near East.

I attended the Yeshivah for a good many years all through my grammar-school days and my first years of high school, and I have pleasant memories of a number of my fellow students. Several of my predecessors, whom I admired and even idolized, went on to carve out notable careers for themselves in later life. One was Gershon Agronsky, who became a fervent Zionist and left America for Palestine, where he founded the outstanding English language newspaper, the *Palestine Post*, and became one of the first Jewish mayors of Jerusalem. On the other hand, there was Louis Fisher, who became a well-known journalist deeply sympathetic to atheistic Russian communism, only to reject it later in bitter disillusionment. Two others were Louis Leventhal, who became one of the first Jewish judges in Phildelphia, and Israel Goldstein, who for many years was the spiritual leader of Bene Jeshurun, one of the outstanding synagogues of Conservative Judaism in New York City.

After graduating from grammar school, I matriculated in Southern High. There were very few high schools in Philadelphia at the time. The most prestigious was Central High, but this institution of learning was chiefly attended by richer, more Americanized, and more sophisticated students. Most of the poorer and more recently immigrated Jews lived in South Philadelphia and sent their children to Southern High, which began as a manual-training center but was soon transformed into a liberal-arts school. It was here that I began to get some idea of the scope, content, and importance of secular education. The courses in mathematics, history, literature, and foreign languages opened my eyes, and I began to realize the parochialism and limitations of my Biblical and Talmudic learning. So much so, that when I was midway through the high-school years I persuaded my father to permit me to leave the Yeshivah and instead to attend Gratz College, a Jewish educational institution where the teachers were college graduates who taught in English rather than Yiddish.

Here, in courses scheduled for evenings and Sundays, I first learned Hebrew grammar in a systematic fashion and Jewish history from a relatively secular perspective. I was very much taken with this new approach to Jewish studies, and graduated with high honors, not to mention two prizes of one hundred dollars each, a welcome contribution to the family finances. The Gratz College sojourn was not without influence on my later choice of an academic career, and when, years later, I was invited to prepare an article for the volume commemorating its seventy-fifth jubilee, I did so with a feeling of deep gratitude. My contribution, however, dealt with a Sumerian goddess and idolatrous temples, and I fear revealed how far I had strayed from the college's Jewish-oriented disciplines.

After my graduation from Southern High, there was no question but that I would continue with some form of higher education. There was no money, however, for college tuition, and I decided to matriculate in the Philadelphia School of Pedagogy, which provided two years of free preparatory education for men who wished to become teachers in the Philadelphia elementary-school system. There was a special Normal School for women, who far outnumbered men in the school system. It was a rather unusual teacher-training college, in which the liberal arts, rather than courses in education, were the center of instruction. Its head was a Dr. Brandt, who taught philosophy, and the small faculty included several mavericks who were a very real source of inspiration to the students. The one I remember best was Hugh Mearns who, I believe, later became a professor at Columbia University. In his courses in English, he had us write compositions and short stories which he read with great care and evaluated in considerable detail in private sessions with the students. It was Mearns who aroused in me an appetite for American literature, as well as the notion of becoming a writer, a profession for which, I gradually realized, I was not at all qualified.

Another subject taught in the school that influenced me profoundly was philosophy, and especially the course in the history of Western Philosophy, my favorites being Locke and Hume. Throughout the years of attendance at the School of Pedagogy, I was the diligent, enthusiastic, and not unappreciated secretary of the Philosophy Club under the aegis of Dr. Brandt. What all this did to my Jewish orthodoxy is not difficult to imagine, and it became obvious to me that I could no longer perform the daily prayers with phylacteries bound tight about head and arms. Nor could I attend synagogue or keep the Sabbath without feeling like a hypocrite. It became ever more clear that I would have to come to some compromise arrangement with my father, and that sooner or later I would have to leave home.

In the year 1917, I graduated from the School of Pedagogy. The First World War was then raging, and I enlisted in the Student Army Training Corps. But the war soon came to an end, and I was almost immediately discharged when the SATC was disbanded. During the army training I lived in the dormitories of the University of Pennsylvania, which gave me a taste of living away from home. In the course of the next year I rented an apartment in the Bohemian center-city section, Philadelphia's Latin Quarter, as it were. I was still not free of the writer-complex. Money was no serious problem at the time since my father's Hebrew School in South Philadelphia had become quite popular and was well attended. I now did most of the teaching.

Young, energetic, college-trained, at least in part, I taught the Bible and even the Talmud in the English language, so that the pupils understood and, at least to some extent, appreciated what they were learning. It was this Hebrew School that supported my father and myself—mother had died rather unexpectedly following a stomach operation—throughout the twenties; in fact, the school was so successful that I could employ one of my close friends, Max Scarf, who was studying medicine, as an associate.

The hours at the Hebrew School were from four to nine in the evening, which left me free during the day. I could now think of continuing my higher education from where it had stopped in the School of Pedagogy. I therefore matriculated in Temple University, Philadelphia's "poor man's" college, where I obtained a Bachelor of Science in Education after two years of study. The courses that attracted and affected me most were those concerned with the history of the novel and drama as taught by a man whose name I vaguely recollect as Robertson. He was a lean, shy professor, soft of voice and sad of face; all of which helped to bring conviction to his constantly repeated melancholy theme that great literature reflected the tragedy of life and the pathos of the human condition.

The inspiration of Mearns and Robertson kindled in me a burning desire to become a novelist and dramatist. Since my days were free, I read avidly the works of the current and classic American and English novelists and dramatists. At the time, the acknowledged *guru* of the American literary scene was H. L. Mencken, and the *Smart Set* magazine which he and the drama critic George Jean Nathan edited was the Bible of young would-be writers. I read it assiduously. It took some years and many rejection slips to convince me that I had no literary talent and had better settle for something less creative and more suited to my rather literal, factual, unimaginative mind. However, those groping years of unwarranted literary expectations did help me understand myself and my mentality.

On looking back I realize that some of the virtues and failings of my scholarship were already apparent in those days of literary dilettantism. For example, my favorite author was Theodore Dreiser, a novelist whose style is dense and unattractive, but who was a master at building and depicting character. On the other hand, I never took to James Branch Cabell, a master of form and style, in spite of Mencken's encomiums and exhortations. This preference for content over form has influenced my scholarship. In studying the Sumerian literary documents, I tend to stress their context and content to the neglect of their formal features, though these are also quite significant. . . .

The years passed, and I was approaching thirty. Having been unsuccessful as a writer, I began looking around for more practical ways of meeting the future. In the Yeshivah days I had a good friend, Herman Silver, whom chance and circumstance led into the printing business where he was doing quite well. Because of our close friendship, he suggested that I join him as a partner. But it took only a year or so to realize that the business would go bankrupt if I continued as partner; I had no business sense whatsoever. I therefore turned once again to academe. For a few weeks I tried the Law School of the University of Pennsylvania. But when the professor of torts began to lecture on his specialty, it sounded so much like the Talmud of Yeshivah days, that I was loath to continue.

I next tried the Department of Philosophy, but after listening to several of the professor's lectures on Kant, I lost my appetite for philosophy. Finally it came to me that I might well go back to my beginnings and try to utilize the Hebrew learning on which I had spent so much of my youth, and to relate it in some way to an academic future. And so in 1925, at the age of twenty-eight, I matriculated in one of America's unique educational institutions, the Dropsie College of Philadelphia for Hebrew and Cognate Learning.

The college building was a rather charming, many-windowed, small two-story structure with a broad impressive lawn in front—I had often passed it admiringly in the years when I was attending nearby Gratz College. Its president at the time was Cyrus Adler, a well-known and highly respected leader of the German Jewish community. Its small and distinguished faculty included one of the world's most renowned Biblical scholars, Max Margolis; Solomon Zeitlin, the learned but controversial Talmudist and historian of the Hebrews at the time of the birth and growth of Christianity; the Arabist Solomon Skoss, a scholar devoted primarily to Judaeo-Arabic studies, and editor of a unique Karaite commentary on the Bible; and Nathaniel Reich, an Austrian Egyptologist who had been invited to the newly established chair of Eyptology. These men opened new horizons for me in Hebrew studies and in their Oriental background. With Margolis, for example, I learned of the existence and importance of the Greek, Latin, and Syriac translations of the Bible. Skoss introduced me to Judaeo-Arabic—that is, medieval Hebrew manuscripts written in Arabic characters. But what attracted me most was Egyptology, and for two years I studied it assiduously and enthusiastically—I well-nigh knew by heart the contents of the remarkable, pedagogically superb, Egyptian grammar published by the great British Egyptologist Alan Gardiner in 1923.

Fate, the inscrutable, however, did not approve of my becoming an Egyptologist—it had other plans for my future. For reasons that are trivial, and need not be gone into here, the professor of Eyptology and I had a falling out, and I left Dropsie College without obtaining a doctorate in Egyptology. By this time, however, I was no stranger to the Philadelphia academic halls of learning. Immediately upon my rupture with Dropsie College I matriculated in the Oriental Department of the Graduate School of the University of Pennsylvania, which included in its faculty George Barton, a prolific but, as I learned later, not very trustworthy contributor to such facets of Oriental research as Sumerian, Egyptian, and Biblical archaeology; Alan Montgomery, one of the finest American scholars of Hebrew and Aramaic; and a brilliant young scholar, Ephraim Avigdor Speiser, who was to become a leading figure in Near Eastern studies and make fundamental contributions in archaeology, cuneiform literature, and the Bible.

When I came to the department, Speiser, five years my junior, had already published several articles relating to Hebrew linguistics. But his main interest at the time was the cuneiform documents excavated at Nuzi, an ancient site close to the modern city of Kirkuk, in the oil-rich region of northern Iraq. Most of the tablets, dating from about 1300 B.C., had been excavated by his predecessor at the University of Pennsylvania, Edward Chiera, with whom Speiser had collaborated closely as a Fellow in the Oriental Department. These ancient Nuzi documents were written in Akkadian, a Semitic language, although the native population were not Akkadians, but a non-Semitic people, the Hurrians, about whom virtually nothing was known at the time. . . . When I joined the department as a graduate student in 1928, I decided to work with Speiser for my doctorate, and because of his involvement with the Nuzi tablets, it was inevitable that my dissertation would be related to them.

After two years of diligent study under inspiring tutelage, I completed my dissertation, which bore the title "The Verb in the Kirkuk Tablets"; accepted and approved toward the end of 1929, it was published in 1931 in the *Annual* of the American Schools of Oriental Research. . . .

In 1930, I found myself to be the proud possessor of a Ph.D. degree in Oriental studies from the Graduate School of the University of Pennsylvania. The problem was, however, what to do with it. There were very few universities in America with Oriental departments at that time, and available academic positions were minimal. But then there occurred the first of a series of what might be termed "minor miracles"—strokes of luck, if you like—that came to the rescue of my scholarly career whenever it seemed to be on the verge of collapsing. In 1919 there had come into being the American Council of Learned Societies (ACLS), a sort of central exchange of all American societies concerned with humanistic research. In 1930, the very year my post-doctoral career began, ACLS instituted a new program of fellowship awards to young scholars, especially those who had only recently graduated and were eager to broaden their studies. At the suggestion of the Oriental Department of the University of Pennsylvania and with the warm recommendation and blessing of its faculty, I applied for and was awarded one of these post-doctoral Fellowships—the amount, if I am not mistaken, was two thousand dollars, enough to keep me for a year in comfort, if not in luxury.

That same year, 1930, my erstwhile professor and mentor, E. A. Speiser, was going to northern Iraq to excavate one of the tells he had surveyed several years earlier, a mound known as Tell Billah, which he hoped would turn out to be the capital of his favorite people, the ancient Hurrians. The ACLS fellowship enabled me to join his expedition as epigrapher, although this is hardly what Speiser needed, since he could read the tablets far better than I could. It was agreed that the members of the expedition were to meet in Baghdad in the fall of 1930 and from there proceed as a group to Tell Billah, some two hundred miles to the north. But I left Philadelphia several months earlier in order to acquaint myself with some of the museums abroad and learn something firsthand about the archaeology of the ancient Near East, before joining the expedition in Baghdad.

2. *Tell Billah and Tell Farah: A Timid Epigraphist in Iraq (1930–1931)*

Making plans, as I had occasion to learn more than once in the course of my scholarly career, is relatively easy and painless, but carrying them out is quite another matter. Timid and shy by nature, introspective and withdrawn, I failed to take full advantage of my trip through Europe and the archaeologically informative opportunities it provided. In London, for example, I visited the British Museum several days in a row, but I was too timorous to ring the bell of its famous Student Room, where in later years I spent many a summer, and ask for the Keeper of the department or one of his colleagues to discuss with them the history and significance of the museum's archaeological and epigraphic activities.

In Paris, I stood with palpitating heart before the vast collection of statues and inscriptions excavated some four decades earlier in ancient Lagash, but I dared not ask the whereabouts of the conservateurs and excavators and try to learn something of their plans and projects. Only in Berlin, where I stood enthralled before the fabled Ishtar Gate of Babylon as restored in its *Vorderasiatische* Museum by the river Spree, did I have the courage to ask for an appointment with its director, Walther Andrae, the excavator of Babylon, Ashur, and Farah (ancient Shuruppak), home of the Sumerian Flood-hero. Though I did not know it at the time, it was in the roofless, broken-down excavation house built at Farah by Andrae and his colleagues, that I would make my bed a few months later. And how could I anticipate that one day in the distant future Andrae would honor me with his attendance at one of my lectures on the Sumerians delivered in that very museum then still partially bombed out? Sick in body and almost blind, he had somehow survived Nazi rule and the Second World War. In 1930 he was at the peak of his career. Nevertheless he received me, nonentity that I was, with courtesy and grace, and I left his presence happy and starry-eyed.

From Berlin I journeyed to Istanbul, where I lingered some days in order to visit the archaeological museums situated beside the historic Bosphorus, in the palace grounds of the former sultans. I had no inkling then that Istanbul and its Museum of the Ancient Orient, especially the rooms devoted to its tablet collections, would in later years become a second home to me, Sumerologically speaking. From Istanbul I hastened on to holy Jerusalem, visiting the Jewish sacred places about which I had studied in my youth, little dreaming that one day it would become the capital of Israel, and that I would lecture in its Hebrew University on Sumerian echoes in the Hebrew Bible. From Jerusalem I journeyed to charming, verdant Damascus, and from there by bus over the harsh desert to Baghdad.

In September of 1930 I arrived in Baghdad full of hopes, dreams, and visions. There I was in the fabled city of the caliph Haroun al-Rashid, the capital of Iraq, the land where the mighty empires of Assyria and Babylonia had risen, flourished, and fallen. At first, however, I felt nothing but disappointment and disenchantment. As I trudged the narrow, muddy streets of the shabby Baghdad of forty years ago and traveled the dreary, dilapidated roads of its desolate hinterland, my dreams turned into nightmares and my visions into phantoms. Could this sun-parched, wind-riven, desert-like land have been the home of heroic Gilgamesh, the celebrated ruler of ramparted, broad-marted Erech? Or of the energetic ruler and statesman Hammurabi, immortalized by his pre-Mosaic law code? Or of the mighty kings of Assyria, the scourge of Yahweh, who led their conquering, ravaging armies all the way from remote, mountainous and barbarous Urartu to the southernmost reaches of effete, over-refined Egypt? Or of the powerful Nebuchadnezzar who destroyed Jerusalem and exiled Yahweh's people to pagan, carnal Babylonia? Surely, I thought, there must be some misunderstanding here, some error in tradition, perhaps even a fatuous hoax perpetrated by some spurious archivist or pseudo-historian.

Fortunately for my scholarly peace of mind, I spent several weeks visiting some of the excavations going on at that time in various parts of Iraq and learned something about their exciting finds. . . .

With my faith in the unique significance of Mesopotamian history and culture restored, I came to Tell Billah with romantic hopes and expectations of world-resounding discoveries that turned out to be baseless and deceptive. Tell Billah was not the ruined remains of the ancient capital of the Hurrians, with potentially rich archaeological and historical treasures, but of a rather poor provincial town dating back only to the ancient second millennium B.C. During the two months of my stay there, not a single inscription was uncovered, and I began to feel like a supernumerary, a man with useless expertise, a tablet-reader without tablets to read. To make matters worse, I fell ill with an attack of acute appendicitis, perhaps due in part to frustration and disappointment. I was taken hurriedly to the small, poorly equipped hospital in Mosul, where, fortunately for me, there was a Canadian doctor and an Armenian nurse. There was of course a much larger and better equipped hospital in Baghdad, but my condition was serious, and it was feared that the two-hundred-mile journey might prove fatal. I was operated on in a small dark room in the Mosul hospital, and the doctor told me later that he had me so long under ether that he had not time to sew up the wound with aesthetic care, and I am proud to report that the Mosul scar across my stomach can meet any competition for size and zigzagging. After several weeks of convalescence in Mosul, I was all set to depart once again for Tell Billah, with no appendix and very little enthusiasm, when from a quarter entirely unforeseen and unexpected, the second of my minor miracles came to the rescue and turned melancholy resignation into enthusiastic anticipation.

I mentioned that I traveled to Iraq as a paid Fellow of the American Council of Learned Societies, but I should have added that I was also an unpaid Fellow of the American Schools of Oriental Research (ASOR) in Jerusalem and Baghdad. This body, founded in 1900, was supported largely by dues paid by American universities and divinity schools interested in Biblical archaeology. In Jerusalem, the ASOR actually had a building and library. In Baghdad, the ASOR had no building; its presence in Iraq was made manifest only by a professor appointed annually to participate in any American excavations being conducted that year. Sometimes the ASOR also appointed an Honorary Fellow—Honorary, in this case, meaning without honorarium. For the year 1930–1931, Theophile Meek of the University of Toronto was the paid annual professor, and I had the privilege of being Honorary Fellow.

Meek was one of the leading Orientalists of those days, a top-rank Hebrew and Biblical scholar, and a cuneiformist of note. As annual professor of the ASOR he was acting as epigraphist to the Nuzi expedition and was very busy and happy there, because it was unearthing hundreds of tablets dating back to the third millennium B.C., earlier by close to a millennium than the Nuzi documents known till then, for example those that constituted the source material for my dissertation. It was a very exciting, unexpected discovery, and it took all his time to clean the tablets and to try to read and interpret their contents for his preliminary report to be published in the *Bulletin* of the ASOR.

In the midst of this intense and concentrated epigraphic activity, he received a telegram from Eric Schmidt that put him in a quandary. Schmidt had just begun working at Farah, the southern site that had been excavated almost thirty years earlier by Andrae and his associates, and was finding Sumerian tablets, but had no one on his staff to read and study their contents. He wired Meek requesting him to come down to Farah to act as epigraphist. Reluctant to leave Nuzi and the newly discovered third-millennium tablets, Meek turned to me at Tell Billah and asked whether I would not take his place.

I needed no urging. Early in February 1931, I took the train from Mosul to Baghdad, hired a car to take me to Farah, some hundred miles to the south, and was welcomed by my new "boss" with no little enthusiasm. Quite a number of Sumerian tablets had already been excavated, and unlike Tell Billah, there was an urgent need for an epigraphist to interpret their contents and help to clarify some of the problems besetting the excavators, especially those relating to stratigraphic chronology.

Eric Schmidt, who died in 1964, was a first-generation German of considerable personal charm, who came to America in 1923. After participating in archaeological excavations in Arizona and Anatolia, he organized an expedition under the joint auspices of the Oriental Institute of the University of Chicago and the Philadelphia Museum of Art, for the purpose of excavating in Iran—he is best known for his excavations at the world-renowned ruins of Persepolis. His excavations at Farah were only a stopover, so to speak, on the road to Iran; he undertook them at the request of Horace Jayne, the director of the University Museum of the University of Pennsylvania, who was interested in sending a permanent expedition to the site—a project that never materialized. The expedition staff lived in tents that were reasonably comfortable. Because an epigraphist had not been planned for, there was no tent for me, and I had to bed down in the roofless ruins of the expedition house built by the Germans close to three decades earlier.

The sandstorms in the Farah region were so savage that when I awoke in the early morning I was literally buried in sand up to my neck. Even eating was often a serious problem. The expedition had on its staff a competent Iranian cook, but cooking was almost impossible because of the constant unremitting storms. Often the food taken from the cans was no sooner placed on the plates than it became sand-covered and inedible. Still I remember the Farah experience as one of the happiest of my life. When Friday, the Moslem day of rest, came and we took our lukewarm showers from improvised perforated cans, sipped a cocktail hopefully free of sand, read our mail, which included an occasional "love letter," and reflected on the week's archaeological finds, we were a merry, contented crew—*mutatis mutandis*, this Friday celebration was almost as hallowed as that of the eve of the Sabbath in my Zashkov youth.

Scattered over the Farah mound were ancient wells full of clay and sand, and some of these had cuneiform tablets imbedded in them. It was my job to dig out these tablets carefully, clean them, and study their contents. By the time the expedition closed, about three hundred Sumerian tablets had been excavated, and I had only a vague idea of their import. The only professor in the Oriental Department who had claimed to know Sumerian was George Barton, but he really knew very little of what it was all about, and I did not get much from his courses. I was therefore deeply troubled lest the reading and interpretation of these documents would prove too difficult for my limited scholarship and I would fail in this, my first fully independent attempt at cuneiform research.

Therefore, when Schmidt and his associates departed for Iran, I turned my face west and journeyed once again to Istanbul and its Museum of the Ancient Orient, which had among its collections a large group of tablets from Farah excavated earlier by Andrae. Permission to study these was given me readily by the Turkish authorities, and after immersing myself for several weeks in the study of their contents, I acquired a deeper understanding of the nature and scope of the Farah documents in general and felt ready to publish the results of my study of the newly found tablets from the Schmidt excavations.

Still, I was quite green and hesitant about some of the formal Sumerological conventions used by recognized cuneiformists in those days—George Barton's system of transliteration, for example, was not accepted by the majority of cuneiformists. From Istanbul, therefore, I decided to journey to the Leipziger Semitisches Institut, which, in those pre-Nazi days, was the world's outstanding institution for cuneiform research. Its head, Benno Landsberger, was one of the keenest minds in the history of Assyriology, and he attracted a group of students that in future years were to excel in cuneiform studies. Landsberger was gracious enough to give me some help in preparing the Farah material for publication, and my study "New Tablets from Farah," appeared in 1932 in the *Journal of the American Oriental Society*. It was no trail-blazing contribution, but it did help to shed some light on the results of Schmidt's excavations and made me a bit more confident and secure in my calling.

By this time my ACLS Fellowship was beginning to run out, and I had to leave Leipzig for Philadelphia to face the future. Before doing so, however, I became a small-time philanthropist. While in Baghdad I had visited several antique dealers who in those days were uncontrolled agents buying and selling antiquities at will. For some reason that I can no longer recall, one of these took a fancy to me, and seeing how excitedly I was examining some of his tablets that I did not have the money to buy, he put his hand into a baggy receptacle like that carried on the back of a donkey, pulled out about fifty small tablets that he had bought for a couple of pennies each from Arabs digging illicitly on various tells, and presented them to me with his compliments. Planning to bring them with me to America and treasure them as sweet memorabilia of my first Mesopotamian archaeological and epigraphic experience, I took them with me to Leipzig. There I learned that despite its fame, the Semitisches

Institut had not a single cuneiform tablet in its possession, and I donated most of the precious gift to it, as a token of appreciation and gratitude.

In the decades that have passed since, the Leipziger Semitisches Institut has undergone some drastic changes. First came the Nazis and "der Jude Landsberger" had to leave Germany together with two of his best students who were half-Jews. After the Second World War, it came under the control of the East Germans who preferred to make it a center of modern rather than ancient Near Eastern studies. In spite of all the changes, however, rumor has it that the tablets I donated are still there in show cases, a dim reminder of its earlier scholarly interests and achievements.

In June 1931 I returned to Philadelphia, where I could have well used a bit of philanthropy, myself, since the ACLS Fellowship was at an end, and I was penniless and jobless. But not hopeless—it never crossed my mind to give up the scholarly career. . . . One sweet day, another of those minor miracles came to pass, and I packed my bags for Chicago and its Oriental Institute. There I was to stay from 1932 to 1936 as a member of the staff of its Assyrian Dictionary project—a bittersweet experience that gave direction and focus to my scholarly future. I came to the Institute as a groping young Assyriologist and left it five years later as a specialist in Sumerology.

3. *Arno Poebel and Sumerian Grammar (Chicago, 1932–1934)*

. . . On arrival in Chicago, I immediately went to the newly built and impressive Oriental Institute structure where I was interviewed by Chiera and Poebel. I no longer recollect the exact nature of the interview, but in one way or another I must have expressed a strong desire for the Sumerian role in the Assyrian Dictionary, minor though that was. In any case I soon found myself under the guidance and tutelage of Arno Poebel, rather than Edward Chiera, and was assigned an office usually shared with another young colleague, close to Poebel's office and to the large "Dictionary" room where the innumerable word-cards were filed in metal cabinets. . . . It was my task to go through the transliterations and translations of these documents prepared by the senior scholars from America and abroad, to examine carefully their renderings of the Sumerian logograms into Assyrian, and to note these on cards, making sure of their consistency and accuracy before they were utilized in any passage quoted in the dictionary. I found it a very real joy to work on this material, since it provided training in both Sumerian and Assyrian, not to mention that the contents of these documents were new to me, thus enriching my knowledge of aspects of Mesopotamian culture of which I was quite ignorant at the time.

As if this gratifying scholarly labor was not enough to fill my days and nights—the evenings, too, were often spent in the Institute office—I was further enriched by an unexpected and unanticipated bonus that sharpened my scholarly focus and determined my career. The two editors of the Assyrian Dictionary, Chiera and Poebel, were also teaching members of the Department of Near Eastern Languages and Literatures, which was part of the Humanities Faculty of the University of Chicago. Poebel, who was professor of Sumerology—to my knowledge, the only such chair in the world—taught classes in Sumerian grammar and in the translation of Sumerian texts. The junior members of the Assyrian Dictionary staff were permitted, and even encouraged, to attend these classes. Pedagogically speaking, Poebel was a terrible teacher, no better in some ways than my Talmud teachers of Yeshivah days. But in other respects he was stimulating and inspiring, at least for me—and I was at times the only one attending his classes. His speech was rather slow, low, and monotonous; his English was far from idiomatic; he was given to numerous and prolonged digressions and tended to be repetitive and diffuse. But none of these pedagogical failings was a defect as far as I was concerned. Blessed with neither a quick, brilliant mind or a superior memory, I found that Poebel's repetitions, digressions, and *obiter dicta* were just what I needed to help me understand and digest the principles of Sumerian grammar underlying the intricate and often misleading cuneiform system of writing, as well as the methodology of transforming the dead inscriptions into living informants.

Arno Poebel was in some respects a self-made Sumerologist. In his early years he studied theology and philosophy in Germany and Switzerland. In 1905, he was awarded a Harrison Research Fellowship to the University of Pennsylvania where he acquired his Ph.D. under the supervision of Professor H. V. Hilprecht, who was an eminent Assyriologist, but hardly a Sumerologist of note. In 1907, Poebel returned to Germany and continued his researches, but without a university affiliation. In 1911 he was invited to be a teaching Fellow at the Johns Hopkins University, which provided him with the opportunity to spend much time in nearby Philadelphia at the University Museum where he copied many Sumerian literary, historical, lexical, legal, and administrative texts—this University Museum experience was one of the most fruitful of his career. In 1914 he returned to Germany, where he became a professor at the University of Rostock. There he stayed until 1930 when he was called to the Oriental Institute at the suggestion and recommendation of Edward Chiera, who knew of his pioneering and fundamental Sumerological researches from first-hand personal contact at the University Museum, where he too had been copying cuneiform documents.

In 1923, one of those bitter postwar inflationary years in Germany, Poebel published his *Grundzüge der Sumerischen Grammatik*—he had to publish it at his own expense, since he could find no publisher who would accept it. Based on a painstakingly thorough and minutely detailed study of the Sumerian inscriptions of all periods, from the classical of the third millennium B.C. to the late post-Sumerian of the first millennium, it set down with compelling logic the fundamental rules and principles that govern Sumerian grammar and illustrated them profusely and pertinently whenever possible. Subsequent grammatical studies by Peobel and other scholars have resulted in a number of additions and corrections. But by and large, Poebel's *Grundzüge* has stood the test of time, and has continued to be the cornerstone of all constructive research in the area of Sumerian grammar. As a result of assiduously attending Peobel's classes, I had learned his grammar virtually by heart and mastered its intricacies, complexities, and peculiarities. Over the next several years I published several articles explaining and demonstrating its methodology and significance, and gradually it came to be recognized for the valuable contribution that it is. . . .

My relationship to Poebel evolved into that of a disciple to his master, and on the scholarly level, there developed a friendly intimacy that was a source of gratification to both of us, though I profited most from it. But in 1933, Hitler came to power in Germany, and our relationship deteriorated. I cannot say whether Poebel ever became a "true" Nazi, but there is no doubt that he was a German superpatriot ready to accept whatever anti-Jewish feelings this involved, and the tension between us became inevitable and unbearable. Not only did I no longer attend his classes, but we each tried to avoid the other as much as possible, and if by accident we met in the hallway, we lowered our eyes and passed without greeting. It was not until long after the Second World War that our relationship warmed up once again, though by this time we were separated by the distance between Chicago and Philadelphia. When my first popular work *From the Tablets of Sumer* was published in 1956, I deemed it a privilege to be permitted to dedicate it in these words: "To the Master of Sumerological Method, My Teacher and Colleague, Arno Poebel." Poebel died in 1957, and I traveled to Chicago to bid him goodby forever. But only physically speaking. On the spiritual level, Poebel's hesitating, stuttering, diffident voice still haunts my mind and memory, and my heart is filled with deep gratitude for the debt I owe this unassuming, pioneering scholar.

The rupture of scholarly collaboration with Poebel was a serious blow to me, and I was gravely troubled about my Sumerological future. But in 1933, to lift me out of depression, occurred the third of those minor miracles that played so decisive a role in promoting my career, although unfortunately this began with a tragic event: the unexpected death of Edward Chiera.

4. *Edward Chiera and Sumerian Literature (Chicago, 1934–1936)*

. . . Edward Chiera had, in 1923, traveled to Istanbul as a Crozer Fellow, and copied fifty important Sumerian literary tablets from its Nippur collection. On his return to Philadelphia he devoted every minute he could spare to the study of the Sumerian literary pieces in the Nippur collection of the University Museum. Between 1924 and 1927 he succeeded in preparing admirable copies of two hundred and seventy tablets and fragments inscribed with a varied assortment of the Sumerian literary works, identified the contents of a good many more that he intended to copy at some future date, and began to prepare a glossary of key Sumerian words to enable him to recognize additional crucial duplications that could lead to the restoration of the texts of quite a number of the compositions to which these belonged—in short, Chiera may be said to have laid the groundwork for the recovery and restoration of Sumerian literature, and had he not died unexpectedly he might well have played a leading role in this ongoing process.

In 1927, when he was called to the Oriental Institute to become the editor of the Assyrian Dictionary, Chiera carried with him the copies of the Sumerian literary pieces on which he had labored in the University Museum, and Breasted agreed to have the Oriental Institute publish them in two volumes in one of its publication series. But then death came suddenly, before Chiera was able to complete his notes and prepare the introduction to the books that would help to identify and illuminate their contents, at least to some extent. His copies were thus left stranded and "orphaned," and the editorial department of the Institute in charge of publications was in a quandary. George Allen, the Egyptologist who was head of that department, asked me, a budding Sumerologist, to undertake the preparation of the two volumes for publication.

At the time, I actually knew very little about Sumerian literature and its significance or about the complex problems relating to its recovery and restoration, since I had been working with Poebel mostly on Sumerian grammar. I therefore began to read avidly everything I could lay my hands on that had been said on this subject by earlier scholars, especially those who had already copied and published some of the Nippur literary pieces from Istanbul and Philadelphia. But I soon realized that this area of cuneiform research was virtually untouched. Not only had relatively few Sumerian literary texts been copied and published thus far, but hardly any of the attempts at the translation and interpretation of their contents were reasonably trustworthy or enlightening. This inspired me to greater zeal and determination. I worked day and night trying to read and understand the documents copied by Chiera, which I had undertaken to edit, regarding it as a task that must not be allowed to fail. I had to make at least enough sense out of Chiera's copied material to enable me to arrange it meaningfully and intelligently for publication and to prepare an Introduction which would be of some help to future researches. Chiera's list of duplicates which he had prepared when working on the Nippur material in the University Museum proved to be most helpful, as did his scattered notes and provisional, tentative glossary. In June 1934, two volumes, *Sumerian Epics and Myths* and *Sumerian Texts of Varied Contents*, appeared as volumes III and IV of the Oriental Institute's Cuneiform Series, and I breathed a sigh of relief.

But not for long! I was now taken by Sumerian literature, totally and obsessively, and there was so much to learn and do in this virtually unknown field of humanistic research. Copies of tablets, such as those in the Chiera volumes, were only the roots of the tree; its trunk and branches were the translations and interpretations that would make their contents available to interested humanists the world over. As soon as I had finished preparing Chiera's copies for publication, therefore, I concentrated all my attention and efforts to piecing together with the help of Chiera's list of duplicates the extant text of several Sumerian literary compositions that seemed to be of unusual interest and significance and to try to translate and interpret their contents.

First came a myth which I entitled "Inanna's Descent to the Nether World," a rather melancholy tale of the gods that was nevertheless responsible for one of the happier events of my scholarly career. What made this study possible at the time was Chiera's discovery that a tablet inscribed with the first half of this myth had been broken either before or during the Nippur excavations, and one half had gone to Istanbul and the other to Philadelphia. This "long-distance" join provided a partially preserved text of around two hundred lines and enabled me to place in their correct position in the story eight other published pieces, including three that appeared in *Sumerian Epics and Myths*. The resulting edition of the extant text, still quite incomplete, consisting of transliteration, translation, and commentary, was eventually published in the *Revue d'Assyriologie* of 1937.

The second text upon which I concentrated was part of an epic tale that I published under the title "Gilgamesh and the Huluppu-tree" as *Assyriological Study No. 10* of the Oriental Institute. It appeared in 1938, though I had begun working on it as early as 1934. At that time there had already been published eight pieces of tablets inscribed with parts of this poem, but I was unable to place them in their proper position in the text until I gradually learned to utilize certain stylistic clues.

One of the more somber genres of the Sumerian literary repertoire is the lamentation type of composition that bewails and bemoans the sporadic destruction of Sumer and its cities. Among the Nippur pieces copied by Chiera and published in *Sumerian Texts of Varied Content*, there were eight inscribed with parts of a composition that I entitled "Lamentation over the Destruction of Ur." In 1930 the French scholar Henri de Genouillac had copied and published a large tablet in the possession of the Louvre which was originally inscribed with the entire text of this composition, but now had a considerable number of breaks that left large gaps in the body of the poem. By piecing together the texts of these nine pieces, I was able to reconstruct the contents of the lamentation almost, but not quite, in their entirety.

The Sumerian literary research that began in 1933 with the preparation of Chiera's posthumous volumes for publication filled me with happiness and joy. My personal life, too, was fulfilled by my marriage, in that same year, to Milly Tokarsky, a Chicago schoolteacher and by the birth of our son Daniel in the following year. The future looked rosy and promising, and in my imagination I saw myself traveling as a member of the Oriental Institute staff to the University Museum in Philadelphia, and to the Museum of the Ancient Orient in Istanbul, in order to identify, copy, and study their unpublished Nippur literary tablets and fragments, and thus bring to fruition Chiera's inspiring vision. But Fate played it altogether differently. Eventually, I did travel to Philadelphia and Istanbul, and I did bring Chiera's vision to fruition, at least to a considerable extent; but not as a member of the Oriental Institute. My connection with that institution was severed to all intents and purposes in 1936, after I had suffered one humiliating blow after another, and the days that had dawned in sweet hope, ended in bitter despair.

The first blow came toward the end of 1934. The Department of Near Eastern Languages and Literatures that was part of the Humanities Faculty of the University of Chicago, had its offices in the Oriental Institute, and most of its professors were connected in one way or another with that institution. As a junior member of the Assyrian Dictionary staff, I was part of the Institute, but not of the Department, although I did teach a course in introductory Sumerian, but without stipend or standing in the Department. The chairman of the department was the Arabist, Martin Sprengling, a rather blunt, direct, but not overly sensitive or subtle academic. One day he summoned me to his office, and after a rather warm and expansive greeting, said something like the following: "Sam, we all like you here and think highly of your scholarship. We have therefore decided to appoint you as an instructor in the Department." At this point my heart began to beat with excitement, and my face to shine with joy; then I heard his booming voice continue: "But I must warn you, Sam, that as a Jew you cannot rise in the Department above the position of Assistant Professor. What's more, to balance your appointment, we shall also appoint a gentile as instructor in the Department."

I could hardly believe my ears, and fearing that I would lose control of my emotions, I hurriedly said goodby and rushed out of the office. That night my wife and I spent many an hour discussing this bitter development, and we decided that I should "take it on the chin," and go along as before, and try not to let this matter interfere with my research. This was easier said than done, however. The Institute was no longer a "promised land," and I walked its bare and gloomy halls with averted eye. The denouement to this rather crude bit of anti-Semitism was even more disheartening. When the appointments to the Department were annnounced, the gentile was appointed an instructor, and I was simply renewed as a research assistant on the Assyrian Dictionary staff.

But a more severe blow struck in 1936. Breasted had died in December 1935, and the Oriental Institute was in dire financial difficulty. This was only in part because of his death. The troubles had begun earlier in 1935, when as a result of the ongoing depression in the land, Mr. Rockefeller and the Rockefeller Board, the financial angels of the institution, decided to withdraw their support from almost all its activities, except for one large terminal grant.

As one of the lowest men on the Institute's hierarchical totempole, I knew virtually nothing of all this turmoil until some weeks before the end of the academic year of 1935–1936, when I received a notice of immediate dismissal from the Institute staff. I was among the very last hired by the Institute, and it was therefore not unreasonable that I should be among the first to be fired. But what made this action seem to me most unfair, and even illegal, though the University lawyers did not think so, was the fact that I had not received the dismissal notice in sufficient time to look for another academic position, or even to apply for a grant from some foundation. Milly was expecting our second child at the time, and this made the situation so distressing and intolerable that I decided to do something about it. As I recollect it, I wrote a letter to Wilson stating my case with no little anger and indignation and vowed to picket the Institute with an explanatory sign on my shoulder unless I was appointed for one more year, and given the opportunity to look about for some other academic opening.

To this day I cannot decide whether I would have had the temerity to carry out this one-man demonstration. I am not an activist by nature, and far from aggressive—"Your arms are broken at the elbows," said one dear friend to me—and I might never have been able to lift and hold the accusing wooden post. But fortunately it did not reach that embarassing stage. From some friends in the University I learned that there was a chapter of the American Association of University Professors on the campus, and that its chairman was the distinguished scientist Anton Carlson, of Nobel-prize fame. I turned to him with my complaint and he arranged a meeting with Wilson that resulted in the withdrawal of the dismissal notice, with the understanding that this was to be my terminal year. I immediately applied to the Guggenheim Foundation for one of its fellowships, to enable me to travel to Istanbul and copy some of the Sumerian literary tablets and fragments in the Museum of the Ancient Orient. And miracle of miracles, the application was acted upon favorably and I was awarded a grant of two thousand dollars, if I recollect correctly, for the year 1937–1938. And so in June 1937, the Kramer family—Milly, Daniel aged four, and Judy aged one, pulled up stakes in Chicago and left by freighter for Istanbul.

5. *The Gods: Sumerian Mythology (Istanbul and Philadelphia, 1937–1944)*

The freighter took about a month for its leisurely journey to Istanbul, making several stops in the Mediterranean before docking at the Golden Horn. The weather was summery and pleasant. The Kramer family of four constituted more than half the passenger list, and the crew seemed to make a special effort to please. The two children were favorites, and the sailors took time out to teach Judy to walk the deck on her wobbly little legs. Upon arrival in Istanbul we rented a comfortable apartment in Bebek with a Greek family. There was, of course, no central heating—and Istanbul can be quite cold and nasty in winter—and the bathroom and toilet facilities were not exactly modern. The house was situated high up on a hill that had to be climbed several times a day, but the view of the Bosphorus was breath-taking. I traveled to work by ferry, a boat that meandered dreamily from continent to continent along the history-laden Bosphorus.

Not long after our arrival, I paid a courtesy call on the Director of the Archaeological Museums, a building complex that is beautifully situated in a part of Istanbul known as Saray-burnu or "Palace-Nose," where the Sea of Marmara branches out into the gulflike Golden Horn and the winding Bosphorus.

The Director of the Archaeological Museums at that time was Aziz Bey, a member of a distinguished Turkish family—his uncle was the eminent Halil Bey who was largely responsible for metamorphosing the caliph palaces and kiosks into archaeological treasure-houses. Aziz Bey received me cordially and welcomed me warmly. I had of course written to the Turkish Directorate of Antiquities in some detail about the nature and purpose of my visit and had received permission to carry on my research in the museum. What worried me deeply, however, was how to do so effectively and without too many delays. The tablet collection of the Istanbul museum is enormous, second only to that of the British Museum. From ancient Lagash alone it had in its cupboards more than fifty thousand tablets, and in addition it had many thousands from Nippur and other sites that had been excavated in Iraq when it was part of the Turkish empire. I was interested only in a tiny fraction of this vast collection, the Sumerian literary tablets from Nippur, that at the time could be estimated to be not much more than a thousand or so. Where were these stored? Would I have to examine thousands upon thousands of tablets in order to locate them? If so, this in itself would be an immense and laborious task that might well consume the entire year of the Guggenheim Fellowship. It was with these disturbing thoughts that I followed the guard whom Aziz Bey had instructed to take me to the small building alongside the Museum of the Ancient Orient that housed the tablet collections. There I was met by a young cuneiformist from Leipzig, Rudolph Kraus, and I soon realized that my troubles were over, at least with regard to the location and partial identification of the source material for my researches.

Upon becoming Curator of the Tablet Collection, Kraus had begun cataloguing all its myriad tablets and fragments in order to inform cuneiformists of their contents, a laborious but essential task occupying many years. Fortunately for me, Kraus began with the Nippur collection, and when I arrived at the museum, I was happy to learn that he had already identified roughly, and set aside, several hundred Nippur literary pieces which I could begin to study and copy at once.

Before I did so, however, it was agreed between us that there was a rather unappealing but very useful scholarly chore to perform in connection with the museum's Nippur literary tablets, the task of "collation," that is, the correction of copies made by earlier scholars who for one reason or another had misread or missed altogether some signs on the original. In 1914, almost a quarter of a century before my arrival in Istanbul, the eminent Anglo-American scholar Stephen Langdon had copied and published some fifty of the Nippur literary pieces in the Istanbul museum. Langdon was an energetic and enthusiastic cuneiformist who made numerous important contributions to the discipline. But he was a fast and careless copyist, and many misreadings crept into his copies, errors that were to confuse and bedevil future translators and interpreters of the texts. I therefore spent several months collating his copies with the originals, and the resulting additions and corrections were published in 1940 in the *Journal of the American Oriental Society*.

The collation of Langdon's copies proved useful in another respect—it helped to prepare me for the main task of copying originals. Until this time, the Sumerian literary texts that I had studied were copies, published or unpublished, prepared by other scholars, and these are much easier and smoother to read than the original tablets and fragments. Unlike Poebel and Chiera, I was not blessed with particularly good handwriting and it took weeks of concentrated practice to learn to copy adequately and accurately. Time was passing and I was becoming somewhat panicky—soon the year of the Guggenheim Fellowship would come to an end, and I had made only a few copies of the original tablets. I therefore applied to the Guggenheim Foundation for a renewal of the Fellowship, and to my surprise, the application was again acted upon favorably; the grant was even increased by five hundred dollars to help pay our traveling expenses.

Encouraged by this show of faith in such an esoteric and specialized project, I continued the work with renewed zest and energy, and by the end of the second Guggenheim year, in June 1939, I had copied one hundred and sixty-seven tablets and fragments whose contents ranged over the entire spectrum of Sumerian literary genres. These were not published, however, until 1944, when they appeared under the title "*Sumerian Literary Texts from Nippur*" as an *Annual* of the American Schools of Oriental Research, with an introduction in English and Turkish, the Turkish translation having been prepared as a labor of love by two young Turkish conservators. By 1944, I had become an associate curator in the Babylonian Section of the University Museum, something I did not even dream of in 1939, when we left Istanbul to return to Philadelphia.

Upon returning to Philadelphia after two Guggenheim years in Istanbul, I found myself once again virtually penniless, and without a job, or the prospects of one. My wife's father, a retired carpenter, had bought a small farm near Niles, Michigan, and Milly and the children left immediately for that welcome haven. I stayed in Philadelphia with my friends. My object in Philadelphia was twofold: to see if I could get permission from University Museum authorities to study, copy, and publish the Nippur literary pieces in the tablet collection of its Babylonian Section and to try to obtain some financial support for this research activity. And so one day in the fall of 1939 I climbed with fluttering heart the majestic steps of the University Museum and knocked timidly on the door of the office of its Director, Horace Jayne.

Horace Howard Furness Jayne ("Hoddy" to his friends), a specialist in Chinese art and archaeology, was a warm-hearted, and despite his impressive prenomen that indicated high Philadelphia lineage, unpretentious man. He received me cordially, listened sympathetically to my enthusiastic description of the projected research and its importance, and responded favorably to my request. Most of the Nippur tablets, he informed me, were numbered and arranged in metal cases in a room in the basement. A desk and chair would be provided for me, and I could carry on my researches there to my heart's content. The matter of a stipend, or any other source of financial support, was not mentioned throughout our conversations.

I next proceeded to the office of Leon Legrain, the Curator of the Babylonian Section, Hilprecht's successor as Clark Research Professor of Assyriology, to obtain his blessing for the project. He, too, was not unfavorably disposed. In the 1930s, he had represented the Museum in the Joint British-American excavations at Ur, and at the moment was concentrating on preparing copies, indices, and glossaries of about eighteen hundred Ur tablets, virtually all administrative in content. He had lost all enthusiasm for the Nippur material and was only too happy to have it studied by a younger cuneiformist who seemed to be deeply interested and immersed in it.

I had thus achieved the first objective and immediately began to work zealously and ardently in the tablet-lined basement that was destined to be my happy workshop for the next four years. As for the second objective, someone in the Museum suggested that I apply to the American Philosophical Society for one of its research grants. Rumor had it that this august Society had recently come into some millions, and that it was awarding small research grants to scholars in need of limited financial help. I obtained and filled out one of the Society's application forms, in which I described the project, as well as my qualifications for carrying it out, and asked for a modest stipend of eighteen hundred dollars for the year 1939–1940. To my delight, the grant came through. Solvent once again, I immediately rented an apartment, and the family joined me in Philadelphia, which became our permanent home.

The American Philosophical Society awarded me grants ranging from fifteen hundred to three thousand dollars for the next four years, and this enabled me to continue my researches without interruption. It was not until much later, after I had been elected a member of the Society, that I learned who, among its members, was the Sumerological Santa Claus. The Society is virtually run by committees, one of the most important of which is the Committee on Research. It consists of a dozen or more scholars, each representing a major scientific or humanistic discipline. The scholar responsible for the archaeology of "Bible Lands," which included Mesopotamia, was William Foxwell Albright, whose popular books such as *From the Stone Age to Christianity* and the *Archaeology of Palestine* had made his name a household word.

There were roughly about fifteen thousand in number in the museum's basement; but only a small fraction was inscribed with Sumerian literary texts. It was therefore necessary to work my way through this immense mass of tablets and fragments, to handle each individual piece and scan its contents, in order to identify and put aside for later study those inscribed with texts belonging to one or another of the Sumerian literary works. This was a slow process though not especially difficult, since the Sumerian literary pieces could often be recognized at first glance by their shape and script. After several months of this preparatory labor, I succeeded in identifying six hundred and seventy-five pieces as literary. Of these, approximately one hundred and seventy-five were inscribed with parts of myths and epic tales; about three hundred and fifty were hymns and laments; one hundred and fifty were "wisdom" texts of one sort or another. I now had to decide on which of these literary categories to start working in earnest. But this quandary was soon resolved for me from an unexpected source.

In the early 1940s, the Department of Oriental Studies in the Graduate School of the University of Pennsylvania, one of the largest and most distinguished in America and abroad, whose courses covered entire Ancient Orient, from the Mediterranean to the Pacific, instituted an Interconnection Seminar. Attended by more professors than students, it had as its goal the bridging of the gap between the various separate Oriental disciplines, as well as the developing of a comparative approach that might uncover some underlying principles applicable to the study of ancient man in general. Every year, a central, pivotal theme was chosen for investigation, and each of the distinguished professors participating, was committed to prepare a comprehensive survey of whatever was known about it in his own geographical area, including and stressing the results of his most recent relevant researches.

I was not a member of the Department at the time, but as one of its former graduates, and a guest-researcher in the Museum, not to mention my continued tenuous connection with the Oriental Institute as "honorary,"—that is, unsalaried—Research Associate on the Assyrian Dictionary staff, I was invited to participate in the educative and illuminating program of this seminar. The theme selected for the year 1940–1941 was cosmogony and cosmology: the ideas, notions, and concepts of the ancient Oriental peoples related to the creation of the universe, the birth of the gods, and the organization of the cosmos. Fred Speiser, my Ph.D. mentor a decade earlier, was to report on the Assyrians and Babylonians; Herman Ranke, an eminent German Egyptologist then teaching in the Department, was to analyze and elucidate the Egyptian views on this elusive and enigmatic theme; the distinguished Sanskritist Norman Brown, was to do the same for the peoples of India, and Derk Bodde, the author in later years of *Peking Diary*, for the peoples of China. I was not an eminent professor or even a member of the Department, but as the only available Sumerologist, it fell to my lot to report on Sumerian cosmogony and cosmology, and this plunged me into the study of the myths of Sumer that was to result in the publication of my first "popular" book, *Sumerian Mythology*.

* * * * * * * * * * *

14. *Postscript (1975)*

The future, however, now (1975) that I am approaching my seventy-eighth birthday, is hardly my favorite province of concern; and a more appropriate note on which to close this book is my scholarly past: its promises and disappointments, its accomplishments and setbacks, its successes and failures. As I see it, my more enduring contributions to cuneiform research were threefold. First, and most important, is the key role I played in the recovery, restoration and resurrection of Sumerian literature, or at least a representative cross section of it. To be sure I was by no means the first to be concerned with this humanistic endeavor, nor have I brought it to fruition. But it is through my efforts that several thousand Sumerian literary tablets and fragments have been made available to cuneiformists the world over, a basic reservoir of pure unadulterated data that will endure for many a decade, if not for centuries to come. Secondly, I endeavored, consciously and purposefully, and with a fair degree of success, to make available reasonably reliable translations of many of these documents to the academic community, and especially to the anthropologist, historian, and humanist. Third, I have helped to spread the name of Sumer to the world at large, and to make people aware of the crucial role the Sumerians played in the ascent of civilized man.

As the academic title "Clark Research Professor of Assyriology" indicates, research was always my main interest and concern. But I did not neglect teaching altogether, especially in the form of seminars where I guided younger colleagues and graduate students in the copying, restoring, and translating of one or another of the Sumerian compositions. In my later years for example, I had as many as seven graduate students in close succession who went on to obtain their doctorates with me or my successor, Ake Sjöberg, not to mention one volunteer of mature age, Jane Heimerdinger, who has devoted much of her time to the preparation of copies of hundreds of small fragments that will make many a future Sumerologist happy, by filling in a missing sign, word, or phrase in the text of the composition he happens to be piecing together.

From time to time I also gave courses in Sumerian mythology designed for undergraduates, but I must admit that these were not overly successful. Often the class would start with as many as twenty or more students, but the number would be considerably reduced as the weeks passed. This is one failure, however, of which I am not particularly ashamed. For, as I realized in due course, many of these students came to this course with exaggerated and extravagant notions about the profound cosmic insights of the ancients, and even with some hope for psychiatric therapy for troubled minds and hearts. Instead, they found a rather hard-nosed common-sense agnostic and skeptic who offered them disturbing ambiguities and uncertainties regarding historical *truth*, rather than reassuring and consoling words regarding *salvation*. I would have liked to help and heal their troubled spirits, but I could not think of compromising my scholarly integrity, and had to be satisfied with the few students who persisted, either to amass University credit, or because they were temperamentally attuned to my non-oracular, non-cabbalistic approach to the study of myth.

Throughout this book I have mentioned the Sumerian *lama*, the good angel that came to my rescue in time of need. In two matters dear to my heart, however, I must sadly report, he has failed me. One concerns the hope, or rather the vision of establishing an American Institute of Sumerology, preferably on the campus of the University of Pennsylvania, that would promote research and teaching on all aspects of Sumerian language, history, and culture. But though I have done much to publicize the Sumerians and their crucial role in the history of civilization, I have lacked the charisma to attract and inspire American "angels" to help make this dream a reality, and the *lama* seemed unable to help.

Nor did he serve me better in a more personal desire that I had cherished over the years: to have my ashes buried in Ur, the Sumerian city where—so at least the Bible tells us—Father Abraham was born, as a symbol and as a reminder of Arab-Jewish fellowship and fraternity. This, I fear, is now quite impossible; the political struggle between the two related peoples has become so embittered that even a well-meaning, innocent Sumerian *lama* cannot make this symbolic wish come true. But a Sumerian sage once said, "Friendship lasts a day, kinship lasts forever" and I will therefore not give up the hope that one day ancient Sumer and Ur, resurrected out of dust and ashes by the spade of modern archaeologists, will help revive the spiritual and familial bonds between Arab and Jew.

[*Wayne State University Press will now be publishing the complete version of Sam's autobiography. J.M.S.*]

[This listing is a continuation of the bibliography published in AOAT 25.451–61, and it was compiled with the help of Julia Hardy, to whom I am beholden.]

A. BOOKS

24. *Sumerian Literary Tablets and Fragments in the Archeological Museum of Istanbul, II.* Ankara: Türk-Tarih-Kurumu Basimevi, 1976.

25. *Sumerian Literary Texts in the Ashmolean Museum.* (*OECT* 5.) New York: Oxford University Press, 1976. Co-author: Oliver Gurney.

26. *From the Poetry of Sumer: Creation, Glorification, Adoration.* (*UNA*'s Lectures 2.) Berkeley: University of California Press, 1979.

27. *History Begins at Sumer: Thirty-nine Firsts in Man's Recorded History.* (Third Revised Edition.) Philadelphia: University of Pennsylvania Press, 1981.

In press:

Inanna: Stories of the Love-Goddess of Sumer (title is tentative). New York: Harper and Row. Co-author Diane Wolkstein.

French Edition of *The Sacred Marriage Rite* (Revised). Translation and Addenda by Jean Bottéro

Ur Excavation Texts. Part III.

In preparation:

La Mythologie suméro-accadienne. Paris: Gallimard. (Projected publication in 1983.) Co-author: Jean Bottéro.

B. ARTICLES

141. "Kingship in Sumer and Akkad: The Ideal King," *Comptes rendus, Rencontre assyriologique internationale* 19 (1971), 163–176. [Appeared in 1974.]

142. "CT XXXVI: Corrigenda and Addenda," *Mallowan Festschrift: IRAQ* 36 (1974), 93–102

143. "Prolegomena to a Comparative Study of the Book of Psalms and Sumerian Literature," *Beth Mikra* 56 (1974), 136–59. Co-author: Moshe Weinfeld. [In Hebrew.]

144. "Die Tempel und Götterschreine von Nippur," *Orientalia* 44 (1975), 96–102. Co-author: Inez Bernhardt.

145. "Thorkild Jacobsen: Philologist, Archaeologist, Historian," *Jacobsen Festschrift: Assyriological Studies* 20 (1975), 1–7.

146. "Two British Museum iršemma 'Catalogues'," *Salonen Festschrift: Studia Orientalia* 46 (1975), 141–166.

147. "Sumerian Culture and Society: The Cuneiform Documents and their Cultural Significance," Cummings Modules in Anthropology, 58. Menlo Park, CA: Cummings Publishing Co., 1975.

148. "The Ur Excavations and Sumerian Literature," *Expedition* 20 (1978), 41–47.

149. "Commerce and Trade: Gleanings from Sumerian Literature," *IRAQ* 39 (1977) 59–66.

150. "The *Gir*$_5$ and the *ki-sikil*: A New Sumerian Elegy," *Essays on the Ancient Near East in Memory of Jacob Joel Finkelstein.* Connecticut: Archon Books, 1977, 139–142.

151. "Poets and Psalmists: Goddesses and Theologians," *The Legacy of Sumer.* (Bibliotheca Mesopotamica 4.) Malibu: Undena Publications, 1976, 3–21.

152. "Die Sumerische Literatur: der Menscheit älteste Belletristic," *Der Garten in Eden.* Berlin: Museum für Vor- und Frühgeschichte. 1978.

153. "Preface," *Kingship and the Gods: A Study of Ancient Near Eastern Religion as the Integration of Society and Nature.* By Henri Frankfort. Chicago: University of Chicago Press, Phoenix Edition, 1978.

154. "Sumerian Literature: Recovery and Restoration," *Essays on the Occasion of the Seventieth Anniversary of the Dropsie University.* Philadelphia: The Dropsie University, 1979, 307–315.

155. "Sumerian Literature and the British Museum: The Promise of the Future," *Proceedings of the American Philosophical Society* 124, #4 (1980), 295–312.

156. "Inanna and the *numun*-plant: A New Sumerian Myth," *The Biblical World: Essays in Honor of Cyrus H. Gordon.* New York: KTAV Publishing House, 1980, 87–97.

157. "The Death of Dumuzi: A New Sumerian Version," *Anatolian Studies* 30 [Festschrift Oliver Gurney] (1981), 5–13.

158. "BM 29616: The Fashioning of the gala," *Acta Sumerologica* 3 [Festschrift Yokomuro Nikahara] (1981), 1–11.

159. "Lisin, the Weeping Goddess," *Zikir Šumim: Assyriological Studies Presented to F. R. Kraus.* Leiden: B. J. Brill, 1982, 133–144.

160. "Binning 3," in C. B. F. Walker & S. N. Kramer, "Cuneiform Tablets in the Collection of Lord Binning," *IRAQ* 44 (1982), 71–86.

161. "Three Old Babylonian *balag*-catalogues from the British Museum," in *Diakonoff Festschrift*: *Societies and Languages of the Ancient Near East*. Warminster: Aris & Phillips, 1981/2, 206-213.

162. "BM 98396: A Sumerian Prototype of the *Mater-Dolorosa*," *Orlinsky Festschrift: Eretz-Israel* 16 (1982), 141*–146*.

163. "The Weeping Goddesses: Sumerian Prototypes of the MATER-DOLOROSA," *Biblical Archaeologist* 46 (1983), 69–80.

In preparation:

"The Marriage of Martu," Volume Commemorating the Founding of the Assyriological Institute of Bar-Ilan University, Jacob Klein, editor.

C. REVIEWS AND REVIEW ARTICLES

The following were omitted from the 1975 listing:

Francis Henry Taylor, *Babel's Tower: The Dilemma of the Modern Museum*. New York, 1945.
—Reviewed in *Crozer Quarterly* 22 (1945), 268–271.

Edith Porada, *Seal Impressions of Nuzi*. New Haven, 1947.
—Reviewed in *Crozer Quarterly* 25 (1948), 268–269.

Thorkild Jacobsen, *Toward the Image of Tammuz and Other Essays on Mesopotamian History and Culture*. Cambridge, 1970.
—Reviewed in *Catholic Biblical Quarterly* 33 (1971), 266–268.

Willem H. Ph. Römer, *Das Sumerische Kurzepos 'Bilgameš und Akka.'* (*Alter Orient und Altes Testament* 209/1.) Neukirchen-Vluyn, 1980.
—Reviewed in the *Journal of the American Oriental Society*, 102 (1982), 655.

INDEX

*[In the following series of indexes, page numbers refer to **first** citation of a vocable within each article. In other words, were one to look for mention of "Marduk" in the listings of divine names, the index would direct only to the initial occurrence of this deity within **each** article.*

When using the "Texts Cited" entries, please note that I list only those texts which receive appreciable attention in a given article.

*To be noted also is the convention by which vocables within a footnote are cited as "**n**," following a specific page number. I do not give the precise footnote number within that page wherein is embedded a specific vocable.*

*The indexes of Sumerian and Akkadian words depended completely on the compilation of Dr. Margaret W. Green (The University of Pennsylvania), and the listing of Hittite vocabulary was enormously facilitated by Dr. Galina Kellerman's (The Hebrew University) preliminary draft. It is a pleasure for me to recognize their part in preparing this **Index**.*

*I should warn that I have never excelled in such ventures; but I do hope that the following pages will allow the reader easier access to the rich harvest of information found within this, the "Simcha" Kramer **Volume**.* J. M. S.]

A. VOCABULARY

1. SUMERIAN

A 84
A.BAR.EDIN 64
a-da-al 319
A.EDIN 64
a-lum 194
a-pa$_4$ 320
ad 278
al-lib 320
alim/elum 194
alan-sù 319
am-si$_{(4)}$-si$_{(4)}$ 179
àm 85
ama-dùg-bad 63
ama-é-šà-ba 65
ama-tu-ud-da 63
^{urudu}ama-TÙN 81
ama$_5$ 195
an-bar-sù 178
anše 87
as-lum 194
/aš/ 84ff
AŠ-*tenû* 84
bad-bad 63
BAHAR.BAR 64
bán 86
bar—tab 64
bú 277
BUL 66
BULUG 277f
BÚR 101, 197f
bùr 86
da 79
DAG.KISIM$_5$×GA 61
dah 207
dam 311
dam-kaskal-la 311
dam-nitadam 63
dam-sì-ga 63
dam-šà-ga-ni 63
dam-tam-(ma) 63
de$_6$/di$_6$ 195
dedle 86
dele 86ff
dèm-me-er 86
deš 85ff
dim 319
dím-dím 66
dím-ma ma-da 244
dìm 319
dingir 86
dingir-kur-ra 320
dingir-nam-ti-la 259
du$_6$ 63
dub-zu 319
dùg—nir 63
dug$_4$ 207
dur-gun-na 196
dúr 179
e/dug$_4$ 194
^{kuš}E.ÍB 100
^{kuš}E.ÍB-ùr 95ff
e-ne 63
e-ri-ib 62
E.ÙR 100

2. AKKADIAN

napāhu 196, 319
naparkû 62f
napištu 6
napšuru 256
nasāhu 277
nassihu 276
naṣābu 61
našāku 80
našarbuṭ / ṣu 277
natāru 177
naṭālum 284, 291
nazāru 33
neperdû 257
nēru 86
nisannu 86, 179
nissabu 64
nišū 4
padānu 64
pahāru 62
palû 36
parakku 8
parāku 62, 290
parāmu 213
pâru 259
parzillu 178
pasāmu 33, 199
pašāru 256
pasuttu / pasuntu 33
pašru 257
patar šibbi 178
paṭāru 33
pēmtu 179
pe / indû 179
petû 32, 63
pīhātu 63n, 194
pilšu 64
pû 180
pu / arkullu 213
puṭṭuru 33
puzru 79
qabû 207
qadištu 65
qalālu 259
qâmu 290
qarrādu 33
qaštum malītum 101
qibītu 9
qubūru 136
qullulu 259
quttû 213
rabiān amurrim 240f
râbu 224
raʾīmu 33
rakābu 290
rakāmu 12
ramānu 32, 124
rapādu 100
raṭāpum 288
rāṭu 81
rigmu 224f, 278
rikis bilti 196
sahāru 260
sahāšu 195
salāʾu 138
sarru 33
sêru 213
siliʾtu 138
simtu 127
siqar 208
sûm 177
supû 208
surqinnu 220
ṣabātum 208
ṣâhu 29
ṣalālu 224
ṣalmu 287
ṣâlum 291
ṣarāpu 179
ṣerru 178
ṣīru 9
ṣurru 137, 177
ša abāri 178
š / sabāsu 224
šabsūtu 65
šadādu 193
šahrartu 224
šahtu 219
(*ša*) *inūma* 284n
šajjamānu 276n
šakānu 12
šaknum 289
šalāšu 206
šalāṭu 177
šamû 179
šâmu 276
šanānu 195
šāninu 195
šanītu 289
šanû 206
šanūdu 33
šapāku 81
šāpir bīti 33
šaqāru 101
šarāṭu 177

3. HITTITE

4. HEBREW

5. GREEK

B. NAMES

1. DIVINE NAMES

2. ROYAL AND PERSONAL NAMES

3. PLACE NAMES

C. TEXTS

1. CUNEIFORM TEXTS

2. BIBLICAL CITATIONS

3. OTHER CITATIONS

D. SUBJECT